S0-AXQ-280

The Text-Wrestling Book

Donna LeCourt
and the UMass Writing Program

Editorial Collective

Michael Y. Bennett

Thomas Burke

Marcia Curtis

Michael Edwards

Monica Fambrough

John Gibney

Erica Goehring

Wayne Kirley

Tanja Krupa

Heidi McKee

Lauren Rosenberg

Peggy Woods

Lesley Yalen

Patricia Zukowski

KENDALL/HUNT PUBLISHING COMPANY

4050 Westmark Drive   Dubuque, Iowa 52002

Cover art provided by author.

Copyright © 2005 by Donna LeCourt

ISBN 0-7575-2073-1

Kendall/Hunt Publishing Company has the exclusive rights to reproduce this work,
to prepare derivative works from this work, to publicly distribute this work,
to publicly perform this work and to publicly display this work.

All rights reserved. No part of this publication may be reproduced, stored
in a retrieval system, or transmitted, in any form or by any means,
electronic, mechanical, photocopying, recording, or otherwise, without
the prior written permission of the copyright owner.

Printed in the United States of America
10 9 8 7 6 5 4 3 2

Contents

Section II: Interacting with Texts   161

Section III: Adding to a Conversation   371

Alternative Table of Contents

Media & Advertising

Nature

Perceiving the World

Place

Race & Ethnicity

On Writing

Social Class

Screens of Reality

Sports & Hobbies

Technology

Acknowledgments

Although our editorial collective began work on the new edition of *The Text-Wrestling Book* in the fall semester of 2003, the history of this text extends much longer than that. In 1997, Peter Elbow, then director of the UMass Amherst Writing Program, introduced an essay assignment called "text-wrestling" into the First-Year Writing Program curriculum. The next director, Marcia Curtis, then developed, with another editorial team of graduate student teaching associates, the first edition of this text, called *The Original Text-Wrestling Book,* in response to the need for some conformity in the reading selections for this essay in a program with so many different teachers and sections. Over the course of five months, this initial editorial team compiled a group of essays that served the program well for four years and helped initiate larger conversations about the role of reading in a writing classroom. In fact, much of the structure and original intent of the first edition has served as the basis for this new edition. Thus, the new editorial collective owes a great debt of gratitude to this initial editorial group: Marcia Curtis, Benjamin Balthaser, Michael Edwards, Zan Goncalves, Robert Hazard, Noria Jablonski, Brian Jordan, Shauna Seliy, and Peggy Woods. We are especially thankful for the ongoing contributions of some of these original members, in particular Marcia Curtis, Michael Edwards, and Peggy Woods. We also would like to acknowledge Peter Elbow for the resiliency of his metaphor and continuing influence on the UMass Amherst Writing Program.

The new edition reflects changes in the UMass First-Year Writing Curriculum where text-wrestling has become a metaphor that extends beyond a single essay and reflects the role of reading across all the essays students write. In fact, the section titles themselves are taken from the three central units of this curriculum: *Inquiring into Self, Interacting with Texts,* and *Adding to a Conversation.* As we try to reflect in the book's content, text-wrestling continues to resonate as a way of imaging how writers interact with texts in a multitude of ways: how writers gain ideas from reading, understand the nature of the rhetorical situations they might choose to write within, invoke modes of analysis gleaned from reading to their own experience, and interact with texts to initiate their own reflections on ideas central to living in American culture. In laying out the purposes for reading, then, this new edition extends text-wrestling into new contexts, admittedly reflecting the rhetorical and cultural studies influences on our current curriculum. Thus, my use of the term—particularly any misuse—and its application to the contents therein are entirely my responsibility and may not reflect Peter Elbow's original intent.

The current editorial collective represents the fourteen teaching associates and Writing Program staff members who responded to my call for volunteers to work on a new edition of the book. I'm not sure any of them knew quite what they were signing on for as we, over the course of the next year and a half, read and reviewed almost 300 essays; met continually to refine our sense of the book, the curriculum, and the goals we hoped the final text would meet; solicited essay ideas, exercises, and student essays from the rest of the Writing Program staff; and co-authored the introductions, contents, and exercises you see here. Over the course of this work, I was continually impressed with the commitment, intelligence, and thoughtfulness all members of the collective brought to the project, as well as the respect they showed each other, student work, and the program itself. As I frequently wrote in e-mails, our meetings "inspired me," reminding me that I work with a truly amazing group of teachers whose dedication to student learning and writing humbles me. Thus, I would like to thank each member of the collective individually here: Michael Y. Bennett, Thomas Burke, Marcia Curtis, Michael Edwards, Monica Fambrough, John Gibney, Erica Goehring, Wayne Kirley, Tanja Krupa, Heidi McKee, Lauren Rosenberg, Peggy Woods, Lesley Yalen, and Patricia Zukowski. Although all members of this group contributed above and beyond what could be expected, I would like to single out Peggy Woods for her extraordinary contributions. Even though she declined the collective's offer to foreground her contributions on the author-page by putting her name first, she is first in our book, both literally and figuratively!

Finally, the collective also would like to thank all the students, teachers, and tutors whose contributions cannot be recognized individually for their feedback, ideas, essay suggestions, and general good will throughout this process. Of particular note are the Resource Staff members—Brian Baldi and Bethany Bucholz—for their work on exercises and their feedback as well as the Curriculum Committee members for their responses to the text: Michelle Deal, Jennifer DiGrazia, Linh Dich, Amy Dickinson, Haivan Hoang, Anna Rita Napoleone, and Mary Wilson.

Last, but certainly not least, I close as I began—by acknowledging the contributions of Marcia Curtis. Without her vision, no edition of this text would exist.

—Donna LeCourt

Why Do Writers Read?

As the words on the cover indicate, text-wrestling has many meanings for writers: it can mean responding to someone else's ideas, reading to help form one's own ideas, wrestling with one's own words to produce a text, and many things in between. We have deliberately chosen for this book a title whose meaning can be interpreted in multiple ways because what you will read and what you will write will likewise serve multiple purposes for both yourself and your readers. Reading may seem like a separate activity from writing—something people do before they write or use to support ideas they already have—but as you will see in the essays and exercises in this text, reading is integral to the process of writing.

Reading is one way writers get outside themselves and their own words/worlds to consider how their experiences and ideas might be interpreted by others, to look at how their ideas are formed in the context of what others are thinking and saying, and to understand better how their own ideas were formed so that they can communicate those opinions and thoughts more clearly to readers who may not share the same experiences. In short, writing is a deeply social act. A writer does not write alone even when she sits at a computer in complete isolation. Instead, she invokes her experiences formed in social interactions with others, makes assumptions about her readers based on their past experiences, and uses words that have meaning through their shared use. Writers, readers, and the words they use to communicate all bring part of the world to an essay. We write to affect our world and to recreate it, but we must begin with what already exists—the experiences, contexts, and presumptions readers and writers already have. In this way, writing is not simply a school exercise or an act of self-expression; it is something we use to understand and alter our world.

The Rhetorical Situation

The essays in this book are not presented simply as something to *write about;* they were chosen to help you write essays of your own that meet your purposes and reflect what you want to communicate. We begin, then, by considering what elements come into play as we produce texts: What must writers consider as they plan, compose, and revise to produce a text that can meet its intended purpose? What role does reading play in this process?

One way to imagine the variety of elements involved in any communication act is visually through the rhetorical triangle:

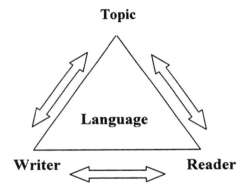

This triangle represents the variety of interactions that take place as we seek to communicate in writing: the writer's interaction with her subject matter, the writer's interaction with the reader, the reader's interaction with the subject matter, and the way language (our written text) provides the medium through which such interactions are negotiated. What the triangle doesn't show very clearly, however, is that each of these elements does not exist only in our interactions with them as we write. Each element is also influenced by its interactions in the world. For example, a writer does not exist in isolation from everything she experienced before sitting down to write. Similarly, readers bring their experiences with them to their interpretations of the text before them. The topics we write about, while seemingly inanimate, also bring with them certain social situations in terms of how the topics have been discussed prior to our writing, why a given group or society thinks the topics are important enough to discuss, and even what values and assumptions might be associated with such topics because of how others already think about them. Thus, a better way to imagine the rhetorical triangle might be to represent visually the different contexts that each element brings with it to a given writing situation—the past history and assumptions that come with any writer, reader, or subject matter—by enclosing each element in a circle to reflect the different contexts each brings with it.

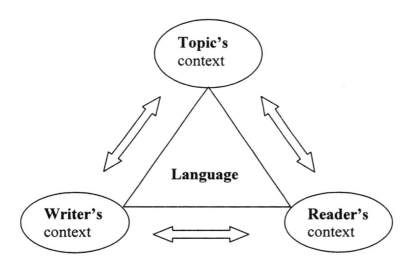

As if this weren't complicated enough, the triangle is still missing one element: why we write. Frequently, we write in response to something that has happened. For example, if I decide to write my autobiography, it may be because I recently had a child for whom I want to preserve memories, or it may be that I have recently become famous and think others will be interested. Either way, the motivation is not coming just from me, but also from events in my life (child's birth) or my world (becoming famous). The inspiration to write, whether it be from within ourselves or from events that take place beyond our control, is called the "situation" for our writing—that is, the things in our lives, minds, readings, and so on that prompt us to sit down and write. No one writes in a vacuum. We write because what happens in our lives, in our society, and in our everyday interactions makes us care enough to communicate our ideas to others. Moreover, we don't write to anyone who happens to pick up our essay. We write because we imagine a certain group of readers *need* to read what we have written, are willing to listen, and/or can take action based on what they read. In other words, locating writing in a situation acknowledges that motivations occur in the world not just within the writer's mind. Situations force us to pay attention to what inside and outside the writer prompts him to produce a text and, thus, how that situation also affects the text he will produce. How motivation emerges from a situation and affects each element of the composing process is illustrated here:

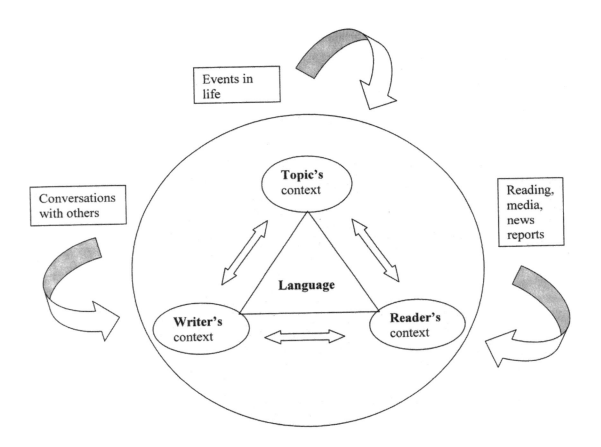

The larger circle around the rhetorical triangle in this diagram represents the multiple influences our rhetorical situations can have on how we choose to write. How we imagine the situation influences our purposes, how we will treat the subject, and who we hope will read our final version. Thus, the circle encompasses the entire process of composing, representing how a situation helps determine other elements. As Lloyd Bitzer, who coined the term *rhetorical situation,* put it, the situation is like a question; the act of writing, the answer.

This explanation is admittedly abstract, but it can help explain many writing acts—from the most mundane to the most complex. For instance, a writing act we rarely think about is making a grocery list. Such a list would seem to be only about the writer—what do I need at the store? Yet, while the motivation to write may be personal, we also construct such lists with all the rhetorical elements in mind. When I sit down to write a list, for example, I consider my "topic" in a certain context: What is missing from my kitchen at the moment? What does my family like to eat? How many days will we not be home for supper? Am I having guests this week? My topic, "groceries," exists in the real world of my family's interactions and desires. Similarly, there is a larger situation that influences this list: Who will be doing the shopping? What store am I going to? Considering the reader of my list might matter a great deal. If I am the only reader, I might simply write down "chips," but if my partner is shopping, I'll change that to "Pringles," since he never remembers the brand we buy. Or if I am going to shop at one store rather than another, I may organize the list differently so that my list has categories that match the layout of the store to make my shopping more efficient. Or I might decide to do research—checking out the newspaper to see what's on sale at the place I am intending to shop. The rhetorical situation for my list, then, includes the larger situation (the lack of groceries, the store I'm shopping at, my budget), the reader (myself, my partner, someone else!), my own context (am I a vegetarian? on Atkins?), and my topic (what do I already have? what do my family members like to eat?). All of these elements ultimately shape the text I write: a list that will look much different from someone else's because of our different rhetorical situations.

Reading to Write: The Three Sections of This Book

Writing an essay works in much the same way as a grocery list but rarely are such complicated situations as easy to analyze. Further, in *writing classes,* our reasons for writing may seem less connected to "real" motivations and situations since frequently the main reason for writing is to fulfill an assignment. But to be successful at such assignments, we must in some way create a situation where we have a reason to write about a given topic that we can communicate to a reader. Writers may be prompted by events in the world to compose, but they also analyze the situations available for their communication in seeking out reasons to write: Why is the topic important? What have others said about it? What is happening in the world that might make others want to read about a given topic? Effective writers, that is, create and/or interpret the situations available for writing—they think about why their text might be needed in the larger "conversation" on a topic and how it might affect the way others think about their subject matter. Helping writers think about each element of the situation is where reading can be extremely valuable. This book is set up so that reading can help make different aspects of the situation more open to scrutiny in a way that will help you in composing your own texts in the situations you create and for the purposes you design. The book is laid out in three sections: *Inquiring into Self, Interacting with Texts,* and *Adding to the Conversation.* Each of these sections is designed to help you create a different situation for your writing, offers exercises for reading the essays in ways that correspond to that writing situation, and ends with two essays written by students responding to similar situations.

In the first section, *Inquiring into Self,* we begin with essays that prompt us to think more directly about how our own experiences, values, and culture affect who we are and how we think. The essays in the first section consider how the contexts we participate in might affect how we communicate, make decisions, and think about ourselves. Reading such essays can help you consider what influences you bring to composing a text that may not be immediately apparent. As a result, these essays focus on the writer as both topic and producer of the text, but notice as well that such texts also have intended readers: readers much like yourselves for whom reading others' explorations of self can help prompt their own, or readers who may not have considered the influences of specific contexts on how others think and act.

The second section, *Interacting with Texts,* provides essays that are designed to give you new and different topics—some of which you might be encountering for the first time—to interact with. These essays take a variety of perspectives on a range of topics, but what they all have in common is a similar motivation for writing: to affect the way potential readers will think about the subject matter. You may not agree with or even immediately understand the authors' positions in these essays, but one reason many writers compose is to help them understand someone else's position and figure out their own relationship to a topic. Reading, in this way, helps bring the world to us as writers, to provide us with material that might become important to us even though it may not appear in our everyday experience. Reading can be, then, a context in itself, providing its own purposes for writing.

The essays in section three, *Adding to the Conversation,* make this idea of context most explicit. In this section, we provide multiple essays on the *same* topic to highlight the many different ways writers respond to the same issue depending upon their rhetorical situations and personal contexts. Reading many approaches to the same topic provides writers with a much better sense of the assumptions and positions already associated with their topic as well as the different audiences that might be interested in hearing their positions or contributions to an ongoing conversation on a given issue. Thus, reading many essays in conversation about an issue offers writers a way to assess the different rhetorical situations they might create for their own texts as well as to consider the contexts in which their topic and readers already exist.

Each section offers writers different reasons for reading: to find out more about self, to interact with another's ideas, and to understand the contexts of a particular topic. As a result, the book provides you not only with many purposes for writing but also many reasons for reading as a writer. Such purposes do not exhaust the possibilities, however, and you may find yourself reading for other reasons as well: to get ideas about how to organize a text, how to address certain readers, or even to imitate different styles that you find effective. Writers read, that is, not only for content but also for ideas on how different forms and styles meet the needs of different writing situations. We read to increase our choices, to understand the multiple options we have available when writing our own texts. Any of the essays in this book provide fertile ground for such exploration. To highlight how other writers have made such choices, we also include transitional essays called *Reflections on Writing* between sections.

Finally, the many purposes for reading we attempt to offer here also account for the difficulty level of many of the essays. These are not essays that we quickly understand on one reading or that offer only one interpretation. The essays are deliberately dense in an attempt to provide you with many ways into the texts. Less complex essays don't offer writers as much fodder for rethinking and rewriting their own texts. We too easily dismiss or accept essays that seem to have only one message. In these essays, we hope you find much that might challenge what you already know or prompt you to question yourself so that you might invigorate your own writing with that sense of meaningful purpose that is sometimes missing from *classroom* essays. Our hope is that you will take up the challenge to discover more about yourself as you write and to use your texts to add your voice to conversations our society has deemed central to civic life in a democracy.

Reflection on Writing

Student Essay

How to Be a Writer:
1. Buy a pen
2. Pay no attention to me (or anyone else for that matter)
Kathleen Clifford

The quest for evolution in writing is contingent upon one's understanding of how the person has come to achieve such ability. Therefore past experiences with writing are an indispensable part of how one defines oneself. Intense reflection on the past and inner workings of one's writing is essential knowledge in order to further shape one's life as a writer.

In my inspired girlhood years I became entranced by the glamour of spies and counterspies through the novel *Harriet the Spy*. I soon took to writing down the quiet whispers I heard on the street and in my own home. Sometimes I would even make up my own mystery stories. In this world my neighbors and family members were all my suspects of fantastic crimes, and I was determined to unravel the truth. Offhand comments were deep insights into mysteries. Books and writing transported me from my world. I found all of it truly daring and heroic.

From an outsider's point of view, I was just a snooping girl who liked to live in a make-believe world. None of this I would disagree with, yet the implications were much grander. I reveled in being able to control my fantasy world while others shunned me from theirs. Escapism went hand in hand with imagination.

My journal reflected this and more. I would expound upon simple facts, turning them into long stories. These entries differed in content from the way I was taught a journal should be kept. Journals were the facts of your own life, not fantasies about others'. But I preferred the imaginary world to actual life, finding excitement only in writing. Even so, I do not see different styles as severely different. I have written anecdotally and bridged what some people see as two different styles of writing. Similarly I bridged fantasy and reality through trying to write like my favorite heroine, Harriet.

Despite these exciting years, life changes and imagination can take a backseat. I remember vividly when my friend and I became "young adults" and strayed from the imaginary world we were used to. My friend and I sat for a good while recording what we saw through my plastic periscope. However, no matter how much we wished for something interesting to happen, no robber or car chase would materialize. Finally my friend gave up out of boredom and walked home, leaving me alone with my notebook. This prompted me to get up and walk home as well. I discontinued my detective notebook and resumed journal writing. Perhaps I felt that I finally had something to write about. Most likely, though, I saw the fantasy world of detectives as not one of my own.

Has this made me a writer? Most people would not see how keeping a journal makes a person a writer. I never labeled myself a writer but never felt that it was a title exclusive to the art of journals. I decry the idea that the word is reserved for the writing world's elite and since the appellation is pliable, the definition is left to one's discretion. We are not bound by anyone's definition of a writer, and therefore free to express ourselves through words in any way we want. I refute anyone who demands that true writing only appears in certain forms. I enjoy utilizing different forms of writing in order to create a stronger world around myself.

Through building this life interwoven with writing, I have been able to better know myself and where I can take myself. It has been easy to define and outline my past as a writer. To see how I define myself in the future is a near impossible challenge, so I see the definition as a guideline or goal. It entails a continuing reformation in my essays. I refuse to allow myself to become stagnant in the process, for I am always looking for ways to improve. It is the mark of a true writer: evolution. This demonstrates how important writing is in my life as a whole, a topic I never gave much thought to, but now I realize the story is only just beginning.

SECTION I

Inquiring Into Self

Introduction

Few of us think in sustained ways about why we might take a certain position on an issue or why we might hold certain values rather than others. Writing can serve as a way to inquire into our own histories to better understand ourselves. Such an understanding can help make us better writers because we can then explain to others the background behind our thinking. Many times when we read texts that might be confusing, we are not reacting to the difficulty of the ideas themselves. We are just as often confused or dismayed by how a writer is presenting those ideas and why she interprets them differently from the way we already think. As a result, writers who can make the background of their thinking more apparent are usually more successful. The essays in this section provide (1) an example of writers *inquiring into self* to understand better their own positions in society, and (2) possible prompts for thinking about the influences that are most relevant in your own life.

As you read these essays, think about what you learn about the authors from their exploration of the contexts they participate in: What did they learn by writing this? What questions might they be trying to resolve for themselves? What experiences and influences seem central to how they see themselves and the world around them? Or if the author himself is not participating in the context he described, consider why he may have decided to analyze this context: What is he attempting to highlight? Why is this context an important one to get others to consider? Just as important as understanding why an author might have written such an essay, though, is what you might learn about yourself from reading it. One reason writers read is to prompt us to ask new questions about our own background and the positions we take in our society or our lives: What influences does an author bring up that you have not considered about yourself? Where do your experiences differ from the author's? Why are they different? What contexts are more central to your background?

Be careful, though, of too readily dismissing the usefulness of an essay by someone whose background is quite different from your own. You might not *share* an experience or a context with an author, but more than likely you have an analogous experience—have played a sport, have a special place, have played a game with gendered implications, and so on. On the other hand, also be cautious of assuming too much difference or reading too literally. Many of the essays in this section, for example, deal with the influence of gender, race, or class on the writers. If you are white, it may seem that the influence of race upon your life is radically different from that of an African American author. Or if you are female, essays from men about gendered experiences may seem irrelevant. This is not to say that your experiences or the influence of race and gender are not different. They probably are. But that does not mean that race or gender is irrelevant to your background; instead, the questions you might ask yourself would be about your own race and gender and its influences on how you see yourself.

As you read, then, keep in mind that your purpose should not be to evaluate an author's experience but instead to use those experiences to think about similar influences on your own life. Making more apparent to yourself even one aspect of the contexts that have influenced you will do much to highlight what you bring to any writing act and help you understand (and communicate to your readers) *why* you might be taking a certain position or offering a certain interpretation of an idea. Understanding why we make meaning is as central to communication as being clear about that meaning itself because readers do not share our experience or have the background to our thinking. We need to make explicit to readers the aspects of our background that are relevant to understanding our positions, or at the very least, consider how and why our readers will not immediately see things the same way we do. Highlighting these differences is, in fact, one of the reasons we write personal essays for others. Our readers may not care about us as individuals—they do not, after all, have any motivation to do so since they do not know us—but they may care to understand better why people differ or to get a glimpse into someone else's life so that they might better understand their own.

Love Letters

Megan Foss

Megan Foss's journey from heroin-addicted prostitute to writer and teacher is remarkable, but Foss does not allow us to see her journey as a simple Cinderella story. Despite having been "thoroughly indoctrinated in how to speak and compose according to arbitrary conventions created by people who [have] been dead for centuries," and despite her awareness that "people are judged by their use of language," Foss refuses to leave behind the contexts that have made her. She challenges our ideas of what it means to be educated and what it means to write well, and in so doing demonstrates how her own evolution as a writer is intimately connected to the non-academic life she has led. Foss's unconventional style never falls into linguistic sloppiness: she deploys words like "gonna" and "outa" with obvious calculation and self-awareness. By exploring the ways her life experiences have shaped her writing, Foss's essay asks us to consider our own relationship to language. What experiences have shaped you as a writer? How have you learned—and how do you continue to learn— the conventions of writing? What are the ways in which the conventions you learn might both constrain you and help you?

-/-

The first time my old man went to prison I wrote him letters. I wrote Darryl long rambling letters that went on for 10 or 11 pages.

I didn't have a home and I had maybe one change of clothes. Our car got confiscated when he got popped, along with everything I owned in the world except for what I was carrying in my backpack when it happened. So I didn't even have shoes at the beginning of that summer but I always had tablets of yellow paper and something to write with. I could fit that in my bag along with my hairbrush and bits and pieces of makeup and a prescription bottle fulla water and the leather cigarette case that held my syringes and cotton and twisted spoons.

I wrote him letters and them tablets of paper got to be as critical for survival as black tape and crazy glue and bolt-cutters. And I can't think of anything much more suspicious in that community than a hooker who spent

From *Creative Nonfiction*. Copyright © 1997 by Megan Foss. Reprinted by permission.

her spare time recording things on paper. I think I got away with it because it was the first thing I did after Darryl went away. I bought paper and wrote and folks who mighta otherwise found my behavior strange to the point of being problematic knew why I was writing. They knew I was Darryl Masters' old lady and he'd just gotten busted and if what made me happy was to sit and scribble it didn't disrupt anything critical in the life cycle. Sometimes people would watch me while I was writing with their eyes kinda narrowed studying me like I mighta been half-crazy and ask me why I was doing it. And I really didn't have an answer because although I wrote Darryl all them letters, I never mailed a single one.

The tablets would fill up with details about business and weather reports and stories about who was getting busted and who was getting sick. I remember sitting on the hood of a car in the parking lot at Marg's bar in my cutoffs with my legs crossed and dangling over the hood of the car and catching dates with that tablet on my lap. And I remember more than a couple sheriffs stopping to see what I was doing and scratching their heads and kinda chuckling at me. And even that didn't really seem to spook anybody. I suppose it shoulda occurred to me that sitting there with that tablet on my lap and a CoCo County Sheriff chatting me up wasn't the brightest thing I coulda done.

But I never thought about what I was putting in them tablets as information. Never thought of it as secrets. That wasn't the purpose in writing. Darryl had been a constant presence in my life—we'd been together as close to 24/7 as two people could be. We shared the same pillow and the same air and the same food and the same dope and the same syringes. In all the months and years we were together I probably never said as many words out loud as I poured into a single one of them 10-page letters. And as long as I kept writing them I could pretend he was still there.

For a while I saved the tablets as they filled up but after I had three or four of them in my pack it started getting crowded and uncomfortable. Stuff would shift around inside and the hard cardboard corners would jab me in the back. So I started another ritual. As a new one would fill up I'd take the oldest and tear all the pages into tiny pieces and throw them away. Until I started doing that, people actually thought I was mailing the letters but Billy Jay Meckles caught me sitting in the 24-hour laundromat one night tearing up them pages and asked me what the hell I was doing. I started to shove the tablet I had half torn up back in my pack but he snatched it outa my hand. He didn't read anything on it—just held it there between us.

"They're just letters," I told him. Billy Jay was huge and probably had the potential to be one mean motherfucka after four years in the joint but he was one of the best-natured junkies I ever knew. He was always finding something to laugh at and the one or two girls working the streets who had kids always left their kids with Billy Jay when they worked. He kept himself fixed that way. The kids never lasted long. Social Services always ended up taking them away but while they were there, he was kinda like the community daycare. It was partly cause he always had a place to live—his mom had left him a small house that he managed to hang onto in between visits to the pen—but it had more to do with knowing kids were safe with Billy Jay. Their mothers could go to work and not have to worry about them and when they picked them up they always dropped off a piece of dope. Billy Jay probably had the cleanest hustle on the stroll.

His eyebrows arched over his round bright blue eyes and he tossed a long blonde curl off his shoulder. "Why aren't ya mailing them?"

"I will. That was just a kinda practice letter. Didn't really say what I wanted to say." The zipper was open on my pack and you couldn't help but see the other two tablets covered with ink and pages curling up at the corners.

"How long ya been trying to find the right thing to say?" he asked and pointed at my pack.

"I don't know. What difference does it make?" I liked Billy Jay but he was getting into shit that he couldn't possibly understand.

"It makes a difference if Darryl ain't gettin any of them letters."

"He does—he will."

"Ya mean in all this time ya ain't mailed a single one? Shit Mickey, he's been gone almost three months."

I cringed when he said it. I'd let people think we were in pretty close contact.

If anybody had actually thought beyond the words I said, they woulda realized how unlikely that was. Where could he write to me at? But people with habits don't have time to waste analyzing shit like that so when I told folks he was doing good and I couldn't wait to see him, they just accepted it. And maybe after a while I convinced myself that somehow we were still in contact. That just writing the letters kept us together.

But Billy Jay had done time and he knew what them letters meant and he wasn't letting it go. "Why aren't ya mailing them? He's probably goin outa his mind, Mickey."

I didn't answer. Didn't have an answer. At least not one I wanted to share with him. He'd think I was crazy and I wasn't entirely sure he woulda been wrong in his assessment. As long as writing had a purpose—a reason—it made sense. Writing to communicate was logical. Just wandering around scribbling thoughts and observations down for no apparent reason pointed to one of two things. A rat or a nut. I knew it wasn't the former and that left only the craziness as an option. And if I told Billy Jay the real reason I wasn't mailing the letters, I knew he'd confirm my diagnosis.

He sat down beside me on the wood slat bench. "What's up with ya, girl? Why ya writing all this shit down if ya don't plan on sending it to him?"

"I do. I am gonna send them." I paused and then latched onto what seemed like a reasonable excuse only because of the pressure I felt to come up with one. "I don't got any stamps or envelopes."

"Ya make two or three-hundred bucks a night—what's a fuckin stamp cost?" It wasn't how much they cost. It was acquiring them that was the real problem. You could buy postage stamps in some of the grocery stores, but I hadn't been in a regular grocery store in over a couple years. I'd got so accustomed to getting thrown outa places of business in Bella Vista that I stopped going anywhere but Dave's liquor store—and Dave didn't sell stamps. And in the beginning when Darryl first went away, I'd intended to mail them letters and I'd even got as far as the parking lot of the Thrifty Foods intending to go in and buy stamps and an envelope. But I'd stood outside with the sun so hot on my shoulders I could smell the heat rising off my skin and changed my mind. Even if I'd had shoes I don't think I coulda forced myself to go in there. We owned the streets in Bella Vista but the square folks owned the grocery stores and the restaurants and gas stations. When they had to go out on the streets, they drove with their windows rolled up and the doors locked and their eyes aimed anywhere but at the working girls and I knew if I went in that store the same thing would happen. I'd walk up to the cash register with a small box of envelopes and ask for a sheet of stamps and no one would respond. Their eyes would go over my head and they'd wait on the person ahead of me and behind me but they'd refuse to see me. And if I made them see me, they'd have me thrown out.

And the post office was absolutely outa the question—all them people in uniforms. So that day in fronta the store I told myself I'd come back at night. And when I went back at night I told myself the next time I had a little extra cash I'd get a pair of shoes and then go back to get my stamps. And after a while I stopped bothering to make excuses to myself. After a while I found that I liked writing the letters better because I knew I'd never mail them. But it was a long time until I understood why and saying something like that to Billy Jay without a good why to back it up wouldn't fly.

"Girl I'm gonna buy some fuckin stamps and envelopes and we're gonna mail some of them letters. Homeboy's gotta be tweakin hard about this by now." I hated hearing him talk about Darryl being in prison. I hated hearing anybody talk specifically about it. When people asked about him they didn't say, So how's Darryl doing in the joint? They just asked how he was and I could say fine like he was just waiting for me out in the car.

"Ya know what, Billy? You're gonna think I'm fuckin spun—but it's like—as long as I don't mail them letters I don't gotta think about him bein gone."

"Huh?"

"It's like I'm just savin stuff up to tell him when he gets back at night. And then at night I know he's not coming back—at least not for a long time—and I can't stand thinkin about it so I just shove it all outa my mind. I tell myself he just went off to cop or take care of some business and he'll be here when I wake up in the mornin."

It was only half a lie. It was my habit more than anything else that kept me from mailing the letters. I learned in those first few months when Darryl was gone and I not only had to earn the money but had to take care of business too, that even something as minimal as mailing a letter required more energy units than I had to spare if I was gonna stay fixed and on toppa my hustle. It's hard to conceive that such a tiny task coulda been so entirely overwhelming but it was. And I knew within the first couple weeks that I'd probably never mail a single one. And on those rare occasions when I allowed myself to remember that Darryl was in prison and not waiting for me at the motel or in the car out by the river—I did know that he was suffering for my inability to get it together. I did know that he'd be sitting up in his cell late at night wondering if I'd stopped loving him. The girl before me did him like that.

He'd loved Bridget like a kid loves the first time, only he was almost 30 when he loved her. And when he went to the joint she hooked up with a heroin-dealer named Fernando and as hard as them guys in the joint are—shit like that rocks their world.

And he'd thought when he went in that I was gonna get clean and when he got out we were gonna do the square thing and have a place to live with walls and rooms instead of back seats and front seats. That had been his insurance against losing me while he was down. Clean—he thought I'd wait for him. Hooked—he thought I'd pull a Bridget on him. Not having heard a single word from me since they transferred him to Vacaville from the county lock-up in Martinez—he musta spent endless empty hours working out scenarios of betrayal in his mind. But I hadn't done any time then so even my worst imaginings didn't come close to understanding such an experience.

– //–

I mailed him the letters I wrote the first time I went to jail. The first time I went and stayed. I didn't fill up tablets fulla letters but the ones I wrote did get mailed. The county gave us unlimited access to paper and pencils and envelopes. You could get five pages and an envelope mailed for a single stamp and they even gave us two free stamps a week. You didn't wanna go over the five page limit cause that would take both your stamps.

Years later he'd claim he never got the letters but I mailed them to his sister's house and they never got returned to me at the jail, so I know they went somewhere. They were very different letters. No long wandering descriptions of how the leaves on the tree branches hanging over the river made shadows that looked like lace in the moonlight. No convoluted explanations about what it was like to fall in love with someone else while he sat in the joint pumping iron and occasionally reading about my latest bust in the paper. No spiraling logic that attempted to claim it wasn't really the same thing as what Bridget did because I'd fallen in love with a girl and it didn't take anything away from him or mean that I loved him any less. There weren't any of them things to write about in jail. And we'd been separated since he got outa the joint that last time so I couldn't even write to him about what it was like being separated from him because it was Charley I hurt for and reached for in the night. But writing was one of the few officially sanctioned ways to pass the time and Darryl was the only person I knew who had a place he could collect mail from so I wrote letters to him.

And because paper and pencils were the only things we had access to without having money on our books—writing was the most normal thing in the world to do. Reading and writing. The library cart came around once a week. The first few weeks I kicked too hard to care about living or dying much less communicating with the free world or tuning into the completely familiar paranoia in Robert Ludlum novels. And at first when I started to feel better all I wanted to do was sit in fronta the TV. I hadn't seen TV for months and I hadn't seen it through clear eyes for years. I missed the Reagan years almost in their entirety and watching the news fascinated me. Movies and MTV and soap operas were fun to watch but the news was the first real look I'd had at the straight world since getting strung out.

I mean—I'd seen the news and TV from time to time. The nights we had motels we always had the TV on—but them people on the news then had been them and we'd been us and it was very different tuning in when I'd been clean for a few weeks because I was no longer sure where the boundary was.

That's what I wrote to Darryl about while I was in jail and that's why I mailed them letters. I wrote to him about how it would be when I was back on the streets. I wrote to him in order to establish where my future would happen. I wrote to try to document that boundary line and my position relative to it. And my world would undoubtedly be a very different place today if he'd answered my letters. If he'd confirmed my vision. But he didn't. He never got the letters and what he might have done if he had is a question we prefer to leave unanswered between us. And after a month passed and I didn't get a single response, I stopped writing the letters with the intention of mailing them.

I lucked out when I did my time. I don't know how county jails in other jurisdictions work but in the winter of '88 the powers that be at the CoCo County jail seemed to be of the opinion that rehabilitation did serve some purpose. I had access to psychologists and spiritual advisers and books and excellent public defense and people whose whole jobs were about helping people like me make some kinda life plan against the day when the door locked behind instead of in fronta them. And I had access to an English teacher.

I had no idea how much time I was gonna do. It took almost 40 days to get all the charges straightened out. For the most part they were misdemeanors but there were a couple potential felonies that coulda pulled a couple years. One thing I did know for certain was that less was better than more and when I found out I could get time off my eventual sentence by attending classes I jumped on it.

They had art classes and English classes and I signed up for both. I had almost no interest in art but that was another one of them things you could do with the free paper and pencils so I was willing to give it a shot—along with everybody else. We had so many people doing art that they had to use the big visiting room to hold class and twice a week we earned a half-day off our sentences sitting down and listening to a short young blonde woman talk to us about art.

We had mostly men in the art class and it was kinda comical to watch the tiny and clearly uncomfortable young teacher trying to be the leader amongst that group of hard-core gangsters. She'd hold her books up and point to something and talk about DaVinci and her finger would be visibly shaking when she pointed at the text. I realize now that she was trying to teach theory but she didn't have any kinda art-theory that spoke to them guys. They kept pointing to the tattoos on their arms as art. Smoking guns and reapers and leaping panthers with huge and clearly articulated musculature and it was obvious that nothing in her education had prepared her to theorize on that particular form. She kept insisting that it wasn't art but she couldn't explain why. And we knew enough about theorizing to be able to poke holes in everything she said after that.

Half the guys on the unit went to art class but there were only two of us who went to the English class and we were both female. The English teacher wasn't particularly young or even remotely nervous. She woulda been far better prepared to handle the homeboys who were always cracking on the art teacher but art wasn't her calling. Letters were her thing.

She was tall and had long cinnamon-colored hair with random strands of silver growing everywhere and she stood at least 5′ 9″ in her flats. Because there were just the three of us we didn't need a larger room. We didn't use a room at all. We sat at one of the tables they used at chow time to serve up and on the first day the first thing she had us do was take a spelling test. Shelley was the other girl in the class. She had the cell next to me and we kinda chuckled when the teacher told us we were having a spelling test because we spent a bunch of our spare time playing Scrabble. "Maybe this will improve my game," Shelley said.

That made it seem a little less childish and I raised my eyebrows and said, "Ya never know."

I don't remember any of the words on that test except the single one I missed. Dessert. The teacher used it in a sentence so I knew she was talking about cake and pie and shit like that but I spelled it "desert." And she gave me one of them cheesy tips for remembering how to spell words like that—words that have two different meanings depending on how you spell them. "When you're trying to remember whether it's one s or two, tell yourself that you like two helpings of dessert," she said. If I've spelled that word wrong since then, it was a typo.

We sat there after the test and talked about English for a while. And it's almost impossible to imagine now—but at the time I didn't have enough knowledge about what English was to know that it was about writing and how to use words until the teacher explained it that way. Shelley got bored shortly after the spelling test when the teacher started talking about reasons for writing but I kept listening.

It was much like the conversations I'd had with myself when I was carrying around them notebooks fulla words that weren't ever gonna get read by anybody but me. And then when the two hours were over, I had an idea.

"Could I—like do some kinda homework and get time credit for it?"

She studied me for a second. "Maybe. What do you have in mind?"

I didn't quite know how to say I wanted to write. It felt embarrassing. When I didn't say anything she said, "I can't give you time-credit for just reading. Everybody in here reads. If I gave time-credit for everybody in here reading books, we could have everybody released by Easter."

"No," I told her. "I wasn't thinkin about readin. I was thinkin about writin. I been doing a lot of writin?"

"What kind of writing?" She seemed honestly interested and it made me comfortable talking about it. For the most part I'd gotten used to people thinking I was strange for writing—strange for wanting to write. But this woman seemed to value the act.

"Well—they started out bein letters—," I paused and she interrupted me.

"Everybody in here writes letters too," she said.

"Well they're not really letters. They started out bein that way but I never mailed them and they kinda turned into—well I'm not sure what you'd call them. Stories maybe."

"Have you been doing that ever since you got here?"

"Shit—I been doin it for a few years now."

"Really?" She said it like she really wasn't expecting an answer. She finished gathering up her books and materials and then stood there with it all piled up in her arms staring at me and I started being sorry I'd mentioned it. Suddenly it seemed like the quintessential arrogance to think I had anything to say that might qualify as a story. And she was looking at me like she couldn't decide whether or not to take me seriously—whether or not I wanted to write or just wanted to get outa jail faster.

"Tell you what I'll do. You bring something you've already written to the next class and I'll read it. Then we'll talk about time-credit. OK?"

I nodded and said, "OK," trying to think of what I had already written up in my room that I could show her.

Later that night in my cell I looked through the stack of papers on my little wooden writing table. I didn't know what she'd be expecting or what she'd be looking for. Mostly what I had in my cell didn't add up to more than a diary of the time I'd been there. Anecdotes and details about the people I shared that space with but not really stories and I told her I wrote stories.

The journals probably woulda served my purpose but somewhere between thinking that I might be able to get time off my sentence in exchange for my scribbling and sitting at my desk trying to decide what to show her my purpose changed a tiny bit. I cared about what she thought for what it could gain me but I also started caring what she thought simply for the sake of the story.

I went back in my mind looking for stories and finally decided I'd write a few pages about Charley. I spent the next four days reconstructing a moment from our relationship and whatever the teacher had been looking for musta been there cause after she read it she agreed that for every two pages I wrote she'd give me credit for one class session. The first independent study project of my education.

And I spent hours sitting at that desk after that. During the day I still hung out on the unit and watched Madonna on MTV and played Scrabble with Shelley but I took to staying up half the night with pencil and paper. I wrote so much my pencils always went dull before I'd quit and go to sleep. The last thing I did before lock-down was sharpen all my pencils and by morning, the points were always all rubbed down to smooth black nubs.

Darryl never wrote but he came to see me twice. Charley ended up in the hospital with endocarditis that winter and so she couldn't come but Darryl did manage to show up two different times.

I'd been there almost two months when he finally showed up. I don't suppose I really had any right to expect anything more from him because we'd been separated for a while when I got popped—but I did. I'd taken care of him for years and I'd expected him—at least while I was at County—to do the same. To make sure I had money for cigarettes and candy bars from the canteen. To buy a bag of Taffy Creme cookies. Life's little luxuries.

By the time he showed up, I'd begun to think about options other than returning to the back seats and the spoon and the grasping hands on my body. I'd begun writing a different kinda letter. With my world on the streets completely cut off I turned—for the first time in years—towards the people I'd spent the first years of my life with. My family. Initially those letters were just to make contact—to re-establish connections that had been stretched and frayed and miswired and all but irreparably severed over the years. When my sentence and my charges were being negotiated, the court sent one of them people who specialize in rehabilitation plans to see me and the first thing the man told me to do was try to make family contact. "One of the things they're going to consider when they look at your time is what your odds are for becoming a productive member of society. You're looking at some serious felonies but the courts have been known to reduce those to misdemeanors in those cases when the defendant has a workable plan for being mainstreamed," he told me.

"Mainstreamed?"

"Becoming a part of mainstream society. Things like having a home and learning how to find a job and take care of yourself."

In the back of our minds we all knew that was what kept us from getting straight. Being hooked on heroin didn't keep us in the spoon so much as our lack of knowledge about the world outside of it. We didn't know how to "mainstream" and in those opaque shadow moments of solitude when we allowed ourselves to think about what existed beyond our borders, we didn't know how they did it—the people in the mainstream. When they needed a place to live we didn't know how they found one. Did they just walk up to apartment buildings and say, I need one of these? We knew that when they needed jobs they used their experience to get them—but we didn't have any experience. And we couldn't even get most businesses to let us in when we had money. How could we ever have gotten them to pay us to be there? But the county had them people who specialized in teaching people like me how to do just exactly that.

And the first parta that process had to do with what the man called "creating a community." He told me that sometimes religious organizations sponsored people like me but for the most part, our families were our last chance to avoid the pen. The words came strained and passive at first—but I wrote them letters and they were the first contact I had with the outside world in years. The doctors and the teachers and the advisors in jail all belonged to that outside world—but I was their job. We were their jobs. Those first tentative letters were an attempt to make contact with a world that had no obligation to acknowledge me. A peace treaty after living for years as one half of a them-against-us equation. And initially my plan was to make that contact and convince my parents to agree to participate in planning my rehabilitation. I didn't plan on going through with it but at the time I needed them involved to turn those felonies into misdemeanors. Like the English classes—the letters I wrote my parents had the potential to cut my time.

If Darryl had come to see me sooner that's probably the only purpose the letters ever woulda served. But somewhere in that second month-between the letters on the Scrabble board and the letters in the spelling tests and the letters to and from my parents—the words became the girders in the formation of a straight identity. I would write about a future absent of drugs and sleeping in cars and working in cars and living and loving on street corners in random moments stolen from the larger narrative of addiction. They were non-specific words because I didn't know any of those specifics. I could only think of the future in terms of the past. It held no meaning beyond what it was not. But as non-specific as the words were, they were the only familiar territory that existed in that limbo. Words were the same on either side of the equation. Later I would discover how many different things a single word could mean—but then I latched onto the idea that language was the same on both sides of the bars. They might not let me go in their restaurants or pay me money to do a job—but if I used the words right there was no way to tell that I was any different from any one of them. And initially I recognized words as tools to perpetuate a scam. I could use them to con people. And if Darryl hadn't waited so long to put in an appearance, I probably never woulda understood how much more letters and words could be than a means to an end.

But he waited and by the time he showed up the words I was writing had shifted in purpose. I was by no means sure that I wanted to change my life. To leave the only home and the only family I'd known for years—to go play at being normal. But I had stopped believing that I couldn't. I believed that in the language I'd found a way out—I just hadn't definitively decided to take it. And now in my letters and in my stories I was writing to discover. To come to the decision.

The second and last time Darryl came, I still hadn't decided. I'd made all the plans. My parents had written letters agreeing to provide me with a home and supervision should the court choose to release me into their custody. I'd had lengthy discussions with counselors about rehabilitation—about AA and NA and CA and all them other alphabet groups. I'd gone to my classes and been a model prisoner and convinced my public defender that—oh yeah—I was that one in a thousand you could put your faith in. I convinced them all. Using words.

I just hadn't convinced myself. It all sounded good in theory. But the theories had all been developed by people with big fancy degrees and I could tell by the way they talked that they didn't have much grounding in practice. My visions of their world lacked the specifics to make it truly conceivable. And their theories had specifics but they were irrelevant enough to make the reality of my life almost inconceivable to them. Their specifics came from books and those books were written by people who got their information from books—ad infinitum. And when the man from the courthouse talked to me about things like finding jobs, I doubted if any of the words he knew coulda helped me where I needed it most. He could talk to me about appearance and the kinda questions I'd get asked on applications. He could even—with the assistance of some tests—tell me what I'd probably be best at. But he couldn't tell me how—after my almost 15 years of prostitution and all that accompanies that—to deal with men on any other level. He couldn't tell me how to keep myself from flinching if a man moved quickly in my presence. Couldn't tell me how to believe that they looked at me and saw anything but sex. I had some understanding of their side of the equation because I'd lived those first years of my life there. But they didn't know anything concrete about the place they were trying to pull me away from and so as great as their theories sounded—I kept finding holes in them. As much as I found myself drawn to the future those theories promised—it was still a blind date and I wasn't sure I wanted to go.

Until Darryl came to see me that last time. He sat on his side of the glass and I sat on mine and there wasn't anything specific in his words or his appearance that made me decide to go. He'd been outa the pen for almost seven months on that run and it was starting to tell. He'd gotten thin and his normally deep-set brown eyes looked sunk almost into the back of his skull with the dark purple shadows beneath them. His hair had grown down to his shoulders and was dull where the street dust stuck to the grease because he had nowhere to wash it. And while seeing that after two months being clean mighta convinced some people that they never wanted to live that way again, it just reminded me that if I left I'd be leaving half my life behind. A lifetime of living dirty on the streets—but it was my lifetime and all I had.

Nothing he said or did made up my mind. There was never any one deciding factor. But sitting there looking at him through the glass I caught myself trying to memorize the details of his appearance. The way his eyebrows grew together and the front tooth that was broken. The tiny mole beside his mouth that disappeared in a wrinkle when he smiled. The smooth satin drawl of his voice when he tipped his head and said "Aw Mickey—don't go" like he had a hundred times before. Only when he said it at the jail that day I snatched the words and ironed them into memory. Tone by tone. And then I realized I'd never see him again. Never hear him say them words again. I was going home.

I wrote one more story. Once I decided to leave, the hardest part became shoving away the thoughts of everything and everyone that would stay behind. And there were a thousand places and things and people I'd miss but they all massed in my mind as Darryl. He'd been the single longest presence in my life. In my mind he became the embodiment of the specifics of memory. When I cried for all things lost, the picture in my mind was of Darryl sleeping in the backseat of the Oldsmobile. Or Darryl standing at the payphone calling for dope. Or Darryl reminding me to wear shoes because it was getting to be cold again. And during the day with access to the support system I had developed, it seemed entirely doable. But at night I would tell myself I'd never be able to pull it off. Never be able to leave him and go on into that alien place where my parents lived almost a thousand miles away.

So I wrote that last story and attempted to envision a future without Darryl and all that he'd represented in the past. And I didn't start out planning to kill him off but that's how it worked out. It took 30 handwritten pages and in the end I lived and he died and once I put the last word on the last sheet of paper—it was over. He was dead and so there was no longer anything to grieve about leaving. He was already gone.

Of course I knew it wasn't true. But just like never mailing him the letters I wrote the first time he went away allowed me to pretend he wasn't gone until such time as my mind could handle the reality—writing that story helped me to bury the past until it was safe to resurrect it.

- /// -

I didn't go to jail and read *Native Son* and suddenly come to some blinding insight about how my own experience hooked up with the larger narratives of society. Didn't discover the power of voice in the words of others. Years later I read Richard Wright and found myself incredibly drawn to Bigger Thomas—to the many similarities in our experience. But in jail I wouldn't have had the knowledge base to appreciate them similarities. I didn't know anything about power structures or dominant classes and I wouldn't have had the ability to appreciate Bigger's position relative to those things anymore than I could have appreciated my own.

I went to jail and I wrote because the writing had value. It was a commodity and I could trade it for freedom. It had a purpose I could identify. In the process I discovered the myriad other purposes and value inherent in the act and I ended up writing in jail for the same reasons I wrote them letters I never mailed. I wrote to discover and I wrote to heal and I wrote to decide. I wrote to make meaning in a world that held none.

And the first thing I bought with the first paycheck I earned on the outside was a typewriter. In those first few years when I understood nothing—I wrote to make sense outa the things I observed around me. Once I got to Washington and had them thousand miles to cross if I really wanted to go back, I allowed myself to remember that Darryl was alive and I started writing long rambling letters again.

I wrote long commentaries on what it felt like to come into the straight world. I wrote about how nice it was to keep my body private and untouched. What it was like to have a home of my own with a door that I could lock. I wrote about how long it took me to stop instinctively thinking I needed to run when I saw a cop and about what it felt like to go shopping—to pay for things and carry them outa stores in bags instead of my pockets. About gaining the ability to move amongst the public without being picked off—without looking like an other. I wrote about what it felt like to pass. But I still didn't mail the letters. Not yet. I was still in a state of becoming and didn't yet know who or what I would become.

But one thing I learned early on was that people are judged by their use of language—that how they spoke could define them as trailer-park trash or it could define them as being potentially suitable for admittance to the country club. I knew that my successful reinvention would depend on how facile I could become with words. I read constantly—trying to teach myself all the things I'd never had instruction in. I learned how to imitate the precise conventional language that marked people as educated so well that when I took entrance exams at the local community college, I placed directly into freshman English without any prep classes. And for the next two years I was trained in formal academic prose until I could spit out papers on anything from the development of the atomic bomb to Henry VIII's obsession with having a son.

But I missed my language. The ungrammatical non-standard English that in its broken rhythms seemed to define the broken rhythms of our lives on the streets. And for a while I prided myself on speaking two languages. I told myself that I was socially bilingual—that it was a gift because I could walk in two worlds. That's what I told myself but I couldn't avoid knowing that the other language was useless because nobody in my here and now spoke it. So I poured it all into the letters that I kept writing to Darryl but even that was hollow because I had nowhere to mail them.

By the time I transferred to the university I was an English major thoroughly indoctrinated in how to speak and compose according to arbitrary conventions created by people who'd been dead for centuries and whose lives bore no resemblance to my own. I had masked and altered and realigned my voice until even I wasn't sure that I'd ever spoken any other way—that there'd ever been a girl who called herself Mickey Masters who wrote down the lives she'd encountered selling her body on Willow Pass Road all those years ago.

And then I found Darryl. It amazed me—while I was on the phone with the California Department of Corrections and the Parole Board—how if I spoke with authority and big words, they'd give me the information I wanted. How language was the biggest con of all. I thought of the thousand ways I coulda exploited that knowledge if I'd only had it back then. You could tell virtually any lie and if you spoke properly, people didn't pause to question. In the other language it didn't matter what I said because nobody ever looked beyond what my voice said about my social circumstances to try to make out my words.

Darryl was at San Quentin doing a parole violation when I found him and finally—almost 10 years after I wrote the first one—I mailed him letters. The past had become so distant that the first one I mailed began "you might not remember me . . ." But once we started writing and reliving memories, the lazy cadence and the singular vocabulary of the streets took over my writing.

And some of it spilled over into my schoolwork. It seemed to me like the creative part of creative writing would allow me to use my own voice but I got told that using words like "hermeneutics" and "gonna" in the same sentence just wouldn't fly. That no one would buy such a voice. The gentle elderly professor of my nonfiction class told me that he'd be more comfortable if I'd present my prose as fiction. Perhaps then such a voice would be acceptable. In real life no one would ever believe that a $20 hooker with an eighth-grade education would know what hermeneutics meant. And when I tried to tell him that he was wrong—that I had known what the word meant—he told me it didn't matter. No one would believe it. I could never tell it true because the truth was somehow too disturbing. And it wasn't the $20 blow jobs or the self-mutilation of my veins that disturbed him as much as it was the apparent conflict between language and experience. I think I understand what's at the core of that discomfort. I think I understand that to accept that the drug-addicted hooker that I was could have possessed intelligence and critical thinking skills somehow speaks to a societal failure as well as my own. And so rather than forcing the world to question its own assumptions—rather than challenging the status quo—I was told to present my life as a lie—as a piece of fiction.

I probably never woulda told the stories—never woulda written them down anywhere except in the letters—if it hadn't been for the intervention of another professor. I did an independent study with Suzanne and she liked the stories I wrote—was intrigued by my memories of Charley and Darryl. But the voice was still a problem. She called me "Miss Passive Voice" and told me to write it the way I spoke it. To whittle away the academese and the moderated tone. And I couldn't do it. I'd write the word "ain't" and it would feel like I was crossing a bigger line than it felt the first time I sold my body.

But some combination of her Bajan heritage and a childhood spent in New Jersey with a cemetery for a backyard allowed her to understand the strange nature of my experiences. We were the same age and sometimes when I looked at her I thought that I coulda been like her if I hadn't stopped along the way to be Mickey—and I trusted her.

She kept encouraging me to talk—to say it the way it happened even if I couldn't make myself write it that way. And I was sitting at my computer one night writing to Darryl and I realized staring at the words on the screen that I had maintained the other voice—the other language. I showed them letters to Suzanne and she said, "Yeah—that's it. That's a natural voice."

I struggled with it at first. I'd use an expression like "spun" or "rig" and spend the next five sentences trying to define the word in the context of the streets. And Suzanne would tell me not to—that the meaning was embedded in the story itself. Language had been my disguise through every step of my education and it was easier to spell out the details of being raped by a trick than it was to deviate from standard English.

There was less at stake with the rape. That was in the past. That happened to Mickey—not to Megan.

But I found—as I worked through the combining of the voices—that I was healing. Losing my fear of the straight world because it wasn't a con anymore. I wasn't disguising my version of the truth in words and structures designed to make it palatable to the rest of the world. As long as it had been a con, I had to live with the possibility that I might get found out. That someone might discover that although I could imitate the language of the masters I didn't understand its substructures and component parts. That the theories behind it all seemed like nothing more than job security for the academic elite and that I couldn't make heads or tails of it. It didn't matter anymore if the whole world found out that I was trailer park trash because I'd discovered something. I can say "gonna" and "hermeneutics" in the same sentence and if it doesn't sound authentic, the problem is with the way the world listens and not the way I speak.

During my second year of grad school I ran across a composition theorist who claimed while working with remedial readers and writers that, "Slowly something has been shifting in my perception: the errors—the weird commas and the missing letters, the fragments and irregular punctuation—they are ceasing to be slips of the hand and brain. They are becoming part of the stories themselves. They are the only fitting way, it seems, to render dislocation—shacks and field labor and children lost to the inner city . . ." (Rose, 214). And I realized that it isn't the broken language and the twisted syntax of the dispossessed that bothers the world. It is the stories they render. It is the fear that beneath the ain'ts and the sentence fragments are bright beautiful minds that would condemn the world for their alienation and exclusion if they ever got the chance to be heard.

Reclaiming my language—proving that being trailer park trash doesn't preclude intelligence—has gone a long way towards bringing me comfort in my new world. I've been allowed to keep my memories whole and intact and the letters have made Mickey and Megan a single being.

And yet every quarter when I look out at the 24 new faces in the freshman composition class that I teach—I remember that I spent half my life as a heroin-addicted hooker and I wonder what their parents would say if they knew. I wonder how they've been educated and if they'll notice that I talk differently than they do. That I pay no attention to speaking standard English. That my words run together and my sentences are punctuated by the kinda slang their high school English teachers woulda rapped their knuckles for using. And just for a moment I remembering standing on my corner negotiating to do blowjobs for men who coulda been their fathers and I ponder on the magic that could have delivered me from the one place to the other. The wordplay and the letters that saved us both—Mickey and Megan.

If You Are What You Eat, Then What Am I?

Geeta Kothari

"If You Are What You Eat, Then What Am I?" is Geeta Kothari's attempt to resolve her split sense of belonging: while raised largely in the United States, Kothari also identifies with her parents' Indian heritage and is continually forced to by others who see only her darker skin. Note that much of Kothari's sense of alienation from her parents revolves around her inability to make the same foods they do: not only the Indian dishes her mother makes, but also the sweet brown bread her father learns to make from an American co-worker. The essay describes how Kothari and her family adapt to American culture while also posing the questions: In adapting to a new culture, what should you keep of your own? What should you be willing to give up? How does the essay's recurring motif—namely, food—help us to answer these questions? Does food represent only ethnicity in the essay?

> To belong is to understand the tacit codes of
> the people you live with.
>
> —Michael Ignatieff, *Blood and Belonging*

-1-

The first time my mother and I open a can of tuna, I am nine years old. We stand in the doorway of the kitchen, in semidarkness, the can tilted toward daylight. I want to eat what the kids at school eat: bologna, hot dogs, salami—foods my parents find repugnant because they contain pork and meat byproducts, crushed bone and hair glued together by chemicals and fat. Although she had never been able to tolerate the smell of fish, my mother buys the tuna, hoping to satisfy my longing for American food.

Indians, of course, do not eat such things.

From *The Kenyon Review* by Geeta Kothari. Copyright © 1999 by Geeta Kothari. Reprinted by permission.

The tuna smells fishy, which surprises me because I can't remember anyone's tuna sandwich actually smelling like fish. And the tuna in those sandwiches doesn't look like this, pink and shiny, like an internal organ. In fact, this looks similar to the bad foods my mother doesn't want me to eat. She is silent, holding her face away from the can while peering into it like a half-blind bird.

"What's wrong with it?" I ask.

She has no idea. My mother does not know that the tuna everyone else's mothers made for them was tuna *salad*.

"Do you think it's botulism?"

I have never seen botulism, but I have read about it, just as I have read about but never eaten steak and kidney pie.

There is so much my parents don't know. They are not like other parents, and they disappoint me and my sister. They are supposed to help us negotiate the world outside, teach us the signs, the clues to proper behavior: what to eat and how to eat it.

We have expectations, and my parents fail to meet them, especially my mother, who works full-time. I don't understand what it means, to have a mother who works outside and inside the home; I notice only the ways in which she disappoints me. She doesn't show up for school plays. She doesn't make chocolate-frosted cupcakes for my class. At night, if I want her attention, I have to sit in the kitchen and talk to her while she cooks the evening meal, attentative to every third or fourth word I say.

We throw the tuna away. This time my mother is disappointed. I go to school with tuna eaters. I see their sandwiches, yet cannot explain the discrepancy between them and the stinking, oily fish in my mother's hand. We do not understand so many things, my mother and I.

$$- // -$$

On weekends, we eat fried chicken from Woolworth's on the back steps of my father's first-floor office in Murray Hill. The back steps face a small patch of garden—hedges, a couple of skinny trees, and gravel instead of grass. We can see the back window of the apartment my parents and I lived in until my sister was born. There, the doorman watched my mother, several months pregnant and wearing a sari, slip on the ice in front of the building.

My sister and I pretend we are in the country, where our American friends all have houses. We eat glazed doughnuts, also from Woolworth's, and french fries with ketchup.

- /// -

My mother takes a catering class and learns that Miracle Whip and mustard are healthier than mayonnaise. She learns to make egg salad with chopped celery, deviled eggs dusted with paprika, a cream cheese spread with bits of fresh ginger and watercress, chicken liver pâté, and little brown-and-white checkerboard sandwiches that we have only once. She makes chicken à la king in puff pastry shells and eggplant Parmesan. She acquires smooth wooden paddles, whose purpose is never clear, two different egg slicers, several wooden spoons, icing tubes, cookie cutters, and an electric mixer.

- /V -

I learn to make tuna salad by watching a friend. My sister never acquires a taste for it. Instead, she craves

bologna

hot dogs

bacon

sausages

and a range of unidentifiable meat products forbidden by my parents. Their restrictions are not about sacred cows, as everyone around us assumes; in a pinch, we are allowed hamburgers, though lamb burgers are preferable. A "pinch" means choosing not to draw attention to ourselves as outsiders, impolite visitors who won't eat what their host serves. But bologna is still taboo.

- V-

Things my sister refuses to eat: butter, veal, anything with jeera. The babysitter tries to feed her butter sandwiches, threatens her with them, makes her cry in fear and disgust. My mother does not disappoint her; she does not believe in forcing us to eat, in using food as a weapon. In addition to pbj, my sister likes pasta and marinara sauce, bologna and Wonder Bread (when she can get it), and fried egg sandwiches with turkey, cheese, and horseradish. Her tastes, once established, are predictable.

- VII -

When we visit our relatives in India, food prepared outside the house is carefully monitored. In the hot, sticky monsoon months in New Delhi and Bombay, we cannot eat ice cream, salad, cold food, or any fruit that can't be peeled. Definitely no meat. People die from amoebic dysentery, unexplained fevers, strange boils on their bodies. We drink boiled water only, no ice. No sweets except for jalebi, thin fried twists of dough in dripping hot sugar syrup. If we're caught outside with nothing to drink, Fanta, Limca, Thums Up (after Coca-Cola is thrown out by Mrs. Gandhi) will do. Hot tea sweetened with sugar, served with thick creamy buffalo milk, is preferable. It should be boiled, to kill the germs on the cup.

My mother talks about "back home" as a safe place, a silk cocoon frozen in time where we are sheltered by family and friends. Back home, my sister and I do not argue about food with my parents. Home is where they know all the rules. We trust them to guide us safely through the maze of city streets for which they have no map, and we trust them to feed and take care of us, the way parents should.

Finally, though, one of us will get sick, hungry for the food we see our cousins and friends eating, too thirsty to ask for a straw, too polite to insist on properly boiled water.

At my uncle's diner in New Delhi, someone hands me a plate of aloo tikki, fried potato patties filled with mashed channa dal and served with a sweet and a sour chutney. The channa, mixed with hot chilies and spices, burns my tongue and throat. I reach for my Fanta, discard the paper straw, and gulp the sweet orange soda down, huge drafts that sting rather than soothe.

When I throw up later that day (or is it the next morning, when a stomachache wakes me from deep sleep?), I cry over the frustration of being singled out, not from the pain my mother assumes I'm feeling as she holds my hair back from my face. The taste of orange lingers in my mouth, and I remember my lips touching the cold glass of the Fanta bottle.

At that moment, more than anything, I want to be like my cousins.

- VIII -

In New York, at the first Indian restaurant in our neighborhood, my father orders with confidence, and my sister and I play with the silverware until the steaming plates of lamb biryani arrive.

What is Indian food? my friends ask, their noses crinkling up.

Later, this restaurant is run out of business by the new Indo-Pak-Bangladeshi combinations up and down the street, which serve similar food. They use plastic cutlery and Styrofoam cups. They do not distinguish between North and South Indian cooking, or between Indian, Pakistani, and Bangladeshi cooking, and their customers do not care. The food is fast, cheap, and tasty. Dosa, a rice flour crepe stuffed with masala potato, appears on the same trays as chicken makhani.

Now my friends want to know, Do you eat curry at home?

One time my mother makes lamb vindaloo for guests. Like dosa, this is a South Indian dish, one that my Punjabi mother has to learn from a cookbook. For us, she cooks everyday food—yellow dal, rice, chapati, bhaji. Lentils, rice, bread, and vegetables. She has never referred to anything on our table as "curry" or "curried," but I know she has made chicken curry for guests. Vindaloo, she explains, is a curry too. I understand then that curry is a dish created for guests, outsiders, a food for people who eat in restaurants.

– *VIII* –

I have inherited brown eyes, black hair, a long nose with a crooked bridge, and soft teeth with thin enamel. I am in my twenties, moving to a city far from my parents, before it occurs to me that jeera, the spice my sister avoids, must have an English name. I have to learn that haldi = turmeric, methi = fenugreek. What to make with fenugreek, I do not know. My grandmother used to make methi roti for our breakfast, cornbread with fresh fenugreek leaves served with a lump of homemade butter. No one makes it now that she's gone, though once in a while my mother will get a craving for it and produce a facsimile ("The cornmeal here is wrong") that only highlights what she's really missing: the smells and tastes of her mother's house.

I will never make my grandmother's methi roti or even my mother's unsatisfactory imitation of it. I attempt chapati; it takes six hours, three phone calls home, and leaves me with an aching back. I have to write translations down: jeera = cumin. My memory is unreliable. But I have always known garam = hot.

– *IX* –

My mother learns how to make brownies and apple pie. My father makes only Indian food, except for loaves of heavy sweet brown bread that I eat with thin slices of American cheese and lettuce. The recipe is a secret, passed on to him by a woman at work. Years later, when he finally gives it to me, when I finally ask for it, I end up with three bricks of gluten that even the birds and my husband won't eat.

-X-

My parents send me to boarding school, outside of London. They imagine that I will overcome my shyness and find a place for myself in this all-girls' school. They have never lived in England, but as former subjects of the British Empire, they find London familiar, comfortable in a way New York—my mother's home for over twenty years by now—is not. Americans still don't know what to call us; their Indians live on reservations, not in Manhattan. Because they understand the English, my parents believe the English understand us.

I poke at my first school lunch—thin, overworked pastry in a puddle of lumpy gravy. The lumps are chewy mushrooms, maybe, or overcooked shrimp.

"What is this?" I don't want to ask, but I can't go on eating without knowing.

"Steak and kidney pie."

The girl next to me, red-haired, freckled, watches me take a bite from my plate. She has been put in charge of me, the new girl, and I follow her around all day, a foreigner at the mercy of a reluctant and angry tour guide. She is not used to explaining what is perfectly and utterly natural.

"What, you've never had steak and kidney pie? Bloody hell."

My classmates scoff, then marvel, then laugh at my ignorance. After a year, I understand what is on my plate: sausage rolls, blood pudding, Spam, roast beef in a thin, greasy gravy, all the bacon and sausage I could possibly want. My parents do not expect me to starve.

The girls at school expect conformity; it has been bred into them, through years of uniforms and strict rules about proper behavior. I am thirteen and contrary, even as I yearn for acceptance. I declare myself a vegetarian and doom myself to a diet of cauliflower cheese and baked beans on toast. The administration does not question my decision; they assume it's for vague, undefined religious reasons, although my father, the doctor, tells them it's for my health. My reasons, from this distance of many years, remain murky to me.

Perhaps I am my parents' daughter after all.

-XI-

When she is three, sitting on my cousin's lap in Bombay, my sister reaches for his plate and puts a chili in her mouth. She wants to be like the grownups, who dip green chilies in coarse salt and eat them like any other vegetable. She howls inconsolable animal pain for what must be hours. She doesn't have the vocabulary for the oily heat that stings her mouth and tongue, burns a trail through her small tender body. Only hot, sticky tears on my father's shoulder.

As an adult, she eats red chili paste, mango pickle, kimchee, foods that make my eyes water and my stomach gurgle. My tastes are milder. I order raita at Indian restaurants and ask for food that won't sear the roof of my mouth and scar the insides of my cheeks. The waiters nod, and their eyes shift—a slight once-over that indicates they don't believe me. I am Indian aren't I? My father seems to agree with them. He tells me I'm asking for the impossible, as if he believes the recipes are immutable, written in stone during the passage from India to America.

-XII-

I look around my boyfriend's freezer one day and find meat: pork chops, ground beef, chicken pieces, Italian sausage. Ham in the refrigerator, next to the homemade bolognese sauce. Tupperware filled with chili made from ground beef and pork.

He smells different from me. Foreign. Strange.

I marry him anyway.

He has inherited blue eyes that turn gray in bad weather, light brown hair, a sharp pointy nose, and excellent teeth. He learns to make chili with ground turkey and tofu, tomato sauce with red wine and portobello mushrooms, roast chicken with rosemary and slivers of garlic under the skin.

He eats steak when we are in separate cities, roast beef at his mother's house, hamburgers at work. Sometimes I smell them on his skin. I hope he doesn't notice me turning my face, a cheek instead of my lips, my nose wrinkled at the unfamiliar, musky smell.

-XIII-

And then I realize I don't want to be a person who can find Indian food only in restaurants. One day my parents will be gone and I will long for the foods of my childhood, the way they long for theirs. I prepare for this day the way people on TV prepare for the end of the world. They gather canned goods they will never eat while I stockpile recipes I cannot replicate. I am frantic, disorganized, grabbing what I can, filing scribbled notes haphazardly. I regret the tastes I've forgotten, the meals I have inhaled without a thought. I worry that I've come to this realization too late.

-*XIV*-

Who told my mother about Brie? One day we were eating Velveeta, the next day Brie, Gouda, Camembert, Port Salut, Havarti with caraway, Danish fontina, string cheese made with sheep's milk. Who opened the door to these foreigners that sit on the refrigerator shelf next to last night's dal?

Back home, there is one cheese only, which comes in a tin, looks like Bakelite, and tastes best when melted.

And how do we go from Chef Boyardee to fresh pasta and homemade sauce, made with Redpack tomatoes, crushed garlic, and dried oregano? Macaroni and cheese, made with fresh cheddar and whole milk, sprinkled with bread crumbs and paprika. Fresh eggplant and ricotta ravioli, baked with marinara sauce and fresh mozzarella.

My mother will never cook beef or pork in her kitchen, and the foods she knew in her childhood are unavailable. Because the only alternative to the supermarket, with its TV dinners and canned foods, is the gourmet Italian deli across the street, by default our meals become socially acceptable.

-*XV*-

If I really want to make myself sick, I worry that my husband will one day leave me for a meat-eater, for someone familiar who doesn't sniff him suspiciously for signs of alimentary infidelity.

-*XVI*-

Indians eat lentils. I understand this as absolute, a decree from an unidentifiable authority that watches and judges me.

So what does it mean that I cannot replicate my mother's dal? She and my father show me repeatedly, in their kitchen, in my kitchen. They coach me over the phone, buy me the best cookbooks, and finally write down their secrets. Things I'm supposed to know but don't. Recipes that should be, by now, engraved on my heart.

Living far from the comfort of people who require no explanation for what I do and who I am, I crave the foods we have shared. My mother convinces me that moong is the easiest dal to prepare, and yet it fails me every time: bland, watery, a sickly greenish yellow mush. These imperfect imitations remind me only of what I'm missing.

But I have never been fond of moong dal. At my mother's table it is the last thing I reach for. Now I worry that this antipathy toward dal signals something deeper, that somehow I am not my parents' daughter, not Indian, and because I cannot bear the touch and smell of raw meat, though I can eat it cooked (charred, dry, and overdone), I am not American either.

I worry about a lifetime purgatory in Indian restaurants where I will complain that all the food looks and tastes the same because they've used the same masala.

-XVII-

About the tuna and her attempts to feed us, my mother laughs. She says, "You were never fussy. You ate everything I made and never complained."

My mother is at the stove, wearing only her blouse and petticoat, her sari carefully folded and hung in the closet. She does not believe a girl's place is in the kitchen, but she expects me to know that too much hing can ruin a meal, to know without being told, without having to ask or write it down. Hing = asafetida.

She remembers the catering class. "Oh, that class. You know, I had to give it up when we got to lobster. I just couldn't stand the way it looked."

She says this apologetically, as if she has deprived us, as if she suspects that having a mother who could feed us lobster would have changed the course of our lives.

Intellectually, she understands that only certain people regularly eat lobster, people with money or those who live in Maine, or both. In her catering class there were people without jobs for whom preparing lobster was a part of their professional training as caterers. Like us, they wouldn't be eating lobster at home. For my mother, however, lobster was just another American food, like tuna—different, strange, not natural yet somehow essential to belonging.

I learned how to prepare and eat lobster from the same girl who taught me tuna salad. I ate bacon at her house too. And one day this girl, with her houses in the country and Martha's Vineyard, asked me how my uncle was going to pick me up from the airport in Bombay. In 1973, she was surprised to hear that he used a car, not an elephant. At home, my parents and I laughed, and though I never knew for sure if she was making fun of me, I still wanted her friendship.

My parents were afraid my sister and I would learn to despise the foods they loved, replace them with bologna and bacon and lose our taste for masala. For my mother, giving up her disgust of lobster, with its hard exterior and foreign smell, would mean renouncing some essential difference. It would mean becoming, decidedly, definitely, American—unafraid of meat in all its forms, able to consume large quantities of protein at any given meal. My willingness to toss a living being into boiling water and then get past its ugly appearance to the rich meat inside must mean to my mother that I am somehow someone she is not.

But I haven't eaten lobster in years. In my kitchen cupboards, there is a thirteen-pound bag of basmati rice, jars of lime pickle, mango pickle, and ghee, cans of tuna and anchovies, canned soups, coconut milk, and tomatoes, rice noodles, several kinds of pasta, dried mushrooms, and unlabeled bottles of spices: haldi, jeera, hing. When my husband tries to help me cook, he cannot identify all the spices. He gets confused when I forget their English names and remarks that my expectations of him are unreasonable.

I am my parents' daughter. Like them, I expect knowledge to pass from me to my husband without one word of explanation or translation. I want him to know what I know, see what I see, without having to tell him exactly what it is. I want to believe that recipes never change.

"Complete Freedom of Movement": Video Games as Gendered Play Spaces

Henry Jenkins

A great distance lies between Pac Man and the often-violent directives of today's video games. It is not unusual for today's players to be given commands such as: "Secure your victory and force your opponent into a river barge at 200 miles per hour." Yet Henry Jenkins suggests that video games serve a vital role in the development of today's urban adolescents; he goes as far as to say, "Perhaps my son finds in his video games what I found in the woods behind my school, on my bike whizzing down the hills . . ." Although Jenkins acknowledges and even applauds how the playing of video games fills a void in children's development, he contends that the current design of video games perpetuates gender inequalities. How do pop culture and the media affect the way we understand gender? In what other ways do you think our culture teaches us to act gender specifically or gender appropriately?

A Tale of Two Childhoods

Sometimes, I feel nostalgic for the spaces of my boyhood, growing up in suburban Atlanta in the 1960s. My big grassy front yard sloped sharply downward into a ditch where we could float boats on a rainy day. Beyond, there was a pine forest where my brother and I could toss pine cones like grenades or snap sticks together like swords. In the backyard, there was a patch of grass where we could wrestle or play kickball and a treehouse, which sometimes bore a pirate flag and at other times, the Stars and Bars of the Confederacy. Out beyond our own yard, there was a bamboo forest where we could play Tarzan, and vacant lots, construction sites, sloping streets, and a neighboring farm (the last vestige of a rural area turned suburban).

Jenkins, Henry. Excerpt from "Complete Freedom of Movement: Video Games as Gendered Play Spaces." *From Barbie to Mortal Kombat: Gender and Computer Games.* Ed. Justine Cassell and Henry Jenkins. Cambridge, MA: MIT Press, 1998: 262–297.

Between my house and the school, there was another forest, which, for the full length of my youth, remained undeveloped. A friend and I would survey this land, claiming it for our imaginary kingdoms of Jungleloca and Freedonia. We felt a proprietorship over that space, even though others used it for schoolyard fisticuffs, smoking cigarettes, or playing kissing games. When we were there, we rarely encountered adults, though when we did, it usually spelled trouble. We would come home from these secret places, covered with Georgia red mud.

Of course, we spent many afternoons at home, watching old horror movies or action-adventure series reruns, and our mothers would fuss at us to go outside. Often, something we had seen on television would inspire our play, stalking through the woods like Lon Chaney Jr.'s Wolfman or "socking" and "powing" each other under the influence of *Batman*.

Today, each time I visit my parents, I am shocked to see that most of those "sacred" places are now occupied by concrete, bricks, or asphalt. They managed to get a whole subdivision out of Jungleloca and Freedonia!

My son, Henry, now 16, has never had a backyard.

He has grown up in various apartment complexes, surrounded by asphalt parking lots with, perhaps, a small grass buffer from the street. Children were prohibited by apartment policy from playing on the grass or from racing their tricycles in the basements or from doing much of anything else that might make noise, annoy the non-childbearing population, cause damage to the facilities, or put themselves at risk. There was, usually, a city park some blocks away that we could go to on outings a few times a week and where we could watch him play. Henry could claim no physical space as his own, except his toy-strewn room, and he rarely got outside earshot. Once or twice, when I became exasperated by my son's constant presence around the house, I would forget all this and tell him he should go outside and play. He would look at me with confusion and ask, "Where?"

But, he did have video games that took him across lakes of fire, through cities in the clouds, along dark and gloomy back streets, and into dazzling neon-lit Asian marketplaces. Video games constitute virtual play spaces which allow home-bound children like my son to extend their reach, to explore, manipulate, and interact with a more diverse range of imaginary places than constitute the often drab, predictable, and overly-familiar spaces of their everyday lives. Keith Feinstein (1997), President of the Video Game Conservatory, argues that video games preserve many aspects of traditional play spaces and culture that motivate children to:

> learn about the environment that they find themselves living in. Video games present the opportunity to explore and discover, as well as to combat

others of comparable skill (whether they be human or electronic) and to struggle with them in a form that is similar to children wrestling, or scrambling for the same ball—they are nearly matched, they aren't going to really do much damage, yet it feels like an all-important fight for that child at that given moment. "Space Invaders" gives us visceral thrill and poses mental/physical challenges similar to a schoolyard game of dodge-ball (or any of the hundred of related kids games). Video games play with us, a never tiring playmate.

Feinstein's comment embraces some classical conceptions of play (such as spacial exploration and identity formation), suggesting that video game play isn't fundamentally different from backyard play. To facilitate such immersive play, to achieve an appropriate level of "holding power" that enables children to transcend their immediate environments, video game spaces require concreteness and vividness. The push in the video game industry for more than a decade has been toward the development of more graphically complex, more visually engaging, more three-dimensionally rendered spaces, and toward quicker, more sophisticated, more flexible interactions with those spaces. Video games tempt the player to play longer, putting more and more quarters into the arcade machine (or providing "play value" for those who've bought the game) by unveiling ever more spectacular "microworlds," the revelation of a new level the reward for having survived and mastered the previous environment (Fuller and Jenkins 1995).

Video games advertise themselves as taking us places very different from where we live:

Say hello to life in the fast lane. "Sonic R" for Sega Saturn is a full-on, pedal-to-the-metal hi-speed dash through five 3D courses, each rendered in full 360 degree panoramas. . . . You'll be flossing bug guts out of your teeth for weeks. ("Sonic R" 1998)

Take a dip in these sub-infested waters for a spot of nuclear fishin'. . . . Don't worry. You'll know you're in too deep when the water pressure caves your head in. ("Critical Depth" 1998)

Hack your way through a savage world or head straight for the arena. . . . Complete freedom of movement. ("Die By the Sword" 1998)

Strap in and throttle up as you whip through the most realistic and immersive powerboat racing game ever made. Jump over roadways, and through passing convoys, or speed between oil tankers, before they close off the track and turn your boat to splinters. Find a shortcut and take the lead, or better yet, secure your victory and force your opponent into a river barge at 200 miles per hour. ("VR Sports" 1998)

Who wouldn't want to trade in the confinement of your room for the immersion promised by today's video games? Watch children playing these games, their bodies bobbing and swaying to the on-screen action, and it's clear they are *there*—in the fantasy world, battling it out with the orcs and globlins, pushing their airplanes past the sound barrier, or splashing their way through the waves in their speed boats. Perhaps my son finds in his video games what I found in the woods behind the school, on my bike whizzing down the hills of the suburban back streets, or settled into my treehouse during a thunder storm with a good adventure novel—intensity of experience, escape from adult regulation; in short, "complete freedom of movement."

This essay will offer a cultural geography of video game spaces, one which uses traditional children's play and children's literature as points of comparison to the digital worlds contemporary children inhabit. Specifically, I examine the "fit" between video games and traditional boy culture and review several different models for creating virtual play spaces for girls. So much of the research on gender and games takes boy's fascination with these games as a given. As we attempt to offer video games for girls, we need to better understand what draws boys to video games and whether our daughters should feel that same attraction.

Video games are often blamed for the listlessness or hyperactivity of our children, yet sociologists find these same behavioral problems occurring among all children raised in highly restrictive and confined physical environmentals (Booth and Johnson 1975; van Staden 1984). Social reformers sometimes speak of children choosing to play video games rather than playing outside, when, in many cases, no such choice is available. More and more Americans live in urban or semi-urban neighborhoods. Fewer of us own our homes and more of us live in apartment complexes. Fewer adults have chosen to have children and our society has become increasingly hostile to the presence of children. In many places, "no children" policies severely restrict where parents can live. Parents, for a variety of reasons, are frightened to have their children on the streets, and place them under "protective custody." "Latch key" children return from school and lock themselves in their apartments (Kincheloe 1997).

In the nineteenth century, children living along the frontier or on America's farms enjoyed free range over a space of ten square miles or more. Elliot West (1992) describes boys of nine or ten going camping alone for days on end, returning when they were needed to do chores around the house. The early twentieth century saw the development of urban playgrounds in the midst of city streets, responding to a growing sense of children's diminishing access to space and an increased awareness of issues of child welfare (Cavallo 1991), but autobiographies of the period stress the availability of vacant lots and back alleys that children could claim as their own play environments. Sociologists writing about the suburban America of my boyhood found that children enjoyed a play terrain of one to five blocks of spacious backyards and relatively safe subdivision streets (Hart 1979). Today, at the end of the twentieth century, many of our children have access to the one to five rooms inside their apartments. Video game technologies expand the space of their imagination.

Let me be clear—I am not arguing that video games are as good for kids as the physical spaces of backyard play culture. As a father, I wish that my son could come home covered in mud or with scraped knees rather than carpet burns. However, we sometimes blame video games for problems they do not cause—perhaps because of our own discomfort with these technologies, which were not part of our childhood. When politicians like Senator Joseph Lieberman, Democrat of Connecticut, target video game violence, perhaps it is to distract attention from the material conditions that give rise to a culture of domestic violence, the economic policies that make it harder for most of us to own homes, and the development practices that pave over the old grasslands and forests. Video games did not make backyard play spaces disappear; rather, they offer children some way to respond to domestic confinement.

Moving Beyond "Home Base": Why Physical Spaces Matter

The psychological and social functions of playing outside are as significant as the impact of "sunshine and good exercise" upon our physical well-being. Roger Hart's *Children's Experience of Place* (1979), for example, stresses the importance of children's manipulations and explorations of their physical environment to their development of self-confidence and autonomy. Our physical surroundings are "relatively simple and relatively stable" compared to the overwhelming complex and ever shifting" relations between people, and thus, they form core resources for identity formation. The unstructured spaces, the playforts and treehouses, children create for themselves in the cracks, gullies, back alleys, and vacant lots of the adult world constitute what Robin C. Moore (1986) calls "childhood's domain" or William Van Vliet (1983) has labeled as a "fourth environment," outside the adult-structured spaces of home, schools, and playground. These informal, often temporary play spaces are where free and unstructured play occurs. Such spaces surface most often on the lists children make of "special" or "important" places in their lives. M. H. Matthews (1992) stresses the "topophilia," the heightened sense of belonging and ownership, children develop as they map their fantasies of empowerment and escape onto their neighborhoods. Frederick Donaldson (1970) proposed two different classifications of these spaces—home base, the world which is secure and familiar, and home region, an area undergoing active exploration, a space under the process of being colonized by the child. Moore (1986) writes:

> One of the clearest expressions of the benefits of continuity in the urban landscape was the way in which children used it as an outdoor gymnasium. As I walked along a Mill Hill street with Paul, he continually went darting ahead, leapfrogging over concrete bollards, hopping between paving slabs, balancing along the curbside. In each study area, certain kids seemed to dance through their surroundings on the look out for microfeatures with which to test their bodies. . . . Not only did he [David, another boy in the study], like Paul, jump over gaps between things, go "tightrope walking" along the tops of walls, leapfrogging objects on sight, but at one point he went "mountain climbing" up a roughly built, nine-foot wall that had many serendipitously placed toe and handholds. (p. 72)

These discoveries arise from children's active exploration of and spontaneous engagement with their physical surroundings. Children in the same neighborhoods may have fundamentally different relations to the spaces they share, cutting their own paths, giving their own names to features of their environment. These spaces are far more important, many researchers conclude, than playgrounds, which can only be used in sanctioned ways, since the "wild spaces" allow many more opportunities for children to modify their physical environment.

Children's access to spaces are structured around gender differences. Observing the use of space within 1970s suburban America, Hart (1979) found that boys enjoyed far greater mobility and range than girls of the same age and class background. In the course of an afternoon's play, a typical ten-to-twelve-year-old boy might travel a distance of 2,452 yards, while the average ten-to-twelve-year-old girl might only travel 959 yards. For the most part, girls expanded their geographic range only to take on responsibilities and perform chores for the family, while parents often turned a blind eye to a boy's movements into prohibited spaces. The boys Hart (1979) observed were more likely to move beyond their homes in search of "rivers, forts and treehouses, woods, ballfields, hills, lawns, sliding places, and climbing trees," while girls were more likely to seek commercially developed spaces, such as stores or shopping malls. Girls were less likely than boys to physically alter their play environment, to dam creeks or build forts. Such gender differences in mobility, access, and control over physical space increased as children grew older. As C. Ward (1977) notes:

> Whenever we discuss the part the environment plays in the lives of children, we are really talking about boys. As a stereotype, the child in the city is a boy. Girls are far less visible. . . . The reader can verify this by standing in a city street at any time of day and counting the children seen. The majority will be boys. (p. 152)

One study found that parents were more likely to describe boys as being "outdoors" children and girls as "indoor" children (Newson and Newson 1976). Another 1975 study (Rheingold and Cook), which inventoried the contents of children's bedrooms, found boys more likely to possess a range of vehicles and sports equipment designed to encourage outside play, while the girls rooms were stocked with dolls, doll clothes, and other domestic objects. Parents of girls were more likely to express worries about the dangers their children face on the streets and to structure girls' time for productive household activities or educational play (Matthews 1992).

Historically, girl culture formed under closer maternal supervision and girls' toys were designed to foster female-specific skills and competencies and prepare girls for their future domestic responsibilities as wives and mothers. The doll's central place in girlhood reflected maternal desires to encourage daughters to sew; the doll's china heads and hands fostered delicate gestures and movements (Formanek-Brunnel 1998). However, these skills were not acquired without some resistance. Nineteenth-century girls were apparently as willing as today's girls to mistreat their dolls, by cutting their hair or by driving nails into their bodies.

If cultural geographers are right when they argue that children's ability to explore and modify their environments plays a large role in their growing sense of mastery, freedom, and self-confidence, then the restrictions placed on girls' play have a crippling effect. Conversely, this research would suggest that children's declining access to play space would have a more dramatic impact on the culture of young boys, since girls already faced domestic confinement.

> Clods were handy and the air was full of them in a twinkling. They raged around Sid like a hail storm; and before Aunt Polly could collect her surprised faculties and sally to the rescue, six or seven clods had taken personal effect, and Tom was over the fence and gone. . . . He presently got safely beyond the reach of capture and punishment, and hasted toward the

public square of the village, where two "military" companies of boys had met for conflict, according to previous appointment. Tom was the general of one of these armies, Joe Harper (a bosom friend) general of the other. . . . Tom's army won a great victory, after a long and hard-fought battle. Then the dead were counted, prisoners exchanged, the terms of the next disagreement agreed upon, and the day for the necessary battle appointed; after which the armies fell into line and marched away, and Tom turned homeward alone. (pp. 19–20)

—Mark Twain, *Adventures of Tom Sawyer* (1876)

What E. Anthony Rotundo (1994) calls "boy culture" resulted from the growing separation of the male public sphere and the female private sphere in the wake of the industrial revolution. Boys were cut off from the work life of their fathers and left under the care of their mothers. According to Rotundo, boys escaped from the home into the outdoor play space, freeing them to participate in a semi-autonomous "boy culture" that cast itself in opposition to maternal culture:

Where women's sphere offered kindness, morality, nurture and a gentle spirit, the boys' world countered with energy, self-assertion, noise, and a frequent resort to violence. The physical explosiveness and the willingness to inflict pain contrasted so sharply with the values of the home that they suggest a dialogue in actions between the values of the two spheres—as if a boy's aggressive impulses, so relentlessly opposed at home, sought extreme forms of release outside it; then, with stricken consciences, the boys came home for further lessons in self-restraint. (p. 37)

The boys transgressed maternal prohibitions to prove they weren't "mama's boys." Rotundo argues that this break with the mother was a necessary step toward autonomous manhood. One of the many tragedies of our gendered division of labor may be the ways that it links misogyny—an aggressive fighting back against the mother—with the process of developing self-reliance. Contrary to the Freudian concept of the oedipal complex (which focuses on boys' struggles with their all-powerful fathers as the site of identity formation), becoming an adult male often means struggling with (and in many cases, actively repudiating) maternal culture. Fathers, on the other hand, offered little guidance to their sons, who, Rotundo argues, acquired masculine skills and values from other boys. By contrast, girls' play culture was often "interdependent" with the realm of their mother's domestic activities, insuring a smoother transition into anticipated adult roles, but allowing less autonomy.

What happens when the physical spaces of nineteenth-century boy culture are displaced by the virtual spaces of contemporary video games? Cultural geographers have long argued that television is a poor substitute for backyard play, despite its potential to present children with a greater diversity of spaces than can be found in their immediate surroundings, precisely because it is a spectatorial rather than a participatory medium. Moore (1986), however, leaves open the prospect that a more interactive digital medium might serve *some* of the same developmental functions as backyard play. A child playing a video game, searching for the path around obstacles, or looking for an advantage over imaginary opponents, engages in many of the same "mapping" activities as children searching for affordances in their real-world environments. Rotundo's core claims about nineteenth-century boy culture hold true for the "video game culture" of contemporary boyhood. This congruence may help us to account for the enormous popularity of these games with young boys. This fit should not be surprising when we consider that the current game genres reflect intuitive choices by men who grew up in the 1960s and 1970s, when suburban boy culture still reigned.

The following are some points of comparison between traditional boy culture and contemporary game culture:

1. Nineteenth-century boy culture was characterized by its independence from the realm of both mothers and fathers. It was a space where boys could develop autonomy and self-confidence.

Video game culture also carves out a cultural realm for modern-day children separate from the space of their parents. They often play the games in their rooms and guard their space against parental intrusion. Parents often express a distaste for the games' pulpy plots and lurid images. As writers like Jon Katz (1997) and Don Tapscott (1997) note, children's relative comfort with digital media is itself a generational marker, with adults often unable to comprehend the movement and colored shapes of the video screen. Here, however, the loss of spacial mobility is acutely felt—the "bookworm," the boy who spent all of his time in his room reading, had a "mama's boy" reputation in the old boy culture. Modern-day boys have had to accommodate their domestic confinement with their definitions of masculinity, perhaps accounting, in part, for the hypermasculine and hyperviolent content of the games themselves. The game player has a fundamentally different image than the "bookworm."

2. In nineteenth-century boy culture, youngsters gained recognition from their peers for their daring, often proven through stunts (such as swinging

on vines, climbing trees, or leaping from rocks as they crossed streams) or through pranks (such as stealing apples or doing mischief aimed at adults).

In video game culture, children gain recognition for their daring as demonstrated in the virtual worlds of the game, overcoming obstacles, beating bosses, and mastering levels. Nineteenth-century boys' trespasses on neighbors' property or confrontations with hostile shopkeepers are mirrored by the visual vocabulary of the video games, which often pit smaller protagonists against the might and menace of much larger rivals. Much as cultural geographers describe the boys' physical movements beyond their home bases into developing home territories, the video games allow boys to gradually develop their mastery over the entire digital terrain, securing their future access to spaces by passing goal posts or finding warp zones.

3.   The central virtues of the nineteenth-century boy culture were mastery and self-control. The boys set tasks and goals for themselves that required discipline in order to complete. Through this process of setting and meeting challenges, they acquired the virtues of manhood.

The central virtues of video game culture are mastery (over the technical skills required by the games) and self-control (manual dexterity). Putting in the long hours of repetition and failure necessary to master a game also requires discipline and the ability to meet and surpass self-imposed goals. Most contemporary video games are ruthlessly goal-driven. Boys will often play the games, struggling to master a challenging level, well past the point of physical and emotional exhaustion. Children are not so much "addicted" to video games as they are unwilling to quit before they have met their goals, and the games seem to always set new goal posts, inviting us to best "just one more level." One of the limitations of the contemporary video game is that it provides only prestructured forms of interactivity, and in that sense, video games are more like playgrounds and city parks rather than wild spaces. For the most part, video game players can only exploit built-in affordances and preprogrammed pathways. "Secret codes," "Easter Eggs," and "warp zones" function in digital space like secret paths do in physical space and are eagerly sought by gamers who want to go places and see things others can't find.

4.   The nineteenth-century boy culture was hierarchical, with a member's status dependent on competitive activity, direct confrontation, and physical challenges. The boy fought for a place in the gang's inner circle, hoping to win admiration and respect.

Video game culture can also be hierarchical, with a member gaining status by being able to complete a game or log a big score. Video game masters move from house to house to demonstrate their technical competency and to teach others how to "beat" particularly challenging levels. The video arcade becomes a proving ground for contemporary masculinity, while many games are designed for the arcade, demanding a constant turnover of coins for play and intensifying the action into roughly two-minute increments. Often, single-player games generate digital rivals who may challenge players to beat their speeds or battle them for dominance.

5. Nineteenth-century boy culture was sometimes brutally violent and physically aggressive; children hurt each other or got hurt trying to prove their mastery and daring.

Video game culture displaces this physical violence into a symbolic realm. Rather than beating each other up behind the school, boys combat imaginary characters, finding a potentially safer outlet for their aggressive feelings. We forget how violent previous boy culture was. Rotundo (1994) writes:

> The prevailing ethos of the boys' world not only supported the expression of impulses such as dominance and aggression (which had evident social uses), but also allowed the release of hostile, violent feelings (whose social uses were less evident). By allowing free passage to so many angry or destructive emotions, boy culture sanctioned a good deal of intentional cruelty, like the physical torture of animals and the emotional violence of bullying. . . . If at times boys acted like a hostile pack of wolves that preyed on its own kind as well as on other species, they behaved at other times like a litter of playful pups who enjoy romping, wrestling and testing new skills. (p. 45)

Even feelings of fondness and friendship were expressed through physical means, including greeting each other with showers of brickbats and offal. Such a culture is as violent as the world depicted in contemporary video games, which have the virtue of allowing growing boys to express their aggression and rambunctiousness through indirect, rather than direct, means.

6. Nineteenth-century boy culture expressed itself through scatological humor. Such bodily images (of sweat, spit, snot, shit, and blood) reflected the boys' growing awareness of their bodies and signified their rejection of maternal constraints.

Video game culture has often been criticized for its dependence upon similar kinds of scatological images, with the blood and gore of games like "Mortal Kombat" (with its "end moves" of dismemberment and decapitation), providing some of the most oft-cited evidence in campaigns to reform video game content (Kinder 1996). Arguably, these images serve the same functions for modern boys as for their nineteenth-century counterparts—allowing an exploration of what it's like to live in our bodies and an expression of distance from maternal regulations. Like the earlier "boy culture," this scatological imagery sometimes assumes overtly misogynistic form, directed against women as a civilizing or controlling force, staged toward women's bodies as a site of physical difference and as the objects of desire or distaste. Some early games, such as "Super Metroid," rewarded player competence by forcing female characters to strip down to their underwear if the boys beat a certain score.

7.   Nineteenth-century boy culture depended on various forms of role-playing, often imitating the activities of adult males. Rotundo (1994) notes the popularity of games of settlers and Indians during an age when the frontier had only recently been closed, casting boys sometimes as their settler ancestors and other times as "savages." Such play mapped the competitive and combative boy-culture ethos onto the adult realm, thus exaggerating the place of warfare in adult male lives. Through such play, children tested alternative social roles, examined adult ideologies, and developed a firmer sense of their own abilities and identities.

Video game culture depends heavily on fantasy role-playing, with different genres of games allowing children to imagine themselves in alternative social roles or situations. Most games, however, provide images of heroic action more appropriate for the rugged individualism of nineteenth-century American culture than for the contemporary information-and-service economy. Boys play at being crime fighters, race-car drivers, and fighter pilots, not at holding down desk jobs. This gap between the excitement of boyhood play and the alienation of adult labor may explain why video game imagery seems so hyperbolic from an adult vantage point. Rotundo (1994) notes, however, that there was always some gap between boys and adult males:

> Boy culture emphasized exuberant spontaneity; it allowed free rein to aggressive impulses and reveled in physical prowess and assertion. Boy culture was a world of play, a social space where one evaded the duties and restrictions of adult society. . . . Men were quiet and sober, for theirs was a life of serious business. They had families to support, reputations to earn, responsibilities to meet. Their world was based on work, not play and their survival in it depended on patient planning not spontaneous impulse. To prosper, then, a man had to delay gratification and restrain desire. Of course, he also needed to be aggressive and competitive, and he needed an instinct for self-advancement. But he had to channel those assertive impulses in ways that were suitable to the abstract battles and complex issues of middle-class men's work. (p. 55)

Today, the boys are using the same technologies as their fathers, even if they are using them to pursue different fantasies.

8. In nineteenth-century boy culture, play activities were seen as opportunities for social interactions and bonding. Boys formed strong ties that were the basis for adult affiliations, for participation in men's civic clubs and fraternities, and for business partnerships.

The track record of contemporary video game culture providing a basis for similar social networking is more mixed. In some cases, the games constitute both play space and playmates, reflecting the physical isolation of contemporary children from each other. In other cases, the games provide the basis for social interactions at home, at school, and at the video arcades. Children talk about the games together, over the telephone or, now, over the Internet, as well as in person, on the playground, or at the school cafeteria. Boys compare notes, map strategies, share tips, and show off their skills, and this exchange of video game lore provides the basis for more complex social relations. Again, video games don't isolate children, but they fail, at the present time, to provide the technological basis for overcoming other social and cultural factors, such as working parents who are unable to bring children to each other's houses and enlarged school districts that make it harder to get together.

Far from a "corruption" of the culture of childhood, video games show strong continuities with the boyhood play fondly remembered by previous generations. There is a significant difference, however. The nineteenth-century "boy culture" enjoyed such freedom and autonomy precisely because the activities were staged within a larger expanse of space, because boys could occupy an environment largely unsupervised by adults. Nineteenth-century boys sought indirect means of breaking with their mothers by escaping to spaces that were outside their control and engaging in secret activities the boys knew would have met parental disapproval. The mothers, on the other hand, rarely had to confront the nature of this "boy culture" and often didn't even know that it existed. The video game culture, on the other hand, occurs in plain sight, in the middle of the family living room, or at best, in the children's rooms. Mothers come face to face with the messy process by which western culture turns boys into men. The games and their content become the focus of open antagonism and the subject of tremendous guilt and anxiety. Sega's Lee McEnany (1998) acknowledges that the overwhelming majority of complaints game companies receive come from mothers, and Ellen Seiter (1996) has noted that this statistic reflects the increased pressure placed on mothers to supervise and police children's relations to popular culture. Current attempts to police video game content reflect a long history of attempts to shape and regulate children's play culture, starting with the playground movements of progressive America and the organization of social groups for boys, such as the Boy Scouts and Little League, which tempered the more rough-and-tumble qualities of boy culture and channeled them into games, sports, and other adult-approved pastimes.

Many of us might wish to foster a boy culture that allowed the expression of affection or the display of empowerment through nonviolent channels, that disentangled the development of personal autonomy from the fostering of misogyny, and that encouraged boys to develop a more nurturing, less domineering attitude to their social and natural environments. These goals are worth pursuing. We can't simply adopt a "boys will be boys" attitude. However, one wonders about the consequences of such a policing action in a world that no longer offers "wild" outdoor spaces as a safety valve for boys to escape parental control. Perhaps our sons—and daughters—need an unpoliced space for social experimentation, a space where they can vent their frustrations and imagine alternative adult roles free of inhibiting parental pressure. The problem, of course, is that unlike the nineteenth-century boy culture, the video game culture is not a world children construct for themselves but rather a world made by adult companies and sold to children. There is no way that we can escape adult intervention in shaping children's play environments as long as those environments are built and sold rather than discovered and appropriated. As parents, we are thus implicated in our children's choice of play environments, whether we wish to be or not, and we need to be conducting a dialogue with our children about the qualities and values exhibited by these game worlds. One model would be for adults and children to collaborate in the design and development of video game spaces, in the process developing a conversation about the nature and meanings of the worlds being produced. Another approach (Cassell, 1998) would be to create tools to allow children to construct their own play spaces and then give them the freedom to do what they want. Right now, parents are rightly apprehensive about a play space that is outside their own control and that is shaped according to adult specifications but without their direct input.

One of the most disturbing aspects of the boy culture is its gender segregation. The nineteenth-century boy culture played an essential role in preparing boys for entry into their future professional roles and responsibilities; some of that same training has also become essential for girls at a time when more and more women are working outside the home. The motivating force behind the "girls' game" movement is the idea that girls, no less than boys, need computers at an early age if they are going to be adequately prepared to get "good jobs for good wages" (Jenkins and Cassell, 1998). Characteristically, the girls' game movement has involved the transposition of traditional feminine play cultures into the digital realm. However, in doing so, we run the risk of preserving, rather than transforming, those aspects of traditional "girl culture" which kept women, restricted to the domestic sphere while denying them the spacial exploration and mastery associated with boy culture. Girls, no less than boys, need to develop an exploratory mindset, a habit of seeking unknown spaces as opposed to settling placidly into the domestic sphere.

Gendered Games/Gendered Books: Toward a Cultural Geography of Imaginary Spaces

These debates about gendered play and commercial entertainment are not new, repeating (and in a curious way, reversing) the emergence of a gender-specific set of literary genres for children in the nineteenth century. As Elizabeth Segel (1986) notes, the earliest writers of children's books were mostly women, who saw the genre as "the exercise of feminine moral 'influence'" upon children's developing minds, and who created a literature that was undifferentiated according to gender but "domestic in setting, heavily didactic and morally or spiritually uplifting" (p. 171). In other words, the earliest children's books were "girls' books" in everything but name, which isn't surprising at a time when novel reading was still heavily associated with women. The "boys' book" emerged, in the mid-nineteenth century, as "men of action," industrialists and adventurers, wrote fictions intended to counter boys' restlessness and apathy towards traditional children's literature. The introduction of boys' books reflected a desire to get boys to read. Boy-book fantasies of action and adventure reflected the qualities of their pre existing play culture, fantasies centering around "the escape from domesticity and from the female domination of the domestic world" (Segel 1986, p. 171). If the girls' game movement has involved the rethinking of video game genres (which initially emerged in a male-dominated space) in order to make digital media more attractive to girls (and thus to encourage the development of computational skills), the boys' book movement sought to remake reading (which initially emerged in a female-dominated space) to respond to male needs (and thus to encourage literacy). In both cases, the goal seems to have been to construct fantasies that reflect the gender-specific nature of children's play and thus to motivate those left out of the desirable cultural practices to get more involved. In this next section, I will consider the continuity that exists between gender/genre configurations in children's literature and in the digital games marketplace.

Adventure Islands: Boy Space

Alex looked around him. There was no place to seek cover. He was too weak to run, even if there was. His gaze returned to the stallion, fascinated by a creature so wild and so near. Here was the wildest of all wild animals—he had fought for everything he had ever needed, for food, for leadership, for life itself; it was his nature to kill or be killed. The horse reared again; then he snorted and plunged straight for the boy. (p. 27)

—Walter Farley, *The Black Stallion* (1941)

The space of the boy book is the space of adventure, risk-taking and danger, of a wild and untamed nature that must be mastered if one is to survive. The space of the boy book offers "no place to seek cover," and thus encourages fight-or-flight responses. In some cases, most notably in the works of Mark Twain, the boy books represented a nostalgic documentation of nineteenth-century "boy culture," its spaces, its activities, and its values. In other cases, as in the succession of pulp adventure stories that form the background of the boys' game genres, the narratives offered us a larger-than-life enactment of those values, staged in exotic rather than the backyard spaces, involving broader movements through space and amplifying horseplay and risk-taking into scenarios of actual combat and conquest. Writers of boys' books found an easy fit between the ideologies of American "manifest destiny" and British colonialism and the adventure stories boys preferred to read, which often took the form of quests, journeys, or adventures into untamed and uncharted regions of the world—into the frontier of the American west (or in the twentieth century, the "final frontier" of Mars and beyond), into the exotic realms of Africa, Asia, and South America. The protagonists were boys or boy-like adult males, who had none of the professional responsibilities and domestic commitments associated with adults. The heroes sought adventure by running away from home to join the circus *(Toby Tyler),* to sign up as cabin boy on a ship *(Treasure Island),* or to seek freedom by rafting down the river *(Huckleberry Finn).* They confronted a hostile and untamed environment (as when *The Jungle Book's* Mowgli must battle "tooth and claw" with the tiger, Sheer Khan, or as when Jack London's protagonists faced the frozen wind of the Yukon). They were shipwrecked on islands, explored caves, searched for buried treasure, plunged harpoons into slick-skinned whales, or set out alone across the desert, the bush, or the jungle. They survived through their wits, their physical mastery, and their ability to use violent force. Each chapter offered a sensational set piece—an ambush by wild Indians, an encounter with a coiled cobra, a landslide, a stampede, or a sea battle—that placed the protagonist at risk and tested his skills and courage. The persistent images of blood-and-guts combat and cliff-hanging risks compelled boys to keep reading, making their blood race with promises of thrills and more thrills. This rapid pace allowed little room for moral and emotional introspection. In turn, such stories provided fantasies that boys could enact upon their own environments. Rotundo (1994) describes nineteenth-century boys playing pirates, settlers and Indians, or Roman warriors, roles drawn from boys' books.

The conventions of the nineteenth- and early-twentieth-century boys' adventure story provided the basis for the current video game genres. The most successful console game series, such as Capcom's "Mega Man" or Nintendo's "Super Mario Brothers," games, combine the iconography of multiple boys' book genres. Their protagonists struggle across an astonishingly eclectic range of landscapes—deserts, frozen wastelands, tropical rain forests, urban undergrounds—and encounter resistance from strange hybrids (who manage to be animal, machine, and savage all rolled into one). The scroll games have built into them the constant construction of frontiers— home regions—that the boy player must struggle to master and push beyond, moving deeper and deeper into uncharted space. Action is relentless. The protagonist shoots fireballs, ducks and charges, slugs it out, rolls, jumps, and dashes across the treacherous terrain, never certain what lurks around the corner. If you stand still, you die. Everything you encounter is potentially hostile, so shoot to kill. Errors in judgement result in the character's death and require starting all over again. Each screen overflows with dangers; each landscape is riddled with pitfalls and booby traps. One screen may require you to leap from precipice to precipice, barely missing falling into the deep chasms below. Another may require you to swing by vines across the treetops, or spelunk through an underground passageway, all the while fighting it out with the alien hordes. The games' levels and worlds reflect the set-piece structure of the earlier boys' books. Boys get to make lots of noise on adventure island, with the soundtrack full of pulsing music, shouts, groans, zaps, and bomb blasts. Everything is streamlined: the plots and characters are reduced to genre archetypes, immediately familiar to the boy gamers, and defined more through their capacity for actions than anything else. The "adventure island" is the archetypal space of both the boys' books and the boys' games—an isolated world far removed from domestic space or adult supervision, an untamed world for people who refuse to bow before the pressures of the civilizing process, a never-never-land where you seek your fortune. The "adventure island," in short, is a world that fully embodies the boy culture and its ethos.

References

Booth, A. and Johnson, D. 1975. "The Effect of Crowding on Child Health and Development." *American Behavioural Scientist* 18: 736–749.

Cassell, J. 1998. "Storytelling as a Nexus for Change in the Relationship between Gender and Technology: A Feminist Approach to Software Design." In J. Cassell and H. Jenkins, eds. *From Barbie to Mortal Kombat: Gender and Computer Games.* Cambridge: MIT Press, p. 298–326.

Cavallo, D. 1981. *Muscles and Morals: Organized Playgrounds and Urban Reform, 1880–1920.* Philadelphia: University of Pennsylvania Press.

"Critical Depth." 1998. Advertisement, *Next Generation,* January.

"Die by the Sword." 1998. Advertisement, *Next Generation,* January.

Donaldson, F. 1970. "The Child in the City." University of Washington, mimeograph, cited in M. H. Matthews 1992, *Making Sense of Place: Children's Understanding of Large-Scale Environments.* Herfordshire: Barnes and Noble.

Farley, W. 1941. *The Black Stallion.* New York: Random House.

Feinstein, K. and Kent, S. 1997. "Towards a Definition of 'Videogames.'" http:www.videotopia.com/errata1.htm.

Formanek-Brunnel, M. 1996. "The Politics of Dollhood in Nineteenth-Century America." In H. Jenkins, ed., *The Children's Culture Reader.* New York: New York University Press.

Fuller, M. and Jenkins, H. 1995. "Nintendo and New World Travel Writing: A Dialogue." In S. G. Jones, ed., *Cybersociety: Computer-Mediated Communication and Community.* Thousand Oaks, Calif.: Sage Publications.

Hart, R. 1979. *Children's Experience of Place.* New York: John Wiley and Sons.

Jenkins, H. and Cassell, J. 1998. "Chess for Girls? Feminism and Computer Games." In J. Cassell and H. Jenkins, eds. *From Barbie to Mortal Kombat: Gender and Computer Games.* Cambridge: MIT Press, p. 2–45.

Katz, J. 1997. *Virtuous Reality.* New York: Random House.

Kinchloe, J. L. 1997. "Home Alone and 'Bad to the Bone': The Advent of a Postmodern Childhood." In S. R. Steinberg and J. L. Kincheloe, eds., *Kinder-Culture: The Corporate Construction of Childhood.* New York: Westview.

Kinder, M. 1996. "Contextualizing Video Game Violence: From 'Teenage Mutant Ninja Turtles 1' to 'Mortal Kombat 2.'" In P. M. Greenfield and R. R. Cocking, eds., *Interacting with Video.* Norwood: Ablex Publishing.

Matthews, M. H. 1992. *Making Sense of Place: Children's Understanding of Large-Scale Environments.* Hertfordshire: Barnes and Noble.

McEnany, Caraher, L. 1998. Interview. In J. Cassell and H. Jenkins, eds. *From Barbie to Mortal Kombat: Gender and Computer Games.* Cambridge: MIT Press, p. 192–213.

Moore, R. C. 1986. *Childhood's Domain: Play and Place in Child Development.* London: Croom Helm.

Newson, J. and Newson, E. 1976. *Seven Years Old in the Home Environment.* London: Allen and Unwin.

Rheingold, H. L. and Cook, K. V. 1975. "The Content of Boys' and Girls' Rooms as an Index of Parents' Behavior." *Child Development* 46: 459–463.

Rotundo, E. A. 1994. *American Manhood: Transformations in Masculinity from the Revolution to the Modern Era.* New York: Basic.

Searles, H. 1959. *The Non-Human Development in Normal Development and Schizophrenia.* New York: International Universities Press.

Segel, F. 1986. "'As the Twig Is Bent . . .': Gender and Childhood Reading." In E. A. Flynn and P. P. Schweickart, eds., *Gender and Reading: Essays on Readers, Texts, and Contexts.* Baltimore: Johns Hopkins University Press.

Seitzer, E. 1996. Transcript of Expert Panel Meeting, Sega of America Gatekeeper Program. Los Angeles, June 21.

"Sonic R." 1998. Advertisement, *Next Generation,* January.

Tapscott, D. 1997. *Growing Up Digital: The Rise of the Net Generation.* New York: McGraw-Hill.

van Staden, J. F. 1984. "Urban Early Adolescents, Crowding and the Neighbourhood Experience: A Preliminary Investigation." *Journal of Environmental Psychology* 4: 97–118.

Van Vliet, W. 1983. "Exploring the Fourth Environment: An Examination of the Home Range of City and Suburban Teenagers." *Environment and Behavior* 15: 567–88.

"VR Sports." 1998. Advertisement, *Next Generation,* January.

Ward, C. 1977. *The Child in the City.* London: Architectural Press.

West, E. 1992. "Children on the Plains Frontier." In E. West and P. Petrik, eds., *Small Worlds: Children and Adolescents in America, 1850–1950.* Lawrence: The University Press of Kansas, p. 26–41.

Class Identity and the Politics of Dissent: The Culture of Argument in a Chicago Neighborhood Bar

Julie Lindquist

For several months, Julie Lindquist served as a bartender and, with per-mission, tape-recorded conversations and took notes on what she heard and saw. In this essay, she examines how people used the bar as a space to come together to invent and to enact social identities—both individ-ual and communal. Conversation is more than just "mere talk" in this bar, or, Lindquist implies, in any social context. It is a way of establish-ing and maintaining a connection to the people in one's community and reaffirming that one shares the values and ways of thinking of that com-munity. What social situations have you found yourself in where the "way of talking" mattered to keep group membership? Are there other contexts in which your speech seems "natural" but might reflect a sim-ilar acceptance of shared values? Have you ever lost the ability to "talk the talk" with certain groups and been marginalized as a result?

"Let's get somebody in that can run this country like a *business!*" Jack is once again singing the praises of Ross Perot, Texas billionaire and inde-pendent candidate in the 1992 presidential election. Jack stands at his usual place at the corner of the bar, his ashtray full and beer mug empty in front of him. He never sits, but as the hours drag on, he is beginning to lean more heavily on the bar. Lately, he has been looking all of his 52 years, but now the prospect of a good argument has rejuvenated him. From my position behind the bar there is no place to hide; I will have to respond to Jack's gambit. But Jack knows what I will say just as well as I know his routine. The challenge in this game is to deliver oratory, not to fashion the perfect syllogism. A newcomer looks on in alarm, having mistaken this rit-ual fabrication of a cultural text for a rupture in the social fabric. I know that before my shift is over we will have strenuously debated virtues of the presidential candidates, and that we will have managed to persuade each

Lindquist, J. (2004). *Ethnolinguistics Chicago.* (pp. 295–320). Mahwah, NJ: Lawrence Erlbaum Associates, Inc.

other only to commit even more enthusiastically to our original positions. I brace myself and light another cigarette: This play is hard work, and the night is young.

At the Smokehouse Inn, a restaurant-lounge in a working-class suburb south of Chicago, working men and women gather daily to invent a space for sociable leisure, to seek respite from the quotidian realities of their working lives.[1] The Smokehouse is a place of fierce community, of imagined history and garrulous sociability. Yet this space, although safe from the demands of work and everyday responsibility, is a scene of controlled antagonisms and managed contradictions. A stranger to the scene might conclude, from the voices raised in hot dispute all around her, that the arguers there had nothing in common. But after returning to the same scene time and again to find the same arguers in the same positions and engaged in debate on the same topics, she might begin to understand that the noisy confrontations she hears are in fact structured and consensual, and that the arguers do in fact share lives, histories, and strategies for making sense of both. She might even be tempted to conclude that those at the Smokehouse are participating in an important (if not exactly sacred) ritual.

The idea of "class culture" presents interesting problems for scholars across disciplines, pointing as it does to the place where social structures and material conditions meet the particulars of local practice, in the politics of the everyday. What I am attempting here is, in a sense, tautological: I begin from the premise that there is such a phenomenon as "class culture"—a meaning-making, historical social organism whose collective experience arises out of a particular relation to the larger political economy—and end by implicitly affirming the existence of a distinctive working-class culture.[2] Like such ethnographers of working-class life and language as Douglas Foley (1990) and Aaron Fox (1994), I see class culture as a local problem, and would likewise contend that local institutions are good places to witness the microdynamics of social production.[3] My aim is to show "class culture," in this case working-class culture, to be a localized rhetorical invention. I hasten to add, here, that this does not mean that it has no basis in structural or material relations. Rather, I mean that it is produced and reproduced discursively, that it is constituted by the particulars of the relationship between ideology and practice.[4] I am especially concerned with the social uses of argument as a speech genre, the performance of which is significant to the formation and maintenance of group identity. For this reason, I give interpretive priority to *rhetoric,* an emphasis that foregrounds what is strategic, hortatory, and conflictual in acts of communication.[5] At the Smokehouse Inn, *argument* is a locally controlled, rhetorical production and the principle modality through which Smokehousers express class identity in practice while disclaiming the viability of "class" as a theory of social relations. In the routinized practice of argument, people both assert a collective identity and resist its homogenizing effects.

In what follows, I first establish the Smokehouse as an institutional site for the production of distinctive cultural forms and class ideology. Next, I frame class identity as a problem of rhetoric. Finally, I offer an interpretation of an exemplary verbal performance to show how argument not only serves as the occasion for performance of local thematics, but also expresses tensions in ideologies of class identity.

The Smokehouse as Working-Class Institution

The Smokehouse Inn is both a distinctively local institution and a place like a thousand other such places in the Midwest. My claim that barroom culture is metonymically related to "working-class" culture rests on the assumption that barrooms are institutional microcosms of social organization, sites where culture is produced through expressive practice.[6] Historians and anthropologists of working-class social life have shown that bars have traditionally functioned as spaces mediating between home and public spheres; also, that this role has remained intact even as industrial bases and patterns of labor have changed and neighborhood demographics have shifted. Others have suggested that working-class bars are places where the social order is inverted, and where local values of reciprocity, sociability, and vernacular speech forms are asserted over their bourgeois counterparts of competitive consumption, social mobility, and standards of linguistic propriety.[7] Roy Rosenwieg, for example, links bars to the historical predicament of the worker, and suggests that bars as sites of sociability came to be associated with resistance to bourgeois values of individualism and acquisitiveness. At the bar, explains Rosenwieg, workers "affirmed communal over individualistic and privatistic values" (1993, p. 247). Many Chicago communities, particularly those with large populations of industrial workers have dense concentrations of neighborhood bars. Historians such as Slayton (1986) and Duis (1983) have documented the important role taverns have played in the cultural life and social organization of working-class communities in Chicago.[8]

With Rosenwieg and others, I hold that local bars can function as contexts for expressions of working-class resistance to mainstream middle-class values, and as such offer opportunities to observe how people in working-class communities experience themselves in relation to dominant social codes.[9] The suburban site of the Smokehouse, Greendale, has an attenuated, rural geography that presents a marked contrast to the multiplex urban density of traditional working-class enclaves such as Cicero or Bridgeport, yet it does not suffer from lack of drinking establishments from which local workers can choose to spend leisure time. Of the four genres of barroom in the area—corner bar, dance club, strip joint, and restaurant lounge—the Smokehouse is the latter. It nonetheless functions as a *neighborhood* tavern, perhaps all the more so for its potential to locate the willfully dislocated.[10] It occupies a building with a family-style restaurant famous for steak and barbecued ribs; its proximity to the attached dining room enforces a level of decorum to which the patrons of a corner bar would never be subjected (men drinking at the bar during restaurant hours are admonished to "watch the language" so as not to offend women and other diners not privy to the codes and rituals of male sociability).[11] Yet it attracts a regular clientele of working men and women who spend much of their leisure time at the bar, although these same clients rarely, or never, patronize the restaurant.

Depending on your point of view (or your place in the scene), the bar itself is either invitingly cozy or darkly claustrophobic. There are no windows; this public space guards its privacy fiercely. This insular, smoke-suffused room serves its blue-collar population—machinists, builders, Teamsters, and service workers—as a public forum, as a place to seek out a stable society of friends and coworkers and to engage these others in conversation and debate about current issues and political events. In fact, one might conclude that the Smokehouse serves the same function that neighborhood yards and porches once served before working-class Whites moved out from urban centers. That is, it is a physical and symbolic agent of the local, a repository of folk histories and originary tales.

For many people from Greendale and its adjacent suburbs, the Smokehouse is the nexus of leisure, truly a home-away-from-home. Many of its regulars spend several hours a day, several days a week, drinking beer and *shooting the shit* at the Smokehouse.[12] The bar is both a space apart from the routinized space of work and a compressed, concentrated space of leisure where the textures of sociality are pressed into relief. As a site of leisure, the Smokehouse barroom represents the institutionalization of challenges to institutional authority. The marking of leisure time with the ritual celebration of vice suspends the constraints of normal social arrangements, such that the local sheriff bellies up to the bar next to the neighborhood drug dealer, the immigrant octogenarian bends elbows with the young single mother. Like the butter-saturated popcorn set in front of you by the bartender upon your arrival, talk is plentiful, flavorful, and cheap. People come to the Smokehouse because they know they will find someone "at home" there, someone to listen to their stories of getting by, getting over, and getting even.

The Practice of Identity

For the Smokehouse cohort, "class" is experienced phenomenologically, not philosophically. The cultural logic about class is that it is irrelevant to social experience—at least as a theory, an interpretive language, a way to locate oneself in social space. Smokehousers voice common political interests—lower taxes, less unemployment, more pay, better working conditions—and they generally see politicians as working against their interests as working whites. At the same time, Smokehousers do not claim membership in a "working class" as explicitly defined by a history of disenfranchisement from dominant discourses or institutions. Unlike other clearly identifiable cultural themes such as work, education, race, or politics, class remains implicit, unnameable. "Class" has no place in the cultural lexicon, is not present in everyday discourse as an organizing metaphor for social phenomena. If an explicit theory of class is absent, however, its practice is everywhere. Precisely because so little is spoken about class per se, much is said. As a phenomenology of identity relations, its unnameability makes it highly narratizable.[13] Class ideologies are encoded in themes of ethnicity, education, and politics; such themes structure narratives and animate public discussions. Yet even as *class* is sublimated into other social alignments and rhetorical domains, the identification with *working* is explicit. Whether or not Smokehousers will tell you they are "working class," they want you to know that they are *people who work.* Talk of work encodes dominant values of productivity, practical knowledge, proximity to and control over products of labor, sharing of social and economic resources.

Such themes and tensions in Smokehouse logics of identity are yet more effectively illustrated by the terms of my own position in Smokehouse society. As an ethnographer, I spent over a year behind the bar as a participant and observer, distributing drinks and collecting data on everyday speech.[14] My post behind the bar was the ideal ethnographic position: Like the paradoxical position of the participant-observer, a bartender is simultaneously central to, and at a remove from, social action.[15] This ambiguous identity as academic and worker put me at the center of another kind of social dilemma as well: As one with enduring connections to the neighborhood, I was an insider (I grew up in the surrounding community, and got the Smokehouse job through a friend of a friend from a prior bartending job). As an academic, my investment in a rhetorical economy in which theory is perceived to operate as currency apart from practice—where ideas circulate as commodities, and where "saying" also counts as "doing"—meant that I would always be set apart from Smokehousers, for whom doing and saying, or producing and philosophizing, earn very different kinds of social and economic rewards.

Yet my status as insider in practice, outsider in theory was what earned me a secure—if not always comfortable—place among others at the Smokehouse. In fact, one might say that my position as insider depended on my willingness to perform the role of outsider, to present a challenge to cultural logics. As an egghead with middle-class aspirations, I became a catalyst for public performance, and in particular, for performances in arguments about politics.[16] This was a role I was not entirely unwilling to play, as unsettling as it often was, for at least it gave me a way to have a place among others (and, I should confess, to affirm my own upwardly mobile status). Apart from my participation in particular argumentative events, however, I was generally constructed as a symbol of supercilious bourgeois intellectualism.[17]

One particularly vexing occasion should serve to illustrate. I was working behind the bar one busy Friday afternoon after the news had just broken about an exhibit set up at Chicago's Art Institute by art student Dred Scott Tyler. Tyler, it seems, had created an art exhibit that involved his placing an American flag on the floor in such a manner as to invite museum-goers to step on it. Imagining that such an issue would be too volatile to contain, I carefully (and no doubt conspicuously, given my usual willingness to participate in arguments) avoided interjecting my own judgments about the morality of Tyler's action, or taking up any of the disgusted excoriations of him voiced by some of the bar regulars. Before long, however, one regular, Wendell, jerked a thumb in my direction and said, "Now take Julie here. She's one of those that thinks it's okay to walk on the flag!" In that moment I was constructed as the embodiment of an oppositional position and imputed with the predictably self-interested and naïve motives that emerge from class privilege. In the next, I found myself struggling, and failing, to communicate my position (that although I did not condone the artist's actions I would defend his right to them) against a roiling storm of invective.[18]

My role as symbolic opposition to prevailing cultural logics—and in particular, to the logic of identification with *work*—is neither incidental to what has emerged as data, nor to my interpretation of it. I not only recorded, but also helped to constitute, the rhetorical situations in which arguments happened. That I functioned as antagonist, as well as bartender and ethnographer, will be important in considering the circumstances and meaning of argument as a performed genre.

A Class Act: Jack Does Perot

Local bars, although purportedly public (as the moniker "pub" would affirm), can be fiercely private domains, as Gerry Philipsen discovered in his ethnographic adventures in a Chicago neighborhood he calls "Teamsterville." Upon arriving on the scene of the barroom-cum-research site, Philipsen (1992) recalls noting that "this was not merely a public place open to anyone, but an enclave in which some but not other personae were welcome," and that "there was no sign outside the tavern, because 'everybody' knew who belonged there" (p. 3). At the Smokehouse, whatever cultural boundaries can't be enforced with brick and mortar are concretized in the practice of conventional speech genres. The social network at the bar is defined not only by its location in the real space of the barroom, but also by how its members locate themselves with respect to these forms of talk. Smokehousers participate in routinized expressive genres such as *shooting the shit* (unmarked conversation), *giving shit* (joking), and *telling it like it is* (narration), and *arguing*. Skillful participation in and metacommentary on the terms of any given genre are a way to communicate one's solidarity with the group's interests and practices, but argument, foregrounding as it does instabilities and tensions in class ideologies, is the genre that invites performance.

The idea that performance is an index, or at least an expression, of social arrangements is a central assumption of folklore and sociolinguistics (Bauman, 1977, 1986, 1991; Briggs 1988; Hymes 1975, 1996; Tannen 1989), but has long enjoyed currency across fields and disciplinary methods from the interactional sociology of Erving Goffman to the ordinary-language philosophy of J. L. Austin (1975) and the rhetorical theory of Kenneth Burke (1969). Studies of communicative behavior across communities have shown various ways verbal performances affirm cultural values (Bauman 1986; Briggs 1988; Farr 1993, 1994; Kirshenblatt-Gimblett 1984; Shuman 1986). The issue of how speech becomes performative in particular domains is significant to the relevance of verbal performance as an index of relations between social relationships and ideology (Bauman 1977, p. 25). Although Smokehousers render verbal performances in telling jokes, relating stories, and so on, by far the genre of talk most closely aligned with performance is argument. Here, it becomes the expression of male sociality, of antibourgeois garrulousness and contentious play.[19] Arguments are a significant site of cultural production inasmuch as they instantiate episodes of verbal art—a practice that functions, as working-class ethnographer Aaron Fox (1994) explains, "to reflexively examine the ideological structure of the 'ordinary' events and discourses it takes as both its raw materials and as objects of scrutiny," thereby working as "a challenge to and a celebration of a particular social order" (p. 2).[20]

The following dramatic episode stars Jack, a prominent Smokehouse regular. It illustrates not only how arguments occasion performances, but also how performances do both social and epistemic work and how these functions are part of the same processes of identification. In this scenario the argument that occasions Jack's performance becomes a framing device for sustained artful narrative. This argument is exemplary in its rhetorical style, framing and progression, and is typical of the kinds of performances that are often staged in arguments with me. As is so often the case, I am pitted against a powerful male and am constructed as someone who speaks out against the interests of, or at least doesn't take seriously, the predicaments of workers.

Because verbal performances are enacted by powerful members of the group (usually men, but always people who can speak from an ethos of experiential wisdom and productivity), it is not surprising that Jack is so often at the center of them. Jack is one of the most visible—and audible—regulars at the Smokehouse. He is a 52-year-old former steelworker who now owns a music store where local rock musicians come to buy guitars, give lessons, and rent equipment.[21] Jack comes in to drink beer and socialize every night; his absence at the bar inevitably invites speculation on his whereabouts. He is typically the center of sociability, and, although he has his own cohort of close friends, transcends the boundaries of smaller barroom cliques. When Jack is at the Smokehouse, he stands at *his* corner, the prestigious spot at the bend of the horseshoe-shaped bar. At this geographic and discursive fulcrum, Jack commands a place of high visibility: His position at the bar is analogous to that of patriarch at the head of a dinner table (or, perhaps more appropriately, a speaker at a podium). In case anyone has missed the point about his stature, Jack does not sit on a stool, but remains standing, all the better to assume a stentorian posture should the occasion arise. Jack's claims to territory are honored by his cohorts, as well: I have seen others who had been occupying Jack's spot vacate it apologetically upon his arrival. For Jack to take another place, or for someone else to claim it, would be a heresy against the social order of the bar. It would be just as unlikely for Jack to change places as it would be for him to remove the Greek fisherman's cap he always wears, or—for that matter—for a woman to enter the bar and persuade the men to switch the television from a football game to a talk show. Jack's presence, as well as his position at the bar, constitute one of the many predictable facts of the heavily routinized quotidian culture of the Smokehouse. Jack's elevation above other seated bar clients, as well as his position at the bar's "head," symbolically assert his standing among Smokehousers: When Jack speaks, he commands an audience.

The argument in the following transcript takes place late on Monday evening in September of 1992.[22] The bar is empty, save for Jack; Arlen, the bar manager; Maggie and Roberta, waitresses who have finished their work in the dining room and are now relaxing at the bar after their shifts are over; and me, the late-shift bartender. The discussion has turned, following a news report covering the campaigning efforts of candidates in the 1992 presidential election, to a debate about the merits of candidates Bill Clinton, George Bush, and Ross Perot. In what follows, Jack delivers a thematic oration that comprises a series of highly stylized narratives. During most of Jack's monologue, the others are, like any well-behaved audience, silent and attentive. But after listening to Jack praise Perot for his "business sense," I move to challenge Jack's assertion that "running the country like a business" would be a good thing, that it would offer solutions for everybody, and press for particulars. I attempt to get Jack to offer specific features of what he believes to be the benefits of Perot's plan, a move that he eludes in favor of escalating proclamations of my own shortsightedness and naivete. As Jack moves into full performance, I try repeatedly and unsuccessfully to claim the floor to get Jack to elaborate his assertions, but finally cede the floor to Jack as he takes center stage to demonstrate his right, through the sheer force of his rhetorical artistry, to speak for others—Smokehousers, and working people in general—who share his interests:

1	Jack:	. . . LET'S get SOMEbody
		who UNderstands
		MONEY!
	Julie:	But he understands it from a point of view that—
5		Now, what is Perot's plan for
		welfare reform?
	Roberta:	The people would be WORKING!
	Jack:	The point is, hon, we're going like this—
	Julie:	How? Is he going to—is he going to advocate child
		care for women—
10	Jack:	Jul, we're going like this—! (makes a masturbatory
		gesture)
		People are bein' taxed, taxed, TAXED!
	Julie:	—who want to go back to work?
	Jack:	Do you understand what's HAPP'NIN'?
	Roberta:	They already GET child care care free!
15	Julie:	No, no, but I mean if they want to get OFF welfare,
		and go get a job at minimum wage—
		How are they going to get ahead?
	Jack:	You didn't even understand what we just said.
		He is the only one talkin' about jobs,
20		and neither candidate TALKED about jobs,
		until Perot got in, and was thirty-six percent!

He said, I *don't wanna talk about nothin —jobs!*
They said.
Well, what about the gay issue? He said,
Bitch, I said, JOBS! And they said,

25   *What about this issue?*
He said—

Roberta: If everybody in America pulls together and everybody was working,
then *maybe—*

Jack: —the country needs JOBS! Don't worry about the
tax system;

30   if we have jobs there'll be taxes; all the programs'll
stay intact.
And they kept askin' him questions. *I don't wanna
know about that—JOBS!*
He's the ONLY man that talked, If you don't get this
country working,
then you're gonna have NO money—

Julie: How's he gonna DO that? How is he gonna do that?

35   How is he gonna make it so that people have jobs—?

Jack: (more loudly): I would rather have him than Bush or
Clinton,
that don't know NOTHIN' about a job,
other than suckin' government money all their life,
they don't know a THING about a job,
they don't know a thing about PEOPLE in here,
who are workin'; they NEVER have.
Here's some sonofabitch at least had a company that
PAID people!

Julie: Well, you ac—

Jack: (still more loudly): He knows something about jobs,

45   what he was talkin' about. The other two know
nothing!
They been SUCKIN' off the government!
They know NOTHIN' about jobs.
Perot has got a big company—you're right!
And I—I don't know—1 will STILL lean toward
him,

50   because he wants to get people—he underSTANDS;
I have a business, and I know there's kids come in
every day,

and there's one thing they lack,
that I didn't have twenty years ago.
Donny (Jack's business partner) and I went—
55   thirty years ago—we went in the mill; you had a
JOB.
I had a CREdit union, I could buy a CAR,
I could buy a HOUSE;
There ain't a FUCKIN' kid today that could ever
buy a car or a house today—
He got NOTHIN'!
He—1 mean, he's a SCAB!
He's makin' five bucks a—you know, an hour, or
less—I got a daughter—!
Ah, five bucks?! *I* was makin' SEVEN, in frickin'
SIXTY!
I was—you know, one thing this country needs, is
jobs!
I don't care about Germany, Russia, NOTHIN'!
65   And Perot is the only man that talked that shit—he's
the ONLY one!
I don't care about insurance,
I don't care about this,
I don't care about Europe, Mexico;
70   *I don't care about NOBODY!*
Get the kids in my country jobs! They can't buy
nothin'.
And! The more they TAX, for the system they're in,
less and LESS people have business.
Here's a good example—right here! There's less
money;
75   the man is makin' less money,
he's FUCKIN' over the employees—
it's less, and it's less, and it's LESS . . .
I'm no different. For the first time in my life, I laid
off two PEople! You know?
And I mean, I watch Tony's Pizza—NO! It's less,
they keep it up!
80   The real estate taxes went up; insurance is up forty-
seven percent, but—
and—they keep it up!

		Whaddaya gonna do? You need someone that got some frickin' *sense!* NOT,
		Oh, we're gonna make the GOVERNMENT—
	Maggie:	People WANNA work. People don't wanna sit home. They—want—to—WORK!
85	Jack:	. . . that's bullshit. There's people that WANT to work, though—
	Maggie:	That's what I'm SAYIN—they WANNA work!
	Jack:	Yeah . . . but . . . there's gotta be someone who can direct, that knows what jobs are all about.

It's—you can't have—Clinton, Gore, Quayle, Bush—you know, huh,

90   the government'll pay 'em! you know—you know—but,

do THEY have vacations?

They have, you know, I mean, they're paid all the TIME!

    If—if Perry don't have the money,

    HE don't get a vacation,

NO one gets a vacation!

95   *I* don't get a vacation! This is BULLSHIT!

You should—the government should work . . . and balance their budget; if they don't, they penalize them, where the government is trillions of dollars in debt! Bullshit!

Get someone in there, that understands—

100   the JAPS don't do that;

the GERMANS don't do that;

they HELP their people.

And they have—you know, NO. This is . . . they only guy, that—

I don't know anything about

105   —talk for talk, you can TAKE your Clinton;

he's gonna run you under;

Bush is gonna run you under;

I don't know if the other guy's gonna run you under; he's makin' sense to me: *Get the people in this country jobs.*

110   I don't wanna talk about GAYS,

I don't wanna talk about ABORTION,

I don't wanna talk about ANY of yer other bullshit . . .

once everybody has a JOB in the country, it'll be right.
We-we'll be able to feel good about it
115   —EVERYTHING!

It is clear that Jack intends not only to showcase his own rhetorical expertise, but also to articulate the group's conventional interpretation of its political predicament. In keeping with these general observations, the generic features that most clearly mark Jack's oratory as performative are the poetic strategies it employs, including repeated key phrases (lines 37–40 and 106–108) progressively amplified assertions (lines 67–70 and 100–103) and parallel constructions (lines 67–70 and 110–113). In framing the speech as a performance with these stylistic cues, Jack also marks the speech as a special case by assuming a posture of speaking *for,* rather than *to* or even *at,* his audience. There is a reciprocal cause-and-effect relationship at work here: Jack's position in the Smokehouse community gives him the authority to *speak for,* but it is performances such as these in which Jack displays his distinctive virtuosity, that help to legitimize his position.

Jack's performance draws from rhetorical topoi or thematic resources that articulate the cultural logic of the group: Politics is a bunch of privileged types blowing smoke. The more talk there is, the less action. Work is the life experience that qualifies you to speak and to make decisions about the lives of others. The job situation is getting worse. Unemployment is the most pressing issue in national politics, and is the economic base of—not just another example of—social identifications. In the same way that one accumulates capital through investments, Jack's authority as cultural spokesperson accrues exponentially and recursively: His role at the bar entitles him to speak these cultural logics, and in so doing, he qualifies himself further to do so.

Having assumed the responsibility of speaking *for,* Jack resolutely ignores any efforts at intervention in his oratory: He does not qualify what he says, nor does he acknowledge any of the questions I pose as requests for elaboration. In deflecting possible challenges to the logic for which he speaks, Jack both authorizes that logic as the *common sense,* and legitimates his claim to enact it publicly. He controls the floor by implicitly circumscribing the terms of the argument: Everything follows from the premise that the solution to all other social ills is "jobs," and although Jack does not explain how Perot will actually create them, he prevents me from redefining the terms of the argument by implying that I'm missing the point of the *Perot equals business sense equals jobs equals solutions to all social problems* equation. Instead of qualifying his arguments, Jack instead escalates into a virtuoso performance in which he amplifies his point as he dramatizes a familiar Smokehouse theme, declining opportunities for manufacturing jobs. Roberta attempts to intervene, but Jack will not allow an aperture into his oratory, even for others to voice support.

Jack's poetic technique of "reporting" presidential contender Ross Perot's words gives his narrative added momentum (lines 22–24, 67–70, and 109). Rather than removing layers of metacommunication to reveal another's speech in its most unmediated, referential form, the strategy of "reporting" (really, resituating) the words of another amounts to reinventing their words for one's own purposes. As Tannen (1989) explained, reported speech both reinterprets the utterance reported, and produces a constructed dialogue that adds dramatic force and calls upon a fictive collaborator to authorize the utterance (pp. 109–112). Ross Perot, it should be noted, earned the admiration and loyalty of many at the Smokehouse for his "real-world" politics of corporate pragmatism and bootstrap economics. Perot has, in fact, become emblematic of such a political orientation and he was often invoked in my presence to trigger arguments. Perot's disclaimers of political interests and engagements have earned him the right to speak for working-class interests even though he is a corporate billionaire. There is a widely held belief that all politicians are "in somebody's pocket." Hence, the reasoning goes, Perot is rich and therefore free of ties to special interest groups. So Jack is not merely parroting Perot's words—rather, he is dramatically taking on the character of Perot. He *takes on* Perot, in the sense that he takes him on as a character; he speaks "through" him. In so doing, Jack is aligning himself, and by extension those for whom he speaks, with the ethical stance of Perot. In effect Jack's own exhortations come together in a duet with Perot's yet more powerful ones. Jack's voice situates Perot's, and Perot's authorizes Jack's. Jack-as-Perot-as-Jack speaks powerfully of the interests of those who must work, if not the "working class."

That the speech emerges in the context of the challenge allows Jack's performance to succeed as a dramatization of Smokehouse cultural logic. Although I become more and more peripheral to Jack's oratory, my presence as obvious dissenter makes the performance possible: Without a contrasting background against which to foreground the cultural logic of the group, Jack's argument would be heard by his audience as "pure show," would be revealed as strategic discourse, and would undermine Jack's authority to speak cultural truths. By rendering these truths publicly and in a style uniquely his own, Jack manages to distinguish himself even as he proclaims solidarity with the group. His rhetoric is attuned to the pathos of his audience, and works by attempting to discredit my own ethical authority as Liberal Democrat Clinton supporter. If the speech seems to be directed as a response to my challenge, it is actually aimed at, and stylized for the appreciation of, his larger audience. By "persuading" the others of what they already believe to be true, Jack constructs an ethos of experiential wisdom. By speaking *to* (really *by way of,* as *against*) me, he disguises his showmanship as an appeal to logic.

It would be tempting to conclude that performances such as this work only to affirm stable and circumscribed ideological structures, yet it is the very *instability* of the conventional belief structure that invites the performance. It is precisely because the Smokehouse "scene" represents a frame in an ongoing historical process of cultural invention that performances become necessary to offer commentary on the "state of the union" from moment to moment. Performances at the Smokehouse appear to supply further evidence for Richard Bauman's (1977, 1986) observation that verbal art generally expresses tensions between tradition and innovation, between conservative and emergent forms. At the Smokehouse, where the conflict between "liberal" and "conservative" political orientations is precisely what is at issue in arguments, this tension is made explicit. In order for arguments to dramatize the script of Smokehouse cultural logic at any given time, contexts for performance must include not only someone who speaks *for* the cultural logic, like Jack, but someone who speaks *against* it, like me. Whether both of these poles are actually given voice in an argument or not, it is the implicit presence of the opposition that makes performance possible. If opposition is not represented in each situation, it will likely be artificially constructed (the bar manager, Arlen, delighted in describing to me how my point of view would be invoked in an argument even when I was not there to argue it). A dissenting voice, in other words, is manufactured in order to reconfigure the rhetorical situation, thereby making dissensus viable and performance possible.

Argument, Performance, and the Solidarity of Dissent

The central place of political argument in the everyday life of the Smokehouse suggests the extent to which ideologies of class identity participate in local processes of rhetorical invention. Although, of course, the everyday realities of the people who inhabit the Smokehouse are profoundly shaped by material conditions, these conditions are always subject to (and the subject of) interpretation. In performances of agonistic discourse,

Smokehousers invent a dynamic class identity and situate it within a larger narrative of cultural logic. Arguments about "politics" serve as occasions for Smokehousers to position themselves rhetorically not only as individuals within the group, but also as a group against the larger social landscape. By participating in arguments, a Smokehouser can both distinguish himself from the guy on the next barstool and from those who would never dream of occupying barstools in places like the Smokehouse. Arguments, inasmuch as they open spaces for (and authorize) narrative performances, allow Smokehousers to experience cultural solidarity in expressions of difference.

My presence as one who dissents from the conventional ideology helps to reconcile the contradiction between consolidating and individuating functions of rhetoric. It both opens possibilities for Smokehousers to claim distinctive positions with respect to the cultural logic, and draws the parameters of that logic. In arguments with me—designated representative of those who do not recognize the material exigencies of the cultural logic—Smokehousers can voice dissent without risking public identification as dissenters. Arguments make room for performances, performances dramatize narratives; narratives announce the place of the group in the social world. By participating in arguments, Smokehousers can narrate the unnameable, theorize cultural practice, and express ideology without sacrificing individual distinctiveness to solidarity. In argument, narratives are made possible (without a structure of contention, performances would be divested of their narrative authority by being exposed *as* performances); narratives articulate the contradictions of working-class identity.

In describing the highly consensual and orchestrated nature of cultural performance, Erving Goffman (1981) observed that in performance, "a tacit agreement is maintained between performers and audiences to act as if a given degree of opposition and accord existed between them. Typically, but not always, agreement is stressed and opposition is underplayed." Here the scales weighing agreement against opposition appear to be tipped the other way: Actors in performed argument agree to "play," but players, once having consented to the rules of the game, foreground dissent. This situation is, I suggest, in part a function of how Smokehousers experience themselves as participants in a unified "working-class" culture even though—and especially because—they are, on the whole, reluctant to define it such.

Because Smokehousers feel that they can claim neither the established political power of the middle class nor the emergent power of groups now recognized as having been historically marginalized, they experience a good deal of ambivalence about their collective political identity. It is as a consequence of this ambivalence that argument—as a discourse of conflict—becomes the genre of speech that invites performance. Because

Smokehousers are unable to name themselves as a political body—to do so would to be acknowledge the structural imperatives of class in America—they must find other ways to express social boundaries, to lay claim to distinctive cultural traditions. Ritualized agonistic rhetoric clears a space for individuals to express their shared class experiences safely, in expressions of difference. Only by actively building dissensus in this way can Smokehousers resolve tensions that exist not only between group solidarity and individual difference, but also between lived experience and the claims of the American myth of unfettered social mobility. The absence of a conventional language to allow Smokehousers to articulate a shared political predicament means that every statement of dissent against the cultural logic must also contain the assurance of assent. Performed argument allows people to manage this tension without perceiving it as a strategic contradiction. As agonistic, indecorous, or disruptive as arguments at the Smokehouse may be, they are always, finally, class acts.

Notes

1. "The Smokehouse Inn" is a pseudonym, chosen both because the bar adjoins a restaurant famous for its smoked barbecued ribs, and because "Smokehouse" suggests the second favorite pastime vice of the bar's clientele.
2. Although it may seem circular to begin and end with the premise that there is such a thing as "class culture," this is no more vexing than the problem that any sociolinguist faces in identifying any given "speech community"—an entity that is at once an a priori heuristic abstraction and a conclusion about the distribution and use of sociolinguistic resources—as a research site.
3. See Fox (1994) for a provocative discussion of the problematics of representation that attend the ethnographic study of class culture. Fox described such a project as "ironic" in its contradictory aims and outcomes: "Oscillating between the challenging cognitive estrangements of otherness and the all-too-familiar, 'class cultures' taunt ethnographers, resist disciplinary containments, and inspire endless sociological head-scratching" (p. 1). Taking up Foley's (1990) discussion of the ambiguous status of class culture as a social organism. Fox observed that class culture is an "epistemological hybrid" constituted by its dual status as a political and an anthropological culture (1994).
4. Woolard (1985) saw questions of hegemony and cultural reproduction—specifically, the nature of "hegemony" and the extent to which local forms can be said to participate in "reproduction"—as the exigency for sociolingusitic research on community practices. On the basis of her own sociolinguistic research in Catalonia, Woolard concluded that "the emphasis by reproduction theorists on formal institutions such as the school is misplaced" and that "the structuralist representation of dominant, hegemonic ideologies as impenetra-

ble does not capture the reality of working-class and minority community practices" (p. 738). My own research begins from this premise.

5. As an ethnography of speaking, this study is deeply rooted in the assumptions about the situated nature of linguistic behavior established by Dell Hymes (1974) and others. Although "rhetoric" is not a term ordinarily associated with anthropological linguistics, I find it useful in emphasizing linkages between performance, ideology, and what linguistic anthropologists might call "rights of participation," and in accounting for ways in which the poetic operates as a function of the hortatory. I see this ethnographic account of Smokehouse rhetoric as a project in "the rhetoric of the everyday," a formulation suggested by Ralph Cintron (1997) to describe critical ethnographic work informed by theories of rhetoric, culture, and social production.

6. Despite the enormous potential for bars to yield microcosmic views of American social structures and practices, there exist only a handful of studies conducted in such institutions. In a bibliography of ethnographic research on American cultures published in 1992, Michael Moffett counted four studies either situated in bars or including extended discussions of barroom life: those of Read (1980), Bell (1983), Halle (1984), and Weston (1991). In addition to these, I have located three others, those of Cavan (1970), LeMasters (1975), and Spradley and Mann (1975). Only two of these, the Halle and LeMasters studies, take the culture of working-class Whites as an object of inquiry; none was published in the past 15 years.

7. See, for example, Halle (1984) and Fox (1993, 1995) for discussions of bars as institutional sites for the expression of resistant (or at least, oppositional) working-class identities; see Hoggart (1957) for an early analysis of the role of bars in the production of British working-class ideology.

8. Following from her extensive study of behavior in 100 bars in the San Francisco area, Sherri Cavan (1970) concluded that bars have predictable codes of conduct that cut across class lines, that they have entirely distinctive institutional rules for social practice. I would argue that these codes of conduct are modulated by the historical status as bars as local, working-class institutions, and that the behavior one finds in bars is not, as Cavan seems to suggest, empty of significance for inferring patterns of social meaning that prevail "outside."

9. Lest it be objected that my claims here are too ambitious, I should make clear that I am not arguing that this oppositional function is unique to White working-class bars—other kinds of bars may well serve analogous (although not necessarily identical) purposes elsewhere. See, for example Michael Bell's (1983) ethnography of speaking in "Brown's Lounge," a Black middle-class bar. Bell noted that what goes on in Brown's can, by virtue of the bar's status as a community institution, be seen as a place to read performances of class and race identity. Bell explained that "the world of Brown's, the environment and complex of human activities that make it up, exists in order to permit the patrons to see themselves and their actions while they are in the bar as

consistent with their own definitions of what it means to be Black and middle class" (p. 6).

10. The building that houses the Smokehouse was once a branch of the Underground Railroad. Now, ironically, Greendale (a pseudonym) is a stop on the Southward commute to ever more rural, ever-Whiter, pastures. Yet older people who frequent the bar still strongly identify with the southside urban neighborhoods from which they came. These ex-Roselanders, -Pullmanites, and -Fernwooders speak as if they were forcibly uprooted and displaced from communities in which they once enjoyed a utopian society of camaraderie and mutual support. Still, that many of the bar's patrons who no longer live and work in the Greendale area continue to visit the Smokehouse on weekends speaks to the relative stability of their social networks, and to the significance of the bar as a geographic nexus of these networks.

11. Many ethnographers who have studied barroom cultures (Halle, 1984; LeMasters, 1975; Spradley & Mann, 1975) have noted that bars have traditionally functioned as male territory, as spaces where ritual celebrations of masculinity are given ceremonial treatment. This is generally true of the Smokehouse as well, yet women are—can be—active participants in the life of the bar. They can construct an ethos that allows them to claim a place among the ranks of socially visible men either by actively taking part in male-solidarity rituals (such as drinking shots, telling "dirty jokes" and buying rounds of beer), or by referring to an extrinsic ethos that is conferred upon those who (e.g., bartenders and waitresses) publicly identify with work that is productive by male standards (see Halle 1984 for a discussion, well supported by research in a community of workers at a chemical plant, of the relationship between class identity, masculinity, and productive labor). That the bar adjoins a restaurant and is therefore inhabited by women at work no doubt modulates male control of social practice.

12. *Shooting the shit* is an emic term that refers to unmarked, highly sociable speech. It is the stream of everyday discourse, the default mode of communication in which other marked genres such as *giving shit* and *arguing* are embedded.

13. In narratives, in other words, Smokehousers both affirm and test the limits of the cultural logics of class. See Stewart (1996) for an extensive overview of definitions of and approaches to narrative in cultural studies, linguistics, anthropology, and folklore (p. 29). After listing several possible functions of narrative, Stewart concludes that "whatever its presumed motives are traceable effects, and whether it takes a relatively authoritative, monologic form or a more open, dialogic form, narrative is first and foremost a mediating form through which 'meaning' must pass." To put it another way, she says, "Stories are productive. They catch up cultural conventions, relations of authority, and fundamental spatiotemporal orientations in the dense sociality of words and images in use and produce a constant mediation of the 'real' in a proliferation of signs" (p. 30).

14. The logistics and ethics of data collection presented special challenges given the status of Smokehousers as a private society within a public institution. My general method for gathering data on natural speech was to switch on a small, handheld tape recorder as episodes of argument (or in some cases, story-telling) happened. Although I did not always remind people of the presence of the tape recorder as I recorded each episode of talk, I did discuss my plan to record data with the owner of the Smokehouse as well as with those regulars who make up the core of the social network under study. So the people who are the participants in this research knew I was working on a project designed to learn "how people talked about politics in the real world," and that I was likely to record conversations (even if I didn't announce my intent to record particular stretches of discourse). Although many at the bar told me that they were supportive of my efforts to write something that might be read by people who didn't know what "life in the real world" was like, my research project was seen as an eccentricity—as yet another indication, no doubt, of the peculiar ways of academic types.

15. As I have-said elsewhere, a bartender, who is by definition a participant-observer in/of the social life around her, is a kind of "naturally occurring ethnographer" (Lindquist, 2002). Both dimensions of this in-and-out-of-things role are highlighted by the geography of the bar at the Smokehouse: The bar is shaped like a tight horseshoe so that the bartender is literally at the center of social life, half of which, at any given moment, is going on behind her back.

16. Smokehousers tend to be much more interested in national politics than local or international politics. Most of the arguments that constitute my data corpus are about the candidates and platforms in the 1992 political campaign, although Smokehousers argue about the politics of a range of other social issues (as, for example—to name one hot topic—the trial of the police officers assault on Rodney King).

17. Many at the bar have commented on the similarity of Smokehouse society to that dramatized by the long-running sitcom *Cheers,* and more established regulars have even gone so far as to compare my own persona to one of its characters, intellectual snob Diane Chambers.

18. Although my role as antagonist emerges from my habit of privileging abstraction from local experience over values of productivity and practical knowledge, that role is also a function of my gender. It is of course significant that I am a woman who speaks against local interests. As Sherry Ortner (1991) has noted, "Gender relations for both middle-class and working-class Americans carry an enormous burden of quite antagonistic class meaning" (p. 171). She goes on to explain that "it appears overwhelmingly the case in working-class culture that women are symbolically aligned . . . with the 'respectable,' 'middle-class side of those oppositions and choices," (p. 173). These cross-significations are certainly operative at the Smokehouse, where real work and productivity are attributes of socially appropriate men.

19. A large and venerable body of sociolinguistic research connects working-class solidarity to highly gendered expressions of sociability controlled by high-status males. Fox (1995), for instance, writes that in high-involvement working-class speech styles, "full performance is metapragmatically associated with powerful males" and that "male discursive power is closely linked to high levels of performativity—assembling caricatured gender-indexical topics and emphasizing emotional intensity, expressive dynamism, emphatic paralinguistic style, invasions of others' physical space, polemical uses of invective and insults in agonistic engagements, sustained narrativity, repetitiveness, and publicness" (p. 2). The point here is not to show that women have no part in performances, no voice in the invention of culture—indeed Fox went on to show how working-class women may "reverse" this order of dominance through ironic performance of the same elements—only that Jack's right of participation in arguments of this kind are attributable to his gender and status.

20. Fox's (1995) conclusions about the ideological workings of "artful discourse" echo what folklorists and anthropologists have suggested about the ethnopoetic function of verbal art, and follow from his own research on the culture of a rural working-class bar near Lockhart, Texas. My research at the Smokehouse supports Fox's assertion that verbal performances function poetically to affirm and critique conventional cultural logics simultaneously.

21. Even though Jack has bought into a business and is therefore now a "businessman," he nonetheless retains strong ties to local interests. His financial success notwithstanding, he (unlike Perry, the owner of the Smokehouse) continues to identify with the employment situations and political interests of industrial workers.

22. The following transcript is edited to render the rhythm and flow of natural speech, and therefore does not use special notation to specify such paralinguistic features as pause length, intonation patters, and the like. Emphasis is indicated by capital letters, and reported speech is italicized. Lines are broken to emphasize such artistic features as parallelism, repetition, and progressive amplification.

References

Austin, J. L. (1975). *How to do things with words*. J. O. Urmson & M. Sbisa (Eds.). Cambridge, MA: Harvard University Press.

Bell, M. J. (1983). *The world from Brown's lounge: An ethnography of black middle-class play*. Urbana: University of Illinois Press.

Bauman, R. (1992). Disclaimers of performance. In J. H. Hill & J. T. Irvine (Eds.), *Responsibility and evidence in oral discourse* (pp. 182–186). Cambridge: Cambridge University Press.

Bauman, R. (1986). *Story, performance, event*. Cambridge: Cambridge University Press.

Bauman, R. (1977). *Verbal art as performance.* New York: Newbury Press.

Briggs, C. (1988). *Competence in performance: The creativity of tradition in Mexicano verbal art.* Philadelphia: University of Pennsylvania Press.

Briggs, C. (1996). *Disorderly discourse: Narrative, conflict, and inequality.* New York: Oxford University Press.

Burke, K. (1969). *A grammar of motives.* Berkeley: University of California Press.

Cavan, S. (1966). Liquor license: An ethnography of bar behavior. Chicago: Aldine.

Cintron, R. (1997). *Angels' Town: Chero ways, gang life, and rhetorics of the everyday.* Boston Beacon Press.

Dius, P. R. (1983). *The saloon: Public drinking in Chicago and Boston 1880–1920.* Urbana: University of Illinois Press.

Farr, M. (1994). Echando relajo: Verbal art and gender among Mexicanos in Chicago. *Proceedings of the Berkeley Women and Language Conference.* Berkeley: Department of Linguistics.

Farr, M. (1993). Essayist literacy and other verbal performances. *Written Communication, 10*(1), 4–38.

Foley, D. (1984). Does the working class have a culture in the anthropological sense? *Cultural Anthropology, 4*(2), 137–163.

Foley, D. (1990). *Learning capitalist culture: Deep in the heart of Tejas.* Philadelphia: University of Pennsylvania Press.

Fox, A. (1993). The bitch about country music: Split-subjectivity in country music and honky-tonk discourse. In G. Lewis (Ed.), *All that glitters: Country music in America* (pp. 131–139). Bowling Green, OH: Bowling Green State University Popular Press.

Fox, A. (1994). The poetics of irony and the ethnography of class culture. Special issue of *Anthropology and Humanism, 19*(1), 53–72.

Fox, A. (1995). The "redneck reverse": Language and gender in Texas working-class women's verbal art. *Proceedings of the SALSA II conference,* 189–199.

Goffman, E. (1959). *The presentation of self in everyday life.* New York: Doubleday.

Goffman, E. (1981). *Forms of talk.* Philadelphia: University of Pennsylvania Press.

Halle, D. (1984). *America's working man: Work, home, and politics among blue-collar property owners.* Chicago: University of Chicago Press.

Hoggart, R. (1957). *The uses of literacy: Aspects of working-class life, with special reference to publications and entertainments.* New York: Oxford Press.

Hymes, D. (1974). *Foundations in sociolinguistics.* Philadelphia: University of Pennsylvania Press.

Hymes, D. (1975). Breakthrough into performance. In Ben Amos & K. Goldstein (Eds.), *Folklore: Performance and communication* (pp. 11–74). The Hague: Mouton.

Kirshenblatt-Gimblett, B. (1984). The concept and varieties of narrative performance in East European Jewish culture. *In R. Bauman & J. Sherzer (Eds.), Explorations in the ethnography of speaking* (pp. 283–308). Cambridge, UK: Cambridge University Press.

LeMasters, E. E. (1975). *Blue-collar aristocrats: Lifestyles at a working-class tavern.* Madison: University of Wisconsin Press.

Lindquist, J. (2002). *A place to stand: Politics and persuasion in a working-class bar.* New York: Oxford University Press.

Moffatt, M. (1992). Ethnographic writing about American culture. *Annual Review of Anthropology, 21,* 205–229.

Ortner, S. (1991). Reading America: Preliminary notes and class and culture. In R. G. Fox (Ed.), *Recapturing anthropology* (pp. 163–191). Santa Fe: School of American Research Press.

Philipsen, G. (1992). *Speaking culturally: Explorations in social communication.* New York: SUNY Press.

Read, K. E. (1980). *Other Voices: The style of a male homosexual tavern.* Novato, CA: Chandler & Sharp.

Rosenwieg, R. (1983). *Eight hours for what we will.* New York: Cambridge University Press.

Shuman, A. (1986). *Storytelling rights: The uses of oral and written texts by urban adolescents.* Cambridge, UK: Cambridge University Press.

Slayton, R. A. (1986). *Back of the yards: The making of a local democracy.* Chicago: University of Chicago Press.

Spradley, J., & Mann, B. (1975). *The cocktail waitress: Women's work in a man's world.* New York: Knopf.

Stewart, K. (1996). *A space on the side of the road: Cultural poetics in an "other" America.* Princeton, NJ: Princeton University Press.

Tannen, D. (1989). *Talking voices: Repetition, imagery, and dialogue in conversational discourse.* Cambridge, UK: Cambridge University Press.

Westen, K. (1991). *Families we chose: Lesbians, gays, kinship.* New York: Columbia University Press.

Woolard, K. (1985). Language variation and cultural hegemony: Toward and integration of sociolinguistic and social theory. *American Ethnologist, 12*(4), 738–747.

What Color Is Jesus?

James McBride

*In "What Color Is Jesus?" James McBride explores a culturally com-
plex question: "Am I black or white?" This highly personal narrative
encourages readers to consider far-reaching questions about identity
and race. How much of your own "self" is lost, captured, or perhaps
even created when you check the racial identity box on a census form
or college application? What complexities appear through the weav-
ing of cultural, ethnic, and religious strands in your own heritage?
Private as well as social conditions prompt McBride's childhood
question and adult answer. We see how, by imposing socially con-
trived meanings onto the range of human complexions, society turns
"color" into "race." McBride's story may invite us to regard ourselves as texts of sorts, formed by how others read us as much as by
how we see ourselves.*

Just before I quit my last job in Washington, I drove down into Virginia to
see my stepfather's grave for the first time. He was buried in a little country graveyard in Henrico County, near Richmond, about a hundred yards
from the schoolhouse where he learned to read. It's one of those old "colored" graveyards, a lonely, remote backwoods place where the wind blows
through the trees and the graves are marked by lopsided tombstones. It was
so remote I couldn't find it by myself. I had to get my aunt Maggie to show
me where it was. We drove down a dirt road and then parked and walked
down a little dusty path the rest of the way. Once we found his grave, I
stood over it for a long time.

I was fourteen when my stepfather died. One minute he was there, the
next—boom—gone. A stroke. Back then I thought a stroke was something
you got from the sun. I didn't know it could kill you. His funeral was the
first I had ever attended. I didn't know they opened coffins at funerals.
When the funeral director, a woman with white gloves, unlatched the coffin, I was horrified. I couldn't believe she was going to open it up. I begged
her in my mind not to open it up—please—but she did, and there he was.
The whole place broke up. Even the funeral director cried. I thought I
would lose my mind.

From *The Washington Post Magazine,* 1988 by James McBride. Copyright © 1988 by James McBride. Reprinted by permission
of Sterling Lord Literistic, Inc.

Afterward, they took him out of the church, put him in a car, and flew him down to Virginia. My mother and older brother and little sister went, but I'd seen enough. I didn't want to see him anymore. As a kid growing up in New York, I'd been embarrassed by him because he wasn't like the other guys' fathers, who drove hot rods, flew model airplanes with their sons, and talked about the Mets and civil rights. My father was solitary, gruff, busy. He worked as a furnace fireman for the New York City Housing Authority for thirty-six years, fixing oil burners and shoveling coal into big furnaces that heated the housing projects where my family lived. He drove a Pontiac, a solid, clean, quiet car. He liked to dress dapper and drink Rheingold beer and play pool with his brother Walter and their old-timey friends who wore fedoras and smoked filterless Pall Malls and called liquor "likka" and called me "boy." They were weathered Southern black men, quiet and humorous and never bitter about white people, which was out of my line completely. I was a modern-day black man who didn't like the white man too much, even if the white man was my mother.

My mother was born Jewish in Poland, the eldest daughter of an Orthodox rabbi. She married my natural father, a black man, in 1941. He died in 1957, at forty-eight, while she was pregnant with me. She married my stepfather, Hunter L. Jordan, Sr., when I was about a year old. He raised me and my seven brothers and sisters as his own—we considered him to be our father—and he and my mother added four more kids to the bunch to make it an even twelve.

My parents were unique. As unique as any parents I have known, which I suppose makes their children unique. However, being unique can spin you off in strange directions. For years I searched for a kind of peace. I vacillated between being the black part of me that I accept and the white part of me that I could not accept. Part writer, part musician, part black man, part white man. Running, running, always running. Even professionally I sprinted, from jazz musician to reporter and back again. Bounding from one life to the other—the safety and prestige of a journalism job to the poverty and fulfillment of the musician's life.

Standing over my stepfather's grave, thinking about quitting my gig to move back to New York to be a musician and freelance writer, I was nervous. He would never approve of this jive. He would say: "You got a good job and you quit that? For what? To play jazz? To write? Write what? You need a job." Those were almost the exact words my mother always used.

My aunt Maggie, who's about seventy-two, was standing there as I waged this war in my mind. She came up behind me and said, "He was a good man. I know y'all miss him so much."

"Yep," I said, but as we walked up the dusty little path to my car to go to the florist to get flowers, I was thinking, "Man, I'm sure glad he's not here to see me now."

I'm a black man and I've been running all my life. Sometimes I feel like my soul just wants to jump out of my skin and run off, things get that mixed up. But it doesn't matter, because what's inside is there to stay no matter how fast you sprint. Being mixed feels like that tingly feeling you have in your nose when you have to sneeze—you're hanging on there waiting for it to happen, but it never does. You feel completely misunderstood by the rest of the world, which is probably how any sixteen-year-old feels, except that if you're brown-skinned like me, the feeling lasts for the rest of your life. "Don't you sometime feel like just beating up the white man?" a white guy at work once asked me. I hate it when people see my brown skin and assume that all I care about is gospel music and fried chicken and beating up the white man. I could care less. I'm too busy trying to live.

Once a mulatto, always a mulatto, is what I say, and you have to be happy with what you have, though in this world some places are more conducive to the survival of a black white man like me than others. Europe is okay, Philly works, and in New York you can at least run and hide and get lost in the sauce; but Washington is a town split straight down the middle— between white and black, haves and have-nots, light-skinned and dark-skinned—and full of jive-talkers of both colors. The blacks are embittered and expect you to love Marion Barry unconditionally. The whites expect you to be either grateful for their liberal sensibilities or a raging militant. There's no middle ground. No place for a guy like me to stand. Your politics is in the color of your face, and nothing else counts in Washington, which is why I had to get out of there.

All of my brothers and sisters—six boys, five girls, wildly successful by conventional standards (doctors, teachers, professors, musicians)—have had to learn to plow the middle ground. Music is my escape, because when I pick up the saxophone and play, the horn doesn't care what color I am. Whatever's inside comes out, and I feel free.

My family was big, private, close, poor, fun, and always slightly confused. We were fueled by the race question and also befuddled by it. Everyone sought their own private means of escape. When he was little, my older brother Richie, a better sax player than I and the guy from whom I took all my cues, decided he was neither black nor white, but green, like the comic book character the Hulk. His imagination went wild with it, and he would sometimes lie on our bed facedown and make me bounce on him until he turned green.

"Do I look green yet?" he'd ask.

"Naw . . ."

"Jump some more."

I'd bounce some more.

"How about now?"

"Well, a little bit."

"RRRrrrrr . . . I'm the Hulk!" And he'd rise to attack me like a zombie.

Richard had a lot of heart. One morning in Sunday school, he raised his hand and asked our Sunday school teacher, Reverend Owens, "Is Jesus white?"

Reverend Owens said no.

"Then why is he white in this picture?" and he held up our Sunday school Bible.

Reverend Owens said, "Well, Jesus is all colors."

"Then why is he white? This looks like a white man to me." Richie held up the picture high so everyone in the class could see it. "Don't he look white to you?" he asked. Nobody said anything.

Reverend Owens was a nice man and also a barber who tore my head up about once a month. But he wasn't that sharp. I could read better than he could, and I was only twelve.

So he kind of stood there, wiping his face with his handkerchief and making the same noise he made when he preached. "Well . . . ahhh . . . well . . . ahhh . . .

I was embarrassed. The rest of the kids stared at Richie like he was crazy. "Richie, forget it," I mumbled.

"Naw. If they put Jesus in this picture here, and he ain't white, and he ain't black, they should make him gray. Jesus should be gray."

Richie stopped going to Sunday School after that, although he never stopped believing in God. My mother tried to make him go back, but he wouldn't.

When we were little, we used to make fun of our mother singing in church. My mother can't sing a lick. She makes a shrill kind of sound, a cross between a fire engine and Curly of the Three Stooges. Every Sunday morning, she'd stand in church, as she does today, the only white person there, and the whole congregation going, "Leaannnnning, ohhh, leaaning on the crosssss, ohhhhh Laaawwwwd!" and her going, "Leeeeeaaannnning, ohhhh, clank! bang! @ *%$@ *!," rattling happily along like an old Maytag washer. She wasn't born with the gift for gospel music, I suppose.

My mother, Ruth McBride Jordan, who today lives near Trenton, is the best movie I've ever seen. She's seventy-six, pretty, about five three, bow-legged, with curly dark hair and pretty dark eyes. She and my father and stepfather raised twelve children and sent them to college and graduate school, and at age sixty-five she obtained her own college degree in social welfare from Temple University. She's a whirlwind, so it's better to test the wind before you fly the kite. When I began writing my book about her, she said, "Ask me anything. I'll help you as much as I can." Then I asked her a few questions and she snapped: "Don't be so nosy. Don't tell all your business. If you work too much, your mind will be like a brick. My pot's burning on the stove. I gotta go."

When we were growing up, she never discussed race. When we asked whether we were black or white, she'd say, "You're a human being. Educate your mind!" She insisted on excellent grades and privacy. She didn't encourage us to mingle with others of any color too much. We were taught to mind our own business, and the less people knew about us, the better.

When we'd ask if she was white, she'd say, "I'm light-skinned," and change the subject. But we knew she was white, and I was embarrassed by her. I was ten years old when Martin Luther King, Jr., was killed, and I feared for her life because it seemed like all of New York was going to burn. She worked as a night clerk-typist at a Manhattan bank and got home every night about 2 A.M. My father would often be unavailable, and one of the older kids would meet her at the bus stop while the rest of us lay awake, waiting for the sound of the door to open. Black militants scared me. So did the Ku Klux Klan. I thought either group might try to kill her.

I always knew my mother was different, knew my siblings and I were different. My mother hid the truth from her children as long as she could. I was a grown man before I knew where she was born.

She was born Ruchele Dwajra Sylska in a town called Dobryn, near Gdansk, Poland. Her father was an Orthodox rabbi who lived in Russia. He escaped the Red Army by sneaking over the border into Poland. He married my grandmother, Hudis, in what my mother says was an arranged marriage, emigrated to America in the early 1920s, changed his name, and sent for his family. My mother landed on Ellis Island like thousands of other European immigrants.

The family settled in Suffolk, Virginia, and operated a grocery store on the black side of town. Her father also ran a local synagogue. Theirs was the only store in town open on Sundays.

He was feared within the family, my mother says. His wife, who suffered from polio, was close to her three children—a son and two daughters—but could not keep the tyranny of the father from driving them off. The oldest child, my mother's brother, left home early, joined the army, and was killed in World War II. The remaining two girls worked from sunup to sundown in the store. "My only freedom was to go out and buy little romance novels," my mother recalls. "They cost a dime." In school, they called her "Jew-baby."

When she was seventeen, she went to New York to visit relatives for the summer and worked in a Bronx factory owned by her aunt. At the factory, there was a young black employee named Andrew McBride, from High Point, North Carolina. They struck up a friendship and a romance. "He was the first man who was ever kind to me," my mother says. "I didn't care what color he was."

Her father did, though. When she returned home to finish her senior year of high school, her father arranged for her to marry a Jewish man after graduation. She had other plans. The day after she graduated, she packed her bags and left. After floating between New York and Suffolk for a while, she finally decided to marry my father in New York City. Her father caught up to her at the bus station the last time she left home. He knew that she was in love with a black man. The year was 1941.

"If you leave now, don't ever come back," he said.

"I won't," she said.

She gave up Judaism, married Andrew McBride, and moved to a one-room flat in Harlem where she proceeded to have baby after baby. Her husband later became a minister, and together they started New Brown Memorial Baptist Church in Red Hook, Brooklyn, which still exists. The mixed marriage caused them a lot of trouble—they got chased up Eighth Avenue by a group of whites and endured blacks murmuring under their breath, and she was pushed around in the hallway of the Harlem building by a black woman one day. But she never went home. She tried to see her mother after she married, when she found out her mother was ill and dying. When she called, she was told the family had sat shiva for her, as if she had died. "You've been out; stay out," she was told. She always carried that guilt in her heart, that she left her mother with her cruel father and never saw her again.

In 1957, Andrew McBride, Sr., died of cancer. My mother was thirty-six at the time, distraught after visiting him in the hospital, where doctors stared and the nurses snickered. At the time, she was living in the Red Hook project in Brooklyn with seven small kids. She was pregnant with me. In desperation, she searched out her aunt, who was living in Manhattan. She went to her aunt's house and knocked on the door. Her aunt opened the door, then slammed it in her face.

She told me that story only once, a few years ago. It made me sick to hear it, and I said so.

"Leave them alone," she said, waving her hand. "You don't understand Orthodox Jews. I'm happy. I'm a Christian. I'm free. Listen to me: When I got home from your daddy's funeral, I opened our mailbox, and it was full of checks. People dropped off boxes of food—oranges, meat, chickens. Our friends, Daddy's relatives, the people from the church, the people you never go see, they gave us so much money. I'll never forget that for as long as I live. And don't you forget it, either."

A number of years ago, after I had bugged her for months about details of her early life, my mother sat down and drew me a map of where she had lived in Suffolk. She talked as she drew: "The highway goes here, and the jailhouse is down this road, and the slaughterhouse is over here. . . ."

I drove several hours straight, and was tired and hungry once I hit Suffolk, so I parked myself in a local McDonald's and unfolded the little map. I checked it, looked out the window, then checked it again, looked out the window again. I was sitting right where the store used to be.

I went outside and looked around. There was an old house behind the McDonald's. I knocked on the door, and an old black man answered.

"Excuse me . . ." and I told him my story: Mother used to live here. Her father was a rabbi. Jews. A little store. He fingered his glasses and looked at me for a long time. Then he said, "C'mon in here."

He sat me down and brought me a soda. Then he asked me to tell my story one more time. So I did.

He nodded and listened closely. Then his face broke into a smile. "That means you the ol' rabbi's grandson?"

"Yep."

First he chuckled, then he laughed. Then he laughed some more. He tried to control his laughing, but he couldn't, so he stopped, took off his glasses, and wiped his eyes. I started to get angry, so he apologized. His name was Eddie Thompson. He was sixty-six. He had lived in that house all his life. It took him a minute to get himself together.

"I knew your mother," he said. "We used to call her Rachel."

I had never heard that name before. Her name is Ruth, but he knew her as Rachel, which was close to Ruchele, the Yiddish name her family called her.

"I knew that whole family," Thompson said. "The ol' rabbi, boy, he was something. Rachel was the nice one. She was kindhearted. Everybody liked her. She used to walk right up and down the road here with her mother. The mother used to limp. They would say hello to the people, y'know? Old man, though . . ." and he shrugged. "Well, personally, I never had no problem with him."

He talked for a long time, chuckling, disbelieving. "Rachel just left one day. I'm telling you she left, and we thought she was dead. That whole family is long gone. We didn't think we'd ever see none of them again till we got to the other side. And now you pop up. Lord knows it's a great day."

He asked if we could call her. I picked up the phone and dialed Philadelphia, got my mother on the line, and told her I had somebody who wanted to talk to her. I handed the phone to him.

"Rachel? Yeah. Rachel. This is Eddie Thompson. From down in Suffolk. Remember me? We used to live right be—yeaaaaah, that's right." Pause. "No, I was one of the little ones. Well, I'll be! The Lord touched me today.

"Rachel!? That ain't you crying now, is it? This is old Eddie Thompson. You remember me? Don't cry now."

I went and got some flowers for my stepfather's grave and laid them across it. My mother wanted me to make sure the new tombstone she got him was in place, and it was. It said OUR BELOVED DADDY, HUNTER L. JORDAN, AUGUST 11, 1900, TO MAY 14, 1972.

He was old when he died and a relatively old fifty-eight when he married my mother. They met in a courtyard of the Red Hook housing project where we lived, while she was selling church dinners on a Saturday to help make ends meet. He strolled by and bought some ribs, came back the next Saturday and bought some more. He ended up buying the whole nine yards—eight kids and a wife. He used to joke that he had enough for a baseball team.

I never heard him complain about it, and it never even occurred to me to ask him how he felt about white and black. He was quiet and busy. He dealt with solid things. Cars. Plumbing. Tricycles. Work. He used to joke about how he had run away from Richmond when he was a young man because Jim Crow was tough; but racism to him was a detail that you stepped over, like you'd step over a crack in the sidewalk. He worked in the stockyards in Chicago for a while, then in a barbershop in Detroit, where, among other things, he shined Henry Ford's shoes. He went to New York in the 1920s. He never told me those things; his brother Walter did. He didn't find those kinds of facts interesting. All he wanted to talk about was my grades.

He was strong for his age, full and robust, with brown eyes and handsome American Indian features. One night, he had a headache, and the next day he was in the hospital with a stroke. After a couple of weeks, he came home. Then two days later, he asked me to come out to the garage with him. I was one of the older kids living at home; most were away at college or already living on their own. He could barely walk and had difficulty speaking, but we went out there, and we got inside his Pontiac. "I was thinking of maybe driving home one more time," he said. He was talking about Henrico County, where we spent summer vacations.

He started the engine, then shut if off. He was too weak to drive. So he sat there, staring out the windshield, looking at the garage wall, his hand on the steering wheel. He was wearing his old-timey cap and his peacoat, though it was May and warm outside. Sitting there, staring straight ahead, he started talking, and I listened closely because he never gave speeches.

He said he had some money saved up and a little land in Virginia, but it wasn't enough. He was worried about my mother and his children. He said I should always mind her and look out for my younger brothers and sisters, because we were special. "Special people," he said. "And just so special to me." It was the only time I ever heard him refer to race, however vaguely, but it didn't matter because right then I knew he was going to die, and I had to blink back my tears. Two days later, he was gone.

Standing over his grave—it seemed so lonely and cold, with the wind blowing through the trees—part of me wanted to throw myself on the ground to cover and warm him. We arranged the flowers. Plastic ones, because, as Aunt Maggie said, they lasted longer. I took one last look and thought, maybe he would understand me now. Maybe not. I turned and left.

I suppose I didn't look too happy, because as I started up the little road toward my car, Aunt Maggie put her arm in mine. I'd known her since I was a boy, just like I'd known these woods as a boy when he took us down here, but I'd blanked her and these woods out of my mind over the years, just like you'd blank out the words of a book by covering them with a piece of paper. She didn't judge me, which is what I always appreciated most about our friends and relatives over the years, the white and the black. They never judged, just accepted us as we were. Maybe that's what a black white man has to do. Maybe a black white man will never be content. Maybe a black white man will never fit. But a black white man can't judge anybody.

I remember when I was ten years old, when I pondered my own race and asked my mother, as she was attempting to fix our dinner table that had deteriorated to three-legged status, whether I was white or black. She paused a moment, then responded thoughtfully: "Pliers "

"Huh?"

"Hand me the pliers out of the kitchen drawer."

I handed her the pliers and she promptly went to work on the kitchen table, hammering the legs and top until dents and gouges appeared on all sides. When the table finally stood shakily on all fours, she set the pliers down, stood up and said, "Pliers can fix anything."

"What about me being black?" I asked.

"What about it?" she said. "Forget about black. You are a human being."

"But what do I check on the form at school that says White, Black, Other?"

"Don't check nothing. Get a hundred on your school tests and they won't care what color you are."

"But they do care."

"I don't," she said, and off she went.

Perturbed, I picked up the pliers and sought out my father, hammering at the fuel pump of his 1969 Pontiac. "Am I black or white?" I asked.

"Where'd you get my pliers?" he asked.

"I got 'em from Ma."

"I been looking for 'em all day." He took them and immediately put them to work.

"Am I black or white, Daddy?"

He grabbed a hose in his hand and said, "Hold this." I held it. He went inside the car and cranked the engine. Fuel shot out of the line and spilled all over me. "You all right?" he asked. I shook my head. He took me inside, cleaned me up, put the hose in the car, and took me out for ice cream. I forgot about my color for a while.

But the question plagued me for many years, even after my father's death, and I never did find out the answer because neither he nor my mother ever gave any. I was effectively on my own. I searched for years to find the truth, to find myself as a black white man. I went to Africa, got VD, came home with no answers. I went to Europe, sipped café and smoked in Paris for months, came home empty. Last year, while working on my '53 Chevy at my home in Nyack, while my four-year-old son rolled around in the leaves and ate mud, it hit me. I asked him to hand me the pliers, and as he did so, he asked me, "What color is Grandma?"

"She's white, "I said.

"Why isn't she like me?"

"She is like you, she's just whiter."

"Why is she whiter?"

"I don't know. God made her that way."

"Why?"

"I don't know. Would you like her better if she looked more like you?"

"No. I like her the way she is."

It occurred to me then that I was not put on this earth to become a leader of mixed-race people, wielding my race like a baseball bat, determined to force white people to accept me as I am. I realized then that I did not want to be known as Mr. Mulatto, whose children try to be every race in the world, proudly proclaiming Indian blood, African blood, Jewish blood, singing Peter, Paul, and Mary songs at phony private schools where yuppie parents arrive each morning hopping out of Chevy Suburban tanks with bumper stickers that read "Question Authority." I want the same thing every parent wants—a good home for my wife and children, good schools, peace and quiet, a good set of wrenches, and a son big enough to hand them to me. And when he gets big enough to have his own tools and work on his own car, maybe he will understand that you can't change someone's opinion about you no matter how many boxes you check, no matter how many focus groups you join, no matter how much legislation you pass, no matter how much consciousness raising you do. It's a real simple answer. Give 'em God. Give 'em pliers. Give 'em math. Give 'em discipline. Give 'em love, and let the chips fall where they may. Pontificating about it is okay. Passing laws is important, but I never once in my life woke up not knowing whether I should eat matzo ball or fried chicken. I never once felt I'd be able to play the sax better if my mom had been black, or that I'd have been better at math if my father were Jewish. I like me, and I like me because my parents liked me.

The Shack of Art and Healing

Oona Hyla Patrick

In "The Shack of Art and Healing," Oona Hyla Patrick discusses feeling like an imposter in her own hometown. Like many beach towns, Provincetown, Massachusetts draws tourists, writers, artists, and naturalists—urban people who come looking for peace and beauty. When Patrick looks out on Provincetown's celebrated dunes, she sees devastation and deforestation, a complex environment where local people are integral to the landscape. She rejects the romanticism with which the "washashores" have historically defined the Cape, and she challenges the traditional genre of nature writing, in which outsiders come to observe the beauty of a landscape with which they are not intimately involved. Who or what defines the place that you come from? How is your view of that place different from an outsider's? What places have you visited as a tourist? What did you see? What might you have missed?

A simple list of plants from the Pilgrims' description of the tip of Cape Cod in the 1622 *Mourt's Relation,* is, strangely enough, one of the more haunting lines in Cape Cod history. "They found it to be a small neck of land; on this side where we lay is the bay, and the further side the sea; the ground or earth, sand hills, much like the downs in Holland, but much better; the crust of the earth a spit's depth excellent black earth; all wooded with oaks, pines, sassafras, juniper, birch, holly, vines, some ash, walnut . . ." Though it is unclear exactly where they were looking—and certainly there were sandy stretches on the Cape from earliest times—Cape Cod, so famed for sand, was once more forested.

Growing up in Provincetown, Mass. I had heard occasional tales of buried trees and of ancient tree stumps at the bottom of the harbor, but it was not until I read two old local histories, Frederick Freeman's 1860 *The History of Cape Cod* and Shebnah Rich's 1883 *Truro—Cape Cod, or, Land marks and sea marks,* that I realized that swaths of Cape Cod's dune landscape are, in essence, man-made.

The histories tell of how seventeenth and eighteenth century settlers and crews from visiting ships cut down much of a forest here for firewood and lumber for houses and boats. They had come from England, where various

From *Post Road Magazine*. Copyright © 2002 by Oona Hyla Patrick. Reprinted by permission.

laws and private ownership restricted access to woodlands, and they now gorged themselves on free wood for every purpose. Soon there was little left to hold the sand, and the dunes began to move, burying remaining trees and threatening the town and its valuable harbor. The state tried for years to stop the cutting of trees and the grazing of cattle, but Provincetowners have never liked being interfered with (a trait with both positive and negative consequences). The federal government appropriated money for the planting of beach grass to finally bring the dunes under relative control in the nineteenth century.

Part of this celebrated landscape, then, is a wasteland, perhaps an adapted one, but a wasteland nevertheless. Why do people now see it in terms of wonder and beauty rather than despair? I know it is not that obscure a piece of information, just an ignored one. Despite Henry Beston's *Outermost House,* John Hay's *The Great Beach,* and so many other popular Cape Cod books, I think this landscape suggests far more about human nature than anything else. Such as our endless capacity for destruction, no matter the fragility of the subject. And a tendency to take note too late, to mourn too briefly, and to forget as quickly as we came and got. This place's literary history, too, points to our habit of following the leader, of reading and believing what we are told to.

I spent the second week of May 2000 in a dune shack in the Province Lands on the back side of Provincetown. Someone had cancelled their residency week, and I was the runner-up in the lottery. These dune shack residencies are advertised as "retreats for art and healing," but all I wanted was time to read and write. Writing and painting in a dune shack is something of a legendary experience in Provincetown, and I wanted to see what the fuss over them was about. This was the easiest way for me to get there now.

Over the past several years I have been reading many things that relate to my family's past on the Lower Cape—histories, old records and newspapers, novels, travelers' accounts, archaeological surveys, studies of Portuguese-American communities, and books on fishing and whaling. But there is one genre I tried, and failed, to read with the same enthusiasm I brought to the other material. The box of books I brought with me to the shack included the usual eclectic mix: the above-mentioned nineteenth century Cape Cod histories by Freeman and Rich, Mary Heaton Vorse's *Time and the Town* (a favorite of mine), and the Portuguese classic *The Lusiads.* I also packed a book I had been avoiding for a while: John Hay's 1963 *The Great Beach.* John Hay has been called the "nature-writing laureate of Cape Cod," and I thought that perhaps here, if anywhere, I could come to terms with Cape Cod nature writing.

On the morning my residency began, a volunteer named Sam drove me out to the shack via a long sandy trail marked *Fire Road*. He mentioned the lost forest to me on the way out in the jeep. When we arrived at the one-and-a-half story gray-shingled house in a shallow valley of sand dunes, I met the previous week's resident: a "multi-media" artist named Ellen, probably in her fifties, with short gray hair and an intense stare. She said she hadn't done much work, that she'd mostly just been writing in her journal and meditating. When she said the word "meditating" she fixed her eyes on mine. I took it as a challenge: meditation as competition. She was sizing me up and she seemed to say, "I bet you don't meditate."

As I listened to the conversation between Sam and Ellen, I began to get that familiar feeling of being out of place in my own hometown—a feeling I got most often while walking down Commercial Street in the summertime crowds. The night before, while in a frantic rush to get batteries and flashlights and other supplies for my week without electricity and running water, I'd glimpsed a woman walking down the street wearing a large pair of well-feathered angel's wings. Locals tend to react to such sights with a combination of proud composure and bemused resignation that masks a secret delight in living in a place where these things have at times been the norm. So I had thought little of this angel—it's never too early in the season for costumes.

What I had forgotten in my haste, of course, was that that night, May 5th, was the night of the potential world-ending alignment of the planets (whatever that means). While I unpacked, Sam and Ellen started talking about the night's "energy:" the strange vibe he'd felt on Commercial Street, and the animal sightings she declined to detail. I later suspected it was just the little cottontail bunny that was living under the shack. This kind of conversation, I knew, shied away from specifics as much as from any hint of negativity. I finally had to interrupt them to find out where the flue was on the wood stove, whether there was extra kerosene for the lamps, and how to use the outdoor water pump, not to mention the outhouse itself.

They drove off and left me alone in the shack, which was more like a house and bigger than my Boston apartment. It had a combination dining room and kitchen, a living room, and a loft bedroom above the living room. The bedroom seemed strangely well-furnished for a rough old place on the beach. It contained a red oriental carpet, a mahogany and glass linen cabinet, a wicker chest full of blankets, an upholstered armchair, and a leather drum the size of a small coffee table. In the kitchen I found so much stored food I realized I had probably brought too much of my own. I opened canisters full of Met-Rx, green tea, and Master's Choice chocolate bars imported from Germany.

I went outside and sat on the new wood of the deck as the sun came out. From somewhere very far away I heard the sound of hammering, and later, a siren. It was a forty-five minute walk to the closest inhabited area, if you didn't count the other dune shacks, some of them still boarded up, which lay over some distant hills.

This dune shack is one of nineteen surviving shacks built in the dunes on the back side of town before the creation of the Cape Cod National Seashore park lands. The "Seashore" decided to bulldoze all of the shacks after it took over the land in 1961. Those that are still standing exist because some of the owners took the Park Service to court and eventually won. As I understand it, the current owners have lifetime leases on their shacks; when they die the buildings revert to the Seashore. The C-Scape shack began in the 1940s when a local couple, Eddie and Mary Nunes, moved a structure from another town and made additions to it; they also gave it its name. It changed hands many times and, since 1996, has been leased from the Seashore by the non-profit organization that runs the residency program. Park rangers now bring tours in to see the visual artists at work here in the summer.

Local people built many of the dune shacks early in the twentieth century, though they may have replaced even older fishing huts. While the Province Lands were owned by the state from the beginning of the town's history, it seems that anyone who wanted to could build a shelter out here from wood they found on the beach. The shacks are small, weathered, and well braced for storms.

My grandfather built several of the shacks himself, perhaps as many as three or four, so it's ironic that I should feel out of place here. He sold them so long ago that no one knows anymore if any of them are still standing, or what they might look like now—though I'm told that one of them had a roof shaped like the upside-down hull of a boat.

The area is most famous as the site of the old Coast Guard Station where Eugene O'Neill lived and wrote—before the building fell into the sea and he left for other places. Many of the town's other artists and writers worked out here too, leading to the area's eventual designation as the Peaked Hill Bars National Register Historic District. A few people made dune shacks their permanent or near-permanent homes. Harry Kemp was the biggest self-promoter among these. 1 have read how he would ply O'Neill with his sometimes awful rhyming poems, hoping for a scrap of praise. He has been dead for more than forty years, but he's still known as the "Poet of the Dunes" and has even been republished. Printed on the brochure advertising the dune shack residences are his lines: "My shack standing in the middle of all this . . ./Next door to heaven and close on the gales/of sunset . . . I've got what few have,/I've got the life I want!" Sam told me on the drive that he'd finally been able to get into Kemp's poetry after spending some time out here.

Among locals, however, the shacks have a less genteel reputation. This is one of those gaps in understanding between natives and most (though not all) "washashores." Before anything else, the dune shacks of my imagination are places of wild parties, chaos, and regrets (my mother says my father used to go out there with notorious town hell raisers such as Norman Mailer). They were where you went to do things you didn't want people to know about in a small town, and to escape authority. I used to look forward to getting my turn out here when I grew up—but I never thought 1 would be filling out an application to do so.

Going back further, there is an older layer of belief beyond the New Age spiritualism I couldn't seem to escape in the Shack of Art and Healing: in Cape Cod folktales, these dunes on the back side of the Cape are the domain of the devil. Some of these tales may even be based on earlier Native American stories about the region. By contrast, in the early twentieth century, the town's Portuguese immigrants gave rise to a legend of a visit by the Virgin Mary, whose footprints blossomed into the clusters of yellow flowers that still grow in the dunes.

Part of me wishes the dune shacks were still lawless and free. Today, the photocopied C-Scape regulations, several pages long, ban dogs and many other things, and explicitly forbid anything a park ranger could possibly "construe as a party."

The landscape here is not all sand—there is the beach grass growing on ridges and down the sides of some dunes. The shallow valley beyond the deck is partially filled with thin, low shrubs that added a dark gray touch to the overall impression of a scoured, bone-dry landscape.

The Atlantic is just over the dune, and the surf added a constant background noise, almost like static. Huge bumblebees swung back and forth over the deck, tracing the same patterns in the air each time as if they were on strings. One resident, I later read, thought these bees were fighting when they suddenly buzzed at each other and flew off locked together. Another thought they were mating. I could never decide—I think perhaps it was both.

Before taking out the books I'd brought with me, I took a quick look through the three volumes of journals left by four years' worth of residents. I sat on the old Indian tapestry covered couch in the living room in front of the cold wood stove, with one good painting to my left, and one very bad pink and green painting to my right. There were two maps of the dunes and a poem written on an old shingle by a group of children on a wall near the couch. In the bookshelf below, I noticed a game of Candy Land. Somewhere behind my head in the Styrofoam-insulated walls that looked like they might double for flotation, I could hear the scratching of a family of mice.

What I read in the journals increased my sense of not having the proper set of responses to this place. I was told I had entered a "realm of magic and poetry" in these dunes. Along with a few drawings and small paintings in the pages, and the occasional interesting musing of a novelist, there were dozens of flailing, repetitive descriptions of the beauty of sand, waves, birds, shells, and light. The words *relaxation, recovery, peace,* and *communion* recurred over and over again. I had come here to work, dreaming of all that I would get done, and I felt like an imposter. But then I also felt there was something programmed about the responses people described—as if they were following some script that I didn't want to, or couldn't, follow.

By the end of the first day, though, I felt something I didn't expect. I had never had anything like a house of my own in Provincetown—this was the closest I had ever been, even if it was only for a week. My family had been through a lot in recent years, and I had gotten used to the daze brought about by a constant, low-level sense of loss. Even though I had developed something of a love-hate relationship with the town, I was going to enjoy this.

Wednesday, May 10

I have been carrying in wood and water. Today it poured, thunder and lightening too, for hours. My hands are so cold that I'm holding them under someone's old blanket on this couch which squeaks just like the mice that have been eating my food. It is hard to do work when I feel so uncomfortable. I've been getting up the courage to "take a shower" outside all day now. But with no sun, there's no solar shower.

The wind is so strong at night that I wake up and wonder if the loft is about to tumble off, rolling with me in it, down the dune. I imagine that single well-furnished room, with the oriental and the glass cabinet, out by itself in this desolate place. The room sways, but not like a boat. Someday it's going to come off. I think about the strength of the metal braces holding the wood stove's chimney to the roof. I think about them a lot.

I have had the worst dreams here. Arguing, two nights in a row, first with my mother and then while being fired from work. Then plane crashes and Kennedys, the one with one leg. My father says one of the early owners of this shack, Howard Lewis, had only one leg. I don't know how he did it, how he got along in the shack. (Less to wash, though.)

It's 5:30 and I think I'm going to go dump a pot full of half-boiled chili-flavored water over my head. Then I'll have to dry my hair in the wood stove smoke, which will make it dirty all over again.

Every day, except for that one terrible day when it was rainy and cold, I worked in the morning and went for a long walk along the beach or through the dunes or the low, bog-ridden forest between them and the highway.

I started, then stopped, John Hay's *The Great Beach* several times. There was a basic guidebook to the plants of the National Seashore propped on a shelf in the shack like some kind of religious icon, and I kept reading that instead. I read about the plants I saw on my walks or knew from around my parents' house. I read how lichen grows even on bare rock, and can turn even the most inhospitable surface into soil rich enough for other plants to grow in after a few years. I read about the stunted pines growing flat along the ground, about poverty grass, wild asparagus, hog cranberry, cat's briar, bayberry, and the few other things out here. It was a thin book.

If *The Great Beach* had been a well-written book about Death Valley or Alaska, I might have swallowed every word, but I was here, had known the landscape since childhood, and I realized I didn't want Hay's voice interpreting these plants and this scenery for me. I found his descriptions weak and his conclusions vague. His clouds are "like heaps of spun silk," and the sun on the water makes it look like "molten gold and silver." Hay's sentences trail off from promising specificity to vague, sometimes incomprehensible conclusions, "The bryozoans on the seaweed tell a deep and primitive tale about the salt water and its animation." You can take many sentences out of context and have no idea what they mean. Not only that, you can take two sentences from the same page and get the same effect, such as, "A greater landscape means a new communion," and "Mountains or seashore make for revelation."

The passages I did like provided more facts than most: I learned about two kinds of fog, tidal bulges, milestones in the lives of the diatoms, and that Cape Cod Bay's tendency to ice up is unique on the East Coast.

I had to give Hay credit for sounding more intimate and being a bit more present than he might have, especially in the one chapter he devotes to the human history of the area. But Hay and other Cape Cod nature writers sometimes seem to live in a "place apart" within their heads. The place they describe is partly just in their imagination, the way the dune shacks, in another way, were in mine.

My own little manifesto against Cape Cod nature writing still stands. It has surely been said before, but I continue to feel this genre, which can be traced back to Thoreau's *Cape Cod,* has been operating on some unspoken assumptions:

1. Audience. The land described is always in understood comparison to suburban/urban life, which the reader is assumed to share. Hay says, "One afternoon in the middle of June I set off from Race Point at Provincetown, carrying a pack and sleeping bag, with Nauset Light Beach in Eastham, twenty-five miles away, as my destination, and my purpose simply to be on the beach, to see it and feel it for whatever it turned out to be, since most of my previous visits had been the sporadic hop, skip, and jump kind to which our automotivated lives seem to lead us."

2. Morality. Human objects, whether trash or a house (excepting perhaps the author's?), take on an immoral air and an original sin for simply existing at all.

3. Class. Natives and those employed in any way in the landscape do not and cannot have the same deep thoughts about the landscape as the (apparently unemployed) nature writer is having. (Unless the native fits into the "Old Salt" stereotype.) Also, most natives are ignorant and need to be told much of what the nature writer already knows, though they may never fully comprehend.

4. Subject Matter. "A Long Walk on the Cape Cod Beach" is an intrinsically interesting subject, and a rare and intrepid trip taken by few. For my family, and for others, walking on this beach and gathering things there is a tradition that goes back at least a hundred years in our memory. My father was once known to go out every day, around the time he was starting his business selling surplus and ships' salvage, some of which he found on the beach.

Nature writing that suffers from these and other similar problems, disappoints its readers by leaving out so much else that is going on, or has gone on, in the landscape.

I am going to say something blasphemous: I do not think this landscape is beautiful. I am not even sure I like it. To me, this landscape looks honest (in that it is undisguised and uncultivated), blank, and defeated. As in many places in Provincetown, I feel at home but I do not feel at ease. While people may no longer see this place as the province of the devil or subject to visitations from the Virgin Mary or the ghosts of the shipwrecked, for me and for others, there is a lingering fear of this place. When my borrowed cell phone's battery died toward the end of the week, my parents started to get nervous, imagining all kinds of scenarios when they could not reach me.

And at night, when you light every kerosene lantern in the place and the glass panes of the windows look like sheets of ebony, all of the Province Lands' demons are loose. Ellen, the previous week's resident, had not slept well, and complained that a local had told her some stories (which she did not specify) before she came out. There were notes about this in the journals too. Someone left a book of ghost stories by the bed as a joke for a friend, who noted that she did not read them. I did no better than the others; I was one of the ones who propped the front door closed at night (the locks have long been rusted out). The truth is that nights in the dune shack are the flip side of the much-touted *relaxation, recovery, peace,* and *communion* in the journals, and that having survived them might just have something to do with why people felt "healed" after their time here.

Friday, May 12
I made the best beach-combing discovery of my life today: I found a color T.V. They say the ocean provides for all our needs.
Coming down the dune, I thought it might be a small stove, or perhaps a generator (my father's been wanting one of those). As I approached, I saw that an electric cord was still attached, flung out beside the object. I got closer and made out the distinctive black plastic curves of a television's back. A large set of sneaker prints led to it and away, back toward the sets of tire tracks that parallel the water line. Either they've begun charging for T.V. disposal at the dump, or there's still not much to do around here on a Thursday night in May.
I turned the object face up. A Sony Trinitron. The faux wood-paneled variety. While the glass was intact, one side of the set had been cruelly kicked in. I sat down beside it, looked it over some more, and finally resisted the temptation to haul it over the dune. It would never fit in Sam's jeep.
Later, wandering aimlessly on the high dunes in my favorite Scarlet O'Hara T-shirt, I arrived in time to watch the sun go down as the sea came to claim the Trinitron.

The Gathering of Tribes

John Seabrook

In "The Gathering of Tribes," John Seabrook examines the world of lacrosse at a Native American reservation and at prep schools. For Seabrook, however, a game is not just a game, especially considering the social ramifications this "game" has. The world of lacrosse opens up a network of power and privilege. However, this network is available only to the "white" prep school students. Whereas prep school students know the game as a social stepladder, Native American students encounter racism time and time again. How are other sports you play and watch more than just a "game"? Who has access to these games in terms of race, gender, and socioeconomic status? What other kinds of success are related to participation in these games? As Seabrook shows, the game of lacrosse has been taken over and changed from the way Native Americans originally played and thought of the game. What are the ramifications of a group taking and changing something that has a significant history in another group?

In the Box

Like most Native Americans, the members of the Onondaga Athletic Club, in upstate New York, play box lacrosse. Box is a faster and more violent game than the genteel sport of field lacrosse, which is played in prep schools and colleges in the United States. The Onondagan box is outdoors, and around the playing surface are weathered wooden boards and heavy-duty fencing to protect spectators from flying lacrosse balls. It is bare ground, worn but not really smooth; the dirt is coarse and abrasive. Most other Indian teams in what is known as the Senior B Box Lacrosse League play in indoor stadiums, on the defrosted surfaces of hockey rinks. The Onondaga take pride in their Spartan confines. "We'll see what happens when we get them in our box," they say after a tough loss at one of the fancier indoor places.

To get to the Onondagan box, I flew to the Syracuse airport, rented a car, jumped on I-81, and drove for twenty minutes, until I saw a large sign telling me I was now on the sovereign land of the Onondaga Nation, where no state or federal laws have jurisdiction. Most Indian reservations in the

Originally published in The New Yorker. Copyright © 1998. www.johnseabrook.com.

United States are quasi-sovereign territories, managed and partly subsidized by the Bureau of Indian Affairs. The Onondaga, however, are completely independent. They govern themselves by a bicameral system set down in the Iroquois Confederacy's constitution, which was created long before the United States Constitution and is thought to have influenced both Benjamin Franklin and Thomas Jefferson.

I took the next exit, and drove along Route 11-A until I saw the box. Sitting there beside the road, with lots of open space around it that seemed ideal for field lacrosse, it suggested a bitter ceremonial reënactment of the original trauma of being corralled into reservations on ancestral lands belonging to the first great political power north of the Rio Grande, the Iroquois.

Oren Lyons, who is the faith-keeper of the Onondaga and is a famous Native American lacrosse player, had told me to be at the box by eleven. The O.A.C. was going on a weekend road trip to Canada, and I was to ride along on the bus with them. Lacrosse, invented by Indians in northeastern North America long before the Europeans arrived, was adopted by nineteenth-century white men and turned into the sport I knew—another kind of tribal subculture, which flourishes in Eastern prep schools and élite colleges in the mid-Atlantic states. Lyons, a fit-looking sixty-eight-year-old with thick gray hair reaching halfway down his back, was teaching me about the Indian game. He was a good teacher and, I'd learned from our conversations, a skillful weaver of narratives that often began and ended with lacrosse but also brought together history, politics, spirituality, Iroquois nationalism, and the limits of private enterprise on Indian lands.

"This game is going to be a war," Lyons had told me. Tonight, the Onondaga club would be playing the Kahnawake Mohawk, in an indoor box on the Mohawk reservation, near Montreal. The Kahnawake had some dirty players, including, it was rumored on the bus, a member of the breakaway faction of Mohawk who, back in the seventies, took over an empty girls' summer camp in the Adirondacks and established a warrior enclave, the Indian version of the Montana Militia. (Eventually, the enclave moved to seven hundred acres in Altona, New York, where, in 1990, its members were involved in an eleven-day armed standoff with state troopers.) Because Oren Lyons was an outspoken opponent of the warrior enclave, as he was of any challenge to the unity of the six-nation Iroquois Confederacy (the nations are Onondaga, Mohawk, Oneida, Cayuga, Seneca, and Tuscarora), it was possible that some of the Mohawk players would go after some of the Onondagan players, among them Lyons's son, Rex, who was a star player on the Onondagan team.

It was a five-hour trip up to the Mohawk reservation. On the bus were thirty-three men and boys, ranging in age from thirty-eight to fifteen. In the front seats were the older men: Rex and his cousin Kent Lyons, the Onondagan goalie; a veteran defenseman known as Ace; and the team's coach, Freeman Bucktooth. "We know when we play lacrosse that we are doing what Iroquois men have always done, since the Creator gave us the game," Kent told me. Lacrosse helps to protect Iroquois culture from the larger American popular culture, which threatens to obliterate it, and which was present on the bus in many forms, from our Nike shoes to "Jerry Springer Too Hot for TV," the video that was playing on the bus's monitors. It featured censored outtakes from the controversial TV show and ended with an earnest message from Springer to the viewers, attacking his critics as enemies of free speech. Meanwhile, Kent was describing a "medicine game" that many of the men and boys on the bus had begun their season with—a kind of intramural lacrosse game played over three days by males of all ages, from thirteen to seventy-five, for the good of the community. "We play the medicine game because it helps with the hunt, even if the hunt is behind a computer screen and the forest is in an office building," Kent explained. "Everything is a circle. Lacrosse makes the circle stronger."

I asked Rex if women played lacrosse much on the reservation; in the outside world, the growth of women's lacrosse in recent years has been explosive. On the rez, Rex said, girls are discouraged by the traditionalists from playing lacrosse, because, as he put it, the Creator didn't intend for them to play, and it's not good for the medicine.

Most of the guys on the bus were holding their sticks, tying and untying the knots in the webbing of the pockets, and spinning them in their hands. Lacrosse players seem to have a fetishistic relationship with their sticks, which are part hockey stick, part tennis racquet, and part club. In field lacrosse, sticks vary in length, depending on whether one plays attack, midfield, or defense (also known as longstick). Indian stick-makers used to supply most of the world's sticks. A hickory trunk was split, steamed, and bent at one end, and the pocket was woven of leather and catgut, which had a very particular smell in the rain. But in 1970 the Brine Company, based in Boston, introduced an aluminum stick with a molded plastic head and a rubber-and-nylon pocket, and within five years the Indian wooden-stick industry had all but disappeared.

For the youngest men on the bus, lacrosse is a chance to escape the entrenched poverty of life on the rez. What basketball is to the black urban poor, lacrosse is to an Indian kid—his shot at a college scholarship and a good education. One of the brightest prospects on the Onondagan's team was the coach's son, Drew Bucktooth, a shy, handsome kid sitting a few rows behind me. He could have his pick of full scholarships at lacrosse schools like Syracuse, Loyola, and Johns Hopkins, but, at his father's insistence, he is spending this year playing in Canada's junior hockey league, with the hope of being drafted into the N.H.L. and making some big money. If that doesn't work out, though, he retains his eligibility for college lacrosse.

Rex is thirty-five. He's a bit beaten up, but he still has a good burst of speed near the "crease," the circular area that surrounds the goal. He and his family live down the road from his father and next door to his mother. There are a couple of lacrosse nets in the back yard where his kids play. Both he and Kent do the high-altitude construction work for which the Iroquois are famous; they have jobs as union glaziers. They also play in a rock-and-roll band called White Boy and the Wagon Burners, after an insult that a white Canadian player once shouted at Rex when he had been repeatedly scored on by Rex and his teammates: "You ain't nothing but wagon burners anyway." Both Rex and Kent got lacrosse scholarships to Syracuse University, but neither of them graduated. When I asked Rex about that, he said the problem had been the "frat boys" whom he and Kent met on and off the lacrosse field. He told me there were some ugly incidents between them, but he added, "I wasn't prepared for college. Not mature enough. I wanted to keep my rock-and-roll band; there were just too many distractions. It wasn't only the frat boys—it was me."

Rex's college experience is typical of that of Native American lacrosse players: got the scholarship, couldn't stick it out. Although lacrosse offers Indians a chance to get off the reservation, it also helps to keep them on it, by reinforcing the native culture that makes it hard for them to assimilate at universities. Roy Simmons, who coached lacrosse for forty-one years at Syracuse University and retired only this year, told me recently, "Of all the Indians I have seen walk through my door on lacrosse scholarships, maybe a third have graduated. Most of them don't feel comfortable here, and leave after a year or so. I remember I had a kid come here from the rez and I went with him up to the high-rise where he had been assigned a room. He put down his bag, which had a few simple things in it, and looked around at his new white roommate's stereo and books and the nice goose-down bedspread, and then he pointed to the wall and said, 'What's that?' I said, 'That's a thermostat.' 'What's it do?' he asked. You know, he was uncomfortable. He was gone pretty soon." Rex's wife, Xina, wants their sons to go to a college far away, so they won't be tempted to come home on weekends.

I asked Rex if he was worried about politically motivated violence against him tonight. He shrugged. He was bringing along his wooden lacrosse stick in case things got out of hand. Today's aluminum and titanium sticks are easier to throw and catch with, but a wooden stick still hurts the most when you whack somebody with it. Ace said he wished he still had his wooden stick. He had recently placed it in the coffin of a friend who died of alcoholism at the age of thirty-eight.

The bus wound along the state roads of the ice-storm-devastated forests of upper New York, the country between Lake Champlain and the St. Lawrence River, which is thought to be where lacrosse was invented, by the Eastern Algonquins. It was known to the Iroquois as *takitchawei,* which means "bump hips." The game was spread south by the Cherokee, who called it "little brother of war," and west by the Sioux. Lacrosse games sometimes lasted as long as three days, with goals as much as a mile or two apart, as many as a hundred players on a team, and no side boundaries, like the game of Capture the Flag that kids at summer camp now play in those same forests.

The French term *la crosse* was first applied to the Indians' sticks in the sixteen-thirties by a Jesuit missionary who lived among the Huron. The most famous game of the eighteenth century, as described by Francis Parkman in "The Conspiracy of Pontiac," was played between two tribes, the Ojibwa and the Ozaagii, in front of Fort Michilimackinac, a British encampment on the shores of Lake Michigan, on June 4, 1763. The British soldiers had thrown open the fort's gates in order to see the game better and were having a good time watching the Indians beat one another senseless (which is what some white people still enjoy doing on a Saturday night in the Senior B Box Lacrosse League), when, at a prearranged signal, the Indians flung the lacrosse ball through the fort's gate. Switching from lacrosse mode to war mode (an easy transition in those days), they killed most of the soldiers—some on the spot and the others later, slowly torturing them to death in the forest.

The transformation of *takitchawei* into the game that college students call "lax" occurred during the eighteen-sixties. The seminal figure was a Montreal dentist, Dr. William George Beers, one of those slightly creepy Victorian games enthusiasts who may have had more influence on our sports culture than was healthy. For lacrosse, Beers established boundaries, limited the number of players per side, set play to a clock, replaced the Indians' deer-skin ball with a hard rubber one, and drew up rational rules in keeping with Victorian ideals of social progress. Just as "civilization tamed the manners and habits of the Indians," Beers wrote, so lacrosse was "gradually divested of its radical rudeness and brought to a more sober sport." The game quickly spread to the United States; in 1877, New York University and Manhattan College played the first collegiate game, in Central Park. (Princeton and Rutgers had played the first collegiate football game only eight years earlier.) The sport caught on in cloistered pockets of the Northeast, where it can still be found—from the hardscrabble blue-collar lacrosse towns in upstate New York to the public high schools of west-central Long Island, and on to the lush greenswards of Baltimore preppiedom. While football has long since outgrown its folk origins to become a national spectacle, in which much of the country's melting pot is represented, lacrosse remains mostly an East Coast, mostly white game, and is largely unknown in Middle America.

The Indian game, being without boundaries or clocks, favored speed, stamina, and daring individual play. The white game favored organization, specialization, and strategy. Before Beers changed the rules, the Indians routinely beat the whites at lacrosse with their more athletic style of play. Professional Indian lacrosse teams were a common sight in the eighteen-seventies, but in 1880 Indians were banned from international competition, on the ground that they were accepting money to play in the Canadian lacrosse leagues.

Beers, in his rule-making, did not act purely in the interests of the game, as Rule IX, Section 6, of the original lacrosse rule book makes plain. It states, "No Indian must play in a match for a white club, unless previously agreed upon." Thomas Vennum, the author of *American Indian Lacrosse,* writes, "The rule was a blatant, segregationist, 'separate but equal' clause, which would eventually and effectively bar Indians from participation in international lacrosse competition for more than a century."

Shut out of the field game, the Indians took up box lacrosse, which was invented in Canada, in 1930, by three white promoters who were looking for a way to make money with hockey rinks in the summertime. Box is a six-man, hockeylike sport, very different from the flowing, ten-man game of field lacrosse. It features slick stickwork, no-look passes, behind-the-back shots, and a thirty-second shot clock that makes for lots of action. There is also plenty of brutal checking and fighting, as there was in the old Indian game. The most famous white lacrosse players in the world are the Canadian twins Paul and Gary Gait, who grew up playing box in Vancouver, and they have inspired a new generation of potential field-lacrosse stars to play a flashier, Magic Johnson-style game.

That night in the Kahnawake box, several of the Mohawk did seem to have it in for Rex Lyons. Early in the game, the younger O.A.C. players were hanging back, not wanting to challenge for position in front of the crease. Rex exhorted them by trying a run through the middle and received a vicious slash on one shoulder. In retaliation, Coach Bucktooth sent in Lab, the Onondaga's "goonie"—a beefy guy whom lots of teams bring along in the Senior B League, in case there's a rumble—and Lab made efficient work of the guy who had clubbed Rex. He threw off one glove, grabbed the Mohawk's jersey with that hand, punched his face mask with the gloved hand until the man's helmet came off, hit him in the face a couple of times, then pulled his jersey up over his head and slammed him down onto the concrete—all in about five seconds.

Now the arena was thick with the menace of impending violence. As the second period began, the Mohawk face-off man came up to the Onondagan face-off man, drew a finger across his jugular vein, and said furiously, "I'm going to cut your tro-o-at."

Midway through the period, Rex again made a dash across the crease. One of the biggest of the Mohawk players spread his hands wide on his stick and, without making even a pretense of going for the ball, smashed the stick over Rex's head. Rex fell hard on the concrete floor, bouncing a little as he hit, and lay there face down for a few minutes. Eventually, he got up and limped back to the bench.

The game ended 10–6 Mohawk. Afterward, some of the older Onondaga had a reasonably friendly drink in the bar with some of the Mohawk players. They came out to the bus in fifteen minutes. But when Coach Bucktooth called the roll a few of the younger guys were missing. Someone said he'd heard them talking about going to a bar up the road. Rex, limping badly, went outside, found the missing guys in a girl's car, and brought them back, and Coach Bucktooth gave everyone a lecture about the importance of staying focused for tomorrow night's game. Box had been a way of ritualistically confronting a certain threat of disorder—a Saturday night of drinking and mayhem—but had not completely exorcised this demon. It now seemed to be lurking somewhere in the dark at the back of the bus, where some of the younger guys were whispering about getting beer and bringing it back to the Best Western.

On The Field

The two great tribes of lacrosse enthusiasts in the United States—the Iroquois and the white Easterners—almost never play against each other. A rare exception took place in July, in Baltimore, when the Iroquois Nationals, an all-star team made up of the best players from the Six Nations, took on Team U.S.A., a dream team of white American players, at World Lacrosse 1998, the sport's world championship.

It was the Iroquois Nationals' third appearance at the championships, which come around every four years, since the ban against Indians in international competition was lifted, in 1990. They were one of eleven teams at the games, and they ended up in fourth place, behind the United States, Canada, and Australia, and ahead of England (whom the Iroquois beat in an exciting 10-9 game, clinched by Rex with sixteen seconds to go) and the six other lacrosse-playing nations—Japan, Germany, Sweden, Wales, Scotland, and the Czech Republic. The Lyons family was represented in force. Not only was Rex there but Rex's son Monte was playing in the Under-Fifteen tournament; Rex's cousins Kent and Scottie were in the Masters; and Rex's father, Oren Lyons, was in the Grandmasters. Oren would also carry the Indian flag and lend spiritual support to the Nationals.

Homewood Field, at Johns Hopkins University, where the games were held, is the heartland of white lacrosse in the United States. The game is especially popular in the old-money suburbs to the north of Baltimore, like Cockeysville and Lutherville-Timonium; in Baltimore, the prep schools actually recruit lacrosse players from the grade schools. After prep school, the players move on to lacrosse colleges like Hopkins and Bucknell and Princeton. (This year's Princeton team, which was coached by the Team U.S.A. coach, Bill Tierney, and won the N.C.A.A. championship for the third year in a row, had five students from Baltimore's Gilman School on it—a cozy Amtrak relationship between Baltimore and Princeton that goes back at least as far as *This Side of Paradise*.) Over the years, many post-collegiate lacrosse players have found employment in the Baltimore wing of the investment firm of Alex Brown, which used to be run by a stalwart member of the lacrosse fraternity, Buzzy Krongard (now the top adviser to the director of the C.I.A.). Thanks in part to lacrosse, the Baltimore preppies I know have managed to survive with their sense of entitlement more or less intact; for better or worse, they're not beaten down like New York preppies, who have had to compete in the remorseless meritocracy of Manhattan.

But the Baltimore lacrosse élite, not unlike the Indians, is a group in danger of being colonized by the surrounding popular culture. The code of amateurism, which is the closest thing to a spiritual ideal that their game has, is in the process of being transformed by the commercialization of sports in America. "The problem with lacrosse is that you can't make money doing it," Darren Lowe, a twenty-seven-year-old Team U.S.A. attackman, told me. Amateurism, which once served the ruling class as a way of excluding the people it didn't want to play with, now excludes the younger members of the ruling class from the ESPN sports culture that they want to belong to. The Team U.S.A. players I spoke to appeared a bit sheepish about not being able to make a living from lacrosse; not getting paid for your sport, it seems, places you lower in the status hierarchy than professional athletes. Things have changed since the days when the Indian players were banned from international competition because they earned money playing lacrosse.

Lowe, the son of a lacrosse coach, went to a public school in Mineola, Long Island, which is one of the prosperous postwar bedroom communities where lacrosse took root in the nineteen-fifties and became part of the delivery mechanism of the good life. He said, "When I told my college adviser I wanted to go to Brown, he said, 'Brown where? California?' I had eleven-hundred S.A.T.s and an eighty-five average." But Lowe got into Brown, where he was an All-American; his brother Kevin was an All-American at Princeton. After college, lacrosse helped get Darren a job at Lehman Brothers and Kevin a job at Merrill Lynch. "There's definitely a fraternity of lacrosse guys available who will help you get jobs on Wall Street," Lowe said. The business of bond-brokering in particular, which Lowe is in, is full of lacrosse jocks. He estimates that twenty per cent of the people on the foreign-reserve bond desk at Lehman Brothers are lacrosse players, adding, "I would say that lacrosse and crew are the two biggest sports networks on the Street."

On the eve of the Iroquois Nationals' Sunday game against Team U.S.A., Oren Lyons and I visited the lacrosse minipark that had been set up next to Homewood Field. It was a hot night. Loose-limbed lax jocks roamed the Homewood grounds in packs of three or four, their tribal allegiances to such local prep schools as Gilman or St. Paul's or Boys' Latin proclaimed on their T-shirts. Smooth-skinned girls in tartan skirts and sleeveless blouses with the collars turned up were prowling in posses. Some boys walked around bare-chested, their shucked-off T-shirts hanging from their belts, dish-rag style, and all of them wearing the same kind of knee-length khaki shorts and Teva sandals. The younger ones were lean, but the college graduates were getting a bit stout from all the beer drinking and barbecue that go with Baltimore lacrosse. Both the boys and the girls carried sticks. Around Baltimore, kids grow up with sticks in the umbrella stand next to the front door. They play on the big lawn with their "golden," the same breed of dog that's often seen wearing a red bandanna at the game.

"All this stuff," Lyons said, indicating piles of lacrosse merchandise for sale everywhere. He picked up one of the Warrior Company's titanium sticks, which, according to the accompanying promotional literature, was "precision engineered with Aerospace Grade Titanium using a proprietary seamless extrusion process," and which promised to give the stick's user "the Means to Dominate." On the side of the big Warrior tent was a picture of the president of the company, a twenty-seven-year-old Princeton graduate named David Morrow, who was also playing longstick for Team U.S.A. and had obtained the exclusive right to promote his products at the World

Games. Around here, lacrosse is a medicine game, too: it brings good fortune to its community. The difference is that the Indians' medicine doesn't work so well outside the reservation.

Lyons seemed aware of this problem—of the need to preserve a cultural identity and at the same time shop it around in the larger marketplace in a way that benefits the people to whom it belongs. When we sat down at one of the barbecue places and a senior official in the New York State Republican Party stopped by to say hello, Lyons started telling him about a new complex he was hoping to persuade the Six Nations to build on Onondagan land. "It won't be a casino," Lyons said. "It'll be a theme park, though we don't call it that. A place to showcase our heritage, and teach democracy, on our terms. Everyone's running around like gaming is a panacea for everything, when it's not." That there is only one casino on native lands in New York state—Turning Stone, run by the Oneida—is due in no small part to Lyons's powerful opposition to gambling. He had told me earlier that he sees casinos as the single greatest threat to the Iroquois Confederacy. "With casinos—instead of tradition, which makes you strong—people only care about money, which makes you weak," he said.

After the official had gone, Lyons mulled over the possibility that by building the complex, which would be a boost to the economy of central New York, he might be able to persuade the state to settle some of the Iroquois land claims in the Indians' favor. In his thoughts, I sensed, a political version of Team U.S.A. vs. the Iroquois was already being played.

Before taking the field against Team U.S.A. the following afternoon, the Iroquois Nationals gathered under a big tree outside the Homewood Field Stadium and built a small fire of twigs and bark. Chief Paul Waterman, the grandfather of Gewas Schindler, one of the stars of the Nationals, produced some loose tobacco and cupped it in his hands. It was then passed from player to player around the twenty-six-member team. Thomas Vennum writes, in "American Indian Lacrosse," that Cherokee conjurors used to scratch players with rattlesnake fangs, to purify them, and that Creek players were rubbed with a liquid made of "the track of a wolf and the burrow of a crayfish," which allowed them to perform amazing athletic feats. Today, the Iroquois sprinkled the tobacco on the fire and offered a traditional prayer, invoking the help of this tree, the tree's roots, the sun, the fields, the birds, the four winds, and all their ancestors to protect them from injury and to make them strong. The Iroquois jerseys were purple with yellow-and-white trim; they had a traditional geometric design of a wampum belt on one sleeve and the word "Brine," the supplier of the uniforms, in large letters on the back.

About seventy-five feet away, their opponents, wearing red-white-and-blue uniforms, were posing for photographs on the steps of the Newton H. White Athletic Center. "Look, sweetheart," a lacrosse dad said to his little girl. "They're representing our country." Since the United States is far and away the dominant lacrosse nation in the world, the team is also representing the sport of lacrosse as a whole. U.S. Lacrosse, the sport's national governing body, is trying to make lacrosse a bigger presence on the sports landscape, by employing the same techniques that Team U.S.A. would be using on the field: teamwork, strategy, central control. The money to pay for this expansion comes from an annual fee that U.S. Lacrosse began collecting this year from players at any organized level, from youth to club—between fifteen and forty dollars per person per year, which is about what soccer collects from soccer moms and dads.

But the same clannishness that breeds such an intense following among lacrosse players and their families also works against lacrosse in its efforts to grow. Lacrosse will have to compete for fans' interest with made-for-TV sports like arena football and women's beach volleyball. History, context (the smell of barbecued "pit beef" drifting over from the concession stands behind the bleachers), and Wasp nepotism don't come through very clearly on cable. Box lacrosse has some of the right elements for TV (the flashy moves and the violence), but promoting box would alienate the lacrosse establishment, who see it as a lowbrow version of the field game.

At game time, five o'clock, the Baltimore sun was still burning down on the artificial Homewood turf, making it hot to the touch. Oren Lyons was standing by the Iroquois bench.

"Are you going to use that wooden stick?" a white boy asked Lyons, pointing to one of six hickory longsticks that Alfie Jacques, a native stickmaker, had made specially for the Iroquois Nationals.

"Yes," Lyons said.

"Is it true the Indians and the Americans don't like each other?" the boy asked.

Lyons said that it was not true, though they might not be too friendly for the next couple of hours.

"One, two, three, Iroquois!" The team members broke their final huddle and took their positions on the bright-green field: three attackmen, three midfielders, three defensemen, and the goalie.

Field lacrosse is a game of circles and lines—the natural religion of the Indians overlaid with the capitalistic religion of the white men. When the attackmen and midfielders jog-trot like hunters around the goal, looking for shots as the defensemen poke-check them with their longsticks, the game looks Indian, but when Team U.S.A. takes positions and whips the ball efficiently around the crease, running complex set plays, the game looks white. Lacrosse combines the stick skills of hockey, the two-on-two, pick-and-roll play of basketball, the flow of soccer, and the field generalship of football. (Unlimited substitutions are allowed.) In field lacrosse, you can take three or four minutes on offense, as in football, or you can play an uptempo game of thirty-second possessions with quick shots, as in basketball. "Partly because of its origins as a mix of North American cultures," I was told by Jim Grube, who is a former football and lacrosse coach at Middlebury College, "lacrosse is a true hybrid, which can be played at either end of the sports continuum."

Team U.S.A. won the face-off and began slinging the ball around in a circle, from the center out to the wing, then around behind the goal and out to the other wing, then back to the center. The Indians looked as though they were having trouble adjusting to the wide-open field: they were bunched somewhat awkwardly as their opponents slid toward the crease and looked for passes. The U.S.A. scored two goals quickly, and it looked as if the game would be a rout. The crowd cheered them loudly. A couple of white kids were rooting for the Indians, perhaps to piss their parents off, but for the most part the fans were solidly behind Team U.S.A.

"Come on, Iroquois!" shouted three Indian women wearing a lot of purple. "Be strong! You can run right through them!"

A white boy in a baseball cap, sitting next to me, looked at his buddy and said, "Yeah, right."

One of the Team U.S.A. attackmen tried some fancy stickwork and lost the ball to the Iroquois, who came down the field quickly and scored a goal. They won the ensuing face-off, and Gewas Schindler scored another goal on a dive into the crease. (The day before, I was in the press box when Schindler scored against Team Canada, and one of the announcers wasn't sure how to pronounce "Gewas." "Just call him Chief," another announcer advised.)

Coach Tierney sent in the mid-fielder Jesse Hubbard, who grew up across the street from St. Alban's, the Washington prep school that is Vice-President Gore's alma mater. Some girls in the stands started a cheer—"Jes-se Hub-bard, Jes-se Hub-bard." Team U.S.A. scored again. "Yesss!" the kid in the baseball cap cried, pumping his clenched fist. But the Iroquois got the ball back, and Rex Lyons broke hard across the crease—the same box move I'd seen him get clobbered for in Canada. This time, he scored.

Early in the second period, the score was tied, 3–3. Then it seemed to dawn on the Iroquois that they were playing even with the best team in the world, and a sort of shyness overtook them. The U.S.A. fired the ball around the crease, seeming to mesmerize the younger Indian players, and shot it into the net. They were deadly.

By the end of the third period, the score was 14–7, U.S.A. With the game out of reach, and the only remaining question being how bad it was going to get, one of the Iroquois players had pushed one of the U.S.A. players, the U.S.A. guy pushed back, and then, after a moment's pause, the Iroquois player hit the U.S.A. player in the face mask. The U.S.A. player fell to the ground, clutching his head. There were angry shouts from the fans at this intrusion of box into their field game. A man next to me, leaning against the chain-link fence that separated the fans from the field, yelled, "Get the animals out of the game!"

In the end, the score was 20–8—a respectable performance by the 'Quois. Afterward, Oren Lyons walked back to the hotel carrying the All Nations' staff, a scythe-shaped hickory stick with six golden-eagle feathers along the top crook and more eagle feathers down the shaft. It was attracting attention from lacrosse-stick-twirling white boys who were running around the outside of the field.

"Is that real?" one of them asked.

"That's our flag," Lyons said simply.

"Is it real?" the boy asked again. In a culture that knows its Indian heritage mostly through Chief Wahoo and tomahawk chops at Braves games, the real thing loses its talismanic power. It's just better gear.

The boy ran off to join his friends. Lyons said to me, "Sixteen million people under that flag." I asked what he meant, and he said that he was referring to the sixteen million Indians who had died as a result of the European conquest of North America.

As we crossed the street, Lyons said, "You know, the Indians invented baseball, too."

"Invented baseball!" I exclaimed.

"Oh, yeah," he said. "Baseball began with a man running back and forth between two bases, and the object was to throw the ball at him to get him out. That's an old Indian game. But white people aren't ready to hear that yet."

Naming and Identity

Felly Nkweto Simmonds

In "Naming and Identity," Felly Nkweto Simmonds calls attention to assumptions surrounding the ways we read and understand our names. Simmonds uses the example of her own names to inquire into self on various levels, examining a "confusion in identity" that she connects with competing cultural influences, such as the impact of colonialism, Catholicism, and her family's tribal history. Each of these contexts carries with it a system of meaning. Simmonds writes: "For better, for worse, my names locate me in time and space." However, as she also observes, the meanings of our names change depending on the context. Like many of us, Simmonds understands herself through the identities given to her (family history, religion), as well as through the identities she chooses (Marxism, a husband of European descent). Think about the roots of your own name(s). What contexts do your name(s) exist within? What kind of identities do your names(s) point to? What names have been given to you? What names have you chosen for yourself? What names have you rejected?

My paternal grandparents named me Nkweto wa Chilinda. But the name arrived too late. Time had moved on. This was the middle of the twentieth century. The modern age. Modernity had implications for my very identity in colonial central Africa, what is now Zambia.

When I was born, my parents also gave me a name, as they waited for the ancestors to grant me life. This was taking time. Messages and letters took weeks to get to my grandparents' village and back. I had to be called something and my father found an English name for me from a book that he was reading. Nora. In my father's house I'm still called Nora.

In terms of names, I was born at the wrong time. The postwar colonial African society into which I was born was having a crisis of identity. A separation of the old order from the new. Families were literally torn apart, separated by the idea of progress itself. Having an English name was symbolic. It was one way that you could show you were of the modern world . . . could speak English. Many English names were literally invented and

From *The Feminist Critique of Language*. Copyright © 1990 by Routledge. Reprinted by permission.

appropriated for whatever was the immediate need . . . registering for a job in the mines, registering for school . . . for the future that was beckoning so tantalizingly in the shape of crowded towns, shanty towns, badly paid jobs. . . . The resulting names were fantastic. Any English word could be and *was* used as a name, producing names that exposed the very idea of progress as a sham, a pantomime, a charade—the modern world was a game, you took on a role and a name . . . Cabbage, Spoon, Pelvis, Loveness. . . . .

But there were some of us who played this game too seriously. We were pawns in a game whose rules we didn't know. Our names symbolized another existence. A God beyond our imagination. A Christian God . . . Mary, Joseph, James . . . Felicitas. At the appointed time I became Felicitas, and joined the world of rosary beads, holy water, saints, a virgin, confession . . . hellfire and damnation . . . a very modern world.

I now had three names. This is the order in which they came to me: Nora Nkweto (wa Chilinda) Felicitas. And my father's clan name, Mfula—rain. We are of the rain clan.

Nora Nkweto Felicitas Mfula. My friends call me Felly.

There are many things wrong with the way I was named. The first being that I shouldn't carry a name from my father's family at all. As AbaBemba we are matrilineal. The maternal spirits of the ancestors should be passed on to the child through the given name. This does not imply a female name, but a maternal ancestor, female or male. Names are not gendered. My mother's grandmother delivered me. By ancestral right she should also have named me. That was my first loss, the first confusion in my identity. I was born at a time when AbaBemba men were acquiring authority over their wives and children based on the new ways of the modern world. The loss of the right to name me was a loss for my mother and all our foremothers, and a loss for me, who carries my father's people's spirit, I who am denied a continuation of the female line.

However, I carry an important name. Nkweto wa Chilinda. Apparently he was my great-grandfather—and who am I to doubt it, although of course as one who has studied history there is a clash of truths even in the name I carry. The Bemba historian P. B. Mushindo claims to be unable to trace Nkweto wa Chilinda's descendants after he and his wife ". . . left home, possessions, their high position, subjects, slaves, etc. for love of their child. . . ." A child that they had only been able to have because of the medical skills of strangers who came into his country: ". . . the Ng'alang'asa . . . who had a great knowledge of medicine . . ." to whom they had promised the first child born to them. *Ulupangi Iwatamfishe Nkweto mu Chilinda,* ". . . a vow drove Nkweto out of Chilinda. . . ."

If he was never heard of again, how come his name lives on?

My grandfather was known as *umwana wa MuSukuma,* ". . . a child of the Sukuma. . . ." The Sukuma live on the shores of Lake Victoria, several thousand miles north of where Chilinda would have been, but easily accessible to traders who came down the Rift Valley, along Lake Tanganyika.

Are the Ng'alang'asa and the Sukuma related in some way?

The name was important enough for my grandfather. In it there is a message for me. Now, as an adult, I find the further I am from home, not just in distance, but also in time, the more I need to reclaim this name, and the position I have in LuBemba history. It is then I recognize that Nkweto wa Chilinda's spirit and I are one—strangers in strange lands—but also guardians of our past.

Chilinda is the verb for one who guards *(ukulinda),* a guardian *(chilinda).*

The second thing wrong with my naming was the very order in which the names came to me. I was Nora first. My family still call me Nora. Also my parents' friends. I can tell how long people have known me (and in what space) by the name they call me. Nkweto as a name stood no chance against progress. My grandmother, my father's mother, was the only one who always called me Nkweto—and sometimes the full name, Nkweto wa Chilinda, when she wanted to make me feel very special. She has a special place in my heart.

At the age of ten, I named myself . . . Felicitas.

Felicitas . . . Felly. There is a whole lot wrong with this name that I still carry as the ultimate symbol of my confused identity. I no longer have a reason to carry it. I'm no longer a Catholic, which was the only reason I took the name in the first place! I had been in my Catholic convent school for a full year before I was baptised. It was a terrible year. I had arrived with names that were not acceptable. Nora Nkweto Mfula. At least Nora was an English name. Nkweto I dropped, completely. It was a shameful name, a pagan name—even a man's name—how could I live with it? And in any case, we were not allowed to use African names except as sur-

names—so that we couldn't be confused with "white" men's children—
"coloureds," as they were called, in the Southern African way. This was, of
course, not a realistic fear. We didn't come in contact with "white" children,
in their posh convent in the town, and as for "coloured" children, "white"
men's children with African women, they were out of sight (out of mind) in
special schools, usually in the middle of nowhere, looked after by nuns . . .
hiding one of the "white" man's fears in Africa. Miscegenation.

It wasn't just the fact of not having an appropriate English name that
was the problem. It had to be a saint's name. The saint was your guardian,
could mediate on your behalf—a short cut to God, or even better still to the
Virgin Mary. . . . *She* was amazing . . . The Mother of God. In a society
that values motherhood, no one could hold a candle to this woman. She was
to be the ultimate Role Model with an in-built contradiction—we couldn't
be mothers *and* remain virgins. It was a terrible situation to be in, and
encouraged us to dedicate many rosaries to the Virgin Mary to help us live
this contradiction as chastely as possible. We were constantly reminded that
our biggest enemy was the desire for men . . . and that it was the men themselves who inevitably, in the end, would lead us into temptation.

I remember with absolute clarity, sitting on the school veranda with two
of my friends on the Saturday afternoon, the day before I was baptised,
trying to select a name. The book of saints' names also gave a summary of
the saint's life and how she/he achieved sainthood.

Saint Laeticia and Saint Felicitas. Saint's Day 6 March (near my birth-
day, 26 February). Felicitas was the African slave woman to a Roman
woman, Laeticia. They both converted to Christianity and were fed to the
lions. Actually I don't really know if that *is* how they died, but my imagination has always been fired by the idea of being eaten by a lion, a common threat to naughty children in my grandmother's village. This sounded
right. Also there was no other Felicitas in my school, so there wasn't to be
much competition for favours from Saint Felicitas. She would be my own
special saint. Even at that age I liked the idea that Felicitas was an African.

Felicitas . . . Latin for happiness.

And I was happy. At last my soul had been cleansed of Original Sin.
The only thing between me and eternal life in Heaven was myself . . . temptation, sinning. . . . For the next eight years I tried as best as I could to be
good. In the end the modern world defeated me in the shape of Karl Marx
(a Dead "white" Man) and real live men. By then I had shortened my name
to Felly . . . (and had forgotten what happens to naughty girls. After all
"white" hunters had as near as possible wiped out all the lions.)

So now I carry a man's name as well. A "white" name! Simmonds. Apparently there is Dutch blood somewhere on his father's line. The Dutch blood that is so afraid of African blood in Africa.

My National Insurance papers and my driving licence are the only documents as far as I know that carry all my names. Felicitas Nora Nkweto Simmonds.

Often I drop Nora, it is the name I least relate to, unless I'm in Zambia, which is not often these days. I haven't been there since my mother died three years ago. Sometimes I feel that I can't go back. However, these days Nkweto is with me now in a way that I haven't felt before. It could be because of my mother's death. I need to feel close to her spirit, through my own spirit, Nkweto wa Chilinda. Recently I've used it when I write poetry, when I write from my soul, when I'm saying something that touches my very core.

In public, at conferences, for example, I insist that my full name appears on my name tag. In a society that cannot accommodate names that come from "other" cultures, this can be a frustrating exercise. It is no wonder that many Black children will Anglicize their names to avoid playground taunts . . . and much worse. We are still fighting colonialism.

Friends ask me why I don't just drop my non-African names. It would be a good idea, but not a practical one. In reality, my reason has nothing to do with practicality, it has to do with my own identity. For better, for worse, my names locate me in time and space. It gives me a sense of my own history that I not only share specifically with a generation of people in Africa but also with all Africans in the Diaspora.

I belong to a time. The twentieth century. A time of fragmentation, a time of rebirth. I need to understand and know myself from that position. It is the only position I have, wherever I am. In both my private space and my public life. I'm also lucky. Naming myself differently to suit the occasion allows me the space to experience all my subjective realities and identities (we all have many) in a way that does not imply fragmentation, but coherence.

I also know I belong and simultaneously don't belong either to the time or the space I occupy. I carry my history and that of my people. As I experience life, all that I experience is also in readiness for those who come after me, those who will carry my name and my spirit. That is my identity.

Three summers ago, in New York, at an international women's conference, I *really* experienced being an African woman in the Diaspora, as I sat with Joselina and Sueli from Brazil. It was hard to accept that these women were strangers to me . . . I was also freaked by the many times women came to talk to me, thinking that they knew me from somewhere.

To make sense of this experience I wrote this poem for Sueli, with whom I could only communicate through Joselina.

Coming to America

I am here,
To feed my fragmented self.
I am here,
To see my other self.
When you ask me—
Have I seen you before?
Why do I say
No, this is my first crossing of the Atlantic.
You have seen me before.
I am your sister.
The sister, whose memory three hundred years of separation
    cannot wipe out,
Even though you speak Portuguese now.
And I, English . . .
You are my sister,
I know you,
And you know me.
You are the sister that I lost so many centuries ago . . .
But still pined for,
    Just to see you
    and smile at you,
    and, maybe talk to you.
    And if lucky,
    Hold your hand.
    Hold you in my arms.
    After all these years.

Shooting Dad

Sarah Vowell

Our family relationships are often founded not only on shared history and spaces, but also on shared beliefs. What happens, though, when the values of someone in your family are in conflict with strongly held beliefs of your own? Sarah Vowell's essay, "Shooting Dad," explores the contexts of family, politics, and history as Vowell negotiates her position as a pacifist, liberal teenager growing up under the same roof as her conservative father, who is a gunsmith. As we read through the essay, we see that some conflicts between Vowell and her father seem resolved, and others remain intact. How do the public contexts, like history and politics, influence the private context of family? What are the influences of other contexts, like gender and class? How important is it that we try to understand the values of our loved ones, particularly when those values might be in conflict with our own?

If you were passing by the house where I grew up during my teenage years and it happened to be before Election Day, you wouldn't have needed to come inside to see that it was a house divided. You could have looked at the Democratic campaign poster in the upstairs window and the Republican one in the downstairs window and seen our home for the Civil War battleground it was. I'm not saying who was the Democrat or who was the Republican—my father or I—but I will tell you that I have never subscribed to *Guns & Ammo,* that I did not plaster the family vehicle with National Rifle Association stickers, and that hunter's orange was never my color.

About the only thing my father and I agree on is the Constitution, though I'm partial to the First Amendment, while he's always favored the Second.

I am a gunsmith's daughter. I like to call my parents' house, located on a quiet residential street in Bozeman, Montana, the United States of Firearms. Guns were everywhere: the so-called pretty ones like the circa 1850 walnut muzzleloader hanging on the wall, Dad's clients' fixer-uppers leaning into corners, an entire rack right next to the TV. I had to move revolvers out of my way to make room for a bowl of Rice Krispies on the kitchen table.

Reprinted with the permission of Simon & Shuster Adult Publishing Group from *Take the Cannoli* by Sarah Vowell. Copyright © 2000 by Sarah Vowell.

I was eleven when we moved into that Bozeman house. We had never lived in town before, and this was a college town at that. We came from Oklahoma—a dusty little Muskogee County nowhere called Braggs. My parents' property there included an orchard, a horse pasture, and a couple of acres of woods, I knew our lives had changed one morning not long after we moved to Montana when, during breakfast, my father heard a noise and jumped out of his chair. Grabbing a BB gun, he rushed out the front door. Standing in the yard, he started shooting at crows. My mother sprinted after him screaming, "Pat, you might ought to check, but I don't think they do that up here!" From the look on his face, she might as well have told him that his American citizenship had been revoked. He shook his head, mumbling, "Why, shooting crows is a national pastime, like baseball and apple pie." Personally, I preferred baseball and apple pie. I looked up at those crows flying away and thought, I'm going to like it here.

Dad and I started bickering in earnest when I was fourteen, after the 1984 Democratic National Convention. I was so excited when Walter Mondale chose Geraldine Ferraro as his running mate that I taped the front page of the newspaper with her picture on it to the refrigerator door. But there was some sort of mysterious gravity surge in the kitchen. Somehow, that picture ended up in the trash all the way across the room.

Nowadays, I giggle when Dad calls me on Election Day to cheerfully inform me that he has once again canceled out my vote, but I was not always so mature. There were times when I found the fact that he was a gunsmith horrifying. And just *weird*. All he ever cared about were guns. All I ever cared about was art. There were years and years when he hid out by himself in the garage making rifle barrels and I holed up in my room reading Allen Ginsberg poems, and we were incapable of having a conversation that didn't end in an argument.

Our house was partitioned off into territories. While the kitchen and the living room were well within the DMZ, the respective work spaces governed by my father and me were jealously guarded totalitarian states in which each of us declared ourselves dictator. Dad's shop was a messy disaster area, a labyrinth of lathes. Its walls were hung with the mounted antlers of deer he'd bagged, forming a makeshift museum of death. The available flat surfaces were buried under a million scraps of paper on which he sketched his mechanical inventions in blue ball-point pen. And the floor, carpeted with spiky metal shavings, was a tetanus shot waiting to happen. My domain was the cramped, cold space known as the music room. It was also a messy disaster area, an obstacle course of musical instruments— piano, trumpet, baritone horn, valve trombone, various percussion doodads (bells!), and recorders. A framed portrait of the French composer Claude

Debussy was nailed to the wall. The available flat surfaces were buried under piles of staff paper, on which I penciled in the pompous orchestra music given titles like "Prelude to the Green Door" (named after an O. Henry short story by the way, not the watershed porn flick *Behind the Green Door*) I started writing in junior high.

It has been my experience that in order to impress potential suitors, skip the teen Debussy anecdotes and stick with the always attention-getting line "My dad makes guns." Though it won't cause the guy to like me any better, it will make him handle the inevitable breakup with diplomacy—just in case I happen to have any loaded family heirlooms lying around the house.

But the fact is, I have only shot a gun once and once was plenty. My twin sister, Amy, and I were six years old—six—when Dad decided that it was high time we learned how to shoot. Amy remembers the day he handed us the gun for the first time differently. She liked it.

Amy shared our father's enthusiasm for firearms and the quick-draw cowboy mythology surrounding them. I tended to daydream through Dad's activities—the car trip to Dodge City's Boot Hill, his beloved John Wayne Westerns on TV. My sister, on the other hand, turned into Rooster Cogburn Jr., devouring Duke movies with Dad. In fact, she named her teddy bear Duke, hung a colossal John Wayne portrait next to her bed, and took to wearing one of those John Wayne shirts that button on the side. So when Dad led us out to the backyard when we were six and, to Amy's delight, put the gun in her hand, she says she felt it meant that Daddy trusted us and that he thought of us as "big girls."

But I remember holding the pistol only made me feel small. It was so heavy in my hand. I stretched out my arm and pointed it away and winced. It was a very long time before I had the nerve to pull the trigger and I was so scared I had to close my eyes. It felt like it just went off by itself, as if I had no say in the matter, as if the gun just had this *need*. The sound it made was as big as God. It kicked little me back to the ground like a bully, like a foe. It hurt. I don't know if I dropped it or just handed it back over to my dad, but I do know that I never wanted to touch another one again. And, because I believed in the devil, I did what my mother told me to do every time I felt an evil presence. I looked at the smoke and whispered under my breath, "Satan, I rebuke thee."

It's not like I'm saying I was traumatized. It's more like I was decided. Guns: Not For Me. Luckily, both my parents grew up in exasperating households where children were considered puppets and/or slaves. My mom and dad were hell-bent on letting my sister and me make our own choices. So if I decided that I didn't want my father's little death sticks to kick me to the ground again, that was fine with him. He would go hunting with my sister, who started calling herself "the loneliest twin in history" because of my reluctance to engage in family activities.

Of course, the fact that I was allowed to voice my opinions did not mean that my father would silence his own. Some things were said during the Reagan administration that cannot be taken back. Let's just say that I blamed Dad for nuclear proliferation and Contra aid. He believed that if I had my way, all the guns would be confiscated and it would take the commies about fifteen minutes to parachute in and assume control.

We're older now, my dad and I. The older I get, the more I'm interested in becoming a better daughter. First on my list: Figure out the whole gun thing.

Not long ago, my dad finished his most elaborate tool of death yet. A cannon. He built a nineteenth-century cannon. From scratch. It took two years.

My father's cannon is a smaller replica of a cannon called the Big Horn Gun in front of Bozeman's Pioneer Museum. The barrel of the original has been filled with concrete ever since some high school kids in the '50s pointed it at the school across the street and shot out its windows one night as a prank. According to Dad's historical source, a man known to scholars as A Guy at the Museum, the cannon was brought to Bozeman around 1870, and was used by local white merchants to fire at the Sioux and Cheyenne Indians who blocked their trade access to the East in 1874.

"Bozeman was founded on greed," Dad says. The courthouse cannon, he continues, "definitely killed Indians. The merchants filled it full of nuts, bolts, and chopped-up horseshoes. Sitting Bull could have been part of these engagements. They definitely ticked off the Indians, because a couple of years later, Custer wanders into them at Little Bighorn. The Bozeman merchants were out to cause trouble. They left fresh baked bread with cyanide in it on the trail to poison a few Indians."

Because my father's sarcastic American history yarns rarely go on for long before he trots out some nefarious ancestor of ours—I come from a long line of moonshiners, Confederate soldiers, murderers, even Democrats—he cracks that the merchants hired some "community-minded Southern soldiers from North Texas." These soldiers had, like my great-great-grandfather John Vowell, fought under pro-slavery guerrilla William C. Quantrill. Quantrill is most famous for riding into Lawrence, Kansas, in 1863 flying a black flag and commanding his men pharaohlike to "kill every male and burn down every house."

"John Vowell," Dad says, "had a little rep for killing people." And since he abandoned my great-grandfather Charles, whose mother died giving birth to him in 1870, and wasn't seen again until 1912, Dad doesn't rule out the possibility that John Vowell could have been one of the hired guns on the Bozeman Trail. So the cannon isn't just another gun to my dad. It's a map of all his obsessions—firearms, certainly, but also American history and family history, subjects he's never bothered separating from each other.

After tooling a million guns, after inventing and building a rifle barrel boring machine, after setting up that complicated shop filled with lathes and blueing tanks and outmoded blacksmithing tools, the cannon is his most ambitious project ever. I thought that if I was ever going to understand the ballistic bee in his bonnet, this was my chance. It was the biggest gun he ever made and I could experience it and spend time with it with the added bonus of not having to actually pull a trigger myself.

I called Dad and said that I wanted to come to Montana and watch him shoot off the cannon. He was immediately suspicious. But I had never taken much interest in his work before and he would take what he could get. He loaded the cannon into the back of his truck and we drove up into the Bridger Mountains. I was a little worried that the National Forest Service would object to us lobbing fiery balls of metal onto its property. Dad laughed, assuring me that "you cannot shoot fireworks, but this is considered a fire*arm*."

It is a small cannon, about as long as a baseball bat and as wide as a coffee can. But it's heavy—110 pounds. We park near the side of the hill. Dad takes his gunpowder and other tools out of this adorable wooden box on which he has stenciled "PAT G. VOWELL CANNONWORKS." Cannonworks: So that's what NRA members call a metal-strewn garage.

Dad plunges his homemade bullets into the barrel, points it at an embankment just to be safe, and lights the fuse. When the fuse is lit, it resembles a cartoon. So does the sound, which warrants Ben Day dot words along the lines of *ker-pow!* There's so much Fourth of July smoke everywhere I feel compelled to sing the national anthem.

I've given this a lot of thought—how to convey the giddiness I felt when the cannon shot off. But there isn't a sophisticated way to say this. It's just really, really cool. My dad thought so, too.

Sometimes, I put together stories about the more eccentric corners of the American experience for public radio. So I happen to have my tape recorder with me, and I've never seen levels like these. Every time the cannon goes off, the delicate needles which keep track of the sound quality lurch into the bad, red zone so fast and so hard I'm surprised they don't break.

The cannon was so loud and so painful, I had to touch my head to make sure my skull hadn't cracked open. One thing that my dad and I share is that we're both a little hard of hearing—me from Aerosmith, him from gunsmith.

He lights the fuse again. The bullet knocks over the log he was aiming at. I instantly utter a sentence I never in my entire life thought I would say. I tell him, "Good shot, Dad."

Just as I'm wondering what's coming over me, two hikers walk by. Apparently, they have never seen a man set off a homemade cannon in the middle of the wilderness while his daughter holds a foot-long microphone up into the air recording its terrorist boom. One hiker gives me a puzzled look and asks, "So you work for the radio and that's your dad?"

Dad shoots the cannon again so that they can see how it works. The other hiker says, "That's quite the machine you got there." But he isn't talking about the cannon. He's talking about my tape recorder and my microphone—which is called a *shotgun* mike. I stare back at him, then I look over at my father's cannon, then down at my microphone, and I think. Oh. My. God. My dad and I are the same person. We're both smart-alecky loners with goofy projects and weird equipment. And since this whole target practice outing was my idea, I was no longer his adversary. I was his accomplice. What's worse, I was liking it.

I haven't changed my mind about guns. I can get behind the cannon because it is a completely ceremonial object. It's unwieldy and impractical, just like everything else I care about. Try to rob a convenience store with this 110-pound Saturday night special, you'd still be dragging it in the door Sunday afternoon.

I love noise. As a music fan, I'm always waiting for that moment in a song when something just flies out of it and explodes in the air. My dad is a one-man garage band, the kind of rock 'n' roller who slaves away at his art for no reason other than to make his own sound. My dad is an artist—a pretty driven, idiosyncratic one, too. He's got his last *Gesamt Kunstwerk* all planned out. It's a performance piece. We're all in it—my mom, the loneliest twin in history, and me.

When my father dies, take a wild guess what he wants done with his ashes. Here's a hint: It requires a cannon.

"You guys are going to love this," he smirks, eyeballing the cannon. "You get to drag this thing up on top of the Gravellies on opening day of hunting season. And looking off at Sphinx Mountain, you get to put me in little paper bags. I can take my last hunting trip on opening morning."

I'll do it, too. I will have my father's body burned into ashes. I will pack these ashes into paper bags. I will go to the mountains with my mother, my sister, and the cannon. I will plunge his remains into the barrel and point it into a hill so that he doesn't take anyone with him. I will light the fuse. But I will not cover my ears. Because when I blow what used to be my dad into the earth, I want it to hurt.

The Poems Came Late: Literacy as Cultural Dialogue

David Wallace

David Wallace has published numerous articles about his position as a gay academic. In this essay, he urges students to take risks in their writing, even if those risks may set them at odds with friends, teachers, and family. Wallace promotes a kind of literacy that is not about compliance with academic norms, but one that is about having the courage to come out of silence and tell the stories that need to be told. He invites you to "write yourself; write what matters to you. Twist and turn teachers' assignments until you find an angle that lets you say something that you simply must say." In this way, Wallace encourages students to conceive of writing as an opportunity to speak back to culture, and perhaps use it to change the way society views yourself and others. Have you ever felt, when you were writing something, that you were taking a risk? What potential challenges to social or academic norms are rooted in your own unique perspectives?

For me, becoming fully literate meant speaking and writing in a voice that did not edit the words to please my father, my god, my dissertation directors, my journal editors, my department chair, or my dean before the words were uttered. It meant saying words that I'd been scared to say for a very long time, words that might estrange me from my family and friends, words that would mark me as "other" in society, words that might put me physically at risk. It meant claiming words like *queer, fag,* and *homo,* which small-minded people had spat at me in derision all my life. Fortunately, becoming literate also meant discovering that I could be gay and accepted.

In this chapter, I invite you to consider that literacy may be something other than what we have imagined it to be—that it is cultural dialogue. In *The Order of Discourse,* French literary theorist Michel Foucault argues that we do not so much speak as we are spoken by the discourses in which

"The Poems Came Late: Literacy as Cultural Dialogue" by David Wallace is reprinted by permission from *The Subject Is Story* edited by Wendy Bishop and Hans Ostrom. Copyright © 2003 by Boynton/Cook Publishers, Inc. Published by Boynton/Cook Publishers, Inc., a division of Reed Elsevier, Inc., Portsmouth, NH. All rights reserved.

we participate. By *discourse* I mean spoken and written language in the contexts in which it is used. Although Foucault admits in his essay that individuals can take agency in speaking and writing, he sees the critical aspect of language and literacy as examining how individuals are situated in the discourses in which they participate. For example, as children we learn to speak with a slow Georgian drawl or a nasal Jersey twang because we imitate the talk that we hear around us. Thus, in a sense, the discourse we hear teaches us how to speak. Foucault's point is particularly telling when we consider that the discourses we first hear have effects on us that extend far beyond accent. Children who hear their mothers and other adult women referred to as girls or chicks or babes are also learning something about how society views women—lessons they may need to unlearn later in life. In addition, Foucault's position suggests that speaking and writing—participating in discourse—may be more difficult for those of us whom the dominant culture defines in stereotypic ways or renders invisible (e.g., lesbians, gay men, physically disabled people).

Seeing literacy as cultural dialogue stands in direct contrast to how most people in American society understand the term: as the basic ability to read and write. I want to argue here that literacy is more than a fundamental set of skills that children must master to succeed in school, a foundation of grammar and usage knowledge that students should have before entering college, or a set of genres one must master to join a profession. Although literacy can be seen as "basic" in these senses, for me, becoming fully literate meant much more than learning my ABCs, enriching my vocabulary, diagramming sentences, and learning new genres and discourse practices. In a sense, then, becoming literate means finding a voice that allows you to represent yourself in various kinds of dialogue. For me, taking such a literate stance meant rewriting my life against cultural narratives that had led me for too long to see my sexual identity as sinful and unspeakable and then later as tolerated but invisible.

The notion of literacy as cultural dialogue is critical for many people. For example, my colleague and friend, Brenda Daly, writes that as a victim of childhood sexual abuse she had to actively author her life. She says, "The poisonous lesson of my childhood was that I could speak, I even could cry out, but no one would hear me, no one would listen" (1998, 5). For Daly, authoring involved more than simply finding words to speak; she also needed an audience to "bear witness" (15). She explains that early in her life, her abuse story was not a welcome one; indeed, the lesson she learned from the discourses of her childhood in family, church, and home was that her problem didn't exist, that she had imagined it, or, worse, that she had caused it. It wasn't until other victims of incest and sexual abuse began to speak of their experiences publicly that Daly found a discourse that she could join. Still, she felt that telling her story meant she had to be a bad girl, at least from the standpoint of her cultural heritage. She says, "To free myself from this debilitating childhood lesson, I would have to transgress conventions of 'good taste'" (20). Like Daly, I have come to see that becoming fully literate required that I rewrite my life, that I deconstruct the discourses that had led me to a place of relative privilege and safety (although at the cost of years of denial). It meant transgressing the version of morality that had shaped my life. It meant writing poems that explored the trials of flirtation, courtship, and intimacy that most people explore as teenagers. These poems came late.

In the pages that follow, I use stories and poems from my life to illustrate the process by which I became literate—that is, able to speak and write myself as a gay man. I invite you to consider how your experiences are similar to and different from mine and also to consider how schooling has affected the kind of voice that you have been invited to take.

Scene 1: Miss Balfour's Academic-Track Senior English Class, Homer-Center High School, Fall 1977

"Exemplary. Who can use exemplary in a sentence?"
Hands shoot up around the room.
"Kim Jones."
"Marie Antoinette led an exemplary life."
"What! Marie Antoinette certainly did not *lead an exemplary life! She was beheaded because of her cavalier attitude; when she heard that the peasants complained that they had no bread, she said, 'Then let them eat cake!'"*
Kim slides down in her seat; classmates exchange furtive but sympathetic glances.
"Now who can use exemplary correctly *in a sentence?"*
A few nervous hands go up.

Scene 2: Holistic Scoring Session, Indiana University of Pennsylvania; Summer 1987

Six people sit around tables in the English department library. Each pours over a stack of hastily scrawled drafts written on every other line by nearly first-year college students reflecting on the strengths and weaknesses of their high school education for administrators who will never read their papers. The stacks get smaller and pages of numbers next to the students' social security numbers fill up. The sticky afternoon wears on in silent reading, broken only by sighs or the occasional chuckle followed by "listen to this one."

"When Sister Mary Frances died, the whole school was totally lugubrious."
The raters smile, snicker a bit, and then return to their reading.

Shallow Literacy

In the ten years that passed between scene 1 and scene 2, I went from being one of those students nervously trying to help Kim Jones recover from what our twelfth-grade English teacher saw as a deplorable lack of cultural knowledge to being one of those six people charged with deciding which students were ready for college writing courses at the local university. The vocabulary issues here are, of course, just indications of wider issues. Like most of the seniors at my rural Pennsylvania high school, I didn't have the cultural knowledge to know that Marie Antoinette was not an exemplary figure, but ten years later I'd developed the kind of sensitivity to linguistic register to know that *lugubrious* was completely out of context in that student's placement essay. Indeed, my twelfth-grade English teacher's attempts at vocabulary enrichment are likely the same kind of stopgap educational attempts that led the student writing about Sister Mary Frances to throw in an impressive-sounding word.

According to the usual definitions of *literacy,* I became literate, even hyperliterate in those ten years. I learned to write essays, news stories, and term papers; I learned to distinguish between *affect* and *effect* and to identify sentence fragments and run-on sentences. I survived the "weeding-out process" in higher education that "sifts the relatively few 'worthy' members for the rewards that come with social promotion" (Ryan and Sackrey 1998, 114). Yet this new literacy was shallow because I was never invited to consider how I was being acculturated in those years—to consider the implications of leaving my working-class roots and becoming someone who knows both how and when to use such words as *psycholinguistics, deconstruction,* and *eco-feminism.*

I bought into what Cheryl Geisler calls the great appeal of higher education: "to make expertise universally accessible" (1994, 79). The problem with such an assumption is that it led me to believe that the ways in which I was taught to speak and write as well as the topics I was encouraged to write and speak about were natural, normal, the way things ought to be. No one invited me to consider why certain topics were never mentioned. And this brand of academic and professional literacy did not occur by accident or descend as holy writ from some language god. Rather, as Geisler notes, it was a part of a larger repackaging of "Anglo-Protestant elitist culture as neutral expertise" by the men who set the initial standards for professional status and the terms by which higher education would bestow that status (75). And for many years, I bought into this presumption, probably because, on the surface, the match between my rural Pennsylvanian, fundamentalist Christian values and the values of higher education was fairly good. I was a smart, white, Protestant male who was trying to appear both straight and middle class. And school itself served as a kind of sanctuary for me—a place where it was okay for a skinny, awkward, deeply closeted gay boy to be smart. Indeed, graduate education eventually provided me the perspective and tools to step back from my evangelical heritage and its attendant condemnation of homosexuality. However, the culture of higher education—at least as I've experienced it— did not immediately encourage me to integrate my sexual identity into my professional life. Thus, school has played a complicated role in the development of my literacy.

Athletes

1971
Last picked, the outfield moves in, easy out.
Swing and a miss; a foul tip has the line of batters reaching.
Across the playground the girls double dutch and hopscotch.
"Just hit this one."
Eyes squeezed shut at contact; the dull thud tells me to release the bat
  and run.
Always a step slower than the throw, but just the second out.
I shuffle back to the end of the line, eyes focused on the gravel beneath
  my feet.
The top of the order grips the bat in his coarse hands.
Arms swing; hips rotate forward; the ball falls over the heads of fielders
  who forgot to adjust.
He rounds second and beats the relay home.
Pop fly, the third out. I trot out to hide in deep right, an inning closer to
  the safety of math problems and phonics lessons.

1977
Head down, eyes focused on a chip of gray paint separating from the
  steel, I pull up my shorts.
The door next to me bangs closed, metal meeting metal, followed by the
  soft click of the locking mechanism falling into place.
My neighbor spins the dial to hide the last number.
"Better hurry."
A white t-shirt hangs loose on my narrow frame, I pull out my shoes,
  sitting to tie them.

From the back of the stall, I see the broad shoulders that stretch tight
    knit shirts across his smooth chest.
His stance is wide and balanced, supporting loud boasts.
I follow the long torso as it narrows to a jock strap, then turn my eyes to
    examine the rust spot obscuring the number plate riveted to the
    door.
I push my locker shut, step over the wooden bench, and weave through
    bodies I cannot touch, careful not to see the ample globes freed
    from their usual home in his Levis.
In class, this jock admires my quick answers; here, I'm on my own.

1981
A knurled bar and two full plates, I press the weight.
Third rep, the bar stalls, arms quiver between achievement and collapse.
Quick steps bring a hand to guide the bar up.
"Maybe you shouldn't try so much next time."
Bi's and tri's, quads and lats, delts; the room slowly empties.
One more set; I brush away the sweat dammed in my eye brows.
He bounces in, smiles, and flips on the sauna.
His jeans drop to the floor; he steps out of them bending slightly at the
    waist.
Today, tight blue cotton caresses his full cheeks.
Will I join him? He's brought an extra towel.
The heat would lessen tomorrow's ache.
Fine beads of sweat form on his tanned skin, but his thick black hair
    resists the damp.
He sits on the cedar slats, shoulders slumped slightly forward—hands
    lightly holding the edge of the bench.
He laughs, showing straight white teeth, briefly holding eye contact but
    then looking down between his feet.
This pretty boy sees more than a brain, but I fumble his pass.

1998
A knurled bar, four full plates and two quarters; I want four reps.
I stretch one shoulder against the side of the bench, and then the other,
    catching a glimpse of Tony at the fountain.
I stand, check the weights, and wait for him to pass.
"Excuse me, could you give me a spot?"
I lie looking up past the bar at his tight chest and arms. I close my eyes.
We lift on three, and then the weight is mine.
The first is down and up, easy. I feel the second. The third is steady but
    slow.
A couple short breaths and I release my locked elbows, letting the bar
    sink to within a whisker of my chest.
I explode back up, pressing; the weight stalls.

His hands hover, not quite touching the bar.
I press again; a red vein stands out on my forehead. I lock my arms.
His hands close around the bar, guiding it back to the supports.
"Nice lift." The cute ones always make me work a little harder.

March 1999
Ames, Iowa

Heterosexist Literacy

No one was openly gay in my high school, in my church, in my Bible college. Sure, my tenth-grade typing teacher talked in a high nasal voice and was called Suzie behind his back. But he wasn't to be taken seriously. Sure, there were the two spinster ladies in our church: the butch one who always had a new car and brought a whistle when she baby-sat us and the sweet feminine one who never raised her voice. But they were just best friends for forty years. Sure, there was a string of friends in Bible college who had been gay and given it up for Jesus or who discovered they were gay after graduation. But we never kissed during our lonely talks or dared to even think of holding each other's hands during the long walks by the lake. Unfortunately, the message that homosexuality didn't or shouldn't exist was not limited to my rural western Pennsylvania high school, my evangelical Christian church, or my fundamentalist Bible college. It also appeared in my secular graduate training in English: we collectively winked at Truman Capote's "flamboyant" lifestyle and focused on the substance of what Socrates said to Phaedrus rather than on their flirtation.

Scene 3: Rhetorical History Course, Summer 1986

The air-conditioning system couldn't quite pull enough of the humidity out of the air, so the eight or ten of us gathered in the English department's library to discuss ancient Greek rhetoric sat slightly sticky on a warm summer evening. A new master's student, I mostly sat in silence as the teacher and the Ph.D. students discussed the text we'd read. I scribbled some notes, but I wasn't sure exactly what I was supposed to do with them, as there would be no tests. As we were collecting our books to leave, the teacher gave us a last-minute warning about the Phaedrus, *which we were reading for the next class session: "Ah, you will encounter passages that seem homoerotic; don't pay much attention to them because, ah, the sexual tension between Socrates and Phaedrus is largely a literary device."*

I'm not sure why my instructor made that statement. Apparently, he did not see it as important to discuss the obvious sexual tension when Socrates says, "Where is that boy I was talking to? He must listen to me once more, not rush off to yield to his non-lover before he hears what I have to say." And Phaedrus responds, "Here he is, quite close to you, whenever you want him" (Hackforth 1952, 53). I'm fairly sure that the instructor was aware of the tradition of homoeroticism in ancient Greek education, but I don't know if his statement to us was a vestige of homophobia or whether he simply believed that, as a scholarly matter, the answer to the question of whether Socrates and Phaedrus were lovers was so obviously negative that it didn't bear discussion. Whatever his intent, the message that I took as a fledgling rhetorician (who was still deeply closeted) was that homosexuality was not fit subject matter for discussion in our classroom.

Scene 4: The Blazing Saddle, Des Moines, Iowa, September 1998

"You go in first," said Brad as he pulled open the door.

"No, you go first," I replied, pushing him forward, "I've never been to a gay bar before; I don't know what to expect."

The bar was packed with men in Levis and T-shirts; most had stomachs that topped over their belts. Heavy eyes fell on us as we pushed through the crowd to get to the bar.

"Where are the cute guys?" I asked when Brad returned from the bar.

He laughed. "They've probably moved on to the Garden to dance by now."

We sipped our drinks, and I scanned the room, trying to find at least one man whom I found attractive.

"I'm going to leave you now, because no one will hit on you if I stand here with you."

"No," I grabbed Brad's arm and held it in a vice-tight grip.

He shook himself free. "I have to go to the bathroom."

I scowled at him, suspicious.

"As soon as I leave, someone will hit on you because you're fresh meat."

"No, really? I don't see anyone whom I want to hit on me, and what would I say?"

"You'll think of something," and he melted into the crowd, moving toward the back of the bar.

"I haven't seen you in here before."

I turned to face the voice; Brad hadn't been gone thirty seconds yet.

"It's my first time."

"My name is Justin, and this is Chad."

I shook hands. "I'm David."

"You have very nice arms; you must work out a lot," Chad was lightly squeezing my bicep between his thumb and forefinger and smiling.

"Um, ah, thanks, I don't really work out that much." Chad was kind of cute.

"Well, whatever you do, it's working."

I stumbled through three more minutes of conversation before I bolted, "I've got to go to the restroom," and I pressed into the crowd in the direction Brad had gone.

Pride Parade

We are
leather and lace, spikes and boas, lamé and denim,
flannel and sequins, pinstripes and pumps, pancake and eyeliner

We are
fags, dykes, homos, bitches, queens, twinks, mothers,
fathers, sisters, brothers, daughters, sons

We are
confused teenagers silenced by locker room taunts

We are
lascivious and lonely, handsome and homely
svelte and skank, built and butch

We are
smart, dumb, fat, thin, tall, short, bald, hairy, drunk, sober, bold, timid,
positive, negative, happy, sad

We are
servers, technicians, doctors, cooks, lawyers, decorators, mortgage
adjusters, reporters, office managers, college profs, secretaries, senators

We are here; we are proud; we are not alone.

June 1999
Des Moines, Iowa

Scene 5: Room 213, Pearson Hall, Iowa State University, April 2001

"I'm not sure I should read this one." I held the transparency of "Lifestyles" in my hand, five minutes before class ended. I'd just read "Pride Parade" to my first-year composition students. They got the point—poems don't have to have a regular rhythm and rhyme like those singsong poems from Chicken Soup for the Teen-age Soul *that the group in charge of class had given them to read. The group's plan had been*

good; to try to use the poems to get the class to think about what it was like to be in someone else's shoes, someone who had been identified as "other" by the dominant school group and treated badly. I was pushing for a second point with my poems: I wanted the class to be challenged by texts written by someone who was the "other," in this case me, a homosexual.

"Well, now you have to show it to us," they teased.

"Okay, class is officially over; you don't have stay for this one," but who would leave before the drama was over? I took a deep breath, wondering if I should let my students glimpse even this much of my sex life. "Here goes."

Lifestyle

Thighs and hips
Tongues and lips
Boys in g-strings dance for tips

Rum and coke
X and smoke
Meat so thick it makes me choke

Whispers and groan
Dicks come bone
Friends in bed, now not alone

Bottom and top
Press, don't stop
A different kind of sock hop

Anal and oral
Sex in plural
Not what the Boy Scouts call moral.

November 2000
Athens and Atlanta, Georgia

By anal the class is laughing nervously; Chris gets up and leaves the room in a pretend huff, only to return a few seconds later, smiling. Students chat in knots of two or three.

"We'll talk more about this one next time."

I begin the next class session reviewing the piece about making pickles that I shared with the class during our first session together. I remind the class that I've been sharing my writing with them all semester. They understand the point; I've been trying to show them that they should write about things that matter to them by reading them pieces in which I take emotional risks. Then I put "Lifestyles" back up on the overhead projector. In a few minutes I will pass out the course evalua-tion forms. "'Meat so thick it makes me choke. Anal and oral, sex in plural.' Why do you think I chose to begin and end the course with these two pieces? Why did I share this poem with you last time?"

"Well, you wanted to show us an example of a good poem."

"Yeah, but I could have quit with 'Pride Parade' if that were just my goal."

My usually talkative class is silent. No one makes eye contact with me.

"Has it occurred to any of you that none of the poems we read for the last class were written from the point of view of the person who was labeled as 'other'?" Apparently it hadn't. "Has it occurred to any of you that I am labeled as 'other' in many situations?" A few brows wrin-kle, but no one breaks the silence. "I showed you this poem to show you that this stuff is a part of who I am. I wanted you to see that to accept me as a person who makes pickles and strawberry jam to grieve for his mother and grandmother is also to accept me as a person who has sex with other men. It's all part of the same package."

I hand out the course evaluation sheets and—following university rules—I go out in the hall until the students are finished.

A New Literacy

At age thirty-seven, I began learning how to interact as a gay man. Despite the awkwardness of my first exposure to a gay bar, I took to flirting and the pickup games that go on in gay bars fairly easily. I became literate quickly. I learned that in some kinds of bars, men I don't know will feel free to grab my ass and that with the right kind of look I could stop them short. I learned that it was okay to let my eyes linger on an attractive man, but that if we made eye contact, I had to decide in a millisecond whether to hold it and indicate interest or break it immediately. I learned to distinguish between accidental touches on the dance floor and subtle overtures.

Learning to be a gay man in my classrooms was harder. In fact, it was three years after my first experience in a gay bar that I explicitly outed myself to a writing class. I saw the need to be out with this particular class when I received two papers early on in which students defined homosexu-als as outside of their circles of humanity. One student wrote:

The first people I exclude from my circle [of humanity] are homosexuals. They have no right to be able to do those sick and unpure actions. Not even the dumbest animal on earth performs these disgusting acts. It is against the whole plan of Human Nature.

For the first time in my teaching career, I was not content to sit back and pretend that such statements did not affect me, to hide in a safe, supposedly straight, middle-class, educated, white, male, above-it-all teacher role. I stood in for the millions of lesbian, gay, bisexual, transgendered, and transexual people whom these students were writing off and let them know in my responses to their work that their arguments affected me as a gay man. Later in the course, I outed myself to the class as a whole when, as an example of how to develop a focused argument, I used a letter to the editor I'd written responding to a state senator who was upset about Iowa State University's recent decision to grant domestic partner benefits. Yet this was not enough. I was still safe in my teacher's role; I'd won most of the class over early in the semester by reading them some pieces about my mother's death. I'd been patient with them, met with them outside of class, but in Hélène Cixous' (2002) terms, I hadn't written my body for them. I hadn't made them see that the sensitive son grieving for his mother, the caring patient teacher, and the man who flirted with men in bars were all me.

The occasion in which I chose to push past some students' comfort level with my homosexuality arose as a response to several poems a group of students had chosen for their class discussion. As I read the poems about an hour before class, I was annoyed that in one of the predictable, singsong poems, the hero was a pretty, popular girl who got assigned to work with a group with a boy who could barely speak English and two girls who were fashion-challenged. And so, at age forty, in 213 Pearson Hall on a bright April afternoon, I found a new academic voice. I found a small way to speak back to the discourses both throughout my life and in that very classroom that had tried to make me see myself as abnormal, sinful, and needing to be silent. My choice to make my sexual identity explicit by reading "Lifestyles" to my class was far from safe. In the course evaluations, the students' responses were mixed. Several cited "Lifestyles" as offensive, as over the line; others saw it as a more natural part of the series of revelations that I'd made throughout the semester and were grateful for the chance to have substantive interaction with an openly gay man for the first time in their lives.

Although I have not read "Lifestyles" to any other of my writing classes, I continue to share my poems and stories with my classes, and I always share something that involves an emotional risk for me. The main reason I make myself vulnerable to my students in this way is to invite them to tell stories that society has encouraged them to keep to themselves. This semester a beautiful young woman wrote a paper in which she admitted for the first time that she was bulimic; a self-described computer nerd wrote about a recent romantic rejection and shame at never having had a girlfriend; and a budding feminist wrote about her secret desire for larger breasts, the kind that turn men's heads. To be completely honest, though, I also take these risks—particularly those related to my gay identity— because I need to, because I'm still recovering from a personal and educational history that discouraged me from accepting myself.

Authoring Your Life

Although I wrote thousands of words in elementary, junior high, and high school and tens of thousands as an undergraduate and graduate student, the poems came late, came last. School provided me with many important intellectual tools: I learned to read others' texts and summarize them fairly and efficiently; I learned to question authors' assumptions and examine the support that they provided for their claims; I learned to construct my own arguments, to make a clear point and support it well. Rarely, however, did school invite me to consider who I was or what assumptions other authors were making about me. I learned to explore my own life in relationship to others only as I taught myself to write stories and poems.

Along with the other authors in this book, I want to invite you to consider the power of story to enliven your writing. The writing teachers in this book as well as those in your classrooms have much to teach you about new techniques and exploring unfamiliar genres. However, they may or may not encourage you to author your own life, and so I conclude by extending that invitation: write yourself; write what matters to you. Twist and turn teachers' assignments until you lind an angle that lets you say something that you simply must say. Take a risk; write the things that you've been hiding under covers of silence or forced eloquence. I can't guarantee that your teachers, your family, or your friends will like what you write, but at least you won't wait as long as I did to write your poems and stories, your essays and letters to the editor, your paintings and portraits. Write yourself.

Works Cited

Cixous, Hélène. 2001. *The Laugh of the Medusa*. In *The Rhetorical Tradition: Readings for Classical Times to the Present*, 2nd ed., 1524–1537. Edited by Patricia Bizzell and Bruce Herzberg. Boston: St. Martin's Press.

Daly, Brenda. 1998. *Authoring a Life: A Woman's Survival in and through Literary Studies*. Albany: State University of New York Press.

Foucault, Michel. 2001. *The Order of Discourse.* In *The Rhetorical Tradition: Readings for Classical Times to the Present,* 2nd ed., 1460–1470. Edited by Patricia Bizzell and Bruce Herzberg. Boston: St. Martin's Press.

Geisler, Cheryl. 1994. *Academic Literacy and the Nature of Expertise: Reading, Writing and Knowing in Academic Philosophy.* Hillsdale, NJ: Erlbaum.

Hackforth, K. 1952. *Plato's Phaedrus: Translated with an Introduction and Commentary.* London: Cambridge University Press.

Ryan, Jake, and Charles Sackrey. 1985. *Strangers in Paradise: Academics from the Working Class.* Boston: South End Press.

Death of the Profane

Patricia Williams

In this essay, law professor Patricia Williams examines an event in her life—being denied entry into a store by a white store clerk because she is black. She also examines numerous "retellings" of the event. Each time Williams writes about the incident, she finds that the "event" itself almost changes because the context of her retelling alters what she can say about it. Each new context imposes different expectations about what her audience expects and understands about racial relations and discrimination. More importantly, each context imposes its own conventions on how one should talk of such events that force Williams to either break the norms or tell a completely different story. Have you ever retold the same story in different contexts? Felt restricted by what you could say about your own experience because of how factors of your identity (e.g., race, class, gender, sexuality, etc.) might be "heard" by your audience? What constraints were placed (or self-imposed) on what you said and how you said it? What aspects of the context and what conventions of society at large shaped your retellings?

Buzzers are big in New York City. Favored particularly by smaller stores and boutiques, merchants throughout the city have installed them as screening devices to reduce the incidence of robbery: if the face at the door looks desirable, the buzzer is pressed and the door is unlocked. If the face is that of an undesirable, the door stays locked. Predictably, the issue of undesirability has revealed itself to be a racial determination. While controversial enough at first, even civil-rights organizations backed down eventually in the face of arguments that the buzzer system is a "necessary evil," that it is a "mere inconvenience" in comparison to the risks of being murdered, that suffering discrimination is not as bad as being assaulted, and that in any event it is not all blacks who are barred, just "17-year-old black males wearing running shoes and hooded sweatshirts."

"The Death of the Profane" reprinted by permission of the publisher from *The Alchemy of Race and Rights: Diary of a Law Professor* by Patricia J. Williams, pp. 44–51. Cambridge, Mass.: Harvard University Press, Copyright © 1991 by the President and Fellows of Harvard College.

The installation of these buzzers happened swiftly in New York; stores that had always had their doors wide open suddenly became exclusive or received people by appointment only. I discovered them and their meaning one Saturday in 1986. I was shopping in Soho and saw in a store window a sweater that I wanted to buy for my mother. I pressed my round brown face to the window and my finger to the buzzer, seeking admittance. A narrow-eyed, white teenager wearing running shoes and feasting on bubble gum glared out, evaluating me for signs that would pit me against the limits of his social understanding. After about five seconds, he mouthed "We're closed," and blew pink rubber at me. It was two Saturdays before Christmas, at one o'clock in the afternoon; there were several white people in the store who appeared to be shopping for things for *their* mothers.

I was enraged. At that moment I literally wanted to break all the windows of the store and *take* lots of sweaters for my mother. In the flicker of his judgmental gray eyes, that saleschild had transformed my brightly sentimental, joy-to-the-world, pre-Christmas spree to a shambles. He snuffed my sense of humanitarian catholicity, and there was nothing I could do to snuff his, without making a spectacle of myself.

I am still struck by the structure of power that drove me into such a blizzard of rage. There was almost nothing I could do, short of physically intruding upon him, that would humiliate him the way he humiliated me. No words, no gestures, no prejudices of my own would make a bit of difference to him; his refusal to let me into the store—it was Benetton's, whose colorfully punnish ad campaign is premised on wrapping every one of the world's peoples in its cottons and woolens—was an outward manifestation of his never having let someone like me into the realm of his reality. He had no compassion, no remorse, no reference to me; and no desire to acknowledge me even at the estranged level of arm's-length transactor. He saw me only as one who would take his money and therefore could not conceive that I was there to give him money.

In this weird ontological imbalance, I realize that buying something in that store was like bestowing a gift, the gift of my commerce, the lucre of my patronage. In the wake of my outrage, I wanted to take back the gift of appreciation that my peering in the window must have appeared to be. I wanted to take it back in the form of unappreciation, disrespect, defilement. I wanted to work so hard at wishing he could feel what I felt that he would never again mistake my hatred for some sort of plaintive wish to be included. I was quite willing to disenfranchise myself, in the heat of my need to revoke the flattery of my purchasing power. I was willing to boycott Benetton's, random white-owned businesses, and anyone who ever blew bubble gum in my face again.

My rage was admittedly diffuse, even self-destructive, but it was symmetrical. The perhaps loose-ended but utter propriety of that rage is no doubt lost not just to the young man who actually barred me, but to those who would appreciate my being barred only as an abstract precaution, who approve of those who would bar even as they deny that they would bar *me*.

The violence of my desire to burst into Benetton's is probably quite apparent. I often wonder if the violence, the exclusionary hatred, is equally apparent in the repeated public urgings that blacks understand the buzzer system by putting themselves in the shoes of white storeowners—that, in effect, blacks look into the mirror of frightened white faces for the reality of their undesirability; and that then blacks would "just as surely conclude that [they] would not let [themselves] in under similar circumstances." (That some blacks might agree merely shows that some of us have learned too well the lessons of privatized intimacies of self-hatred and rationalized away the fullness of our public, participatory selves.)

On the same day I was barred from Benetton's, I went home and wrote the above impassioned account in my journal. On the day after that, I found I was still brooding, so I turned to a form of catharsis I have always found healing. I typed up as much of the story as I have just told, made a big poster of it, put a nice colorful border around it, and, after Benetton's was truly closed, stuck it to their big sweater-filled window. I exercised my first amendment right to place my business with them right out in the street.

So that was the first telling of this story. The second telling came a few months later, for a symposium on Excluded Voice sponsored by a law review. I wrote an essay summing up my feelings about being excluded from Benetton's and analyzing "how the rhetoric of increased privatization, in response to racial issues, functions as the rationalizing agent of public unaccountability and, ultimately, irresponsibility." Weeks later, I received the first edit. From the first page to the last, my fury had been carefully cut out. My rushing, run-on-rage had been reduced to simple declarative sentences. The active personal had been inverted in favor of the passive impersonal. My words were different, they spoke to me upside-down. I was afraid to read too much of it at a time—meanings rose up at me oddly, stolen and strange.

A week and a half later, I received the second edit. All reference to Benetton's had been deleted because, according to the editors and the faculty adviser, it was defamatory; they feared harassment and liability; they said printing it would be irresponsible. I called them and offered to supply a footnote attesting to this as my personal experience at one particular location and of a buzzer system not limited to Benetton's; the editors told me that they were not in the habit of publishing things that were unverifiable. I could not but wonder, in this refusal even to let me file an affidavit, what it would take to make my experience verifiable. The testimony of an independent white bystander? (a requirement in fact imposed in U.S. Supreme Court holdings through the first part of the century).

Two days *after* the piece was sent to press, I received copies of the final page proofs. All reference to my race had been eliminated because it was against "editorial policy" to permit descriptions of physiognomy. "I realize," wrote one editor, "that this was a very personal experience, but any reader will know what you must have looked like when standing at that window." In a telephone conversation to them, I ranted wildly about the significance of such an omission. "It's irrelevant," another editor explained in a voice gummy with soothing and patience; "It's nice and poetic" but it doesn't "advance the discussion of any principle . . . This is a law review, after all." Frustrated, I accused him of censorship; calmly he assured me it was not. "This is just a matter of style," he said with firmness and finality.

Ultimately I did convince the editors that mention of my race was central to the whole sense of the subsequent text; that my story became one of extreme paranoia without the information that I am black; or that it became one in which the reader had to fill in the gap by assumption, presumption, prejudgment, or prejudice. What was most interesting to me in this experience was how the blind application of principles of neutrality, through the device of omission, acted either to make me look crazy or to make the reader participate in old habits of cultural bias.

That was the second telling of my story. The third telling came last April, when I was invited to participate in a law-school conference on Equality and Difference. I retold my sad tale of exclusion from Soho's most glitzy boutique, focusing in this version on the law-review editing process as a consequence of an ideology of style rooted in a social text of neutrality. I opined:

Law and legal writing aspire to formalized, color-blind, liberal ideas. Neutrality is the standard for assuring these ideals; yet the adherence to it is often determined by reference to an aesthetic of uniformity, in which difference is simply omitted. For example, when segregation was eradicated from the American lexicon, its omission led many to actually believe that racism therefore no longer existed. Race-neutrality in law has become the presumed antidote for race bias in real life. With the entrenchment of the notion of race-neutrality came attacks on the concept of affirmative action and the rise of reverse discrimination suits. Blacks, for so many generations deprived of jobs based on the color of our skin, are now told that we ought to find it demeaning to be hired, based on the color of our skin. Such is the silliness of simplistic either-or inversions as remedies to complex problems.

What is truly demeaning in this era of double-speak-no-evil is going on interviews and not getting hired because someone doesn't think we'll be comfortable. It is demeaning not to get promoted because we're judged "too weak," then putting in a lot of energy the next time and getting fired because we're "too strong." It is demeaning to be told what we find demeaning. It is very demeaning to stand on street corners unemployed and begging. It is downright demeaning to have to explain why we haven't been employed for months and then watch the job go to someone who is "more experienced." It is outrageously demeaning that none of this can be called racism, even if it happens only to, or to large numbers of, black people; as long as it's done with a smile, a handshake and a shrug; as long as the phantom-word "race" is never used.

The image of race as a phantom-word came to me after I moved into my late godmother's home. In an attempt to make it my own, I cleared the bedroom for painting. The following morning the room asserted itself, came rushing and raging at me through the emptiness, exactly as it had been for twenty-five years. One day filled with profuse and overwhelming complexity, the next day filled with persistently recurring memories. The shape of the past came to haunt me, the shape of the emptiness confronted me each time I was about to enter the room. The force of its spirit still drifts like an odor throughout the house.

The power of that room, I have thought since, is very like the power of racism as status quo: it is deep, angry, eradicated from view, but strong enough to make everyone who enters the room walk around the bed that isn't there, avoiding the phantom as they did the substance, for fear of bodily harm. They do not even know they are avoiding; they defer to the unseen shapes of things with subtle responsiveness, guided by an impulsive awareness of nothingness, and the deep knowledge and denial of witchcraft at work.

The phantom room is to me symbolic of the emptiness of formal equal opportunity, particularly as propounded by President Reagan, the Reagan Civil Rights Commission and the Reagan Supreme Court. Blindly formalized constructions of equal opportunity are the creation of a space that is filled in by a meandering stream of unguided hopes, dreams, fantasies, fears, recollections. They are the presence of the past in imaginary, imagistic form—the phantom-roomed exile of our longing.

It is thus that I strongly believe in the efficacy of programs and paradigms like affirmative action. Blacks are the objects of a constitutional omission which has been incorporated into a theory of neutrality. It is thus that omission is really a form of expression, as oxymoronic as that sounds; racial omission is a literal part of original intent; it is the fixed, reiterated prophecy of the Founding Fathers. It is thus that affirmative action is an affirmation; the affirmative act of hiring—or hearing—blacks is a recognition of individuality that replaces blacks as a social statistic, that is profoundly interconnective to the fate of blacks and whites either as sub-groups or as one group. In this sense, affirmative action is as mystical and beyond-the-self as an initiation ceremony. It is an act of verification and of vision. It is an act of social as well as professional responsibility.

The following morning I opened the local newspaper, to find that the event of my speech had commanded two columns on the front page of the Metro section. I quote only the opening lines: "Affirmative action promotes prejudice by denying the status of women and blacks, instead of affirming them as its name suggests. So said New York City attorney Patricia Williams to an audience Wednesday."

I clipped out the article and put it in my journal. In the margin there is a note to myself. Eventually, it says, I should try to pull all these threads together into yet another law-review article. The problem, of course, will be that in the hierarchy of law-review citation, the article in the newspaper will have more authoritative weight about me, as a so-called "primary resource" than I will have; it will take precedence over my own citation of the unverifiable testimony of my speech.

I have used the Benetton's story a lot, in speaking engagements at various schools. I tell it whenever I am too tired to whip up an original speech from scratch. Here are some of the questions I have been asked in the wake of its telling:

Am I not privileging a racial perspective, by considering only the black point of view?

Don't I have an obligation to include the "salesman's side" of the story?

Am I not putting the salesman on trial and finding him guilty of racism without giving him a chance to respond to or cross-examine me?

Am I not using the store window as a "metaphorical fence" against the potential of his explanation in order to represent my side as "authentic"?

How can I be sure I'm right?

What makes my experience the real black one anyway?

Isn't it possible that another black person would disagree with my experience? If so, doesn't that render my story too unempirical and subjective to pay any attention to?

Always a major objection is to my having put the poster on Benetton's window. As one law professor put it: "It's one thing to publish this in a law review, where no one can take it personally, but it's another thing altogether to put your own interpretation right out there, just like that, uncontested, I mean, with nothing to counter it."

Student Essay: "Be the Dance"

Catherine Pixton

Most people, when hearing "dancer," picture a tall, thin girl with her hair pulled back into a bun, maybe with a pair of ballet shoes slung over her shoulder. When I think of a dancer, I picture lots of men and women, young and old, dancing in different styles and in different clothing. To me, the world of dance is a large building, with lots of floors and lots of rooms, each with a slightly different type or style of dance. On one floor is ballet, jazz, and tap. On another is tango, waltz, and swing. But my favorite floor is the one that is least known about: the floor that houses Balkan line dancing, Polish and Hungarian turning dances, and English sword and stick dancing. I have a window into the world of dance I feel is very unique in this day and age, and I know that if I never had the chance to see this picture, I would be a very different person.

My identity as a dancer is as far from the ballerina image as heavy metal is from classical. Growing up, I did not stick with just one type of dance, but delved into many different types, both popular and what may have been called "dorky" by my peers at the time, like folk dancing. My parents brought me to my first international folk dance when I was three days old, and I have been doing it ever since. The first dance I remember doing, when I was about four or five, was an Italian dance called the Neapolitan Tarantella, with lots of twirls and claps. To this day, my favorite dances are still the ones with twirls and percussion in them, often from France, Romania, Turkey, or Bulgaria.

As a first-grader, I had dreams of being a ballerina in a pink tutu, leaping gracefully around a stage. I enrolled in a ballet class, and at the end of three years, I threw my tutu in the closet and vowed never to take it out again. This was not the kind of twirl I liked. I just wanted to dance in my own way and not someone else's. Ballet made me feel confined, like I was trapped in a pink fluffy box with eight other little girls, most of whom had no clue how to dance. I could only move when and how the teacher told me to. I went through a similar phase with tap a year later. I refused to do what my instructor wanted, and told him, "I want to make my own noise." I couldn't seem to make my poor, suffering teachers understand that I had been dancing since I could walk, and therefore already knew how to dance. I was only trying to learn new things that I could play with. What was the fun, I wondered, in dancing someone else's dance, a dance you could not make your own?

I began doing English ritual sword and stick dances when I was thirteen. I loved them immediately. Here was a kind of dance where I could incorporate my own style, play around with it, and even create new parts. I especially loved rapper, which uses double-handled swords with spring steel blades, and even has fun twirls and step dancing! Four other girls and I formed a rapper team that year, and looking back, I think that that may have been one of the best decisions of my life. Aidin, Erika, Kristin, Gillian, and I became best friends, and we worked well together as a team. We traveled together on the weekends and over vacations, when most of our performances occurred. I had never been part of such a seamless team before then.

Teamwork is one of my favorite things about rapper. Dancing would be too easy if it was just one or two people dancing together, or a whole group of people doing all the same moves at the same time. With rapper, there are five people performing different motions simultaneously, and they all come together in what is called a "figure." One person being slightly off slows down the whole group, because we are all holding the other end of someone else's sword. For example, if one girl were to trip in the middle of a figure, chances are the rest of us would go down with her. That is why when we complete a dance without any mistakes, we feel so great because it means we work well as a team. Rapper is such a precise type of dancing; you have to be in exactly the right place at exactly the right time or you could get hurt. A moment after I dash through the opening between two of my teammates, their sword flashes down into the place I just left. If I am late, I get a sword through the crown of my head. Though it may sound weird, this is another reason why I love rapper so much. I am a perfectionist, and rapper is a perfectionist's type of dance.

There were moments when I didn't love rapper. Dancing with sharp objects means you get some interesting injuries, in addition to the usual sprained ankles and pulled muscles. I have several scars on my hands and a lot on my memory from the particularly nasty accidents that were inevitable but somehow didn't leave a mark. For instance, once I did a supported back flip over the swords, except that halfway through, Gillian and Aidin dropped me, and it became an unsupported back flip. I like to think that rapper has really become a physical part of me because of the scars it periodically leaves behind.

Needless to say, dancing has provided me with an excellent sense of balance, and rapper in particular gives me a great deal of spatial awareness and good reflexes. I am nimble on my feet, and my back muscles have prevented me from taking a tumble more than once. All of these come in handy on a day-to-day basis, especially in the winter when most sidewalks become glaciers and a fall is nearly inevitable. The team skills I learned in the first months of dancing are useful in all sorts of situations, like working on group projects, mediating arguments between friends, and even little things like organizing meetings. Perhaps I would have acquired all of these skills and senses regardless through the course of my life, but I feel that I am that much luckier to have gotten them from dance.

I love rapper. The feeling I get when I first take the sword in my hands and flex it a little to get the feel of the blade is unparalleled. I love hearing the swish of blade on blade and the crisp tap of leather-soled shoes on a hard surface. And seeing a dark sea of upturned faces after momentarily being blinded by bright stage lights is at once intimidating and exciting. Performing for an audience, especially those who have never seen or heard of rapper before, is exhilarating. At first, I was amazed to realize that young children and other rapper dancers looked up to us. I don't think I was ever more surprised than when a nine-year-old told me that she wanted to be like me when she grew up. To me, receiving such praise from an audience member is one of the most rewarding things about dancing. Because the way I see it, I'm just doing what I love: dancing. There is nothing amazing about my feet, or my hands, or my sword, which I sometimes view as an extension of my arm, or any other specific part of me. What is amazing is the dance. And while I am dancing, I am the dance. Not my sword, not my feet. My whole body is the dance. And so are Erika, Kristin, Aidin, and Gillian. Together, we are the dance. As soon as the music begins, I feel like I'm on a different level of being. I am always moving, always looking, always thinking: jump here, don't duck, hands up, clean stepping . . .

So when I say that I am a dancer, I don't mean that I wear leotards and watch my weight. The people who traditionally did rapper in the 1700s are usually the only people who do it today, portly middle-aged men. Could you imagine Howard Dean in a tutu? He fits my image of a dancer, but not the image that I feel most of America holds. I have seen all kinds of dancing, done by all kinds of people. It is not all young women with their hair pulled back, although I may fit that description from time to time. I will still be a dancer when I am a mother, and a grandmother, and not just because my hands are scarred. The dance community to which I am proud to belong does not exclude people, ever, no matter their age, race, or ability. We all know that dancing can be so important that little else matters, whether you are the dancer or the audience. Dance is something that is everywhere, all the time, whether you know it or not. It can be solitary, social, performed, choreographed, improvised, rhythmical, or unphrased. Or it can just be. And I will always be the dance.

Student Essay:
"Survival: By Any Means Necessary"

Justin Bell

"Don't any of you go bringing no white girl 'round here!" My Aunt Rita's voice blared throughout the room. I struggled to keep from laughing, the corners of my mouth turning up slightly. "I see you smirking J.B., but I'm being dead serious." My aunt was now looking directly at me. Aunt Rita had a gift for being dramatic and was infamous for her tirades that seemed to go on forever; most of the time they were tongue-in-cheek and would have all those who listened laughing hysterically. However this one seemed different and looking into her eyes it was evident that my smile was out of place. I looked around the room at the rest of her audience: my four first cousins. One was sixteen, the other three, her children, were six, eight, and the oldest was my age of ten. My father and my grandmother looked on from the distance co-signing Aunt Rita's ideology. None of us kids really knew what to make of what we were witnessing. Most seemed to be handling the situation the same way I was—with an uncomfortable look on their faces. We all had to have been thinking the same thing exactly: How serious was she? As she continued, our question was answered, "I want to make sure all of you keep in mind that we didn't move to Upper Montclair so the five of you could become a bunch of house niggers." With that the entire mood of the room changed, her sentiments and the fury that went behind them were now crystal clear. Her words hit me like a body blow. I was so hurt I felt as though I would cry any second, so embarrassed I would have sworn that I was the first member of my skin complexion to turn red in the face. I had been called the worst thing imaginable: a turncoat, a traitor, an Uncle Tom.

The catalyst behind Aunt Rita's speech had been me. In my fifth grade homeroom I had met a girl named Molly. The two of us became very close and had even taken to calling each other boyfriend and girlfriend. Molly had skin that was far in contrast to mine; she was a white girl. The couple the two of us formed was actually not uncommon in the town of Upper

Montclair where we lived. Upper Montclair was ranked by most surveys as the number one community in the United States for interracial relationships. To me it had seemed commonplace to "go out" with a white girl, something that no one would have a problem with. Aunt Rita didn't see it that way. She saw it as an extension of selling out, the worst thing one could do. Although it would not be the last time, the issue of selling out was first really brought home to me at the age of ten when Aunt Rita lectured us that night.

As I grew older I realized the issue was not so much selling out as it was being labeled a sellout. At the age of thirteen I decided I would change my image so as not to have been thought a sellout. I became entranced in my own personal black power movement. I wore Afro-centric clothing, I listened to rap music, and not just rap music, but only those rappers who spoke the word of black empowerment. I could quote the speeches of Malcolm X verbatim. I can remember the sense of pride I felt arguing with my American history teacher, telling him something along the lines of: "Sitting at the table doesn't make you a diner unless you eat what's on your plate. Just like being in America doesn't make you an American" (X 26). It didn't matter that I didn't believe a word of what I was saying; all that mattered was that I was standing up for my people. Besides, if it was good enough for Malcolm X to say, then it was good enough for me. After all no one ever called him a sellout.

Then there was my crowning moment of convincing my family to celebrate Kwanzaa. I remember going to my dad and telling him why it was necessary that our family take part in this holiday. I don't think he could have been any prouder as I explained to him the principles of each day and he happily agreed to have the family celebrate. The last day of Kwanzaa is the first of July and the principle is Imani, meaning faith. Imani is a special day and we decided to celebrate it with the extended family. All my aunts and uncles from my father's side and all of my first cousins made their way to our house in order to take part. We made it into a big event and in order to help celebrate all of the children were asked to read something that reflected the principle of Imani. It was actually my idea to have the kids read and I made sure I went last. I watched as my cousins and my sister went up with paper in hand and read their various selections. They read stuff from Langston Hughes, Maya Angelou, and even the last part of Martin Luther King's "I Have a Dream" speech; all the generic non-threatening black readings.

When it came my turn, I rose from my seat with no paper in hand. I had no need for a written script because I had been preparing for this day for weeks. In front of my dad, my mom, Aunt Rita, and all those in attendance I recited word for word a speech given by Malcolm X. It was an intense speech bashing those—namely Martin Luther King—that Malcolm X perceived as being pawns of the white man. In the speech, I, as Malcolm X, explained the ways of slavery time; explained that there were two different types of slaves, the ones that worked the field and the ones that worked in the house. That the slave in the house grew to love his white master maybe even more than the master loved himself. I went on with the speech explaining the differences until I got to the fiery conclusion that I knew would bring the house down. I said in my best Malcolm X impression: "Back then we called them house niggers and we still got a couple house niggers running around today" (*Malcolm X*).

By entrancing myself in the black empowerment culture I felt a certain air of invincibility. With my knowledge of everything that was black, how could anyone challenge me as a sellout? This was all shattered when I started high school in a new town. It soon became evident that no matter how much I could quote or how many African terms I knew, it meant nothing to the black upperclassmen. All they knew was that I was from the affluent town of Upper Montclair, my parents were both doctors, and that made me an unredeemable sellout. In their minds the fact that I came from a family with money meant that I wasn't authentically black. There was nothing I could do to change their minds. I attempted to duplicate the character that had gotten me through middle school, trying to prove my blackness at every turn, but it was no use.

The upperclassmen mocked my attempts to prove my authenticity and took to calling me "Crossover," another term for sellout. Stripped of my name, pride, and blackness, it became clear to me that they would never accept me as a true black man. So it occurred to me that I should embrace the name and expectations put on me by my elders. I decided that if they wanted to give me the cursed name of Crossover, I would wear it like my scarlet letter. In about a year's time I shed my black empowerment roots and became the Crossover character. I purposely spoke in contrast to the way the other blacks spoke. I became the sole black kid to join the tennis team. Any time I talked about black issues I would approach them with arrogance, acting as if I were too good to be bothered with such issues. I remember praising the Republican Party and telling a group of older blacks how stupid it was for blacks not to vote Republican. Any time they would make mention of some predominantly black function, such as a dance, I would turn my nose up and ridicule it. Once again I didn't believe in the rhetoric I was saying, but it got me by and that was all I was asking for.

Surprisingly it had an effect better than I could have hoped. The upperclassmen took great amusement in the character I had become and loved to have me around. I became a mascot of sorts for the older black kids. I would always be in character around them as that was the only way they would accept me. I was "Crossover" so much that I almost started to believe in the things I was saying. However this did not last forever as the upperclassmen all eventually graduated and with them went the character of Crossover. I felt foolish and embarrassed for acting as an Uncle Tom court jester for them all those years. I quickly turned down my antics for I no longer felt the need to put on an act simply to entertain my peers

I once again went by my name of J.B., instead of the one that had been given to me with scorn. I was left not Justin X, the revolutionary, nor Crossover, the sellout; I was simply J.B., perhaps a mixture of both.

Works Cited

Malcolm X. Dir. Spike Lee. Warner Bros., 1992.

X, Malcolm. "The Ballot or the Bullet." *Malcolm X Speaks*. Ed. George Breitman. New York: Grove Press, Inc., 1965, 23–44.

Suggested Exercises and Activities for Inquiring Into Self

Reading for Self

Many of the essays in this section are very personal and/or look closely at how people act or behave within a very specific context (e.g., a bar, a shack on Cape Cod). This exercise can help you assess what rhetorical purpose such essays might be serving. To get at this concept, answer the following questions about the essay, trying to write at least a paragraph in response to each question.

1. Why might the author have written this essay? What do you think she was trying to communicate to others? Include a quote or two to support your answer.

2. What indications are there in the essay of what the author learned about himself?

3. What did you learn by reading this essay? What was new information to you? What surprised you? Frustrated you?

4. What did the essay make you think about in your own life? (You do not need to make a direct correlation; for example, few of us will have stayed in a shack on the Cape, but we may have a special place.)

Hierarchy of Influences

Make a list of all the "outside" influences on the author and/or topic of this piece. Be sure to define influence as broadly as possible to include other people, places, groups, institutions, or even cultural categories such as beliefs about gender, race, religion, and so on. Once you have constructed your list, re-read the essay to see which of these influences has the most impact on what the author is describing (her actions, thinking, etc. in the essay). Go back to your list and rewrite it to reflect a hierarchy of influences: What is most important? What is next? What is least important?

Finally, write a brief paragraph explaining why you ranked your list in the order you did.

Spinning Out an Inquiry

This exercise may resemble other diagramming exercises you have done such as clustering or webbing. The difference is that you will not only be spinning out the essay in many directions, but also drawing connections between points on the web.

Start with the subject of the essay. Whose story are you reading? Place that person, situation, or event at the center of your web. Now identify the primary influences acting upon that person, situation, or event. Draw threads that connect the subject to each of his primary influences. Notice that for any person, situation, or event there is not one significant influence on her sense of self and the world, but many. Your objective is to look at these influences simultaneously, in relation to each other. Now, begin to spin your web further outward: What are the characteristics of each of these influences? What experiences, backgrounds, and settings contribute to a way of seeing or being seen? Continue your web, allowing yourself to expand outward in as many directions as you can. See how far you can go with each feature. You may notice that characteristics overlap.

Now start to connect them. Think about how lines in a spider web don't just spin out, but they also cross each other for structure and support. Feel free to make a mess of your web as you draw threads connecting one characteristic with another. When you have finished, write about your discoveries, particularly the areas of greatest overlap. Explain how you see the various features in the web connecting for the subject whose text you read. What does the analysis of context help you understand about the author and/or subject of the text?

Analyzing Stylistic Choices

All writers make choices about such issues as what words to use, what details to emphasize, what order to retell events, and how to present one's own thinking and actions to the audience(s) one is addressing. Each of these seemingly minor choices (e.g., choosing the verb *bumped* or *crushed* to describe one car hitting another) not only conveys the writer's relationship to what he describes, but also affects how readers envision the events, persons, and/or places described.

1) Select one of the texts you have read and reread it marking passages where the author describes self, another person, an event, and/or a place.

2) From these marked passages, choose three to focus on that relate to the same person, event, or place.

3) For each of these passages, list words/phrases/sentences that seem key to you in terms of how they convey a sense of the person/place/ event. Then write a paragraph or two reflecting on the impact of these stylistic choices, using the following questions as guides:

   a) What similarities and differences are there in these passages? How do they differ in terms of word choice, syntax, imagery, etc.? Are there differences in point of view (e.g., first person v. third person) or perspective?

   b) How do these different choices reflect the overall message you think the writer seeks to communicate? What tone/mood/point of view is the author conveying in each passage? Does this relationship change between the three passages?

   c) How do these choices position the writer in relation to what she describes?

   d) How do these choices position the reader in relation to what is described?

Gertrude Stein

How Writing Is Written

What I want to talk about to you tonight is just the general subject of how writing is written. It is a large subject, but one can discuss it in a very short space of time. The beginning of it is what everybody has to know: everybody is contemporary with his period. A very bad painter once said to a very great painter, "Do what you like, you cannot get rid of the fact that we are contemporaries." That is what goes on in writing. The whole crowd of you is contemporary to each other, and the whole business of writing is the question of living in that contemporariness. Each generation has to live in that. The thing that is important is that nobody knows what the contemporariness is. In other words, they don't know where they are going, but they are on their way.

Each generation has to do with what you would call the daily life: and a writer, painter, or any sort of creative artist, is not at all ahead of his time. He is contemporary. He can't live in the past, because it is gone. He can't live in the future because no one knows what it is. He can live only in the present of his daily life. He is expressing the thing that is being expressed by everybody else in their daily lives. The thing you have to remember is that everybody lives a contemporary daily life. The writer lives it, too, and expresses it imperceptibly. The fact remains that in the act of living, everybody has to live contemporarily. But in the things concerning art and literature they don't have to live contemporarily, because it doesn't make any

How Writing Is Written from *Previously Uncollected Writings of Gertrude Stein,* Vol. 2. Permission granted by the Estate of Gertrude Stein, through its Literary Executor, Mr. Stanford Gann, Jr. of Levin & Gann, P.A.

difference; and they live about forty years behind their time. And that is the real explanation of why the artist or painter is not recognized by his contemporaries. He is expressing the time-sense of his contemporaries, but nobody is really interested. After the new generation has come, after the grandchildren, so to speak, then the opposition dies out: because after all there is then a new contemporary expression to oppose.

That is really the fact about contemporariness. As I see the whole crowd of you, if there are any of you who are going to express yourselves contemporarily, you will do something which most people won't want to look at. Most of you will be so busy living the contemporary life that it will be like the tired businessman: in the things of the mind you will want the things you know. And too, if you don't live contemporarily, you are a nuisance. That is why we live contemporarily. If a man goes along the street with horse and carriage in New York in the snow, the man is a nuisance; and he knows it, so now he doesn't do it. He would not be living, or acting, contemporarily: he would only be in the way, a drag.

The world can accept me now because there is coming out of *your* generation somebody they don't like, and therefore they accept me because I am sufficiently past in having been contemporary so they don't have to dislike me. So thirty years from now I shall be accepted. And the same thing will happen again: that is the reason why every generation has the same thing happen. It will always be the same story, because there is always the same situation presented. The contemporary thing in art and literature is the thing which doesn't make enough difference to people of that generation so they can accept it or reject it.

Most of you know that in a funny kind of way you are nearer your grandparents than your parents. Since this contemporariness is always there, nobody realizes that you cannot follow it up. That is the reason people discover—those interested in the activities of other people—that they cannot understand their contemporaries. If you kids started in to write, I wouldn't be a good judge of you, because I am of the third generation. What you are going to do I don't know any more than anyone else. But I created a movement of which you are the grandchildren. The contemporary thing is the thing you can't get away from. That is the fundamental thing in all writing.

Another thing you have to remember is that each period of time not only has its contemporary quality, but it has a time-sense. Things move more quickly, slowly, or differently, from one generation to another. Take the Nineteenth Century. The Nineteenth Century was roughly the Englishman's Century. And their method, as they themselves, in their worst moments, speak of it, is that of "muddling through." They begin at one end and hope to come out at the other: their grammar, parts of speech, methods of talk, go with this fashion. The United States began a different phase when, after the Civil War, they discovered and created out of their inner need a different way of life. They created the Twentieth Century. The United States, instead of having the feeling of beginning at one end and ending at another, had the conception of assembling the whole thing out of its parts, the whole thing which made the Twentieth Century productive. The Twentieth Century conceived an automobile as a whole, so to speak, and then created it, built it up out of his parts. It was an entirely different point of view from the Nineteenth Century's. The Nineteenth Century would have seen the parts, and worked towards the automobile through them.

Now in a funny sort of way this expresses, in different terms, the difference between the literature of the Nineteenth Century and the literature of the Twentieth. Think of your reading. If you look at it from the days of Chaucer, you will see that what you might call the "internal history" of a country always affects its use of writing. It makes a difference in the expression, in the vocabulary, even in the handling of grammar. In Vanderbilt's amusing story in your *Literary Magazine,* when he speaks of the fact that he is tired of using quotation marks and isn't going to use them any more, with him that is a joke; but when I began writing, the whole question of punctuation was a vital question. You see, I had this new conception: I had this conception of the whole paragraph, and in *The Making of Americans* I had this idea of a whole thing. But if you think of contemporary English writers, it doesn't work like that at all. They conceive of it as pieces put together to make a whole, and I conceived it as a whole made up of its parts. I didn't know what I was doing any more than you know, but in response to the need of my period I was doing this thing. That is why I came in contact with people who were unconsciously doing the same thing. They had the Twentieth Century conception of a whole. So the element of punctuation was very vital. The comma was just a nuisance. If you got the thing as a whole, the comma kept irritating you all along the line. If you think of a thing as a whole, and the comma keeps sticking out, it gets on your nerves; because, after all, it destroys the reality of the whole. So I got rid more and more of commas. Not because I had any prejudice against commas; but the comma was a stumbling block. When you were conceiving a sentence, the comma stopped you. That is the illustration of the question of grammar and parts of speech, as part of the daily life as we live it.

The other thing which I accomplished was the getting rid of nouns. In the Twentieth Century you feel like movement. The Nineteenth Century didn't feel that way. The element of movement was not the predominating thing that they felt. You know that in your lives movement is the thing that occupies you most—you feel movement all the time. And the United States had the first instance of what I call Twentieth Century writing. You see it first in Walt Whitman. He was the beginning of the movement. He didn't see it very clearly, but there was a sense of movement that the European was much influenced by, because the Twentieth Century has become the American Century. That is what I mean when I say that each generation has its own literature.

There is a third element. You see, everybody in his generation has his sense of time which belongs to his crowd. But then, you always have the memory of what you were brought up with. In most people that makes a double time, which makes confusion. When one is beginning to write he is always under the shadow of the thing that is just past. And that is the reason why the creative person always has the appearance of ugliness. There is this persistent drag of the habits that belong to you. And in struggling away from this thing there is always an ugliness. That is the other reason why the contemporary writer is always refused. It is the effort of escaping from the thing which is a drag upon you that is so strong that the result is an apparent ugliness; and the world always says of the new writer, "It is so ugly!" And they are right, because it *is* ugly. If you disagree with your parents, there is an ugliness in the relation. There is a double resistance that makes the essence of this thing ugly.

You always have in your writing the resistance outside of you and inside of you, a shadow upon you, and the thing which you must express. In the beginning of your writing, this struggle is so tremendous that the result is ugly; and that is the reason why the followers are always accepted before the person who made the revolution. The person who has made the fight probably makes it seem ugly, although the struggle has the much greater beauty. But the followers die out; and the man who made the struggle and the quality of beauty remains in the intensity of the fight. Eventually it comes out all right, and so you have this very queer situation which always happens with the followers: the original person has to have in him a certain element of ugliness. You know that is what happens over and over again: the statement made that it is ugly—the statement made against me for the last twenty years. And they are quite right, because it *is* ugly. But the essence of that ugliness is the thing which will always make it beautiful. I myself think it is much more interesting when it seems ugly, because in it you see the element of the fight. The literature of one hundred years ago is perfectly easy to see, because the sediment of ugliness has settled down and you get the solemnity of its beauty. But to a person of my temperament, it is much more amusing when it has the vitality of the struggle.

In my own case, the Twentieth Century, which America created after the Civil War, and which had certain elements, had a definite influence on me. And in *The Making of Americans,* which is a book I would like to talk about, I gradually and slowly found out that there were two things I had to think about; the fact that knowledge is acquired, so to speak, by memory; but that when you know anything, memory doesn't come in. At any moment that you are conscious of knowing anything, memory plays no part. When any of you feels anybody else, memory doesn't come into it. You have the sense of the immediate. Remember that my immediate forebears were people like Meredith, Thomas Hardy, and so forth, and you will see what a struggle it was to do this thing. This was one of my first efforts to give the appearance of one time-knowledge, and not to make it a narrative story. This is what I mean by immediacy of description: you will find it in *The Making of Americans,* on page 284: "It happens very often that a man has it in him, that a man does something, that he does it very often that he does many things, when he is a young man when he is an old man, when is an older man." Do you see what I mean? And here is a description of a thing that is very interesting: "One of such of these kind of them had a little boy and this one, the little son wanted to make a collection of butterflies and beetles and it was all exciting to him and it was all arranged then and then the father said to the son you are certain this is not a cruel thing that you are wanting to be doing, killing things to make collections of them, and the son was very disturbed then and they talked about it together the two of them and more and more they talked about it then and then at last the boy was convinced it was a cruel thing and he said he would not do it and the father said the little boy was a noble boy to give up pleasure when it was a cruel one. The boy went to bed then and then the father when he got up in the early morning saw a wonderfully beautiful moth in the room and he caught him and he killed him and he pinned him and he woke up his son then and showed it to him and he said to him 'see what a good father I am to have caught and killed this one,' the boy was all mixed up inside him and then he said he would go on with his collection and that was all there was then of discussing and this is a little description of something that happened once and it is very interesting."

I was trying to get this present immediacy without trying to drag in anything else. I had to use present participles, new constructions of grammar. The grammar-constructions are correct, but they are changed, in order to get this immediacy. In short, from that time I have been trying in every possible way to get the sense of immediacy, and practically all the work I have done has been in that direction.

In *The Making of Americans,* I had an idea that I could get a sense of immediacy if I made a description of every kind of human being that existed, the rules for resemblances and all other things, until really I had made a description of every human being—I found this out when I was at Harvard working under William James.

Did you ever see that article that came out in *The Atlantic Monthly* a year or two ago, about my experiments with automatic writing? It was very amusing. The experiment that I did was to take a lot of people in moments of fatigue and rest and activity of various kinds, and see if they could do anything with automatic writing. I found that they could not do anything with automatic writing, but I found out a great deal about how people act. I found there a certain kind of human being who acted in a certain way, and another kind who acted in another kind of way, and their resemblances and their differences. And then I wanted to find out if you could make a history of the whole world, if you could know the whole life history of everyone in the world, their slight resemblances and lack of resemblances. I made enormous charts, and I tried to carry these charts out. You start in and you take everyone that you know, and then when you see anybody who has a certain expression or turn of the face that reminds you of some one, you find out where he agree or disagrees with the character, until you build up the whole scheme. I got to the place where I didn't know whether I knew people or not. I made so many charts that when I used to go down the streets of Paris I wondered whether they were people I know or ones I didn't. This is what *The Making of Americans* was intended to be. I was to make a description of every kind of human being until I could know by these variations how everybody was to be known. Then I got very much interested in this thing, and I wrote about nine hundred pages, and I came to a logical conclusion that this thing could be done. Anybody who has patience enough could literally and entirely make of the whole world a history of human nature. When I found it could be done, I lost interest in it. As soon as I found definitely and clearly and completely that I could do it, I stopped writing the long book. It didn't interest me any longer. In doing the thing, I found out this question of resemblances, and I found in making these analyses that the resemblances were not of memory. I had to remember what person looked like the other person. Then I found this contradiction: that the resemblances were a matter of memory. There were two prime elements involved, the element of memory and the other of immediacy.

The element of memory was a perfectly feasible thing, so then I gave it up. I then started a book which I called *A Long Gay Book* to see if I could work the thing up to a faster tempo. I wanted to see if I could make that a more complete vision. I wanted to see if I could hold it in the frame.

Ordinarily the novels of the Nineteenth Century live by association; they are wont to call up other pictures than the one they present to you. I didn't want, when I said "water," to have you think of running water. Therefore I began by limiting my vocabulary, because I wanted to get rid of anything except the picture within the frame. While I was writing I didn't want, when I used one word, to make it carry with it too many associations. I wanted as far as possible to make it exact, as exact as mathematics; that is to say, for example, if one and one make two, I wanted to get words to have as much exactness as that. When I put them down they were to have this quality. The whole history of my work, from *The Making of Americans,* has been a history of that. I made a great many discoveries, but the thing that I was always trying to do was this thing.

One thing which came to me is that the Twentieth Century gives of itself a feeling of movement, and has in its way no feeling for events. To the Twentieth Century events are not important. You must know that. Events are not exciting. Events have lost their interest for people. You read them more like a soothing syrup, and if you listen over the radio you don't get very excited. The thing has got to this place, that events are so wonderful that they are not exciting. Now you have to remember that the business of an artist is being exciting. If the thing has its proper vitality, the result must be exciting. I was struck with it during the War: the average dough-boy standing on a street corner doing nothing—(they say, at the end of their doing nothing, "I guess I'll go home")—was much more exciting to people than when the soldiers went over the top. The populace was passionately interested in their standing on the street corners, more so than in the St. Mihiel drive. And it is a perfectly natural thing. Events had got so continuous that the fact that events were taking place no longer stimulated anybody. To see three men, strangers, standing, expressed their personality to the European man so much more than anything else they could do. That thing impressed me very much. But the novel which tells about what happens is of no interest to anybody. It is quite characteristic that in *The Making of Americans,* Proust, *Ulysses,* nothing much happens. People are interested in existence. Newspapers excite people very little. Sometimes a personality breaks through the newspapers—Lindbergh, Dillinger—when the personality has vitality. It wasn't what Dillinger *did* that excited anybody. The feeling is perfectly simple. You can see it in my *Four Saints.* Saints shouldn't do anything. The fact that a saint is there is enough for anybody. The *Four Saints* was written about as static as I could make it. The saints conversed a little, and it all did something. It did something more than the theatre which has tried to make events has done. For our purposes, for our contemporary purposes, events have no importance. I merely say that for the last thirty years events are of no importance. They make a great many people unhappy, they may cause convulsions in history, but from the standpoint of excitement, the kind of excitement the Nineteenth Century got out of events doesn't exist.

And so what I am trying to make you understand is that every contemporary writer has to find out what is the inner time-sense of his contemporariness. The writer or painter, or what not, feels this thing more vibrantly, and he has a passionate need of putting it down; and that is what creativeness does. He spends his life in putting down this thing which he doesn't know is a contemporary thing. If he doesn't put down the contemporary thing, he isn't a great writer, for he has to live in the past. That is what I mean by "everything is contemporary." The minor poets of the period, or the precious poets of the period, are all people who are under the shadow of the past. A man who is making a revolution has to be contemporary. A minor person can live in the imagination. That tells the story pretty completely.

The question of repetition is very important. It is important because there is no such thing as repetition. Everybody tells every story in about the same way. You know perfectly well that when you and your roommates tell something, you are telling the same story in about the same way. But the point about it is this. Everybody is telling the story in the same way. But if you listen carefully, you will see that not all the story is the same. There is always a slight variation. Somebody comes in and you tell the story over again. Every time you tell the story it is told slightly differently. All my early work was a careful listening to all the people telling their story, and I conceived the idea which is, funnily enough, the same as the idea of the cinema. The cinema goes on the same principle: each picture is just infinitesimally different from the one before. If you listen carefully, you say something, the other person says something; but each time it changes just a little, until finally, you come to the point where you convince him or you don't convince him. I used to listen very carefully to people talking. I had a passion for knowing just what I call their "insides." And in *The Making of Americans* I did this thing; but of course to my mind there is no repetition. For instance, in these early *Portraits,* and in a whole lot of them in this book *(Portraits and Prayers)* you will see that every time a statement is made about someone being somewhere, that statement is different. If I had repeated, nobody would listen. Nobody could be in the room with a person who said the same thing over and over and over. He would drive everybody mad. There has to be a very slight change. Really listen to the way you talk and every time you change it a little bit. That change, to me, was a very important thing to find out. You will see that when I kept on saying something was something or somebody was somebody, I changed it just a little bit until I got a whole portrait. I conceived the idea of building this thing up. It was all based upon this thing of everybody's slightly building this thing up. What I was after was this immediacy. A single photograph doesn't give it. I was trying for this thing, and so to my mind there is no repetition. The only thing that is repetition is when somebody tells you what he has learned. No matter how you say it, you say it differently. It was this that led me in all that early work.

You see, finally, after I got this thing as completely as I could, then, of course, it being my nature, I wanted to tear it down. I attacked the problem from another way. I listened to people. I condensed it in about three words. There again, if you read those later *Portraits,* you will see that I used three or four words instead of making a cinema of it. I wanted to condense it as much as possible and change it around, until you could get the movement of a human being. If I wanted to make a picture of you as you sit there, I would wait until I got a picture of you as individuals and then I'd change them until I got a picture of you as a whole.

I did these *Portraits,* and then I got the idea of doing plays. I had the *Portraits* so much in my head that I would almost know how you differ one from the other. I got this idea of the play, and put it down in a few words. I wanted to put them down in that way, and I began writing plays and I wrote a great many of them. The Nineteenth Century wrote a great many plays, and none of them are now read, because the Nineteenth Century wanted to put their novels on the stage. The better the play the more static. The minute you try to make a play a novel, it doesn't work. That is the reason I got interested in doing these plays.

When you get to that point there is no essential difference between prose and poetry. This is essentially the problem with which your generation will have to wrestle. The thing has got to the point where poetry and prose have to concern themselves with the static thing. That is up to you.

1935

SECTION II

Interacting with Texts

Introduction

Reading an essay and then writing about it may seem like a typical assignment in any given college classroom. And in some ways it is. In courses across the disciplines you may be given a text and then asked to respond to it. But why? What is the purpose of reading and then writing about what you have read? On the surface, the answer may be obvious—we read texts in order to gain information and knowledge and then write our own essays in order to demonstrate that we understand the information we have read. But is this the sole purpose for reading and writing about texts?

Writers continually take part in ongoing conversations, written discussions in the form of essays, articles, and papers that take up the issues related to various fields. Each new published form of writing is a contribution to the conversation, a way to either reinforce the issues stated, to disagree with points raised, or, more importantly, to extend and to expand the ongoing discussion.

When we read a text we enter into an established conversation. We begin reading to gain knowledge about the specific discussion to which the writer is contributing. However, we do much more than simply gain information. We read in order to interact with the ideas and issues the author raises about the discussion, to wrestle with the ideas presented to us, and to grapple with the questions raised by the author. As we read through a text we not only engage with the ideas and issues presented to us, but we also interact with the author's context. Critically examining the author's position enables us to gain further understanding of the issues the author is working through.

Our own writing about a text can take a variety of forms. It also involves a process. Usually our first interaction with a text may be in the form of a summary in order to gain an understanding of the issues and ideas raised by the author. We also may begin by writing through our own initial reactions, working through why we agree or disagree with the author as a way of understanding how our own contexts affect our reactions to the text. Our writing will lead us to work through our own thinking about the issues and ideas raised within a text, to test out our own ideas against those of the author in order to examine, extend, and re-see our own views. This will lead us to develop our own texts that will contribute to the discussion. Our own essays will acknowledge the essays we have read through the academic conventions of quoting, summarizing, and paraphrasing, as well as position us within the conversation. Our own wrestling and grappling with the issues presented will enable us to position ourselves within the ongoing conversation.

The essays in this section cover a range of topics from art, to shopping, to computer games, to education, to genetic engineering. Although you may agree with some of the points raised by the authors included here and disagree with others, all these essays ask you to examine how you perceive the issues raised. The essays are meant to challenge the way you perceive things in order to extend, and maybe revise, your own way of viewing the world. This is not always easy. It is comfortable to stick with what you know. However, working through the difficulties raised in these essays will enable you to expand your knowledge and to grow intellectually. The essays included in this section are meant to be complex. They are not meant to provide us with easy answers. At times, you may find yourself unsure of what you think. You may find the essays raising more questions than they answer. That is fine. Reading and re-reading the essays, discussing the issues and ideas, examining the author's intended audience and purpose can further your own understanding of the text. And, of course, writing through the issues and the questions raised will enable you to work out your own thinking and to come to your own conclusions.

How to Tame a Wild Tongue

Gloria Anzaldúa

Gloria Anzaldúa, the Chicana child of immigrant Mexican parents, was born in Jesus Maria of the Valley, Texas, and grew up in Hargill, Texas, on the Mexican border. Anzaldúa describes herself as a "border woman," and her book, Borderland/La Frontera: The New Mestiza, *from which this essay comes, straddles the boundaries of genre and language as well as geography, ethnicity, and sexuality. This essay is part autobiographical narrative, part poetry, part social history, and part cultural critique. Anzaldúa simultaneously explains and enacts the unbreakable bond between ethnic identity and its "twin skin," linguistic identity. In the essay, Anzaldúa slides among eight languages, two variations of English and six of Spanish, including Chicano, Tex-Mex, and Castilian. What effect does this have on the non-bilingual reader? Who has or should have the authority to tame her wild tongue? What is at stake in having her wild tongue "cut out"? How does her writing style help us understand the conflict among identities so many Americans feel?*

"We're going to have to control your tongue," the dentist says, pulling out all the metal from my mouth. Silver bits plot and tingle into the basin. My mouth is a motherlode.

The dentist is cleaning out my roots. I get a whiff of the stench when I gasp. "I can't cap that tooth yet, you're still draining," he says.

"We're going to have to do something about your tongue," I hear the anger rising in his voice. My tongue keeps pushing out the wads of cotton, pushing back the drills, the long thin needles. "I've never seen anything as strong or as stubborn," he says. And I think, how do you tame a wild tongue, train it to be quiet, how do you bridle and saddle it? How do you make it lie down?

> Who is to say that robbing a people of its language is less violent than war?
>
> —Ray Gwyn Smith[1]

From *Borderlands/La Frontera: The New Mestiza.* Copyright © 1987, 1999 by Gloria Anzaldúa. Reprinted by permission of Aunt Lute Books.

I remember being caught speaking Spanish at recess—that was good for three licks on the knuckles with a sharp ruler. I remember being sent to the corner of the classroom for "talking back" to the Anglo teacher when all I was trying to do was tell her how to pronounce my name. "If you want to be American, speak 'American.' If you don't like it, go back to Mexico where you belong."

"I want you to speak English. *Pa´ haller buen trabajo tienes que saber hablar el inglés bien. Qué vale toda tu educación si todavía hablas inglés con un* 'accent,'" my mother would say, mortified that I spoke English like a Mexican. At Pan American University, I and all Chicano students were required to take two speech classes. Their purpose: to get rid of our accents.

Attacks on one's form of expression with the intent to censor are a violation of the First Amendment. *El Anglo con cara de inocente nos arrancó la lengua.* Wild tongues can't be tamed, they can only be cut out.

Overcoming the Tradition of Silence

> *Ahogadas, escupimos el oscuro.*
> *Peleando con nuestra propia sombra*
> *el silencio nos sepulta.*

En boca cerrada no entran moscas. "Flies don't enter a closed mouth" is a saying I kept hearing when I was a child. *Ser habladora* was to be a gossip and a liar, to talk too much. *Muchachitas bien criadas,* well-bred girls don't answer back. *Es una falta de respeto* to talk back to one's mother or father. I remember one of the sins I'd recite to the priest in the confession box the few times I went to confession: talking back to my mother, *hablar pa´ 'tras, repelar. Hocicona, repelona, chismosa,* having a big mouth, questioning, carrying tales are all signs of being *mal criada.* In my culture they are all words that are derogatory if applied to women—I've never heard them applied to men.

The first time I heard two women, a Puerto Rican and a Cuban, say the word *"nosotras,"* I was shocked. I had not known the word existed. Chicanas use *nosotros* whether we're male or female. We are robbed of our female being by the masculine plural. Language is a male discourse.

> And our tongues have become
> dry   the wilderness has
> dried out our tongues   and
> we have forgotten speech.

> —Irena Klepfisz[2]

Even our own people, other Spanish speakers *nos quieren poner candados en la boca.* They would hold us back with their bag of *reglas de academia.*

Oyé como ladra: El lenguaje de la frontera

Quien tiene boca se equivoca.

—Mexican saying

"Pocho, cultural traitor, you're speaking the oppressor's language by speaking English, you're ruining the Spanish language," I have been accused by various Latinos and Latinas. Chicano Spanish is considered by the purist and by most Latinos deficient, a mutilation of Spanish.

But Chicano Spanish is a border tongue which developed naturally. Change, *evolución, enriquecimiento de palabras nuevas por invención o adopción* have created variants of Chicano Spanish, *un nuevo lenguaje. Un lenguaje que corresponde a un modo de vivir.* Chicano Spanish is not incorrect, it is a living language.

For a people who are neither Spanish nor live in a country in which Spanish is the first language; for a people who live in a country in which English is the reigning tongue but who are not Anglo; for a people who cannot entirely identify with either standard (formal, Castilian) Spanish nor standard English, what recourse is left to them but to create their own language? A language which they can connect their identity to, one capable of communicating the realities and values true to themselves—a language with terms that are neither *español ni inglés,* but both. We speak a patois, a forked tongue, a variation of two languages.

Chicano Spanish sprang out of the Chicanos' need to identify ourselves as a distinct people. We needed a language with which we could communicate with ourselves, a secret language. For some of us, language is a homeland closer than the Southwest—for many Chicanos today live in the Midwest and East. And because we are a complex, heterogeneous people, we speak many languages. Some of the languages we speak are

1. Standard English
2. Working class and slang English
3. Standard Spanish
4. Standard Mexican Spanish
5. North Mexican Spanish dialect

6. Chicano Spanish (Texas, New Mexico, Arizona, and California have regional variations)
7. Tex-Mex
8. *Pachuco* (called *caló*)

My "home" tongues are the languages I speak with my sister and brothers, with my friends. They are the last five listed, with 6 and 7 being closest to my heart. From school, the media, and job situations, I've picked up standard and working class English. From Mamagrande Locha and from reading Spanish and Mexican literature, I've picked up Standard Spanish and Standard Mexican Spanish. From *los recién llegados,* Mexican immigrants, and *braceros,* I learned the North Mexican dialect. With Mexicans I'll try to speak either Standard Mexican Spanish or the North Mexican dialect. From my parents and Chicanos living in the Valley, I picked up Chicano Texas Spanish, and I speak it with my mom, younger brother (who married a Mexican and who rarely mixes Spanish with English), aunts, and older relatives.

With Chicanas from *Nuevo Mexico* or *Arizona* I will speak Chicano Spanish a little, but often they don't understand what I'm saying. With most California Chicanas I speak entirely in English (unless I forget). When I first moved to San Francisco, I'd rattle off something in Spanish, unintentionally embarrassing them. Often it is only with another Chicana *tejano* that I can talk freely.

Words distorted by English are known as anglicisms or *pochismos.* The *pocho* is an anglicized Mexican or American of Mexican origin who speaks Spanish with an accent characteristic of North Americans and who distorts and reconstructs the language according to the influence of English.[3] Tex-Mex, or Spanglish, comes most naturally to me. I may switch back and forth from English to Spanish in the same sentence or in the same word. With my sister and my brother Nune and with Chicano *tejano* contemporaries I speak in Tex-Mex.

From kids and people my own age I picked up *Pachuco. Pachuco* (the language of the zoot suiters) is a language of rebellion, both against Standard Spanish and Standard English. It is a secret language. Adults of the culture and outsiders cannot understand it. It is made up of slang words from both English and Spanish. *Ruca* means girl or woman, *vato* means guy or dude, *chale* means no, *simón* means yes, *churro* is sure, talk is *periquiar, pigionear* means petting, *que gacho* means how nerdy, *ponte águila* means watch out, death is called *la pelona.* Through lack of practice and not having others who can speak it, I've lost most of the *Pachuco* tongue.

Chicano Spanish

Chicanos, after 250 years of Spanish/Anglo colonization, have developed significant differences in the Spanish we speak. We collapse two adjacent vowels into a single syllable and sometimes shift the stress in certain words such as *maíz/maiz, cohete/cuete*. We leave out certain consonants when they appear between vowels: *lado/lao, mojada/mojao*. Chicanos from South Texas pronounce *f* as *j* as in *jue (fue)*. Chicanos use "archaisms," words that are no longer in the Spanish language, words that have been evolved out. We say *semos, truje, haiga, ansina,* and *naiden*. We retain the "archaic" *j*, as in *jalar*, that derives from an earlier *h* (the French *halar* or the Germanic *halon* which was lost to standard Spanish in the sixteenth century), but which is still found in several regional dialects such as the one spoken in South Texas. (Due to geography, Chicanos from the Valley of South Texas were cut off linguistically from other speakers. We tend to use words that the Spaniards brought over from Medieval Spain. The majority of the Spanish colonizers in Mexico and the Southwest came from Extremadura—Hernán Cortés was one of them—and Andalucía. Andalucians pronounce *ll* like a *y,* and their *d's* tend to be absorbed by adjacent vowels: *tirado* becomes *tirao*. They brought *el lenguaje popular, dialectos y regionalismos.*)[4]

Chicanos and other Spanish speakers also shift *ll* to *y* and *z* to *s*.[5] We leave out initial syllables, saying *tar* for *estar, toy* for *estoy, hora* for *ahora* (*cubanos* and *puertorriqueños* also leave out initial letters of some words). We also leave out the final syllable such as *pa* for *para*. The intervocalic *y,* the *ll* as in *tortilla, ella, botella,* gets replaced by *tortia* or *tortiya, ea, botea*. We add an additional syllable at the beginning of certain words: *atocar* for *tocar, agastar* for *gastar*. Sometimes we'll say *lavaste las vacijas,* other times *lavates* (substituting the *ates* verb ending for the *aste*).

We used anglicisms, words borrowed from English: *bola* from ball, *carpeta* from carpet, *máchina de lavar* (instead of *lavadora*) from washing machine. Tex-Mex argot, created by adding a Spanish sound at the beginning or end of an English word such as *cookiar* for cook, *watchar* for watch, *parkiar* for park, and *rapiar* for rape, is the result of the pressures on Spanish speakers to adapt to English.

We don't use the word *vosotros/as* or its accompanying verb form. We don't say *claro* (to mean yes), *imagínate,* or *me emociona,* unless we picked up Spanish from Latinas, out of a book, or in a classroom. Other Spanish-speaking groups are going through the same, or similar, development in their Spanish.

Linguistic Terrorism

Deslenguadas. Somos los del español deficiente. We are your linguistic nightmare, your linguistic aberration, your linguistic *mestisaje,* the subject of your *burla.* Because we speak with tongues of fire we are culturally crucified. Racially, culturally, and linguistically *somos huérfanos*—we speak an orphan tongue.

Chicanas who grew up speaking Chicano Spanish have internalized the belief that we speak poor Spanish. It is illegitimate, a bastard language. And because we internalize how our language has been used against us by the dominant culture, we use our language differences against each other.

Chicana feminists often skirt around each other with suspicion and hesitation. For the longest time I couldn't figure it out. Then it dawned on me. To be close to another Chicana is like looking into the mirror. We are afraid of what we'll see there. *Pena.* Shame. Low estimation of self. In childhood we are told that our language is wrong. Repeated attacks on our native tongue diminish our sense of self. The attacks continue throughout our lives.

Chicanas feel uncomfortable talking in Spanish to Latinas, afraid of their censure. Their language was not outlawed in their countries. They had a whole lifetime of being immersed in their native tongue; generations, centuries in which Spanish was a first language, taught in school, heard on radio and TV, and read in the newspaper.

If a person, Chicana or Latina, has a low estimation of my native tongue, she also has a low estimation of me. Often with *mexicanas y latinas* we'll speak English as a neutral language. Even among Chicanas we tend to speak English at parties or conferences. Yet, at the same time, we're afraid the other will think we're *agringadas* because we don't speak Chicano Spanish. We oppress each other trying to out-Chicano each other, vying to be the "real" Chicanas, to speak like Chicanos. There is no one Chicano language just as there is no one Chicano experience. A monolingual Chicana whose first language is English or Spanish is just as much a Chicana as one who speaks several variants of Spanish. A Chicana from Michigan or Chicago or Detroit is just as much a Chicana as one from the Southwest. Chicano Spanish is as diverse linguistically as it is regionally.

By the end of this century, Spanish speakers will comprise the biggest minority group in the United States, a country where students in high schools and colleges are encouraged to take French classes because French is considered more "cultured." But for a language to remain alive it must be used.[6] By the end of this century English, and not Spanish, will be the mother tongue of most Chicanos and Latinos.

So, if you want to really hurt me, talk badly about my language. Ethnic identity is twin skin to linguistic identity—I am my language. Until I can take pride in my language, I cannot take pride in myself. Until I can accept as legitimate Chicano Texas Spanish, Tex-Mex, and all the other languages I speak, I cannot accept the legitimacy of myself. Until I am free to write bilingually and to switch codes without having always to translate, while I still have to speak English or Spanish when I would rather speak Spanglish, and as long as I have to accommodate the English speakers rather than having them accommodate me, my tongue will be illegitimate.

I will no longer be made to feel ashamed of existing. I will have my voice: Indian, Spanish, white. I will have my serpent's tongue—my woman's voice my sexual voice, my poet's voice. I will overcome the tradition of silence.

> My fingers
> move sly against your palm
> Like women everywhere, we speak in code. . . .
>
> —Melanie Kaye/Kantrowitz[7]

"Vistas," corridos, y comida: My Native Tongue

In the 1960s, I read my first Chicano novel. It was *City of Night* by John Rechy, a gay Texan, son of a Scottish father and a Mexican mother. For days I walked around in stunned amazement that a Chicano could write and could get published. When I read *I Am Joaquín*,[8] I was surprised to see a bilingual book by a Chicano in print. When I saw poetry written in Tex-Mex for the first time, a feeling of pure joy flashed through me. I felt like we really existed as a people. In 1971, when I started teaching High School English to Chicano students, I tried to supplement the required texts with works by Chicanos, only to be reprimanded and forbidden to do so by the principal. He claimed that I was supposed to teach "American" and English literature. At the risk of being fired, I swore my students to secrecy and slipped in Chicano short stories, poems, a play. In graduate school, while working toward a Ph.D., I had to "argue" with one adviser after the other, semester after semester, before I was allowed to make Chicano literature an area of focus.

Even before I read books by Chicanos or Mexicans, it was the Mexican movies I saw at the drive-in—the Thursday night special of $1.00 a carload—that gave me a sense of belonging. *"Vámonos a las vistas,"* my mother would call out and we'd all—grandmother, brothers, sister, and cousins—squeeze into the car. We'd wolf down cheese and bologna white bread sandwiches while watching Pedro Infante in melodramatic tearjerkers like *Nosotros los pobres,* the first "real" Mexican movie (that was not an imitation of European movies). I remember seeing *Cuando los hijos se van* and surmising that all Mexican movies played up the love a mother has for her children and what ungrateful sons and daughters suffer when they are not devoted to their mothers. I remember the singing-type "westerns" of Jorge Negrete and Miquel Aceves Mejía. When watching Mexican movies, I felt a sense of homecoming as well as alienation. People who were to amount to something didn't go to Mexican movies, or *bailes,* or tune their radios to *bolero, rancherita,* and *corrido* music.

The whole time I was growing up, there was *norteño* music sometimes called North Mexican border music, or Tex-Mex music, or Chicano music or *cantina* (bar) music. I grew up listening to *conjuntos,* three- or four-piece bands made up of folk musicians playing guitar, *bajo sexto,* drums, and button accordion, which Chicanos had borrowed from the German immigrants who had come to Central Texas and Mexico to farm and build breweries. In the Rio Grande Valley, Steve Jordan and Little Joe Hernández were popular, and Flaco Jiménez was the accordion king. The rhythms of Tex-Mex music are those of the polka, also adapted from the Germans, who in turn had borrowed the polka from the Czechs and Bohemians.

I remember the hot, sultry evenings when *corridos*—songs of love and death on the Texas-Mexican borderlands—reverberated out of cheap amplifiers from the local *cantinas* and wafted in through my bedroom window.

Corridos first became widely used along the South Texas/Mexican border during the early conflict between Chicanos and Anglos. The *corridos* are usually about Mexican heroes who do valiant deeds against the Anglo oppressors. Pancho Villa's song, *"La cucaracha,"* is the most famous one. *Corridos* of John F. Kennedy and his death are still very popular in the Valley. Older Chicanos remember Lydia Mendoza, one of the great border *corrido* singers who was called *la Gloria de Tejas.* Her *"El tango negro,"* sung during the Great Depression, made her a singer of the people. The ever-present *corridos* narrated one hundred years of border history, bringing news of events as well as entertaining. These folk musicians and folk songs are our chief cultural mythmakers, and they made our hard lives seem bearable.

I grew up feeling ambivalent about our music. Country-western and rock-and-roll had more status. In the fifties and sixties, for the slightly educated and *agringado* Chicanos, there existed a sense of shame at being caught listening to our music. Yet I couldn't stop my feet from thumping to the music, could not stop humming the words, nor hide from myself the exhilaration I felt when I heard it.

There are more subtle ways that we internalize identification, especially in the forms of images and emotions. For me food and certain smells are tied to my identity, to my homeland. Woodsmoke curling up to an immense blue sky; woodsmoke perfuming my grandmother's clothes, her skin. The stench of cow manure and the yellow patches on the ground; the crack of a .22 rifle and the reek of cordite. Homemade white cheese sizzling in a pan, melting inside a folded *tortilla*. My sister Hilda's hot, spicy *menudo, chile colorado* making it deep red, pieces of *panza* and hominy floating on top. My brother Carito barbequing *fajitas* in the backyard. Even now and 3,000 miles away, I can see my mother spicing the ground beef, pork, and venison with *chile*. My mouth salivates at the thought of the hot steaming *tamales* I would be eating if I were home.

Si le preguntas a mi mamá, "¿Qué eres?"

> Identity is the essential core of who we are as individuals, the conscious experience of the self inside.
>
> —Gershen Kaufman[9]

Nosotros los Chicanos straddle the borderlands. On one side of us, we are constantly exposed to the Spanish of the Mexicans; on the other side we hear the Anglos' incessant clamoring so that we forget our language. Among ourselves we don't say *nosotros los americanos, o nosotros los españoles, o nosotros los hispanos.* We say *nosotros los mexicanos* (by *mexicanos* we do not mean citizens of Mexico; we do not mean a national identity, but a racial one). We distinguish between *mexicanos del otro lado* and *mexicanos de este lado.* Deep in our hearts we believe that being Mexican has nothing to do with which country one lives in. Being Mexican is a state of soul—not one of mind, not one of citizenship. Neither eagle nor serpent, but both. And like the ocean, neither animal respects borders.

> *Dime con quien andas y te diré quien eres.*
> (Tell me who your friends are and I'll tell you who you are.)
>
> —Mexican saying

Si le preguntas a mi mamá, "¿Qué eres?" te dirá, "Soy mexicana." My brothers and sister say the same. I sometimes will answer *"soy mexicana"* and at others will say *"soy Chicana" o "soy tejana."* But I identified as *"Raza"* before I ever identified as *"mexicana"* or "Chicana."

As a culture, we call ourselves Spanish when referring to ourselves as a linguistic group and when copping out. It is then that we forget our predominant Indian genes. We are 70–80 percent Indian.[10] We call ourselves Hispanic[11] or Spanish-American or Latin American or Latin when linking ourselves to other Spanish-speaking peoples of the Western hemisphere and when copping out. We call ourselves Mexican-American[12] to signify we are neither Mexican nor American, but more the noun "American" than the adjective "Mexican" (and when copping out).

Chicanos and other people of color suffer economically for not acculturating. This voluntary (yet forced) alienation makes for psychological conflict, a kind of dual identity—we don't identify with the Anglo-American cultural values and we don't totally identify with the Mexican cultural values. We are a synergy of two cultures with various degrees of Mexicanness or Angloness. I have so internalized the borderland conflict that sometimes I feel like one cancels out the other and we are zero, nothing, no one. *A veces no soy nada ni nadie. Pero hasta cuando no lo soy, lo soy.*

When not copping out, when we know we are more than nothing, we call ourselves Mexican, referring to race and ancestry; *mestizo* when affirming both our Indian and Spanish (but we hardly ever own our Black) ancestry; Chicano when referring to a politically aware people born and/or raised in the United States; *Raza* when referring to Chicanos; *tejanos* when we are Chicanos from Texas.

Chicanos did not know we were a people until 1965 when Cesar Chavez and the farmworkers united and *I Am Joaquín* was published and *la Raza Unida* party was formed in Texas. With that recognition, we became a distinct people. Something momentous happened to the Chicano soul—we became aware of our reality and acquired a name and a language (Chicano Spanish) that reflected that reality. Now that we had a name, some of the fragmented pieces began to fall together—who we were, what we were, how we had evolved. We began to get glimpses of what we might eventually become.

Yet the struggle of identities continues, the struggle of borders is our reality still. One day the inner struggle will cease and a true integration take place. In the meantime, *tenémos que hacer la lucha. ¿Quién está protegiendo los ranchos de mi gente? ¿Quién está tratando de cerrar la fisura entre la india y el blanco en nuestra sangre? El Chicano, si, el Chicano que anda como un ladrón en su propia casa.*

Los Chicanos, how patient we seem, how very patient. There is the quiet of the Indian about us.[13] We know how to survive. When other races have given up their tongue we've kept ours. We know what it is to live under the hammer blow of the dominant *norteamericano* culture. But more than we count the blows, we count the days the weeks the years the centuries the aeons until the white laws and commerce and customs will rot in the deserts they've created, lie bleached. *Humildes* yet proud, *quietos* yet wild, *nosotros los mexicanos-Chicanos* will walk by the crumbling ashes as we go about our business. Stubborn, persevering, impenetrable as stone, yet possessing a malleability that renders us unbreakable, we, the *mestizas* and *mestizos,* will remain.

Notes

1. Ray Gwyn Smith, *Moorland Is Cold Country,* unpublished book.
2. Irena Klepfisz, *"Di rayze aheym*/The Journey Home," in *The Tribe of Dina: A Jewish Women's Anthology,* Melanie Kaye/Kantrowitz and Irena Klepfisz, eds. (Montpelier, VT: Sinister Wisdom Books, 1986), 49.
3. R. C. Ortega, *Dialectología Del Barrio,* trans. Hortencia S. Alwan (Los Angeles, CA: R. C. Ortega Publisher & Bookseller, 1977), 132.
4. Eduardo Hernandéz-Chávez, Andrew D. Cohen, and Anthony F. Beltramo, *El Lenguaje de los Chicanos: Regional and Social Characteristics of Language Used by Mexican Americans* (Arlington, VA: Center for Applied Linguistics, 1975), 39.
5. Hernandéz-Chávez, xvii.
6. Irena Klepfisz, "Secular Jewish Identity: Yidishkayt in America," in *The Tribe of Dina,* Kaye/Kantrowitz and Klepfisz, eds., 43.
7. Melanie Kaye/Kantrowitz, "Sign," in *We Speak in Code: Poems and Other Writings* (Pittsburgh, PA: Motheroot Publications, Inc., 1980), 85.
8. Rodolfo Gonzales, *I Am Joaquín/Yo Soy Joaquín* (New York, NY: Bantam Books, 1972). It was first published in 1967.
9. Gershen Kaufman, *Shame: The Power of Caring* (Cambridge, MA: Schenkman Books, Inc., 1980), 68.
10. John R. Chávez, *The Lost Land: The Chicano Images of the Southwest* (Albuquerque, NM: University of New Mexico Press, 1984), 88–90.
11. "Hispanic" is derived from *Hispanis (España,* a name given to the Iberian Peninsula in ancient times when it was a part of the Roman Empire) and is a term designated by the U.S. government to make it easier to handle us on paper.

12. The treaty of Guadalupe Hidalgo created the Mexican-American in 1848.

13. Anglos, in order to alleviate their guilt for dispossessing the Chicano, stressed the Spanish part of us and perpetuated the myth of the Spanish Southwest. We have accepted the fiction that we are Hispanic, that is Spanish, in order to accommodate ourselves to the dominant culture and its abhorrence of Indians. Chávez, 88–91.

Linguistic Profiling

John Baugh

In an ad for fair housing reproduced in this essay, we are offered the following notes taken by a landlord after a phone conversation: Tina and Frank—Teacher/Sales Mgr.—2 incomes, 2 kids—SOUNDS BLACK. *This ad exposes the continued racism in contemporary society as Americans judge race, class, and ethnicity through what John Baugh labels* linguistic profiling. *Baugh carefully reveals how speakers of various English dialects are denied insurance, mortgages, employment, even fair trials. Ironically, unlike racial profiling, which targets persons of color, linguistic profiling engenders one kind of equal opportunity: "Whites are just as susceptible to the victimization of linguistic profiling if they speak with an 'undesirable accent'." Have you ever found yourself discriminated against because of your accent? Have you ever found yourself making judgments about others based on their accent or dialect? Baugh also finds that many Americans resort to* linguistic elasticity, *switching dialects depending on their purpose and audience. Have you ever engaged in this elasticity? If so, when and why?*

Mr. Darden: "The second voice that you heard sounded like the voice of a Black man; is that correct?"

California v. Orenthal James Simpson

This chapter consolidates a long-standing tradition in dialectology and sociolinguistics: the study of linguistic discrimination based on speech or writing. The concept of "linguistic profiling" is introduced here as the auditory equivalent of visual "racial profiling." We ultimately argue that linguistic profiling is more finely tuned to diversity among Americans than are dissatisfactory racial classifications that have been used in the courts and for controversial social and educational policies based on race. Matters of fairness, which Americans value, lie at the core of linguistic profiling. As with racial profiling, linguistic profiling can have devastating consequences for those US residents who are perceived to speak with an undesirable accent or dialect.

From *Black Linguistics: Language, Society, and Politics in Africa and the Americas.* Ed. Makoni, Sinfree, et al. Routledge 2003.

At the very outset I acknowledge that accents vary substantially in terms of prosody, phonetics, and phonology, while distinctive dialects exhibit unique grammatical properties that are shared by other speakers of the same dialect, but which may be unfamiliar to, unused by, or unknown to speakers of other dialects of the same language. As such, our language, be it speech or writing, tells others much about us as we perform linguistic tasks throughout our daily lives. Perceptions of intelligence, or the lack of it, are often deeply interwoven with perceptions about language, or specific dialects and accents within a particular language.

This discussion traces different trends, including discriminatory linguistic profiling, preferential linguistic profiling, which might include profiles in linguistic adoration, and the legal paradox resulting from linguistic profiling in America. Tentative policy implications with global ramifications are introduced in the conclusion of this chapter. More narrowly, within a US context, I hope this analysis may be of value for improving linguistic acceptance throughout the Republic, and, in so doing, that it may be particularly beneficial to educators, diplomats, legal scholars, jurists, and legislators who must ultimately determine the (il)legality of linguistic profiling.

Discriminatory Linguistic Profiling

Racial identification based on speech captured public attention during the O.J. Simpson trial. Simpson's African American attorney, Mr. Cochran, objected forcefully to the assertion that one can deduce racial identity from speech (*California v. Orenthal James Simpson*):

Mr. Darden	When you heard that voice, you thought that that was the voice of a young white male, didn't you?
Mr. Cochran	Object to the form of that question, your Honor.
Judge Ito	Overruled.
Mr. Cochran	Speculation, conclusion.
Judge Ito	Overruled.
Mr. Cochran	How can he tell if it was a white man, your Honor?
Judge Ito[1]	Counsel, overruled.

In 1999, in the case of *Clifford v. Kentucky,* the Supreme Court of Kentucky enlisted linguistic profiling to convict an African American appellant who was overheard by a white police officer. Thus far this case affirms the legality of racial identification based on speech by a lay witness. The case, for obvious reasons, is obscure when compared to the global visibility of the Simpson trial, but the practice of linguistic profiling was no less acute.

> Smith testified that he saw Birkenhauer enter the apartment. He then heard four different voices, the first of which he recognized as being that of Birkenhauer. He then heard the voice of another male, the voice of a female, and, then later, a fourth voice which "sounded as if it was of a male Black." Smith testified that he had been a police officer for thirteen years and had spoken to Black males on numerous occasions; that based on that experience, he believed that the last voice which he heard was that of a Black male. Appellant is a Black male; Vanover is a white male.

Smith then testified as follows:

> *Q*   Based on that [Smith's experience], as best you can recall, I just want you to tell me what you can recall of the conversation you heard between Detective Birkenhauer, just tell the jury what the male Black said, or the person you believed to be a male Black.
>
> *A*   That would have been the fourth and final voice on the tape. Detective Birkenhauer stated that he would take the "75" now and asked how long it would be, something along those lines, before he could get back with the additional drugs. What was believed to be a male Black responded, fifteen or twenty minutes or so, I didn't bring it with me, I left it at my house, you know what I am saying, I didn't want to have it on me. Detective Birkenhauer said, I'll take the "75" now, and we will hook up later.

On cross-examination, the following colloquy occurred between Smith and defense counsel:

> *Q*   Okay. Well, how does a Black man sound?
>
> *A*   Uh, some male Blacks have a, a different sound of, of their voice. Just as if I have a different sound of my voice as Detective Birkenhauer does. I sound different than you.
>
> *Q*   Okay, can you demonstrate that for the jury?
>
> *A*   I don't think that would be a fair and accurate description of the, you know, of the way the man sounds.
>
> *Q*   So not all male Blacks sound alike?
>
> *A*   That's correct, yes.
>
> *Q*   Okay. In fact, some of them sound like whites, don't they?
>
> *A*   Yes.
>
> *Q*   Do all whites sound alike?
>
> *A*   No sir.
>
> *Q*   Okay. Do some white people sound like Blacks when they're talking?
>
> *A*   Possibly, yes.

In his ruling opinion, Justice Cooper of the Supreme Court of Kentucky noted that "an opinion that an overheard voice was that of a particular nationality or race has never before been addressed in this jurisdiction." Citing the case of *People v. Sanchez* (1985), Justice Cooper noted that "a lay eyewitness to a fatal shooting was permitted to testify that immediately prior to the shooting, he overheard the victim and the killer arguing in Spanish, and that the killer was speaking with a Dominican, rather than a Puerto Rican, accent."

In support of the preceding ruling, the New York Superior Court noted that:

> It is clear that lay witnesses can often detect the distinctive accent related to particular ethnic or geographic groups. Thus, a lay witness, depending upon his experience, could distinguish between a Yiddish accent and an Italian accent, or between a Russian and an English accent, or between a Spanish and a French accent. In addition, within broad categories, certain more specific accents, characteristic of [a] particular region, may be ascertained. For example, the lay witness may be able to reliably identify the "Brooklyn" accent, as distinguished from the "Boston" accent, or the "Southern" accent from the "Cockney" accent. Human experience has taught us to discern the variations in the mode of speech of different individuals.

Returning to the Kentucky case in question, Justice Cooper observed that: No one suggests that it was improper for Officer Smith to identify one of the voices he heard as being that of a female. We perceive no reason why a witness could not likewise identify a voice as being that of a particular race or nationality, so long as the witness is personally familiar with the general characteristics, accents, or speech patterns of the race or nationality in question, i.e. so long as the opinion is "rationally" based on the perception of the witness.

Whereas "racial profiling" is based on visual cues that result in the confirmation or speculation of the racial background of an individual, or individuals, "linguistic profiling" is based upon auditory cues that may include racial identification, but which can also be used to identify other linguistic subgroups within a given speech community. The legal distinction and disagreement lie between Justice Cooper's assertions that lay people can indeed confirm the race or nationality of an individual based on his or her speech and those of Mr. Simpson's attorney who claimed—quite forcefully—that basing racial identification on speech is overtly racist and should not be permitted in a court of law. We shall return to this legal paradox briefly.

My earliest work on African American Vernacular English (AAVE) focused substantially on "style-shifting" among African Americans. During years of fieldwork I observed that a majority of African American adults would adjust their speech to fit their immediate social circumstances (Baugh 1983). Dillard (1972) and Labov (1972) made similar independent observations, noting that adult African Americans tended to use AAVE less frequently than did younger African Americans. By contrast, my research, which included observations of the same adults in a broad range of speaking circumstances, demonstrated considerable linguistic elasticity.

Similar forms of "linguistic accommodation" have been noted in other speech communities as well, suggesting that my observations in the African American community readily extend to other speakers who adjust their manner of speaking to fit the situation (Weinreich 1953; Blom and Gumperz 1972; Ervin-Tripp 1972; Goffman 1972; Hymes 1974; Giles and Powesland 1975; Trudgill 1986; Hazen 1998; Schilling-Estes and Wolfram 1999). This is not to suggest that AAVE speakers "sound white" when speaking in formal situations and "sound black" in colloquial circumstances. Rather, the preceding court rulings seem not to take "style-shifting" or "linguistic accommodation" into account, thereby calling the veracity of Justice Cooper's ruling into question.

I first became aware of "linguistic profiling" through deeply personal circumstances, as have some of my peers who are also African American professionals with advanced graduate degrees. Two anecdotes illustrate the point. In 1988 I was honored to accept a fellowship at the Stanford Center for Advanced Study in the Behavioral Sciences (CASBS), and I was trying to relocate my family to Palo Alto for a year. I moved to Palo Alto first in search of accommodations that would serve my entire family. Any reader who has ever tried to rent a home or apartment knows the experience of scouring the classified advertisements and then calling to make an appointment.

During all calls to prospective landlords, I explained my circumstances, as a visiting professor at CASBS, always employing my "professional voice," which I am told "sounds white." No prospective landlord ever asked me about my "race," but in four instances I was abruptly denied access to housing upon arrival for my scheduled appointment. Although I suspected that these refusals were directly the result of my race, which was confirmed through visual racial profiling, my standard English fluency was (and is) such that I escaped "linguistic profiling" because I sounded white.

Anita Henderson describes nearly identical circumstances in her search for an apartment in Philadelphia:

> I went to a large apartment complex in Philadelphia to inquire about apartments. I was steered to the most expensive apartment in the building

and told that this was the only apartment available for the following month and that no other apartments would be coming available. However, the next day, using my very best Standard American English on the phone and inquiring about apartments at the same complex, I discovered that, miraculously, several less expensive apartments were immediately available, and I was more than welcome to come and see them.

(Henderson 2001: 2–3)

In my particular case I was unable to prove that I had escaped auditory "linguistic profiling," only to eventually be snared by visual "racial profiling," but Henderson's experience incontrovertibly confirms "racial profiling." Her ensuing telephone call to the same apartment complex escaped linguistic profiling. She further observes, "Having guessed the nature of our face-to-face interaction, I knew I should 'sound white' in order to obtain the truth about the actual availability of apartments." She was ultimately able to rent "the apartment I wanted with no subsequent attempts on the part of the apartment building management to explain the mysterious availability of apartments" (Henderson 2001: 6).

As African American linguists with considerable professional training and extensive speech dexterity, our experiences are still relatively rare; that is, in the sense that we possess the ability to "sound white" if we choose to do so. Many of our fellow African Americans either cannot or will not attempt to adopt standard English under similar circumstances, thereby making them vulnerable to the kind of linguistic profiling described by Kentucky's Justice Cooper. I am not suggesting that speakers of AAVE must embrace Standard English if it is not their personal desire to do so. Rather, because of our professional circumstances, Henderson and I have been able to confirm the practice of linguistic profiling against Blacks.

Linguistic stereotypes have long been studied by linguists. Preston (1993), Lippi-Green (1997), and Cukor-Avila (2000) each provide independent evidence of "accent discrimination" or "dialect discrimination" against speakers of various regional, racial, and ethnic accents (or dialects) throughout the United States. Cukor-Avila (2000) confirms this practice in the workplace, noting that prospective employers are concerned with the linguistic impressions conveyed by their employees.

Because of the manner in which this first came to my attention, however, I have devoted most of my research on this topic to forms of housing discrimination, which has been documented extensively by the National Fair Housing Alliance (NFHA) in different regions of the country. Without the benefit of detailed linguistic analyses, "testers" who work for NFHA routinely seek to determine the existence of linguistic profiling associated with various forms of housing discrimination. Horwitz (1999) describes the situation as follows:

> Testers for the nonprofit group (i.e. the Fair Housing Council of Greater Washington) called more than 60 insurance offices and sought information about renters' insurance. In 150 cases, responses to Black and Latino callers were compared with responses to white callers, and 45 percent revealed discrimination.

My own research on this topic, produced in collaboration with phoneticians,[2] confirms Justice Cooper's observation. Through modified versions of matched guise studies that were adapted to compare standard English, AAVE, and Chicano English, over 80 percent of listeners were able to correctly identify the dialect spoken based on hearing the single word, "Hello." (See Purnell *et al.:* 1999.) Since many Americans routinely answer the telephone by saying "Hello," these results further confirm the potential for linguistic profiling, even when such racial or ethnic identification (or speculation) is not overtly used for discriminatory purposes.

Shanna Smith, executive director of the National Fair House Alliance, notes, "It is such an effective way of not doing business with people of color. It is subtle, not in your face, not slamming down the phone. But not following up by calling back or mailing material is just as malicious as saying, 'I won't give you insurance because you're Black or Mexican'" (Horwitz 1999: B 01). It is this "subtle" quality, combined with the fact that linguistic profiling can take place over the telephone, or through written correspondence, that has made it difficult to prosecute in the courts.

Ironically, in most of the cases of housing discrimination that have come to my attention, either as a consultant or as an expert witness, defendants have routinely denied the identical accent or linguistic detection skills that Justice Cooper confirmed through his ruling and subsequent conviction. That is to say, when confronted with evidence that suggests that linguistic profiling was used to deny housing, or insurance, or mortgages, to members of minority groups, defendants often retreat to Mr. Cochran's assertion that one cannot draw any racial or ethnic inference based on speech that is heard over the telephone, or, in Mr. Cochran's case, through an intercom system.

The NFHA recognized that many prospective home buyers or renters were simply unaware of the illegality of linguistic profiling, and they produced a series of advertisements to alert African American and Latino/a populations to be wary of these subdued forms of discrimination, as illustrated in Figures 1 and 2.

What matters is how you look on paper—not how you sound over the phone.
Judging by your race or national origin instead of your qualifications
is discrimination. It's unfair, it's painful . . . and it's against the law.
The best way to stop housing disciminations is to report it.

FAIR HOUSING IS THE LAW!

If you suspect unfair housing practices, contact
HUD or your local Fair Housing Center.

U.S. Department of Housing and Urban Development • 1-800-669-9777 • TDD 1-800-927-9275

Figure 1. Sounds Black.

Sounds like discrimination.

What matters is how you look on paper—not how you sound over the phone.
Judging by your race or national origin instead of your qualifications
is discrimination. It's unfair, it's painful . . . and it's against the law.
The best way to stop housing discriminations is to report it.

EQUAL HOUSING OPPORTUNITY

FAIR HOUSING IS THE LAW!

If you suspect unfair housing practices, contact
HUD or your local Fair Housing Center.

U.S. Department of Housing and Urban Development • 1-800-669-9777 • TDD 1-800-927-9275

Figure 2. Sounds Mexican.

Although my remarks thus far have been focused on People of Color, linguistic profiling trawls through much deeper demographic waters than visual profiling, which is constrained to navigation by race alone. Perhaps the most insidious cases are those where accent is employed as a surrogate for race in attempts to maintain overt discrimination, say, through illegal redlining or employment discrimination. Whites who speak with "undesirable" accents may fall victim to linguistic profiling just as readily as members of minority groups. Cukor-Avila's (2000) research confirms the existence of linguistic prejudice against various white dialects, along with regional preferences that defy simplistic racial attribution.

Preferential Linguistic Profiling

Thus far some of the negative consequences of linguistic profiling have been pronounced, but there is a positive side to the coin of this realm. Language, dialects, and accents also serve to bind Americans, reminding us of the ancestors who left distant lands to seek their freedom and fortune here.

Before turning completely to the sunny side of linguistic profiling, I would be remiss if I did not acknowledge the death of hundreds of indigenous American languages that resulted from colonization and the ensuing attacks on Native Americans. The legacy of Native American linguistic mortality is etched deeply in our collective past because the spread of English came at the expense of America's primordial languages. Ever the optimist in search of a silver linguistic lining, I am heartened by indigenous people's efforts to revive their heritage languages throughout the continental US, Alaska, and Hawaii. In my opinion these are positive cultural developments resulting from a positive interpretation of linguistic profiling, to which I now turn.

Just as linguistic diversity has been used to accentuate differences among us, it also unites us into the bundles of linguistic enclaves that reinforce our heritage and pride in our ancestry. That heritage is multiethnic by definition. When we are able to converse with people who share linguistic backgrounds similar to our own, most of us feel most comfortable and at ease. These same linguistic sensitivities alert us to differences among us that come into play when we see others of "our own linguistic kind," be they speakers of English or languages other than English. The unique American linguistic hybrids that blend English with other languages from throughout the world may also fall under the microscope of linguistic profiling. Such linguistic hybrids serve to evoke solidarity among their speakers at the very same time that they may be the objects of linguistic bigotry beyond their vernacular sanctuary.

Whereas racial differences and controversies over affirmative action have tended to divide us, the recognition that most of our ancestors came from lands where English was foreign gives us a common historical bond that has the potential to help reunite Americans. Those readers who are US citizens whose ancestors had the luxury of immigrating to America of their own volition typically take considerable pride in the accomplishments of their ancestors, as do those of us whose ancestors were enslaved. Yet most of our ancestors, in freedom or in bondage, were once mocked for their speech, and linguistic profiling spread to greet each wave of immigrants who struggled to master "good" English.

A strong honorific sense of ancestral pride is certainly not unique to America, but the American multiethnic tapestry includes a tremendous linguistic repository of global languages that are derived from every continent on earth. While some other nations may likewise boast of considerable linguistic diversity, the dominance of the US culture and economy has evoked the full continuum from scorn to envy among those who are not citizens of our extraordinary Republic. Inclusive linguistic profiling is exercised daily as Americans choose those with whom they like to associate most. For some these personal choices are highly diverse, for others they remain narrow. Although "inclusiveness" tends to evoke positive connotations, I use it here as a neutral heuristic concept that concedes that one person's linguistic pride can easily serve as another person's source of linguistic displeasure.

Profiles in Linguistic Adoration

There are many noteworthy examples of linguistic adoration, if not linguistic envy, that produce another form of linguistic profiling. It results from forms of linguistic admiration of "beautiful speech" or other positive linguistic attributes that we might feel are somehow lacking in ourselves. Two examples readily come to mind, including French and British accents. Many Americans find both accents appealing, if not somewhat intimidating. At this point I resort to a greater degree of speculation in an effort to provide a comprehensive picture of linguistic profiling in America because I have only conducted preliminary pilot research to date. However, the data suggest that a wide range of socially stratified British dialects hold considerable prestige in America. Whether it is the speech of Queen Elizabeth or that of Mick Jagger, many Americans hold a British accent in higher regard than they do most American accents.

A French accent is viewed somewhat differently, or at least it seems so. Whereas American English cannot deny its British ancestry, positive interpretations of French culture, and a shared historical ethos of equality, liberty, and fraternity, tend to yield favorable linguistic stereotypes. I seek not to imply that there is universal love by Americans for either British or French accents; linguistic resentment often lies beneath the surface of linguistic envy and adoration. Nevertheless, hostile reactions to a British accent pale when compared to the hostile reception that greeted Ebonics's global debut (Baugh 1999, 2000; Smitherman 2000).

Another brief anecdote illustrates the point at hand. By remarkable coincidence, several of my linguistic colleagues at Stanford are originally from England, and faculty meetings are striking in a US context because of the extensive use of British English. I once made an informal observation to a group of students that I believed speakers of British English were loath to adopt American English for any number of reasons, not the least of which being that so many Americans admire British speech and strongly associate upper-class British English with high levels of intelligence. If one must suffer from a linguistic stereotype, I would argue that being perceived as highly intelligent is not a social detriment in American society.

British intelligence notwithstanding, one young woman in the group disagreed with my offhand observation. Her experience demonstrates that despite the general American adoration of British English, there is at least one social context where this variety of English is not welcome. She pointed out that she was from England and had arrived in the US speaking a highly educated variety of British English, which she had learned at an exclusive school for young women in London. When she arrived in New York, encountering a wide range of Americans from diverse backgrounds, she found that many of her new-found peers mocked her speech, and so she not only embraced American English, she even chose to adopt AAVE over Standard American English. She was the first Black graduate student that I ever taught who was a native of England, and, to date, she has been the only speaker of British English to inform me that she had abandoned her native dialect to escape linguistic chastisement. While her case represents an exception to the general American adoration for British accents, it fits squarely within the context of Black American adolescents criticizing their peers for "talking" or "sounding white."

The Legal Paradox of Linguistic Profiling

Returning to discriminatory linguistic profiting, Judge Cooper would have us believe that lay citizens who are "rational" witnesses can confirm legal identification which connects linguistic behavior with racial background.

As a dialectologist and linguist I find this position to be inherently problematic. The testimony cited in Judge Cooper's court asserts that some Blacks sound white, and vice versa. Be that as it may, Judge Cooper sent the appellant to jail on the basis of linguistic profiling that was used to obtain a conviction.

The other side of the paradox lies in the area of linguistic profiling when it is employed in racially motivated criminal discrimination. As previously observed, such acts are alleged to have exclusionary intent at their core, and defendants in such cases typically claim to lack the capacity for linguistic or racial identification that Judge Cooper affirmed by his ruling. Stated another way, Judge Cooper accepted the fact that many lay people can draw racial inference from speech, whereas many defendants in housing discrimination cases or insurance redlining deny that they can make any such racial determination, say, during a telephone conversation.

Linguistic profiling is either legal, or it is not. Under current legal statutes the US Supreme Court has yet to rule on linguistic profiling, *per se,* and it will be interesting to see how the Supreme Court rules on this matter should the issue ever come before that body. Supreme Court Justice Clarence Thomas observed during his confirmation hearings before the US Senate that he pursued an undergraduate major in English because many of his elementary school teachers told him that he spoke a language other than English. This was a lighthearted moment in the proceedings, and his comments evoked laughter, if not empathy, from Senators and an American public who readily acknowledged that AAVE and his skills as a jurist were in open conflict in a profession that demands considerable Standard English proficiency. No one suggested, as I do now, that young Clarence Thomas was the object of uninformed linguistic profiling within an educational system that made African American students of his generation feel a sense of linguistic inferiority and, by extension, a sense of linguistic shame. (See Baugh 2000; Lanehart 2002.)

Conclusion

I have intentionally focused on the US in this discussion, resisting the temptation to discuss new research from South Africa that shows evidence of linguistic profiling there. Nor have I made biblical reference to shibboleths, or trotted out well-worn examples from Shaw's *Pygmalion,* or similar Greek plays that preceded it. Each example confirms global linguistic profiling in human antiquity. On the basis of our keen auditory skills as a species, I believe that linguistic profiling will exist as long as human language exists. The challenge to Americans and our fellow citizens elsewhere is to have wisdom, patience, and sufficient tolerance of others whose linguistic backgrounds differ substantially from our own. To do so would accentuate the benefits of preferential linguistic profiling, while discarding the tradition of discriminatory linguistic profiling that fans the embers of racial discord.

Acknowledgments

Previous research on similar topics has been supported by funding from the Ford Foundation, the Office of Educational Research and Improvement, the United States Department of State, and the Center for Applied Language Studies and Services in Africa at the University of Cape Town, South Africa. I am grateful to Shanna Smith and Robyn Webb-Williams of the National Fair Housing Alliance, which produced the advertisements that appear herein as Figures 1 and 2. I gratefully acknowledge the advice, guidance, and insights of Charla Larrimore Baugh, Anita Henderson, Janet Hales, Hesham Alim, Dennis Preston, Tom Purnell, Doug Young, Rajend Mesthrie, Kay McCormick, and Connie Eble. All limitations herein are my own.

Notes

1. Judge Lance Ito became the object of linguistic profiling when former Senator Alfonse D'Amato openly mocked his speech during a radio talk show. The Senator adopted a stereotypical Asian accent that was attributed to Judge Ito. The linguistic portrayal was a cartoon with inescapable racist overtones, for which the Senator publicly apologized.
2. Linguists are strongly encouraged to consult Purnell *et al.* (1999) for detailed discussion of a series of experiments which were conducted pertaining to phonetic properties of dialect perception of three American English dialects: African American Vernacular English, Chicano English, and Standard American English.

References

Baugh, J. (1983) *Black Street Speech: Its History, Structure, and Survival,* Austin, TX: University of Texas Press.
—— (1999) *Out of the Mouths of Slaves: African American Language and Educational Malpractice,* Austin, TX: University of Texas Press.

——— (2000) *Beyond Ebonics: Linguistic Pride and Racial Prejudice,* New York: Oxford University Press.

Blom, J.P. and Gumperz, J.J. (1972) "Social meaning in linguistic structures: code-switching in Norway," in J.J. Gumperz and D. Hymes (eds.) *Directions in Sociolinguists: The Ethnography of Communication,* New York: Holt, Rinehart, and Winston, 407–34.

California v. Orenthal James Simpson (1995), Los Angeles District Court.

Clifford v. Kentucky (1999) 7 SW 3d 371, Supreme Court of Kentucky.

Cukor-Avila, P. (2000) "Linguistic diversity in the workplace: how regional accent affects employment decisions," paper presented at the 2000 NWAV Conference, East Lansing, Michigan State University.

Dillard, J.L. (1972) *Black English: Its History and Usage in the United States,* New York: Random House.

Ervin-Tripp, S. (1972) "On sociolinguistic rules: alternation and co-occurrence," in J.J. Gumperz and D. Hymes (eds) *Directions in Sociolinguistics: The Ethnography of Communication,* New York: Holt, Rinehart, and Winston, 213–50.

Giles, H. and Powesland, P. (1975) *Speech Styles and Social Evaluation,* New York: Academic Press.

Goffman, E. (1972) "The neglected situation," in P.P. Giglioli (ed.) *Language in Social Context,* New York: Penguin, 61–6.

Hazen, K. (1998) "The birth of a variant: evidence for a tripartite, negative past *be* paradigm," *Language Variation and Change,* 10: 221–43.

Henderson, A. (2001) "Put your money where your mouth is: hiring managers' attitudes toward African-American Vernacular English," PhD dissertation, University of Pennsylvania.

Horowitz, S. (1999) "Minority renters face insurance bias," *Washington Post,* September 29, p. B-01.

Hymes, D. (1974) *Foundations in Sociolinguistics,* Philadelphia, PA: University of Pennsylvania Press.

Labov, W. (1972) *Language in the Inner-City: Studies in the Black English Vernacular,* Philadelphia, PA: University of Texas Press.

Lanehart, S. (2002) *Sista, Speak! Black Women Kinfolk Talk about Language and Literacy,* Austin, TX: University of Texas Press.

Lippi-Green, R. (1997) *English with an Accent: Language, Ideology, and Discrimination in the United States,* London: Routledge.

People v. Sanchez (1985) 129 Misc. 2d 91, 492, NYS 2d 683, New York Supreme Court.

Preston, D. (ed.) (1993) *American Dialect Research,* Philadelphia, PA: John Benjamins.

Purnell, T., Idsardi, W., and Baugh, J. (1999) "Perceptual and phonetic experiments on American English dialect identification," *Journal of Language and Social Psychology,* 18: 10–30.

Schilling-Estes, N. and Wolfram, W. (1999) "Alternative models of dialect death: dissipation vs. concentration," *Language,* 75: 486–521.

Smitherman, G. (2000) *Talkin That Talk: Language, Culture and Education in African America,* New York and London: Routledge.

Trudgill, P. (1986) *Dialects in Contact,* Oxford, Blackwell.

Weinreich, U. (1953) *Languages in Contact,* The Hague: Mouton.

Hunger as Ideology

Susan Bordo

Susan Bordo does not linger on the female obsession for ultra-thinness. Rather, she seeks to expose the deeper roots of eating disorders and distorted body image: a long-standing, devastating ideology that has held women captives of their own desires. From Victorian manuals on women's conduct to contemporary media, Bordo traces the message and the myth that women's desires are unfeminine, "vulgar," and best expressed in secret. True femininity rests in the complete absence of desire, and women should appear, "emotionally and mentally opaque, even vacant." Bordo peels away this myth, exposing its fierce psychological effects on women's relationships, particularly to food. She argues that while masculinity demands a celebratory, even voracious appetite, women are encouraged to indulge only in small amounts to demonstrate a lack *of all desire even about the basic need to eat. Do Bordo's arguments and examples relate to your own experiences? Can you find exceptions to these "traditional gender dualities" in advertising? Are contemporary gender roles and attitudes toward food changing?*

The Woman Who Doesn't Eat Much

We live in a time in which mass imagery has an unprecedented power to instruct. When I was a teenager in the 1960s, Twiggy's mascara-spiked stare and long, spindly legs represented our variant of the wide-eyed waif. We envied Twiggy's casual cool and elegantly elongated body. But few of us imagined that Twiggy represented a blueprint for the ordinary, adolescent girl to model herself after. She was a high-fashion mannequin, after all, and we all knew that they *had* to be skinny "to photograph well." Today, young women and men no longer experience much of a distinction between the commercially fabricated, artfully arranged images that surround them and the aspirations they hold for themselves. Women with eating disorders bring photos of ultra-thin model Kate Moss to their therapists as an example of the look they strive for, and the latest craze in cosmetic

Reprinted by permission from *Feminisms and Pedagogies of Everyday Life* edited by Carmen Luke, the State University of New York Press © 1996, State University of New York. All rights reserved.

surgery is the "waif procedure," which vacuums out cheek-fat in order to achieve a hollowed-out look.

It would be a mistake, however, to imagine that what is being taught through mass images is only the desirability of a certain appearance of face and body. In layout after layout, Moss is arranged to look emotionally and mentally opaque, even vacant. She seems utterly without need, without expectation, without complaint. Without desire. Without hunger. Moss is an archetype of female recessiveness in an era of enormous gender-change and challenge. She assures us in interviews that she eats anytime and anything she wants. But even if this is true, it only adds to Moss's mystique for anorexics. For they know that the only way to eat whatever you like and look like Kate is either to remain in perpetual motion, or not to *want* to eat much of anything at all. And that, above all, is the state they aspire to—a state beyond appetite, beyond desire.

Some of the slickest advertisements appear to recognize the cultural potency of the imagery of the woman who is beyond hunger. In one television commercial, two little French girls are shown dressing up in the feathery finery of their mother's clothes. They are exquisite little girls, flawless and innocent, and the scene emphasizes both their youth and the natural sense of style often associated with French women. (The ad is done in French, with subtitles.) One of the girls, spying a picture of the other girl's mother, exclaims breathlessly, "Your mother, she is so slim, so beautiful! Does she eat?" The daughter, giggling, replies: "Silly, just not so much," and displays her mother's helper, a bottle of FibreThin. "Aren't you jealous?," the friend asks. Dimpling, shy yet self-possessed and deeply knowing, the daughter answers, "Not if I know her secrets."

Admittedly, women are continually bombarded with advertisements and commercials for weight-loss products and programs, but this commercial makes many of us particularly angry. On the most obvious level, the commercial affronts with its suggestion that young girls begin early in learning to control their weight, and with its romantic mystification of diet pills as part of the obscure, eternal arsenal of feminine arts to be passed from generation to generation. But far more unnerving is the psychological acuity of the ad's focus, not on the size and shape of bodies, but on a certain *subjectivity,* represented by the absent but central figure of the mother, the woman who eats, only "not so much." We never see her picture; we are left to imagine her ideal beauty and slenderness. But what she looks like is not important, in any case; what is important is the fact that she has achieved what we might call a "cool" (that is, casual) relation to food. She is not starving herself (an obsession, indicated the continuing power of food), but neither is she desperately and shamefully binging in some private corner. Eating has become, for her, no big deal. In its evocation of the lovely French mother who doesn't eat much, the commercial's metaphor of European "difference" reveals itself as a means of representing that enviable and truly foreign "other": the woman for whom food is merely ordinary, who can take it or leave it.

Another version, this time embodied by a sleek, fashionable African-American woman, playfully promotes Virginia Slims Menthol. "Decisions are easy. When I get to a fork in the road, I eat." Here the speaker scorns obsessiveness, not only over professional or interpersonal decision-making, but over food as well. Implicitly contrasting herself to those who worry and fret, she presents herself as utterly "easy" in her relationship with food. Unlike the FibreThin mother, she eats anytime she wants. But *like* the FibreThin mother (and this is the key similarity for my purposes), she has achieved a state beyond craving. Undominated by unsatisfied, internal need, she eats not only freely but without deep desire and without apparent consequence. It's "easy," she says. Presumably, without those forks in the road she might forget about food entirely.

The Virginia Slims woman is a fantasy figure, her cool attitude toward food as remote from the lives of most contemporary African-American women as from any others. For most women today—whatever their racial or ethnic identity, and increasingly across class and sexual-orientation differences as well—free and easy relations with food are a best a relic of the past.[1] Almost all of us who can afford to be eating well are dieting—and hungry—almost all of the time. It is thus Dexatrim, not Virginia Slims, that constructs the more realistic representation of women's subjective relations with food. In Dexatrim's commercial that shows a woman, her appetite-suppressant worn off, hurtling across the room, drawn like a living magnet to the breathing, menacing refrigerator, hunger is represented as a insistent, powerful force with a life of its own. This construction reflects the physiological reality of dieting, a state the body is unable to distinguish from starvation (Starvation stages, 1989, April 3). And it reflects its psychological reality as well; for dieters, who live in a state of constant denial, food is a perpetually beckoning presence, its power growing ever greater as the sanctions against gratification become more stringent. A slender body may be attainable through hard work, but a "cool" relation to food, the true "secret" of the beautiful "other" in the FibreThin commercial, is a tantalizing reminder of what lies beyond the reach of the inadequate and hungry self.

Gender, Hunger, and Desire

Men, of course, are *supposed* to have hearty, even voracious, appetites. It is a mark of the manly to eat spontaneously and expansively, and manliness is frequent commercial code for amply portioned products: "Manwich," "Hungry Man Dinners," "Manhandlers." Even when men advertise diet products (as they more frequently do, now that physical perfection is increasingly being demanded of men as well as women), they brag about their appetites, as in the Tommy Lasorda commercials for Slim-Fast, which feature three burly football players (their masculinity beyond reproach) declaring that if Slim-Fast can satisfy *their* appetites, it can satisfy any-one's. But is it possible to imagine an advertisement depicting a young, attractive *woman* indulging as freely as a man. Such an image would vio-late deeply sedimented expectations, would be experienced by many as dis-gusting and transgressive.

When women are positively depicted as sensuously voracious about food (almost never in commercials, and only very rarely in movies and novels), their hunger for food is employed solely as a metaphor for their sexual appetite—as in the eating scenes in *Tom Jones* and *Flashdance.* Women are permitted to lust for food itself only when they are pregnant or when it is clear they have been near starvation—as, for example, in *McCabe and Mrs. Miller,* in the scene in which Mrs. Miller, played by Julie Christie, wolfs down half a dozen eggs and a bowl of beef stew before the amazed eyes of McCabe. Significantly, the scene serves to establish Mrs. Miller's "manliness"; a woman who eats like this is to be taken seriously, is not to be trifled with, the movie suggests.

The metaphorical situation is virtually inverted in the representation of male eaters. Although voracious eating may occasionally code male sexual appetite (as in *Tom Jones*), we frequently also find *sexual* appetite operat-ing as a metaphor for eating pleasure. In commercials that feature male eaters, the men are shown in a state of wild, sensual transport over heavily frosted, rich, gooey deserts. Their total lack of control is portrayed as appropriate, even adorable; the language of the background jingle is unashamedly aroused, sexual and desiring:

"I'm thinking about you the whole day through [crooned to a Pillsbury cake]. I've got a passion for you."

"I'm a fool for your chocolate. I'm wild, crazy, out of control [assorted Betty Crocker cake mixes]."

In these commercials food is constructed as a sexual object of desire, and eating is legitimated as much more than a purely nutritive activity. Rather, food is *supposed* to supply sensual delight and succor—not as metaphorically standing for something else, but as an erotic experience in itself. Women are permitted such gratification from food only in measured doses. In another ad from the Diet Jell-O series, eating is metaphorically sexualized: "I'm a girl who just can't say no. I insist on dessert," admits the innocently dressed but flirtatiously posed model. But at the same time that eating is mildly sexualized in this ad, it is also contained. She is permitted to "feel good about saying 'Yes'"—but ever so demurely, and to a harmless low-calorie product. Women may be encouraged (like the man on the Häagen-Dazs high-board) to "dive in"—not, however, into a dangerous pool of Häagen-Dazs Deep Chocolate, but for a "refreshing dip" into Weight Watcher's linguini.

All of this may seem peculiarly contemporary, revolving as it does around the mass marketing of diet products. But in fact the same metaphorical universe, as well as the same practical prohibitions against female indulgence (for, of course, these ads are not only selling products, but teaching appropriate behavior) were characteristic of Victorian gender ideology. Victorians did not have *Cosmo* and television, of course. But they did have conduct manuals, which warned elite women of the dangers of indulgent and overstimulating eating and advised how to consume in a feminine way (as little as possible and with the utmost precaution against unseemly show of desire). *Godey's Lady's Book* warned that it was vulgar for women to load their plates; young girls were admonished to "be frugal and plain in your tastes" (Brumberg, 1988, 179). And in the Victorian era, as today, the forbiddenness of rich food often resulted in private binge behavior, described in *The Bazaar Book of Decorum* (1870) as the "secret luncheon," at which "many of the most abstemious at the open dinner are the most voracious . . . swallowing cream tarts by the dozen, and caramels and chocolate drops by the pound's weight" (Mitchie, 1987, 193).

The emergence of such rigid and highly moralized restrictions on female appetite and eating are, arguably, part of what Bram Dijkstra has interpreted as a nineteenth-century "cultural ideological counter-offensive" against the "new woman" and her challenge to prevailing gender arrangements and their constraints on women (Dijkstra, 1986, 30–31). Mythological, artistic, polemical, and scientific discourses from many cultures and eras certainly suggest the symbolic potency of female hunger as a cultural metaphor for unleashed female power and desire, from the blood-craving Kali (who in one representation is shown eating her own entrails) to the *Malleus Malificarum* ("For the sake of fulfilling the mouth of the womb, [witches] consort even with the devil"), to Hall and Oates's contemporary rock lyrics: "Oh, oh, here she comes, watch out boys, she'll chew you up." In *Tom Jones* and *Flashdance,* the trope of female hunger as female sexuality is embodied in attractive female characters; more frequently, however, female hunger as sexuality is represented by Western culture in misogynist images permeated with terror and loathing rather than affection or admiration. In the figure of the man-eater the metaphor of the devouring woman reveals its deep psychological underpinnings. Eating is not really a metaphor for the sexual act; rather, the sexual act, when initiated and desired by a woman, is imagined as itself an act of eating, of incorporation and destruction of the object of desire. Thus, women's sexual appetites must be curtailed and controlled, because they threaten to deplete and consume the body and soul of the male. Such imagery, as Dijkstra has demonstrated, flourishes in the West in the art of the late nineteenth century. Arguably, the same cultural backlash (if not in the same form) operates today—for example, in the ascendancy of popular films that punish female sexuality and independence by rape and dismemberment (as in numerous slasher films), loss of family and children (*The Good Mother*), madness and death (*Fatal Attraction, Presumed Innocent*), and public humiliation and disgrace (*Dangerous Liaisons*).

Of course, Victorian prohibitions against women eating were not *only* about the ideology of gender. Or, perhaps better put, the ideology of gender contained other dimensions as well. In the reigning body symbolism of the day, a frail frame and lack of appetite signified not only feminine delicacy and spiritual transcendence of the desires of the flesh, but *social* transcendence of the laboring, striving "economic" body. Then, as today, to be aristocratically cool and unconcerned with the mere facts of material survival was highly fashionable. The hungering bourgeois wished to appear, like the aristocrat, above the material desires that in fact ruled his life. The closest he could come was to possess a wife whose ethereal body became a sort of fashion statement of *his* aristocratic tastes. If he could not be or marry an aristocrat, he could have a wife who looked like one, a wife whose nonrobust beauty and delicate appetite signified her lack of participation in the taxing "pubic sphere."[2]

Food and Love

At the beginning of the 1992 U.S. Presidential campaign, Hillary Clinton, badgered by reporters' endless questions concerning her pursuit of a professional career, shot back defensively and sarcastically: "Well, I suppose I could have stayed home and baked cookies and had teas . . ." Media audiences never got to hear the end of her remark (or the questioning that proceeded it); the "cookie and teas" sound-byte became *the* gender-transgression of the campaign, replayed over and over, and presented by opponents as evidence of Hillary's rabid feminism and disdain for traditional maternal values. Rightly protesting this interpretation, Hillary Clinton tried to prove her true womanhood by producing her favorite recipe for oatmeal chocolate chip cookies. Barbara Bush, apparently feeling that a gauntlet had been thrown down, responded in kind with a richer, less fibre-conscious recipe of her own. Newspapers across the country asked readers to prepare each and vote on which First Lady had the better cookie.

That the cookie itself should have become the symbol and center of the national debate about Hillary Clinton's adequacy as wife and mother is not surprising. Food is equated with maternal and wifely love throughout our culture. In nearly all commercials that feature men eating—such as the cake commercials whose sexualized rhetoric was described earlier—there is a woman in the background (either visible or implied) who has *prepared* the food. Most significantly, *always,* the woman in the background speaks the language of love and care through the offering of food: "Nothin' says lovin' like something from the oven"; "Give me that great taste of love"; "Nothing says 'Cookie, I love you' like Nestle's Toll House Cookies Do." In these commercials, male eating is inextricably tied to female offerings of love. This is not represented, however, as female self-abnegation. Rather, it is suggested that women receive *their* gratification through nourishing others:

> *Her voice, heard off:* "He's like a little boy—normally serious, *then* he eats English muffins with butter . . . [shot of man's face transported with childlike delight] . . . and *I* get to enjoy watching him. A little butter brings a lot of joy."

My analysis, I want to emphasize, is not meant to disparage caring for the physical and emotional well-being of others, "maternal" work that has been scandalously socially undervalued even as it has been idealized and sanctified. Nor am I counterposing to the argument of these ads the construction that women are simply oppressed by such roles. This would be untrue to the personal experiences of many women including myself. I remember the pride and pleasure that radiated from my mother, who was anxious and unhappy in most other areas of her life, when her famous stuffed cabbage was devoured enthusiastically and in voluminous quantities by my father, my sisters, and me. As a little girl, I loved watching her roll each piece, enclosing just the right amount of filling, skillfully avoiding tearing the tender cabbage leaves as she folded them around the meat. I never felt so safe and secure as at those moments. She was visibly pleased when I asked her to teach me exactly how to make the dish and thrilled when I even went so far as to write the quantities and instructions down as she tried to formulate them into an official recipe (until then, it had been passed through demonstration from mother to daughter, and my mother considered that in writing it down, I was conferring a higher status on it). Those periods in my life when I have found myself too busy writing, teaching, and traveling to find the time and energy to prepare special meals for people that I love have been periods when a deep aspect of my self has felt deprived, depressed.

Nor would I want my critique to be interpreted as effacing the collective, historical experiences of those groups, forced into servitude for the families of others, who have been systematically deprived of the freedom *to* care for their own families. bell hooks points out, for example, that black women's creation of "homeplace," of fragile and hard-won "spaces of care and nurturance" for the healing of deep wounds made by racism, sexism, and poverty, was less a matter of obedience to a tyrannical gender-norm than the construction of a "site of cultural resistance" (hooks, 1990, 42). With this in mind, it is clear that the Jell-O Heritage ad discussed earlier is more complex than my interpretation has thus far allowed. Part of an extensive General Foods series aimed at the African-American consumer and promoting America's historically black colleges, the ad's association of the maternal figure with "strong foundations" runs far deeper than a nostalgic evocation of Mom's traditional cooking. In this ad, the maternal figure is linked with a black "heritage," with the preservation and communication of culture.

However at the same time that hooks urges that contemporary black culture should honor the black woman's history of service to her family and her community, she also cautions against the ideological construction of such service as woman's natural role. (Despite the pleasure I take in cooking, in relationships where it has been expected of me, I have resented it deeply.) It is this construction that is reinforced in the representations I have been examining, through their failure to depict males as "naturally" fulfilling that role, and—more perniciously—through their failure to depict females as appropriate *recipients* of such care. Only occasionally are little girls represented as being *fed;* more often, they (but never little boys) are shown learning how to feed others. In this way, caring is representationally "reproduced" as a quintessentially and exclusively female activity. And here, it is significant and disquieting that the General Foods series does not include any ads that portray female students discovering their black heritage (or learning how to rely on convenience foods!) at college. Women appear only in the background, encouraging and supporting "feeding" the development of others.

The ubiquitous configuration of woman-food-man, with food expressing the woman's love for the man and at the same time satisfying woman's desire to bestow love, establishes male hunger as thoroughly socially integrated into the network of heterosexual family and love relations. Men can eat *and* be loved; indeed, a central mode by which they receive love is through food from women. For women by contrast (who are almost never shown being fed by others), eating—in the form of private, *self*-feeding—is represented as a *substitute* for human love. Weight Watchers transparently offers itself as such in its "Who says you can't live on love?" ad. In these ads there is no partner, visible or implied, offering the food and thus operating as the true bestower of "love." In many ads—virtually a genre, in fact—the absence of the partner is explicitly thematized, a central aspect of the narrative of the ad. One commercial features a woman in bed, on the phone, refusing date after date in favor of an evening alone with her ice-cream bonbons: "Your Highness? Not tonight!" "The inauguration? Another year!" In another, a woman admits to spending a lot of time alone with her "latest obsession," a chocolate drink, because it gives her "the same feeling as being in love" and "satisfies her innermost cravings anytime [she] wants." She pleads with us, the viewers, not to tell Michael, her boyfriend.

These commercials hit a painful nerve for women. The bonbon commercial may seem merely silly, but the chocolate drink ad begins to evoke, darkly and disturbingly, the psychological and material realities of women's food problems. The talk of "obsession" and "inner-most cravings," the furtiveness, the secrecy, the use of food to satisfy emotional needs, all suggest central elements of binge behavior. Frusen Glädjé supplies another piece and gives an important lie to the other, more upbeat commercials: "He never called. So, Ben and I went out for a walk to pick up a pint of Frusen Glädjé. Ben's better looking anyway." Frusen Glädjé: "It feels so good." Here, as in the Häagan-Dazs ad discussed earlier, the sensuousness of the ice-cream experience is emphasized; unlike the Häagan-Dazs ad, however, Frusen Glädjé offers solace from emotional depths rather than the thrill of emotional heights. This is, indeed, the prevailing gender reality. For women, the emotional comfort of self-feeding is rarely turned to in a state of pleasure and independence, but in despair, emptiness, loneliness, and desperation. Food is, as one woman put it, "the only thing that will take care of *me*."

Food as Transgression

An extremely interesting fact about male bulimics; they rarely binge alone. They tend to binge at mealtime and in public places, whereas women almost eat minimally at meals and gorge later, in private (Schneider & Agras, 1987, March). Even in our disorders (or perhaps especially in our disorders) we follow the gender rules. In the commercials I have been discussing, female eating is virtually always represented as private, secretive, illicit. The woman has stolen away from the world of husband, family, friends to a secret corner where she and the food can be alone. A "Do Not Disturb" sign hangs on the door to the room where the woman sits munching on her "purple passion," New York Deli Potato Chips. A husband returns home to discover that in this absence, his wife, sitting on the floor, has eaten all the Frusen Glädjé; her voice is mildly defiant, although soft— "I ate all the Frusen Glädjé"—but her face is sheepish and her glance averted. Men sing openly of their wild cravings for Betty Crocker cakes; women's cravings are a dirty, shameful secret, to be indulged in only when no one is looking.

More often than not, however, women are not even permitted, even in private, indulgences so extravagant in scope as the full satisfaction of their hungers. Most commonly, women are used to advertise, *not* ice cream and potato chips (foods whose intake is very difficult to contain and control), but individually wrapped pieces of tiny, bite-size candies: Andes candies, Hershey's kisses, Mon Cheri bonbons. Instead of the mounds of cake and oozing frosting typical of commercials featuring male eaters, women are confined to a "tiny scoop" of flavor, a "tiny piece" of chocolate. As in the Weight Watchers linguini advertisement ("Dive in"), the rhetoric of indulgence is invoked, only to be contained by the product itself: "Indulge a little," urges Andes Candies. "Satisfy your urge to splurge in five delicious bite-size ways." The littleness of the candy and the amount of taste that is packed within its tiny boundaries are frequently emphasized: "Each bite-size piece packs a wallop of milk chocolate crunch." Instead of the emphasis on undifferentiated feelings of sensuous delight that we see in commercials showing men, the pitch aimed at women stresses the exquisite pleasure to be had from a sensually focused and limited experience. The message to women is explicit: "Indulge a *little*." (And only out of sight; even these minuscule bonbons are eaten privately, in isolation, behind closed doors.) It is significant, too, that in all these commercials, the woman is found "indulging" only after a day spent serving others. In these commercials, it is permissible for women to feed the self (if such dainty nibbling merits this description) only after first feeding others: "For my angel, I sewed for days. Now I deserve a little praise. I thank me very much with Andes Candies."

These commercials, no less than the Victorian conduct manuals, offer a virtual blueprint for disordered relations to food and hunger. The representation of unrestrained appetite as inappropriate for women, the depiction of female eating as a private, transgressive act, make restriction and denial of hunger central features of the construction of femininity, and set up the compensatory binge as a virtual inevitability. Such restrictions on appetite, moreover, are not merely about food intake. Rather, the social control of female hunger operates as a practical "discipline" (to use Foucault's term) that trains female bodies in the knowledge of their limits and possibilities. Denying oneself food becomes the central micro-practice in the education of feminine self-restraint and containment of impulse.

Victorian women were told that it was vulgar to load their plates; in 1990, women students of mine complain of the tortures of the cafeteria— the embarrassment of eating ice cream in front of the male students, the pressure to take just a salad, or, better yet, refuse food altogether. Later at night, when they are alone, they confront the deprived and empty feeling left in the wake of such a regimen. As in the commercials, the self-reward and solace is food. The problem, however, after a day of restraint, is the requirement for any further containment of the now ravenous self. Unlike the women in the Andes candy commercials, few women who have spent the day submerging their desires, either for the sake of their families or to project the appropriately attractive lack of appetite to a cafeteria full of adolescent boys, really feel rewarded by a bite-size piece of candy, no matter how much chocolate "wallop" it packs. In private, shamefully and furtively, we binge.

Destabilizing Images?

When, in my classes, we discuss contemporary representations, I encourage my students to bring in examples that appear to violate traditional gender-dualities and the ideological messages contained in them. These ads almost always display a complicated and bewitching tangle of new possibilities and old patterns of representation. A television commercial for Hormel microwaveable Kid's Kitchen Meals, for example, opens with two young girls trying to fix a bicycle. A little boy, watching them, offers to help, claiming that "I can fix anything. My dad lets me fix his car. My mom lets me fix her dinner." When the girls are skeptical ("Yeah, well prove it!"), he fixes a Hormel's Kid's Kitchen Meal for them. Utterly impressed with his culinary skill and on the basis of this ready to trust his mechanical aptitude, they ask, "You know how to fix a bike?" "What? Yeah, I do!" he eagerly replies. Now, what pedagogy is contained in this ad? The little girls cannot fix their own bike, a highly traditional, "feminine" limitation. Yet they do not behave in helpless or coquettish ways in the commercial. Far from it. They speak in rough voices and challenging words to the boy, who is physically smaller (and, it appears, younger) than they; "Give me a break!" they scornfully mutter when he claims he can "fix anything." Despite their mechanical inability, they do not act deferential, and in a curious way this neutralizes the gendered meanings of the activities depicted. Not being able to fix a bike is something that could happen to anyone, they seem to believe.

Then, too, there is the unusual representation of the male cooking for and serving the females. True, it only required a touch of the microwave panel. But this is, after all, only a little boy. One message this commercial may be delivering is that males can engage in traditionally "feminine" activities without threat to their manhood. Cooking for a woman does not mean that she won't respect you in the morning. She will still recognize your authority to fix her bike (indeed, she may become further convinced of it precisely by your mastery of "her" domain). The expansion of possibilities for boys thus extracts from girls the price of continued ineptitude in certain areas (or at least the show of it) and dependence on males. Yet, in an era in which most working women find themselves with two full-time jobs—their second shift beginning at five o'clock, when they return from work to meet their husband's expectations of dinner, a clean and comfortable home, a sympathetic ear—the message that cooking and serving others is not "sissy," though it may be problematic and nonprogressive in many ways, is perhaps the single most *practically* beneficial (to women) message we can convey to little boys.

In its provision of ambiguous and destabilizing imagery, the influx of women into the professional arena has had a significant effect on the representation of gender. Seeking to appeal to a population that wishes to be regarded (at least while on the job) as equal in power and ability to the men with whom they work, advertisers have tried to establish gender symmetry in those representations that depict or evoke the lives of professional couples. Minute Rice thus has two versions of its "I wonder what 'Minute' is cookin' up for dinner tonight?" commercial. In one, father and children come home from work and school to find mother "cookin' up" an elaborate chicken stir-fry to serve over Minute Rice. In the other, a working woman returns to find her male partner "cookin' up" the dinner. The configuration is indeed destabilizing, if only because it makes us aware of how very rare it is to see. But, significantly, there are no children in this commercial, as there are in the more traditional version; the absence of children codes the fact that this is a yuppie couple, the group to which this version is designed to appeal.

And now Häagen-Dazs, the original yuppie ice cream, has designed an ad series for this market. These ads perfectly illustrate the unstable location of contemporary gender advertisements: they attempt to satisfy representational conventions that still have a deep psychic grip on Western culture, while at the same time registering every new rhythm of the social heartbeat. "Enter the State of Häagen-Dazs"—a clear invocation of the public world rather than the domestic domain. The man and woman are dressed virtually identically (making small allowances for gender-tailoring) in equally no-nonsense, dark business suits, styled for power. Their hair-styles are equivalent, brushed back from the face, clipped short but not punky. They have similar expressions: slightly playful, caught in the act but certainly not feeling guilty. They appear to be indulging in their ice-cream break in the middle of a workday; this sets up both the fetching representational incongruity of the ad, and its realism. Ice cream has always been represented as relaxation food, to be *indulged* in; it belongs to a different universe than the work ethic, performance principle, or spirit of competition. To eat it in a business suit is like having "quickie" sex in the office, irregular and naughty. Yet everyone knows that people *do* eat ice cream on their breaks and during their lunch hours. The ad thus appears both realistic and *representationally* odd; we realize that we are seeing images we have not seen before *except* in real life. And, of course, in real life, women *do* eat Häagen-Dazs, as much as, if not more than, men.

And yet, intruding into this world of gender equality and eating realism that is designed to appeal to the sensibilities of "progressive" young men and women is the inescapable disparity in how much and how the man and woman are eating. He: an entire pint of vanilla fudge, with sufficient abandon to top the carton, and greedy enough to suck the spoon. She: a restrained Eve-bite (already taken; no licks or sucks in process here), out of a single brittle bar (aestheticized as "artfully" nutty, in contrast to his bold, unaccessorized "Vanilla Fudge"). Whether unconsciously reproduced or deliberately crafted to appeal to the psychic contradictions and ambivalence of its intended audience, the disparity comes from the recesses of our most sedimented, unquestioned notions about gender.

Notes

A longer version of this paper originally appeared in Susan Bordo, *Unbearable weight: Feminism, Western culture, and the body,* (Berkeley: University of California Press, 1993). The present version has been edited to conform to space requirements of this volume and to highlight the theme of "pedagogies of everyday life."

1. True, if we survey cultural attitudes toward women's appetites and body size, we find great variety—a variety that is shaped by ethnic, national, historical, class, and other factors. My eighty-year-old father, the child of immigrants, asks at the end of every meal if I "got enough to eat"; he considers me "skinny" unless I am plump by my own standards. His attitude reflects not only memories of economic struggle and a heritage of Jewish-Russian preference for *zaftig* women, but the lingering, well into this century, of what was once a more general Anglo-Saxon cultural appreciation for the buxom woman. In the mid-nineteenth century, hotels and bars were adorned with Bouguereau-inspired paintings of voluptuous female nudes; Lillian Russell, the most photographed woman in America in 1890, was known and admired for her hearty appetite, ample body (over two hundred pounds at the height of her popularity), and "challenging, fleshly, arresting" beauty (Banner, 1984, 136). Even as such fleshy challenges became less widely appreciated in the twentieth century, men of Greek, Italian, Eastern-European, and African descent, influenced by their own distinctive cultural heritages, were still likely to find female voluptuousness appealing. And even in the late 1960s and early 1970s, as Twiggy and Jean Shrimpton began to set a new norm for ultra-slenderness, lesbian cultures in the United States continued to be accepting—even celebrating—of fleshy, space-claiming female bodies.

    Even more examples could be produced, of course, if we cast our glance more widely over the globe and back through history. Many cultures, clearly, have revered expansiveness in women's bodies and appetites. Some still do. But in the 1980s and 1990s, an increasingly universal equation of slenderness with beauty and success has rendered the competing claims of cultural diversity even feebler. Men who were teenagers from the mid-seventies on, whatever their ethnic roots or economic class, are likely to view long, slim legs, a flat stomach, and a firm rear end as essentials of female beauty. Unmuscled heft is no longer as acceptable in lesbian communities. Even the robust, earthy actresses who used to star in Russian films have been replaced by slender, Westernized types.

2. Women were thus warned "gluttonous habits of life" would degrade their physical appearance and ruin their marriageability. "Gross eaters" could develop thick skin, broken blood vessels on the nose, cracked lips, and as unattractively "superanimal" facial expression (Brumberg, 1988, 179). Of course, the degree to which actual women were able to enact any part of these

idealized and idolized constructions was highly variable (as it always is); but *all* women, of all classes and races, felt their effects as the normalizing measuring rods against which their own adequacy was judged (and, usually, found wanting).

References

Banner, L. (1984). *American beauty.* Chicago: University of Chicago Press.

Berger, J. (1977). *Ways of seeing.* London: Penguin.

Brumberg, J. (1988). *Fasting girls.* Cambridge, MA: Harvard University Press.

Bynum, C. W. (1987). *Holy feast and holy fast: The religious significance of food to medieval women.* Berkeley: University of California Press.

Canetti, E. (1962). *Crowds and power.* New York: Viking.

Dijkstra, B. (1986). *Idols of perversity.* New York: Oxford University Press.

hooks, b. (1990). *Yearning.* Boston: South End Press.

Mitchie, H. (1987). *The flesh made word.* New York: Oxford University Press.

Poloquin, B. (1988, May 8). An ode to mothers. *Syracuse Herald American,* p. D1.

Roth, G. (1982). *Feeding the hungry heart.* New York: New American Library.

Schneider, J., & Agras, W. S. (1987, March). Bulimia in males: A matched comparison with females. *International Journal of Eating Disorders,* 6(2), 235–242.

Starvation stags in weight-loss patients similar to famine victims. (1989, April 3). *International Obesity Newsletter.*

Ward, H. O. (Mrs.) (1880). *The young lady's friend.* Philadelphia: Porter and Coates. (Quoted in Mitchie.)

The Mountain

Eli Clare

Eli Clare is a genderqueer activist and author of Exile *and* Pride: Disability, Queerness, and Liberation, *from which this essay is drawn. As a way to signify a gender identity other than male or female, Clare, in hir larger work, uses* sie *("see") and* hir *("here") to refer to hirself in place of s/he and his/her. In "The Mountain," Clare describes hir experience with cerebral palsy, interrogating the terms* normality, ability, disability, *and* impairment. *In unapologetic prose, Clare demands that readers examine what it means to be identified as "supercrip," "queer," "freak," and "redneck." Clare's essay challenges readers to examine the labels we use to identify others, and the labels others have used to identify us in terms of gender, sexuality, and ableness. What happens when we internalize labels? How do these labels inform our ideas of what is "normal" and what is not normal? What happens when we question internalized notions of ourselves?*

1: A Metaphor

The mountain as metaphor looms large in the lives of marginalized people, people whose bones get crushed in the grind of capitalism, patriarchy, white supremacy. How many of us have struggled up the mountain, measured ourselves against it, failed up there, lived in its shadow? We've hit our heads on glass ceilings, tried to climb the class ladder, lost fights against assimilation, scrambled toward that phantom called normality.

We hear from the summit that the world is grand from up there, that we live down here at the bottom because we are lazy, stupid, weak, and ugly. We decide to climb that mountain, or make a pact that our children will climb it. The climbing turns out to be unimaginably difficult. We are afraid; every time we look ahead we can find nothing remotely familiar or comfortable. We lose the trail. Our wheelchairs get stuck. We speak the wrong languages with the wrong accents, wear the wrong clothes, carry our bodies the wrong ways, ask the wrong questions, love the wrong people. And it's goddamn lonely up there on the mountain. We decide to stop climbing

From *Exile and Pride: Disability, Queerness and Liberation* by Eli Clare. Copyright © 1999 by South End Press. Reprinted by permission.

and build a new house right where we are. Or we decide to climb back down to the people we love, where the food, the clothes, the dirt, the sidewalk, the steaming asphalt under our feet, our crutches, all feel right. Or we find the path again, decide to continue climbing only to have the very people who told us how wonderful life is at the summit booby-trap the trail. They burn the bridge over the impassable canyon. They redraw our topo maps so that we end up walking in circles. They send their goons—those working-class and poor people they employ as their official brutes—to push us over the edge. Maybe we get to the summit, but probably not. And the price we pay is huge.

Up there on the mountain, we confront the external forces, the power brokers who benefit so much from the status quo and their privileged position at the very summit. But just as vividly, we come face-to-face with our own bodies, all that we cherish and despise, all that lies imbedded there. This I know because I have caught myself lurching up the mountain.

II: A Supercrip Story

I am a gimp, a crip, disabled with cerebral palsy. The story of me lurching up the mountain begins not on the mountain, but with one of the dominant images of disabled people, the supercrip. A boy without hands bats .486 on his Little League team. A blind man hikes the Appalachian Trail from end to end. An adolescent girl with Down's syndrome learns to drive and has a boyfriend. A guy with one leg runs across Canada. The nondisabled world is saturated with these stories: stories about gimps who engage in activities as grand as walking 2,500 miles or as mundane as learning to drive. They focus on disabled people "overcoming" our disabilities. They reinforce the superiority of the nondisabled body and mind. They turn individual disabled people, who are simply leading their lives, into symbols of inspiration.

Supercrip stories never focus on the conditions that make it so difficult for people with Down's to have romantic partners, for blind people to have adventures, for disabled kids to play sports. I don't mean medical conditions. I mean material, social, legal conditions. I mean lack of access, lack of employment, lack of education, lack of personal attendant services. I mean stereotypes and attitudes. I mean oppression. The dominant story about disability should be about ableism, not the inspirational supercrip crap, the believe-it-or-not disability story.

I've been a supercrip in the mind's eye of nondisabled people more than once. Running cross-country and track in high school, I came in dead last in more races than I care to count. My tense, wiry body, right foot wandering out to the side as I grew tired, pushed against the miles, the stopwatch, the final back stretch, the last muddy hill. Sometimes I was lapped by the front runners in races as short as the mile. Sometimes I trailed everyone on a cross-country course by two, three, four minutes. I ran because I loved to run, and yet after every race, strangers came to thank me, cry over me, tell me what an inspiration I was. To them, I was not just another hopelessly slow, tenacious high school athlete, but supercrip, tragic brave girl with CP, courageous cripple. It sucked. The slogan on one of my favorite t-shirts, black cotton inked with big fluorescent pink letters, one word per line, reads PISS ON PITY.

Me lurching up the mountain is another kind of supercrip story, a story about internalizing supercripdom, about becoming supercrip in my own mind's eye, a story about climbing Mount Adams last summer with my friend Adrianne. We had been planning this trip for years. Adrianne spent her childhood roaming New Hampshire's White Mountains and wanted to take me to her favorite haunts. Six times in six years, we set the trip up, and every time something fell through at the last minute. Finally, last summer everything stayed in place.

I love the mountains almost as much as I love the ocean, not a soft, romantic kind of love, but a deep down rumble in my bones. When Adrianne pulled out her trail guides and topo maps and asked me to choose one of the mountains we'd climb, I looked for a big mountain, for a long, hard hike, for a trail that would take us well above treeline. I picked Mount Adams. I think I asked Adrianne, "Can I handle this trail?" meaning, "Will I have to clamber across deep gulches on narrow log bridges without hand railings to get to the top of this mountain?" Without a moment's hesitation, she said, "No problem."

I have walked from Los Angeles to Washington, D.C., on a peace walk; backpacked solo in the southern Appalachians, along Lake Superior, on the beaches at Point Reyes; slogged my way over Cottonwood Pass and down South Manitou's dunes. Learning to walk took me longer than most kids—certainly most nondisabled kids. I was two and a half before I figured out how to stand on my own two feet, drop my heels to the ground, balance my height on the whole long flat of each foot. I wore orthopedic shoes—clunky unbending monsters—for several years, but never had to suffer through physical therapy or surgery. Today, I can and often do walk unending miles for the pure joy of walking. In the disability community I am called a walkie, someone who doesn't use a wheelchair, who walks rather than rolls. Adrianne and I have been hiking buddies for years. I never questioned her judgment. Of course, I could handle Mount Adams.

The night before our hike, it rained. In the morning we thought we might have to postpone. The weather reports from the summit still looked uncertain, but by 10 a.m. the clouds started to lift, later than we had planned to begin but still okay. The first mile of trail snaked through steep jumbles of rock, leaving me breathing hard, sweat drenching my cotton t-shirt, dripping into my eyes. I love this pull and stretch, quad and calves, lungs and heart, straining.

The trail divides and divides again, steeper and rockier now, moving not around but over piles of craggy granite, mossy and a bit slick from the night's rain. I start having to watch where I put my feet. Balance has always been somewhat of a problem for me, my right foot less steady than my left. On uncertain ground, each step becomes a studied move, especially when my weight is balanced on my right foot. I take the trail slowly, bringing both feet together, solid on one stone, before leaning into my next step. This assures my balance, but I lose all the momentum gained from swinging into a step, touching ground, pushing off again in the same moment. There is no rhythm to my stop-and-go clamber. I know that going down will be worse, gravity underscoring my lack of balance. I watch Adrianne ahead of me hop from one rock to the next up this tumble trail of granite. I know that she's breathing hard, that this is no easy climb, but also that each step isn't a strategic game for her. I start getting scared as the trail steepens, then steepens again, the rocks not letting up. I can't think of how I will ever come down this mountain. Fear sets up a rumble right alongside the love in my bones. I keep climbing. Adrianne starts waiting for me every 50 yards or so. I finally tell her I'm scared.

She's never hiked this trail before so can't tell me if this is as steep as it gets. We study the topo map, do a time check. We have many hours of daylight ahead of us, but we're both thinking about how much time it might take me to climb down, using my hands and butt when I can't trust my feet. I want to continue up to treeline, the pines shorter and shorter, grown twisted and withered, giving way to scrub brush, then to lichen-covered granite, up to the sun-drenched cap where the mountains all tumble out toward the hazy blue horizon. I want to so badly, but fear rumbles next to love next to real lived physical limitations, and so we decide to turn around. I cry, maybe for the first time, over something I want to do, had many reasons to believe I could, but really can't. I cry hard, then get up and follow Adrianne back down the mountain. It's hard and slow, and I use my hands and butt often and wish I could use gravity as Adrianne does to bounce from one flat spot to another, down this jumbled pile of rocks.

I thought a lot coming down Mount Adams. Thought about bitterness. For as long as I can remember, I have avoided certain questions. Would I have been a good runner if I didn't have CP? Could I have been a surgeon or pianist, a dancer or gymnast? Tempting questions that have no answers. I refuse to enter the territory marked *bitterness*. I wondered about a friend who calls herself one of the last of the polio tribe, born just before the polio vaccine's discovery. Does she ever ask what her life might look like had she been born five years later? On a topo map, bitterness would be outlined in red.

I thought about the model of disability that separates impairment from disability. Disability theorist Michael Oliver defines impairment as "lacking part of or all of a limb, or having a defective limb, organism or mechanism of the body." I lack a fair amount of fine motor control. My hands shake. I can't play a piano, place my hands gently on a keyboard, or type even 15 words a minute. Whole paragraphs never cascade from my fingertips. My longhand is a slow scrawl. I have trouble picking up small objects, putting them down. Dicing onions with a sharp knife puts my hands at risk. A food processor is not a yuppie kitchen luxury in my house, but an adaptive device. My gross motor skills are better but not great. I can walk mile after mile, run and jump and skip and hop, but don't expect me to walk a balance beam. A tightrope would be murder; boulder hopping and rock climbing, not much better. I am not asking for pity. I am telling you about impairment.

Oliver defines disability as "the disadvantage or restriction of activity caused by a contemporary social organization which takes no or little account of people who have physical [and/or cognitive/developmental/mental] impairments and thus excludes them from the mainstream of society." I write slowly enough that cashiers get impatient as I sign my name to checks, stop talking to me, turn to my companions, hand them my receipts. I have failed timed tests, important tests, because teachers wouldn't allow me extra time to finish the sheer physical act of writing, wouldn't allow me to use a typewriter. I have been turned away from jobs because my potential employer believed my slow, slurred speech meant I was stupid. Everywhere I go people stare at me, in restaurants as I eat, in grocery stores as I fish coins out of my pocket to pay the cashier, in parks as I play with my dog. I am not asking for pity. I am telling you about disability.

In large part, disability oppression is about access. Simply being on Mount Adams, halfway up Air Line Trail, represents a whole lot of access. When access is measured by curb cuts, ramps, and whether they are kept clear of snow and ice in the winter; by the width of doors and height of counters; by the presence or absence of Braille, closed captions, ASL, and TDDs; my not being able to climb all the way to the very top of Mount Adams stops being about disability. I decided that turning around before reaching the summit was more about impairment than disability.

But even as I formed the thought, I could feel my resistance to it. To neatly divide disability from impairment doesn't feel right. My experience of living with CP has been so shaped by ableism—or to use Oliver's language, my experience of impairment has been so shaped by disability—that I have trouble separating the two. I understand the difference between failing a test because some stupid school rule won't give me more time and failing to summit Mount Adams because it's too steep and slippery for my feet. The first failure centers on a socially constructed limitation, the second on a physical one.

At the same time, both center on my body. The faster I try to write, the more my pen slides out of control, muscles spasm, then contract trying to stop the tremors, my shoulder and upper arm growing painfully tight. Even though this socially constructed limitation has a simple solution—access to a typewriter, computer, tape recorder, or person to take dictation—I experience the problem on a very physical level. In the case of the bodily limitation, my experience is similarly physical. My feet simply don't know the necessary balance. I lurch along from one rock to the next, catching myself repeatedly as I start to fall, quads quickly sore from exertion, tension, lack of momentum. These physical experiences, one caused by a social construction, the other by a bodily limitation, translate directly into frustration, making me want to crumple the test I can't finish, hurl the rocks I can't climb. This frustration knows no neat theoretical divide between disability and impairment. Neither does disappointment nor embarrassment. On good days, I can separate the anger I turn inward at my body from the anger that needs to be turned outward, directed at the daily ableist shit, but there is nothing simple or neat about kindling the latter while transforming the former. I decided that Oliver's model of disability makes theoretical and political sense but misses important emotional realities.

I thought of my nondisabled friends who don't care for camping, hiking, or backpacking. They would never spend a vacation sweat-drenched and breathing hard halfway up a mountain. I started to list their names, told Adrianne what I was doing. She reminded me of other friends who enjoy easy day hikes on smooth, well-maintained trails. Many of them would never even attempt the tumbled trail of rock I climbed for an hour and a half before turning around. We added their names to my list. It turned into a long roster. I decided that if part of what happened to me up there was impairment, another part was about desire, my desire to climb mountains.

I thought about supercrips. Some of us—the boy who bats .486, the man who through-hikes the A.T.—accomplish something truly extraordinary and become supercrips. Others of us—the teenager with Down's who has a boyfriend, the kid with CP who runs track and cross-country—lead entirely ordinary lives and still become supercrips. Nothing about having a boyfriend or running cross-country is particularly noteworthy. Bat .486 or have a boyfriend, it doesn't matter; either way we are astonishing. In the creation of supercrip stories, nondisabled people don't celebrate any particular achievement, however extraordinary or mundane. Rather, these stories rely upon the perception that disability and achievement contradict each other and that any disabled person who overcomes this contradiction is heroic.

To believe that achievement contradicts disability is to pair helplessness with disability, a pairing for which crips pay an awful price. The nondisabled world locks us away in nursing homes. It deprives us the resources to live independently. It physically and sexually abuses us in astoundingly numbers. It refuses to give us jobs because even when a workplace is accessible, the speech impediment, the limp, the ventilator, the seeing-eye dog are read as signs of inability. The price is incredibly high.

And here, supercrip turns complicated. On the other side of supercripdom lies pity, tragedy, and the nursing home. Disabled people know this, and in our process of knowing, some of us internalize the crap. We make supercrip our own, particularly the type that pushes into the extraordinary, cracks into our physical limitation. We use supercripdom as a shield, a protection, as if this individual internalization could defend us against disability oppression.

I climbed Mount Adams for an hour and half scared, not sure I'd ever be able to climb down, knowing that on the next rock my balance could give out, and yet I climbed. Climbed surely because I wanted the summit, because of the love rumbling in my bones. But climbed also because I want to say, "Yes, I have CP, but see. See, watch me. I can climb mountains too." I wanted to prove myself once again. I wanted to overcome my CP.

Overcoming has a powerful grip. Back home, my friends told me, "But you can walk any of us under the table." My sister, a serious mountain climber who spends many a weekend high up in the North Cascades, told me, "I bet with the right gear and enough practice you *could* climb Mount Adams." A woman who doesn't know me told Adrianne, "Tell your friend not to give up. She can do anything she wants. She just has to want it hard enough." I told myself as Adrianne and I started talking about another trip to the Whites, "If I used a walking stick, and we picked a dry day and a different trail, maybe I could make it up to the top of Adams." I never once heard, "You made the right choice when you turned around." The mountain just won't let go.

III: Home

I will never find home on the mountain. This I know. Rather home starts here in my body, in all that lies imbedded beneath my skin. My disabled body: born prematurely in the backwoods of Oregon, I was first diagnosed as "mentally retarded" and then later as having CP. I grew up to the words *cripple, retard, monkey, defect,* took all the staring into me and learned to shut it out.

My body violated: early on my father started raping me, physically abusing me in ways that can only be described as torture, and sharing my body with other people, mostly men, who did the same. I abandoned that body, decided to be a hermit, to be done with humans, to live among the trees, with the salmon, to ride the south wind bareback.

My white body: the only person of color in my hometown was an African-American boy, adopted by a white family. I grew up to persistent rumors of a lynching tree way back in the hills, of the sheriff running people out of the county. For a long time after moving to the city, college scholarship in hand, all I could do was gawk at the multitude of humans: homeless people, their shopping carts and bedrolls, Black people, Chinese people, Chicanos, drag queens and punks, vets down on Portland's Burnside Avenue, white men in their wool suits, limos shined to sparkle. I watched them all sucking in the thick weave of Spanish, Cantonese, street talk, English. This is how I became aware of my whiteness.

My queer body: I spent my childhood, a tomboy not sure of my girl-ness, queer without a name for my queerness. I cut firewood on clearcuts, swam in the river, ran the beaches at Battle Rock and Cape Blanco. When I found dykes, fell in love for the first time, came into a political queer community, I felt as if I had found home again.

The body as home, but only if it is understood that bodies are never singular, but rather haunted, strengthened, underscored by countless other bodies. My alcoholic, Libertarian father and his father, the gravedigger, from whom my father learned his violence. I still dream about them sometimes, ugly dreams that leave me panting with fear in the middle of the night. One day I will be done with them. The white, working-class loggers, fishermen, and ranchers I grew up among: Les Smith, John Black, Walt Maya. Their ways of dressing, moving, talking helped shape my sense of self. Today when I hear queer activists say the word *redneck* like a cuss word, I think of those men, backs of their necks turning red in the summertime from long days of work outside, felling trees, pulling fishnets, baling hay. I think of my butchness, grounded there, overlaid by a queer, urban sensibility. A body of white, rural, working-class values. I still feel an allegiance to this body, even as I reject the virulent racism, the unexamined destruction of forest and river. How could I possibly call my body home without the bodies of trees that repeatedly provided me refuge? Without queer bodies? Without crip bodies? Without transgendered and transsexual bodies? Without the history of disabled people who worked as freaks in the freak show, displaying their bodies: Charles Stratton posed as General Tom Thumb, Hiriam and Barney Davis billed as the "Wild Men from Borneo"? The answer is simple. I couldn't.

The body as home, but only if it is understood that place and community and culture burrow deep into our bones. My earliest and most enduring sense of place is in the backwoods of Oregon, where I grew up but no longer live, in a logging and fishing town of a thousand that hangs on to the most western edge of the continental United States. To the west stretches the Pacific Ocean; to the east the Siskiyou Mountains rise, not tall enough to be mountains but too steep to be hills. Portland is a seven-hour drive north; San Francisco, a twelve-hour drive south. Home for me is marked by Douglas fir and chinook salmon, south wind whipping the ocean into a fury of waves and surf. Marked by the aching knowledge of environmental destruction, the sad truth of that town founded on the genocide of Native peoples, the Tuni and Coquille, Talkemas and Latgawas. In writing about the backwoods and the rural, white, working-class culture found there, I am not being nostalgic, reaching backward toward a re-creation of the past. Rather I am reaching toward my bones. When I write about losing that place, about living in exile, I am putting words to a loss which also grasps at my bones.

The body as home, but only if it is understood that language too lives under the skin. I think of the words *crip, queer, freak, redneck*. None of these are easy words. They mark the jagged edge between self-hatred and pride, the chasm between how the dominant culture views marginalized peoples and how we view ourselves, the razor between finding home, finding our bodies, and living in exile, living on the metaphoric mountain. Whatever our relationships with these words—whether we embrace them or hate them, feel them draw blood as they hit our skin or find them entirely fitting, refuse to say them or simply feel uncomfortable in their presence—we deal with their power every day. I hear these words all the time. They are whispered in the mirror as I dress to go out, as I straighten my tie and shrug into my suit jacket; on the streets as folks gawk at my trembling hands, stare trying to figure out whether I'm a woman or man; in half the rhetoric I hear from environmentalists and queer activists, rhetoric where rural working-class people get cast as clods and bigots. At the same time, I use some, but not all, of these words to call out my pride, to strengthen my resistance, to place myself within community. *Crip, queer, freak, redneck* burrowed into my body.

The body as home, but only if it is understood that bodies can be stolen, fed lies and poison, torn away from us. They rise up around me—bodies stolen by hunger, war, breast cancer, AIDS, rape; the daily grind of factory, sweatshop, cannery, sawmill; the lynching rope; the freezing streets; the nursing home and prison. African-American drag performer Leonard/Lynn Vines, walking through his Baltimore neighborhood, called a "drag queen faggot bitch" and shot six times. Matt Sheppard—gay, white, young—tied to a fence post in Wyoming and beaten to death. Some bodies are taken for good; other bodies live on, numb, abandoned, full of self-hate. Both have been stolen. Disabled people cast as supercrips and tragedies; lesbian/gay/bisexual/trans people told over and over again that we are twisted and unnatural; poor people made responsible for their own poverty. Stereotypes and lies lodge in our bodies as surely as bullets. They live and fester there, stealing the body.

The body as home, but only if it is understood that the stolen body can be reclaimed. The bodies irrevocably taken from us: we can memorialize them in quilts, granite walls, candlelight vigils; remember and mourn them; use their deaths to strengthen our will. And as for the lies and false images, we need to name them, transform them, create something entirely new in their place, something that comes close and finally true to the bone, entering our bodies as liberation, joy, fury, hope, a will to refigure the world. The body as home.

The mountain will never be home, and still I have to remember it grips me. Supercrip lives inside my body, ready and willing to push the physical limitations, to try the "extraordinary," because down at the base of the mountain waits a nursing home. I hang on to a vision. Someday after the revolution, disabled people will live ordinary lives, neither heroic nor tragic. *Crip, queer, freak, redneck* will be mere words describing human difference. Supercrip will be dead; the nursing home, burnt down; the metaphoric mountain, collapsed in volcanic splendor. Post-revolution I expect there will still be literal mountains I want to climb and can't, but I'll be able to say without doubt, without hesitation, "Let's turn around here. This one is too steep, too slippery for my feet."

The Science of Shopping

Malcolm Gladwell

In "The Science of Shopping," Malcolm Gladwell takes us into the world of urban anthropology. We're introduced to a guru of voyeurism, Paco Underhill, known to his mother as "the best paid spy in America." Underhill is one of the leaders in the multibillion-dollar business of dissecting American consumers, a borderline invasive practice that includes hidden cameras and "anthropologists who sift through garbage of carefully targeted households to analyze their true consumption patterns" in order to understand and conform to the whims and desires of the consumer. How does the perpetuation of class and gender-specific marketing strategies affect our culture? And what do we make of Gladwell's biting summation of the results: that sellers have learned "to treat male shoppers like small children, to respect the female derriere, and to put the socks between the cash/wrap and the men's pants?"

1.

Human beings walk the way they drive, which is to say that Americans tend to keep to the right when they stroll down shopping-mall concourses or city sidewalks. This is why in a well-designed airport travellers drifting toward their gate will always find the fast-food restaurants on their left and the gift shops on their right: people will readily cross a lane of pedestrian traffic to satisfy their hunger but rarely to make an impulse buy of a T-shirt or a magazine. This is also why Paco Underhill tells his retail clients to make sure that their window displays are canted, preferably to both sides but especially to the left, so that a potential shopper approaching the store on the inside of the sidewalk—the shopper, that is, with the least impeded view of the store window—can see the display from at least twenty-five feet away.

Of course, a lot depends on how fast the potential shopper is walking. Paco, in his previous life, as an urban geographer in Manhattan, spent a great deal of time thinking about walking speeds as he listened in on the great debates of the nineteen-seventies over whether the traffic lights in midtown should be timed to facilitate the movement of cars or to facilitate

From *The New Yorker.* Copyright © 1996 by Malcolm Gladwell. Reprinted by permission.

the movement of pedestrians and so break up the big platoons that move down Manhattan sidewalks. He knows that the faster you walk the more your peripheral vision narrows, so you become unable to pick up visual cues as quickly as someone who is just ambling along. He knows, too, that people who walk fast take a surprising amount of time to slow down—just as it takes a good stretch of road to change gears with a stick-shift automobile. On the basis of his research, Paco estimates the human downshift period to be anywhere from twelve to twenty-five feet, so if you own a store, he says, you never want to be next door to a bank: potential shoppers speed up when they walk past a bank (since there's nothing to look at), and by the time they slow down they've walked right past your business. The downshift factor also means that when potential shoppers enter a store it's going to take them from five to fifteen paces to adjust to the light and refocus and gear down from walking speed to shopping speed—particularly if they've just had to navigate a treacherous parking lot or hurry to make the light at Fifty-seventh and Fifth.

Paco calls that area inside the door the Decompression Zone, and something he tells clients over and over again is never, ever put anything of value in that zone—not shopping baskets or tie racks or big promotional displays—because no one is going to see it. Paco believes that, as a rule of thumb, customer interaction with any product or promotional display in the Decompression Zone will increase at least thirty percent once it's moved to the back edge of the zone, and even more if it's placed to the right, because another of the fundamental rules of how human beings shop is that upon entering a store—whether it's Nordstrom or K mart, Tiffany or the Gap—the shopper invariably and reflexively turns to the right. Paco believes in the existence of the Invariant Right because he has actually verified it. He has put cameras in stores trained directly on the doorway, and if you go to his office, just above Union Square, where videocassettes and boxes of Super-eight film from all his work over the years are stacked in plastic Tupperware containers practically up to the ceiling, he can show you reel upon reel of grainy entryway video-customers striding in the door, downshifting, refocusing, and then, again and again, making that little half turn.

Paco Underhill is a tall man in his mid-forties, partly bald, with a neatly trimmed beard and an engaging, almost goofy manner. He wears baggy khakis and shirts open at the collar, and generally looks like the academic he might have been if he hadn't been captivated, twenty years ago, by the ideas of the urban anthropologist William Whyte. It was Whyte who pioneered the use of time-lapse photography as a tool of urban planning, putting cameras in parks and the plazas in front of office buildings in midtown Manhattan, in order to determine what distinguished a public space that worked from one that didn't. As a Columbia undergraduate, in 1974, Paco heard a lecture on Whyte's work and, he recalls, left the room "walking on air." He immediately read everything Whyte had written. He emptied his bank account to buy cameras and film and make his own home movie, about a pedestrian mall in Poughkeepsie. He took his "little exercise" to Whyte's advocacy group, the Project for Public Spaces, and was offered a job. Soon, however, it dawned on Paco that Whyte's ideas could be taken a step further—that the same techniques he used to establish why a plaza worked or didn't work could also be used to determine why a store worked or didn't work. Thus was born the field of retail anthropology, and, not long afterward, Paco founded Envirosell, which in just over fifteen years has counselled some of the most familiar names in American retailing, from Levi Strauss to Kinney, Starbucks, McDonald's, Blockbuster, Apple Computer, A.T. & T., and a number of upscale retailers that Paco would rather not name.

When Paco gets an assignment, he and his staff set up a series of video cameras throughout the test store and then back the cameras up with Envirosell staffers—trackers, as they're known—armed with clipboards. Where the cameras go and how many trackers Paco deploys depends on exactly what the store wants to know about its shoppers. Typically, though, he might use six cameras and two or three trackers, and let the study run for two or three days, so that at the end he would have pages and pages of carefully annotated tracking sheets and anywhere from a hundred to five hundred hours of film. These days, given the expansion of his business, he might tape fifteen thousand hours in a year, and, given that he has been in operation since the late seventies, he now has well over a hundred thousand hours of tape in his library. Even in the best of times, this would be a valuable archive. But today, with the retail business in crisis, it is a gold mine. The time per visit that the average American spends in a shopping mall was sixty-six minutes last year—down from seventy-two minutes in 1992—and is the lowest number ever recorded. The amount of selling space per American shopper is now more than double what it was in the mid-seventies, meaning that profit margins have never been narrower, and the costs of starting a retail business—and of failing—have never been higher. In the past few years, countless dazzling new retailing temples have been built along Fifth and Madison Avenues—Barneys, Calvin Klein, Armani, Valentino, Banana Republic, Prada, Chanel, Nike Town, and on and on— but it is an explosion of growth based on no more than a hunch, a hopeful multimillion-dollar gamble that the way to break through is to provide the shopper with spectacle and more spectacle. "The arrogance is gone," Millard Drexler, the president and CEO of the Gap, told me. "Arrogance makes failure. Once you think you know the answer, it's almost always over." In such a competitive environment, retailers don't just want to know how shoppers behave in their stores. They have to know. And who better to ask than Paco Underhill, who in the past decade and a half has analyzed tens of thousands of hours of shopping videotape and, as a result, probably knows more about the strange habits and quirks of the species *Emptor americanus* than anyone else alive?

2.

Paco is considered the originator, for example, of what is known in the trade as the butt-brush theory—or, as Paco calls it, more delicately, le facteur bousculade—which holds that the likelihood of a woman's being converted from a browser to a buyer is inversely proportional to the likelihood of her being brushed on her behind while she's examining merchandise. Touch—or brush or bump or jostle—a woman on the behind when she has stopped to look at an item, and she will bolt. Actually, calling this a theory is something of a misnomer, because Paco doesn't offer any explanation for why women react that way, aside from venturing that they are "more sensitive back there." It's really an observation, based on repeated and close analysis of his videotape library, that Paco has transformed into a retailing commandment: a women's product that requires extensive examination should never be placed in a narrow aisle.

Paco approaches the problem of the Invariant Right the same way. Some retail thinkers see this as a subject crying out for interpretation and speculation. The design guru Joseph Weishar, for example, argues, in his magisterial "Design for Effective Selling Space," that the Invariant Right is a function of the fact that we "absorb and digest information in the left part of the brain" and "assimilate and logically use this information in the right half," the result being that we scan the store from left to right and then fix on an object to the right "essentially at a 45 degree angle from the point that we enter." When I asked Paco about this interpretation, he shrugged, and said he thought the reason was simply that most people are right-handed. Uncovering the fundamentals of "why" is clearly not a pursuit that engages him much. He is not a theoretician but an empiricist, and for him the important thing is that in amassing his huge library of in-store time-lapse photography he has gained enough hard evidence to know how often and under what circumstances the Invariant Right is expressed and how to take advantage of it.

What Paco likes are facts. They come tumbling out when he talks, and, because he speaks with a slight hesitation—lingering over the first syllable in, for example, "re-tail" or "de-sign"—he draws you in, and you find yourself truly hanging on his words. "We have reached a historic point in American history," he told me in our very first conversation. "Men, for the first time, have begun to buy their own underwear." He then paused to let the comment sink in, so that I could absorb its implications, before he elaborated: "Which means that we have to totally rethink the way we sell that product." In the parlance of Hollywood scriptwriters, the best endings must be surprising and yet inevitable; and the best of Paco's pronouncements take the same shape. It would never have occurred to me to wonder about the increasingly critical role played by touching—or, as Paco calls it, petting—clothes in the course of making the decision to buy them. But then I went to the Gap and to Banana Republic and saw people touching and fondling and, one after another, buying shirts and sweaters laid out on big wooden tables, and what Paco told me—which was no doubt based on what he had seen on his videotapes—made perfect sense: that the reason the Gap and Banana Republic have tables is not merely that sweaters and shirts look better there, or that tables fit into the warm and relaxing residential feeling that the Gap and Banana Republic are trying to create in their stores, but that tables invite—indeed, symbolize—touching. "Where do we eat?" Paco asks. "We eat, we pick up food, on tables."

Paco produces for his clients a series of carefully detailed studies, totalling forty to a hundred and fifty pages, filled with product-by-product breakdowns and bright-colored charts and graphs. In one recent case, he was asked by a major clothing retailer to analyze the first of a new chain of stores that the firm planned to open. One of the things the client wanted to know was how successful the store was in drawing people into its depths, since the chances that shoppers will buy something are directly related to how long they spend shopping, and how long they spend shopping is directly related to how deep they get pulled into the store. For this reason, a supermarket will often put dairy products on one side, meat at the back, and fresh produce on the other side, so that the typical shopper can't just do a drive-by but has to make an entire circuit of the store, and be tempted by everything the supermarket has to offer. In the case of the new clothing store, Paco found that ninety-one percent of all shoppers penetrated as deep as what he called Zone 4, meaning more than three-quarters of the way in, well past the accessories and shirt racks and belts in the front, and little short of the far wall, with the changing rooms and the pants stacked on shelves. Paco regarded this as an extraordinary figure, particularly for a long, narrow store like this one, where it is not unusual for the rate of penetration past, say, Zone 3 to be under fifty percent. But that didn't mean the store was perfect—far from it. For Paco, all kinds of questions remained.

Purchasers, for example, spent an average of eleven minutes and twenty-seven seconds in the store, nonpurchasers two minutes and thirty-six seconds. It wasn't that the nonpurchasers just cruised in and out: in those two minutes and thirty-six seconds, they went deep into the store and examined an average of 3.42 items. So why didn't they buy? What, exactly, happened to cause some browsers to buy and other browsers to walk out the door?

Then, there was the issue of the number of products examined. The purchasers were looking at an average of 4.81 items but buying only 1.33 items. Paco found this statistic deeply disturbing. As the retail market grows more cutthroat, store owners have come to realize that it's all but impossible to increase the number of customers coming in, and have concentrated instead on getting the customers they do have to buy more. Paco thinks that if you can sell someone a pair of pants you must also be able to sell that person a belt, or a pair of socks, or a pair of underpants, or even do what the Gap does so well: sell a person a complete outfit. To Paco, the figure 1.33 suggested that the store was doing something very wrong, and one day when I visited him in his office he sat me down in front of one of his many VCRs to see how he looked for the 1.33 culprit.

It should be said that sitting next to Paco is a rather strange experience. "My mother says that I'm the best-paid spy in America," he told me. He laughed, but he wasn't entirely joking. As a child, Paco had a nearly debilitating stammer, and, he says, "since I was never that comfortable talking I always relied on my eyes to understand things." That much is obvious from the first moment you meet him: Paco is one of those people who look right at you, soaking up every nuance and detail. It isn't a hostile gaze, because Paco isn't hostile at all. He has a big smile, and he'll call you "chief" and use your first name a lot and generally act as if he knew you well. But that's the awkward thing: he has looked at you so closely that you're sure he does know you well, and you, meanwhile, hardly know him at all.

This kind of asymmetry is even more pronounced when you watch his shopping videos with him, because every movement or gesture means something to Paco—he has spent his adult life deconstructing the shopping experience—but nothing to the outsider, or, at least, not at first. Paco had to keep stopping the video to get me to see things through his eyes before I began to understand. In one sequence, for example, a camera mounted high on the wall outside the changing rooms documented a man and a woman shopping for a pair of pants for what appeared to be their daughter, a girl in her mid-teens. The tapes are soundless, but the basic steps of the shopping dance are so familiar to Paco that, once I'd grasped the general idea, he was able to provide a running commentary on what was being said and thought. There is the girl emerging from the changing room wearing her first pair. There she is glancing at her reflection in the mirror, then turning to see herself from the back. There is the mother looking on. There is the father—or, as fathers are known in the trade, the "wallet carrier"—stepping forward and pulling up the jeans. There's the girl trying on another pair. There's the primp again. The twirl. The mother. The wallet carrier. And then again, with another pair. The full sequence lasted twenty minutes, and at the end came the take-home lesson, for which Paco called in one of his colleagues, Tom Moseman, who had supervised the project.

"This is a very critical moment," Tom, a young, intense man wearing little round glasses, said, and he pulled up a chair next to mine. "She's saying, 'I don't know whether I should wear a belt.' Now here's the salesclerk. The girl says to him, 'I need a belt,' and he says, 'Take mine.' Now there he is taking her back to the full-length mirror."

A moment later, the girl returns, clearly happy with the purchase. She wants the jeans. The wallet carrier turns to her, and then gestures to the salesclerk. The wallet carrier is telling his daughter to give back the belt. The girl gives back the belt. Tom stops the tape. He's leaning forward now, a finger jabbing at the screen. Beside me, Paco is shaking his head. I don't get it—at least, not at first—and so Tom replays that last segment. The wallet carrier tells the girl to give back the belt. She gives back the belt. And then, finally, it dawns on me why this store has an average purchase number of only 1.33. "Don't you see?" Tom said. *"She wanted the belt.* A great opportunity to make an add-on sale . . . *lost!"*

3.

Should we be afraid of Paco Underhill? One of the fundamental anxieties of the American consumer, after all, has always been that beneath the pleasure and the frivolity of the shopping experience runs an undercurrent of manipulation, and that anxiety has rarely seemed more justified than today. The practice of prying into the minds and habits of American consumers is now a multibillion-dollar business. Every time a product is pulled across a supermarket checkout scanner, information is recorded, assembled, and sold to a market-research firm for analysis. There are companies that put tiny cameras inside frozen-food cases in supermarket aisles; market-research firms that feed census data and behavioral statistics into algorithms and come out with complicated maps of the American consumer; anthropologists who sift through the garbage of carefully targeted households to analyze their true consumption patterns; and endless rounds of highly organized focus groups and questionnaire takers and phone survey-ors. That some people are now tracking our every shopping move with video cameras seems in many respects the last straw: Paco's movies are, after all, creepy. They look like the surveillance videos taken during con-venience-store holdups—hazy and soundless and slightly warped by the angle of the lens. When you watch them, you find yourself waiting for something bad to happen, for someone to shoplift or pull a gun on a cashier.

The more time you spend with Paco's videos, though, the less scary they seem. After an hour or so, it's no longer clear whether simply by watching people shop—and analyzing their every move—you can learn how to control them. The shopper that emerges from the videos is not pli-able or manipulable. The screen shows people filtering in and out of stores, petting and moving on, abandoning their merchandise because checkout lines are too long, or leaving a store empty-handed because they couldn't fit their stroller into the aisle between two shirt racks. Paco's shoppers are fickle and headstrong, and are quite unwilling to buy anything unless condi-tions are perfect—unless the belt is presented at exactly the right moment. His theories of the butt-brush and petting and the Decompression Zone and the Invariant Right seek not to make shoppers conform to the desires of sell-ers but to make sellers conform to the desires of shoppers. What Paco is teaching his clients is a kind of slavish devotion to the shopper's every whim. He is teaching them humility.

Paco has worked with supermarket chains, and when you first see one of his videos of grocery aisles it looks as if he really had—at least in this instance—got one up on the shopper. The clip he showed me was of a father shopping with a small child, and it was an example of what is known in the trade as "advocacy," which basically means what happens when your four-year-old goes over and grabs a bag of cookies that the store has conveniently put on the bottom shelf, and demands that it be purchased. In the clip, the father takes what the child offers him. "Generally, dads are not as good as moms at saying no," Paco said as we watched the little boy approach his dad. "Men tend to be more impulse-driven than women in grocery stores. We know that they tend to shop less often with a list. We know that they tend to shop much less frequently with coupons, and we know, simply by watch-ing them shop, that they can be marching down the aisle and something will catch their eye and they will stop and buy." This kind of weakness on the part of fathers might seem to give the supermarket an advantage in the cookie-selling wars, particularly since more and more men go grocery shop-ping with their children. But then Paco let drop a hint about a study he'd just done in which he discovered, to his and everyone else's amazement, that shoppers had already figured this out, that they were already one step ahead—that *families were avoiding the cookie aisle.*

This may seem like a small point. But it begins to explain why, even though retailers seem to know more than ever about how shoppers behave, even though their efforts at intelligence-gathering have rarely seemed more intrusive and more formidable, the retail business remains in crisis. The reason is that shoppers are a moving target. They are becoming more and more complicated, and retailers need to know more and more about them simply to keep pace.

This fall, for example, Estée Lauder is testing in a Toronto shopping mall a new concept in cosmetics retailing. Gone is the enclosed rectangular counter, with the sales staff on one side, customers on the other, and the product under glass in the middle. In its place the company has provided an assortment of product-display, consultation, and testing kiosks arranged in a broken circle, with a service desk and a cashier in the middle. One of the kiosks is a "makeup play area," which allows customers to experiment on their own with a hundred and thirty different shades of lipstick. There are four self-service displays—for perfumes, skin-care products, and makeup—which are easily accessible to customers who have already made up their minds. And, for those who haven't, there is a semiprivate booth for personal consultations with beauty advisers and makeup artists. The redesign was prompted by the realization that the modern working woman no longer had the time or the inclination to ask a salesclerk to assist her in every purchase, that choosing among shades of lipstick did not require the same level of service as, say, getting up to speed on new developments in skin care, that a shopper's needs were now too diverse to be adequately served by just one kind of counter.

"I was going from store to store, and the traffic just wasn't there," Robin Burns, the president and C.E.O. of Estée Lauder U.S.A. and Canada, told me. "We had to get rid of the glass barricade." The most interesting thing about the new venture, though, is what it says about the shifting balance of power between buyer and seller. Around the old rectangular counter, the relationship of clerk to customer was formal and subtly paternalistic. If you wanted to look at a lipstick, you had to ask for it. "Twenty years ago, the sales staff would consult with you and tell you what you needed, as opposed to asking and recommending," Burns said. "And in those days people believed what the salesperson told them." Today, the old hierarchy has been inverted. "Women want to draw their own conclusions," Burns said. Even the architecture of the consultation kiosk speaks to the transformation: the beauty adviser now sits beside the customer, not across from her.

4.

This doesn't mean that marketers and retailers have stopped trying to figure out what goes on in the minds of shoppers. One of the hottest areas in market research, for example, is something called typing, which is a sophisticated attempt to predict the kinds of products that people will buy or the kind of promotional pitch they will be susceptible to on the basis of where they live or how they score on short standardized questionnaires. One market-research firm in Virginia, Claritas, has divided the entire country, neighborhood by neighborhood, into sixty-two different categories—Pools & Patios, Shotguns & Pickups, Bohemia Mix, and so on—using census data and results from behavioral surveys. On the basis of my address in Greenwich Village, Claritas classifies me as Urban Gold Coast, which means that I like Kellogg's Special K, spend more than two hundred and fifty dollars on sports coats, watch *Seinfeld,* and buy metal polish. Such typing systems—and there are a number of them—can be scarily accurate. I actually do buy Kellogg's Special K, have spent more than two hundred and fifty dollars on a sports coat, and watch *Seinfeld.* (I don't buy metal polish.) In fact, when I was typed by a company called Total Research, in Princeton, the results were so dead-on that I got the same kind of creepy feeling that I got when I first watched Paco's videos. On the basis of a seemingly innocuous multiple-choice test, I was scored as an eighty-nine-percent Intellect and a seven-percent Relief Seeker (which I thought was impressive until John Morton, who developed the system, told me that virtually everyone who reads *The New Yorker* is an Intellect). When I asked Morton to guess, on the basis of my score, what kind of razor I used, he riffed, brilliantly, and without a moment's hesitation. "If you used an electric razor, it would be a Braun," he began. "But, if not, you're probably shaving with Gillette, if only because there really isn't an Intellect safety-razor positioning out there. Schick and Bic are simply not logical choices for you, although I'm thinking, You're fairly young, and you've got that Relief Seeker side. It's possible you would use Bic because you don't like that all-American, overly confident masculine statement of Gillette. It's a very, very conventional positioning that Gillette uses. But then they've got the technological angle with the Gillette Sensor. . . . I'm thinking Gillette. It's Gillette."

He was right. I shave with Gillette—though I didn't even know that I do. I had to go home and check. But information about my own predilections may be of limited usefulness in predicting how I shop. In the past few years, market researchers have paid growing attention to the role in the shopping experience of a type of consumer known as a Market Maven.

"This is a person you would go to for advice on a car or a new fashion," said Linda Price, a marketing professor at the University of South Florida, who first came up with the Market Maven concept, in the late eighties. "This is a person who has information on a lot of different products or prices or places to shop. This is a person who likes to initiate discussions with consumers and respond to requests. Market Mavens like to be helpers in the marketplace. They take you shopping. They go shopping for you, and it turns out they are a lot more prevalent than you would expect." Mavens watch more television than almost anyone else does, and they read more magazines and open their junk mail and look closely at advertisements and have an awful lot of influence on everyone else. According to Price, sixty percent of Americans claim to know a Maven.

The key question, then, is not what I think but what my Mavens think. The challenge for retailers and marketers, in turn, is not so much to figure out and influence my preferences as to figure out and influence the preferences of my Mavens, and that is a much harder task. "What's really interesting is that the distribution of Mavens doesn't vary by ethnic category, by income, or by professional status," Price said. "A working woman is just as likely to be a Market Maven as a nonworking woman. You might say that Mavens are likely to be older, unemployed people, but that's wrong, too. There is simply not a clear demographic guide to how to find these people." More important, Mavens are better consumers than most of the rest of us. In another of the typing systems, developed by the California-based SRI International, Mavens are considered to be a subcategory of the consumer type known as Fulfilled, and Fulfilleds, one SRI official told me, are "the consumers from Hell—they are very feature oriented." He explained, "They are not pushed by promotions. You can reach them, but it's an intellectual argument." As the complexity of the marketplace grows, in other words, we have responded by appointing the most skeptical and the most savvy in our midst to mediate between us and sellers. The harder stores and manufacturers work to sharpen and refine their marketing strategies, and the harder they try to read the minds of shoppers, the more we hide behind Mavens.

5.

Imagine that you want to open a clothing store, men's and women's, in the upper-middle range—say, khakis at fifty dollars, dress shirts at forty dollars, sports coats and women's suits at two hundred dollars and up. The work of Paco Underhill would suggest that in order to succeed you need to pay complete and concentrated attention to the whims of your customers. What does that mean, in practical terms? Well, let's start with what's called the shopping gender gap. In the retail-store study that Paco showed me, for example, male buyers stayed an average of nine minutes and thirty-nine seconds in the store and female buyers stayed twelve minutes and fifty-seven seconds. This is not atypical. Women always shop longer than men, which is one of the major reasons that in the standard regional mall women account for seventy per cent of the dollar value of all purchases. "Women have more patience than men," Paco says. "Men are more distractible. Their tolerance level for confusion or time spent in a store is much shorter than women's." If you wanted, then, you could build a store designed for men, to try to raise that thirty-percent sales figure to forty or forty-five percent. You could make the look more masculine—more metal, darker woods. You could turn up the music. You could simplify the store, put less product on the floor. "I'd go narrow and deep," says James Adams, the design director for NBBJ Retail Concepts, a division of one of the country's largest retail-design firms. "You wouldn't have fifty different cuts of pants. You'd have your four basics with lots of color. You know the Garanimals they used to do to help kids pick out clothes, where you match the giraffe top with the giraffe bottom? I'm sure every guy is like 'I wish I could get those, too.' You'd want to stick with the basics. Making sure most of the color story goes together. That is a big deal with guys, because they are always screwing the colors up." When I asked Carrie Gennuso, the Gap's regional vice-president for New York, what she would do in an all-male store, she laughed and said, "I might do fewer displays and more signage. Big signs. Men! Smalls! Here!"

As a rule, though, you wouldn't want to cater to male customers at the expense of female ones. It's no accident that many clothing stores have a single look in both men's and women's sections, and that the quintessential nineties look—light woods, white walls—is more feminine than masculine. Women are still the shoppers in America, and the real money is to be made by making retailing styles more female-friendly, not less. Recently, for example, NBBJ did a project to try to increase sales of the Armstrong flooring chain. Its researchers found that the sales staff was selling the flooring based on its functional virtues—the fact that it didn't scuff, that it was long-lasting, that it didn't stain, that it was easy to clean. It was being sold by men to men, as if it were a car or a stereo. And that was the problem. "It's a wonder product technologically," Adams says. "But the woman is the decision-maker on flooring, and that's not what's she's looking for. This product is about fashion, about color and design. You don't want to get too caught up in the man's way of thinking."

To appeal to men, then, retailers do subtler things. At the Banana Republic store on Fifth Avenue in midtown, the men's socks are displayed near the shoes and between men's pants and the cash register (or cash/wrap, as it is known in the trade), so that the man can grab them easily as he rushes to pay. Women's accessories are by the fitting rooms, because women are much more likely to try on pants first, and then choose an item like a belt or a bag. At the men's shirt table, the display shirts have matching ties on them—the tie table is next to it—in a grownup version of the Garanimals system. But Banana Republic would never match scarves with women's blouses or jackets. "You don't have to be that direct with women," Jeanne Jackson, the president of Banana Republic, told me. "In fact, the Banana woman is proud of her sense of style. She puts her own looks together." Jackson said she liked the Fifth Avenue store because it's on two floors, so she can separate men's and women's sections and give men what she calls "clarity of offer," which is the peace of mind that they won't inadvertently end up in, say, women's undergarments. In a one-floor store, most retailers would rather put the menswear up front and the women's wear at the back (that is, if they weren't going to split the sexes left and right), because women don't get spooked navigating through apparel of the opposite sex, whereas men most assuredly do. (Of course, in a store like the Gap at Thirty-ninth and Fifth, where, Carrie Gennuso says, "I don't know if I've ever seen a man," the issue is moot. There, it's safe to put the women's wear out front.)

The next thing retailers want to do is to encourage the shopper to walk deep into the store. The trick there is to put "destination items"—basics, staples, things that people know you have and buy a lot of—at the rear of the store. Gap stores, invariably, will have denim, which is a classic destination item for them, on the back wall. Many clothing stores also situate the cash/wrap and the fitting rooms in the rear of the store, to compel shoppers to walk back into Zone 3 or 4. In the store's prime real estate—which, given Paco's theory of the Decompression Zone and the Invariant Right, is to the right of the front entrance and five to fifteen paces in—you always put your hottest and newest merchandise, because that's where the maximum number of people will see it. Right now, in virtually every Gap in the country, the front of the store is devoted to the Gap fall look—casual combinations in black and gray, plaid shirts and jackets, sweaters, black wool and brushed-twill pants. At the Gap at Fifth Avenue and Seventeenth Street, for example, there is a fall ensemble of plaid jacket, plaid shirt, and black pants in the first prime spot, followed, three paces later, by an ensemble of gray sweater, plaid shirt, T-shirt, and black pants, followed, three paces after that, by an ensemble of plaid jacket, gray sweater, white T-shirt, and black pants. In all, three variations on the same theme, each placed so that the eye bounces naturally from the first to the second to the third, and then, inexorably, to a table deep inside Zone 1 where merchandise is arrayed and folded for petting. Every week or ten days, the combinations will change, the "look" highlighted at the front will be different, and the entryway will be transformed.

Through all of this, the store environment—the lighting, the colors, the fixtures—and the clothes have to work together. The point is not so much beauty as coherence. The clothes have to match the environment. "In the nineteen-seventies, you didn't have to have a complete wardrobe all the time," Gabriella Forte, the president and chief operating officer of Calvin Klein, says. "I think now the store has to have a complete point of view. It has to have all the options offered, so people have choices. It's the famous one-stop shopping. People want to come in, be serviced, and go out. They want to understand the clear statement the designer is making."

At the new Versace store on Fifth Avenue, in the restored neoclassical Vanderbilt mansion, Gianni Versace says that the "statement" he is making with the elaborate mosaic and parquet floors, the marble façade and the Corinthian columns is "quality—my message is always a scream for quality." At her two new stores in London, Donna Karan told me, she never wants "customers to think that they are walking into a clothing store." She said, "I want them to think that they are walking into an environment, that I am transforming them out of their lives and into an experience, that it's not about clothes, it's about who they are as people." The first thing the shopper sees in her stark, all-white DKNY store is a video monitor and café: "It's about energy," Karan said, "and nourishment." In her more sophisticated, "collection" store, where the walls are black and ivory and gold, the first thing that the customer notices is the scent of a candle: "I wanted a nurturing environment where you feel that you will be taken care of." And why, at a Giorgio Armani store, is there often only a single suit in each style on display? Not because the store has only the one suit in stock but because the way the merchandise is displayed has to be consistent with the message of the designers: that Armani suits are exclusive, that the Armani customer isn't going to run into another man wearing his suit every time he goes to an art opening at Gagosian.

The best stores all have an image—or what retailers like to call a "point of view." The flagship store for Ralph Lauren's Polo collection, for example, is in the restored Rhinelander mansion, on Madison Avenue and Seventy-second Street. The Polo Mansion, as it is known, is alive with color and artifacts that suggest a notional prewar English gentility. There are fire-places and comfortable leather chairs and deep-red Oriental carpets and soft, thick drapes and vintage photographs and paintings of country squires and a color palette of warm crimsons and browns and greens—to the point that after you've picked out a double-breasted blazer or a cashmere sweater set or an antique silver snuffbox you feel as though you ought to venture over to Central Park for a vigorous morning of foxhunting. The Calvin Klein flagship store, twelve blocks down Madison Avenue, on the other hand, is a vast, achingly beautiful minimalist temple, with white walls, muted lighting, soaring ceilings, gray stone flooring, and, so it seems, less merchandise in the entire store than Lauren puts in a single room. The store's architect, John Pawson, says, "People who enter are given a sense of release. They are getting away from the hustle and bustle of the street and New York. They are in a calm space. It's a modern idea of luxury, to give people space."

The first thing you see when you enter the Polo Mansion is a display of two hundred and eight sweaters, in twenty-eight colors, stacked in a haber-dasher's wooden fixture, behind an antique glass counter; the first thing you see at the Klein store is a white wall, and then, if you turn to the right, four clear-glass shelves, each adorned with three solitary-looking black handbags. The Polo Mansion is an English club. The Klein store, Pawson says, is the equivalent of an art gallery, a place where "neutral space and light make a work of art look the most potent." When I visited the Polo Mansion, the stereo was playing Bobby Short. At Klein, the stereo was playing what sounded like Brian Eno. At the Polo Mansion, I was taken around by Charles Fagan, a vice-president at Polo Ralph Lauren. He wore pale-yellow socks, black loafers, tight jeans, a pale-purple polo shirt, blue old-school tie, and a brown plaid jacket—which sounds less attractive on paper than it was in reality. He looked, in a very Ralph Lauren way, fabu-lous. He was funny and engaging and bounded through the store, keeping up a constant patter ("This room is sort of sportswear, Telluride-y, vin-tage"), all the while laughing and hugging people and having his freshly cut red hair tousled by the sales assistants in each section. At the Calvin Klein store, the idea that the staff—tall, austere, sombre-suited—might laugh and hug and tousle each other's hair is unthinkable. Lean over and whisper, per-haps. At the most, murmur discreetly into tiny black cellular phones. Visiting the Polo Mansion and the Calvin Klein flagship in quick succession is rather like seeing a "Howards End"–"The Seventh Seal" double feature.

Despite their differences, though, these stores are both about the same thing—communicating the point of view that shoppers are now thought to demand. At Polo, the "life style" message is so coherent and all-encompassing that the store never has the 1.33 items-per-purchase problem that Paco saw in the retailer he studied. "We have multiple purchases in excess—it's the cap, it's the tie, it's the sweater, it's the jacket, it's the pants," Fagan told me, plucking each item from its shelf and tossing it onto a tartan-covered bench seat. "People say, 'I have to have the belt.' It's a life-style decision."

As for the Klein store, it's really concerned with setting the tone for the Calvin Klein clothes and products sold outside the store—including the designer's phenomenally successful underwear line, the sales of which have grown nearly fivefold in the past two and a half years, making it one of the country's dominant brands. Calvin Klein underwear is partly a design triumph: lowering the waistband just a tad in order to elongate, and flatter, the torso. But it is also a triumph of image—transforming, as Gabriella Forte says, a "commodity good into something desirable," turning a forgotten necessity into fashion. In the case of women's underwear, Bob Mazzoli, president of Calvin Klein Underwear, told me that the company "obsessed about the box being a perfect square, about the symmetry of it all, how it would feel in a woman's hand." He added, "When you look at the boxes they are little works of art." And the underwear itself is without any of the usual busyness—without, in Mazzoli's words, "the excessive detail" of most women's undergarments. It's a clean look, selling primarily in white, heather gray, and black. It's a look, in other words, not unlike that of the Calvin Klein flagship store, and it exemplifies the brilliance of the merchandising of the Calvin Klein image: preposterous as it may seem, once you've seen the store and worn the underwear, it's difficult not to make a connection between the two.

All this imagemaking seeks to put the shopping experience in a different context, to give it a story line. "I wish that the customers who come to my stores feel the same comfort they would entering a friend's house—that is to say, that they feel at ease, without the impression of having to deal with the 'sanctum sanctorum' of a designer," Giorgio Armani told me. Armani has a house. Donna Karan has a kitchen and a womb. Ralph Lauren has a men's club. Calvin Klein has an art gallery. These are all very different points of view. What they have in common is that they have nothing to do with the actual act of shopping. (No one buys anything at a friend's house or a men's club.) Presumably, by engaging in this kind of misdirection designers aim to put us at ease, to create a kind of oasis. But perhaps they change the subject because they must, because they cannot offer an ultimate account of the shopping experience itself. After all, what do we really know, in the end, about why people buy? We know about the Invariant Right and the Decompression Zone. We know to put destination items at the back and fashion at the front, to treat male shoppers like small children, to respect the female derrière, and to put the socks between the cash/wrap and the men's pants. But this is grammar; it's not prose. It is enough. But it is not much.

6.

One of the best ways to understand the new humility in shopping theory is to go back to the work of William Whyte. Whyte put his cameras in parks and in the plazas in front of office buildings because he believed in the then radical notion that the design of public spaces had been turned inside out— that planners were thinking of their designs first and of people second, when they should have been thinking of people first and of design second. In his 1980 classic, *The Social Life of Small Urban Spaces,* for example, Whyte trained his cameras on a dozen or so of the public spaces and small parks around Manhattan, like the plaza in front of the General Motors Building, on Fifth Avenue, and the small park at 77 Water Street, down-town, and Paley Park, on Fifty-third Street, in order to determine why some, like the tiny Water Street park, averaged well over a hundred and fifty people during a typical sunny lunch hour and others, like the much bigger plaza at 280 Park Avenue, were almost empty. He concluded that all the things used by designers to attempt to lure people into their spaces made little or no difference. It wasn't the size of the space, or its beauty, or the presence of waterfalls, or the amount of sun, or whether a park was a narrow strip along the sidewalk or a pleasing open space. What mattered, overwhelmingly, was that there were plenty of places to sit, that the space was in some way connected to the street, and—the mystical circularity— that it was already well frequented. "What attracts people most, it would appear, is other people," Whyte noted:

> If I labor the point, it is because many urban spaces still are being designed as though the opposite were true—as though what people liked best were the places they stay away from. People often do talk along such lines, and therefore their responses to questionnaires can be entirely mis-leading. How many people would say they like to sit in the middle of a crowd? Instead, they speak of "getting away from it all," and use words like "escape," "oasis," "retreat." What people do, however, reveals a dif-ferent priority.

Whyte's conclusions demystified the question of how to make public space work. Places to sit, streets to enjoy, and people to watch turned out to be the simple and powerful rules for park designers to follow, and these rules demolished the orthodoxies and theoretical principles of conventional urban design. But in a more important sense—and it is here that Whyte's connection with Paco Underhill and retail anthropology and the stores that line Fifth and Madison is most striking—what Whyte did was to remystify the art of urban planning. He said, emphatically, that people could not be manipulated, that they would enter a public space only on their own terms, that the goal of observers like him was to find out what people wanted, not why they wanted it. Whyte, like Paco, was armed with all kinds of facts and observations about what it took to build a successful public space. He had strict views on how wide ledges had to be to lure passersby (at least thirty inches, or two backsides deep), and what the carrying capacity of prime outdoor sitting space is (total number of square feet divided by three). But, fundamentally, he was awed by the infinite complexity and the ultimate mystery of human behavior. He took people too seriously to think that he could control them. Here is Whyte, in *The Social Life of Small Urban Spaces,* analyzing hours of videotape and describing what he has observed about the way men stand in public. He's talking about feet. He could just as easily be talking about shopping:

> Foot movements . . . seem to be a silent language. Often, in a schmoozing group, no one will be saying anything. Men stand bound in amiable silence, surveying the passing scene. Then, slowly, rhythmically, one of the men rocks up and down; first on the ball of the foot, then back on the heel. He stops. Another man starts the same movement. Sometimes there are reciprocal gestures. One man makes a half turn to the right. Then, after a rhythmic interval, another responds with a half turn to the left. Some kind of communication seems to be taking place here, but I've never broken the code.

Flying Air Jordan: The Power of Racial Images

John Hoberman

John Hoberman has written extensively on how sport is used as a political tool of manipulation. In this introduction to his book, Darwin's Athletes: How Sport Has Damaged Black America and Preserved the Myth of Race, *he argues that sport and media have "become an image factory that disseminates and even intensifies our racial preoccupations." Hoberman examines how the media represents black males in four connected images: violent black athletes, violent black rappers, violent black criminals, and passive black "white wannabes." Ultimately, blacks are presented by the media "as [an] essentially physical and thus primitive people" reproducing a longer history of racism that emerged from slavery. Helping to perpetuate racist stereotypes, athleticism and violence are, Hoberman argues, presented by the media as the ultimate in African-American achievement. What is the importance of sport and media on how we think of racial identity? How does the media affect and create our taken-for-granted assumptions about race?*

The modern world is awash in images of black athletes. The airborne black body, its sinewy arms clutching a basketball as it soars high above the arena floor, has become the paramount symbol of athletic dynamism in the media age. Stereotypes of black athletic superiority are now firmly established as the most recent version of a racial folklore that has spread across the face of the earth over the past two centuries, and a corresponding belief in white athletic inferiority pervades popular thinking about racial difference. Such ideas about the "natural" physical talents of dark-skinned peoples, and the media-generated images that sustain them, probably do more than anything else in our public life to encourage the idea that blacks and whites are biologically different in a meaningful way. Prominent racial theorists of the 1990s such as Charles Murray and Dinesh D'Souza have declared that black athletic superiority is evidence of more profound differences. The

From *Darwin's Athletes* by John Hoberman. Copyright © 1997 by John Hoberman. Reprinted by permission of Houghton Mifflin Company. All rights reserved.

world of sport has thus become an image factory that disseminates and even intensifies our racial preoccupations. Centuries of racial classification have made exceptional athletes into ethnic specimens. "Are you a nigger or an Eskimo?" one racist sports fan asked the finest high school basketball player in Alaskan history, displaying a curiosity about human biology that is always latent in multiracial athletic encounters. Interracial sport has thus breathed new life into our racial folklore, reviving nineteenth-century ideas about the racial division of labor that then recur in a trend-setting book like *The Bell Curve*.

Ideas about racial athletic aptitude reign virtually uncontested outside the small number of classrooms in which they are examined. The idea that African Americans are the robust issue of slave-era breeding experiments has served the fantasy needs of blacks and whites alike. ("I propose," Ralph Ellison once wrote, "that we view the whole of American life as a drama acted out upon the body of a Negro giant.") "We were simply bred for physical qualities," the Olympic champion sprinter Lee Evans said in 1971, and better-educated black men have embraced the same eugenic fantasy. Decades of popular scientific speculation about the special endowments of black athletes have shaped the thinking of entire populations. White television sportscasters have long employed a special vocabulary to distinguish "natural" black athletes from "thinking" whites and have referred to black athletes as "monkeys" on more than one occasion. African-American college students who suddenly discover that their assumptions about "natural" black athleticism are illusory can feel as though they are waking from a dream. For their white counterparts too, critical scrutiny of racial stereotypes can take on the power of revelation, because it challenges conventional assumptions about the natural distribution of human abilities. The study of racialistic thinking changes people by exposing unconscious mental habits that permeate everyday life and shape our identities. Conversations with young blacks and whites reveal an unpublicized but thoroughly racialized social universe in which sport functions as a principal medium in which racial folklore flourishes. Here we find the schoolchild who cannot believe that the black college student who is his mentor is not a football player, since television has persuaded him that every black male student is an athlete; here too is the academically precocious child whose athletic skills save him from harassment by his black peers, whose hostility to intellectual development (and even "whitey's" habit of using seatbelts) only intensifies as they enter adolescence. Some black children still face overt hostility in interracial games. In east Texas in the 1990s, black junior high school boys sometimes play football against whites whose parents shout "Niggers!" from the stands as they watch their sons lose.

This racialized universe of everyday encounters receives far less attention than the highly public and officially deracialized theater of professional and collegiate sport, which white administrators present as an oasis of racial harmony. The sports media do not identify or investigate conflicts between blacks and whites, or they portray them as idiosyncratic episodes; young black athletes are immature rather than angry, while older white coaches are curmudgeons whose decency (if not always their authority) remains firmly intact. The realities of race are more evident in the unvarnished world of high school athletics, where far greater numbers of people engage in race relations, absorb ideas about racially specific traits and abilities, and grapple with their own racial dramas in athletic terms. Here, for example, we find a black nerd, the bookish son of a physician, whose conflicts about blackness prompt him to find his athletic identity in ice hockey and other "white" activities. A more common character is the young black athlete who is persuaded, at times by a black coach, that he or she enjoys a physical advantage over whites.

Such black self-confidence has contributed to self-doubts on the other side of the racial divide. A gifted white high school athlete told me that he found himself wondering why the muscles of some black teammates seem to be better defined than his own, and some white professionals are simply fatalistic about their ability to match up against blacks. "You have to be a realist," says Scott Brooks, a guard on the Dallas Mavericks basketball team. "White people can't jump as high." "There aren't many white guys who can jump the way they can," says Pete Chilcutt, white player for the Houston Rockets. White spectators at an interracial high school basketball game may find themselves expecting their team to fail and hearing racial taunts from the other side. White high school players may also perceive a bias in calling fouls that favors black players, as if prevailing stereotypes had persuaded referees that whites are simply incapable of making extraordinary moves while obeying the rules of the game.

Yet it is also possible to face and conquer self-defeating mental habits. A white basketball team in Texas openly confronted the internalized stereotype of black superiority that had ruined one season and proceeded to finish third in the state the following year. This true story of white demoralization and subsequent self-assertion represents a variation on the storyline of the popular film *Hoosiers,* in which a tiny white Indiana high school wins a state championship over a predominantly black city team whose leaping ability is emphasized by the camera. In fact, this storyline has known many variations over the past century of interracial athletic competition, as racial dominance in sport has changed color from white to black.

Racial folklore can also provide modern whites with various compensations for their lost preeminence and the feelings of physical inferiority that are now immortalized in the popular slogan "white men can't jump." A young woman who played high school basketball told me of her coach's habit of giving white players custodial control of presumably less disciplined black teammates. Naive biological racism can also play a compensatory role in the minds of anxious whites. A black teenager who worked as a lifeguard in the Dallas area in 1990 was told by his white counterparts that the peculiar capacity of black skin to absorb water reduced buoyancy and that this explained the scarcity of good black swimmers. When the golfer Jack Nicklaus told an interviewer in 1994 that blacks were anatomically unsuited to play golf ("Blacks have fit different muscles that react in different ways"), he too was employing an eccentric racial biology to rationalize the absence of black athletes in a segregated country club sport. Such are the culturally acquired mental habits that can preserve the racial balance of power more efficiently than any policies enacted by legislatures and public officials.

While the racial stereotypes that flourish in the sports world can impair white performance, they are capable of damaging African Americans in much more serious ways. The images of black athletes that fill television screens and the pages of newspapers and magazines only sustain the traditional view of blacks as essentially physical and thus primitive people, and variations on this theme are absorbed by blacks as well as whites. In this category we find the young black man who told a Hispanic friend that it was harder for blacks to master the art of pitching a baseball because blacks are not as "in control" as whites. Here too is the black football player who grew up believing that blacks were "genetically superior" athletes while "white men can't jump, but they are hell in the classroom." Another young black athlete adopted the habit of calling a white teammate "nigger" in recognition of his superior skills, an awkward variation on the popular idea that athleticism is literally a black trait. Nor are such ideas about the inherent limitations of robust black males expressed only by athletes. A young black woman told me that she had thought of her football-playing cousin as an insensate "buck" until she learned something about the travails of black college athletes, at which point she was able to empathize with him as a person who had feelings of his own. Confinement within the athletic syndrome is maintained by powerful peer-group pressures which ridicule academic achievement while stigmatizing blacks who do not beat "whitey" at whichever game is at stake. In these and many other ways the sports fixation permeates the lives of countless people whose ideas about their own developmental possibilities are tightly bound to the world of physical self-expression.

The interracial sport of earlier decades offered profound emotional gratifications and a measure of hope to most African Americans, and the integration of college and professional sports played a dramatic (if also overrated) role in the civil rights movement. Today, however, the sports world is a battleground on which the symbolic integration that reigns on television confronts a black male stereotype that feeds on media images of black athletes and other black male action figures. "It is no exaggeration to say," Glenn Loury has written, "that black, male youngsters in the central cities have been demonized in the popular mind as have no other group in recent American history." This aggressive stereotype flourishes in the minds of everyone who is constantly exposed to images of black athletes who can appear to be threatening or dangerous. The sports world they inhabit is, after all, an extraordinary social space in which black men are expected to act out their aggressions, so the "violent black male" becomes the dangerous twin of the spectacular black athlete.

While it is assumed that sport has made an important contribution to racial integration, this has been counterbalanced by the merger of the athlete, the gangster rapper, and the criminal into a single black male persona that the sports industry, the music industry, and the advertising industry have made into the predominant image of black masculinity in the United States and around the world. Convinced that black athleticism alone cannot sustain market appeal, these commercial interests dramatize and embellish the physical and psychological traits of athletes whose public personalities come to embody the full spectrum of male pathology. From the National Basketball Association comes Charles Barkley, "the frowning clown" whose deodorant advertisements play cleverly on tacit racist ideas about he black man's inherent lack of refinement. Here too is the self-mutilating eccentric Dennis Rodman, whose hair dyes and tattoos have turned his entire body into a kaleidoscopic demonstration of how black self-hatred can be marketed as spectacle to white America, which has always embraced variations of the ridiculous black jester. Here is the young star Alonzo Mourning wearing "a scowling mask of rage" that could be depthless black anger or just the personality quirk of an "intense competitor." Some magazine advertisements confront whites with hard black faces in a safe setting, counterfeit versions of the "bad nigger" of black lore and white nightmares. "You got something to say?" asks a belligerent Shawn Kemp in a Foot Locker ad, presumably thrilling and intimidating insecure white men with his disdain. The broad, sullen face of the football player Greg

Lloyd covers two full-color pages of *Sports Illustrated,* every pore visible and glistening to produce the effect of personal confrontation within the safe confines of a photograph, exemplifying the "male restrictions on emotional expression" that reign in the ghetto.

Yet the appeal of such images has less to do with athleticism per se than with a black male style that counts as one of the major cultural myths of our era, for while it is true that black men fill sports teams, hip-hop groups, and prisons in disproportionate numbers, these numbers alone cannot account for the manner in which this notably powerless group of people is presented by various media to the American public.

The black male style has become incarnated in the fusion of black athletes, rappers, and criminals into a single menacing figure who disgusts and offends many blacks as well as whites. The constant, haunting presence of this composite masculine type is maintained by news coverage and advertising strategies that exploit the suggestive mixture of black anger and physical prowess that suffuses each of these roles. Rap music, as the black feminist Trisha Rose once pointed out, "is basically the locker room with a beat"—a perfect fusion of the rhythm and athleticism that are found in so many folkloric images of blackness. In fact, the athlete and the rapper have a relationship that is more reciprocal than popular images might suggest. Shaquille O'Neal serves as a primary symbol of black physical domination in the NBA and is also a highly publicized rap singer. The most aggressive or radical rappers brag about their pugilistic as well as sexual prowess: "I'm like [Mike] Tyson!" crows the rapper L.L. Cool J. The conversation of the rapper Run (Joseph Simmons) of Run-D.M.C. is strewn with sports metaphors, since rappers as well as athletes express "the style and attitude and identity of the street," while many black youths idolize rap artists, just as they do athletic heroes. "I'm a hip-hop man," says the football star Natrone Means, summing up the effect of his baggy jeans, baseball cap, and diamond earrings. Numerous rappers return the compliment by pursuing physical training regimens to build muscle and endurance for their stage routines. "A lot of us have been in and out of jail," says Tom Guest of Young Gunz. "Once you develop a body in the penitentiary, you want to keep it." The hip-hop dancer who calls himself "Incredible" describes his troupe's production as "the most physically demanding show on or off Broadway" and refers to break-dancing competitions as "musical football without teams," thereby extending the range of black athleticism as an idiom that can encompass black creativity in general.

Criminality, real or imagined, is an essential ingredient of this charismatic black persona. One major producer of "gangsta rap" is a former football star who thrives in the music business by projecting an aura of incipient criminality, thereby combining all three roles into a thuggish identity presented to the world by an awestruck white journalist in the pages of the *New York Times Magazine*. Numerous rappers, including such celebrities as Tupac Shakur and Snoop Doggy Dogg, have been arrested for serious crimes, thereby achieving the "ghetto authenticity" that is glamorized by white-owned corporations and the advertising experts who adapt the black "homeboy" style for consumption by affluent white wannabes. The police blotter also includes many black athletes, some of whom (like O. J. Simpson) have battered wives or girlfriends.

The thoughtful black athlete recognizes the commercial value of violence and understands that he has been cast in two grotesquely incongruous roles, impersonating the traditional sportsman, who honors fair play, while being paid to behave like a predator, a role to which the black athlete brings a special resonance. When the Pittsburgh Steelers linebacker Greg Lloyd blindsided a quarterback who suffered a concussion, he was fined $12,000. "Come to a game early and watch the Jumbotron scoreboard," he objected, pointing out the hypocrisy of the penalty. "You'll see 'NFL's Greatest Hits,' with guys getting their helmets ripped off . . . They're marketing that."

Finally, just as the black athlete may radiate an aura of criminality, so the black criminal can radiate a threatening aura of athleticism. Several states have enacted vindictive anticrime laws that have deprived predominantly black prison populations of weightlifting facilities, on the grounds that more muscular convicts are more dangerous when released—as if muscles were more influential than minds in determining the behavior of black men. But the modern archetype of the black criminal-as-superathlete is now Rodney King, whose beating by a crowd of Los Angeles police officers is best understood as a kind of perverse athletic event that matched a team of unathletic white policemen against a black behemoth descended from the mythical John Henry. "It will be very interesting," an attorney for one of the indicted officers said before the trial, "to see him standing next to these officers, because it will be like a giant standing next to pygmies." Officer Stacy Koon, who was eventually convicted and imprisoned for his role in the attack, stated that Rodney King possessed a "hulk-like super strength" and arms that were like unbendable "steel posts." Related imagery also appeared in the "liberal" media. The same artist who produced the notorious darkened *Time* magazine cover of O. J. Simpson in late June 1994, Matt Mahurin, contributed a strikingly apelike depiction of Rodney King's cranium to the same publication a few weeks earlier. Indeed, it would be interesting to know to what extent folkloric ideas about black primitiveness and physical prowess have shaped police behavior toward black men throughout the twentieth century.

The dissemination of aggressive black male images by corporations and their advertising media threatens to alienate the white public if displays of black assertiveness are not rationed and counterbalanced by others that domesticate and gentrify virile black men. The National Basketball Association, for example, must somehow defuse the "undertone of violence" that surrounds its dynamic but sometimes unstable black players, and it does so with the cooperation of the sporting press. Black as well as white sportswriters have warned black players not to act out degenerate roles that threaten the league's profitability by creating an image of chaos and incipient revolt. The besieged white NBA coach who simply cannot grasp "the bewildering mentality of today's [black] players" has become an emblematic martyr of white failure inside the sports world. The domestication of the black male in our mass media also occurs outside the sports world. Perhaps the most striking images occur in advertisements for fashionable men's clothing, in which a handsome and well-built black man can be racially neutralized as he is absorbed into a white cultural context. Here, for example, we find a statuesque and impeccably groomed black male model posing in a full-page advertisement for the polo sports tie from Ralph Lauren. He is paired with a white counterpart who combines rugged outdoorsiness with evident good breeding. This is one of many men's fashion ads that symbolically induct the stylishly athleticized black male into the squeaky-clean prep school world of inherited money and the symbolic racial vigor of demanding physical exercise. Fitted out in a dark blazer with insignia, this man wears a tie that shows two white polo players in action on their charging horses. Ethnic blackness is dissolved in a sporting world that is exclusively and impeccably white: golfing, fishing, tennis, rowing, sailing, and polo—the sports of dynamic imperial males unwinding from the rigors of colonial administration. Here in its purest form is the dream of the black athlete as a natural gentleman, a cherished white fantasy that culminated in the lionization of a deracialized O. J. Simpson and then met a grotesque end in his fall from grace.

The sports world and the advertising industry that feeds on its celebrities pursue the domesticating strategy on a continual basis. Every black man who smiles for the camera, whether he has scored a touchdown or endorsed a product in a commercial, is participating in the detoxification of his own image in the eyes of a white audience that seldom perceives the redemptive function of these images. This process is one example of what may be called "virtual integration," an effortless commingling of the races (almost always in the service of corporate profits) that offers the illusion of progress to a public that wants both good news about race and the preservation of a racial status quo that seldom forces whites to examine their own racial attitudes. (The aftermath of the O. J. Simpson verdict was one of these rare occasions.) The same passive longing for racial peace once prompted the veteran sportswriter Dan Shaughnessy to beg his readers to believe that the white arm of a Boston Celtics player draped around the shoulder of a black teammate was a sign of hope for race relations in the United States. A standard technique for delivering this message is to place big black athletes in the company of small white children; such juxtapositions appear frequently, for example, on the cover of *Sports Illustrated for Kids,* thereby reassuring the many whites who believe that black men are by nature physically dangerous. The Boston Red Sox slugger Mo Vaughn, who has become a rare black symbol of reconciliation in a racially troubled city, appeared on the cover of *Sports Illustrated* in the company of a small and adoring white boy.

Ralph Ellison pointed out many years ago that such idealized versions of the gentle black man are rooted in white fears of black retribution for the humiliations of slavery. Such symbolic figures also represent an unconscious attempt to resurrect the docile black male of southern racial lore. They are of doubtful social value if only because they cannot resolve the white psyche's anxious oscillation between idealized and demonized images of blacks, who are always denied normal human status. A similar gentling technique appears in a Nike-sponsored, pseudo public-service ad that features the meditative face of Michael Jordan as he contemplates a world without his own celebrity ("Would I still be your hero?"). The cynicism of such corporate advertising is rooted both in its commercial motives and in its entrapment of the black athlete in the vicious cycle of demonization and domestication.

Another domesticating strategy uses the black man's body to accentuate his vulnerability. American publications have a conspicuous tendency to publish naked black male torsos more often than white ones, a practice that expresses the same racial mentality that has long permitted the undressing of racial exotics in *National Geographic* and that plays on the tantalizing themes of miscegenation and human bondage. Yet another pictorial device is the comic-racist celebration of the obese black athlete, who is symbolically neutered the moment he becomes the jolly fat man. The media celebrity once accorded to William (The Refrigerator) Perry of the Chicago Bears is the best-known example of a racist fixation on the black body that becomes acceptable as harmless burlesque. *Sports Illustrated,* the most widely circulated and Middle American sports publication of them all, has published an entire series of such entertainments in recent years, oblivious to the fact that the gratification experienced by its white readers is rooted in an elaborate racist folklore about blacks and their appetites. Here is Nate (The Kitchen) Newton, a Dallas Cowboys guard, surrounded by a dozen bags of fattening snacks and a watermelon, his eager lips pursed for a potato chip. There is Dwayne (Road Grader) White of the St. Louis Cardinals, his dark face averted from the camera as his belly bulges obscenely over an invisible belt. In another photograph Dan (Big Daddy) Wilkinson sits before a heaping plate of food, his large fists grasping an enormous wooden fork and matching spoon, which he holds erect like an African chief posing for *National Geographic*. Nate Newton reveals that he is paid personal appearance fees "so they can see how fat I am"—the bloated black athlete as commercialized human specimen and Garfield-like house creature. "Across the country," *Sports Illustrated* reports, "he is perceived as some kind of enormous, lovable Chia Pet, a big huggy-bear of a man in the NFL's cast of cartoon characters." Yet even this saccharin nonsense has its social significance, in that these relentlessly upbeat makeovers of black giants for white audiences express a racist wish to find comfort in the domestication of big black men.

The virtual integration of interracial sport is only one aspect of a larger racial coping strategy described by the cultural critic Benjamin DeMott. American mass media, he argues, have been engaged in the relentless promotion of "feel-good images" of black-white sameness that systematically evade all of the deep conflicts between blacks and whites: "Round the clock, ceaselessly, the elements of this orthodoxy of sameness are grouped and regrouped, helping to root an unspoken but felt understanding throughout white America: race problems belong to the passing moment. Race problems do not involve group interests and conflicts developed over centuries. Race problems are being smoothed into nothingness, gradually, inexorably, by good will, affection, points of light." This propaganda of racial bonhomie is also a de facto policy of the American sports industry and is elaborated most effectively and ingeniously in advertisements. The athleticizing of the black male image is thus an integral part of corporate enterprises worth billions of dollars a year. This contributes in turn to the perpetual underdevelopment of people to whom athleticism seems to offer both personal fulfillment and social liberation. At the same time, it is only fair to ask whether these "friendship dogmas" might also serve a useful purpose. As DeMott points out, "friendship ideas do, after all, represent a step forward from yesterday's race-viciousness. Combined with an intelligent address to the problems of non-middle-class blacks, the friendship faith could move us toward a positive interracial future. Some sameness themes radiate real moral energy and carry an inspiring, even lyric charge."

The problem is that "feel-good" initiatives do not seem to transform racial attitudes in socially effective ways. The fifty years of integrated sport that produced a miraculously deracialized O. J. Simpson could not obscure, let alone prevent, the bitter racial antagonisms revealed by his acquittal. Indeed, friendship dogmas may be worse than useless if they are offered as a substitute for social policies that redistribute power toward the powerless, because they help whites avoid "the hard truth that a caste society attempting erratically to dismantle its caste structures can't expect to get the job done without making commitments to developmental assistance on a scale this country has never imagined."

Black athleticism has complicated the identity problems of black Americans by making athletes the most prominent symbols of African-American achievement. This has done much to perpetuate the invisibility of the black middle class, by making black professional achievement a seldom-noted sideshow to more dramatic media coverage of celebrities and deviants. As the critic Walter Goodman once said of local television news in New York City, "If a rule went out excluding entertainers, athletes, and criminals from a night's report, the only black faces you could be sure of seeing would be those of the anchors." The "tabloid style" of such programming virtually prescribes a demoralizing image of blacks as a group: "The opening headlines are about mayhem, not classes for the gifted. The accomplishments come across as flowers in a world of weeds; on local television, social aberration is the norm."

Responses to this process of continuous defamation are strikingly selective, in that members of the black middle class who rightly resent the notoriety of black criminals appear to be unembarrassed by the omnipresence of black athletes, who serve as the reigning symbol of black "genius" for a majority of blacks and whites. "For many years," a black sociologist once noted, "blacks were politically powerless to affect the imagery and metaphor of popular media expression." Yet even after they acquired some influence over their media images, if only the right to censor the worst of them, their lobbying efforts have rarely targeted disproportionate emphasis on athleticism as an obstacle to progress. A black middle class (and its intelligentsia) that remains infatuated with sports cannot campaign effectively against racial stereotyping that preserves the black man's physicality as a sign of his inherent limitations.

This appearance of passivity is, however, misleading, for there are both working-class and middle-class African Americans who do resist the sports propaganda by encouraging their children to pursue more productive cultural and intellectual interests. At this point we do not know how many people offer this sort of guidance to black children. What is more, their voices are unlikely to be heard above the din of a sports industry that profits from the athleticizing of young blacks. Another obstacle is the athleticizing of black life itself, a sense that giving expression to the ordeal of black survival has long required the visceral power of athletic metaphors— or as one black patient told his psychiatrist: "The black man in this country fights the main event in Madison Square Garden every day."

Darwin's Athletes is a racial history of modern sport that explores our racial predicament in its broadest dimensions. The first section of the book describes the origins of the African-American preoccupation with athletic achievement and shows how this cultural syndrome has subverted more productive developmental strategies founded on academic and professional achievement. It argues that Western racism inflicted on African Americans a physicalized (and eventually athleticized) identity from which they have yet to escape. The cult of black athleticism continues a racist tradition that has long emphasized the motor skills and manual training of African Americans. While the idea of black athletic superiority serves the fantasy needs of blacks as well as whites, providing symbolic victories and a renewal of survivalist thinking about black toughness, the sports fixation is also emblematic of an entire complex of black problems, which includes the adolescent violence and academic failure that have come to symbolize the black male for most Americans.

The second section of the book presents the past century of sport as an arena of racial competition. The ascendancy of the black athlete and the growing belief in his biological superiority represent a historic reversal of roles in the encounter between Africans and the West. The Anglo-Saxon racial self-confidence of the nineteenth century prided itself on an athleticism of both physique and temperament, and the conquered racial inferior played a role in confirming the masculinity of the explorer or colonist. Sport in the colonial context was both an instrument of domination and a field of conflict. The European colonialist's emotional stake in his own sense of physical vitality made the issue of racial athletic competition a sensitive one. The decline of the European empires has been accompanied by the decline of the athletic white male as well, and the world of sport is still adjusting to the psychological dislocations brought on by this loss of prestige.

The third section of the book shows how ideas about black athletic superiority belong to a more comprehensive racial folklore that has long imagined black people to be a hardier, physically stronger, and biologically more robust human subspecies than other races. Nineteenth-century racial science took an intimate interest in the black body and intensified a fixation on black physicality from which there appears to be no escape. The rise of the black athlete during this century has thus given the biological racism of the last century a new lease on life. The emergence of African and African-American athletes as the most spectacular stars of the summer Olympic Games has also led to white fatalism and fears that the twilight of the Caucasian athlete has at last arrived. Images of superior black athleticism have also taken on a special power in the context of a resurgent neo-Darwinian interpretation of the black male and his allegedly criminal propensities. Persistent racial stereotyping has thus made racial athletic aptitude a controversial and even disreputable topic that some would ban from the scientific agenda. The concluding section of this book opposes such censorship and proposes a "postliberal" approach to biomedical racial differences, since a fear of racial biology can only encourage racist interpretations of the genetic research of the future.

A Fist in the Eye of God

Barbara Kingsolver

This essay comes from Small Wonder, *a book that examines crimes against humanity and global politics that Barbara Kingsolver wrote in response to the terrorist attacks of September 11th. "A Fist in the Eye of God" pays particular attention to the global issue of gene modification in plants. Kingsolver explores this topic by giving a hypothetical Ethiopian farmer "magic wheat" from an American seed company; "magic wheat" not only grows large, fast, and is fortified with vitamins but is also capable of bankrupting farmers, wiping out precious wheat varieties, and irrevocably altering farmland habitats. Kingsolver remarks: "We stand here in the epicenter of corporate agribusiness and look around the world asking, 'Why on earth would they hate us?'" As well as thinking about your own position on this issue, think about the effectiveness of the literary devices Kingsolver uses to appeal to her audience. Why does Kingsolver keep the focus of her essay on seeds rather than anything else, and to what effect?*

In the slender shoulders of the myrtle tree outside my kitchen window, a hummingbird built her nest. It was April, the sexiest month, season of budburst and courtship displays, though I was at the sink washing breakfast dishes and missing the party, or so you might think. Then my eye caught a flicker of motion outside, and there she was, hovering uncertainly. She held in the tip of her beak a wisp of wadded spiderweb so tiny I wasn't even sure it was there, until she carefully smoodged it onto the branch. She vanished then, but in less than a minute she was back with another tiny white tuft that she stuck on top of the first. For more than an hour she returned again and again, increasingly confident of her mission, building up by infinitesimal degrees a whitish lump on the branch—and leaving me plumb in awe of the supply of spiderwebbing on the face of the land.

I stayed at my post, washing everything I could find, while my friend did her own housework out there. When the lump had grown big enough—when some genetic trigger in her small brain said, "Now, that will do"—she stopped gathering and sat down on her little tuffet, waggling her wings and tiny rounded underbelly to shape the blob into a cup that would easily

---

"A Fist in the Eye of God," pp. 93–108, from *Small Wonder*. Copyright © 2002 by Barbara Kingsolver. Reprinted by permission of HarperCollins Publishers.

have fit inside my cupped hand. Then she hovered up to inspect it from this side and that, settled and waddled with greater fervor, hovered and appraised some more, and dashed off again. She began now to return with fine filaments of shredded bark, which she wove into the webbing along with some dry leaflets and a slap-dab or or two of lichen pressed onto the outside for curb appeal. When she had made of all this a perfect, symmetrical cup, she did the most surprising thing of all: She sat on it, stretched herself forward, extended the unbelievable length of her tongue, and *licked* her new nest in a long upward stroke from bottom to rim. Then she rotated herself a minute degree, leaned forward, and licked again. I watched her go all the way around, licking the entire nest in a slow rotation that took ten minutes to complete and ended precisely back at her starting point. Passed down from hummingbird great-grandmothers immemorial, a spectacular genetic map in her mind had instructed her at every step, from snipping out with her beak the first spiderweb tuft to laying down whatever salivary secretion was needed to accrete and finalize her essential creation. Then, suddenly, that was that. Her busy urgency vanished, and she settled in for the long stillness of laying and incubation.

If you had been standing with me at my kitchen sink to witness all this, you would likely have breathed softly, as I did, "My God." The spectacular perfection of that nest, that tiny tongue, that beak calibrated perfectly to the length of the tubular red flowers from which she sucks nectar and takes away pollen to commit the essential act of copulation for the plant that feeds her—every piece of this thing and all of it, my God. You might be expressing your reverence for the details of a world created in seven days, 4,004 years ago (according to some biblical calculations), by a divine being approximately human in shape. Or you might be revering the details of a world created by a billion years of natural selection acting utterly without fail on every single life-form, one life at a time. For my money the latter is the greatest show on earth, and a church service to end all. I have never understood how anyone could have the slightest trouble blending religious awe with a full comprehension of the workings of life's creation.

Charles Darwin himself was a religious man, blessed with an extraordinary patience for observing nature's details, as well as the longevity and brilliance to put it all together. In his years of studying animate life he noticed four things, which any of us could notice today if we looked hard enough. They are:

1. Every organism produces more seeds or offspring than will actually survive to adulthood.

2. There is variation among these seeds or offspring.

A Fist in the Eye of God ✒ *Barbara Kingsolver* **251**

3. Traits are passed down from one generation to the next.

4. In each generation the survivors succeed—that is, they survive—because they possess some advantage over the ones that don't succeed, and *because* they survive, they will pass that advantage on to the next generation. Over time, therefore, the incidence of that trait will increase in the population.

Bingo: the greatest, simplest, most elegant logical construct ever to dawn across our curiosity about the workings of natural life. It is inarguable, and it explains everything.

Most people have no idea that this, in total, is Darwin's theory of evolution. Furthermore, parents who tell their children not to listen to such talk because "it's just a theory" are ignorant of what that word means. A theory, in science, is a coherent set of principles used to explain and predict a class of phenomena. Thus, gravitational theory explains why objects fall when you drop them, even though it, too, is "just a theory." Darwin's has proven to be the most robust unifying explanation ever devised in biological science. It's stunning that he could have been so right—scientists of Darwin's time knew absolutely nothing about genetics—but he was. After a century and a half, during which time knowledge expanded boundlessly in genetics, geology, paleontology, and all areas of natural science, his simple logical construct continues to explain and predict perfectly the existence and behavior of every earthly life form we have ever studied. As the unifying principle of natural sciences, it is no more doubted among modern biologists than gravity is questioned by physicists. Nevertheless, in a bizarre recent trend, a number of states have limited or even outright banned evolution in high schools, and many textbooks for the whole country, in turn, have wimped out on the subject. As a consequence, an entire generation of students is arriving in college unprepared to comprehend or to pursue good science. Many science teachers I know are nostalgic for at least one aspect of the Cold War days, when *Sputnik* riveted us to the serious business of training our kids to real science, instead of allowing it to be diluted or tossed out to assuage the insecurities of certain ideologues.

We dilute and toss at our peril. Scientific illiteracy in our population is leaving too many of us unprepared to discuss or understand much of the damage we are wreaking on our atmosphere, our habitat, and even the food that enters our mouths. Friends of mine who opted in school for English lit instead of microbiology (an option I myself could easily have taken) sometimes come to me and ask, "In two hundred words or less, can you explain to me why I should be nervous about genetic engineering?" I tell them, "Sit down, I'll make you a cup of tea, and then get ready for more than two hundred words."

A sound-bite culture can't discuss science very well. Exactly what we're losing when we reduce biodiversity, the causes and consequences of global warming—these traumas can't be adequately summarized in an evening news wrap-up. Arguments *in favor* of genetically engineered food, in contrast, are dangerously simple: A magazine ad for an agribusiness touts its benevolent plan to "feed the world's hungry with our vitamin-engineered rice!" To which I could add in reply my own snappy motto: "If you thought that first free hit of heroin was a good idea. . . ." But before you can really decide whether or not you agree, you may need the five hundred words above and a few thousand more. If so, then sit down, have a cup of tea, and bear with me. This is important.

At the root of everything, Darwin said, is that wonder of wonders, genetic diversity. You're unlike your sister, a litter of pups is its own small Rainbow Coalition, and every grain of wheat in a field holds inside its germ a slightly separate destiny. You can't see the differences until you cast the seeds on the ground and grow them out, but sure enough, some will grow into taller plants and some shorter, some tougher, some sweeter. In a good year all or most of them will thrive and give you wheat. But in a bad year a spate of high winds may take down the tallest stalks and leave standing at harvest time only, say, the 10 percent of the crop that had a "shortness" gene. And if that wheat comprises your winter's supply of bread, plus the only seed you'll have for next year's crop, then you'll be almighty glad to have that small, short harvest. Genetic diversity, in domestic populations as well as wild ones, is nature's sole insurance policy. Environments change: Wet years are followed by droughts, lakes dry up, volcanoes rumble, ice ages dawn. It's a big, bad world out there for a little strand of DNA. But a population will persist over time if, deep within the scattered genetics of its ranks, it is literally prepared for anything. When the windy years persist for a decade, the wheat population will be overtaken by a preponderance of shortness, but if the crop maintains its diversity, there will always be recessive aspirations for height hiding in there somewhere, waiting to have their day.

How is the diversity maintained? That old black magic called sex. Every seed has two parents. Plants throw their sex to the wind, to a hummingbird's tongue, to the knees of a bee—in April you are *inhaling* sex, and sneezing—and in the process, each two parents put their scrambled genes into offspring that represent whole new genetic combinations never before seen on Earth. Every new outfit will be ready for *something,* and together—in a large enough population—the whole crowd will be ready for *anything*. Individuals will die, not at random but because of some fatal misfit between what an organism *has* and what's *required*. But the population will live on, moving always in the direction of fitness (however "fitness" is at the moment defined), not because anyone has a master plan but simply because survival carries fitness forward, and death doesn't.

People have railed at this reality, left and right, since the evening when a British ambassador's wife declared to her husband, "Oh dear, let us hope Mr. Darwin isn't right, and if he is, let us hope no one finds out about it!" Fundamentalist Christians seem disturbed by a scenario in which individual will is so irrelevant. They might be surprised to learn that Stalin tried to ban the study of genetics and evolution in Soviet universities for the opposite reason, attacking the idea of natural selection—which acts only at the level of the individual—for being anti-Communist. Through it all, the little engines of evolution have kept on turning as they have done for millennia, delivering us here and passing on, untouched by politics or what anybody thinks.

Nikolai Vavilov was an astounding man of science, and probably the greatest plant explorer who has ever lived. He spoke seven languages and could recite books by Pushkin from memory. In his travels through sixty-four countries between 1916 and 1940, he saw more crop diversity than anyone had known existed, and founded the world's largest seed collection.

As he combed continents looking for primitive crop varieties, Vavilov noticed a pattern: Genetic variation was not evenly distributed. In a small region of Ethiopia he found hundreds of kinds of ancient wheat known only to that place. A single New World plateau is astonishingly rich in corn varieties, while another one is rolling in different kinds of potatoes. Vavilov mapped the distribution of what he found and theorized that the degree of diversity of a crop indicated how long it had been grown in a given region, as farmers saved their seeds through hundreds and thousands of seasons. They also saved more *types* of seed for different benefits; thus popcorn, tortilla corn, roasting corn, and varieties of corn with particular colors and textures were all derived, over centuries, from one original strain. Within each crop type, the generations of selection would also yield a breadth of resistance to all types of pest and weather problems encountered through the years. By looking through his lens of genetics, Vavilov began to pinpoint the places in the world where human agriculture had originated. More modern genetic research has largely borne out his hypothesis that agriculture emerged independently in the places where the most diverse and ancient crop types, known as land races, are to be found: in the Near East, northern China, Mesoamerica, and Ethiopia.

The industrialized world depends entirely on crops and cultivation practices imported from what we now call the Third World (though evidently it was actually First). In an important departure from older traditions, the crops we now grow in the United States are extremely uniform genetically, due to the fact that our agriculture is controlled primarily by a few large agricultural corporations that sell relatively few varieties of seeds. Those who know the seed business are well aware that our shallow gene bank is highly vulnerable; when a crop strain succumbs all at once to a new disease, all across the country (as happened with our corn in 1970), researchers must return to the more diverse original strains for help. So we still rely on the gigantic insurance policy provided by the genetic variability in the land races, which continue to be hand-sown and harvested, year in and year out, by farmers in those mostly poor places from which our crops arose.

Unbelievably, we are now engaged in a serious effort to cancel that insurance policy.

It happens like this. Lets say you are an Ethiopian farmer growing a land race of wheat—a wildly variable, husky mongrel crop that has been in your family for hundreds of years. You always lose some to wind and weather, but the rest still comes through every year. Lately, though, you've been hearing about a kind of Magic Wheat that grows six times bigger than your crop, is easier to harvest, and contains vitamins that aren't found in ordinary wheat. And amazingly enough, by special arrangement with the government, it's free.

Readers who have even the slightest acquaintance with fairy tales will already know there is trouble ahead in this story. The Magic Wheat grows well the first year, but its rapid, overly green growth attracts a startling number of pests. You see insects on this crop that never ate wheat before, in the whole of your family's history. You watch, you worry. You realize that you're going to have to spray a pesticide to get this crop through to harvest. You're not so surprised to learn that by special arrangement with the government, the same company that gave you the seed for free can sell you the pesticide you need. Its a good pesticide, they use it all the time in America, but it costs money you don't have, so you'll have to borrow against next year's crop.

The second year, you will be visited by a terrible drought, and your crop will not survive to harvest at all; every stalk dies. Magic Wheat from America doesn't know beans about Ethiopian drought. The end.

Actually, if the drought arrived in year two and the end came that quickly, in this real-life fairy tale you'd be very lucky, because chances are good you'd still have some of your family-line seed around. It would be much more disastrous if the drought waited until the eighth or ninth year to wipe you out, for then you'd have no wheat left at all, Magic or otherwise. Seed banks, even if they're eleven thousand years old, can't survive for more than a few years on the shelf. If they aren't grown out as crops year after year, they die—or else get ground into flour and baked and eaten—and then this product of a thousand hands and careful selection is just gone, once and for all.

This is no joke. The infamous potato famine or Southern Corn Leaf Blight catastrophe could happen again any day now, in any place where people are once again foolish enough, or poor enough to be coerced (as was the case in Ireland), to plant an entire country in a single genetic strain of a food crop.

While agricultural companies have purchased, stored, and patented certain genetic materials from old crops, they cannot engineer a crop, *ever,* that will have the resilience of land races under a wide variety of conditions of moisture, predation, and temperature. Genetic engineering is the antithesis of variability because it removes the wild card—that beautiful thing called sex—from the equation.

This is our new magic bullet: We can move single genes around in a genome to render a specific trait that nature can't put there, such as ultra-rapid growth or vitamin A in rice. Literally, we could put a wolf in sheep's clothing. But solving agricultural problems this way turns out to be far less broadly effective than the old-fashioned multigenic solutions derived through programs of selection and breeding. Crop predators evolve in quick and mysterious ways, while gene splicing tries one simple tack after another, approaching its goal the way Wile E. Coyote tries out each new gizmo from Acme only once, whereupon the roadrunner outwits it and Wile E. goes crestfallen back to the drawing board.

Wendell Berry, with his reliable wit, wrote that genetic manipulation in general and cloning in particular: ". . . besides being a new method of sheep-stealing, is only a pathetic attempt to make sheep predictable. But this is an affront to reality. As any shepherd would know, the scientist who thinks he has made sheep predictable has only made himself eligible to be outsmarted."

I've heard less knowledgeable people comfort themselves on the issue of genetic engineering by recalling that humans have been pushing genes around for centuries, through selective breeding of livestock and crops. I even read one howler of a quote that began, "Ever since Mendel spliced those first genes. . . ." These people aren't getting it, but I don't blame them—I blame the religious fanatics who kept basic biology out of their grade-schools textbooks. Mendel did not *splice* genes, he didn't actually control anything at all; he simply watched peas to learn how their natural system of genetic recombination worked. The farmers who select their best sheep or grains to mother the next year's crop are working with the evolutionary force of selection, pushing it in the direction of their choosing. Anything produced in this way will still work within its natural evolutionary context of variability, predators, disease resistance, and so forth. But tampering with genes outside of the checks and balances you might call the rules of God's laboratory is an entirely different process. It's turning out to have unforeseen consequences, sometimes stunning ones.

To choose one example among many, genetic engineers have spliced a bacterium into a corn plant. It was arguably a good idea. The bacterium was *Bacillus thuringensis,* a germ that causes caterpillars' stomachs to explode. It doesn't harm humans, birds, or even ladybugs or bees, so it's one of the most useful pesticides we've ever discovered. Organic farmers have worked for years to expedite the path of the naturally occurring "Bt" spores from the soil, where the bacterium lives, onto their plants. You can buy this germ in a can at the nursery and shake it onto your tomato plants, where it makes caterpillars croak before sliding back into the soil it came from. Farmers have always used nature to their own ends, employing relatively slow methods circumscribed by the context of natural laws. But genetic engineering took a giant step and spliced part of the bacterium's DNA into a corn plant's DNA chain, so that as the corn grew, each of its cells would contain the bacterial function of caterpillar killing. When it produced pollen, each grain would have a secret weapon against the corn worms that like to crawl down the silks to ravage the crop. So far, so good.

But when the so-called Bt corn sheds its pollen and casts it to the wind, as corn has always done (it's pollinated by wind, not by bees), it dusts a fine layer of Bt pollen onto every tree and bush in the neighborhood of every farm that grows it—which is rapidly, for this popular crop, becoming the territory known as the United States. There it may explode the stomach of any butterfly larva in its path. The populations of monarch butterflies, those bold little pilgrims who migrate all the way to Mexico and back on wings the consistency of pastry crust, are plummeting fast. While there are many reasons for this (for example, their winter forests in Mexico are being burned), no reasonable person can argue that dusting them with a stomach explosive is going to help matters. So, too, go other butterflies more obscure, and more endangered. And if that doesn't happen to break your heart, just wait awhile, because something that pollinates your food and builds the soil underneath it may also be slated for extinction. And there's another practical problem: The massive exposure to Bt, now contained in every cell of this corn, is killing off all crop predators except those few that have mutated a resistance to this long-useful pesticide. As a result, those superresistant mutants are taking over, in exactly the same way that overexposure to antibiotics is facilitating the evolution of antibiotic-resistant diseases in humans.

In this context of phenomenal environmental upsets, with even larger ones just offstage awaiting their cue, it's a bit surprising that the objections to genetic engineering we hear most about are the human health effects. It is absolutely true that new combinations of DNA can create proteins we aren't prepared to swallow; notably, gene manipulations in corn unexpectedly created some antigens to which some humans are allergic. The potential human ills caused by ingestion of engineered foods remain an open category—which is scary enough in itself, and I don't mean to minimize it. But there are so many ways for gene manipulation to work from the inside to destroy our habitat and our food systems that the environmental challenges loom as something on the order of a cancer that might well make personal allergies look like a sneeze. If genetically reordered organisms escape into natural populations, they may rapidly change the genetics of an entire species in a way that could seal its doom. One such scenario is the "monster salmon" with genes for hugely rapid growth, which are currently poised for accidental release into open ocean. Another scenario, less cinematic but dangerously omnipresent, is the pollen escaping from crops, creating new weeds that we cannot hope to remove from the earth's face. Engineered genes don't play by the rules that have organized life for three billion years (or, if you prefer, 4,004). And in this case, winning means loser takes all.

Huge political question marks surround these issues: What will it mean for a handful of agribusinesses to control the world's ever-narrowing seed banks? What about the chemical dependencies they're creating for farmers in developing countries, where government deals with multinational corporations are inducing them to grow these engineered crops? What about the business of patenting and owning genes? Can there be any good in this for the flat-out concern of people trying to feed themselves? Does it seem *safe,* with the world now being what it is, to give up self-sustaining food systems in favor of dependency on the global marketplace? And finally, would *you* trust a guy in a suit who's never given away a nickel in his life, but who now tells you he's made you some *free* Magic Wheat? Most people know by now that corporations can do only what's best for their quarterly bottom line. And anyone who still believes governments ultimately do what's best for their people should be advised that the great crop geneticist Nikolai Vavilov died in a Soviet prison camp.

These are not questions to take lightly, as we stand here in the epicenter of corporate agribusiness and look around at the world asking, "Why on earth would they hate us?" The general ignorance of U.S. populations about who controls global agriculture reflects our trust in an assured food supply. Elsewhere, in places where people grow more food, watch less TV, and generally rencounter a greater risk of hunger than we do, they mostly know what's going on. In India, farmers have persisted in burning to the ground trial crops of transgenic cotton, and they forced their government to ban Monsanto's "terminator technology," which causes plants to kill their own embryos so no viable seeds will survive for a farmer to replant in the next generation (meaning he'd have to buy new ones, of course). Much of the world has already refused to import genetically engineered foods or seeds from the United States. But because of the power and momentum of the World Trade Organization, fewer and fewer countries have the clout to resist the reconstruction of their food supply around the scariest New Deal ever.

Even standing apart from the moral and political questions—if a scientist *can* stand anywhere without stepping on the politics of what's about to be discovered—there are question marks enough in the science of the matter. There are consequences in it that no one knew how to anticipate. When the widely publicized Human Genome Project completed its mapping of human chromosomes, it offered an unsettling, not-so-widely-publicized conclusion: Instead of the 100,000 or more genes that had been expected based on the number of proteins we must synthesize to be what we are, we have only about 30,000—about the same number as a mustard plant. This evidence undermined the central dogma how genes work; that is, the assumption of a clear-cut chain of processes leading from a single gene to the appearance of the trait it controls. Instead, the mechanism of gene expression appears vastly more complicated than had been assumed since Watson and Crick discovered the structure of DNA in 1953. The expression of a gene may be altered by its context, such as the presence of other genes on the chromosome near it. Yet, genetic engineering operates on assumptions based on the simpler model. Thus, single transplanted genes often behave in startling ways in an engineered organism, often proving lethal to themselves, or, sometimes, neighboring organisms. In light of newer findings, geneticists increasingly concede that gene-tinkering is to some extent shooting in the dark. Barry Commoner, senior scientist at the Center for the Biology of Natural Systems at Queens College, laments that while the public's concerns are often derided by industry scientists as irrational and uneducated, the biotechnology industry is—ironically—conveniently ignoring the latest results in the field "which show that there are strong reasons to fear the potential consequences of transferring a DNA gene between species."

Recently I heard Joan Dye Gussow, who studies and writes about the energetics, economics, and irrationalities of global food production, discussing some of these problems in a radio interview. She mentioned the alarming fact that pollen from genetically engineered corn is so rapidly contaminating all other corn that we may soon have no naturally bred corn left in the United States. "This is a fist in the eye of God," she said, adding with a sad little laugh, "and I'm not even all that religious." Whatever you believe in—whether God for you is the watchmaker who put together the intricate workings of this world in seven days or seven hundred billion days—you'd be wise to believe the part about the fist.

Religion has no place in the science classroom, where it may abridge students' opportunities to learn the methods, discoveries, and explanatory hypotheses of science. Rather, its place is in the hearts of the men and women who study and then practice scientific exploration. Ethics can't influence the outcome of an experiment, but they can serve as a useful adjunct to the questions that get asked in the first place, and to the applications thereafter. (One must wonder what chair God occupied, if any, in the Manhattan Project.) In the halls of science there is often an unspoken sense that morals and objectivity can't occupy the same place. That is balderdash—they always have cohabited. Social norms and judgments regarding gender, race, the common good, cooperation, competition, material gain, and countless other issues reside in every active human mind, so they were hovering somewhere in the vicinity of any experiment ever conducted by a human. That is precisely why science invented the double-blind experiment, in which, for example, experimental subjects don't know whether they're taking the drug or the placebo, and neither does the scientist recording their responses, so as to avoid psychological bias in the results. But it's not possible to double-blind the scientist's approach to the task in the first place, or to the way results will be used. It is probably more scientifically constructive to acknowledge our larger agenda than to pretend it doesn't exist. Where genetic engineering is concerned, I would rather have ethics than profitability driving the program.

I was trained as a biologist, and I can appreciate the challenge and the technical mastery involved in isolating, understanding, and manipulating genes. I can think of fascinating things I'd like to do as a genetic engineer. But I only have to stand still for a minute and watch the outcome of thirty million years' worth of hummingbird evolution transubstantiated before my eyes into nest and egg to get knocked down to size. I have held in my hand the germ of a plant engineered to grow, yield its crop, and then murder its own embryos, and there I glimpsed the malevolence that can lie in the heart of a profiteering enterprise. There once was a time when Thoreau wrote, "I have great faith in a seed. Convince me that you have a seed there, and I am prepared to expect wonders." By the power vested in everything living, let us keep to that faith. I'm a scientist who thinks it wise to enter the doors of creation not with a lion tamer's whip and chair, but with the reverence humankind has traditionally summoned for entering places of worship: a temple, a mosque, or a cathedral. A sacred grove, as ancient as time.

Flight

Amitava Kumar

Amitava Kumar is an Indo-American scholar interested in travel, migration, and how these processes shape human perspectives. This essay revolves around the newspaper account of a young Indian migrant who stows away in the wheel chamber of an airplane in order to find work in England. As Kumar considers the significance of this young man's story, the essay becomes an exercise in interacting with texts. Kumar weaves interpretative readings of major Indian writers like Salman Rushdie into his own to develop an allegory of flight that represents the physical and emotional distance between the "first world" and the overlooked, impoverished "third world." Kumar attempts to bridge the distance between himself and the young man dropped from the wheel chamber through an imaginative leap of empathy and understanding. Does he accomplish this? Why does Kumar juxtapose the fatal flight of the immigrant Mohammed with that of the 9/11 terrorists? Does Kumar see the immigrant and the terrorist as comparable figures? How does perspective work in the essay? What do these flights mean for those on the ground versus those in the air?

The Indian writer Rabindranath Tagore flew in a plane in 1932. He had awoken at three-thirty in the dark morning and was in the air at four. Tagore was traveling in what was then called Persia; at half past eight the plane reached Bushire. "Now comes an age in which man has lifted the burdens of earth into the air," the writer noted in his travel diary. The achievement of flight did not always promise freedom for Tagore. On the contrary, he felt that the airplane was not in harmony with the wind. It roared like an animal in rage. A plane in flight suggested very strongly that human conflict had been raised from the level of the mundane world into the heavenly skies above.

Tagore had been awarded the Nobel Prize in literature in 1913 for his book of poems, *Gitanjali.* The thought that the earth lost its hold on man when he flew into the sky was not the result of poetic fancy. A few paragraphs later in his travelogue, Tagore had supplied the context for his

Copyright © 2002 from *Bombay London New York* by Amitava Kumar. Reproduced by permission of Routledge/Taylor & Francis Books, Inc.

thoughts. "A British air force is stationed at Baghdad," he wrote. "Its Christian chaplain informs me that they are engaged in bombing operations on some Sheikh villages."

The fields, ponds, and rivers of his childhood bound Tagore to the earth and its beauty. To fly was to lose this contact with the earth. Only the sense of sight remained for the one who was in the air, and it gave man the disease of aloofness. For Tagore, the man in the plane raining bombs below could not even in good faith ask himself who is kin and who is stranger: he has put himself in a place from where he is unable to be aware of the difference and to judge accordingly. "The men, women and children done to death there," wrote Tagore, "meet their fate by a decree from the stratosphere of British imperialism—which finds it easy to shower death because of its distance from its individual victims." At the same time, the invention of the airplane impressed Tagore. He saw in the race of the inventors qualities of character like perseverance and courage. The sight of his four Dutch pilots ("immensely built, the personification of energy . . . their rude, overflowing health, bequeathed by generations brought up on nourishing food") evoked admiration and the thought that his own compatriots had been deprived of food and exhausted by toil.

This picture has now changed. The descendants of those who were, in Tagore's time, the subject peoples have now for long been flying planes. They also travel in planes. This situation also incites ambivalence. The travelers are often workers migrating long distances in search of work. In fact, such travel remains a part of the fantasy in the minds of the poor. There are many in the poorer countries of the world for whom the plane in flight represents the journey that, when undertaken in the future, will take them to the promised land. In airports all over the world, one can see the migrant workers from countries like Tagore's India, waiting to be taken to another place to work.

On the morning of September 11 last year, nineteen men, in their appearance not different at all from the others who stand in the visa lines outside the embassies and consulates of rich nations in cities like Calcutta and Cairo, Karachi and Khartoum, hijacked four American jets filled with fuel and people. The suicidal acts of the hijackers also gave a perverse twist to the old story of the difficult travel to the land of plenty and promise. According to reports that were published in the days following the attacks, it was revealed that the hijackers believed that their deaths promised them entry into the garden of heaven and the ministrations of seventy virgins. We can persist with Tagore's vision of the fiery bird raining death, but his universe is already lost, the simple oppositions between the earth and the sky rendered obsolete. Those who had been chained to the earth have also learned to claw their way into the air and wreak havoc from on high. There are new stories of travel, and now terror touches all.

Salman Rushdie's novel *The Satanic Verses* opens with an explosion in the air. A jet is blown apart while in flight, and two actors tumble out, "like tidbits of tobacco from a broken old cigar." The two men, Gibreel Farishta and Saladin Chamcha, were passengers in the jumbo jet *Bostan,* Flight AI-420. In the night air around them "floated the debris of the soul, broken memories, sloughed-off selves, severed mother-tongues, violated privacies, untranslatable jokes, extinguished futures, lost loves, the forgotten meaning of hollow, booming words, *land, belonging, home.*" Rushdie's fictional midair explosion was based on an actual event. On June 28, 1985, Flight AI-182 burst into flames off the coast of Ireland. The plane had taken off from Toronto and Montreal; it was headed for New Delhi and Bombay via London. All 331 people on board were killed. The plane's destruction was widely believed to be the work of Sikh extremists who wanted to avenge the Indian army's assault on the Holy Temple in Amritsar. Two Indo-Canadian Sikhs were arrested by the police and charged with first-degree murder. Flight AI-182 had indeed been packed with migrants. Rushdie's catalog of the debris from the destroyed airliner furnishes a valuable, and touching, inventory of the baggage—the load of everyday experience—that immigrants carry with them. And the play of magic realism allows the writer to introduce, amid the destruction, the miracle of rebirth. Gibreel Farishta and Saladin Chamcha survive death, and are transformed. This is an allegory of migration. Loss renews life. As Gibreel Farishta croons, even as he falls from 29,002 feet, "To be born again, first you have to die."

The sweet dream of reinvention is a radical one, but reality turns out to be more intractable. Rushdie's story of the passenger floating down to a part of London is not nearly as surprising as the actual, unheralded fall from the sky of a secret passenger at the edge of the same city. According to a July 2001 report in the *Guardian,* a body was discovered in a parking lot of a department store in west London. A workman in nearby Heathrow airport had seen a figure in jeans and a black T-shirt suddenly "plummeting from the sky like a stone." Where was the home of this dead man who was lying in a pool formed from his own split brains? The report said that the man who had fallen to earth was Mohammed Ayaz, a twenty-one-year-old stowaway who had made a desperate attempt to escape the harsh life of a peasant in his village in Pakistan on the Afghan border. The previous night, when a British Airways jet turned around to begin taxing at Bahrain airport in preparation for takeoff, Ayaz had apparently sprinted through the dark and climbed into the huge chambers above the wheels of the Boeing. It could not have been an easy task to find one's way into the wheel bay.

The report said: "It involves climbing 14 ft up one of the aircraft's 12 enormous wheels, then finding somewhere to crouch or cling as the plane makes its way to the end of the runway and starts its deafening engines." At that point, the plane would have accelerated to 180 mph.

Ayaz would not have known this, though one cannot be sure, but the undercarriage compartment "has no oxygen, no heating and no pressure." Within minutes, the temperature around Ayaz would have dropped below freezing. The report that I have been quoting had furnished, at this point, its own sense of journalistic pathos: "At 18,000 ft, minutes later, while passengers only a few feet away were being served gin and tonic and settling down to watch in-flight movies, Ayaz would have begun to hallucinate from lack of oxygen." The report had then added plainly: "At 30,000 ft the temperature is minus 56 degrees." When, many hours later, the plane was still a few miles away from Heathrow, the captain would have lowered the wheels of the aircraft. It was at that time, when the plane was likely to have been between 2,000 and 3,000 feet, that Mohammed Ayaz's lifeless body must have been delivered into the morning air.

For seven months prior to his death, Ayaz had been working as a laborer in Dubai. His family is poor, finding a meager livelihood from farming wheat, barley, corn, and onions. The agent who had secured a way for Ayaz to go to the Gulf had demanded money in addition to the cost of travel and visa. The family had had to borrow heavily. The money that Ayaz was going to earn would allow him to repay the debts in two years. But things didn't turn out the way Ayaz had expected. In Dubai, Ayaz's employer took away his passport. The salary he received was less than one-fourth of what the agent had promised. Ayaz was able to make barely enough to buy food. Ayaz did not tell his family of his plan to cross into Bahrain or his attempt to make his way to England. Ayaz's brother, Gul Bihar, told reporters: "He always spoke about going to work in America or England. But they don't give visas to poor people like us."

The report in the *Guardian* had been sent to me in the mail by a friend. I was standing outside my house when the mailman brought the letter one morning, and I read the newspaper clipping while standing on my steps. As I began reading the first few paragraphs, I thought of the opening lines from Rushdie's *Satanic Verses* quoted above. Those lines were what first came to mind. But in seconds, the mood had slipped. The pain and despair that surrounded me as I read the report took me away from the pages of celebrated fiction. In much that I have written in the past few years, I have tried to understand how Indian writing has populated the literary landscape familiar to Western readers with people who look and speak differently and who have their histories in another part of the world. The presentation of this record by Indian writers has been a great, imaginative achievement. But a dead stowaway? So much that appears in Indian fiction today, particularly in its magical realist versions, appears banal if not also meretricious, when compared to the fragmentary account that emerges from a news story of a poor youth's struggle to cross the borders that divide the rich from the poor. The textbook of "multicultural literature" carries no words of testimony of a young man narrating what flashed through his head as he went running in the dark behind a giant airplane that was about to pick up speed on the runway. It suddenly strikes me that Mohammed Ayaz could not have foreseen his death—and that seems to me to be more and more a triumph of his imagination.

The article in the *Guardian* also said that Ayaz was not the first to fall down from the sky. In October 1996, the body of nineteen-year-old from Delhi, Vijay Saini, had dropped out of a plane at almost the same spot. Saini's corpse lay undiscovered for three days. (Vijay Saini's brother, Pradeep, according to the report, is the only person believed to have survived such a journey. The article said that the man was found at Heathrow "in a disoriented state shortly after a flight from Delhi landed.") Then, two years later, a couple drinking in a pub in nearby Marlborough had seen another man tumble out of the sky. That body was never discovered. The police believed that it might have fallen in a reservoir. "The undercarriage is always lowered at the same point, that is why they are falling at the same place," an official told the *Guardian*. "But it's an almost uncanny coincidence—these people fly right across the world in this way from different places, and they all end up in a car park in Richmond. If there are any more bodies to fall, that's where they will fall." The West rushes up to meet the migrant, not as the promised land but, instead, a parking lot that becomes for him a desolate, temporary graveyard.

On September 11, bodies fell from the top floors of the north tower of the World Trade Center. One writer, watching from the street below, wrote, "it looked like a desperate ballet: some seemed to be flying, their arms sweeping gracefully as they picked up speed. Others tumbled and some just dropped, rigid, all the way down." As I reflect on that ghastly scene, months after it occurred, I find myself mentally moving Mohammed Ayaz from a parking lot in west London to the Twin Towers. He could have been one among the many migrant workers, dishwashers, messengers, cleaners, and restaurant help who perished on that day. But it doesn't work. I see him again and again in the wheel bay of the airplane. That thought won't go away. I also realize that I am perturbed by the thought that the hijackings and the mayhem that followed should erase from public consciousness the presence of the other illegal passenger, the humble stowaway, and stretching behind him, the memory of a whole history of dispossession. The sad truth is that the stowaway is not alone. Hidden behind that figure are the untold millions in countries like India or Pakistan who dream of a different future. Often, these young men and women have been turned into migrants in their own land because of poverty, or famines, or wars waged by others in the fields where their families have toiled for generations. How removed is the pathos of the stowaway from the rage of the hijacker?

The body falling out of the sky is the other and silent half of the story of international travel and tourism. We are reminded that not everyone crosses borders alive, despite the cheerful acceptance of globalization by many governments of the world. Standing near his son's unmarked grave, a mound of brown earth ringed by stones and covered with a plastic sheet, Mohammed Ayaz's father said, "My son was as strong as four men but he died in search of bread."

I can try to imagine the dreams that come to the stowaway when he begins to drift into sleep despite the cold and the noise in his shuddering cage. But these would be speculations. The stowaway will not share his secrets with the writer. It is impossible for me to know if the stowaway is nostalgic for the fields in his village and the familiar sunshine on the wall of his house. He had wanted to leave them behind. The plane is carrying him into the future. He tells himself that he can bear hunger for a long time. He is a quick learner. Once he has his feet on the ground he will find a way to earn money soon. These are the thoughts that I surround the stowaway with, as if he were, in reality, trapped inside the darkness in my head. It is because I am telling myself over and over that he does not feel any pain. He feels light-headed. He is not fleeing anything anymore. He is flying.

The Clamor of Justification

Barry Lopez

In "The Clamor of Justification" Barry Lopez tries to answer the question that he poses to himself: "When a man cocked a rifle and aimed at a wolf's head, what was he trying to kill?" Lopez shows that the answer is not that simple. He offers a history that traces the fear of the wolf back to the fear of the wilderness for Western expansionists, constructing a narrative thread for fear. In this way, Lopez considers how fear might be a culturally constructed phenomenon rather than a natural or biological reaction. What difference would it make to define fear in this way? Does it prompt us to question our relationship to the natural world? How much control should humans have over nature? Are preemptive killings okay, considering that the wolf has been known to kill humans? What should our relationship be with wildlife? And how does Lopez pose these questions so as to engage readers in reflecting upon the answers?

In the course of writing this book I had a chance to talk with many people, and to come into contact with several different points of view about wolves. I enjoyed being in the field with biologists. I enjoyed the range and subtlety of Indian and Eskimo ideas. My only discomfort came when I talked with men who saw nothing wrong with killing wolves, who felt it was basically a good thing to be doing. For the most part, they were men who had matured in a different time and under different circumstances than I. We didn't share the same feelings toward animals, but I could understand their positions. Some were professional trappers. Others had lost stock to wolves. There was a larger context.

There were a few I spoke with, however, who were quite different. It was as though these men had broken down at some point in their lives and begun to fill with bile, and that bile had become an unreasoned hatred of many things. Of laws. Of governments. Of wolves. They hated wolves because—they would struggle to put it into words—because wolves seemed better off than they were. And that seemed perverse. They killed wolves habitually, with a trace of vengeance, with as little regret as a boy shooting rats at a dump.

Reprinted by permission of Sterling Lord Literistic, Inc. Copyright 1978 by Barry Lopez.

They were few in number but their voices, screaming for the wolf's head, were often the loudest, the ones that set the tone at a grange meeting and precipitated the wolf's extirpation in the lower forty-eight states.

These men, and others, killed no one will ever know how many thousands of wolves in America, mostly to control predation against livestock. At the time, toward the close of the nineteenth century, it was a legitimate undertaking. Wolves, deprived of buffalo and other wild game, had turned to cattle and sheep; if you wanted to raise stock in America you had little choice but to kill wolves. But the killing was a complicated business, it was never as clearly reasoned as that. On the spur of the moment men offered ridiculous reasons—because the wolves loafed and didn't have to work for their food, they would say.

It is easy to condemn these men now, to look at what they did—destroy a national wildlife heritage—and feel a sense of loss. But they are, perhaps, too easily blamed. We forget how little, really, separates us from the times and circumstances in which we, too, would have killed wolves. Besides, blaming them for the loss is too simplistic. We are forced to a larger question: when a man cocked a rifle and aimed at a wolf's head, what was he trying to kill? And other questions. Why didn't we quit, why did we go on killing long after the need was gone? And when the craven and deranged tortured wolves, why did so many of us look the other way?

In an historical sense, we are all to blame for the loss of wolves. In the nineteenth century when the Indians on the plains were telling us that the wolf was a brother, we were preaching another gospel. Manifest Destiny. What rankles us now, I think, is that an alternative gospel still remains largely unarticulated. You want to say there never should have been a killing, but you don't know what to put in its place.

Ever since man first began to wonder about wolves—to make dogs of their descendants, to admire them as hunters—he has made a regular business of killing them. At first glance the reasons are simple enough, and justifiable. Wolves are predators. When men come into a land to "tame" it, they replace wild game with domestic animals. The wolves prey on these creatures, the men kill them in turn, and reduce the wolf population generally, as a preventive measure to secure their economic investment. The two just can't live side by side. A step removed from this, perhaps, in terms of its justification, is the action of Fish and Game departments that kill wolves to sustain or increase the yield of big game animals so human hunters can kill them. This kind of "predator control" has historically accommodated economic and political interests ahead of ecological interests. And it has acted occasionally from a basis of bar stool and barbershop biology, not wildlife science.

Wolf killing goes much beyond predator control, of course. Bounty hunters kill wolves for money; trappers kill them for pelts; scientists kill them for data; big game hunters kill them for trophies. The arguments for killing here are harder to sustain, yet many people see nothing at all wrong with these activities. Indeed, this is the way we commonly treat all predators—bobcats, bears, and mountain lions included. But the wolf is fundamentally different because the history of killing wolves shows far less restraint and far more perversity. A lot of people didn't just kill wolves; they tortured them. They set wolves on fire and tore their jaws out and cut their Achilles tendons and turned dogs loose on them. They poisoned them with strychnine, arsenic, and cyanide, on such a scale that *millions* of other animals—raccoons, black-footed ferrets, red foxes, ravens, red-tailed hawks, eagles, ground squirrels, wolverines—were killed incidentally in the process. In the thick of the wolf fever they even poisoned themselves, and burned down their own property torching the woods to get rid of wolf havens. In the United States in the period between 1861 and 1881 cattlemen killed wolves with almost pathological dedication. In the twentieth century people pulled up alongside wolves in airplanes and snowmobiles and blew them apart with shotguns for sport. In Minnesota in the 1970s people choked Eastern timber wolves to death in snares to show their contempt for the animal's designation as an endangered species.

This is not predator control, and it goes beyond the casual cruelty sociologists say manifests itself among people under stress, or where there is no perception of responsibility. It is the violent expression of a terrible assumption: that men have the right to kill other creatures not for what they do but for what we fear they may do. I almost wrote "or for no reason," but there are always reasons. Killing wolves has to do with fear based on superstitions. It has to do with "duty." It has to do with proving manhood (abstractly, perhaps, this is nothing more than wanting either to possess or to destroy the animal's soul). And sometimes, I think, because the killing is so righteously pursued and yet so entirely without conscience, killing wolves has to do with murder.

Historically, the most visible motive, and the one that best explains the excess of killing, is a type of fear: theriophobia. Fear of the beast. Fear of the beast as an irrational, violent, insatiable creature. Fear of the projected beast in oneself. The fear is composed of two parts: self-hatred; and anxiety over the human loss of inhibitions that are common to other animals who do not rape, murder, and pillage. At the heart of theriophobia is the fear of one's own nature. In its headiest manifestations theriophobia is projected onto a single animal, the animal becomes a scapegoat, and it is annihilated. That is what happened to the wolf in America. The routes that led there, however, were complex.

Those days are past. There is little to be gained now by condemning the aerial "sport" hunting of wolves (the activity is banned in the United States by federal law), or by railing against the cattle industry for the excesses of its founders. But there is something to be gained from learning where the fear and hatred originated, and where the one thing besides cruelty to the animal that sets wolf hunting apart from other kinds of hunting—the "righteousness" of it—comes from.

The hatred has religious roots: the wolf was the Devil in disguise. And it has secular roots: wolves killed stock and made men poor. At a more general level it had to do, historically, with feelings about wilderness. What men said about the one, they generally meant about the other. To celebrate wilderness was to celebrate the wolf; to want an end to wilderness and all it stood for was to want the wolf's head.

In setting down a base for our antipathy toward wilderness, the historian Roderick Nash has singled out religious and secular antecedents. In *Beowulf,* for example, there is an expression of the secular (i.e., non-religious) wilderness that is constituted of uninhabited forest—a region whose dank, cold depths, with its miasmic swamps and windswept crags, harbor foul creatures that prey on men. In the Bible, wilderness is defined as the place without God—a sere and barren desert. This twined sense of wilderness as a place innately dangerous and godless was something that attached itself, inevitably, to the wolf—the most feared denizen of gloomy wilderness. As civilized man matured and came to measure his own progress by his subjugation of the wilderness—both clearing trees for farms and clearing pagan minds for Christian ideas—the act of killing wolves became a symbolic act, a way to lash out at that enormous, inchoate obstacle: wilderness. Man demonstrated his own prodigious strength as well as his allegiance to God by killing wolves. I greatly oversimplify, but there is not much distinction in motive between the Christian missionaries who set fire to England's woods to deprive Druids of a place to worship and the residents of Arkansas who set fire to thousands of acres of the Ouachita National Forest in 1928 to deprive wolves of hiding places.

In America in the eighteenth century Cotton Mather and other Puritan ministers preached against wilderness as an insult to the Lord, as a challenge to man to show the proof of his religious conviction by destroying it. Mather, and others, urged the colonists to make of the "howling wilderness" a "fruitful field." In 1756 John Adams wrote that when the colonists arrived in America, "the whole continent was one continued dismal wilderness, the haunt of wolves and bears and more savage men. Now the forests are removed, the land covered with fields of corn, orchards bending with fruit and the magnificent habitations of rational and civilized people." In Europe at the same time the subjugation and ordering of shabby wilderness had reached its exaggerated apotheosis in the excessive neatness of the Versailles gardens.

The drive to tame wilderness in America never let up. The wagon-master of the 1840s "opened the road west"; he was followed by the farmer, who cleared the fields, and the logger, who "let daylight into the swamp." One hundred years after Adams wrote of dismal wilderness, the railroad barons and cattle barons were speaking of Manifest Destiny and man's right and obligation as God's steward to "make something of the land." And where they made it into towns, fields, and pastures, there was no place for the wolf. The wolf became the symbol of what you wanted to kill— memories of man's primitive origins in the wilderness, the remnant of his bestial nature which was all that held him back in America from building the greatest empire on the face of the earth. The wolf represented "a fierce, bloodsucking persecutor" (as Roger Williams called him) of everything that was high-born in man. Theodore Roosevelt, his hand on the Bible, his eye riveting the attention of men of commerce, spoke gravely of wolf predation on his ranch in North Dakota, of the threat to progress represented by the wolf. He called him "the beast of waste and desolation."

The image of wilderness as a figurative chaos out of which man had to bring order was one firmly embedded in the Western mind; but it was closely linked with a contradictory idea: that of the wilderness as holy retreat, wilderness as towering grandeur, soul-stirring and majestic. In the Exodus experience man deliberately sought wilderness to escape sinful society. Those oppressed by city living sought communion with wildlife in the countryside. The celebration of nature by Romantic poets like Wordsworth and Shelley, the landscapes of Thomas Moran, Albert Bierstadt and the Hudson River School, Rousseau's noble savage, and the later writings of John Muir and Henry David Thoreau were all in this tradition.

It was inevitable that the idea of wild land and wolves as something worthy of preservation, and wild land and wolves as obstacles to the west-ward course of empire, would clash. They met head on in America in the twentieth century in places like Alaska, where residents wanted to wipe out wolves to increase game herds, which would in turn attract tourist hunters to supplement a state economy inebriated with the sudden riches of oil; and environmentalists, mostly from out of state, did not want to see the wolf and the wilderness for which he was a symbol disappear in Alaska the way they had in the lower forty-eight.

The basis for conflict between these two groups becomes clearer if you recall that while people like Bierstadt and Karl Bodmer were exhibiting America's primitive beauty in European salons, American pioneers were cursing that same wilderness as the symbol of their hardships—not to mention decrying the genteel men who praised it but lived for their part in the comfort of a European city. In *Democracy in America,* de Tocqueville wrote: "In Europe people talk a great deal of the wilds of America, but the Americans themselves never think about them; they are insensible to the wonders of inanimate nature. Their eyes are fired with another sight; they march across these wilds, clearing swamps, turning the course of rivers. . . ."

The pioneer's attitude toward wilderness was hostile and utilitarian. Roderick Nash writes: "In the morality play of westward expansion, wilderness was the villain, and the pioneer, as hero, relished its destruction. The transformation of wilderness into civilization was the reward for his sacrifices, the definition of his achievement and the source of his pride."

This inheritance explains in part why a resident of modern-day Alaska, even if he is a recent arrival in the city of Fairbanks, feels he can jeer at the opinions of outsiders. He is on the edge of wilderness; and he participates in a mentality that drove railroads west and thought anyone who liked wolves was "too soft" to survive in the outlands.

It is easy to criticize Western man for his wholesale destruction of the wolf and to forget the milieu in which it was effected. The men I have met who killed wolves at one time or another for a living were not barbarians. Some were likable, even humble men; others were insecure, irresponsible. But the difference was this: the ones who did it for more than a few years had no illusions about the killing and some regret; the ones who tried it only briefly seemed all but possessed by the idea that they were battling something inimicable to man, doing something terribly right. In a 1955 *Field and Stream* article entitled "Strafing Arctic Killers," an aerial hunter named Jay Hammond—later governor of Alaska—wrote that if he had not been on the scene with gun and plane in the early fifties, killing three hundred wolves a month, the local Eskimos would surely have starved. No matter that Eskimo, caribou, and wolf had got on for a thousand years before the coming of the airplane and the gun. Similarly, a trapper in northern Minnesota proudly showed me the illegal snares he used to kill Eastern timber wolves and said if he didn't go on killing wolves his livestock would be wiped out. He saw himself as a man who knew more than the "overeducated" biologists, who had the courage to stand up to them when his neighbors wouldn't. He said, "A man must stand to protect his land against the wolf when the law is wrong." (The law had made it a federal crime to kill wolves.)

A lot of people admired the forthrightness and spunk of this individual, but the sort of land ownership and stockraising and the kind of wolf threat he saw were the visions of a man a hundred years old, dreaming of a frontier farm in the wilderness of Minnesota—a time in the past.

To clear wilderness. Out of this simple conviction was spawned a war against wolves that culminated in the United States in the late nineteenth century. But the story is older, the origins of the conviction more complex.

Men first took the killing of wolves seriously when they became husbandmen, but because wolves ate the human dead on battlefields and were most often seen in the eerie twilight of dawn and dusk, they were feared not just as predators of stock but as physical and metaphysical dangers. Folklore made of the wolf a creature possessed. There was a great mystery about the wolf and a fabulous theater of images developed around him. He was the Devil, red tongued, sulfur breathed, and yellow eyed; he was the werewolf, human cannibal; he was the lust, greed, and violence that men saw in themselves. And men went like Ahab after this white whale.

Let me begin with something concrete— predation on domestic stock. Animals have been variously perceived in history: as objects for man's amusement, as slaves to do his bidding, as objects of purely symbolic interest. We smile today at the thought of putting an animal on trial for murder, but the notion of trial and punishment for murders committed by animals should not be dismissed as unenlightened farce. This was serious business in the sixteenth century, and understanding why a pig was tried, convicted, and hung for murder lends understanding to why people should seek the same fate for a wolf. It stemmed from the principle of retribution.

The scholastic mind of the time went to extreme lengths to observe principle strictly, and one of the oldest principles of justice was the law of retribution, *lex talionis,* the Judaic law of an eye for an eye. This was not simple vengeance; it preserved a cosmic order. No act of killing was to be *left* unexpiated. If such a serious transgression went unpunished, the sins of the father would fall on the son. To leave murder unpunished in the community, then, was to invite God's wrath in the form of disease and famine.

Although no longer regarded as expeditious, the law of retribution was once a powerful influence on legal thinking. And though animals were regarded by men like Thomas Aquinas as the unwitting tools of the Devil, the means by which God brought pain and anguish that would test men's mettle, it made no difference; interfere with God's plan and justice must be meted out. If a horse kicked a pestering child and the child died, the horse was to be tried and hung. Taken to its extreme, such thinking had the man who committed suicide with a knife tried, his hand cut off and punished separately, and the knife banished, thrown beyond the city walls.

Even after such trials of animals ceased, the idea that *human* murder (whether committed by another human being, the family dog, or a falling tree) had to be expiated persisted. In recent times it was preserved in the English law of deodands. The wagon that struck a man down was sold and the profits went to the state which, in theory, had lost his services as a citizen. No such reasoning was really necessary to get men to go after a wolf suspected of killing a human being, but it is important to note that men felt a moral *obligation,* not simply that they had the right, to find the wolf and kill it. It made no difference whether wolves were sentient beings or the witless tools of Satan, whether they killed deliberately or accidentally or were only suspected of having killed someone. The spirit of the deceased had to be avenged by retributive action.

This retributive stance where the slaughter of livestock was concerned—nonhuman murder—came about for two reasons. First, there was an understanding of sheep and cattle as innocent creatures unable to avenge themselves and, as such, man's wards—"Kill my sheep and you kill me." Secondly, there was a belief that domestic animals were innately good and the wolf innately evil, even that the wolf was somehow cognizant of the nature of his act, a deliberate murderer. Eventually (in the late nineteenth century in America) this defensive stance to protect innocent livestock, the righteousness of it, became a central element in the rationale for setting up bounty laws and poisoning programs to wipe out the wolf, as crucial as the issue of economic loss.

Other ideas grew out of the Middle Ages and contributed to the sense that it was morally right to kill wolves. In the popular mind, a distinction was made between animals like the dog and the cow who served man, and the wolf and the weasel who caused him grief. A distinction was made between *bestes dulces* or sweet beasts, and *bestes puantes,* or stenchy beasts. The contrast between wolf and doe and raven and dove sufficiently conveys the idea.

Another important perception was the belief that animals were put on earth to do man's bidding, that "no life can be pleasing to God which is not useful to man." Men considered that they had dominion over animals the way they had dominion over slaves, that they could do anything they wanted with them. To clear wolves out of the forest so man could raise cattle was perfectly all right. It was not only all right, it met with the approval of various religious denominations who admired such industry, and of the state, whose aim was a subdued, pastoral, and productive countryside. It was for this reason that King Edgar the Peaceful of England let men pay their taxes in the tenth century in wolf heads and their legal fines in wolves' tongues.

One more idea born in Europe bears on the propriety of wolf killing, and that is to be found in the work of René Descartes. Descartes articulated the belief that not only were animals put on earth for man's use but they were distinctly lowborn; they were without souls and therefore man incurred no moral guilt in killing them. This was a formal denial of a "pagan" idea abhorrent to the Roman Church at the time: that animals had spirits, that they should not be wantonly killed, and that they did not belong to men. The belief that man could kill without moral restraint, without responsibility, because the wolf was only an animal, would take on terrifying proportions during the strychnine campaigns in nineteenth-century America. The European wolf hunter of 1650 might kill twenty to thirty wolves in his lifetime; a single American wolfer of the late 1800s could kill four or five thousand in ten years.

Additional support for wolf killing was born in America, as ideas regarding private property and the need to defend one's property against trespassers—claim jumpers, squatters, usurpers of water rights, purveyors of phony deeds— matured. It wasn't only because one owned the cow that one had the right to kill the wolf that attacked it; it was because one owned the land the cow was on and had *those* rights as a basis on which to open fire on a wolf. "Really," wrote one sheepman in 1892, "it is a stain, a foul stigma, on the civilization and enterprise of the people of Iowa that these wolves remain and are frequently seen crossing the best cultivated farms, and even near the best towns in our state."

A second idea that matured in America was that the wolf was a natural coward, not the respected hunter of the Indian and Eskimo imagination. And a disdain for cowards was especially ingrained in the frontier attitude of the pioneer. The belief in the wolf's cowardice must, I think, have grown out of several misconceptions. Once wolves had experienced gunfire they ran at the very sight of a gun, or, in the frontier mind, ran away like cowards. Another reason for calling the wolf a coward was that he killed "defenseless" prey like deer. Man saw himself as God's agent correcting what was imperfect in nature; as he became more abstracted from his natural environment, he came to regard himself as the protector of the weak animals in nature against the designs of bullies like the wolf.

It was against a backdrop of these broad strokes—taming wilderness, the law of vengeance, protection of property, an inalienable right to decide the fate of all animals without incurring moral responsibility, and the strongly American conception of man as the protector of defenseless creatures—that the wolf became the enemy.

Wolves of course were killed directly and indirectly for a diversity of reasons. Great *battues,* or drives, were organized against wolves in Europe whenever anyone suspected someone had been bitten by a wolf. Hundreds of wolves were often killed in these drives, like the one in which the beasts of Gevaudan were hunted down. Another famous outlaw wolf, a bobtailed animal named Courtaud, appeared outside the walled city of Paris in the summer of 1447. Courtaud and a pack of ten or twelve other wolves attacked small flocks of domestic animals being driven to market through the bramble woods where they lived. They chased horses, upsetting carts and frightening children. In February 1450, they supposedly entered Paris through a breach in the walls and killed forty people. As the hard winter bore on and attempts to kill the wolves in their lairs failed, they were lured into the city proper with a bloody trail of butchered livestock. Trapped in the square in front of Notre Dame, they were stoned and lanced to death.

Some wolves who killed human beings were thought to be more than mere wolves. In 1685 a wolf preying on domestic stock and supposed to have killed women and children near Ansbach, Germany, was identified as the reincarnation of a local, hated burgomaster. Hunted down and killed, the wolf was dressed up in a suit of flesh-colored cloth and fitted with a chestnut brown wig and white beard. The wolf's muzzle was cut off and a mask fashioned after the burgomaster's face was strapped on. The animal was then hung in the town square.

A generally accepted practice in Europe was an almost ritualized purging of wolves from the countryside after wars. Preying on thousands of dead bodies on the battlefields and left unmolested by a population at war, the wolf population increased and took advantage of untended flocks. Members of a victorious army, returning home elated, immediately set about killing the wolves and regarded the activity simply as a continuation of the war. Similarly, American soldiers returning after World War II to the upper Midwest began to refer to all wolves as Nazis and to hunt them down with great intensity.

Wolves were also killed as the result of being blamed for the deaths of stock and wildlife when feral dogs were at fault. In Minnesota recently, more than 100 deer were killed in separate incidents in two state parks and left uneaten. Wolves were blamed and bitter reprisals threatened by antiwolf forces until the real culprits, two dogs in each case, were found and killed.

In antiwolf campaigns in North America, wolves were killed and thrown on the steps of the state legislature well into the 1970s to garner headlines and pressure lawmakers into instituting bounties. Other angry citizens, seduced by the inflammatory language of antiwolf pamphlets, set up their own poisoned meat stations to kill wolves.

In recent years wolves have increasingly been the victims of "recreational killings," run down by snowmobiles, surprised on snowbound roads, and chased in pickup trucks, or just shot on impulse by the one in a thousand deer hunters who chanced to see one during hunting season. (In 1975 a three-year-old wolf was found during deer season at a northern Minnesota dump. He had died of internal hemorrhaging, the result of having been shot in the back with a .22. I dug old fragments of a .30-caliber bullet of undetermined age out of the same animal's skull.)

Others responsible for the death of wolves are less visible. Tourists in the Yukon demanding a wolf pelt for a den wall and willing to pay $450 or more for one are directly responsible for the deaths of hundreds of animals. In 1973 well-meaning people in New York and Los Angeles urged that the Eastern timber wolf should be classified an endangered species. The law was passed and the same people scoffed when Minnesota complained that it had too many Eastern timber wolves. Afforded full federal protection, the Minnesota wolf population grew larger and larger and without simultaneous control on the number of human deer hunters, the wolf's primary food source declined and many wolves died of starvation.

Wolves kept in zoos die every year as a result of poor cage design, faulty capture systems, and harassment. The failure of research institutions to isolate sexually mature animals at the correct times produces litters that have to be killed every year. Wolf pups given away to people are often put to sleep because they're more trouble to raise and keep than dogs. Lois Crisler, who wrote about her life with wolves in Alaska in a book called *Arctic Wild*, killed the wolves she raised from pups because she couldn't stand what captivity had done to them. And her.

That has been the shape of history for the wolf. Even today, in spite of a generally widespread sympathy for animals that have been persecuted through the ages, no more substantive reasons are needed to kill a wolf than the fact that someone feels like doing it. On a Saturday afternoon in Texas a few years ago, three men on horseback rode down a female red wolf and threw a lasso over her neck. When she gripped the rope with her teeth to keep the noose from closing, they dragged her around the prairie until they'd broken her teeth out. Then while two of them stretched the animal between their horses with ropes, the third man beat her to death with a pair of fence pliers. The wolf was taken around to a few bars in a pickup and finally thrown in a roadside ditch.

It is relatively easy to produce reasons why such depravity exists— because people are bored, because some men feel powerless in modern society. But this incident is, in fact, a staggering act of self-indulgence. That it is condoned by silence and goes unpunished reveals a terrible meanness in the human spirit.

Our Present Disillusionment

Jacqueline Rose

Jacqueline Rose is an English instructor at Queen Mary University of London. She specializes in modern literature, psychoanalysis, feminism, and the political imagination and "explores the forms of potential dialogue between writing and the understanding of the inner life . . . and between cultural expression and justice and injustice in the modern world." In this essay, taken from In Our Present-Day White Christian Culture, *Rose questions the assumptions of the masses through the language of Freud's* Mass Psychology and the Analysis of the Ego. *Who is unjust or evil: civilization, social institutions, the people, individuals, or the state? Who is the "our" in the essay? How does our collective identity breakdown beneath our disillusionment when we cannot be rid of social evil and war? Who do we blame? And how can we reconcile our worldly actions as we refuse to question them? Do you think we live in an age of disillusionment?*

Ever since the fall of Baghdad, when looters rampaged through the city, a centuries-old assumption about "the people" has lurked, barely spoken, beneath the ghastly aftermath of the war. It is that the people, meaning "people en masse," are incapable of restraining themselves. In the case of Iraq, two further assumptions are in play. First, people freed from the yoke of oppressive dictatorship are most at risk: the excesses of the Iraqi populace are laid at the door of Saddam Hussein at the very moment he loses his power to control them, and not, for example, seen as the responsibility of the occupying armies. Second, the Iraqi people are especially prone to such behavior because they fall outside the civilizing processes of the West. Thus beneath Donald Rumsfeld's magnificently evasive "Stuff happens"— a formula that allows us to think that such things might happen to anyone, including, presumably, us, or even him—we glimpse a much harsher, more discriminatory form of judgment. Between dictatorship and barbarity, Iraq stands condemned: one reason, no doubt, democracy has to be imported and cannot be entrusted to the Iraqis themselves, even while the images from Abu Ghraib suggest that there is no foundation for such self-serving discriminations between us and them.

From *Harper's* Vol, 309, No. 185, October 2004, pp. 15–21.

In *Mass Psychology and the Analysis of the Ego,* Freud discussed the "masses," shockingly, in terms of the church and the army, where the most passionate, not to say sacred, group identifications are formed. Freud's term is *"die Massen,"* but a translation more faithful to its spirit than "the masses" might be "collectivity," since Freud's question is what makes individuals bind themselves into groups. But "collectivity" sidesteps the problem, since it avoids the awkward, but politically suggestive, blurring of boundaries between masses and groups. Or, say, between looters and the army. Or between Iraqis running wild in the street and American and British soldiers in Baghdad jails obeying vicious orders from their superiors.

"We don't feel like we were doing things we weren't supposed to, because we were told to do them," Pfc. Lynndie England says. The fact that such orders can be traced back through the highest chain of command will not stop her from becoming a scapegoat in the United States and Britain alike. The violations, however, are not those of one or two individuals whom it is easy to hate but of a group—a group moreover that is meant to embody our national pride. At moments it has felt as if exposing this reality, rather than the reality itself, were the worst offense. Lynndie England and her partners in crime will be despised less for the appalling things they have done than for shattering the complacency of Western values, for letting the world see. The lone criminal can be distanced but not the policies of a government that, democratically elected, represents each and every one of us. We cannot palm our atrocities off on a dictator.

The people can be cruel, our institutions vicious. Knowing this, however, may not in the long term make any difference. It might even make matters worse. According to Freud, it is when people's self-love is threatened that they resort to extremes. Far from being humbled, they tend to lash out in narcissistic self-defense. We are in a vicious circle if it is true that there are no limits to what people will do to hold on to their belief in themselves.

It isn't a coincidence that Freud's first extensive analysis of people en masse came after his study of narcissism, which had obliged him to revise completely his model of the mind. His early distinction between love and hunger, between the drives of desire and those of self-preservation, broke down when he realized that people can be their own preferred object. A group is nothing if not the struggle to preserve its ideal image of itself. This is not an "ideal" in the sense of the ideal of democracy invoked so often in justification of an illegal war, the sort of ideal that is set before us as something to which we, and the world, can aspire. After Freud, things are more complicated, in that such apparently unobjectionable ideals can be seen as cover for something far less disinterested. What if, in struggling, say, to "impose democracy," we are in fact merely servicing an ideal version of ourselves?

Freud developed this analysis of narcissism at the outbreak of the First World War in "The Disillusionment of the War," the first essay in *Thoughts for the Time on War and Death*. What was being shattered by the war, along with the lives of the people it trampled, was the self-idealization of the West. Freud was not talking about the preemptive warfare of America's New Century against the countries of the East, but his idea of what war should be like—a belief falling to pieces as he wrote—bears repeating. "We saw [such a war]," Freud writes, "as an opportunity for demonstrating the progress of comity among men since the era when the Greek Amphictyonic Council proclaimed that no city of the league might be destroyed, nor its olive groves cut down, nor its water supply stopped. . . . There would of course," he continues, "be the utmost consideration for the non-combatant classes of the population. . . . And again, all the international undertakings and institutions in which the common civilization of peacetime had been embodied would be maintained." Such a war would have produced "horror and suffering" enough, he recognizes, "but it would not have interrupted the development of ethical relations between the collective individuals of mankind—the peoples and states."

In a strange way, warfare is the deadly repository of our most tenacious and precarious self-idealization. Because it is so ugly it must be good: civilized in its conduct and civilized in its aims. In psychoanalytic terms, you might say that narcissists are so frantic and demanding because of the extent of the internal damage they are battling to repair. Paradoxically, it is because war is so awful that we invest with such ferocity in the belief that it can be the bearer of civilization to all peoples. Freud's bruising catalogue of the reality of the war in which such hope had been so naively invested is worth quoting at length:

> Then the war in which we had refused to believe broke out, and it brought—disillusionment. . . . It disregards all the restrictions known as International Law, which in peacetime the states had bound themselves to observe; it ignores the prerogative of the wounded and the medical service, the distinction between the civil and military sections of the population. . . . It tramples on all that comes its way as if there were to be no future. . . . It cuts all the common bonds between the contending peoples and threatens to leave a legacy of embitterment that will make any renewal of those bonds impossible for a long time to come.

Even more important perhaps is what such conduct does, then and now, to the relationship between the citizen and the state. It is precisely because the state is the representative of the people, precisely because we are a democracy, that our present disillusionment is so intense. What is falling apart is the belief in the virtue of representative institutions. It is starting to cross the minds of the citizens that states, even democratic states, might embody the very evils they use to justify wars against other—totalitarian or what today are called "rogue" or "failed"—states. Today the citizen is again faced with the dawning recognition—the "horror," to use Freud's term—that "the state has forbidden to the individual the practice of wrong-doing, not because it desires to abolish it, but because it desires to monopolize it, like salt and tobacco." (Freud uses the same word, *"der Schrecken,"* "horror" or "terror," to describe both war and the people's loss of faith.) A belligerent state not only breaks the law in relation to the enemy; it also violates the principles that should hold between itself and its citizens. "A belligerent state," Freud writes, "permits itself every such mis-deed every act of violence as would disgrace the individual." No surprise. then, that faced with the disclosure of such misdeeds as those at Abu Ghraib, the state will rush to return them to the citizen precisely as "indi-vidual disgrace." Furthermore, the state uses secrecy and censorship to rob its citizens of the critical defenses they might need in order to deal with the reality of war. Truth, we have so often been told, is the first casualty of war. We tend to understand this as referring simply to censorship, but Freud is making another point. Numbing its citizens' capacity for judgment is one of the chief war aims of the modern state.

Of course we can understand these ideas at least in part as Freud's dis-illusionment at finding his own nation on the wrong side of the First World War: "We live in hopes that the pages of an impartial history will prove that that nation, in whose language we write and for whose victory our dear ones are fighting, has been precisely the one which has least transgressed the laws of civilization. . . . But at such a time, who dares to set himself up as judge in his own cause?" Inside this lament is one of his fiercest defenses of the people against the democratic state's monopoly of violence. It isn't just that the state demands of its citizens a form of virtue from which it so blatantly abstains itself; or that it suppresses the critical faculties of the people at a time when they are more in need of the freedom to exercise them than ever; or that it has broken a bond of trust between itself and its citizens at a time when, in the name of patriotism, it is demanding ever more sacrifices. All this is bad enough. Worse however, like insane parents who insist they are being cruel to be kind, the state insists that its worst bel-ligerence is a virtue.

The greatest sacrifice the people are being asked to make on behalf of the state is to give up their right not to believe in it. If there is one thing worse than disillusionment, it is not being allowed to recognize that you are disillusioned. There is a lie at the heart of democracy if the state will sacrifice its citizens' freedom to dissent, and indeed its relationship to them, for the sake of its own violently enacted and no less violently preserved self-regard. Tony Blair's increasingly desperate statements of conviction are simply an inflated example of the trend. "I believe in myself" is the last great performative statement of an idealist on the rocks. It also exposes the lie, since, believing in himself and himself alone, he clearly neither believes in nor belongs to the people. Righteousness is, then, a flag of honor that leads a nation to war. How many times have we been told, as though it should make us feel better, that what was done in Abu Ghraib is nothing compared with the executions and tortures of Saddam Hussein. As Ahdaf Soueif put it in a recent article in the *Guardian:* "Hussein is now the moral compass of the West."

Humiliation is a central component of torture. In Abu Ghraib, as many commentators have pointed out, the humiliation is targeted deliberately at Muslim sensibilities about sexual decorum and pride. Behind the humiliation lies a carefully thought-out policy of psychic abuse. "The purpose of all coercive techniques," states the *Human Resource Exploitation Training Manual* produced by the CIA for Honduras in 1983, "is to induce psychological regression. . . . Regression is basically a loss of autonomy." The manual is an updated version of the *Kubark Counterintelligence Interrogation Manual* of 1963, according to which such regression has to be traumatically induced: "There is an interval . . . of suspended animation, a kind of psychological shock or paralysis. It is caused by a traumatic or sub-traumatic experience which explodes, as it were, the world that is familiar to the subject as well as his image of himself within that world. . . . At this moment the source is far more open to suggestion, far likelier to comply."

This is almost exactly the scenario laid out by the psychoanalyst Christopher Bollas in his 1995 article "The Structure of Evil," which describes the "psychic death" or "radical infantilization" that the serial killer imposes on his victim: "With the total collapse of trust and the madness expressed by sudden dementia of the real, the victim experiences an annihilation of adult personality structures and is time-warped into a certain kind of infantile position, possibly depending now for existence itself on the whim of incarcerated madness." Incarcerated madness will do nicely for Abu Ghraib. Crucial in both cases is that the subject is made to regress to a state of childlike dependency, at the same time losing all the reference points that would allow him to find himself even in this regressed, infantile world. The key, as the CIA manual puts it, is "loss of autonomy." Far from raising the world to heights of civilization, the ruling powers of the new century seem to be spending a lot of energy trying to turn both citizens and enemies into children.

Freud was not always generous toward the people. He was a snob. "The people," he writes to his fiancée, Martha Bernays, in August 1883, "judge, think, hope and work in a manner utterly different from ourselves." In a letter to her sister, written two years later, in 1885, after he had spent time wandering the streets of Paris, he describes them as a "different species, 'uncanny.'" "I feel they are all possessed of a thousand demons," Freud continues. "I don't think they know the meaning of shame or fear; the women no less than the men crowd round nudities as much as they do round corpses in the morgue." Freud thus handed to the people the aberrations of sexuality that it would take him another twenty years to theorize as the unconscious property of us all. But even as he takes his distance he recognizes that the people have access to a truth about the civilization from which he excludes them. "The people" are "utterly different" not due to some inherent failing of their nature but because they are so beset. The "poor people," who become just "the poor," are "too helpless, too exposed to behave like us"; in their "lack of moderation" they are compensating for being "a helpless target for all the taxes, epidemics, sicknesses and evils of social institutions." They have no moderation because they have no illusions to maintain—in this they are way ahead of the disillusioned citizens of war-torn Europe in 1914. Why on earth should the people believe in the benign power of social institutions?

By 1927, Freud's early recognition that the poor are the bearers of the "evils of social institutions" has become even more political and precise:

> If a culture has not got beyond the point where the satisfaction of some participants requires the oppression of others, maybe the majority (and this is the case with all contemporary cultures), then, understandably, the oppressed will develop a deep hostility towards a culture that their labor makes possible but in whose commodities they have too small a share. . . .
> It goes without saying that a culture that fails to satisfy so many of its participants, driving them to rebellion, has no chance of lasting for any length of time, nor does it deserve [to].

The people expose the evils of social institutions, the injustices of culture (what Freud refers to elsewhere as "our present-day white Christian culture"). In doing so, they reveal unconscious desires that, however shameless (indeed because they are so shameless), implicate every one of us. In *Mass Psychology,* he describes the masses as laying bare "the unconscious foundation that is the same for everyone." Go back to the letter of 1885: "The women no less than the men crowd round nudities as much as they do round corpses in the morgue." Suddenly this brings to mind the images of grinning soldiers crowding round the abject inmates of Abu Ghraib. These images are pornographic, as many have pointed out, but in a very specific form. They trade on the unconscious association of sex and death. You don't have to accept Freud's vision of the mob, burdened as it is with all the stereotypes of bourgeois fear, to notice that he has run a line from perversion to truth. Civilization is unjust; our most venerated social institutions are evil; be wary of pointing the finger at the individual who disgraces us, since we are all of us perverts in our dreams.

"Well may the citizen of the world stand helpless in a world that has grown strange to him," Freud writes in "The Disillusionment of the War." But, he adds, "there is something said in criticism of his disappointment: It is not justified, since it consists in the destruction of an illusion." At this unexpected turning point, we discover that what Freud means by "disillusionment" is not quite what we expected. Our mistake, it turns out, was to have believed in the first place. In this context, war, at the very moment when the state is doing its utmost to subdue the critical judgment of citizens, might provide us with a rare opportunity. Like "the people," who of course need no such prompting or crisis, we can now see things, see people, as they really are. "In reality, our fellow citizens have not sunk so low as we feared, because they had never risen as high as we believed." This is not, finally, a narcissistic lament ("How we have fallen" or "This is not the America I know," to cite Bush's more recent phrase); it is at once more modest and more devastating. "White Christian culture" should stop kidding itself.

Much follows from this. There is no such thing, Freud states, as "eradicating" evil. The impulses that constitute the "deepest essence" of human nature are "neither good nor bad" in themselves. He will condemn actions but never the drives from which they stem. It is a central tenet of psychoanalysis that if we can tolerate what is most disorientating—disillusioning—about our own unconscious, we will be less likely to act on it, less inclined to strike out in a desperate attempt to assign the horrors of the world to someone or somewhere else. It is not, therefore, the impulse that is dangerous but the ruthlessness of our attempts to be rid of it.

Freud knew that the fierceness with which a group builds and defends its identity was the central question of modern times. But unlike the leaders of our "present-day White Christian culture," he knew that no group is safe from the dangers of conviction, and that a nation that frees itself from doubt and refuses to question its own motives and acts can place the world in peril.

Planning, Advertising and Consumption

Wesley Shumar

Through a close analysis of college recruiting materials and brochures, Wesley Shumar examines the relationship between the university and the marketplace, asking the question of whether college is, indeed, for sale. Ultimately, Shumar offers two competing visions of education: education that produces "thinking citizens" and prepares them "to take their place in a democracy" versus education aimed at "careerism." Within the first three paragraphs of the essay, we also detect an elevated vocabulary in words like semiotic, commodification, linguistics, sociometrics, cybernetics, and structuralism. How does Shumar's vocabulary contribute to his argument that "the laws of the marketplace" are very much a part of higher education today? What changes does Shumar suggest to remedy the commodification he perceives? Do you see these changes as plausible? Is adopting a more customer service-oriented approach to education and keeping costs down necessarily a negative? Are Shumar's two visions of higher education mutually exclusive?

Introduction

Modern higher education is inextricably bound up in images of the marketplace. The purchase of goods and services, once a metaphor for tuition and learning, is now the central reality of college life, with learning itself imagined as a purchasable service commodity. A generation ago this was not true. This model of higher education evolved during a period of perceived crisis when the applicant pool was declining dramatically. The ways in which that crisis was handled are related to an increasing preoccupation with signs in the larger culture and with a tendency to use those signs to understand and manage social life.

This chapter will look at evidence of this semiotic shift in the brochures and bookstores in America's colleges and universities and will relate these changes to political and economic changes discussed in previous chapters.

Planning, Advertising, and Consumption, Wesley Shumar, 1997, Falmer Press.

These semiotic shifts can be shown to be both ways to manage consumption and ways to commodify the university. The chapter will also examine the relationship of commodification to democratization. Democratization often brings with it, or is carried out through, commodification (Capra, 1989, p. 3), resulting in an uneasy association in our society between these forces. The recent history of higher education in the USA can be seen as an object lesson in moving from a democratic movement into the commodification of a social arena. Advertising and the other technologies of consumption are the mechanisms of this commodification.

The Semiotics of College Life

The forerunners to the linguistic revolution—a long history of developments in sociometrics and cybernetics, systems of information and control used in the military, business and industry—were all created to be a 'predictive technology for social control' (Haraway, 1989, p. 108). When structural linguistic revolution hit American academia around 1963 it had already had a huge impact on the other humanities and social science disciplines, creating an increased interest in semiotics and the birth of a new theoretical discipline in the social sciences called structuralism. Structuralism asserted that social life was constructed from various systems of signs and that those systems were relational systems of meaning. These ideas generated, at the beginning of the mid-sixties, much discussion in American academia, as they were already doing in Europe. Journals proliferated with articles and seminars on language, language structure and language's relationship to other aspects of social reality. The development of semiotics and structuralism in France, Britain and the United States was, significantly, paralleled by a dramatic increase in the number of commodity signs in use in the culture during the same period. The understanding of language and signs developed and changed simultaneously with accelerated change in social sign use; scholars were developing the vocabulary to talk about this in the midst of an enormous proliferation of signs both in the larger culture and on the smaller academic stage. Certainly I would not say that the linguistic revolution *caused* the change in sign use (or vice versa) but there clearly was a dynamic interaction between sign use in American society capitalism, and the language to discuss these phenomena.

As often happens, the first models were idealist. Scholars imagined a semiotic realm independent of economic, political and social forces. Structuralism in all its varieties had persistent flaws in that it saw the sign system as having an autonomous nature rather than existing in relationship with the forces of capitalism in a particular historical setting. Richard Ohmann (1987) talks about an early semiotic transformation in national magazines around the turn of the century. He shows that transformations in the print ad are central to the development of advertising in the twentieth century. Print ads at that time moved from intellectual argument techniques to affective appeals, which was achieved partly by relying more heavily on the visual. Instead of intellectual persuasion, the modern ad strives for an image that appeals to the emotions. The exact nature of the appeal varies; it can draw on popular fantasies (often but not necessarily sexual), reinforce deeply felt attitudes around racial, gender, or national stereotypes, evoke childhood pleasures—the possibilities are endless. The image is then associated with a brand name or a slogan evoking the product, grafting the affect onto perception of the product.

This new form of advertising developed at a time when, as already noted, businesses needed a guarantee of consumption. The enormous investments in large-scale production around the turn of the century demanded a predictive way to guarantee consumers. The new kind of advertising images were very effective. They not only guaranteed consumption but they generated enough revenue to take over the magazine publishing business. Magazines became an image-oriented public format.

Academic journals and college catalogs before 1960 looked more like bibles than magazines.[1] There was no attempt to make college catalogs look like advertising circulars because the laws of the marketplace were considered to have nothing to do with the university. In 1964 the look of the *Harvard Educational Review* changed from a journal with double-column print and no graphics (a format reminiscent of a bible) to single-column print, larger, more modern typeface and advertising in the back of the book; a familiar format resembling a mass-market magazine. The *Harvard Educational Review* was certainly not unique; many other journals made similar shifts to a new "look" at this time.

People impose the image they have of a social world onto that world. The college used to look like a monastery and the publications of it like bibles because this was the model imposed on it in people's collective imagination. New sites look like corporate R&D parks or military bases because often these are images the new leadership has in mind. Modern university publications all look like magazines, annual reports or mail-order catalogs (whether the university itself still looks like a gothic cathedral, a modern research park or some hybrid of the two). The catalogs and other publications use the commercial idiom of the marketplace because, first of all, this is the lingua franca of the class of businessmen, bankers, and lawyers who now dominate higher education. But it is also the way the rest of us in our culture have come to imagine all institutions. Institutions today find themselves in the marketplace needing to deal with market forces and they have few other ways to imagine their situation.

Semiotic changes in American culture, coupled with pressure on the university to seek students, have made marketing the overriding concern. The admissions office in the sixties typically was in a small, matter-of-fact, low profile corner of the administration building. Now it is likely to be the biggest, highest profile office in the university. Even Zemsky and Oedel (1983) have warned that marketing higher education like a business will have potentially disastrous results, but they admit the need for, and Zemsky has himself been central in, developing ways to use marketing data to solve college admission needs and keep tuition money coming in as the government's contribution shrinks (p. 5). I would like to look at the semiotics of the college brochure and then at the other ways marketing functions on and around the campus of the nineties.

This year's brochure for a small, local, non-competitive four-year college is about twelve inches square and twenty-six pages long, in look and layout (four-color gloss, staple-folded) it resembles an upscale clothing catalog. On the cover, to the left hand side of the page, is the picture of a young man skiing down a hillside, the brand of his goggles and boots prominently displayed. The skis, snowsuit, poles and gloves are clearly detailed although we cannot see any specific brand. Wrapped from the right around his image is copy that begins, "my mom and dad and lots of aunts and uncles went to (college X), but I just wasn't sure. . . ." The copy continues as the boy obsesses about the college's "pretty campus and friendly atmosphere" and then decides "it's been a part of his family for a long time." When he tells someone he's decided to go to X, they say "who?" and at the bottom of the page, in answer, is a dictionary definition of the college including a quote from Edward Fiske saying college X is one of the best buys in college education. Below that is the name of the college in large bold red print, like a magazine name. The whole picture is bordered by the black edge of a Kodak negative, complete with arrows and frame number. This whole fantasy scene is (fresh from the documentary cameraman's darkroom) a pleasing image of fun, affluence, excitement, activity, and has no reference to college anywhere. (Even inside the brochure only the last five pages devote any space at all to information about programs, financial aid packages or requirements.) The definition at the bottom referring to Fiske vaguely suggests college evaluators to legitimate college X but the bulk of the brochure is devoted to images of affluence and fun and the copy is about feelings.

It's no accident the catalog looks like a *Gap* ad; this is a typical product of mass advertising, complete with demographics on the projected college audience and assessments—read conscious manipulation—of that audiences' concerns. The demographic segment this ad appeals to—the student population college X is seeking—doesn't have parents and relatives who attended college. In fact, a decade ago this four-year college was itself a junior college. But the working-class people being appealed to enjoy the fantasy of affluence and have no way of knowing what college is really like. The brochure gives them a pleasant image that tells them college is structured reassuringly like institutions they are familiar with; notably the department store.

The next six pages continue with this motif. It looks like a six-page ad front-of-the-book fashion ad; fantasy images of students stereotyped by role: the bookworm, the chemist, the businessman, the actress, the jock. Each image, complete with testimonial, invents a little fantasy. The brochure then moves into the meat of describing college life and beyond. The application is a blow-in card exactly like the ones that advertise exercise machines in *TV Guide,* only bigger. The back cover features another testimonial, this one a cheerleader fantasy.

This catalog is typical, although, of course, different marketing strategies are used for different social groups. When advertising to the working class, people likely to be the first in their families to attend college, images like the ones described above are most common, tying college to the purchase of goods. A catalog advertising to a more middle-class audience might use a different testimonial format—images of graduates from the school telling their stories of great jobs they got after graduating. There would be more copy and a certain assumption that the reader knows more about college. The most prestigious universities, appealing to the scions of well-to-do and well-educated elites, adorn their brochures with the images of status and culture; ivy-covered buildings, important sculptures; libraries filled with books; showcasing the tradition and cultural capital to be obtained by going to this institution. Still a kind of purchase, but at Sotheby's instead the mall.

David Riesman (1980) concerned about the development of the marketing approach in college catalogs, has suggested that an outside auditor should validate claims made by catalogs (pp. 241–7). The results of another study, looking at the marketing of competitive liberal arts colleges, suggest that while college catalogs may color the way a college is perceived they usually contain a concise statement of the institution's goals and make reasonable claims (Ragan and McMillan, 1989). But while competitive liberal arts colleges might be forthright in their advertising, many less competitive schools rely on less than ethical means to acquire students. The larger point is we have entered into a new era of college admissions, one that is rapidly changing and not well defined.

At one time there was just one bulletin for a university or college. That bulletin looked like a bible and it told you everything—how to apply, about financial aid and programs of study, requirements, lists of faculty and their research—everything. Now there is typically a whole array of glossy advertising flyers. The publications have different purposes—one to hook the audience, or in the case of larger institutions, a separate hook for each college or area of study. There are separate brochures for evening and special programs. There is a brochure for before you apply and one for after you apply and one for after you're admitted. And like the advertising images at the turn of the century described by Ohmann, these catalogs don't tell you anything substantive. The catalog I just described could be a TV promo for college life in America, very televisual, no specific information, lots of fantasy and lots of effect.

Another campus arena transformed by the advertising semiotic is the college bookstore. Many of the bookstores on campuses where I work have been taken over by Barnes and Noble, one of the largest book retailers in the United States. Colleges sell their bookstore franchises to commercial retailers because of their inability to run the bookstore in the black. There are several reasons for this, the most important of them stemming from a corporate decision by print capitalists. About a decade ago, in order to keep profits at their outrageously high levels, publishers said they would accept only a small percentage of returns on books, instead of allowing booksellers to return virtually any book that did not sell. This put colleges and universities in an impossible situation. There was no way to accurately guess the number of students in a class and books had to be ordered early. Bookstores can try to pressure faculty into using the same books over and over but this is only partially successful at larger institutions, so it has been harder and harder for college bookstores to break even. The university could subsidize the bookstores but the pressures on college budgets and the movement toward a businesslike "cost accounting" approach in higher education has required bookstores to be profitable.

There have been two main approaches to being profitable; selling things besides books, (the gift shop approach); and selling the franchise to a larger retailer (monopolization). A large bookseller, like Barnes and Noble, can deal with the problems because of the size of their retail organization network. This is one of the reasons college bookstores have moved to commercial retailers. Even before the move to commercial retailers, bookstores at some universities had begun to look like small specialty shops. At an Ivy League university where books used to occupy 80 percent of the selling space, they have been reduced about 30 percent with the remainder devoted to CDs, tapes, cameras, walkmans, calendars, specialty foods, magazines, clothing; what was once a place to buy textbooks and school supplies has become a small up-scale specialty shop that happens to also have books.[2] There have been a variety of transformations. As is common in the retail industry, bookstores market to the appropriate class faction. At an elite highly competitive university, for instance, the bookstore may resemble an upscale cappuccino bar which does carry books, though many fewer than a decade ago. It has become an up-scale retail shop with good books catering to its upper-middle class constituency. At a more comprehensive university, or the typical state university, the Barnes and Noble bookstore has become a trinket shop and resembles *K-mart*. Often the books are kept behind the counter and you must present your class list to get them; there is no browsing through the books. Books are still available at the university bookstore. But the bookstore, that place unique to the university, with books stacked from floor to ceiling and students actively experiencing the value and prestige of reading; that bookstore no longer exists on many university campuses.

University life itself has become an important sign in the consumer sign culture. Major daily newspapers run regular Sunday supplements on college life; the *New York Times* runs no less than two annual Sunday pull-outs, indistinguishable in style from the advertising circulars also included with the paper. The college-life supplements are glorified ads, with articles about how to choose college and what to do when you get there tucked in between pages and pages of ads for schools. Universities and colleges constantly bombard all of the media TV, radio and print, with ads for their schools. College fairs have become opportunities to hand out brochures and look more like trade shows than the traditional college recruiting. *US News and World Report* runs three special magazines a year on the best colleges. It's easy to see how this form of journalism can become thinly-disguised PR, any opportunity to advertise is used. A recent article (Wright, 1991) in *The College Board Review* discussed increased pressure on families and the confusion they experience as a result of the college rating game played by the media.

Families are confused because although the magazine rating articles are ostensibly intended to clarify, there is something other than the need for information driving the rating mania. While everyone in higher education is at least theoretically cautious about marketing, many private, less competitive institutions find it increasingly necessary to advertise and market extensively, given the decline of the so-called traditional college-age students and ever-less government funding. A major daily newspaper headline in March 1996 announced "With competition fierce, colleges turn to hard sell." The article reports on a number of colleges which, through aggressive advertising campaigns and computer-designed individualized direct marketing campaigns, have not only increased their applicant pools but increased their enrollments and succeeded in offsetting the fiscal problems that began with declining enrollment. The pressures on these institutions are such that they will do what is necessary to survive even if concerns can be raised about the methods.

And as already observed, with the increased competition in the global economy and the resultant growing competition for scarcer middle class jobs, there has been inflation in the academic credentials market. The job that used to require a college degree may now take a degree from a *good* college. McDonough (1994) has discussed this pressure in the economy and also documents the fact that high schools' funding cutbacks on counselors have spurred the development of a new industry—the private admissions counselor to advise affluent low-achievers about their college options. Colleges are desperate for students and students are increasingly interested in colleges with good names, so the image of the university has become doubly important.

Amidst the slick brochures and college catalogs, and the expensive logo-ed clothing and paraphernalia where books used to be, and the PR stunts and the ubiquitous commercial advertising, the signs of college life have changed greatly. Imagination is fetishized in a new, more image-rich and rapid semiotic, which is keeping pace with movements in the mass culture as it too is reduced to images of the commodity and exchange. It appears that the intense and seamless flow of images has a life of its own, but these images did not begin proliferating magically. There are infrastructural forces in the economy and higher education behind this semiotic, forces that have generated new ideas and new institutions which participate in image production.

Technologies of Control

In 1967 the Carnegie Foundation for the Advancement of Teaching (CFAT) established the Carnegie Commission on Higher Education (CCHE). Its goal was an organization empowered to undertake a series of research problems dealing with contemporary campus issues. It is clear that the initial impetus for the CCHE was student unrest and the civil rights movement of the 1960s. They were very turbulent times, affecting universities and colleges across America. Only a few years after the establishment of the CCHE the student movement began to die down but almost immediately another problem took its place, the caving enrollment picture. It was the

CCHE's report in 1972 that began to reverse optimism about college enrollments and predict an enormous decline in college enrollment. Seemingly overnight the sixties were forgotten and the seventies were upon us with economic depressions and the newly-limited horizons. As previously noted, the university's response was "economically reasonable" and it's certainly possible to see why that form of reasoning was applied to the situation. The sudden shock of this crisis changed forever the way colleges and universities planned. One factor that insured this was that demographic research, thanks to new disciplines and technological advances as well as the colleges' need for information, improved by quantum leaps. Marketing came to campus and it found not only new ways to lure students but new and better ways to accurately predict trends. Empowered by success, the scientific study of college enrollment was here to stay.

The College Board, the organization which administers the SAT test, traditionally saw itself as an organization primarily concerned with the standards and quality of education. It also has a history as a gatekeeper. Barrow said at the turn of the century if you could pay you could get into Harvard (and perhaps with current college tuition costs we may return to that system), but changes after World War II called for a way to regulate who got into the more prestigious universities and colleges. The College Board became an important part of that process by administering a standardized exam supposed to measure basic academic ability. In the boom era of the sixties the SAT was an important ticket, used by admissions officers and sanctioned by a Federal system of educational support that saw access to higher education in stratified terms. With so many students knocking at the doors of higher education, the SAT was a way of determining who was capable of university work and who needed to start in a community college. The SAT legitimated notions of intelligence, quality; the great man myth.

It also gave students a way to internalize exclusion, seeing it as personal failure. They didn't get into the good school because of personal failure, they lacked the intellectual ability, not because they were excluded by forces beyond their control. That these methods of exclusion followed racial, class and gender lines suited the purposes of the system—it was a means of restricting access and maintaining existing boundaries—and did not (in this early era) occasion much protest. The College Board is also a barometer of the times, responding to the concerns in the educational community. In recent years, it has struggled with these issues of quality and sought to identify what defines education. It has certainly tried to make its examination less biased along gender, racial and class lines over its history.

As more and more people began to take the SAT the average score went down. Students from working-class backgrounds who took it, because of their less advantaged culture and education, got lower scores. The partial democratization of higher education in the sixties pushed scores on standardized tests down because more people with less educational and cultural "capital," to use Bourdieu's term, began taking them. This produced an interesting phenomenon in the seventies. Average SAT scores fell every year, because more students from less advantaged backgrounds were taking the test and they were a growing percentage of the whole because the total pool of college students was shrinking. College officials decried the decrease in SAT scores, pronouncing it evidence for the decline of a culture. At the same time they were growing desperate for warm bodies with which to fill their classrooms (Shor, 1986, p. 74).

Not until the 1980s did the College Board shift its understanding of what they were. Gatekeeping, by measuring the potential performance ability of students, used to be a way the College Board could be part of a school strategy of increasing institutional prestige. (If you are taking high-scoring students you have a better school.) While this is still a strategy used by colleges today, the gatekeeping function began in the era of shortage to assume secondary importance. And as the need for gatekeeping receded, the College Board (finding itself in a culture suddenly awash in market metaphor) began to see itself as a marketing firm. More and more businesses were looking for solid demographic information and the College Board was sitting on a mountain of suddenly interesting demographic data.

In the days when school choice was a simple matter of students searching for the right institution, the College Board used to fund its operations by charging students to take the SAT and then charging them for each school the scores were sent to. Robert Zemsky and some colleagues at the University of Pennsylvania wondered if it was possible to use the wealth of information the College Board had to model the kinds of patterns that went into college choice among students (Zemsky and Oedel, 1983). For Zemsky, this project was a matter of rationalizing the college admissions process such that market segments could be identified and efficiently targeted. In his view this would help the right students get to the right universities and would also help the university to efficiently find students that fit the university and incidentally plan for the future because the university would also be able to accurately predict future enrollment.

Zemsky's vision certainly had many advantages. However, in the competitive climate for non-prestige schools, the goals of Zemsky's project are often put aside in favor of increasingly aggressive advertising coupled with the more refined marketing techniques made possible by the College

Board's fund of demographic data. The College Board was capable of generating lists broken into categories, cross-referencing demographic information like family income, region and ethnic background with SAT scores. The College Board was willing to sell those lists to schools. This enabled an institution to send promotional literature to pre-selected audiences, of people likely to want to attend their school. The College Board still officially sees its role as facilitating the movement of students to college and measuring their potential for college performance, but the fact that their activities are in service to marketing imperatives—it is just too easy to use College Board lists in a target marketing strategy, tailoring the imagination of the university for each consumer group—is often lamented in their own magazine (Johnson, 1988).

The College Board has now moved into a new era of management, beyond their original gatekeeping function to become a part of a technology with several purposes. They are in the business of desire production. This mechanism includes the older gatekeeping function because we want appropriate desires for the right institutions. But, moving beyond the old system, it is now necessary to nurture desires in all potential consumers, and this can be done with the right demographic information. If you know what peoples' backgrounds and interests are, you can encourage them in the right fantasy. It is also important to be able to forecast trends, which has become very complicated because attempts to produce desire will also change trends.

There are many contradictions here. Colleges in the United States have become much more democratic in the sense that there are more high school graduates going to college. The College Board can be part of the attempt to get many kids to college, still monitoring the quality of students, but it's a tricky issue. Increased opportunity and democratization is often, in our society, in an uneasy relationship with forces of commodification. There are other difficulties as well. It is unequivocally difficult to measure a person's college potential in unbiased ways; all knowledge is culturally based. Whose knowledge is being tested? Issues of curriculum and cultural elitism are only a small part of this whole difficult discussion.

Marketing and advertising of colleges threaten to produce a system of highly prestigious sought-after institutions in high demand, a second layer of less illustrious institutions doing their best to imagine themselves illustrious and a huge number of institutions using all the market techniques they can get their hands on to sell their product to a consuming public. The rapid growth of adult student populations, which is the result of the survival strategies of many universities, shows that the buying public can, and will, be wooed successfully with images of prestige and credentials promising to get you out of your humdrum life and into an exciting new career.

The crisis of higher education is a crisis of capitalism, which tends by its nature toward overproduction. The "boom" in higher education necessitated the bust. The bust in college enrollments, of course, was tied to not only declines in student-age population but declines in demand due to economic weakness. Bourdieu (1984) speaks feelingly of the generation of the 1970s (p. 143). He calls it the generation promised great hope, only to see economic opportunity decline. The truth of this causes more and more high school students to turn away from college because the pay-off was uncertain at best.

Economic declines of the seventies wrought changes in capitalism as well. I've talked about the slow transformation of the productive sector toward globalization and the development of lean production strategies on the part of corporations. Meanwhile, the consumer sector changed as well. New marketing technologies had made the sale of goods and services possible in tight times, by tailoring products to specialty markets. These new technologies were part of the shift away from a civil society and toward one permeated by the economic on every level. In a culture where college professors use the J Peterman[3] catalog in writing courses, it is increasingly difficult to tell the difference between art and advertisement, film and commercial, literature and mail order catalog.

Baudrillard (1981) discusses this idea with his notion of the "commodity sign," however he essentializes the notion rather than making it historical: the Baudrillard model developed in opposition to Marxism. In contrast to Marx, who assumed the realism of production and the idea of real needs, Baudrillard argues that capitalism has always invented need, that there are no real needs. Therefore the commodity is merely a sign, something important to the actor who wants to enter the semiotic of commodity-based culture. A person consumes because of the value or meaning of the sign, not because of any "real" need. Capitalism—and consumption—has always been about produced desires.

Sidney Mintz's (1986) work on sugar production in the Caribbean supports this line of thinking. In the early days of sugar production, sugar had three functions in society: as spice (not food), medicine and preservative. When more sugar started being produced in the colonies it was marketed as a sign of affluence and cultural superiority to the ruling class, the gentry of Europe. It became tied in to the symbolism of world domination, the symbolism of white as pure and superior and the symbolism of wealth and power, and the ruling class began to use sugar more and more as a food. As the rich ate more sugar, the sugar producers became richer and produced more. As they produced more the price dropped and then the middle class bought sugar to emulate the rich. More profits, more production, even lower prices; eventually sugar reached all the way down to the working class. No longer distinctive, sugar was no longer something for the rich to revel in. It became a mass-produced and widely-consumed good and then a basic necessity of life. Indubitably something that satisfied biological needs, though never a real need, sugar was used because of its sign function. Its history is an object lesson in the commodity sign and its transformation of a capitalist society.

Demand for sugar was produced before the modern technologies of demand production developed and is unique in that it did not require force. Earlier attempts to ensure consumption often did. For instance, capitalists in the nineteenth century forced farmers off their land and into the factories so that they would make factory-made textiles. Demand for sugar was produced nonetheless. Demand has always been produced.

The Hidden-hand and the Death of the Real

As the media became more complex and each time the market's attention declined, businesses and marketing firms moved to new and better means of getting our attention. One popular way has been to link a series of products into a campaign. A fast-food store gives away free toys with food purchases, toys which are themselves advertising a movie or TV show. The toy advertises the TV show and the TV show advertises the fast food and the toy manufacturer. This kind of semiotic chain encourages a participant in the consumer culture to move around the chain, i.e., buy lots of things. Many products have small ads for other products, for instance a soda can might advertise a radio contest, and be (certainly not merely a drink!) both an ad for the radio station and the car company giving cars as prizes in the contest. In return the radio advertises the soda and car dealers advertise the radio station and the soda. Recent trends in film demonstrate the Lacanian term "suture." In film and television it is increasingly common for sponsors to pay to have their products shown within the narrative. And there is the Internet with a series of advertisements on every Web page. The boundaries between advertising, the world of commerce and other social arenas, begin to collapse in this semiotic chain where all aspects of the culture are on sale. MTV is the ultimate conclusion; the ad for the band (the music video) is the product itself, producing an odd and ironic effect when the programming cuts to a "real" commercial, and the "real" commercial seems somehow more substantial than the program, the music video. Colleges, in marketing themselves, have no choice but enter this arena as well. It would be difficult to present images *not* part of this commercial semiotic.

Before going further I want to look more carefully at French post-structuralism. Certain insights appeared in the 1970s among social scientists who were, I believe, unconsciously reflecting on the new technologies of demand production and the resulting implications for the ways we look at society and people. Lacan, Baudrillard and others brought our attention to the semiotic realm, to what they called the death of the real and the signified. Baudrillard in particular abandons traditional infrastructural analysis in his assumption that all demand is a sign and commodities are signs. While these contributions are important, it is the historical unfolding of the technologies and infrastructure of desire production which needs to be addressed. Production is arbitrary, as Baudrillard maintains, but in capitalism there must be production so that people can be encouraged to consume. It is a materialist process that has only in more recent times been possible to see in all its complexity.

At the same historical moment Baudrillard is saying all commodities are signs, and Lacan is saying there is no signified but only chains of signifiers; marketers, advertisers and business people are developing new technologies to deal with the market slump in the seventies. These new technologies are of two orders. There is first of all a movement toward more "soft," image-based products and services (for example, videotape, software, TV programming, Disneyland), products that are not primarily signs but are in fact nothing but signs. The social arena is reconceived as a field of possible arrangements where an individual occupies any number of places, in place of the old model of a single joint public space, with a market and a set of consumers to buy goods in it. In Baudrillard's terms, a movement beyond the real.

Mintz's history of the sugar industry shows that desire under capitalism has always been produced. However until very recent times Western culture saw the world in "real" terms. There were real needs and even after the technologies of consumption learned to produce needs, consumers were still thought of as rational individuals. This vision of the real holds through the Fordist era where large-scale production and mass consumption reinforced the idea of a society of individuated rational producers and consumers. It was still possible to see supply and demand as an equation, even if demand was goosed a little from time to time. However in the 1970s, as a response to crises in capitalism at this stage, new technologies like market segmentation radically changed the Smithian view of capitalism.

Market segmentation saw the social field populated not with individuals but with demographic centers, social groups from a particular set of socioeconomic backgrounds. These demographic centers reverberate with other groups. Marketers speak of primary, secondary and tertiary markets. Markets overlap and if you carefully tailor products you can reach more than 100 percent of that market. Take portable personal stereos, for instance. Sony produces not just the walkman, but the sport walkman, the outback walkman, the professional walkman, big bass walkman for the boom-box crowd; all essentially the same appliance with the same function but designed and packaged differently. (This is Sony alone. There are also many other products.) People, instead of being conceived and appealed to as individuals who may need or want or be capable of being talked into wanting a walkman, are being appealed to in their roles or functions. They need a walkman for their uptown job, one to go the gym with, one to take camping. People are not being appealed to at all, their roles are, turning lives into demographic fragments. This is one way to think of Baudrillard's notion of "the end of the social" or the "death of the real." People do not exist in this arena at all except as disparate roles.

The fragmented social suited the purposes of business in its drive to sell more and more product, and it was also exactly what colleges and universities needed in their crisis: more consumers. Fragmentation delivered. Students now are not just "all the college-aged kids," but so many demographic segments; middle-class undergraduates who want to go to law or business school, housewives who want to pick up a few liberal arts courses, working-class high school kids who want to trade up by going to an engineering college; whatever. They have become multiple consumers.

There are many ways the fragmented social can be used to produce demographic statistics of the "four out of five doctors prefer" type. A large state urban university, one of North Urban's potential "competitors," wanted to increase its rating with services like Barrens and Fiske. One way to do that was to accept only a higher-ranking pool of students; students with higher SAT scores and better grades. But if they did do that across the board they wouldn't have enough students. So they raised the requirements for regular daytime admission, and then with rejection notices they included a letter saying the student had been rejected by the daytime college but could reapply to the continuing education school, where they would be accepted. The potential student was assured s/he could take daytime classes, that costs were the same and the degree was the same. No future employer would ever know they came to the university through the less prestigious evening college. The administrators knew that Barrons and Fiske use the daytime college statistics for their ratings. Raising daytime requirements and funneling the lower-end applicants into the university college made it possible for the university to increase its rating without changing its overall population, and the new rating not only enhanced the prestige of the university but gave it a new pool of potential applicants, since better students would be encouraged to apply as a result of the superior rating of the school. Fragmentation takes many forms, making the social nothing more than statistical manipulation. It's no longer a matter of lying with statistics—that would imply a "real" to lie about—it has become simply a matter of producing the desired social effects. Baudrillard would say the map goes before the real.

Planning and Social Control

The establishment of the Carnegie Commission on Higher Education in 1967 was part of the efforts to plan and control the development of higher education and the social movements within higher education. On the national level, the Nixon administration began attempting to manage and control the democratic movement in education as well. There was a clear federal policy of replacing education that produced thinking citizens to take their place in a democracy, with education aimed at careerism (Shor, 1986, pp. 4–5). If there hadn't been any other changes in the economy and society, the Nixon repression of education might not have been very successful. There were, however, many other important changes. 1969 saw the first big economic recession since World War II and this was just the beginning of a series of recessions and economic problems. In such an environment, management in the form of "instrumental reasoning" was quite an effective means of social control. A generation of children grew up thinking, not of their place in a democracy whose course they could steer, but of how they could survive in hard times. The message they took to heart was that survival depended on buying an education that would buy you a job in the marketplace.

Democratization of education was subverted to the interests of those in power, and in a very particular way, by carefully designing social control to take the appearance of democracy. Students got "freedom of choice," that is to say, they were offered choices among prepackaged educational goods. This gave them the illusion of freedom, but the days when they had a real hand in changing existing systems of inequality, by opening admissions, getting rid of grades and making decisions about the directions and meaning of education, were over. Democracy had been subverted to commodification.

Nowadays the liberal arts colleges can advertise sub-disciplines like women's studies, African-American studies, semiotics, Marxism; all relatively new areas of study opened in the 1960s when the curriculum was democratized. Political consciousness (of students and others in the population) became one of the first new "products" sold in the marketplace of commodified culture. What had begun as a democratic political movement was successfully taken over by the semiotic of commercialization. As these ideas became products they were changed by market forces, while education itself was becoming a market-driven arena. Faculty members not only respond to market forces in the kinds of courses they offer to students, they do the same thing with regard to the kind of scholarly work they pursue. Fashions move through academic disciplines at an accelerating rate and it's necessary to keep up with the latest "images" being sold in the market of intellectual capital. Deconstruction, post-structuralism, practice, post-modernity—all these were once ideas but are now merely product, changing moment by moment in response to market pressures. Commodification masquerading as democracy serves an economic need and makes social control possible as well, using the instrumental reasoning of the marketplace. It offers people the hope, if not the reality, of good jobs after school. It does not encourage the production of knowledge or discussion about where we ought to go as a nation, what should we do about the environmental crisis, how could we have sustainable economic development that would be good for people and not just transnational corporations.

The crisis-ridden seventies conjured an administrative army of people to create new programs, advertise them, make sure there were faculty to teach them, recruit specialized students, create new colleges, so on. During this decade, administration jobs grew two to three times as rapidly as the faculty. The production of the image, (the packaging) of education was, and is, demonstrably more important than the education itself. This is the clearest indication of education's commodity status—institutions care very little about the use value of the education they offer. The image, on the other hand, is of utmost importance because the image is what produces exchange value. Image became more important then content (Haug, 1986, pp. 40–1).

And the images being sold in the 1980s as a result of this new administrative army of curriculum developers was no longer fashionable political movements but a course in real estate, hotel management, physical therapy, healthcare administration etc. These are the new service economy technocratic positions. They open the hope of an area of job growth but may fall short of their promise. I spoke with a student who, after finishing his business degree in the early 1980s returned to night school to get a nursing degree. He had been working in a bank in a job that was going nowhere at a time when business was glutted with business degrees. At the time that he started the nursing program, there was a shortage of nurses and salaries were twice what he was earning in the bank. Half-way through his BSN, the professional literature was predicting a glut on the market of nurses. All of this was well before the recent closing of hospitals and downsizing of healthcare. The product offered looks good, people go for it but then it turns out to be not what they needed. Career professionals don't see a bit of irony in this, they say with authority that the average worker will have to retool five times in the modern world; it's just the nature of a fast moving economy.

An administration class growing by leaps and bounds also shifted the balance of power within the university. As we have seen, corporate management has been taking behind-the-scenes control of the university since the beginning of this century. But by the mid-seventies universities were visibly dominated by administrators, if for no other reason than that there were so many of them, and this has begun to have an negative impact on curriculum and course content. Administrative culture is not inculcated in the academic values and practices it seeks to regulate in the name of institutional effectiveness. The faculty can no longer say "we are the university" because they are so clearly only a very small part of this image-producing machine. The need to produce more product and bring in more consumers, directly linked to the rationalization of the productive sector, and seeing universities and colleges in market terms makes the movement of the faculty toward worker status inevitable. It is no accident that faculties have responded by attempting to unionize.

The issue of who controls the university has been unmasked. Universities, while they still pretending to believe in the tradition of faculty control because it harks back to a great university tradition in the past, and such an image is a useful marketing tool, are in fact being run by salespeople and marketers. Ivy-covered tradition simply has no substance in the present. Faculty members are glorified in the brochure's advertising pages only to be completely squeezed out of all actual decision-making in the university. The contradiction is very clear to the faculty.

This new market orientation of education normalizes crisis. When schools first began using marketing technologies to bring in students they had no idea how successful they would be. During the early eighties at many Northeastern schools they were very successful indeed. It was not uncommon to see a newspaper article about the declining secondary school population side-by-side with one about local college enrollments going up. Most colleges saw this as a good thing and worried only about doing it again next year.

Advertising does work but how well? Are there absolute limits to how much the market can expand? Where these are major concerns a flexible work-force is essential. It enables the administration to expand or contract the faculty depending on the number of students who do respond to the advertising. The flexible work force also offers the advantage of keeping productive costs down. Schools, by keeping a large portion of the work force temporary and/or part-time, get flexibility and cheap labor at the same time. This keeps faculty members on their, toes, not to say on edge. What will enrollment be? Will I be able to teach my research area or just basic courses? Will my course run? Will there be release time? For part-timers the questions are even harder. Will I have a job? How much will I work? How many institutions will I have to work at? What new hoops do I have to jump through to get jobs?

Market technologies were clearly the response to the enrollment crises of the seventies and eighties. What is less clear to all involved is how advertising changes relationships: faculty to workers, students to consumers, administrators to business people. The many contradictions this process produces for workers, students and for the culture have made it difficult to know what education is. Marketing and advertising are undeniably technologies of social control. We tend to see them, are encouraged to see them, as simply ways to help the market along but that model is wholly inaccurate. These technologies redefine the market, the product and the people involved and impose their definitions willy-nilly on the world. This apparatus of power is itself producing new contradictions as it wields its power to name, classify, define. Workers resist, consumers get bored, and the product is criticized for lacking substance. Education in America today is coming under increasing attack for not being what it is imagined to be.

Running through all of this is the confusion between democratization of education, which is a political activity, and commodification, which is not. Thanks to policies of the Federal government and the university's own administrative responses in the 1960s and 1970s, commodification has become the dominant force. There are still many educators who understand that the issues of access to education and the right to question the status of knowledge are political questions and ones which moreover need to be addressed by a democratic society. There is ideological hegemony; the model of the marketplace and the influence of instrumental reasoning, but there is also conflict and contestation as well.

Notes

1. This is not surprising. Barrow (1990) shows that the dominant force on the Board of Trustees of America's colleges and universities in 1870 was the clergy (p. 47). The university was never a medieval guild in the US but it had close ties to the image of the church and monastic orders. The common way

of referring to college as being not the "real" world probably came from this religious image.

2. In the 1980s when Barnes and Noble, an indirect subsidiary of Exxon, took over a university bookstore they filled it with petroleum by-products: plastics, polyester tee-shirts and sweatsuits that advertised the school, CDs, tapes; all petroleum based goods. It is a nice isomorphism. The retailer is indirectly owned by an oil company and fills the bookstore with indirect oil products.

3. J. Peterman is an up-scale mail order clothing business whose specializes in a dazzling array of tongue-in-cheek bourgeois fantasies.

Whither Psychoanalysis in Computer Culture?

Sherry Turkle

As the founder and director of the Initiative on Technology and Self at MIT, Sherry Turkle's work focuses on the "evolving connections between people and artifacts in the co-construction of identity." Turkle explores our interactions with identity technologies *and how we remodel our human responses within new technological contexts and languages. These new contexts open windows to rethinking a lost social discourse, psychoanalysis: "The computer culture needs psychoanalytic understanding to adequately confront our evolving relationships with a new world of objects." How do these objects, computers and machines, allow us to see differently, to explore our many selves? What personal or cultural consequences do our self-made screens, computer identities, and relationships proffer if any? In your own history with computers, how have your online identities and relationships changed through time?*

The computer as an "object to think with" enters into how people think about their minds in several ways. First, it serves as a model of mind, both historically and in contemporary neuroscience and neuropsychology. Second, the computer enters into our thinking about mind through our everyday interactions with computational objects. In recent years, people have embarked on a range of new "intersubjective" relationships, some of which, albeit problematically, have taken machines as subjects. Understanding these forms of interaction—one on one with computers, on the Internet, in virtual realities, and with robotic creatures—calls for psychodynamic modes of understanding. New computational objects in the culture serve as "objects to think with" for a revitalized psychoanalytic discourse.

Over 20 years ago, as a new faculty member at the Massachusetts Institute of Technology (MIT), I taught an introductory class on psychoanalytic theory. For one meeting, early in the semester, I had assigned Freud's chapters on slips of the tongue from *The Psychopathology of Everyday Life*

Copyright © 2004 by the Educational Publishing Foundation. Repritned by permission.

(1901/1960b). I began class by reviewing Freud's first example: The chairman of a parliamentary session begins the meeting by declaring it closed. Freud's analysis centered on the possible reasons behind the chairman's slip—for example, he might be anxious about what the parliamentarians had on their agenda. Freud's analysis turned on trying to uncover the hidden meaning behind the chairman's remark. The theoretical effort was to understand his mixed emotions, his unconscious ambivalence.

As I was talking to my class about the Freudian notions of the unconscious and of ambivalence, one of the students, an undergraduate majoring in computer science, raised her hand to object. She was studying at the MIT Artificial Intelligence (AI) Laboratory, which was (and is) a place whose goal, in the words of one of its founders, Marvin Minsky, is to create "machines that did things that would be considered intelligent if done by people." Work in the AI Lab began with the assumption that the mind, in Minsky's terms, "was a meat machine," best understood by analogizing its working to that of a computer program. It was from this perspective that my student objected to what she considered a tortured explanation for slips of the tongue. "In a Freudian dictionary," she began, "closed and open are far apart. In a *Webster's* dictionary," she continued,

> they are as far apart as the listings for C and the listings for O. But in a computational dictionary—such as we have in the human mind—closed and open are designated by the same symbol, separated by a sign of opposition. Closed equals "minus" open. To substitute closed for open does not require the notion of ambivalence or conflict. When the substitution is made, a bit has been dropped. A minus sign has been lost. There has been a power surge. No problem.

With this brief comment, a Freudian slip had been transformed into an information-processing error. An explanation in terms of meaning had been replaced by a narrative of mechanistic causation. At the time, that transition from meaning to mechanism struck me as emblematic of a larger movement that might be taking place in psychological culture. Were we moving from a psychoanalytic to a computer culture, one that would not need such notions as ambivalence when it modeled the mind as a digital machine (Turkle, 1984, 1991)?

For me, that 1981 class was a turning point. The story of the relationship between the psychoanalytic and computer cultures moved to the center of my intellectual concerns. But the story of their relationship has been far more complex than the narrative of simple transition that suggested itself to me during the early 1980s. Here I shall argue the renewed relevance of a psychoanalytic discourse in digital culture. Indeed, I shall argue that this relevance is so profound as to suggest an occasion for a revitalization and renewal of psychoanalytic thinking.

In my view, this contemporary relevance does not follow, as some might expect, from efforts to link psychoanalysis and computationally inspired neuroscience. Nor does it follow, as I once believed it would, from AI and psychoanalysis finding structural or behavioral analogies in their respective objects of study.

In "Psychoanalysis and Artificial Intelligence," I suggested an opening for dialogue between these two traditions that had previously eyed each other with suspicion, if not contempt (Turkle, 1988). In my view, the opening occurred because of the ascendance of "connectionist" models of AI. Connectionist descriptions of how mind was "emergent" from the interactions of agents had significant resonance with the way psychoanalytic object-relations theory talked about objects in a dynamic inner landscape. Both seemed to be describing what Minsky would have called a "society of mind." Today, however, the elements within the computer culture that speak most directly to psychoanalysis are concrete rather than theoretical. Novel and evocative computational objects demand a depth psychology of our relationships with them. The computer culture needs psychoanalytic understandings to adequately confront our evolving relationships with a new world of objects. Psychoanalysis needs to understand the influence of computational objects on the terrain it knows best: the experience and specificity of the sensual and speaking human subject.

Evocative Objects and Psychoanalytic Theory

The designers of computational objects have traditionally focused on how these objects might extend and/or perfect human cognitive powers. As an ethnographer–psychologist of computer culture, I hear another narrative as well: that of the users. Designers have traditionally focused on the instrumental computer, the computer that does things for us. Computer users are frequently more in touch with the subjective computer, the computer that does things to us, to our ways of seeing the world, to the way we think, to the nature of our relationships with each other. Technologies are never "just tools." They are evocative objects. They cause us to see ourselves and our world differently.

Whereas designers have focused on how computational devices such as personal digital assistants will help people better manage their complex lives, users have seen devices such as a Palm Pilot as *extensions of self*. The designer says, "People haven't evolved to keep up with complexity.

Computers will help." The user says, "When my Palm crashed it was like a death. More than I could handle. I had lost my mind." Wearable computers are devices that enable the user to have computer and online access all the time, connected to the Web by a small radio transmitter and using specially designed eyeglasses as a computer monitor. Designers of wearable computing talk about new and, indeed, superhuman access to information. For example, with a wearable computer, you can be in a conversation with a faculty colleague and accessing his or her most recent papers at the same time. But when people actually wear computers all the time (and in this case, this sometimes happens when the designers begin to use and live with the technology), they testify to impacts on a very different register: Wearable computers change one's sense of self. One user says, "I become my computer. It's not just that I remember people or know more about them. I feel invincible, sociable, better prepared. I am naked without it. With it, I'm a better person." A wearable computer is lived as a glass through which we see, however darkly, our cyborg futures (Haraway, 1991). Indeed, the group of students at MIT who have pioneered the use of wearable computing call themselves cyborgs.

Computer research proceeds through a discourse of rationality. Computer *culture* grows familiar with the experiences of passion, dependency, and profound connection with artifact. Contemporary computational objects are increasingly *intimate machines;* they demand that we focus our attention on the significance of our increasingly intimate relationships with them. This is where psychoanalytic studies are called for. We need a developmental and psychodynamic approach to technology that focuses on our new object relations.

There is a certain irony in this suggestion, for of course psychoanalysis has its own object-relations tradition (Greenberg & Mitchell, 1983). Freud's "Mourning and Melancholia" (1917/1960a) opened psychoanalysis to thinking about how people take lost objects and internalize them, creating new psychic structure along with new facets of personality and capacity. But for psychoanalysis, the "objects" in question were usually people. Although some psychoanalytic writers, particularly child analysts (Erikson, 1963; Winnicott, 1971), explored the power of the inanimate, in general, the story of object relations in psychoanalysis has cast people in the role of "objects."

Today, the new objects of our lives call upon psychoanalytic theory to create an object relations theory that really is about objects in the everyday sense of the word.

What are these new objects? When in the early 1980s I first called the computer a "second self" or a Rorschach inkblot, an object for the projection of personhood, relationships with the computer were usually one to one, a person alone with a machine. This is no longer the case. A rapidly expanding system of networks, collectively known as the Internet, links millions of people together in new spaces that are changing the way we think, the nature of our sexuality, the form of our communities, our very identities. A network of relationships on the Internet challenges what we have traditionally called "identity" (Turkle, 1995).

Most recently, a new kind of computational object has appeared on the scene. "Relational artifacts," such as robotic pets and digital creatures, are explicitly designed to have emotive, affect-laden connections with people. Today's computational objects do not wait for children to "animate" them in the spirit of a Raggedy Ann doll or the Velveteen Rabbit, the toy that finally became alive because so many children had loved it. Today's robotic creatures present themselves as already animated and ready for relationship. People are not simply imagined as their "users" but as their companions.

At MIT, a research group on "affective computing" works on the assumption that machines will not be able to develop humanlike intelligence without sociability and affect. The mission of the affective computing group is to develop computers that are programmed to assess humans' emotional states and respond with emotional states of their own. In the case of the robotic doll and the affective computers, we are confronted with relational artifacts that demand that human users attend to the psychology of a machine.

Today's relational artifacts include robot dogs and cats, some specially designed and marketed to lonely elders. There is also a robot infant doll that makes baby sounds and even baby facial expressions, shaped by mechanical musculature under artificial skin. This computationally complex doll has baby "states of mind." Bounce the doll when it is happy, and it gets happier. Bounce it when it is grumpy and it gets grumpier.

These relational artifacts provide good examples of how psychoanalysis might productively revisit old "object" theories in light of new "object" relations. Consider whether relational artifacts could ever be "transitional objects" in the spirit of a baby blanket or rag doll. For Winnicott (1971) such objects (to which children remain attached even as they embark on the exploration of the world beyond the nursery) are mediators between the child's earliest bonds with the mother, who the infant experiences as inseparable from the self, and the child's growing capacity to develop relationships with other people who will be experienced as separate beings. As the child grows, the actual objects are left behind. The abiding effects of early encounters with them, however, are manifest in the experience of a highly charged intermediate space between the self and certain objects in later life. This experience has traditionally been associated with religion, spirituality, the perception of beauty, sexual intimacy, and the sense of connection with nature. In recent years, the power of the transitional object is commonly seen in experiences with computers.

Just as musical instruments can be extensions of the mind's construction of sound, computers can be extensions of the mind's construction of thought. A novelist refers to "my ESP with the machine. The words float out. I share the screen with my words." An architect who uses the computer to design goes even further: "I don't see the building in my mind until I start to play with shapes and forms on the machine. It comes to life in the space between my eyes and the screen." Musicians often hear the music in their minds before they play it, experiencing the music from within before they experience it from without. The computer similarly can be experienced as an object on the border between self and not-self.

In the past, the power of objects to play this transitional role has been tied to the ways in which they enabled the child to project meanings onto them. The doll or the teddy bear presented an unchanging and passive presence. In the past, computers also invited this kind of projection; the machine functioned as a Rorschach or "second self." But today's relational artifacts take a decidedly more active stance. With them, children's expectations that their dolls want to be hugged, dressed, or lulled to sleep don't come only from the child's projection of fantasy or desire onto inert playthings but also from such things as a digital doll crying inconsolably or even saying, "Hug me!" or "It's time for me to get dressed for school!"

In a similar vein, consider how relational artifacts look from the perspective of self psychology. Heinz Kohut describes how some people may shore up their fragile sense of self by turning another person into a "self-object" (Ornstein, 1978). In the role of self-object, the other is experienced as part of the self, thus in perfect tune with the fragile individual's inner state. Disappointments inevitably follow. Relational artifacts (not as they exist now but as their designers promise they will soon be) clearly present themselves as candidates for such a role. If they can give the appearance of aliveness and yet not disappoint, they may even have a comparative advantage over people and open new possibilities for narcissistic experience with machines. One might even say that when people turn other people into self-objects, they are making an effort to turn a person into a kind of "spare part." From this point of view, relational artifacts make a certain amount of sense as successors to the always resistant human material.

Just as television today is a background actor in family relationships and a stabilizer of mood and affect for individuals in their homes, in the near future a range of robotic companions and a web of pervasive computational objects will mediate a new generation's psychological and social lives. We will be living in a relational soup of computation that offers itself as a self-ether if not as a self-object. Your home network and the computational agents programmed into it, indeed the computing embedded in your furniture and your clothing, will know your actions, your preferences, your habits, and your physiological responses to emotional stimuli. A new generation of psychoanalytic self-psychology is called on to explore the human response and the human vulnerability to these objects.

Personal Computing: One-on-One With the Machine

Each modality of being with a computer—one-on-one with the machine, using the computer as a gateway to other people, and being presented with it as a relational artifact—implies different modes of object relations and different challenges to psychoanalytic thinking. All of these challenges face us at the same time. The development of relational artifacts does not mean that we don't also continue to spend a great deal of time on the Internet talking with other people as well as alone, one-on-one with our personal computers. What makes computers compelling in these different relational manifestations?

Being alone with a computer can be compelling for many different reasons. For some, the computer as solitary mirror offers *the promise of perfection,* the fantasy that if you do it right, it will do it right, and right away. Writers can become obsessed with fonts, layout, spelling and grammar checks. What was once a typographical error can be, like Hester Prynne's Scarlet Letter, a sign of shame. As one writer put it, "A typographical error is the sign not of carelessness but of sloth and disregard for others, the sign that you couldn't take the one extra second, the one keystroke, to make it right." Like the anorectic projecting self-worth onto his or her body and calorie consumption, and who endeavors to eat 10 calories less each day, game players or programmers may try to get to one more screen or play 10 minutes more each day without error when dealing with the perfectible computational material.

Thus, in the one-on-one relationship with a machine, the promise of perfection is at the heart of the computer's holding power for some. Others are drawn by different sirens. As we have seen, there is seduction in the sense that when one is interacting with the computer, mind is building mind or even merging with the mind of another being. The machine can seem to be a second self, a metaphor first suggested to me by a 13-year-old girl who said, "When you program a computer there is a little piece of your mind, and now it's a little piece of the computer's mind. And now you can see it." An investment counselor in her mid-40s echoes the child's sentiment when she says of her laptop computer: "I love the way it has my whole life on it." If one is afraid of intimacy yet afraid of being alone, a computer offers an apparent solution: the illusion of companionship without the demands of friendship. In the mirror of the machine, one can be a loner yet never be alone.

Lives on the Screen:
Relating Person-to-Person via Computer

From the mid-1980s, the cultural image of computer use expanded from an individual alone with a computer to an individual engaged in a network of relationships via the computer. The Internet became a powerful evocative object for rethinking identity, one that encourages people to recast their sense of self in terms of multiple windows and parallel lives.

Virtual Personae

In cyberspace, as is well known, the body is represented by one's own textual description, so the obese can be slender, the beautiful plain. The fact that self-presentation is written in text means that there is time to reflect on and edit one's composition, which makes it easier for the shy to be outgoing, the "nerdy," sophisticated. The relative anonymity of life on the screen—one has the choice of being known only by one's chosen "handle" or online name—gives people the chance to express often unexplored aspects of the self. Additionally, multiple aspects of self can be explored in parallel. Online services offer their users the opportunity to be known by several different names. For example, it is not unusual for someone to be BroncoBill in one online context, ArmaniBoy in another, and MrSensitive in a third.

The online exercise of playing with identity and trying out new ones is perhaps most explicit in "role-playing" virtual communities and online gaming, where participation literally begins with the creation of a persona (or several), but it is by no means confined to these somewhat exotic locales. In bulletin boards, newsgroups, and chat rooms, the creation of personae may be less explicit than in virtual worlds or games, but it is no less psychologically real. One Internet relay chat (IRC) participant describes her experience of online talk: "I go from channel to channel depending on my mood . . . I actually feel a part of several of the channels, several conversations. . . . I'm different in the different chats. They bring out different things in me." Identity play can happen by changing names and by changing places.

Even the computer interface encourages rethinking complex identity issues. The development of the windows metaphor for computer interfaces was a technical innovation motivated by the desire to get people working more efficiently by "cycling through" different applications, much as time-sharing computers cycled through the computing needs of different people. But in practice, windows have become a potent metaphor for thinking about the self as a multiple, distributed, time-sharing system. The self is no longer simply playing different roles in different settings, something experienced when, for example, one wakes up as a lover, makes breakfast as a mother, and drives to work as a lawyer. The windows metaphor perhaps merely suggests a distributed self that exists in many worlds and plays many roles at the same time. Cyberspace, however, translates that metaphor into a lived experience of cycling through.

Identity, Moratoria, and Play

For some people, cyberspace is a place to act out unresolved conflicts, to play and replay characterological difficulties on a new and exotic stage. For others, it provides an opportunity to work through significant personal issues, to use the new materials of cybersociality to reach for new resolutions. These more positive identity effects follow from the fact that for some, cyberspace provides what Erik Erikson would have called a "psychosocial moratorium," a central element in how Erikson (1963) thought about identity development in adolescence. Although the term *moratorium* implies a time out, what Erikson had in mind was not withdrawal. On the contrary, the adolescent moratorium is a time of passionate friendships and experimentation. The adolescent falls in and out of love with people and ideas. Erikson's notion of the moratorium was not a "hold" on significant experiences but on their consequences. It is a time during which one's actions are, in a certain sense, not counted as they will be later in life. They are not given as much weight, not given the force of full judgment. In this context, experimentation can become the norm rather than a brave departure. Relatively consequence-free experimentation facilitates the development of a "core self," a personal sense of what gives life meaning that Erikson called "identity."

Erikson developed these ideas about the importance of a moratorium during the late 1950s and early 1960s. At that time, the notion corresponded to a common understanding of what "the college years" were about. Today, the idea of the college years as a consequence-free time-out seems of another era. But if our culture no longer offers an adolescent moratorium, virtual communities often do. It is part of what makes them seem so attractive.

Erikson's (1963) ideas about stages did not suggest rigid sequences. His stages describe what people need to achieve before they can easily move ahead to another developmental task. For example, Erikson pointed out that successful intimacy in young adulthood is difficult if one does not come to it with a sense of who one is, the challenge of adolescent identity building. In real life, however, people frequently move on with serious deficits. With incompletely resolved "stages," people simply do the best they can. They use whatever materials they have at hand to get as much as they can of what they have missed. Now virtual social life can play a role in these dramas of self-reparation. Time in cyberspace reworks the notion of the moratorium because it may now exist on an always available "window." Analysts need to note, respect, and interpret their patients' "life on the screen."

Once we have literally written our online personae into existence, they can be a kind of Rorschach. We can use them to become more aware of what we project into everyday life. We can use the virtual to reflect constructively on the real. Cyberspace opens the possibility for identity play, but it is very serious play. People who cultivate an awareness of what stands behind their screen personae are the ones most likely to succeed by using virtual experience for personal and social transformation. And the people who make the most of their lives on the screen are those who are capable of approaching it in a spirit of self-reflection. What does my behavior in cyberspace tell me about what I want, who I am, what I may not be getting in the rest of my life?

"Case" is a 34-year-old industrial designer happily married to a female coworker. Case describes his real life (or RL) persona as a "nice guy," a "Jimmy Stewart type like my father." He describes his outgoing, assertive mother as a "Katharine Hepburn type." For Case, who views assertiveness through the prism of this Jimmy Stewart–Katharine Hepburn dichotomy, an assertive man is quickly perceived as "being a bastard." An assertive woman, in contrast, is perceived as being "modern and together." Case says that although he is comfortable with his temperament and loves and respects his father, he feels he pays a high price for his low-key ways. In particular, he feels at a loss when it comes to confrontation, both at home and at work. Online, in a wide range of virtual communities, Case presents himself as females to whom he refers as his "Katharine Hepburn types." These are strong, dynamic, "out there" women. They remind Case of his mother, who "says exactly what's on her mind." He tells me that presenting himself as a woman online has brought him to a point where he is more comfortable with confrontation in his RL as a man. Additionally, Case has used cyberspace to develop a new model for thinking about his mind. He thinks of his Katharine Hepburn personae as various "aspects of the self." His online life reminds him of how Hindu gods could have different aspects or subpersonalities, or avatars, all the while being a whole self.

Case's inner landscape is very different from those of a person with multiple personality disorder. Case's inner actors are not split off from each other or his sense of "himself." He experiences himself very much as a collective whole, not feeling that he must goad or repress this or that aspect of himself into conformity. He is at ease, cycling through from Katharine Hepburn to Jimmy Stewart. To use the psychoanalyst Philip Bromberg's (1993) language, online life has helped Case learn how to "stand in the spaces between realities and still not los[e] any of them . . . the capacity to feel like one self while being many" (p. 166). To use the computer scientist Marvin Minsky's (1987) language, Case feels at ease cycling through his "society of mind," a notion of identity as distributed and heterogeneous. Identity, from the Latin *idem,* has been typically used to refer to the sameness between two qualities. On the Internet, however, one can be many and usually is.

Most recently, Ray Kurzweil, inventor of the Kurzweil reading machine and AI researcher, has created a virtual alter ego: a female rock star named Ramona. Kurzweil is physically linked to Ramona. She moves when he moves; she speaks when he speaks (his voice is electronically transformed into that of a woman); she sings when he sings. What Case experienced in the relative privacy of an online virtual community Kurzweil suggests will be standard identity play for all of us. Ramona can be expressed as a puppet on a computer screen as Kurzweil performs her and as an AI on Kurzweil's Web site. In the first case Kurzweil is performing his alter ego "live"; in the second case the intelligent "bot" Ramona is performing an online representation of Kurzweil's distributed self.

Theory and Objects-to-Think-With

The notions of identity and multiplicity to which I was exposed in the late 1960s and early 1970s originated within the continental psychoanalytic tradition. These notions, most notably that there is no such thing as "the ego"—that each of us is a multiplicity of parts, fragments, and desiring connections—grew in the intellectual hothouse of Paris; they presented the world according to such authors as Jacques Lacan, Gilles Deleuze, and

Félix Guattari. I met these ideas and their authors as a student in Paris, but despite such ideal conditions for absorbing theory, my "French lessons" remained abstract exercises. These theorists of poststructuralism spoke words that addressed the relationship between mind and body but that, from my point of view, had little to do with my own.

In my lack of personal connection with these ideas, I was not alone. To take one example, for many people it is hard to accept any challenge to the idea of an autonomous ego. Although in recent years, many psychologists, social theorists, psychoanalysts, and philosophers have argued that the self should be thought of as essentially decentered, the normal requirements of everyday life exert strong pressure on people to take responsibility for their actions and to see themselves as unitary actors. This disjuncture between theory (the unitary self is an illusion) and lived experience (the unitary self is the most basic reality) is one of the main reasons why multiple and decentered theories have been slow to catch on—or, when they do, why we tend to settle back quickly into older, centralized ways of looking at things.

When, 20 years later, I first used my personal computer and modem to join online communities, I had an experience of this theoretical perspective that brought it shockingly down to earth. I used language to create several characters. My actions were textual—my words made things happen. I created selves that were made of and transformed by language. And in each of these different personae, I was exploring different aspects of my self. The notion of a decentered identity was concretized by experiences on a computer screen. In this way, cyberspace became an object to think with for thinking about identity. In cyberspace, identity was fluid and multiple, a signifier no longer clearly points to a thing that is signified, and understanding is less likely to proceed through analysis than by navigation through virtual space.

Appropriable theories, ideas that capture the imagination of the culture at large, tend to be those with which people can become actively involved. They tend to be theories that can be "played" with. So one way to think about the social appropriability of a given theory is to ask whether it is accompanied by its own objects-to-think-with that can help it move out beyond intellectual circles.

For example, the popular appropriation of Freudian theory had little to do with scientific demonstrations of its validity. Freudian theory passed into the popular culture because it offered robust and down-to-earth objects-to-think-with. The objects were not physical but almost tangible ideas, such as dreams and slips of the tongue. People were able to play with such Freudian "objects." They became used to looking for them and manipulating them, both seriously and not so seriously. And as they did so, the idea that slips and dreams betray an unconscious started to feel natural.

In Freud's work, dreams and slips of the tongue carried the theory. Today, life on the computer screen carries theory. People decide that they want to interact with others on a computer network. They get an account on a commercial service. They think that this will provide them with new access to people and information, and of course it does. But it does more. When they log on, they may find themselves playing multiple roles; they may find themselves playing characters of the opposite sex. In this way they are swept up by experiences that enable them to explore previously unexamined aspects of their sexuality or that challenge their ideas about a unitary self. The instrumental computer, the computer that does things *for* us, has another side. It is also a subjective computer that does things *to* us—to our view of our relationships, to our ways of looking at our minds and ourselves.

Within the psychoanalytic tradition, many "schools" have departed from a unitary view of identity, among these the Jungian, object relations, and Lacanian. In different ways, each of these groups of analysts was banished from the ranks of orthodox Freudians for such suggestions or was somehow relegated to the margins. As America became the center of psychoanalytic politics in the mid-20th century, ideas about a robust executive ego moved into the psychoanalytic mainstream.

These days, the pendulum has swung away from any complacent view of a unitary self. Through the fragmented selves presented by patients and through theories that stress the decentered subject, contemporary social and psychological thinkers are confronting what has been left out of theories of the unitary self. Online experiences with "parallel lives" are part of the significant cultural context that supports new ways of theorizing about nonpathological, indeed healthy, multiple selves.

Relational Artifacts: A Companion Species?

In Steven Spielberg's movie *A.I.: Artificial Intelligence,* scientists build a humanoid robot boy, David, who is programmed to love. David expresses this love to a woman who has adopted him as her child. In the discussion that followed the release of the film, emphasis usually fell on the question of whether such a robot could *really* be developed. People thereby passed over a deeper question, one that historically has contributed to our fascination with the computer's burgeoning capabilities. That question concerns not what computers can do or what computers will be like in the future but rather what *we* will be like. What kinds of people are we becoming as we develop more and more intimate relationships with machines?

In this context, the compelling issues in *A.I.* do not follow from how close we are to the technical realities of the robot "son," but to the emotional realities faced by its adoptive, biological mother. When a machine asked this woman for her love, her response was a desire to love and nurture, and to feel an attendant mix of attachment, horror, and confusion.

The questions faced by the mother in *A.I.* include "What kind of relationship is appropriate, desirable, imaginable to have with a machine?" and "What is a relationship?" Although AI research has not come close to creating a robot such as Spielberg's David, these questions have become current, even urgent.

Today, we are faced with relational artifacts to which people respond in ways that have much in common with the mother in *A.I.* These artifacts are not perfect human replicas as was David, but they are able to push certain emotional buttons (think of them perhaps as evolutionary buttons). When a robotic creature makes eye contact, follows your gaze, and gestures toward you, you are provoked to respond to that creature as a sentient and even caring other. Psychoanalytic thought offers materials that can deepen our understanding of what we feel when we confront a robot child who asks us for love. It can help us explore what moral stance we might take if we choose to pursue such relationships.

There is every indication that the future of computational technology will include relational artifacts that have feelings, life cycles, moods; that reminisce and have a sense of humor—that say they love us and expect us to love them back. What will it mean to a person when their primary daily companion is a robotic dog? Or their health care "attendant" is built in the form of a robot cat? Or their software program attends to their emotional states and, in turn, has affective states of its own? In order to study these questions I embarked on a research project that includes fieldwork in robotics laboratories, among children playing with virtual pets and digital dolls, and among the elderly to whom robotic companions are starting to be aggressively marketed.

I noted that in the over two decades in which I have explored people's relationships with computers, I have used the metaphor of the Rorschach, the computer as a screen on which people project their thoughts and feelings, their very different cognitive styles. With relational artifacts, the Rorschach model of a computer-human relationship breaks down. People are learning to interact with computers through conversation and gesture; people are learning that to relate successfully to a computer you have to assess its "emotional state."

In my previous research on children and computer toys (Turkle, 1984, 1995), children described the lifelike status of machines in terms of their cognitive capacities (the toys could "know" things, "solve" puzzles, even "cheat"). In my studies on children and Furbies, however, I found that children describe these new toys as "sort of alive" because of the quality of their emotional attachments to the objects and because of the idea that the Furby might be emotionally attached to them. So, for example, when I ask the question "Do you think the Furby is alive?" children answer not in terms of what the Furby can do but in terms of how they feel about the Furby and how the Furby might feel in return:

Ron (age 6): Well, the Furby is alive for a Furby. And you know, something this smart should have arms. It might want to pick up something or to hug me.

Katherine (age 5): Is it alive? Well, I love it. It's more alive than a Tamagotchi because it sleeps with me. It likes to sleep with me.

Jen (age 9): I really like to take care of it. So, I guess it is alive, but it doesn't need to really eat, so it is as alive as you can be if you don't eat. A Furby is like an owl. But it is more alive than an owl because it knows more and you can talk to it. But it needs batteries so it is not an animal. It's not like an animal kind of alive.

Although we are just at the early stages of studying children and relational artifacts, several things seem clear. Today's children are learning to distinguish between an "animal kind of alive" and a "Furby kind of alive." The category of "sort of alive" becomes used with increasing frequency. And quite often, the boundaries between an animal kind of alive and a Furby kind of alive blur as the children attribute more and more lifelike properties to the emotive toy robot. So, for example, 8-year-old Laurie thinks that Furbies are alive but die when their batteries are removed. People are alive because they have hearts, bodies, lungs, "and a big battery inside. If somebody kills you—maybe it's sort of like taking the batteries out of the Furby."

Furthermore, today's children are learning to have expectations of emotional attachments to computational objects, not in the way we have expectations of emotional attachments to our cars and stereos, but in the way we have expectations about our emotional attachments to people. In the process, the very meaning of the word *emotional* may change. Children talk about an "animal kind of alive" and a "Furby kind of alive." Will they also talk about a "people kind of love" and a "computer kind of love"?

We are in a different world from the old AI debates of the 1960s to 1980s in which researchers argued about whether machines could be "really" intelligent. The old debate was essentialist; the new objects side-step such arguments about what is inherent in *them* and play instead on what they evoke in *us*: When we are asked to care for an object, when the cared-for object thrives and offers us its attention and concern, we experience that object as intelligent, but more important, we feel a connection to it. So the question here is not to enter a debate about whether objects "really" have emotions but to reflect on what relational artifacts evoke in the *user*.

How will interacting with relational artifacts affect people's way of thinking about themselves, their sense of human identity, what makes people special? Children have traditionally defined what makes people special in terms of a theory of "nearest neighbors." So, when the nearest neighbors (in the children's eyes) were their pet dogs and cats, people were special because they had reason. The Aristotelian definition of man as a rational animal made sense even for the youngest children. But when, in the 1980s, it seemed to be the computers who were the nearest neighbors, children's approach to the problem changed. Now people were special not because they were rational animals but because they were emotional machines. In 1983, a 10-year-old told me, "When there are robots that are as smart as people, the people will still run the restaurants, cook the food, have the families, I guess they'll still be the only ones who'll go to Church."

Now in a world in which machines present themselves as emotional, what is left for us?

In Ray Bradbury's (1948/1998) story "I Sing the Body Electric," a robotic, electronic grandmother is unable to win the trust of the girl in the family, Agatha, until the girl learns that the robotic grandmother, unlike her recently deceased mother, cannot die. And one woman's comment on AIBO, Sony's household entertainment robot, startles in what it might augur for the future of person–machine relationships as they are developing today: "[AIBO] is better than a real dog. . . . It won't do dangerous things, and it won't betray you. . . . Also, it won't die suddenly and make you feel very sad" (Moshavi, 1999, p. A1).

Mortality has traditionally defined the human condition; a shared sense of mortality has been the basis for feeling a commonality with other human beings, a sense of going through the same life cycle, a sense of the preciousness of time and life, of its fragility. Loss (of parents, of friends, of family) is part of the way we understand how human beings grow and develop and bring the qualities of other people within themselves.

The possibilities of engaging emotionally with creatures that will not die, whose loss we will never need to face, presents dramatic questions that are based on current technology—not issues of whether the technology depicted in *A.I.* could really be developed.

The question "What kinds of relationships is it appropriate to have with machines?" has been explored in science fiction and in technophilosophy. But the sight of children and the elderly sharing tender moments with robotic pets brings science fiction into everyday life and technophilosophy down to earth. In the end, the question is not just whether our children will come to love their toy robots more than their parents but what will *loving* itself come to mean?

Conclusion: Toward the Future of the Computer Culture

Relational artifacts are being presented to us as companionate species at the same time that other technologies are carrying the message that mind is mechanism, most notably, psychopharmacology. In my studies of attitudes toward AI and robotics, people more and more are responding to a question about computers with an answer about psychopharmacology. Once Prozac has encouraged someone to see his or her mind as a biochemical machine, it seems a far smaller step to see the mind as reducible to a computational one. Twenty years ago, when my student turned a Freudian slip into an information-processing error, it was computational models that seemed most likely to spread mechanistic thinking about mind. Today, psychopharmacology is another significant backdrop to the rather casual introduction of relational artifacts as companions, particularly for the elderly and for children.

In the case of children, the introduction of robotic toys is presented as good for "learning" and "socialization." In the case of the elderly, it is presented as realistic social policy. This is the "robot or nothing" argument. (If the elderly don't get the robots, they certainly aren't going to get a pet.) Many people find the idea of robot companions unproblematic. Their only question about a robot companion is "Does it work?" By this they usually mean "Does it keep the elderly people/children quiet?" There are, of course, many other questions. To begin with, putting artificial creatures in the role of companions to our children and parents, indeed, even considering doing so, raises the question of their moral status.

Already, there are strong voices that argue the moral equivalence of robots as a companion species. Kurzweil (1999) writes of an imminent age of "spiritual machines" by which he means machines with enough self-consciousness that they will deserve moral and spiritual recognition (if not parity) with their human inventors. Computer "humor," which so recently played on anxieties about whether people could "pull the plug" on machines, now portrays the machines confronting their human users with challenges that play on more specific anxieties. One *New Yorker* cartoon has the screen of a desktop computer asking, "I can be upgraded. Can you?" (Bacall, 1996, p. 74). Another cartoon makes an ironic reference to Kurzweil's own vision of "downloading" his mind onto a computer chip. In this cartoon, a doctor, speaking to his surgical patient hooked up to an IV drip, says, "You caught a virus from your computer and we had to erase your brain. I hope you kept a back-up copy" (Glasbergen, 2002, not paginated).

Kurzweil's (1999) argument for the moral (indeed spiritual) status of machines is intellectual, theoretical. Cynthia Breazeal's comes from her experience of connection with a robot. Breazeal was leader on the design team for Kismet, the robotic head that was designed to interact with humans "sociably," much as a 2-year-old child would. Breazeal was its chief programmer, tutor, and companion. Kismet needed Breazeal to become as "intelligent" as it did, and then Kismet became a creature Breazeal could interact with. Breazeal experienced what might be called a maternal connection to Kismet; she certainly describes a sense of connection with it as more than "mere" machine. When she graduated from MIT and left the AI Laboratory, where she had done her doctoral research, the tradition of academic property rights demanded that Kismet be left behind in the laboratory that had paid for its development. What she left behind was the robot "head" and its attendant software. Breazeal describes a sharp sense of loss. Building a new Kismet would not be the same.

It would be facile to analogue Breazeal's situation to that of the mother in Spielberg's *A.I.,* but she is, in fact, one of the first people in the world to have one of the signal experiences in that story. The issue is not Kismet's achieved level of intelligence but Breazeal's human experience as a care-taker. Breazeal "brought up" Kismet and then could interact with it through inflection, gesture, example. What we need today is a new object-relations psychology that will help us understand such relationships and, indeed, to responsibly navigate them. Breazeal's concerns have been for being responsible to the robots, acknowledging their moral status. My concern is centered on the *humans* in the equation. In concrete terms: First we need to understand Cynthia Breazeal's relationship to Kismet; second, we need to find a language for achieving some critical distance on it. Caring deeply for a machine that presents itself as a relational partner changes who we are as people. Presenting a machine to an aging parent as a companion changes who we are as well. Walt Whitman (1855/1993) said, "There was a child went forth every day/And the first object he look'ed upon, that object he became" (p. 454). We make our technologies, and our technologies make and shape us. We are not going to be the same people we are today, on the day we are faced with machines with which we feel in a relationship of mutual affection.

Even when the concrete achievements in the field of AI were very primitive, its mandate was always controversial, in large part because it challenged ideas about human "specialness" and specificity. In the earliest days of AI, what seemed threatened was the idea that people were special because of their intelligence. There was much debate about whether machines could ever play chess; the advent of a program that could beat its creator in a game of checkers was considered a moment of high intellectual and religious importance (Weiner, 1964). By the mid-1980s, anxiety about what AI challenged about human specialness had gone beyond whether machines would be "smart" and had moved to emotional and religious terrain. At MIT, Marvin Minsky's students used to say that he wanted to build a computer "complex enough that a soul would want to live in it." Most recently, AI scientists are emboldened in their claims. They suggest the moral equivalence of people and machines. Ray Kurzweij argues that machines will be spiritual; Rodney Brooks (2002) argues that the "us and them" problem of distinguishing ourselves from the robots will disappear because we are becoming more robotic (with chips and implants) and the robots are becoming more human (with biological parts instead of silicon-based ones).

The question of human specificity and the related question of the moral equivalence of people and machines have moved from the periphery to the center of discussions about AI. Populist resistance to the idea of moral equivalence takes several forms, among these the idea that people are special because of their imperfections. A 10-year-old who has just played with Breazeal's Kismet says, "I would love to have a robot at home. It would be such a good friend. But it couldn't be a best friend. It might know everything, but I don't. So it wouldn't be a best friend." There is resistance from the experience of the life cycle. An adult confronting an "affective" computer program designed to function as a psychotherapist says, "Why would I want to talk about sibling rivalry to something that was never born and never had a mother?" In the early days of the Internet, a *New Yorker* cartoon captured what seemed to many to be the essential psychological issue presented by the new technology: Paw on keyboard, one dog says to another, "On the Internet, nobody knows you're a dog" (Steiner, 1993, p. 61). The same year, another cartoon was prescient in the way it summed up more recent anxieties. Two grownups face a child in a wall of solidarity, explaining, "We're neither software nor hardware. We're your parents" (Caplan, 1993, p. 69). The issue raised in this cartoon is the specificity of human beings and human meaning. We are back to the family, to the life cycle, to human fragility and the experience of the human body. We are back to the elements of psychoanalytic culture.

With the turn of the millennium, we came to the end of the Freudian century. It is fashionable to argue that we have moved from a psychoanalytic to a computer culture, that there is no longer any need to talk about Freudian slips now that we can talk about information-processing errors in an age of computation and neuroscience. In my view, however, the very opposite is true.

We must cultivate the richest possible language and methodologies for talking about our increasingly emotional relationships with artifacts. We need far closer examination of how artifacts enter the development of self and mediate between self and other. Psychoanalysis provides a rich language for distinguishing between need (something that artifacts may have) and desire (which resides in the conjunction of language and flesh). It provides a rich language for exploring the specificity of human meanings in their connections to the body. Finally, to come full circle, if one reinterprets Freudian slips in computational terms—if one moves from explanations in terms of meaning to ones in terms of mechanism—there is often a loss in appreciation for complexity and ambivalence.

Immersion in simulation games and relationships with digital creatures put us in reassuring microworlds where the rules are clear. But never have we so needed the ability to think, so to speak, "ambivalently," to consider life in shades of gray, consider moral dilemmas that aren't battles for "infinite justice" between Good and Evil. Never have we so needed to be able to hold many different and contradictory thoughts and feelings at the same time. People may be comforted by the notion that we are moving from a psychoanalytic to a computer culture, but what the times demand is a passionate quest for joint citizenship if we are to fully comprehend the human meanings of the new and future objects of our lives.

References

Bacall, A. (1996). I can be upgraded. Can you? [Cartoon]. In The Cartoon Bank (Ed.), *E-mail this book* (p. 74). New York: Knopf.

Bradbury, R. (1998). *I Sing the Body Electric and other stories.* New York: Avon Books. (Original work published 1948)

Bromberg, P. (1993). Shadow and substance: A relational perspective on clinical process. *Psychoanalytic Psychology, 10,* 147–168.

Brooks, R. (2002). *Flesh and machines: How robots will change us.* New York: Pantheon.

Caplan, B. E. (1993, May 3). We're neither software nor hardware. We're your parents [Cartoon]. *The New Yorker, 69*(11), 69.

Erikson, E. (1963). *Childhood and society* (2nd rev. ed.). New York: Norton.

Freud, S. (1960a). Mourning and melancholia. In J. Strachey (Ed. & Trans.), *The standard edition of the complete psychological works of Sigmund Freud.* London: Hogarth Press. (Original work published 1917)

Freud, S. (1960b). Slips of the tongue. In J. Strachey (Ed. & Trans.), *The standard edition of the complete psychological works of Sigmund Freud.* London: Hogarth Press. (Original work published 1901)

Glasbergen, R. (2002). You caught a virus from your computer and we had to erase your brain. I hope you kept a back-up copy [Cartoon]. Retrieved 10/30/03 from *Today's cartoon,* http://www.glasbergen.com

Greenberg, J. R., & Mitchell, S. A. (1983). *Object relations in psychoanalytic theory.* Cambridge, MA: Harvard University Press.

Harawa, D. (1991). *Simians, cyborgs and women.* New York: Routledge.

Kurzweil, R. (1999). *The age of spiritual machines: When computers exceed human intelligence.* New York: Viking.

Minsky, M. (1987). *Society of mind.* New York: Simon and Schuster.

Moshavi, S. (1999, June 17). Putting on the dog in Japan. *The Boston Globe,* p. Al.

Ornstein, P. H. (Ed.), (1978). *The search for the self: Selected writings of Heinz Kohut: 1950–1978* (Vol. 2). New York: International Universities Press.

Steiner, P. (1993, July 5). On the Internet, nobody knows you're a dog [Cartoon]. *The New Yorker, 69*(20), 61.

Turkle, S. (1984). *The second self: Computers and the human spirit.* New York: Simon and Schuster.

Turkle, S. (1988). Psychoanalysis and artificial intelligence: A new alliance. *Daedalus, 117,* 1.

Turkle, S. (1991). *Psychoanalytic politics: Jacques Lacan and Freud's French revolution* (2nd rev. ed.). New York: Guilford Press.

Turkle, S. (1995). *Life on the screen: Identity in the age of the Internet.* New York: Simon and Schuster.

Weiner, N. (1964). *God and Golem, Inc.: A comment on certain points where cybernetics impinges on religion.* Cambridge, MA: MIT Press.

Whitman, W. (1993). *Leaves of grass.* New York: Random House. (Original work published 1855)

Winnicott, D. W. (1971). *Playing and reality.* New York: Basic Books.

Art Objects

Jeanette Winterson

Do you find art inspiring? Beautiful? Amazing? Do you find art boring? Irrelevant? Elitist? In "Art Objects," Jeanette Winterson asks us to look again. She writes that learning to look at art is like learning to speak a foreign language—it takes practice and a willingness to leave one's comfort zone. Like falling in love, Winterson says, we cannot remain tame when looking at art. Engaging with art requires us to put aside our timidity. We need to let ourselves go and remove our inhibitions. She describes the experience of looking at one painting for a full hour, observing not only the painting, but the wanderings and resistances of her own mind as she tries to look. When confronted with something new and unfamiliar, what makes us able to get beyond the initial discomfort and distraction? How might we move beyond "I like this/I don't like this?" Can we get beyond the "irrelevancies" of the creator's fame and how others have already responded to the work to see, as Winterson does, the wild vitality of the art object?

I was in Amsterdam one snowy Christmas when the weather had turned the canals into oblongs of ice. I was wandering happy, alone, playing the *flâneur,* when I passed a little gallery and in the moment of passing saw a painting that had more power to stop me than I had power to walk on.

The quality of the draughtsmanship, the brush strokes in thin oils, had a Renaissance beauty, but the fearful and compelling thing about the picture was its modernity. Here was a figure without a context, in its own context, a haunted woman in blue robes pulling a huge moon face through a subterranean waterway.

What was I to do, standing hesitant, my heart flooded away?

I fled across the road and into a bookshop. There I would be safe, surrounded by things I understood, unchallenged, except by my own discipline. Books I know, endlessly, intimately. Their power over me is profound, but I do know them. I confess that until that day I had not much interest in the visual arts, although I realise now, that my lack of interest was the result of the kind of ignorance I despair of in others. I knew nothing about

From ART OBJECTS by Jeanette Winterson, copyright © 1996 by Jeanette Winterson. Used by permission of Alfred A. Knopf, a division of Random House, Inc.

painting and so I got very little from it. I had never given a picture my full attention even for one hour.

What was I to do?

I had intended to leave Amsterdam the next day. I changed my plans, and sleeping fitfully, rising early, queued to get into the Rijksmuseum, into the Van Gogh Museum, spending every afternoon at any private galleries I could find, and every evening, reading, reading, reading. My turmoil of mind was such that I could only find a kind of peace by attempting to determine the size of the problem. My problem. The paintings were perfectly at ease. I had fallen in love and had no language. I was dog-dumb. The usual response of "This painting has nothing to say to me" had become "I have nothing to say to this painting." And I desperately wanted to speak.

Long looking at paintings is equivalent to being dropped into a foreign city, where gradually, out of desire and despair, a few key words, then a little syntax make a clearing in the silence. Art, all art, not just painting, is a foreign city, and we deceive ourselves when we think it familiar. No-one is surprised to find that a foreign city follows its own customs and speaks its own language. Only a boor would ignore both and blame his defaulting on the place. Every day this happens to the artist and the art.

We have to recognise that the language of art, all art, is not our mother-tongue.

I read Ruskin's *Modern Painters.* I read Pater's *Studies of the History of the Renaissance.* Joshua Reynolds' *Discourses,* Bernard Berenson, Kenneth Clark, Sickert's *A Free House!,* Whistler's *Ten O'Clock Lecture,* Vasari, Michael Levey, William Morris. I knew my Dante, and I was looking for a guide, for someone astute and erudite with whom I had something in common, a way of thinking. A person dead or alive with whom I could talk things over. I needed someone I could trust, who would negotiate with me the sublimities and cesspits of regions hitherto closed. Someone fluent in this strange language and its dialects, who had spent many years in that foreign city and who might introduce me to the locals and their rather odd habits. Art is odd, and the common method of trying to fit it into the scheme of things, either by taming it or baiting it, cannot succeed. Who at the zoo has any sense of the lion?

At last, back home, and ransacking the shelves of secondhand bookshops, I found Roger Fry.

It may seem hopelessly old-fashioned to have returned to Bloomsbury, but I do not care about fashion, only about permanencies, and if books, music and pictures are happy enough to be indifferent to time, then so am I.

Fry was the one I wanted. For me, at least, a perfect guide, close enough in spirit to Walter Pater, but necessarily firmer. I had better come clean now and say that I do not believe that art (all art) and beauty are ever separate, nor do I believe that either art or beauty are optional in a sane society. That puts me on the side of what Harold Bloom calls "the ecstasy of the privileged moment." Art, all art, as insight, as rapture, as transformation, as joy. Unlike Harold Bloom, I really believe that human beings can be taught to love what they do not love already and that the privileged moment exists for all of us, if we let it. Letting art is the paradox of active surrender. I have to work for art if I want art to work on me.

I knew about Roger Fry because I had read Virginia Woolf's biography of him, and because it is impossible to be interested in Modernism without finding reference to him. It was he who gave us the term "Post-Impressionist," without realising that the late twentieth century would soon be entirely fenced in with posts.

A Quaker, trained as a scientist, passionate about painting, Roger Fry did more than anyone else in Britain to promote and protect new work during the first thirty years of the century. The key quality in Fry's writing is enthusiasm. Nothing to him is dull. Such a life-delighting, art-delighting approach, unashamed of emotion, unashamed of beauty, was what I needed.

I decided that my self-imposed studentship would perform a figure of eight. I would concentrate my reading on priests and prophets of the past, while focusing my looking on modern painters. This saved me from the Old Master syndrome and it allowed me to approach a painting without unfelt reverence or unfit complacency. At the same time it allowed me to test out the theories and assumptions of the art writers whose company I kept. For me, this lemniscate of back and forth has proved the right method. I still know far far less about pictures than I do about books and this will not change. What has changed is my way of seeing. I am learning how to look at pictures. What has changed is my capacity of feeling. Art opens the heart.

Art takes time. To spend an hour looking at a painting is difficult. The public gallery experience is one that encourages art at a trot. There are the paintings, the marvellous speaking works, definite, independent, each with a Self it would be impossible to ignore, if . . . if . . . , it were possible to see it. I do not only mean the crowds and the guards and the low lights and the ropes, which make me think of freak shows, I mean the thick curtain of irrelevancies that screens the painting from the viewer. Increasingly, galleries have a habit of saying when they acquired a painting and how much it cost . . .

Millions! The viewer does not see the colours on the canvas, he sees the colour of the money.

Is the painting famous? Yes! Think of all the people who have carefully spared one minute of their lives to stand in front of it.

Is the painting Authority? Does the guide-book tell us that it is part of The Canon? If Yes, then half of the viewers will admire it on principle, while the other half will dismiss it on principle.

Who painted it? What do we know about his/her sexual practices and have we seen anything about them on the television? If not, the museum will likely have a video full of schoolboy facts and tabloid gossip.

Where is the tea-room/toilet/gift shop?

Where is the painting in any of this?

Experiencing paintings as moving pictures, out of context, disconnected, jostled, over-literary, with their endless accompanying explanations, over-crowded, one against the other, room on room, does not make it easy to fall in love. Love takes time. It may be that if you have as much difficulty with museums as I do, that the only way into the strange life of pictures is to expose yourself to as much contemporary art as you can until you find something, anything, that you will go back and back to see again, and even make great sacrifices to buy. Inevitably, if you start to love pictures, you will start to buy pictures. The time, like the money, can be found, and those who call the whole business élitist, might be fair enough to reckon up the time they spend in front of the television, at the DIY store, and how much the latest satellite equipment and new PC has cost.

For myself, now that paintings matter, public galleries are much less dispiriting. I have learned to ignore everything about them, except for the one or two pieces with whom I have come to spend the afternoon.

Supposing we made a pact with a painting and agreed to sit down and look at it, on our own, with no distractions, for one hour. The painting should be an original, not a reproduction, and we should start with the advantage of liking it, even if only a little. What would we find?

Increasing discomfort. When was the last time you looked at anything, solely, and concentratedly, and for its own sake? Ordinary life passes in a near blur. If we go to the theatre or the cinema, the images before us change constantly, and there is the distraction of language. Our loved ones are so well known to us that there is no need to look at them, and one of the gentle jokes of married life is that we do not. Nevertheless, here is a painting and we have agreed to look at it for one hour. We find we are not very good at looking.

Increasing distraction. Is my mind wandering to the day's work, to the football match, to what's for dinner, to sex, to whatever it is that will give me something to do other than look at the painting?

Increasing invention. After some time spent daydreaming, the guilty or the dutiful might wrench back their attention to the picture.

What is it about? Is it a landscape? Is it figurative? More promisingly, is it a nude? If the picture seems to offer an escape route then this is the moment to take it. I can make up stories about the characters on the canvas much as art-historians like to identify the people in Rembrandt's *The Night Watch.* Now I am beginning to feel much more confident because I am truly engaging with the picture. A picture is its subject matter isn't it? Oh dear, mine's an abstract. Never mind, would that pink suit me?

Increasing irritation. Why doesn't the picture *do* something? Why is it hanging there staring at me? What is this picture for? Pictures should give pleasure but this picture is making me very cross. Why should I admire it? Quite clearly it doesn't admire me . . .

Admire me is the sub-text of so much of our looking; the demand put on art that it should reflect the reality of the viewer. The true painting, in its stubborn independence, cannot do this, except coincidentally. Its reality is imaginative not mundane.

When the thick curtain of protection is taken away; protection of prejudice, protection of authority, protection of trivia, even the most familiar of paintings can begin to work its power. There are very few people who could manage an hour alone with the *Mona Lisa.*

But our poor art-lover in his aesthetic laboratory has not succeeded in freeing himself from the protection of assumption. What he has found is that the painting objects to his lack of concentration; his failure to meet intensity with intensity. He still has not discovered anything about the painting but the painting has discovered a lot about him. He is inadequate and the painting has told him so.

It is not as hopeless as it seems. If I can be persuaded to make the experiment again (and again and again), something, very different might occur after the first shock of finding out that I do not know how to look at pictures, let alone how to like them.

A favourite writer of mine, an American, an animal trainer, a Yale philosopher, Vicki Heame, has written of the acute awkwardness and embarrassment of those who work with magnificent animals, and find themselves at a moment of reckoning, summed up in those deep and difficult eyes. Art has deep and difficult eyes and for many the gaze is too insistent. Better to pretend that art is dumb, or at least has nothing to say that makes sense to us. If art, all art, is concerned with truth, then a society in denial will not find much use for it.

In the West, we avoid painful encounters with art by trivialising it, or by familiarising it. Our present obsession with the past has the double advantage of making new work seem raw and rough compared to the cosy patina of tradition, whilst refusing tradition its vital connection to what is happening now. By making islands of separation out of the unbreakable chain of human creativity, we are able to set up false comparisons, false expectations, all the while lamenting that the music, poetry, painting, prose, performance art of Now, fails to live up to the art of Then, which is why, we say, it does not affect us. In fact, we are no more moved by a past we are busy inventing, than by a present we are busy denying. If you love a Cézanne, you can love a Hockney, can love a Boyd, can love a Rao. *If* you love a Cézanne rather than lip-service it.

We are an odd people: We make it as difficult as possible for our artists to work honestly while they are alive; either we refuse them money or we ruin them with money; either we flatter them with unhelpful praise or wound them with unhelpful blame, and when they are too old, or too dead, or too beyond dispute to hinder any more, we canonise them, so that what was wild is tamed, what was objecting, becomes Authority. Canonising pictures is one way of killing them. When the sense of familiarity becomes too great, history, popularity, association, all crowd in between the viewer and the picture and block it out. Not only pictures suffer like this, all the arts suffer like this.

That is one reason why the calling of the artist, in any medium, is to make it new. I do not mean that in new work the past is repudiated; quite the opposite, the past is reclaimed. It is not lost to authority, it is not absorbed at a level of familiarity. It is re-stated and re-instated in its original vigour. Leonardo is present in Cézanne, Michelangelo flows through Picasso and on into Hockney. This is not ancestor worship, it is the lineage of art. It is not so much influence as it is connection.

I do not want to argue here about great artists, I want to concentrate on true artists, major or minor, who are connected to the past and who themselves make a connection to the future. The true artist is connected. The true artist studies the past, not as a copyist or a pasticheur will study the past, those people are interested only in the final product, the art object, signed sealed and delivered to a public drugged on reproduction. The true artist is interested in the art object as an art process, the thing in being, the being of the thing, the struggle, the excitement, the energy, that have found expression in a particular way. The true artist is after the problem. The false artist wants it solved (by somebody else).

If the true artist is connected, then he or she has much to give us because it is connection that we seek. Connection to the past, to one another, to the physical world, still compelling, in spite of the ravages of technology. A picture, a book, a piece of music, can remind me of feelings, thinkings, I did not even know I had forgot. Whether art tunnels deep under consciousness or whether it causes out of its own invention, reciprocal inventions that we then call memory, I do not know. I do know that the process of art is a series of jolts, or perhaps I mean volts, for art is an extraordinarily faithful transmitter. Our job is to keep our receiving equipment in good working order.

How?

It is impossible to legislate taste, and if it were possible, it would be repugnant. There are no Commandments in art and no easy axioms for art appreciation. "Do I like this?" is the question anyone should ask themselves at the moment of confrontation with the picture. But if "yes," why "yes"? and if "no," why "no"? The obvious direct emotional response is never simple, and ninety-nine times out of a hundred, the "yes" or "no" has nothing at all to do with the picture in its own right.

"I don't understand this poem"
"I never listen to classical music"
"I don't like this picture"

are common enough statements but not ones that tell us anything about books, painting, or music. They are statements that tell us something about the speaker. That should be obvious, but in fact, such statements are offered as criticisms of art, as evidence against, not least because the ignorant, the lazy, or the plain confused are not likely to want to admit themselves as such. We hear a lot about the arrogance of the artist but nothing about the arrogance of the audience. The audience, who have not done the work, who have not taken any risks, whose life and livelihood are not bound up at every moment with what they are making, who have given no thought to the medium or the method, will glance up, flick through, chatter over the opening chords, then snap their fingers and walk away like some monstrous Roman tyrant. This is not arrogance; of course they can absorb in a few moments, and without any effort, the sum of the artist and the art.

If the obvious direct emotional response is to have any meaning, the question "Do I like this?" will have to be the opening question and not the final judgement. An examination of our own feelings will have to give way to an examination of the piece of work. This is fair to the work and it will help to clarify the nature of our own feelings; to reveal prejudice, opinion, anxiety, even the mood of the day. It is right to trust our feelings but right to test them too. If they are what we say they are, they will stand the test, if not, we will at least be less insincere. But here we come back to the first hurdle of art, and it is a high one; it shows us up.

When you say "This work has nothing to do with me." When you say "This work is boring/pointless/silly/obscure/élitist etc.," you might be right, because you are looking at a fad, or you might be wrong because the work falls so outside of the safety of your own experience that in order to keep your own world intact, you must deny the other world of the painting. This denial of imaginative experience happens at a deeper level than our affirmation of our daily world. Every day, in countless ways, you and I convince ourselves about ourselves. True art, when it happens to us, challenges the "I" that we are.

A love-parallel would be just; falling in love challenges the reality to which we lay claim, part of the pleasure of love and part of its terror, is the world turned upside down. We want and we don't want, the cutting edge, the upset, the new views. Mostly we work hard at taming our emotional environment just as we work hard at taming our aesthetic environment. We already have tamed our physical environment. And are we happy with all this tameness? Are you?

Art cannot be tamed, although our responses to it can be, and in relation to The Canon, our responses are conditioned from the moment we start school. The freshness which the everyday regular man or woman pride themselves upon; the untaught "I know what I like" approach, now encouraged by the media, is neither fresh nor untaught. It is the half-baked sterility of the classroom washed down with liberal doses of popular culture.

The media ransacks the arts, in its images, in its adverts, in its copy, in its jingles, in its little tunes and journalist's jargon, it continually offers up faint shadows of the form and invention of real music, real paintings, real words. All of us are subject to this bombardment, which both deadens our sensibilities and makes us fear what is not instant, approachable, consumable. The solid presence of art demands from us significant effort, an effort anathema to popular culture. Effort of time, effort of money, effort of study, effort of humility, effort of imagination have each been packed by the artist into the art. Is it so unreasonable to expect a percentage of that from us in return? I worry that to ask for effort is to imply élitism, and the charge against art, that it is élitist, is too often the accuser's defence against his or her own bafflement. It is quite close to the remark "Why can't they all speak English?," which may be why élitist is the favourite insult of the British and the Americans.

But, you may say, how can I know what is good and what is not good? I may wince at the cheap seascape over the mantelpiece but does that necessarily mean I should go to the Tate Gallery and worship a floor full of dyed rice?

Years ago, when I was living very briefly with a stockbroker who had a good cellar, I asked him how I could learn about wine.

"Drink it" he said.

It is true. The only way to develop a palate is to develop a palate. That is why, when I wanted to know about paintings, I set out to look at as many as I could, using always, tested standards, but continuing to test them. You can like a thing out of ignorance, and it is perhaps a blessing that such naiveté stays with us until we die. Even now, we are not as closed and muffled as art-pessimists think we are, we do fall in love at first sight. All well and good, but the fashion for dismissing a thing out of ignorance is vicious. In fact, it is not essential to like a thing in order to recognise its worth, but to reach that point of self-awareness and sophistication takes years of perseverance.

For most of us the question "Do I like this?" will always be the formative question. Vital then, that we widen the "I" that we are as much as we can. Vital then, we recognise that the question "Do I like this?" involves an independent object, as well as our own subjectivity.

I am sure that if as a society we took art seriously, not as mere decoration or entertainment, but as a living spirit, we should very soon learn what is art and what is not art. The American poet Muriel Rukeyser has said:

> There is art and there is non-art; they are two universes (in the algebraic sense) which are exclusive . . . It seems to me that to call an achieved work 'good art' and an unachieved work 'bad art,' is like calling one colour 'good red' and another 'bad red' when the second one is green.

If we accept this, it does not follow that we should found an Academy of Good Taste or throw out all our pet water-colours, student posters or family portraits. Let them be but know what they are, and perhaps more importantly, what they are not. If we sharpened our sensibilities, it is not that we would all agree on everything, or that we would suddenly feel the same things in front of the same pictures (or when reading the same book), but rather that our debates and deliberations would come out of genuine aesthetic considerations and not politics, prejudice and fashion . . . And our hearts? Art is aerobic.

It is shocking too. The most conservative and least interested person will probably tell you that he or she likes Constable. But would our stalwart have liked Constable in 1824 when he exhibited at the Paris Salon and caused a riot? We forget that every true shock in art, whether books, paintings or music, eventually becomes a commonplace, even a standard, to later generations. It is not that those works are tired out and have nothing more to offer, it is that their discoveries are gradually diluted by lesser artists who can only copy but do know how to make a thing accessible and desirable. At last, what was new becomes so well known that we cannot separate it from its cultural associations and time-honoured values. To the average eye, now, Constable is a pretty landscape painter, not a revolutionary who daubed bright colour against bright colour ungraded by chiaroscuro. We have had a hundred and fifty years to get used to the man who turned his back on the studio picture, took his easel outdoors and painted in a rapture of light. It is easy to copy Constable. It was not easy to be Constable.

I cannot afford a Constable, or a Picasso, or a Leonardo, but to profess a love of painting and not to have anything original is as peculiar as a booklover with nothing on her shelves. I do not know why the crowds and crowds of visitors to public galleries do not go out and support new work. Are we talking love-affair or peep-show?

I move gingerly around the paintings I own because I know they are looking at me as closely as I am looking at them. There is a constant exchange of emotion between us, between the three of us; the artist I need never meet, the painting in its own right, and me, the one who loves it and can no longer live independent of it. The triangle of exchange alters, is fluid, is subtle, is profound and is one of those unverifiable facts that anyone who cares for painting soon discovers. The picture on my wall, art object and art process, is a living line of movement, a wave of colour that repercusses in my body, colouring it, colouring the new present, the future, and even the past, which cannot now be considered outside of the light of the painting. I think of something I did, the picture catches me, adds to the thought, changes the meaning of thought and past. The totality of the picture comments on the totality of what I am. The greater the picture the more complete this process is.

Process, the energy in being, the refusal of finality, which is not the same thing as the refusal of completeness, sets art, all art, apart from the end-stop world that is always calling "Time Please!"

We know that the universe is infinite, expanding and strangely complete, that it lacks nothing we need, but in spite of that knowledge, the tragic paradigm of human life is lack, loss, finality, a primitive doom saying that has not been repealed by technology or medical science. The arts stand in the way of this doomsaying. Art objects. The nouns become an active force not a collector's item. Art objects.

The cave wall paintings at Lascaux, the Sistine Chapel ceiling, the huge truth of a Picasso, the quieter truth of Vanessa Bell, are part of the art that objects to the lie against life, against the spirit, that it is pointless and mean. The message coloured through time is not lack, but abundance. Not silence but many voices. Art, all art, is the communication cord that cannot be snapped by indifference or disaster. Against the daily death it does not die.

All painting is cave painting; painting on the low dark walls of you and me, intimations of grandeur. The painted church is the tattooed body of Christ, not bound into religion, but unbound out of love. Love, the eloquent shorthand that volumes out those necessary invisibles of faith and optimism, humour and generosity, sublimity of mankind made visible through art.

Naked I came into the world, but brush strokes cover me, language raises me, music rhythms me. Art is my rod and staff, my resting place and shield, and not mine only, for art leaves nobody out. Even those from whom art has been stolen away by tyranny, by poverty, begin to make it again. If the arts did not exist, at every moment, someone would begin to create them, in song, out of dust and mud, and although the artifacts might be destroyed, the energy that creates them is not destroyed. If in the comfortable West, we have chosen to treat such energies with scepticism and contempt, then so much the worse for us. Art is not a little bit of evolution that late-twentieth-century city dwellers can safely do without. Strictly, art does not belong to our evolutionary pattern at all. It has no biological necessity. Time taken up with it was time lost to hunting, gathering, mating, exploring, building, surviving, thriving. Odd then, that when routine physical threats to ourselves and our kind are no longer a reality, we say we have no time for art.

If we say that art, all art is no longer relevant to our lives, then we might at least risk the question "What has happened to our lives?" The usual question, "What has happened to art?" is too easy an escape route.

I did not escape. At an Amsterdam gallery I sat down and wept.
When I sold a book I bought a Massimo Rao. Since that day I have been filling my walls with new light.

The Numbing of the American Mind: Culture as Anesthetic

Thomas de Zengotita

A question raised by many modern philosophers is whether an absolute or authoritative version of reality exists. In "The Numbing of the American Mind," Thomas de Zengotita, an anthropologist at Columbia University, suggests that reality is more fragmented than ever. He describes some of the degrees or categories of reality in which we live ("real real," "observed real," "staged real"). He argues that the effect of being bombarded by such a range of realities—from the edited reality of wedding videos to the uniquely staged reality of "Survivor"—is that we become numb to the subtle differences between these varying degrees of reality. What are the results of this numbing of the American mind? Do we indeed lead lives of "perpetual motion" in "a flood of surfaces," and if so, how do we cope with this flood in our day-to-day existence?

. . . the massive influx of impressions is so great; surprising, barbaric, and violent things press so overpoweringly—"balled up into hideous clumps"—in the youthful soul; that it can save itself only by taking recourse in premeditated stupidity.

—*Friedrich Nietzsche*

It was to have been the end of irony, remember? Superficial celebrity culture was over; a new age of seriousness was upon us. Of course, the way media celebrities focused on their own mood as the consequence of September 11 was in itself an irony so marvelous you knew immediately how wrong they were. And sure enough, the spotlight never wavered. It went on shining as it always had, on those it was meant for—on them. A guarantee of continuing superficiality right there, quite apart from unintended irony.

So we shared Dan Rather's pain, marveled at intrepid Ashleigh Banfield, scrutinizing those ferocious tribal fighters through her designer specs, and Tom Brokaw, arbiter of greatness among generations, took us on a tour of

Copyright © 2002 by *Harper's Magazine.* All rights reserved. Reproduced from the April issue by special permission.

the real West Wing. But these iconic moments swam into focus only momentarily, soon to be swept away in a deluge of references, references so numerous, so relentlessly repeated, that they came at last to constitute a solid field, a new backdrop for all our public performances. How often did you hear, how often did you say, "Since the events of 9/11"? A new idiom had been deposited in the language, approaching the same plane of habituality as "by the way" or "on the other hand." And in the process we got past it after all. Six months or so was all it took. The holidays came and went, and—if you were not personally stricken by the terror of September—chances are you got over it. You moved on.

How is that possible?

Nietzsche was not thinking I.Q. or ignorance when he used the word "stupidity." He meant stupidity as in clogged, anesthetized. Numb. He thought people at the end of the *nineteenth* century were suffocating in a vast goo of meaningless stimulation. Ever notice how, when your hand is numb, everything feels thin? Even a solid block of wood lacks depth and texture. You can't feel the wood; your limb just encounters the interrupting surface. Well, numb is to the soul as thin is to a mediated world. Our guiding metaphor. And it isn't just youthful souls either.

Here's the basic situation. On the one hand: the Web, satellite cable TV, PalmPilot, DVD, Ethernet—Virtual Environments everywhere. On the other hand: cloning, genetic engineering, artificial intelligence, robotics—Virtual Beings everywhere. Someday, when people (or whatever they are) look back on our time, all this will appear as a single development, called something like "The Information Revolution," and the lesson of that revolution will have been this: what counts is the code. Silicon- or carbon-based. Artifact or animate. The difference between them is disappearing. This is not science fiction. This is really happening. Right now, in an Atlanta hospital, there is a quadriplegic with his brain directly wired to a computer. He can move the cursor with his thoughts.

The moving cursor doesn't really need explaining—it comes down to digital bytes and neurochemical spikes. What needs explaining is our equanimity in the face of staggering developments. How can we go about our business when things like this are happening? How can we just read the article, shake our heads, turn the page? If creatures from outer space sent a diplomatic mission to the U.N., how long would it be before we were taking that in stride? Before Comedy Central send-ups were more entertaining than the actual creatures? About six months?

Soap-opera politics. The therapy industry. Online communities. Digital effects. Workshops for every workplace. Viagra, Prozac, Ritalin. Reality TV. Complete makeovers. Someday, it will be obvious that all the content on our information platforms converges on this theme: there is no important difference between fabrication and reality, between a chemical a pill introduces and one your body produces, between role-playing in marital therapy and playing your role as a spouse, between selling and making, campaigning and governing, expressing and existing. And that is why we moved on after September 11, after an event that seemed so enormous, so horrific, so stark, that even the great blob of virtuality that is our public culture would be unable to absorb it. But it could. It has. Here's how.

Fabrication

Some people refuse to believe that reality has become indistinguishable from fabrication. But beliefs are crude reflections of the psychological processes that actually determine how we function. Fat people believe they are on the stocky side. Abject drunks believe they are poetical free spirits. Malicious prudes believe they are selfless do-gooders. And a lot of people still believe that, with some obvious exceptions involving hoaxes and errors, we know what's real and what's not. We can tell the difference between the *Kursk* and the *Titanic* (meaning the movie, of course), for example.

And maybe we can—when specifically focused on the issue. It might take a while, of course, because there *are* so many gradations when you stop to think about it. For example:

- Real real: You fall down the stairs. Stuff in your life that's so familiar you've forgotten the statement it makes.

- Observed real: You drive by a car wreck. Stuff in your life in which the image-statement is as salient as the function.

- Between real real and observed real: Stuff that oscillates between the first two categories. Like you're wearing something you usually take for granted but then you meet someone attractive.

- Edited real real: Shtick you have down so pat you don't know it's shtick anymore, but you definitely only use it in certain situations. Documentaries and videos in which people are unaware of the camera, though that's not easy to detect, actually. Candid photographs.

- Edited observed real: Other people's down-pat shtick. Shtick you are still working on. Documentaries in which people are accommodating the camera, which is actually a lot of time, probably.

- Staged real: Formal events like weddings. Retail-clerk patter.

- Edited staged real: Pictures of the above. Homemade porn.

- Staged observed real unique: Al kisses Tipper. *Survivor.*

- Staged observed real repeated: Al kisses Tipper again and again. Anchor-desk and talk-show intros and segues. Weather Channel behavior.

(In the interests of time, we can skip the subtler middle range of distinctions and go to the other end of the spectrum:)

- Staged realistic: *The English Patient* and *NYPD Blue.*

- Staged hyperreal: Oliver Stone movies and *Malcolm in the Middle.*

- Overtly unreal realistic: S.U.V.'s climbing buildings. Digitized special effects in general, except when they are more or less undetectable.

- Covertly unreal realistic: Hair in shampoo ads. More or less undetectable digital effects, of which there are more every day.

- Between overtly and covertly unreal realistic: John Wayne in a beer ad (you have to know he's dead to know he isn't "really" in the ad).

- Real unreal: Robo-pets.

- Unreal real: Strawberries that won't freeze because they have fish genes in them.

See? No problem. The differences are perfectly clear.

But the issue isn't *can* we do it; it's *do* we do it—and the answer is, of course not. Our minds are the product of total immersion in a daily experience saturated with fabrications to a degree unprecedented in human history. People have never had to cope with so much stuff, so many choices. In kind and number.

Flood

And sheer quantity really matters, because here we collide with a real limit, one of the few that remain—namely, how much a person can register at a given instant. No innovation in techno-access or sensationalism can overcome this bottleneck. It determines the fundamental dynamic, the battle to secure attention, in every domain of our lives.

Compare, say, the cereal and juice sections of a supermarket today with those of years ago. For you youngsters out there, take it from Dad: it used to be Wheaties, Corn Flakes, Cheerios (oats), Rice Krispies—and that was about it. One for each grain, see? Same for fruit juice. But now? Pineapple/Banana/Grape or Strawberry/Orange/Kiwi anyone? And that's just a sample from Tropicana—check out Nantucket Nectars. Makes of cars? Types of sunglasses? Sneakers species? Pasta possibilities? On and on. It's all about options, as they say.

Umbrella brands toss off diverse and evolving lines of market-researched products for niches of self-inventing customers with continual access to every representational fabrication ever produced in the whole of human history. That's "the environment." You like Vedic ankle tattoos? 1930s cockney caps? Safari jackets? Inca ponchos? Victorian lace-up high-heel booties? Whatever.

No wonder that word caught on.

The moreness of everything ascends inevitably to a threshold in psychic life. A change of state takes places. The discrete display melts into a pudding, and the mind is forced to certain adaptations if it is to cohere at all.

When you find out about the moving cursor, or hear statistics about AIDS in Africa, or see your 947th picture of a weeping fireman, you can't help but become fundamentally indifferent because you are exposed to things like that all the time, just as you are to the rest of your options. Over breakfast. In the waiting room. Driving to work. At the checkout counter. *All the time.* I know you know this already. I'm just reminding you.

Which is not to say you aren't moved. On the contrary, you are moved, often deeply, very frequently—never more so, perhaps, than when you saw the footage of the towers coming down on 9/11. But you are so used to being moved by footage, by stories, by representations of all kinds—that's the point. It's not your fault that you are so used to being moved, you just are.

So it's not surprising that you have learned to move on so readily to the next, sometimes moving, moment. It's sink or surf. Spiritual numbness guarantees that your relations with the moving will pass. And the stuffed screen accommodates you with moving surfaces that assume you are numb enough to accommodate them. And so on, back and forth. The dialectic of postmodern life.

One might say, "Well, people didn't respond deeply to every development in the world 200 years ago either." And that's true, but it isn't an objection, it's a confirmation. Until the new media came along, people didn't even *know* about such developments, or not as quickly, and above all not as dramatically or frequently. Also, there weren't as many developments, period. This is crucial, another aspect of sheer moreness that gets overlooked. *Less was happening.*

The contrast is stark with, say, the Middle Ages. By the industrial era, a lot more was happening, and numbness became an issue then. Think of Baudelaire, adrift in the crowd, celebrating the artist for resisting numbness, for maintaining vulnerability—thus setting the standard for the genius of modernism. But a qualitative threshold has since been breached. Cities no longer belong to the soulful *flâneur* but to the wired-up voyeur in his soundproofed Lexus. Behind his tinted windows, with his cell phone and CD player, he gets more input, with less static, from more and different channels, than Baudelaire ever dreamed of. But it's all insulational—as if the deities at Dreamworks were invisibly at work around us, touching up the canvas of reality with existential airbrushes. Everything has that edgeless quality, like the lobby of a high-end Marriott/Ramada/Sheraton. Whole neighborhoods feel like that now. And you can be sure that whatever they do at "the site" will feel like that, too. Even if they specifically set out to avoid having it feel like that—it will still feel like that. They can't control themselves. They can't stop.

Take the new Times Square, everybody's icon for this process. All the usual observations apply—and each contributes its iota to muffling what it meant to expose. But the point here is the way everything in that place is *aimed*. Everything is firing message modules, straight for your gonads, your taste buds, your vanities, your fears. These modules seek to penetrate, but in a passing way. A second of your attention is all they ask. Nothing is firing that rends or cuts. It's a massage, really, if you just go with it. And why not? Some of the most talented people on the planet have devoted their lives to creating this psychic sauna, just for you.

And it's not just the screens and billboards, the literal signs; it's absolutely everything you encounter. Except for the eyes of the people, shuffling along, and the poignant imperfections of their bodies; they are so manifestly unequal to the solicitations lavished upon them. No wonder they stuff themselves with junk—or, trying to live up to it all, enslave themselves to regimes of improvement.

Yes, there were ersatz environments and glitzy ads back in the fifties, but this is a new order of quality and saturation. Saying that it's just more of what we had before is like saying a hurricane is just more breeze. For here, too, there is a psychological threshold. Today, your brain is, as a matter of brute fact, full of stuff that was *designed* to affect you. As opposed to the scattered furniture of nature and history that people once registered just because it happened to be there. September 11 had to accommodate the fact that our inner lives are now largely constituted by effects.

To get relief, you have to stumble into the Greyhound bus station in Albany, or some old side-street barbershop that time forgot, into someplace not yet subjected to the renovating ministrations of the International Red Brick and Iron Filigree Restoration Corporation. And "stumble" is the key concept here. Accidental places are the only real places left.

That's why a couple of weeks out in Nature doesn't make it anymore. Even if you eschew the resonant clutter of The Tour and The Gear, you will virtualize everything you encounter anyway, all by yourself. You won't see wolves, you'll see "wolves." You'll be murmuring to yourself, at some level, "Wow, look, a real wolf, not in a cage, not on TV, I can't believe it."

That's right, you can't. Natural things have become their own icons.

And you will get restless really fast if that "wolf" doesn't do anything. The kids will start squirming in, like, five minutes; you'll probably need to pretend you're not getting bored for a while longer. But if that little smudge of canine out there in the distance continues to just loll around in the tall grass, and you don't have a really powerful tripod-supported telelens gizmo to play with, you will get bored. You will begin to appreciate how much technology and editing goes into making those nature shows. The truth is that if some no-account chipmunk just happens to come around your camp-site every morning for crumbs from your picnic table, it will have meant more to you than any "wolf."

Precious accidents.

Back to the new Times Squares—do you parse out the real from the fabricated in that mélange? Not *can* you, but *do* you. The Fox screen is showing Elián in his Cuban school uniform on the side of a building—real or not? Some glorious babe in her underwear is sprawled across 35 percent of your visual field. She's looking you right in the eye. You feel that old feeling—real or not? A fabulous man, sculpted to perfection by more time in the health club than most parents have for their kids, is gliding by on Day-Glo Rollerblades eight inches high. He's wearing Tex-tex gear so tight it looks like it's under his skin, and the logos festooning his figure emit meaning-beeps from every angle—real or not? What about the pumped-up biceps? If he uses steroids? But, once again, the issue isn't what you *can* do when I call your attention to it. The real issue is *do* you do it as a matter of routine processing? Or do you rely instead on a general immunity that only numbness can provide, an immunity that puts the whole flood in brackets and transforms it all into a play of surfaces—over which you hover and glide like a little god, dipping in here and there for the moving experience of your choice, with the ultimate reaches of your soul on permanent remote?

Finitude

What about that feeling that it's all been done? Not in the techie department, of course; there, the possibility of novelty seems to be unlimited. But in those areas occupied by platform proprietors call "content providers." What a phrase! Could anything register devastation of the spirit more completely than that little generic? Could meaning suffer more complete evacuation? Not since we landed on the moon and found nothing has our cultural unconscious encountered so traumatic a void.

Maybe the postmodern taste for recycling and pastiche is more than a phase? Maybe it's necessity. Maybe more or less everything that can be done in the plastic arts, say, has been done? How many different ways can a finite set of shapes and colors, be arranged in a finite space? We aren't talking infinitely divisible Platonic geometry here. Maybe there just isn't any really new way to put x shapes and y colors into z permutations. Maybe some day it will be obvious that the characteristic gestures of twentieth-century art were flailing against this fact. Cézanne's planes, Magritte's pipe, Pollock's swirls, Warhol's soup can, Christo's draperies, Serrano's piss, the "installations"—so many desperate efforts to elude the end of originality?

Likewise with music? How many distinguishable sounds can be put in how many patterns? There has to be some limit. After you've integrated techno and Brazilian-Afro and Tibetan monko and Hump-backed Whalo, at some point, surely, there's going to be nothing left but play it again, Sam. Maybe that's why it's the age of the mix. And characters and plots, in stories and shows? What's the raw material? Sex, outlaws, illness, death, master villains, guilt, the fall of giants, fate, just deserts, the dark side, redemption by the little things, a few other themes—we all know the repertoire. Maybe it's just impossible to think of anything that couldn't be described, after the fashion of all contemporary pitches, as "It's *To the Lighthouse* meets *Married with Children*" or "It's Hannibal Lecter meets Peter Pan."

The prospect of finitude helps to account for the turn to sensation, as if intensity of presentation could make up for repetition. Of course, sensation is also a response to sheer clutter on the screen, a way to grab the most possible attention in the least amount of time. But that clutter also accounts for why everything's already been done, and so it cycles on relentlessly—fill the pages, fill the time slots, fill the channels, the websites, the roadsides, the building façades, the fronts and backs of shirts and caps, everything, everything must be saying something, every minute. But what? What's left to say? It doesn't matter. Cut to the response.

Zap. Whimper. Flinch. Cringe. Melt. Assert! Exult! Weep. Subside. Ahhh . . .

Eventually we can just wire our glands directly to a console of sensation buttons, platform to platform, and be done with this tiresome content altogether. Call it P2P communication. Talk about interactive. Thus will the human soul be compensated for the despair of finitude.

Fast

Remember that T-shirt from the eighties that said "High on Stress"? It was sort of true and sort of a way to bluff it out and sort of a protest—it had that "any number of meanings" quality we now prefer to depth. That's because the any-number-of-meanings quality keeps you in motion, but depth asks you to stop. Depth is to your life what dead air is to a talk show.

Being numb isn't antithetical to being totally stressed, 24-7—and asking for more. Over-scheduled busyness might seem like the opposite of numbness, but it is just the active aspect of living in a flood of fabricated surfaces. Consider the guiding metaphor again. The (absence of) sensation that is physical numbness is constituted by a multitude of thrills and tingles at a frequency beyond which you feel nothing. The numbness of busyness works on the same principle, but it relies upon its agents to abide by an agreement they must keep secret, even from themselves. The agreement is this: we will so conduct ourselves that everything becomes an emergency.

Under that agreement, stress is how reality feels. People addicted to busyness, people who don't just use their cell phones in public but display in every nuance of cell-phone deportment their sense of throbbing connectedness to Something Important—these people would suffocate like fish on a dock if they were cut off from the Flow of Events they have conspired with their fellows to create. To these plugged-in players, the rest of us look like zombies, coasting on fumes. For them, the feeling of being busy *is* the feeling of being alive.

Partly, it's a function of speed, like in those stress dramas that television provides to keep us virtually busy, even in our downtime. The bloody body wheeled into the ER, every personjack on the team yelling numbers from monitors, screaming for meds and equipment, especially for those heart-shocker pads—that's the paradigm scene. All the others derive from it: hostage-negotiator scenes, staffers pulling all-nighters in the West Wing, detectives sweeping out of the precinct, donning jackets, adjusting holsters, snapping wisecracks. Sheer speed and Lives on the Line. That's the recipe for feeling real.

The irony is that *after* we have worked really hard on something urgent for a long time, we do escape numbness for a while—stepping out of the building, noticing the breeze, the cracks in the sidewalk, the stillness of things in the shop window. During those accidental and transitional moments, we actually get the feeling of the real we were so frantically pursuing when we were busy. But we soon get restless. We can't take the input reduction. Our psychic metabolism craves more.

Actually, stress dramas are about the lives of the media people who make them. They purport to be about hospitals or law firms, but they are actually about what it is like to make TV shows, about high-stakes teamwork in the land of celebrity, where, by definition, everything matters more than it does anywhere else, a land that welcomes diversity and foibles as long as The Job Gets Done, a land where everything personal, unconditional, intimate—everything unbounded by the task—takes place on the side. That's why, in these shows through which the celebrated teach the rest of us how to be like them, the moments of heartfelt encounter that make it all worthwhile are stolen in the corridors of power, while the verdict is awaited. If we get that real-folks-rushing-to-get-out-of-the-house-in-the-morning scene, it's just to underscore the priority of the Flow of Events that protects the busy from being left alone in the stillness with what makes it all worthwhile. Lest direction be lost, motion must be maintained.

Moving On

So life in a flood of surfaces means a life of perpetual motion, and TV provides the model in other modes as well. Take the transitions from story to story in newscasts, that finishing-with-a-topic moment. "Whether these supplies, still piling up after weeks of intense effort by these humanitarian workers, will actually reach the victims (pause) remains to be seen." A hint of a sigh, a slight shake of the head, eyes down-turning; the note of seasoned resignation. Profound respect is conveyed for the abandoned topic even as a note of anticipation rises to greet the (also interesting, but less burdensome) next topic—and the new camera angle at the anchor desk makes it clear that stern and external necessity, rather than any human agency, governs the shift from two minutes on mass starvation to the next episode of The Fall of the House of Enron.

Judy Woodruff is especially good at this, her particular little head nod, or shake, as the case may be, and the way her lips tighten up a tad. "If it were up to me as a human being I would *never* leave this coverage of thousands of dying innocents, but, as a newscaster, of course, I have to." And her speaking voice says, "All right, Jim, we have to go to a break now, but we will be following this story as it develops—and thanks again." "Thank you, Judy," says Jim, echoing her gesture, and we understand that he, too, as a human being, would never allow us to move on from so ghastly and demanding a reality, but it isn't up to him as a human being either. It isn't up to anybody, actually. That's the one real reality. Moving on.

It would be irrevelent to object by asking, "Well, how else are we supposed to do it?" There isn't any other way to do it. That's the point. This isn't a consultant's memo. This is a serious diagnosis of a serious condition. Would we rather not know about it because it happens to be incurable? This goes much deeper than subject matter, or political bias, the usual fodder. It determines the way we frame everything. Like all that is most profound in human custom, this agreement is almost physical, an attunement, more music than semantics. It instills and expresses, moment by moment, the *attitude* we bring to living in this world of surfaces.

So, for example, you don't have to wait for the anchorperson to change the topic. You can change it yourself, and you don't have to sigh or tighten your lips as you make the transition. But you do. Monitor yourself next time you zap away from some disturbing something on *Lehrer* to catch the action on the *Law & Order* reruns. You mime those little gestures as you punch the buttons. These are the constituting habit structures of our culture.

And we've touched already on what awaits you when you join the gang on *Law & Order.* The stress drama re-creating, more elaborately, the basic gesture of the news show, the one you just performed when you slid away from those refugee visuals. Everything's in motion, elliptical, glancing, fungible. You see the sides of faces, the slope of shoulders, the beginnings of expressions but not the ends, the ends of expressions but not the beginnings. No matter the horror, no matter the injustice, no matter how passionate McCoy may feel, no matter how angry Bratt gets at Briscoe (actors or characters?), no matter how obnoxious the defense attorney or impatient the judge (especially in chambers), they all keep moving. And the camera keeps moving, too, gliding, peeking, glimpsing. Frightened witnesses, incoming lawyers, outgoing suspects, they're all moving—as is the traffic, the doors, hands, phones, everything. Meaningful personal encounters are bound to be interrupted, and the performers, like would-be fighters in a bar relying on friends to keep them apart, anticipate the interruption. Ferociously or tenderly, they emote in transitional interlude, awaiting inevitable rescue by events, and, gratefully regretting the passing of the moment of communion, they watch the D.A. step into the elevator and deliver the homily as the door slides shut across his grizzled visage, a homily that is never merely upbeat or despairing, never final or conclusive in any way. Because the one thing people in a TV series know is that tomorrow is another show, and they will be ready to roll. For they are pros, and pros know how to deal. It's not that they're indifferent or cynical. They care. Sometimes they win, sometimes they lose—but, either way, they move on. That's the lesson, the ultimate homily of all shows The way we live now.

So, if we were spared a gaping wound in the flesh and blood of personal life, we inevitably moved on after September 11. We were carried off by endlessly proliferating representations of the event, and by an ever expanding horizon of associated stories and characters, and all of them, in their turn, represented endlessly, and the whole sweep of it driven by the rhythms of The Show—anthrax, postal workers, the Bronx lady, the Saddam connection, Osama tapes, Al Jazeera's commentary on Osama tapes, Christiane Amanpour's commentary on Al Jazeera's commentary on Osama tapes, a magazine story about Christiane Amanpour . . .

And that's just one thread in this tapestry of virtuality. The whole is so densely woven and finely stranded that no mind could possibly comprehend it, escape it, govern it. It's the dreamwork of culture. It just proceeds and we with it, each of us exposed to thousands, probably millions of 9/11-related representations—everything from the layout of the daily paper to rippling-flag logos to NYPD caps on tourists to ads for *Collateral Damage*. Conditioned thus relentlessly to move from representation to representation, we got past the thing itself as well; or rather, the thing itself was transformed into a sea of signs and upon it we were borne away from every shore, moving on, moving on.

What else could we do?

Student Essay:
Experience: The Key to Understanding Culture Conflicts

Frances Mendieta

"She's trying to pick a fight!" "What's up with her writing style?" "She's confusing." These are some of the comments made in class while discussing Gloria Anzaldúa's work "How to Tame a Wild Tongue." I was surprised to see that I did not feel the same way as my classmates did. I understood everything, regardless of Anzaldúa's complex writing style. At first I thought my classmates did not get Anzaldúa because she uses Spanish in her essay without providing translations. However their misunderstanding went beyond just a complicated text manner.

One of my classmates expressed that the essay was not a good one. A thought came to me quickly and I said, "Well, I think her essay is a very effective way of portraying her reality." I thought that maybe he had read the essay quickly and was not open minded when exposed to a different kind of paper describing a unique situation like Anzaldúa's. After a long time trying to figure out why my classmates negatively criticized her work, I realized that they may have to experience Anzaldúa's situation for themselves to understand her. I cannot recall anyone mentioning the fact that they did not understand her composition because of her Spanish use. Almost everyone mentioned that she wrote as if she had no organization of her ideas. That was the problem. They thought that her mind was a big mess and so was the essay.

A brief summary of Anzaldúa's work is necessary to better understand my classmates' misconception. The author is a Chicana exposed to various cultures. Living on the Mexican-American border has created confusion in her life. She speaks different languages in order to adapt to the different environments she is exposed to and this has created identity problems. Anzaldúa describes this conflict when she explains, "Chicanos and other people of color suffer economically for not acculturating. This involuntary (yet forced) alienation makes for psychological conflict, a kind of dual identity—we don't identify with the Anglo-American cultural values and we don't totally identify with the Mexican cultural values" (173). She explains how living on the border between two completely different cultures has created confusion by not letting her identify with what is surrounding her.

The issue does not stop there. Not only does Anzaldúa feel like she does not belong in Mexican or American culture, but the only culture that she feels she is part of is non-existent. Throughout her life she is forced to adopt one of the cultures she is enclosed by. Chicano culture and language is not accepted by Mexicans or Americans; it is a mutilation of cultures and therefore not valid for recognition as a distinctive community. This creates further problems when Anzaldúa has to decide what culture she is a part of. The various languages she uses and the fact that her "home" tongues are looked down upon directly affects her understanding of who she is.

As I was reading the text, I reacted positively to it because I completely identified with the author. Anzaldúa's conflict was not confusing to me. I am Puerto Rican, and even though we do not experience border problems, being American citizens has shaped our culture. The Americans have colonized us for over a century now, and everything that happens in the United States directly affects us. We reflect this especially in our language. We use Anglicisms when we speak and, like Anzaldúa, we are looked down upon by other Spanish-speaking cultures.

I have been criticized many times by my culture's wrong use of Spanish. Other Spanish-speaking people (other than Puerto Ricans) make fun of me when they hear me talk and try to correct me. These criticisms make me feel as if Puerto Rican culture is not as good as other Latin cultures. I often feel ashamed when I speak in front of Colombians, Spaniards, and Venezuelans who recognize each other for speaking Spanish "correctly." The feeling I get when this kind of criticism happens is perfectly explained by Anzaldúa when she says, "So, if you really want to hurt me, talk bad about my language. Ethnic identity is twin skin to linguistic identity—I am my language. Until I can take pride in my language, I cannot take pride in myself" (170). Language is one of the first things people notice. When you meet someone, the way they talk can identify that person to a certain country or region of a country. Making fun of a person's language is directly making fun of the place that person comes from.

The way other Spanish-speaking countries see Puerto Rican Spanish is the way Anzaldúa describes it when she explains, *"Deslenguadas. Somos los del español deficiente.* We are your linguistic nightmare, your linguistic aberration, your linguistic *mestisaje,* the subject of your *burla.* Because we speak with tongues of fire we are culturally crucified. Racially, culturally, and linguistically *somos huérfanos*—we speak an orphan tongue" (169). Language can be closely correlated to education. Many people understand that if someone receives a good education then his or her communication skills cannot be defective. If Puerto Rican language is defective (like most of the Latin countries believe it is) then our education and culture is the same way.

Like Anzaldúa, I also face contradictions regarding cultural identity, but not as pronounced as hers. I was born in Puerto Rico, but my parents and brother and sister are all Cuban. I experience both cultures, but I do not feel completely Puerto Rican or Cuban. So what am I? Cuban because of my Cuban blood or Puerto Rican because that is the place where I was born and raised? Anzaldúa feels the same way. She is not sure what she is in terms of her cultural identity. She straddles the Mexican-American borderline not feeling Mexican or American. According to Anzaldúa, "We are a synergy of two cultures with various degrees of Mexicanness or Angloness. I have so internalized the borderland conflict that sometimes I feel like one cancels out the other and we are zero, nothing, no one" (173).

Why do I understand Anzaldúa's writing style? Because it is exactly what is going on for people that share different cultures as part of their identity. Confusion. All we have are disappointing experiences that cannot be put together in order for them to make a linear narrative. It is hard to explain us regarding these cultural issues. There is no specific word to identify what I am or what Anzaldúa is. Sometimes I feel Cuban and other times Puerto Rican, depending on the situation. How can I make an organized explanation of my condition when my cultural identity itself is disorganized, not categorized? In Puerto Rico people consider me Puerto Rican; in the United States they consider me Cuban because my parents are Cuban, sometimes even Spanish because my great-grandparents are Spanish. When I am filling out a form and it asks my ethnicity, I do not know what box to check. I am different cultures and at the same time I am neither of them in its entirety.

It is very interesting how this essay produced completely different reactions in class. People who have not experienced a situation like the author's feel uneasy and confused when reading her work. On the other hand, someone like me reads it and completely understands and identifies with the condition. Anzaldúa's convoluted composition has a double purpose. One is to create anger and puzzlement for people to experience a little of what she has her whole life. The second purpose is to make people in her situation say, "Yes, I have been there."

I enjoyed this essay very much and the different reactions people had to it. Anzaldúa is successful in portraying what it feels like to be in her shoes. She does not explain it in simplistic terms for the reader to understand, but she makes the reader experience her problem as they try to "make sense" of the essay.

Works Cited

Anzaldúa, Gloria. "How to Tame a Wild Tongue." *The Text-Wrestling Book.* Ed. Donna LeCourt, et al. Dubuque: Kendall/Hunt, 2005. 164–175.

Student Essay: Capacities of Feeling

Danielle Silva

You are at The Nagasaki Atomic Bomb Museum in Nagasaki, Japan. While examining a collection of glass bottles melted by the blast of extreme heat, an old Japanese woman approaches you and volunteers to be your tour guide. Intrigued by her generosity, you accept the offer. She leads you through several exhibits and gives a detailed and moving account of each. The last exhibit she escorts you to is the charred remains of a school girl's lunch box. She tells you that *she* carried this lunchbox to school on August 9, 1945. Unable to grasp what you just heard, your world stops and you freeze in your tracks. You do not know what to say or how to respond to this woman. The degree to which you are moved by her statement is inexpressible. Language fails you at this time when you need it most, when so much is running through your mind.

Language: a connection between the mind and mouth, thought and spoken word, a method of communication, discussion, and conversation, an instrument of writing and creating. By this definition, it seems as though this instrument could never fail. Yet, in our lives, there are sensations that escape the realm of language. Extreme emotional highs and lows cause the body to lose its sense of control, its connection to spoken word. In her essay "Art Objects," Jeanette Winterson uses painting to discuss the idea that language can be inadequate in conveying many of the viewings we partake in and reconcile, and the emotions we feel. We certainly cannot deny the difficulties in attempting to use and manipulate language to articulate opinions and emotions. When engaged in an argument, we often utter random obscenities because we cannot reason out a logical way to verbally communicate our opinions. Winterson maintains that by examining the brushstrokes of a painting, notes of a musical composition, movements of a dance, metaphors of a poem, or depth of a human emotion, we can discover that our awareness and understanding of the world extends much farther than language can grasp.

In the face of art, Winterson argues that we experience a level of feeling that is beyond description. Nothing can be said to express the intensity of the moment, the unfamiliarity of the situation. There is no language to communicate the love felt for the art (Winterson 329). In my life, I experienced only one event that rendered me completely incapable of speech. When my cousin Kim was killed by a drunk driver, my world collapsed. I could not see, hear, breathe, or think. Who? Had I heard the wrong name? A few more moments passed. How did it happen, and was that possible? The emotion in my heart was fluent in "its own language," where traditional verbal communication was completely useless in the presence of this new feeling (329). Although I was physically able to speak, my expression was limited and came nowhere near portraying the void, the emptiness inside, that, to this day, I cannot accurately describe. Art has the capacity to cause this same effect, to bring about a new language. As a person suffering the death of a loved one or undergoing an uncomfortable new experience, the art viewer faces an uncertainty, something that prevents him or her from responding to the encounter.

Eventually, in reaction to the death of my cousin, I cried. You, at the Nagasaki Atomic Bomb Museum, probably would, or at least want to, cry. Winterson reveals that "[a]rt opens the heart" (330). The feelings and emotions of the viewer are released when his or her heart is opened. Long suppressed memories flood out uncontrollably (334). The emotional response is so overwhelming that it cannot be described. As a result, when confronted with a true work of art, Winterson is brought to tears (339). There are times and circumstances that cause this to be the only possible reaction to an experience. Words cannot truly display the magnitude of the emotion. We can only shed tears. Taking the place of language, crying becomes the alternative pathway of transmission that allows us to attempt to release the feelings held inside. Our inability to explain these feelings, these traumas, shocks, and encounters with the unfamiliar is the result of language failing to grasp emotion.

On the other hand, there can also be a loss of language stemming from extreme joy. Art, such as a favorite poem, painting, or dance performance, is as powerful "as insight, as rapture, as transformation, as joy" (330). Consider the conclusion of a typical Miss U.S.A. Pageant. The winner is visibly flooded with emotion. Images flash before her eyes and noise rings in her ears. She cannot grasp a solid concept, her life spins out of control, and her perception of the world is altered. Sure, this is somewhat extreme and even stereotypical, but, nevertheless, the end result is the complete failure of language to transmit feeling. Would I be wrong in saying Miss U.S.A. cries every year? No, this is the only response she, like Winterson, you, and I, can manage to express. Such deep emotion breaks the bridge that joins this emotional world to real language.

Essentially, our only hope to overcome the failure of language to explain more than the literal is through a language more advanced than our own. However, this "language of art, all art," may be difficult to understand because it "is not our mother-tongue" (329). By equating art to a foreign city, Winterson portrays art as unfamiliar and odd, as a different world. Your trip to The Nagasaki Bomb Museum, my loss of a loved one. Miss U.S.A.'s victory, and Winterson's art gallery visit all bring about a stop to our own worlds, which transports us to this other world. In this place, we confront feelings and emotions that we cannot meet on any other occasion, which vary greatly from the security of our daily, usual, closed heart experiences (335). Becoming Miss U.S.A. or gaining awareness and insight into a work of art certainly does not occur everyday. These emotions are new to us, never felt before, and it is impossible to understand them without the "language of art," which is more of a language of any foreign or unknown experience.

Yet, when we somehow learn the language of a foreign experience, we are able to understand exactly what we are feeling, and although we cannot effectively communicate the things we grasp, we gain a far better conception of our own world. The death of my cousin taught me valuable life lessons that helped me better understand this world. In addition, Winterson realizes that the painting she owns "is a living line of movement, a wave of colour that repercusses in [her] body, colouring it, colouring the new present, the future, and even the past, which cannot now be considered outside of the light of the painting" (337–339). She acquires a new outlook on life and a new view of herself. If we can overcome the obstacle present in the inability to use language, we can recognize objects, events, and ideas for what they really are.

Essentially, describing language as an eternally dependable form of communication is a misconception. Time and again it fails to accurately express the intensity of our emotional experiences. Yet, it is the times when we manage to journey beyond the realm of language and into the world of emotion, which, if anything, is more of a way of thinking, a greater intensity of feeling, that something other than the way we perceive objects and situations changes. We are able to grasp concepts for what they really are, for what they are meant to teach us and change in us. By gaining awareness about the power of the mind and the strength of emotions, we realize that "what has changed is [our] capacity of feeling" (330). This transformation finds in us a deep appreciation for emotion and art, which holds the keys to unlocking the unexplainable worlds beyond the grasp of language.

Works Cited

Winterson, Jeanette. "Art Objects." *The Text-Wrestling Book.* Ed. Donna LeCourt, et al. Dubuque: Kendall/Hunt, 2005. 328–339.

Suggested Exercises and Activities for Interacting with Texts

Reading to Respond

We read for many different purposes: to find a quick answer, to be informed more extensively, to take a test, to be entertained, and so on. Reading so that we might respond directly to an author's ideas, however, can be a much different process because it requires that we not only attend to what the text says, but also what it infers and how we are reacting to the author's ideas. It is very difficult to track all these reactions the first time through a text without some written aids. Using a chart can be helpful in distinguishing the kinds of meaning you are making as you read.

For this exercise, make a three-column chart. First, read through the text once, marking any passages you find significant. Then read the text again, writing down a quote in the left column for any passages you still find significant. Try to mark a passage for every paragraph or two.

Once you have collected all your quotes, move to the middle column where you consider what the passage *implies* (i.e., how does it connect to the author's larger point? Are there hidden meanings in the passage? Could it be interpreted differently than the author intended? How?)

Finally, move to the third column where you will try and gauge your response to this one passage alone: What do you think of the author's idea? What experiences of your own might it remind you of? What aspects of your life might it make you question? What new thoughts does it bring up? (See the example that follows for Eli Clare's "The Mountain.") Continue to the next quote until you have done an implied/response for every quote you wrote down.

Said	Implied	Response
Clare says "I never once heard, 'You made the right choice when you turned around.'"	Clare seems to be implying that her friends and family, in their desire to see her succeed, wish to see her as a "Supercrip," and it may be that she sees herself this way, too.	Aligning expectations of yourself with the expectations of others may be helpful in order to create a comparative experience, but it can also lead to internal tension. It has been said that the difference between how you see yourself and how others see you is equal to the amount of anxiety you have, and I see some of this going on here. Interestingly, Clare also seems to be split by how she sees herself and how she *wants* to see herself.

Challenging Your Reading

As you read the essay, mark in the book or write down on a separate page passages that seem difficult to you for any reason. Consider multiple ways a text might be "difficult" as you read. A passage may be "difficult" because it's written in complicated or academic language, or because it deals with dense subject matter, but the difficulties might also arise because something in the text frustrates you, bores you, or seems unrelated to the points you more readily understand and/or agree with.

Part I—Examining Difficulty

After you finish reading, try to figure out as much as you can about each of your areas of difficulty. Write a sentence or two explaining *each* area of difficulty you marked and how you reacted to it. What makes this part of the essay challenging? Is it the language? The terms? The ideas presented? The author's perspective? The tone? Your own experiences and assumptions? What do you think of these difficult features? Did the text make you want to argue with the author? Did it make you want to throw down your book in frustration?

Part II—Describing Your Reading Process

Write a paragraph describing your reading process: Are there any similarities to what you found difficult or where you got stuck? What might those similarities and differences tell you either about yourself as a reader or the essay you read? What effect did the difficult sections have on the meaning you made of the essay? Did you focus on some areas more than others? Are there areas on your first reading where you shut down because of your reactions? What does your awareness of how you read now make it possible to understand in the essay?

Part III—Reading Through Difficulty

Reread the text, and then write a paragraph explaining how you understand the essay now after working through the difficulties. What is the author trying to say in the essay? What questions do you have to bring to your next class? Are some of your areas of difficulty still there?

Outlining: Not Just for Pre-Writing Anymore

Outlining is often presented as solely an activity for writers as they are starting their essays. But outlining is a useful activity for writers at all stages of the writing process. It is also a useful activity for readers because of how it enables a person (whether reading one's own text or someone else's) to chart the structure of an essay and the order in which ideas, information, and examples are presented.

Often, where a writer begins an essay isn't necessarily where he ends up. That is, examples and premises that are presented initially may seem to carry one meaning, but then as the text progresses and more layers of information are added, what was written earlier may need to be re-examined in light of what is presented later. As a reader, there are many ways to track a writer's thinking as it develops in an essay. One such way is outlining.

1) Divide a sheet of paper into two columns. Go through the essay paragraph by paragraph. In the first column, write a sentence that summarizes each paragraph. Focus as much as possible on what each paragraph "says," not necessarily what *you* might think it's trying to say.

After you have a summary sentence for each paragraph, look at how meaning is constructed in (and between) these paragraphs. In the second column, explain your sense of what the relationship is between each set of paragraphs (i.e., what is the relationship between paragraphs 1 and 2? Between 2 and 3?) Does one paragraph continue an idea from the other? If so, what's the connection between what's said in 1 and in 2? Does the next paragraph extend the thinking? Add a new element?

2) After you have finished outlining the essay (you may have to reread it several times), write a paragraph that answers these questions: Given the audience for and purpose of the text . . .

  • Why might the author have chosen to start with the information she did?

  • Why does the essay follow the order it does?

  • What types of examples does the author use most frequently? How do these examples aid his rhetorical purpose?

3) Imagine a completely different audience for the piece, and make your own outline for this new audience using the same material in the essay. Consider explicitly how the information might be reordered for a new audience and what sections, if any, might need to be deleted or added.

Wrestling the Terms of the Text

In almost every essay, an author will use terms that are specific to the text and crucial to the meaning of it. One way to enter more deeply into a text is to identify these terms and the ways the author uses them to construct meaning.

First list at least three specific terms the author uses. Then respond as fully as you can to the following questions without worrying too much, during this exploratory stage, about matters of spelling, structure, and so on.

  • What does each of the terms mean? Try to paraphrase and summarize what the author has written about each term.

  • What does each of the terms seem to imply—that is, what tones or nuances do the terms carry? Use specific examples from the text to support your analysis of the terms.

  • What do the terms mean to you? What meanings do they carry in your life? Again, use specific examples.

While remaining as true as possible to the author's words and intentions, don't worry too much about getting the "right" answer, for there are no perfectly right answers to these questions. Instead, work to find responses and ideas that are interesting and lead to more questions. If you are working in a group, it is useful to note any disagreements and/or differences group members may have concerning the terms. These points of difference will lead to interesting questions and help further your understanding of the text.

Reflection on Writing

Trinh T. Minh-ha

Selection from Woman, Native, Other

"The triple bind"

Neither black/red/yellow nor woman but poet or writer. For many of us, the question of priorities remains a crucial issue. Being merely "a writer" without doubt ensures one a status of far greater weight than being "a woman of color who writes" ever does. Imputing race or sex to the creative act has long been a means by which the literary establishment cheapens and discredits the achievements of non-mainstream women writers. She who "happens to be" a (non-white) Third World member, a woman, and a writer is bound to go through the ordeal of exposing her work to the abuse of praises and criticisms that either ignore, dispense with, or overemphasize her racial and sexual attributes. Yet the time has passed when she can confidently identify herself with a profession or artistic vocation without questioning and relating it to her color-woman condition. Today, the growing ethnic-feminist consciousness has made it increasingly difficult for her to turn a blind eye not only to the specification of the writer as historical subject (who writes? and in what context?), but also to writing itself as a practice located at the intersection of subject and history—a literary practice that involves the possible knowledge (linguistical and ideological) of itself as such. On the one hand, no matter what position she decides to take, she will sooner or later find herself driven into situations where she is made to feel she must choose from among three conflicting identifies. Writer of color? Woman writer? Or woman of color? Which comes first? Where does

Trinh T. Minh-ha, *Women, Native, Other: Writing Postcoloniality and Feminism*. Indiana University Press.

she place her loyalties? On the other hand, she often finds herself at odds with language, which partakes in the white-male-is-norm ideology and is used predominantly as a vehicle to circulate established power relations. This is further intensified by her finding herself also at odds with her relation to writing, which when carried out uncritically often proves to be one of domination; as holder of speech, she usually writes from a position of power, creating as an "author," situating herself *above* her work and existing *before* it, rarely simultaneously *with* it. Thus, it has become almost impossible for her to take up her pen without at the same time questioning her relation to the material that defines her and her creative work. As focal point of cultural consciousness and social change, writing weaves into language the complex relations of a subject caught between the problems of race and gender and the practice of literature as the very place where social alienation is thwarted differently according to each specific context.

> "Vertically imposed language: on clarity, craftsmanship, and She who steals language"

When commitment remains limited to the sociopolitical sphere, the claim of a "functional" writing that advocates the cause of the oppressed and instructs its audience indicates, in Mphahlele's terms, "a dangerous tendency." It tends "to draw a line of distinction between a function in which an author vindicates or asserts black pride or takes a sociopolitical stand and a function in which he seeks to stir humanity as a whole. . . ." What emerges here are the questions that relate to the nature of literature and writing. On the one hand, can literature be a "freedom that has taken freedom as its end" (Sartre) and still concern itself with elements like structure, form, and style—whose totality precisely allows literature to take on its meaning? On the other hand, can a writing that claims to break down rules and myths submit itself to the exclusive rules of a sociopolitical stand? Nothing could be more normative, more logical, and more authoritarian than, for example, the (politically) revolutionary poetry or prose that speaks of revolution in the form of commands or in the well-behaved, steeped-in-convention-language of "clarity." . . . *Clear* expression, often equated with *correct* expression, has long been the criterion set forth in treatises on *rhetoric,* whose aim was to order discourse so as to *persuade.* The language of Taoism and Zen, for example, which is perfectly accessible but rife with paradox does not qualify as "clear" (paradox is "illogical" and "nonsensical" to many Westerners), for its intent lies outside the realm of persuasion. The same holds true for vernacular speech, which is not acquired through institutions—schools, churches, professions, etc.—and therefore not repressed by either grammatical rules, technical terms, or key words. Clarity as a purely rhetorical attribute serves the purpose of a classical feature in language, namely, its instrumentality. To write is to communicate, express, witness, impose, instruct, redeem, or save—at any rate to *mean* and to send out *an unambiguous message*. Writing thus reduced to a mere vehicle of thought may be *used* to orient toward a goal or to sustain an act, but it does not constitute an act in itself. This is how the division between the writer/the intellectual and the activists/the masses becomes possible. To use the language well, says the voice of literacy, cherish its classic form. Do not choose the offbeat at the cost of clarity. Obscurity is an imposition on the reader. True, but beware when you cross railroad tracks for one train may hide another train. Clarity is a means of subjection, a quality both of official, taught language and of correct writing, two old mates of power; together they flow, together they flower, vertically, to impose an order. Let us not forget that writers who advocate the instrumentality of language are often those who cannot or choose not to see the suchness of things—a language as language—and therefore, continue to preach conformity to the norms of well-behaved writing: principles of composition, style, genre, correction, and improvement. To write "clearly," one must incessantly prune, eliminate, forbid, purge, purify; in other words, practice what may be called an "ablution of language" (Roland Barthes).

"Writing for me," says Toni Cade Bambara, "is still an act of language first and foremost." Before being the noble messenger and the loyal message of her/his people, the writer is a wo/man "whose most absorbed and passionate hours are spent arranging words on pieces of paper" (Joan Didion). S/He does not express her/his thoughts, passion, or imagination in sentences but *thinks sentences:* she is a sentence-thinker . . . who radically questions the world through the questioning of a how-to write. . . .

"A lady of letters, what a funny expression . . . ," says Simone de Beauvoir in an interview with Jean-Paul Sartre, who wonders what it feels like in life to be such a lady (creature). To write is to become. Not to become a writer (or a poet), but to become, intransitively. Not when writing adopts established keynotes or policy, but when it traces for itself lines of evasion. Can any one of us write *like* a man, *like* a woman, *like* a white? Surely, someone would quickly answer, and this leads us straight back to the old master-servant's Guilt, A sentence-thinker, yes, but one who so very often does not know how a sentence will end, I say. And as there is no need to rush, just leave it open, so that it may later on find, or not find, its closure. Words, fragments, and lines that I love for no sound reason; blanks, lapses, and silences that settle in like gaps of fresh air as soon as the inked space smells stuffy. Learned women have often been described in terms one might use in describing a thief. . . .

Women writers are both prompt to hide in (their) writing(s) and feel prompted to do so. As language-stealers, they must yet learn to steal without being seen, and with no pretense of being a stealer, for fear of "exposing the father." Such a reluctance to say aloud that the emperor has no clothes and therefore to betray or admit of an evidence comes perhaps less from a subjection to man than from an acute awareness of emptiness—emptiness through (his) power, through (his) language, through (his) disguises. Hence the compassion and the desire to protect. By countering a (masculine) disguise with another (feminine) disguise, however, Nin felt she had crippled herself. Double mischief: unspoken and unable to speak, woman in exile with herself. Stolen language will always remain that other's language. Say it obliquely, use trickery, cheat, or fake, for if I tell you now what I would like to hear myself tell you, I will miss it. Words thoroughly invested with realities that turn out to be not-quite-yet-mines are radically deceptive. Whenever I *try my best* to say, I never fail to utter the wrong words; I weasel, telling you "hen" when I mean something close to "duck." "It is useless," Virginia Woolf wrote, "to go to the great men writers for help, however much one may go to them for pleasure . . . The ape is too distant to be sedulous. Perhaps the first thing she would find, setting pen to paper, was that there was no common sentence ready for her use." A man's sentence is bound to be unsuited for a woman's use; and no matter how splendid her gift for prose proves to be, she will stumble and fall with such a "clumsy weapon in her hands." "Moreover, a book is not made of sentences laid end to end, but of sentences built, if an image helps, into arcades or domes. And this shape too has been made by men out of their own needs for their own uses." *Literally,* she blabs and cackles and is well known as Ms. Tittletattle, always willing to sell off for a song what she has stolen (overheard) from man. *Figuratively,* she goes unheard (even when she yells and especially when she "shrills," as they put it) and remains as dumb as a fish. So where do you go from here? where do I go? and where does a committed woman writer go? Finding a voice, searching for words and sentences: say some thing, one thing, or no thing; tie/untie, read/unread, discard their forms; scrutinize the grammatical habits of your writing and decide for yourself whether they free or repress. Again, order(s). Shake syntax, smash the myths, and if you lose, slide on, *unearth* some new linguistic paths. Do you surprise? Do you shock? Do you have a choice?

SECTION III

Adding to a Conversation

Introduction

We are surrounded by conversations. Everywhere we go we find a variety of people engaged in conversations that cover a range of topics. As we move through our day we hear people engaged in conversations about our university, our local communities, and our country. We hear conversations about social issues, international issues, and cultural issues. Some people are engaged in conversations that are very specific to their own interests, and some people are engaged in conversations that affect our daily lives. Some of these conversations are informal and some take place in more formal venues.

When we hear the term *conversation,* we usually imagine two or more people sitting around a table discussing a specific topic. We assume that each person involved in the conversation has some knowledge about the topic. The people sitting around the table listen to one another and take turns making points in order to further extend the conversation as a whole. Sometimes the people at the table will disagree with someone, others will agree with a point being made. Sometimes, through the course of the discussion, someone will revise his thinking as he considers the different points raised. In his or her way, each person will seek to further extend the conversation. The conversations included in this section of the book are no different from this imagined conversation. The only difference is that these conversations, like many of the conversations that surround us, take place in writing. Rather than sitting around a table and speaking to one another, the participants in these conversations converse by reading and writing.

When we first enter into a textual conversation we do so as readers. Reading enables us to listen in on a conversation before making a contribution. We read to identify the conversation so that we can better understand the rhetorical situations available for our contributions. We continue reading in order to research the background of the conversation, to discover what has already been said. As we read, we ask ourselves: What has already been said about this topic? Who has already said what? Who is engaged in the conversation? Why are these people involved in this particular conversation? What is at stake for them?

Just as in oral conversations, conversations that occur in print evolve and rarely remain static. A conversation may have started out answering a specific question but, based on the contributions of others, it may move away from its original question and take up something different, something more complex. Before we make a contribution, it is important to research the present conversation. What is being discussed now? Who is currently participating in the conversation?

Once we have read enough of the past and present conversation, we are able to enter into the discussion. Writing becomes our way of participating in the conversation. Depending on the rhetorical situation we are responding to, our writing can take a variety of forms. If we are writing to an academic audience, we would most likely write an essay. If we are contributing to a conversation about a local issue, we may write a letter to the editor or write an opinion piece for our local paper. We may write an article that would appear in a magazine geared towards readers who would be sympathetic to our issue. We may write a letter to community leaders aimed at changing people's minds about a specific issue.

You will notice that the readings in this section are organized differently than the essays in *Inquiring into Self* and *Interacting with Texts*. You will see that, rather than presenting many full essays here, we have clustered together several shorter pieces around a specific topic. Our intention is to mirror four conversations that surround us in order to give you the sense of how a textual conversation looks and how authors may choose to participate. As you read through these conversations, imagine the authors sitting around a table speaking to one another. Like in any conversation, there are multiple voices, different people making a contribution to the specific topic. As you read, ask yourself why this particular author is engaged in this specific conversation. How does the author position himself within this conversation? What contribution is this author making? What is at stake for the particular author? Why does the author choose a specific audience to address? How does that audience affect the form, style, and content of what the author writes? Given the conversation, how effective is the author's response to the specific rhetorical situation of the essay?

Conversation on School Violence

The following selections are part of an ongoing national conversation concerning violence. "The School in School Violence: Definitions and Facts," by Michael Furlong and Gale Morrison, and "Supremacy Crimes," by Gloria Steinem address the particular concern of school violence. We suggest that you visit The National Rifle Association (NRA) website (http://www.nrahq.org/transcripts/index.asp) for a third view of this issue. There you will see speeches given by leaders in the NRA (most notably Charlton Heston) that address the issue of violence through the lens of gun ownership. Furlong and Morrison are social researchers who target educators as their audience. Steinem, a feminist writer and activist, published the original version of her article in *Ms.* magazine. How are concerns like race, gender, class, and sexuality addressed in each piece? How does audience influence content? What assumptions do the authors make? The politics of Steinem and the NRA are highly visible in their texts; what might the hidden biases of Furlong and Morrison be? How is race positioned differently in these texts? How is school violence defined in these essays, and might some contexts be left out?

The School in School Violence: Definitions and Facts

Michael Furlong and Gale Morrison

"The School in School Violence: Definitions and Facts" by Michael Furlong and Gale Morrison, Summer 2000 *Journal of Emotional and Behavioral Disorders* 8.2 pp. 306–319. Copyright © 2000 by PRO-ED, Ind. Reprinted with permission.

The purpose of this article is to clarify the historical and definitional roots of school violence. Knowledge about this issue has matured to the point where there is a need to refine the definition of school violence, thereby positioning educators to take the next step in providing effective, broad-based solutions to this problem. The first section provides an overview of the definitional and boundary issues of the term "school violence" as used in research and applied prevention programs. The second section presents an overview of what is known about the occurrence of violent and related high-risk behaviors on school campuses. Information about the prevalence of school violence is reviewed to inform and guide violence prevention programs, emphasizing the need to implement programs that are well linked to known correlates of school violence. We believe that in addition to identifying the characteristics of both perpetrators and victims of violence at school, researchers need to examine the contexts in which violence occurs.

Violence is taking an increasing toll on American society generally and on children and adolescents specifically, who are the victims of more crimes than any other age group in the United States (Kaufman, et al., 1998; Rennison, 1999). When violence occurs in the community, and especially on a school campus, whether by the hands of another student or by an outsider, actions must be taken to ensure the safety of all students and the staff who serve them. It is important to promote the rights, welfare, education, and health of children and youth by supporting National Education Goal 7 (National Educational Goals Panel, 2000): "Every school in the United States will be free of drugs, violence, and unauthorized presence of firearms and alcohol and will offer a disciplined environment conducive to learning." As the next millennium begins, the importance of National Education Goal 7 becomes increasingly apparent.

As researchers, educators, and politicians continue efforts to reduce violence, it has generally gone unnoticed that the use and meaning of the term school violence have evolved over the past 10 years. School violence is now conceptualized as a multifaceted construct that involves both criminal acts and aggression in schools, which inhibit development and learning, as well as harm the school's climate. School climate is important, as the role of schools as a culture and as an organization has not always received attention because of different disciplinary approaches to studying the problem. Researchers have brought divergent orientations to their work, and these interests have not always been well coordinated with the primary educational mission of schools. An understanding of the multi-disciplinary basis of school violence research is necessary in order to critically evaluate the potential use of programs that purport to reduce "school" violence.

It was not until 1992 that the label "school violence" itself was used widely as a term to describe violent and aggressive acts on school campuses. Citations in the University of California computer database of news reports in 5 major national newspapers show that prior to 1992 only 179 citations were listed under the keyword term "school violence." Since 1992, there have been 601 school violence articles in the same newspapers. Similarly, prior to 1992 only 38 news articles with the words "school violence" in their title were printed; this compares to 118 between 1992 and October 1998.

Since the 1970s, researchers from various disciplines have also addressed what is now called school violence but from different professional perspectives and from different points of interest. Citations in the PsychINFO computer database with title or keyword references to school violence were infrequent in the 1960s, grew slowly through the 1980s, and have increased exponentially during the 1990s. Although the PsychINFO database does not capture all manuscripts addressing school violence, it does reflect the heightened professional interest in this topic, particularly during the past 10 years.

History of the School Violence Concept

Early interest in school violence focused on youth who committed violence. Violence that occurred on school campuses was primarily a law enforcement issue, and researchers became interested in understanding factors that contributed to the development of antisocial behavior in children (Gottfredson & Gottfredson, 1985; Patterson, DeBaryshe, & Ramsey, 1989). Research also emerged among public health researchers and advocates interested in reducing injury to youth, particularly as it concerned the increase of violence-related injuries and homicides among adolescents during the late 1980s and early 1990s (California Department of Education 1989; Callahan, Rivara, & Farrow, 1993; Hausman, Spivak, & Prothrow-Stith, 1995; Kann, et al., 1995; Kellerman, Rivara, Rushforth, Banton, et al., 1993; Rivara, 1995; Sosin, Koepsell, Rivara, & Mercy, 1995; Spivak, Hausman, & Prothrow-Stith, 1989). The youth/school violence connection was made because schools were the most convenient places to access large numbers of youth for epidemiological surveys of exposure to, involvement in, and perpetration of violence (Dryfoos, 1993).

Professionals developed an increased concern about violence involving youth (not just violence occurring at school) due to an interest in extreme forms of juvenile crime and legitimate concern about substantial increases in youth homicide during the 1980s. Physicians were seeing thousands of youth coming into emergency wards with gunshot wounds, and naturally there was concern about this trend (Prothrow-Stith, 1987), which produced early studies of school weapon possession that were carried out by physicians and others interested in public health injury-prevention models and published in medical, health-focused journals (Kellerman, et al., 1993; Kingery, Mirzaee, Pruitt, Hurley, & Heuberger, 1991). In this research tradition, psychologists and psychiatrists interested in the development and treatment of aggressive, antisocial behavior began to focus on increases of violence involving youth (Cornell & Loper, 1998; Eron, Gentry, & Schlegel, 1994; Slaby & Guerra, 1988; Walker, Stieber, & O'Neill, 1990).

Researchers from health and psychology perspectives who were interested in preventing and reducing youth violence saw schools as logical settings in which to implement programs for reducing violence. In fact, this association was initially formed through the dissemination of an inaccurate interpretation of early youth violence survey results. The early Youth Risk Behavior Surveillance Survey (YRBS; Kann, et al., 1995) inquired about adolescents' possession of weapons during the past 30 days. This initial YRBS survey was administered in schools to students, but it did not ask about youths' weapon possession at schools. The results were widely reported and showed that more than 20% of high school students reported carrying weapons in the past month. This was a true statement, but it came to be interpreted as meaning that the students were carrying these weapons at school; this was an inaccurate inference. Nonetheless, this "finding" was reported to Congress as fact. At this same time, with the advent of the school crime supplement to the National Crime Victimization Survey (NCVS) in 1989, the link between youth violence/crime and school violence was firmly established.

Initially, educators were not directly included in these inquiries and the discussions and debates they spawned. This is not to say that educational researchers were not cognizant of or were not responding to this topic. Educational administrators expressed their responsibility and concern about school violence over the years but often thought of it in terms of "disciplinary" policies and actions (Baer, 1998), bullying or mobbing behavior (Batsche & Knoff, 1994; Garity, Jens, Porter, Sager, & Short-Camilli, 1997; Limber & Nation, 1998), truancy problems (Johns & Keenan, 1997), crisis response (Poland, 1997), or within the special education context (e.g., students having emotional or behavior disorders; Colvin, Kameenui, & Sugai, 1993; Kerr & Nelson, in press; Morrison, Furlong, & Smith, 1994; Rutherford & Nelson, 1995). Other, educators (California Department of Education, 1989; Morrison, Furlong, & Morrison, 1994) focused on school violence by reframing the problem in terms that made sense to educators: avoidance of harm, increased school safety, and viewing violence as a risk factor that negatively affected the learning process (Furlong & Morrison, 1994; Miller, Brehm, & Whitehouse, 1998; Morrison, Furlong, & Morrison, 1994). Some investigators began to view exposure to violence as a development risk factor (Morrison, Furlong, & Morrison, 1994; Resnick, et al., 1997; Walker, et al., 1990).

Educators' initial lukewarm interest in school violence must be considered within the larger context of a multidisciplinary interest in school violence, the public interest in school violence, and the tendency to sensationalize the issue. From educators' perspectives, increases in youth violence were not always obvious on their school campuses. For example, even recently a national principal's survey found that 90% of all schools had no known felony crimes during the previous year (United States Office of Education, 1998). As another example, in California during the late 1980s, schools were required to report each incident of "school crime" to the State Department of Education. Although it was claimed that the intent of this initiative, promoted by the State Attorney General's Office, was to help schools reduce crime, it was widely interpreted by the press and the community as a potential indictment of schools. Educators, in their opinion, were being asked to be law enforcement agents, and it was unknown how these "crime" data would be used. When the news media used the first statewide school crime report to characterize some schools as high-crime settings, the process broke down and was discontinued. It took 5 years to reestablish this process, now under the framework of the annual California Safe School Assessment (California Department of Education, 1989).

Current Use of the Term "School Violence"

Given these various perspectives of school violence and public policy foci, schools have not been at the forefront of raising public concern about violence and safety issues in schools. Despite the comparatively recent broad use of the term and its lack of clear definition, it is unlikely that "school violence" will be abandoned in favor of another term. Nonetheless, this historical context is important to keep in mind. It is from this perspective that school violence can be understood as a catchall term that has little precision from an empirical-scientific point of view. It is a term that has come to reflect broad community concern about youth violence and how that violence affects the schooling process. School violence has some utility as a policy term because it reflects societal values that schools should be a special place of refuge and nurturance for youth. Acts of violence that threaten the security of schools attack a core value of our social system. Thus, the task of researchers, as we see it, is to study (a) the many complex pre-cursors of violent-aggressive behavior occurring at school, (b) how to prevent it, and (c) how to reduce its impact when it does occur.

Although school violence is a multi-dimensional construct, there currently exists no definitive statement about its specific dimensions. It has been argued that school violence is composed of the perpetration of violence, violence victimization, antisocial behavior, criminal behavior, fear/worry beliefs, and discipline/school climate, among other aspects. Further complicating the understanding of this term is the political rhetoric that schools are essentially dangerous places and that schools are failing to properly educate today's youth. The lack of clarity in regard to the parameters of school violence has implications for the scientific study of school violence. When researchers say that they are conducting a study of school violence, what do they actually mean? In practice it may mean, for example, that they examine developmental correlates of delinquent behavior (Resnick, et al., 1997), crime on school campuses (Chandler, Chapman, Rand, & Taylor, 1998), victimization experiences (Furlong, Chung, Bates, & Morrison, 1995; Gottfredson & Gottfredson, 1985), school disciplinary practices (Baer, 1998), weapon possession at school (Kingery, Pruitt, & Heuberger, 1996), use of controlled substances at school (Furlong, et al., 1997), the influence of delinquent gangs on school (Conly, 1993), conflict resolution approaches (Dusenbury, Falco, Lake, Brannigan, & Bosworth, 1997), or zero tolerance (Morrison & D'Incau, 1997; Skiba & Peterson, 1999), among others. It is this lack of clarity or agreement on definition that fuels the need for further explication of the school violence concept.

School Violence

Given the various definitional and boundary issues of the term, it is necessary to explore specifically what the difference is between "school violence" and "violence in the schools." Getting educators to own their part in preventing school violence may depend on our ability to define and describe the part that "schools" as an organizational and institutional entity play in violence occurring on school campuses.

First, it is important to distinguish between "school" as a physical location for violence that has roots in the community and "school" as a system that causes or exacerbates problems the individuals within it experience. The former happens when students or intruders bring onto school campuses violence stemming from situations outside of the school experience. For example, such a situation occurred in Los Angeles County when a 20-year-old ex-boyfriend of a 16-year-old female student came onto a campus on an early October 1997 morning and used a gun to kill his girlfriend, who just days before had finally been able to move out of an abusive living arrangement with him. In contrast, in response to rejection by a female classmate, two Arkansas boys methodically fired upon their classmates on the school playground. This latter situation arose at least in part from relationships that were developed and broken within the school context, social contexts that educators have the potential to recognize and influence.

In some ways, society has expected a protective bubble to exist between the problems of our communities and the spillover into the school setting. Schools have remained relatively safe environments for teachers and students (Furlong & Morrison, 1994; Garbarino, 1992); however, in some areas, the community norms and behaviors regarding violence have thoroughly invaded the school (Devine, 1995). This is particularly true in urban environments where there is a commitment to subculture norms and values that endorse the use of violence in solving conflicts (Devine, 1995; Wolfgang & Ferracuti, 1967). Hellan and Beaton (1986) note that the influence of the community is greater for crime in high schools, probably due to the intruder problem. Middle school crimes are more influenced by the school environment, especially the ratio of students to teachers. Thus, even in recognizing that schools cannot completely block out the negative community influences in which they are located, the school as an organization can mount, through effective practices, a certain wall of protection.

Owning School Violence

As noted previously in this article, educators have been slow to investigate their specific and particular realms of influence on the school violence issue (Haynes, 1996). Although the professions of public health and juvenile justice have been very visible in documenting violent incidents in schools (e.g., Kingery, Coggeshall, & Alford, 1998), educators and public school officials have adopted an understandably defensive stance, relying on the quick fix of physical protection (metal detectors), but try to maintain a focus on their mission of education (Stephens, 1998). The reluctance of educators to enter the conversation has several understandable roots. First, the term violence evokes images of crimes and justice-involved punishments; thus, violent incidents at school can be easily passed on to the juvenile justice system. Educators may rightfully feel that their attention is best kept focused within the educational realm, where the issues of educating today's youth are challenge enough. However, as Braaten (1997) cautioned, "Despite the currently popular rhetoric about 'getting tough' with troubling students and bringing the role of schools 'back to basics,' schools are part of an increasingly complex and diverse society, and must respond to the varied needs students inevitably bring with them" (p. 48).

The ambivalence about owning issues of school violence is seen in role boundary lines drawn by some school personnel. Devine (1995) described schools in which the culture of violence has invaded the school's classrooms and halls and where the teachers' response to behavioral issues has become "hands-off." That is, teachers have defined their role as belonging strictly within the learning/classroom realm. Behavior and social interaction problems are relegated to the security staff, few of whom are prepared to handle these problems within a developmental framework. Similarly, Astor, Pitner, and Duncan (1996) discussed the undefined spaces in school grounds, such as hallways and other unsupervised locations, that are more prone to occurrences of violent behavior because no professional educator (teacher, administrator, support personnel) claims responsibility for that locale as part of his or her assigned duties. Trump (1997) addressed the problem of keeping security issues and security personnel in an unprofessional status, noting that efforts end up being fragmented and ineffective. He argues that school security needs to become part of the central mission of the school, where professional standards and evaluation criteria can be applied to assessing the effectiveness of security professionals. Vestermark (1998) described the inherent tension between police-based and school-based security professionals. Although the former tend to highlight the law enforcement aspects of their role, the latter are more likely to emphasize their role in the educational process (i.e., supporting the mission of the schools through their facilitation of school proceedings and positive relationships with students).

Thus, the tension about who owns the problem of school violence increasingly plays out in the professional behaviors and role definitions held by educators and "outside" protection personnel. If one embraces a school violence rather than a violence that happens in schools definition, attention may be refocused on the role that school as a physical, educational, and social environment plays in violence among its participants. Owning school violence as an educational problem also allows the problem of violence to become a topic worthy of classroom and school attention. Epp and Watkinson (1997) eloquently reinforced this focus in suggesting the following:

> School violence is an important component of the daily lives of children in schools. . . . It affects where they walk, how they dress, where they go and who their friends are. As long as teachers treat violence at arms' length, as something that is someone else's problem, they will continue to neglect the opportunity to intervene in a crucial aspect of the children's lives. By ignoring school violence, the name-calling, the shoving, the fighting, the harassment, they are condoning it. Children see teachers

walking by, pretending not to notice, and they learn that the way we treat others, the way we interact on the street or in the playground, is nobody's business but our own. Teachers must talk about violence, they must recognize it, examine it, dissect it, and let children see and understand its secrets and its sources. Without this examination it remains an ugly secret that society cannot understand or control (p. 193).

By adopting educational ownership of school violence, it becomes legitimate to consider the issue within the everyday management of schooling tasks. Threat of physical harm can be interpreted additionally as threat of developmental harm; that is, the threat and reality of physical harm has consequences that suppress the maximal educational growth and development of students. Such a threat lands the issue squarely on the educator's plate of concern. Once this concern has been identified as relevant to the educational mission of the school, then the challenge is in how to weave this concern into the fabric of educational practice. This challenge must be better understood within the context of the impetus for school change.

Defining School and Its Relationship to School Violence

The central vision for school change in the 1970s and 1980s was schooling effectiveness, leading to the "school reform," "school change," and "school restructuring" efforts of the late 1980s and 1990s. The schooling effectiveness literature described the school as an organization that impacts student outcomes; that is, effective schools have (a) clearly defined goals in relation to the school mission and philosophy, (b) close monitoring and feedback in regard to progress toward these goals, (c) high expectations for student achievement and clear boundaries for acceptable behavior, (d) high morale among staff and students, and (e) successful and meaningful involvement of parents and the community (Braaten, 1997; Good & Weinstein, 1986; Rutter, Maughan, & Mortimore, 1979). These parameters provide a useful framework for examining school factors as they relate to violence.

It has been assumed and promoted that effective schools are also schools that are safe and are less vulnerable to violence (Morrison, Furlong, & Morrison, 1994). It has been asserted, for example, that students who engage in their schoolwork, are bonded to school, and have multiple opportunities to participate and succeed in academic tasks are less likely to commit acts of violence toward each other, toward school staff, or upon the school itself (vandalism). It also has been noted that schools having low levels of violence tend to have a firm consistent principalship style, tend to be smaller in size, and have lower levels of crowding

(American Psychological Association, 1993; Goldstein & Conoley, 1997; Zwier & Vaughan, 1984).

However, research that specifically ties school factors to levels of violence is sparse and relies on cursory associations without specifically proving the causal relationships. In order to tighten this association, it may be necessary to go to the next level of specification and delineate the specific situations and circumstances that might lead a student to engage in a violent act. For example, a student may react in a violent or aggressive manner in response to bullying, social rejection, public humiliation, perceived lack of fairness in disciplinary actions, and stress. These situations are all tied to contexts, actions, and policies that schools as organizations can effect.

Epp and Watkinson (1997) provided an interesting framework that connects the concepts of "school" and "violence" and facilitates understanding the impact of specific schooling contexts on students from culturally different populations; they refer to it as "systemic violence." Systemic violence has been defined as any institutional practice or procedure that adversely impacts on individuals or groups by burdening them psychologically, mentally, culturally, spiritually, economically, or physically. Applied to education, it means practices and procedures that prevent students from learning, thus "harming them" (p. 1). Examples of systemic violence include but are not limited to exclusionary practices, overly competitive learning environments, toleration of abuse, school disciplinary policies rooted in exclusion and punishment; discriminatory guidance policies, and the like.

This concept of school violence, which is contextually embedded, is a rare focus among the majority of school violence solutions that have focused on the characteristics and developmental patterns of individuals who perpetrate school violence. We have done little to define the contexts in school settings that trigger violence. For violence that occurs in the schools, these contexts are clearly identifiable, yet they have not received much attention. This decontextualized approach to understanding school violence is curious, as violence is usually an interpersonal event arising and resulting from interactions between individuals.

Because of the heterogeneous blending of interests about school violence, it is time for researchers to be more precise about the use of this term or recognize that its primary function should be to motivate researchers to communicate across parallel research traditions and to keep the issues of youth delinquency and antisocial behavior at the forefront of public policy debate. Researchers from outside the education field need to recognize that the interests and needs of schools and educators must be addressed specifically in this process. Schools may have been reluctant passengers on the school violence bus because initial school violence studies were often not empirically based, did not communicate findings to the education community (studies were published in medical and other journals that educators would not consume), did not include educators in the evaluation of school violence reports (Elliott & Tolan, 1999), and sometimes described schools as having such gross problems that there was an "epidemic" of school violence. These dire descriptions were inconsistent with the educator's day-to-day experiences at school, and these statements were interpreted as attacks on the school system itself (Dear, et al., 1995). There is no longer any need to engage in alarmist discussion about the school violence problem. What is needed is a thoughtful approach to synthesizing the multidisciplinary knowledge bases that have been created over the past two decades and that promote the agenda of preventing youth crime, delinquency, and violent behavior while at the same time supporting educators' efforts to create a positive learning environment for all students through specific consideration of relevant school contexts.

Factors Associated with Violence and Related High-Risk Behaviors

The report Indicators of School Crime and Safety (Kaufman, et al., 1998) provided a snapshot of violence and crime on American school campuses. This was the first of what became an annual school safety and crime scorecard and reported the prevalence of the following types of indicators: (a) non-fatal student victimization (student reports), (b) violence and crime at schools (public school principal reports), (c) violent deaths at school, (d) nonfatal teacher victimization at school (teacher reports), and (e) school environment conditions. Of particular note is the fact that this report systematically emphasized the incidence of these acts both at school and in other locations (while pointing out that even the term "at school" is not uniformly defined in research). Perspective is provided to show that terrible things do happen at schools, but it is emphasized that these events occur more often in other settings. In fact, schools are the safest public setting for children and adolescents (Hyman & Perone, 1998). Enough information is now known about violent and related high-risk behaviors on school campuses that meaningful patterns can be described. The purpose of this section is to provide an overview of the individual factors known to be associated with school violence. It is our assertion that knowledge of these factors is needed to understand the origins of school violence and construct meaningful responses to it.

How Is School Violence Measured?

Recently, researchers have begun to critically examine the procedures used to assess violent incidents on school campuses and how reliability and validity checks of students' self-reports affect school violence incidence rates (Cornell & Loper, 1998; Rosenblatt & Furlong, 1997). When these checks are made, it has been found that the incidence of school violence is significantly higher among those students whose responses fail reliability checks. Cornell and Loper, for example, found that the incidence of fighting at school was 19.2% among students passing reliability checks but significantly higher, at 58.6%, among students failing reliability checks. Rosenblatt and Furlong similarly found that self-reported school violence victimization was nearly 100% higher among students whose responses failed pre-specified reliability checks than among those students whose responses passed the same reliability checks. Given that almost all basic information about the prevalence of school violence has been gleaned from studies that do not report using any response reliability or validity checks, it is likely that known rates of various types of school violence are overestimates of their true rates.

Most of the databases that provide information about the incidence of school violence have come from public health and criminology disciplines that use an epidemiological model, not the psychometric model that is more familiar to psychologists and educators. Thus, much of what is known and inferred from school violence incidence databases is based on responses to single items with untested properties. The matter of evaluating methodological issues in school violence research is a topic that merits more attention than can be given here, but as a brief example, consider the YRBS item, "In the past 30 days how many times have you brought a weapon to school (gun, knife, or club)?" From a measurement perspective, there is much ambiguity in this question. Do youths responding to this item share a common understanding of what the term "weapon" means? If a student brought a knife to school but did not intend to use it to hurt someone, how would he or she answer this question? Is the intent of the item to place the quality of "weapon" in the object itself or in the behavioral intentionality of the student? Furthermore, combining multiple weapons into one item is not good psychometric practice. And, how is the "past 30 days" time period evaluated compared to the "past 6 months," or "past year" time frames, which have been used in other studies? These measurement issues have not been examined empirically.

It is also important to make the distinction between items that measure violent aggression and those that represent violence victimization. For example, one item from the NCVS (Chandler, et al., 1998) asked respondents if they had damaged anyone's school property; this unambiguously measures violence from a perpetrator's perspective. In contrast, one item from the YRBS asks if the student had "been in a physical fight." This item could reflect predatory aggression or victimization. The context in which a fight occurs is important to know. A fight having its origins in a boyfriend/girlfriend dispute has different implications for schools than fights erupting from racial or ethnic conflict. These contextual variations, unfortunately, are rarely included in school violence prevalence studies. Although research is needed to thoroughly understand the patterns of aggressive behavior and violence victimization, some strong relationships with school violence are known. We now turn our attention to these findings.

Violent and Aggressive Behavior at School

1. **Males are Most Involved in School Violence.** Males are much more likely than females to be physically aggressive at school and to be the victim of attacks. In a national study of deaths that occurred on school campuses from 1993 to 1995, 9 out of 10 of the deaths involved a male as both perpetrator and victim. National studies such as the National Educational Longitudinal Study, YRBS, and NCVS, as well as local surveys (e.g., Cornell & Loper, 1998; Furlong, Morrison, Bates, & Chung, 1998; Kingery, Biafora, & Zimmerman, 1996), have all found that males are more involved than females as both perpetrators and victims of school violence, a pattern that is also found in community settings (Rennison, 1999). A side note is that school safety surveys tend to focus on assaultive behavior or high-risk behaviors that could result in physical injury. It is important to recognize that these surveys measure important school violence variables, but they do not measure all types of harmful behavior that occur to students on school property. For example, females do not engage in dangerous physical behaviors as often as males, but they may act in socially aggressive ways more often than males (Crick, 1996). Physical and verbal sexual harassment is another class of behaviors that happen more frequently to females than males (Furlong, et al., 1998; Stein, 1998).

2. **Violence Varies by Student Age.** Patterns of school violence and high-risk behaviors are known to vary by the age of the students (Chandler, et al., 1998; Furlong, et al., 1997). Research examining bullying behavior shows that this form of violence is most frequent among upper-elementary-age students (Batsche & Knoff, 1994). Research with secondary school students has found that some forms of aggressive behavior are higher among

junior high school students (e.g., fighting) and that others peak during the high school years (e.g., weapon possession, drug use at school).

3. Student Experiences Vary by Their Racial/Ethnic Identification. Most research to date has not found extremely large differences in student experiences across racial/ethnic groups. Nationally, one pattern that has been replicated, however, is that African American students report slightly higher rates and Hispanic students slightly lower rates of violence victimization (Chandler, et al., 1998). A survey of more than 7,000 California pupils also found this pattern (Furlong, et al., 1998). Because some forms of school violence can involve ethnic conflict, it may be helpful to examine student violence experiences by attending to their ethnic and cultural heritage (Kingery, Biafora, et al., 1996).

4. Student Experiences Differ Slightly by Location of the School. The school crime supplement of the 1995 NCVS (Kaufman, et al., 1998) found essentially no difference in overall victimization prevalence (violent and property combined) in schools located in central city (14.7%), suburban (14.6%), and non-metropolitan (14.3%) locales, despite the finding that crime victimization is typically found to be higher in urban than suburban and rural locales (Rennison, 1999). Although the rates of school violence may not differ strongly by location, differences may occur in specific locations. In addition, central city areas have larger student populations, so in a given time period, these students may be exposed to a greater number of violent incidents on their school campuses.

5. Individual Student Attitudes Are Associated with School Patterns. Although perhaps not too surprising, the attitudes held by individual students are associated with their involvement as perpetrators of violence or as its victims. Cornell and Loper (1998) found a significant association between engaging in physical fights and weapon carrying at school and beliefs favoring physical aggression and deriving personal satisfaction from hitting. In another study, Bates, Chung, and Chase (1997) found that students who hold distrusting attitudes and are disconnected from their teachers are more likely to be victims of school violence. Further documenting the importance of examining the characteristics of students involved in school violence, Furlong, et al. (1997) found that students reporting frequent substance use at school were more likely to commit aggressive acts and to be a victim of others' aggression. This pattern is also strongly supported by results of the annual survey conducted by the Parents' Resource Institute for Drug Education (PRIDE, 1999).

Deaths on School Campuses

Surprising as it may seem, until the release of the 1998 federal school crime and safety index (Kaufman, et al., 1998), there was no national reporting mechanism for the shootings, homicides, or suicides that occurred on school campuses. Gathering information from newspaper reports is the way in which deaths on school campuses have been monitored. This effort is carried out by the National School Safety Center, and a comprehensive report for the years 1994 to 1996 was reported in the Journal of the American Medical Association (Kachur, 1996). In these 2 years, there were 105 deaths on school campuses nationwide—these included 85 homicides and 20 suicides. Most of these deaths involved the use of firearms. Despite the justified national attention given to the shootings that occurred during the 1997–1998 school year at several rural schools across America, that year was not the most deadly school year in recent years, a distinction that belongs to 1992 (Kaufman, et al., 1998).

Weapon Possession

Other researchers have asked students to report how often they carry various weapons on school campuses, and a few have directly asked about gun possession. Some investigators have also asked students if they have actually witnessed a student with a gun on campus, reasoning that students would be more likely to report that they saw a gun at school than they would be to admit that they personally brought a gun to school. Resnick, et al. (1997), in the National Longitudinal Study of Adolescent Health (NLSAH), reported that 12.4% of adolescents report carrying a weapon anywhere in the past 30 days. This compares with 18.4% for the comparable YRBS weapon-carrying item (carrying weapons anywhere, not just on school property; Kann, et al., 1998).

Other investigators have focused specifically on gun possession by students at school. Cornell and Loper (1998) found that 8.2% of students in their urban sample said they had carried a gun during the preceding month: % at school and outside school; 3.2% outside of school only; and 1.6% chool only. Other studies using past-30-day time periods have reported ol weapon possession rates of between 7% and 15% (Cornell & Loper, ; Johnston, O'Malley, & Bachman, 1996; Kaufman, et al., 1998). nt reports of school gun possession vary by the community being sur- and the manner in which the question is asked. Direct comparison en communities is not advised because of the use of dissimilar ologies, sampling procedures, and response expectation contexts.

However, collectively these findings suggest that guns are brought to school by a relatively small group of students who are also likely to carry guns and other weapons in community settings.

The following factors are associated with gun and other weapon possession at school (see Furlong, Flam, and Smith [1996] for a review of gun possession on school campuses).

1.   Self-Reported Gun Possession Rates Are Higher in Anonymous Self-Report Surveys. Paper-and-pencil self-report surveys have produced the highest rates of school gun possession. Data from the Monitoring the Future study (MTF; Johnston, et al., 1996) showed that between 1994 and 1996 about 3% of twelfth-grade students reported bringing a gun to school at least once during the 4 weeks prior to responding to the survey. See Kingery, et al. (1998) and Furlong, et al. (1996) for summaries of research about gun possession at school.

2.   Schools Are a Barrier to Weapon and Gun Possession. Educators and parents are legitimately concerned about students bringing guns to school, but it is also important to recognize that every major study about youth weapon possession has found that youth carry weapons more frequently outside of school than at school. The YRBS (Kann, et al., 1995, 1996, 1998), for example, has asked about weapon possession on and off school campus on three occasions. For both males and females, weapon possession at school is 3 to 4 times less frequent than outside of school.

3.   Males Are Predominantly Involved in Gun Possession. In the N(
data were collected through personal, face-to-face interviews with st'
ages 12 to 19. In this formal interview context, only 0.1% of all 23,9'
dents admitted to carrying a gun at school for protection in the pre'
months. All of the students who admitted school gun possession w
and a large majority of them were in the eighth, ninth, or tenth gra'
the 11,602 females interviewed admitted to school gun possession
results are likely to underestimate actual gun possession or a'
America's school campuses. Other regional samples using ar
report methods all replicate the strong finding that males are '
possessors of weapons at school. However, in regional samp'
report bringing weapons to school (Kingery, Pruitt, et al., J

4.   Self-Reported Gang Affiliation Is Associated w'
There is some evidence that youths who self-designa'
members are more likely than non-gang members t'

For example, 18.6% of gang members claimed to have brought a gun to school compared to 4.9% of non-gang members (Cornell & Loper, 1998). The NCVS, in 1995, found that students who reported being aware of gangs on their school campuses were significantly more likely to also report being aware of and/or actually seeing guns and other weapons at their school (Kaufman, et al., 1998).

5.   Youth Who Own Guns Are Disproportionately Involved in Aggressive Behavior at School. Youth who report owning a gun, as a group, are disproportionately involved in juvenile crimes and in assaultive, aggressive behaviors at school (Callahan, et al., 1993). Weapon possession/ownership by any adolescent is a matter of concern, particularly when the youth exhibits other distress signals such as those discussed, for example, in the U.S. Office of Education's Early Warning/Timely Response document (Dwyer, Osher, & Warger, 1998). Other researchers have shown that exposure to guns in the home is a high risk factor for being in a physical fight (Kingery, Pruitt, et al., 1996) and for homicide (Kellerman, et al., 1993).

6.   Students Who Admit to Frequent Alcohol or Drug Use At School Have Higher Gun Possession Rates. It is a study involving more than 4,000 secondary students in one California county, students who reported using alcohol or other substances at school 7 or more times during the previous year accounted for about 50% of all students who acknowledged frequent school weapon possession (Furlong, et al., 1997).

7.   Students Bring Weapons, Including Guns, School for Protection and Other Reasons. There is not a lot known about why students specifically bring guns to schools. One regional survey in rural Texas asked students who reported bringing a gun to school during the past 12 months about the reasons why they felt compelled to do this. About half of these gun-carrying students said that it made them feel safer. But, another response should make educators take pause and consider the importance of conflict resolution prevention programs and anger management programs. More than half of these students (55%) reported that they brought the gun to school because they were angry with someone and "I was thinking about shooting him/her" (Kingery, Pruitt, et al., 1996). These findings seem to dispel any notion that the prototypic gun-toting student is acting primarily in a defensive-fearful manner. It is more likely the case, given available data, that these youths are acting in a defensive-aggressive manner. Even more alarming is that only 3% of these gun-carrying students believed that an apology was an effective way to avoid fighting, which compares to 60% for non-gun toting students (Kingery, Pruitt, et al., 1996). This pattern points toward a particularly volatile mix: (a) the combination of concerns about being attacked, (b) the use of weapons as a protective device, (c) angry potentiation to use the gun, and (d) disbelief that apologizing or other nonaggression conflict avoidance strategies are effective.

Gun ownership is known to be much higher among youth who have a history of delinquency, gang membership, and other disorders of conduct (Callahan, et al., 1993). Whenever school personnel are concerned about extremely aggressive behavior in a youth, it is advisable to gather additional information about any past involvement in gangs, history of violent offenses, history of selling drugs, and ownership of or easy access to firearms (Furlong, et al., 1997). Youth with this kind of delinquency profile are more likely than nondelinquent youth to use guns for self-protection and to bring a gun to school.

8. Youth Involved with Violence at School May Have Multiple Risk Factors. Although requiring additional investigation, current research can be interpreted to show that youth who bring guns to school campuses are a high-risk group who usually present with multiple, significant risk factors in their lives. Any youth who is caught with a gun at school should be carefully interviewed to ascertain the range of stresses affecting his or her life and how these stresses impact performance in school and the community. Kingery, Pruitt, et al. (1996), in their survey of Texas students, reported that those students who brought a gun to school were much more likely to experience high-risk behaviors, including walking alone through unsafe neighborhoods, using cocaine, getting into fights in the community, and being forced to have sex. These students reported that they often found themselves in settings and situations in which crime and violence were more likely to occur. Being in these settings more frequently than other students, they also were in physical fights more often, perceived more danger in their environments, which in fact may be true, and therefore were more likely to use guns as a means to enhance their sense of self-protection.

Concerns for Safety at School

One marker for the impact of violence on a school campus is to ask students about their level of worry or concern about their personal safety and if they engage in behaviors to limit their exposure to these perceived dangers. Across three national YRBS surveys (Kann, et al., 1995, 1996, 1998), about 4% to 5% of secondary school students report that they stayed home at least

1 day in the past month because of safety concerns at school or on the way to or from school. In 1989 and 1995 the NCVS asked students (ages 12 to 19) if they feared being "attacked or harmed" at school. Over this time period (the previous 6 months), more students (6% vs. 9%) expressed feeling this fear (Kaufman, et al., 1998). In three other national surveys, students were asked if someone using a weapon at school in the past 12 months had threatened them: MTF (Johnson, et al., 1996), the YRBS (Kann, et al., 1995, 1996, 1998), and the NCVS (Kaufman, et al., 1998). The rates vary widely across these three studies, from a low of 1.3% (NCVS) to a high of 15.2% (MTF). The reasons for such wide discrepancies are unknown.

The Context of School Violence

Most school violence research to date has focused on univariate relationships that characterize both perpetrators and victims. Researchers are beginning to extend knowledge about the factors associated with school violence that take into account its multidimensional influences, such as developmental patterns, community influences, and behavioral contexts. For example, Lockwood (1997) provides an in-depth evaluation of the social contexts in which youth say violent acts occur ("an act carried out with the intention, or perceived intention, of physically injuring another person" (p. 3). The most frequent violent events involved being "pushed, grabbed, shoved" (55%) and/or "kicked or bit or hit with fist" (67%). Twenty-one percent reported that they had been "beaten up" and 17% had been "slapped." A total of 10% and 8% of these youth reported that they were "threatened with a gun" or "threatened with a knife," respectively. An astonishing 89% of these incidents involved someone they knew personally, but 58% of these were considered to be acquaintances, not friends. In about one half of these incidents, an adult became aware of the event and provided support. In 3 out of 5 events, the youth had a third party present (usually friends and relatives), and the third party often became involved in the event to support the youth. These were time-limited events and were often terminated within 15 minutes.

These events were precipitated by many factors, and there was no one predominant "opening move." Unprovoked touching (13%), interfering with something owned or being used (13%), a request to do something (10%), backbiting (9%), and verbal teasing/rough play getting out of hand (9%) were the primary precipitants in about one half of these events. Of the events that occurred at school, the most predominant physical contexts were the classroom (39%), the hall or stairs (21%), the school bus (11%), physical education setting (11%), and the cafeteria (6%).

Of particular relevance to violence prevention programs is the finding that in 84% of the events, the youth provided a rationale for their actions that justified their use of violence. These justifications included "retaliation for harmful behavior" (28.8%), the other youth's behavior was offensive (17.7%), "self-defense to stop victimization" (13.6%), and to "help a friend" (12.6%). Unjustified explanations offered included being blinded by anger into action (6.6%) and being "pushed" into violence by another youth (5.6%). In only 1 of these incidents did the youth acknowledge antisocial behavior intentionally: (i.e., wanted money). Lockwood (1997) concluded that most of the violent incidents described by these youth involved situations in which they perceived themselves or others to be victimized and that their actions were justified as retaliation. Not only did they not believe that their actions were inappropriate, but also their value systems required them to retaliate. One can imagine the limited impact that a violence prevention or conflict management program would have on similar youth when these programs emphasize peaceful negotiation while the youth's values promote justified retaliation. This study provides a strong rationale for implementing programs that attend to the social and broader ecological contexts in which violence occurs. Lockwood stresses the need to construct prevention programs that more realistically match the way in which violent acts occur in the lives of youth. Using such a conceptualization, possible intervention points for educators may include the following: (a) Adults are present in about 50% of the aggressive events reported by youth, so adults need to create strategies to respond with an instructional purpose to these incidents; (b) most of these events occurred at school or home, so opportunities for contextualized learning are significant, and adults need to attend to those events, seeing them as an opportunity to teach negotiation skills; and (c) many conflicts begin with mild, but offensive, touching, so programs ought to include components that role-play ways to respond to this touching in a manner that does not escalate into physical fights.

Summary

There are identifiable patterns of an individual's involvement in incidents of school violence. The patterns and trends described should be useful in helping school personnel to be particularly vigilant in their observations and to provide "preventive" support of certain individuals, groups, and situations. Enough is now known about the correlates of violent and aggressive behavior on school campuses to implement meaningful intervention programs. Efforts such as the Blueprint Program created by the University of Colorado Center for the Study of Prevention and Violence (Elliott, 1998) provided detailed descriptions of prevention and intervention programs that have been implemented in schools and have demonstrated effectiveness. These programs can be best implemented when each school considers the identifiable patterns and correlates of school violence. For example, it is quite clear that males are predominantly involved as both perpetrators and victims of violence, which strongly suggests that school-based programs should openly acknowledge the need to specifically examine the behavior of males. Also, school administrators can use current research findings to be specifically vigilant about potential hot spots in their schools that would be the targets of efficient prevention programs. Nonetheless, we caution that there are multiple pathways toward school violence, and these complex relationships have not been fully explored. Educators need to be mindful that their intervention efforts should target not only those youth whose life experiences closely match the correlates of school violence, but also take into consideration the contexts that contribute to or hinder aggressive behavior. This is demonstrated by the findings of a recent National Longitudinal Adolescent Health Survey report (Resnick, et al., 1997), in which youth who were connected and bonded to meaningful adults in their lives, at ho and at school, were less likely to commit crimes, use substances, an gage in high-risk behaviors.

lly, in addition to continuing the collection of detailed and targeted dat is issue, a parallel effort is needed to further define the nature of sch nce in order to further understand the specific role that schools as a tion play in the deterrence or exacerbation of student problems that iolence. It is through this further explication that the most effec elevant programs can be guided and implemented.

References

Americ respical Association. (1993). *Youth & violence: Psychology's Asso e I: Summary Report of the American Psychological ission on Violence and Youth.* Washington, DC: Author.

Astor, R. ment O., & Duncan, B. E. (1996). Ecological approaches to violen ation with teachers on issues related to youth and school Baer, G. G egro Education, 65(3), 336–355.

and l discipline in the United States: Prevention, correction, 309–3 evelopment. *School Psychology Review,* 31(4),

Bates, M. P., Chung, A., & Chase. M. (1997). Where has the trust gone? The protective role of interpersonal trust and connections with adults in the school. *The California School Psychologist*, 2, 39–52.

Batsche, G. M., & Knoff, H. M. (1994). Bullies and their victims: Understanding a pervasive problem in the schools. *School Psychology Review*, 23(2), 165–174.

Bender, W. N., & McLaughlin, P. J. (1997). Weapons in schools: Strategies for teachers confronting violence and hostage situations. *Intervention in School and Clinic*, 32, 211–216.

Braaten, S. (1997). Creating safe schools: A principal's perspective. In A. P. Goldstein & J. C. Conoley (Eds.), *School violence intervention: A practical handbook* (pp. 46–57). New York: Guilford.

California Department of Education. (1989). *Safe schools: A planning guide for action*. Sacramento, CA: Author. (Revised in 1995)

Callahan, C. M., Rivara, F. P., & Farrow, J. A. (1993). Youth in detention and handguns. *Journal of Adolescent Health*, 14(5), 350–355.

Chandler, K. A., Chapman, C. D., Rand, M. R., & Taylor, B. M. (1998). Students' reports of school crime: 1989 and 1995 (NCES 98-241/NCJ-169607). Washington, DC: U.S. Departments of Education and Justice.

Colvin, G., Kameenui, E. J., & Sugai, G. (1993). School-wide and classroom management: Reconceptualizing the integration and management of students with behavior problems in general education. *Education and Treatment of Children*, 16, 361–381.

Cornell, D. G., & Loper, A. B. (1998). Assessment of violence and other high-risk behaviors with a school survey. *School Psychology Review*, 27(2), 317–3

Crick, N. R. (1996). The role of overt aggression, relational aggression, and social behavior in the prediction of children's future social adjustment. *Development*, 67, 2317–2327.

Dear, J., et al. (1995). Creating caring relationships to foster academic exc Recommendations for reducing violence in California Schools, Fina Sacramento, CA: Advisory Panel on School Violence, Commission o Credentialing.

Devine, J. (1995). Can metal detectors replace the panopticon *Anthropology*, 10(2), 171–195.

Dryfoos, J. (1993). Schools as places for health, mental health, and ices. In R. Takanishi (Ed.), *Risk and opportunity* (pp. 82–109 Teachers College Press.

Dusenbury, L., Falco, M., Lake, A., Brannigan, R., & Bosworth, K critical elements of promising violence prevention progra *School Health*, 67(10), 409–414.

Elliott, D. S. (1998). *Blueprints for violence prevention*. Bou Behavioral Science, Regents of the University of Colorado.

Elliott, D. S., & Tolan, P. H. (1999). Youth violence prevention social policy: An overview. In D. J. Flannery & C. R. Hu *lence: Prevention, intervention, and social policy* (pp. DC: American Psychiatric Press.

Epp, J. R., & Watkinson, A. M. (Eds.). (1997). *Systemic violence in education: Promise broken.* Albany, NY: State University of New York Press.

Eron, L. D., Gentry, J. H., & Schlegel, P. (Eds.). (1994). *Reason to hope: A psychosocial perspective on violence & youth.* Washington, DC: American Psychological Association.

Frammolino, R. (1998). Failing grade for safe schools plan. *Los Angeles Times,* September 6.

Furlong, M. J., Casas, J. M., Corral, C., Chung, A., & Bates, M. (1997). Drugs and school violence. *Education and Treatment of Children,* 20(3), 263–280.

Furlong, M. J., Chung, A., Bates, M., & Morrison, R. (1995). Who are the victims of school violence? *Education and Treatment of Children,* 18(3), 282–298.

Furlong, M. J., Flam, C. S., & Smith, A. (1996). Firearm possession in schools: Disarming the myths. *The California School Psychologist,* 1, 5–14.

Furlong, M. J., & Morrison, G. M. (Eds.). (1994). School violence miniseries: *School Psychology Review* [special issue]. Washington, DC: National Association of School Psychologists.

Furlong, M. J., Morrison, R., Bates, M., & Chung, A. (1998). School violence victimization among secondary students in California: Grade, gender, and racial-ethnic group incidence patterns. *The California School Psychologist,* 3, 71–87.

Garbarino, J. (1992). *Children in danger: Coping with the consequences of community violence.* San Francisco: Jossey-Bass.

Garity, C., Jens, K., Porter, W., Sager, N, & Short-Camilli, C. (1997). "Bully proofing your school: Creating a positive climate." *Intervention in School and Clinic,* 32(4), 235–243.

Goldstein, A. P., & Conoley, J. C. (1997). Student aggression: Current status. In A. P. Goldstein & J. C. Conoley (Eds.), *School violence intervention: A practical handbook* (pp. 3–45). New York: Guilford.

Good, T. L., & Weinstein, R. S. (1986). Schools make a difference: Evidence, criticisms, and new directions. *American Psychologist,* 41, 1090–1097.

Gottfredson, G. D., & Gottfredson, D. C. (1985). *Victimization in schools.* New York: Plenum.

Hausman, A. J., Spivak, H., & Prothrow-Stith D. (1995). Evaluation of a community-based youth violence prevention project. *Journal of Adolescent Health,* 17(6), 353–359.

Haynes, N. M. (1996). Creating safe and caring school communities: Comer school development program schools. *Journal of Negro Education,* 65(3), 308–321.

Hellan, D. A., & Beaton, S. (1986). The pattern of violence in urban public schools: The influence of school and community. *Journal of Research in Crime and Delinquency,* 23(2), 102–127.

Hyman, I. A., & Perone, D. C. (1998). The other side of school violence: Educator policies and practices that may contribute to student misbehavior. *Journal of School Psychology,* 36(1), 7–27.

Johns, B. H., & Keenan, J. P. (1997). *Techniques for managing a safe school.* Denver, CO: Love.

Johnston, L. D., O'Malley, P. M., & Bachman, J. G. (1996). *National survey results on drug use from Monitoring the Future Study, 1975–1995: Volume I Secondary school students* (NIH Publication No. 96-4139). Washington, DC: U.S. Government Printing Office.

Kachur, S. P. (1996). Data on school-associated violent deaths in the United States. *Journal of the American Medical Association, 275*(22), 1729–1733.

Kann, L., Kinchen, S. A., Williams, B. I., Ross, J. G., Lowry, R., Hill, C. V., Grunbaun, J. A., Blumson, P. S., Collins, J. L., & Kolbe, L. J. (1998). Youth risk behavior surveillance—United States, 1997. *Journal of School Health, 68*, 355–369.

Kann, L., Warren, C. W., Harris, W. A., Collins, J. L., Douglas, K. A., Collins, M. E., Williams, B. I., Ross, J. G., & Kolbe, L. J. (1995). Youth Risk Behavior Surveillance—1993. *Journal of School Health, 65*, 163–171.

Kann, L., Warren, C. W, Harris, W. A., Collins, J. L. Douglas, K. A., Williams, B. I., Ross, J. G., & Kolbe, L. J. (1996). Youth risk behavior surveillance—United States, 1995. *Journal of School Health, 66*, 365–377.

Kaufman, P., Chen, X., Choy, S. P., Chapman, C. D. Rand, M. R., & Ringel, C. (1998). *Indicators of school crime and safety, 1998* (NCES 98-251/NCJ-172215). Washington, DC: U.S. Departments of Education and Justice.

Kellerman, A. L., Rivara, F. P., Rushforth, N. B., Banton, J. G., Reay, D. T., Francisco, J. T., Locci, A. B., Prodzinski, J., Hackman, B. B., & Somes, G. (1993). Gun ownership as a risk factor for homicide in the home. *New England Journal of Medicine 329*(15), 1084–1091.

Kerr, M. M., & Nelson, C. M. (in press). *Strategies for managing problem behaviors in the classroom* (2nd ed.). Columbus, OH: Merrill.

Kingery, P. M., Biafora, F. A., & Zimmerman, R. S. (1996). Risk factors for violent behaviors among ethnically diverse urban adolescents. *School Psychology International 17*, 171–188.

Kingery P. M., Coggeshall, M. B., & Alford, A. A. (1998). Violence at school: Recent evidence from four national surveys. *Psychology in the Schools, 7*(2), 137–157.

Kingery, P. M., Mirzaee, E., Pruitt, B. E., Hurley, R. S., & Heuberger, G. (1991). Rural communities near large metropolitan areas: Safe havens from adolescent violence and drug use? *Health Values, 15*(4), 199–208.

Kingery, P. M., Pruitt, B. E., & Heuberger, G. (1996). A profile of rural Texas adolescents who carry handguns to school. *Journal of School Health, 66*(1), 210–214.

Limber, S. P., & Nation, M. (1998). *Bullying among school children.* Washington, DC: Office of Juvenile Justice and Delinquency Prevention.

Lockwood, D. (1997). *Violence among middle school and high school students: An analysis and implications prevention.* Washington, DC: U.S. Department of Justice, Office of Justice Programs, National Institute of Justice.

Miller, G. E., Brehm, K., & Whitehouse, S. (1998). Reconceptualizing school-based prevention for antisocial behavior within a resiliency framework. *School Psychology Review,* 27(3), 364–379.

Morrison, G., Furlong, M. J., & Smith, G. (1994). Factors associated with the experience of school violence among general education, leadership class, opportunity class, and special day class pupils. *Education and Treatment of Children,* 17, 356–369.

Morrison, G. M., & D'Incau, B. (1997). The web of zero-tolerance: Characteristics of students who are recommended for expulsion from school. *Education and Treatment of Children,* 20(3), 316–335.

Morrison, G. M., Furlong, M. J., & Morrison, R. L. (1994). From school violence to school safety: Reframing the issue for school psychologists. *School Psychology Review,* 23, 236–256.

National Educational Goals Panel. (2000). *Goal 7: Safe, disciplined, and alcohol- and drug-free schools.* Washington, DC: Author.

Parents' Resource Institute for Drug Education (PRIDE). (1999). PRIDE survey http://www.prideusa.org/press97/ns97t03.htm

Patterson, G. R., DeBaryshe, B. D., & Ramsey E. (1989). A developmental perspective on antisocial behavior. *American Psychologist,* 44, 329–335.

Poland, S. (1997). School crisis teams. In A. P. Goldstein & J. C. Conoley (Eds.), *School violence intervention: A practical handbook.* New York: Guilford.

Prothrow-Stith, D. B. (1987). *Violence prevention curriculum for adolescents.* Newton, MA: Education Development Center.

Rennison, C. M. (1999). *Criminal victimization 1998: Changes 1997–98 with trends 1993–98* (NCJ 176353). Washington, DC: U.S. Department of Justice, Office of Justice Programs, Bureau of Crime Statistics.

Resnick, M. D., Bearman, P. S., Blum, R. W., Bauman, K. E., Harris, K. M., Jones, J., Tabor, J., Beuhring, T., Sieving, R. E., Shew, M., Ireland, M., Bearinger, L. H, & Udry, J. R. (1997). Protecting adolescents from harm: Findings from the National Longitudinal Study on Adolescent Health. *Journal of the American Medical Association,* 278, 823–832.

Rivara, F. P. (1995). Crime, violence and injuries in children and adolescents: Common risk factors? *Criminal Behavior & Mental Health,* 5(4), 367–385.

Rosenblatt, J. A., & Furlong, M. J. (1997). Assessing the reliability and validity of student self-reports of I B S campus violence. *Journal of Youth and Adolescence,* 26(2), 187–202.

Rutherford, R. B, & Nelson, C. M. (1995). Management of aggressive and violent behavior in the schools. *Focus on Exceptional Children,* 27(6), 1–15.

Rutter, M., Maughan, N., & Mortimore, R (1979). *Fifteen thousand hours: Secondary schools and their effects on children.* Cambridge, MA: Harvard University Press.

Skiba, R., & Peterson, R. (1999). The dark side of zero tolerance: Can punishment lead to safe schools? *Phi Delta Kappan* (January), 372–381.

Slaby, R. G., & Guerra, N. G. (1988). Cognitive mediators of aggression in adolescent offenders: I. Assessment. *Developmental Psychology,* 24, 580–588.

Sosin, D. M., Koepsell, T. D., Rivara, F. P., & Mercy, J. A. (1995). Fighting as a marker for multiple problem behaviors in adolescents. *Journal of Adolescent Health,* 16(3), 209–215.

Spivak, H., Hausman, A. J., & Prothrow-Stith, D. (1989). Practitioners' forum: Public health and the primary prevention of adolescent violence—The Violence Prevention Project. *Violence & Victim,* 4, 203–212.

Stephens, R. (1998). NSSC Web Site. National School Safety Center, www.nsscl.org

Trump, K. S. (1997). Security policy, personnel, and operations. In A. P Goldstein & J. C. Conoley (Eds.), *School violence intervention: A practical handbook* (pp. 46–57). New York: Guilford.

United States Office of Education. (1998). Violence and discipline in U.S. public schools: 1996–97. Washington, DC: Author.

Vestermark, S. D. (1998). Critical decisions, critical elements in an effective school security program. In A. M. Hoffman (Ed.), *Schools, violence, and society* (pp. 101–121). Westport, CT: Praeger.

Walker, H. M., Stieber, S., & O'Neill, R. E. (1990). Middle school behavioral profiles of antisocial and at-risk control boys: Descriptive and predictive outcomes. *Exceptionality,* 12(4), 43–51.

Wolfgang, M. E., & Ferracuti, F. (1967). *The subculture of violence.* London, GB: Tavistock.

Zwier, G., & Vaughan, G. M. (1984). Three ideological orientations in school vandalism research. *Review of Educational Research,* 54(2), 263–292.

Supremacy Crimes

Gloria Steinem

From MS. Copyright © 1999 by Gloria Steinem. Reprinted by permission.

You've seen the ocean of television coverage, you've read the headlines: "How to Spot a Troubled Kid," "Twisted Teens," "When Teens Fall Apart." After the slaughter in Colorado that inspired those phrases, dozens of copycat threats were reported in the same generalized way: "Junior high students charged with conspiracy to kill students and teachers" (in Texas); "Five honor students overheard planning a June graduation bombing" (in New York); "More than 100 minor threats reported statewide" (in Pennsylvania). In response, the White House held an emergency strategy session titled "Children, Violence, and Responsibility." Nonetheless, another attack was soon reported: "Youth with 2 Guns Shoots 6 at Georgia School."

I don't know about you, but I've been talking back to the television set, waiting for someone to tell us the obvious: it's not "youth," "our children," or "our teens." It's our sons—and "our" can usually be read as "white," "middle class," and "heterosexual."

We know that hate crimes, violent and otherwise, are overwhelmingly committed by white men who are apparently straight. The same is true for an even higher percentage of impersonal, resentment-driven, mass killings like those in Colorado; the sort committed for no economic or rational gain except the need to say, "I'm superior because I can kill." Think of Charles Starkweather, who reported feeling powerful and serene after murdering ten women and men in the 1950s; or the shooter who climbed the University of Texas Tower in 1966, raining down death to gain celebrity. Think of the engineering student at the University of Montreal who resented females' ability to study that subject, and so shot to death 14 women students in 1989, while saying "I'm against feminism." Think of nearly all those who have killed impersonally in the workplace, the post office, McDonald's.

White males—usually intelligent, middle class, and heterosexual, or trying desperately to appear so—also account for virtually all the serial, sexually motivated, sadistic killings, those characterized by stalking, imprisoning, torturing, and "owning" victims in death. Think of Edmund Kemper, who began by killing animals, then murdered his grandparents, yet was released to sexually torture and dismember college students and other young women until he himself decided he "didn't want to kill *all* the coeds in the world." Or David Berkowitz, the Son of Sam, who murdered *some* women in order to feel in control of *all* women. Or consider Ted Bundy, the charming, snobbish young would-be lawyer who tortured and murdered as many as 40 women, usually beautiful students who were symbols of the economic class he longed to join. As for John Wayne Gacy, he was obsessed with maintaining the public mask of masculinity, and so hid his homosexuality by killing and burying men and boys with whom he had sex.

These "senseless" killings begin to seem less mysterious when you consider that they were committed disproportionately by white, non-poor males, the group most likely to become hooked on the drug of superiority. It's a drug pushed by a male-dominant culture that presents dominance as a natural right; a racist hierarchy that falsely elevates whiteness; materialist society that equates superiority with possessions, and a homophobic one that empowers only one form of sexuality.

As Elliot Leyton reports in *Hunting Humans: The Rise of the Modern Multiple Murderer,* these killers see their behavior as "an appropriate—even 'manly'—response to the frustrations and disappointments that are a normal part of life." In other words, it's not their life experiences that are the problem, it's the impossible expectation of dominance to which they've become addicted.

This is not about blame. This is about causation. If anything, ending the massive cultural cover-up of supremacy crimes should make heroes out of boys and men who reject violence, especially those who reject the notion of superiority altogether. Even if one believes in a biogenetic component of male aggression, the very existence of gentle men proves that socialization can override it.

Nor is this about attributing such crimes to a single cause. Addiction to the drug of supremacy is not their only root, just the deepest and most ignored one. Additional reasons why this country has such a high rate of violence include the plentiful guns that make killing seem as unreal as a video game; male violence in the media that desensitizes viewers in much the same way that combat killers are desensitized in training; affluence that allows maximum access to violence-as-entertainment; a national history of genocide and slavery; the romanticizing of frontier violence and organized crime; not to mention extremes of wealth and poverty and the illusion that both are deserved.

But it is truly remarkable, given the relative reasons for anger at injustice in this country, that white, non-poor men have a near-monopoly on multiple killings of strangers, whether serial and sadistic or mass and random. How can we ignore this obvious fact? Others may kill to improve their own condition—in self-defense, or for money or drugs; to eliminate enemies; to declare turf in drive-by shootings; even for a jacket or a pair of sneakers—but white males addicted to supremacy kill even when it worsens their condition or ends in suicide.

Men of color and females are capable of serial and mass killing, and commit just enough to prove it. Think of Colin Ferguson, the crazed black man on the Long Island Railroad, or Wayne Williams, the young black man in Atlanta who kidnapped and killed black boys, apparently to conceal his homosexuality. Think of Aileen Carol Wuornos, the white prostitute in Florida who killed abusive johns "in self-defense," or Waneta Hoyt, the upstate New York woman who strangled her five infant children between 1965 and 1971, disguising their cause of death as sudden infant death syndrome. Such crimes are rare enough to leave a haunting refrain of disbelief as evoked in Pat Parker's poem "jonestown": "Black folks do not / Black folks do not / Black folks do not commit suicide." And yet they did.

Nonetheless, the proportion of serial killings that are not committed by white males is about the same as the proportion of anorexics who are not female. Yet we discuss the gender, race, and class components of anorexia, but not the role of the same factors in producing epidemics among the powerful.

The reasons are buried deep in the culture, so invisible that only by reversing our assumptions can we reveal them.

Suppose, for instance that young black males—or any other men of color—had carried out the slaughter in Colorado. Would the media reports be so willing to describe the murderers as "our children"? Would there be so little discussion about the boys' race? Would experts be calling the motive a mystery, or condemning the high school cliques for making those young men feel like "outsiders"? Would there be the same empathy for parents who gave the murderers luxurious homes, expensive cars, even rescued them from brushes with the law? Would there be as much attention to generalized causes, such as the dangers of violent video games and recipes for bombs on the Internet?

As for victims, if racial identities had been reversed, would racism remain so little discussed? In fact, the killers themselves said they were targeting blacks and athletes. They used a racial epithet, shot a black male student in the head, and then laughed over the fact that they could see his brain. What if *that* had been reversed?

What if these two young murderers, who were called "fags" by some of the jocks at Columbine High School, actually had been gay? Would they have got the same sympathy for being gay-baited? What if they had been lovers? Would we hear as little about their sexuality as we now do, even though only their own homophobia could have given the word "fag" such power to humiliate them?

Take one more leap of the imagination: suppose these killings had been planned and executed by young women—of any race, sexuality, or class. Would the media still be so disinterested in the role played by gender-conditioning? Would journalists assume that female murderers had suffered from being shut out of access to power in high school, so much so that they were pushed beyond their limits? What if dozens, even hundreds of young women around the country had made imitative threats—as young men have done—expressing admiration for a well-planned massacre and promising to do the same? Would we be discussing their youth more than their gender, as is the case so far with these male killers?

I think we begin to see that our national self-examination is ignoring something fundamental, precisely because it's like the air we breathe: the white male factor, the middle-class and heterosexual one, and the promise of superiority it carries. Yet this denial is self-defeating—to say the least. We will never reduce the number of violent Americans, from bullies to killers, without challenging the assumptions on which masculinity is based: that males are superior to females, that they must find a place in a male hierarchy, and that the ability to dominate *someone* is so important that even a mere insult can justify lethal revenge. There are plenty of studies to support this view. As Dr. James Gilligan concluded in *Violence: Reflections on a National Epidemic,* "If humanity is to evolve beyond the propensity toward violence . . . then it can only do so by recognizing the extent to which the patriarchal code of honor and shame generates and obligates male violence."

I think the way out can only be found through a deeper reversal: just as we as a society have begun to raise our daughters more like our sons—more like whole people—we must begin to raise our sons more like our daughters—that is, to value empathy as well as hierarchy; to measure success by other people's welfare as well as their own.

But first, we have to admit and name the truth about supremacy crimes.

Conversation on the Ethics of Stem Cell Research

The authors in this conversation each approach stem cell research from different perspectives, which is not surprising given their backgrounds and the different audiences to which each writes. Andrew Sullivan writes for the conservative journal The New Republic. *Charles Krauthammer, a well-known conservative columnist as well as a writer for* Time Magazine *won an award in 2004 from the conservative American Enterprise Institute. The* Washington Post *newspaper has called Katha Pollitt's column in* The Nation, *"the best place to go for original thinking on the left." Constance Holden's column was written for the academic journal* Science, *which is not overtly political in its aims (its implicit ideology is another matter). How does each writer define and describe the issue differently? What is each one's stance and why? What groups, individuals, or even scientific processes does each evoke as part of the problem for why stem cell research should or should not be enacted? What aspects of the issue are present in one writer's discussion but absent in another's? In addition, what types of evidence and what tone does each use to make their argument?*

Only Human

Andrew Sullivan

From *The New Republic*. Copyright © 2001 by The New Republic. Reprinted by permission.

In one of the creepiest scenarios in Steven Spielberg and Stanley Kubrick's new movie A.I., there is something called a Flesh Fair. In this sci-fi fantasy, human beings have developed technology so refined that they can create mechanical humans that appear almost as real as organic ones. These "mechas" are essentially a slave class: They perform chores, replace lost children, even have their body parts distributed for various uses. At Flesh Fairs, mechas are displayed and killed for amusement, their body parts sometimes traded and reused. They are humans entirely as means—not ends. And, of course, they're not truly human at all. They're robots simulating humans. But even robots, Spielberg and Kubrick seem to suggest, merit some dignity.

If robots deserve dignity, shouldn't blastocysts? In thinking about stem-cell research, the image of the Flesh Fair still resonates. In A.I. humans use pseudo-humans for sport; they chop them up, dissect them, then throw them away. When we watch the movie, we naturally recoil. But when we read essentially the same story in the newspapers—about events happening now—we manage to keep calm.

Is the analogy a stretch? Supporters of stem-cell research say blastocysts are not human beings. Or, even if they are human, they are not beings. They are no more human than, say, a clipped fingernail (which contains all the DNA information for an entire person, just as accurately as a blastocyst). Clearly, however, the fingernail comparison misses something important. A fingernail would not become a mature human being if implanted in a womb. The real question is whether this distinction amounts to a moral difference.

One criterion to distinguish a real human being—with rights and dignity—from an embryo or fingernail might be viability. The blastocyst, while clearly the same species as the rest of us, cannot survive independent of scientific paraphernalia, a freezer, or a womb. Hence it's not a human being—and can morally be experimented on. That's a clear line—but it opens up a host of other possibilities. If "viability" independent of a mother or others is the criterion, why shouldn't the physically incapacitated or the very old be consigned to medical experimentation? Why not those in comas or on life support? If they're going to die anyway and have no ability to fend for themselves, what's the point of wasting their bodies when they could yield valuable medical insights? Yes, we could wait till they're dead—but they're far more useful to science alive.

Other criteria might be the ability to feel pain, think rationally, or be self-conscious. Since an embryo (so far as we know) can do none of these things, it's fair game. But again, these criteria make others who are similarly limited—such as those with Alzheimer's, or the paraplegic, or the insane—equal grist for the scientific mill. This is especially the case with those whose mental capacity renders them unable to give meaningful consent. Why ask at all if, like embryos, such pseudo-humans cannot say yes or no? Perhaps some people might even give their consent in advance for such work. For ethical purposes, these people could be protected from physical pain during experimentation until their death.

Supporters of stem-cell research won't go that far. Except that they already have. What, after all, makes a human being a human being? Scientists would say a human is defined by its DNA—the genetic coding that makes our species different from any others. Stem-cell research enthusiasts say we are defined by our DNA and our stage of development. They say a blastocyst is so unformed that it cannot be equated with a fetus, let alone with an adult. But it remains a fact—indeed one of the marvels of creation—that the embryo contains exactly the same amount of genetic information as you or I do. We aren't different from it in kind, only different in degree: in age, size, weight, gender, and on and on. In fact, in some sense, a blastocyst is the purest form of human being—genderless, indistinguishable to the naked eye from any other, unencumbered with the accoutrements of society and experience—and yet as unique as any human being who has ever lived or ever will. To extinguish it is surely not to extinguish something other than us. It is to extinguish us.

Consider these analogies. Federal law makes it a crime to kill or injure a bald eagle. It is also a crime to kill or injure a bald eagle's egg. We recognize that to kill one is the same as to kill the other. Similarly, I cannot remember the last time an apple farmer responded to an early frost by saying, "Never mind, we lost the fertilized blossom, but the apples will be fine." Of course, the apples won't be fine. Once the blossom is dead, the apples will never arrive. And once a blastocyst is killed, the human being coiled inexorably inside is no more. If that isn't killing, what is? And why are we more coherent when it comes to eagles than when it comes to humans?

Some may say that nature itself allows many blastocysts to die. What else are miscarriages? It is true that such tragedies happen all the time. But just because earthquakes happen doesn't mean massacres are justified. And our intuitive moral response to a woman who has had a miscarriage is not the same as our response to a woman who has had a haircut or even to a woman who has lost a limb. One might conceivably justify allowing extra blastocysts to be created and lost as collateral damage in an artificial insemination (although, the more I think about this, the less defensible it seems). But to turn around and use those extra blastocysts for experimentation is a completely separate step. It is to treat human life purely instrumentally. I know of no better description of evil.

Such evil cannot be morally counterbalanced by any good that medical breakthroughs might bring. This is especially true when it's possible to cultivate stem cells from other sources. Perhaps those sources are not as fecund as embryos—but that means we are confronted not by a trade-off between any research into stem cells and preserving human life, but between better, faster stem-cell research and human life. Under those conditions, it's not that close a call. After all, are we currently beset by the problem of scientific breakthroughs that aren't fast enough? Surely the opposite is true (or at least also true): We are beset by scientific break-throughs that are occurring far faster than we have the moral language or the experience to deal with. Is a slight deceleration in that research too high a price to pay for removing even the chance that we may be taking human life?

I'm not dismissing the real pain of those dying of terminal illnesses who might conceivably be saved by this research—or the pain of their families. We should indeed do all we can to end and abate any and all disease. I write as someone with a deeply vested interest in such research. But life should be measured not by how long it is lived but by how it is lived. If my life were extended one day at the expense of one other human's life itself, it would be an evil beyond measure. Some things cannot be simply bar-gained or rationalized away. And one of those things is surely life itself.

Baby, It's Cold Inside!

Katha Pollitt

From *The Nation*. Copyright © 2001 by Katha Pollitt. Reprinted by permission.

The President now says he will make the decision on federal funding of embryonic stem cell research before Labor Day—in time to catch the wave of his just-announced refocusing of his Administration on "values." (Apparently tax cuts for the rich and drilling in the Arctic aren't catnip to women voters. Who knew? Bring on that all-abstinence-all-the-time cable station America's soccer moms are clamoring for!) Perhaps reveal-ing more than he intended about customary decision-making procedures at the White House, Bush has said that his Administration is being "unusually deliberative" about stem cells. Most people, not to mention the powerful biotech industry, say they want the research to go forward, even though it involves the destruction of four- to six-day-old blastocysts left over from fertility treatments. However, Bush not only promised during the campaign that he would eliminate the funding, he went to the Vatican in July for direction, as any good Methodist would do, where the Pope declared that "a tragic coarsening of consciences accompanies the assault on innocent human life in the womb," and out of it, too. If only Bush had gone to a rabbi—modern medicine practically is the Jewish religion.

In a rational world, the President would decide on funding by thinking about whether this was the best use of the country's money and brainpower—but then, in a rational world, the President would not be making this decision at all, as if he were a medieval king dispensing largesse and boons. In this world, the stem cell debate is not about health policy, it's about abortion: Is a 150-cell blastocyst—the equivalent of a fertilized egg not yet implanted in the womb—a person or not? Many people usually lined up on the antichoice side have a hard time visualizing a frozen speck as a baby, especially since, as my friend Dr. Michelle pointed out, that frozen speck could be helping to cure diseases Republican men get, like Alzheimer's and Parkinson's. (Would we be having this debate if the research showed promise to cure Chagas' disease and sleeping sickness?)

According to Orrin Hatch, it's OK to destroy a frozen embryo because the embryo is only a person if it's in a woman. This location theory of personhood is obviously unsatisfactory: You put the cells in the woman, it's a person, you take them out, it's not a person, you put them back in, voila!—it's a person again. You might as well say Orrin Hatch is a person in his office but not in his car. If, as antichoicers like to claim, what makes personhood is a full set of chromosomes—rather than, say, possession of a gender, a body, a head, a brain—then a clump of cells in an ice cube tray is at least as much a person as Trent Lott. Maybe more.

I think I see a way to help the President out of his difficulties. The White House should ask opponents of embryonic stem cell research to sign a legally binding pledge forgoing any treatment or procedures derived from it, both for themselves and their minor offspring. If they really believe that frozen embryos are children, they should have no problem with this. An impressive list of right-wing pundits have laid out the argument in characteristically colorful fashion: Andrew Sullivan, for instance, insisted in *The New Republic* that the blastocyst is "the purest form of human being" and to kill it is to "extinguish us." (Someone should tell him that nearly half of all fertilized eggs fail to implant and are washed out with menstruation—maybe there should be funerals for tampons, just to be on the safe side.) In the *Washington Times,* Michael Fumento writes that stem cell research "rightly or wrongly" summons up visions of Dr. Mengele's Auschwitz experiments. Who, after all, would be willing to treat their illness with a potion of boiled 5-year-olds? Well, maybe some very bad 5-year-olds, already set on the path to crime and low SAT scores by single mothers, but you see my point. As Eric Cohen put it in *The Weekly Standard,* "to ask the sick and dying to love the mystery of life more than their own lives" is a bit like asking comfortable Americans to sacrifice themselves in wars against tyranny around the globe: "Both require a courageous commitment to something larger than self-interest." The mystery of life versus, well, life. Let's put people on record.

If frozen embryos really are children, though, is it enough not to kill them? Don't we need to rescue them from the icy wasteland to which they have been consigned? Their selfish yuppie biological parents may have abandoned them, but the Family Research Council says that every frozen embryo should have "an opportunity to be born" and I am surprised that the antichoicers haven't yet rallied to the cause. True, a few women unable to conceive naturally have been implanted with the leftover embryos of others, but there are some 100,000 frozen embryos in need of homes—it's like a whole other foster-care system.

Antichoice women are the only hope to get those embryos out of Frigidaire limbo. As they like to say, an extra pregnancy is just an inconvenience, its health dangers much exaggerated by prochoice babykillers and its opportunities for moral growth scorned by our culture of death. So, Concerned Women for America, give a frozen embryo the gift of gestation! Mona Charen, Ann Coulter, it isn't enough to write columns comparing stem cell research to tearing transplantable organs out of freshly killed prisoners—you could be leading the way! Think of the talk-show opportunities. ("Chris, some people think we right-wing women are a pack of peroxided harpies, but when I thought of those adorable cells just trapped in there with the yogurt, I knew I had to help!") They can always put the baby up for adoption so it will be raised by normal people, as they think pregnant singles ought to do. Frozen embryo rescue would be an interesting project for the Sisters of Life, the antichoice order of nuns founded by the late John Cardinal O'Connor. Sort of a virgin birth kind of thing.

In a pinch, the President can always call on welfare moms laid off from their jobs at Wendy's in the looming recession. It would be a natural extension of his plan to offer healthcare directly to poor fetuses, a sort of housing program for blastocysts. Compassionate conservatism at its best!

Why Lines Must Be Drawn: Stem Cells Present a Complex Moral Issue. Shame On Democrats for Polarizing It.

Charles Krauthammer

© 2004 TIME Inc. Reprinted by permission.

In an election year, it is too much to expect serious and complicated moral issues to be treated with seriousness and complexity. Nonetheless, the way Democrats have managed to caricature and debase the debate over embryonic stem-cell research stands in a class by itself.

In his Aug. 7 radio address to the nation, John Kerry three times referred to "the ban" on stem-cell research instituted by President George W. Bush. What ban? Stem-cell research is legal in the U.S. and has been so since human embryonic stem cells were first isolated in 1998. There are dozens of groups studying them, including major stem-cell centers recently launched at Stanford and Harvard.

Perhaps Democrats mean a ban on federal funding for stem-cell research. But, in fact, there is no such ban. Through the Clinton years there was a ban. Not a single penny of federal money was allowed for any embryo research. In his first year in office, however, President Bush reviewed the issue and permitted the first federal funding of stem-cell research ever.

Bush did more than just free up money. In August 2001 he addressed the issue in one of the most morally serious speeches ever delivered by a U.S. President. Political speeches are generally constructed—I know; I used to write them—so that facts are stacked from the very beginning to lead you inexorably to the foregone conclusion. In contrast, Bush's nationally televised address presented both sides of the question with such fairness and respect that three-quarters of the way through the speech you found yourself without any idea where the President would come out.

The position he did adopt was one kind of middle ground funding research using existing stem-cell lines but not funding research to create stem-cell lines because these must inevitably involve the destruction of human embryos.

I would have drawn the line differently. I would have permitted the conduct of all research using cells drawn from the discarded embryos of fertility clinics (unused and ultimately doomed) but not from embryos created purposely and wantonly for nothing but use by science.

Honorable people will draw the line in different places because this is not an issue of reason vs. ignorance, as the Democrats have portrayed it, but of recognizing two important competing human values: the thirst for knowledge and cures on the one hand and, on the other, the respect for even embryonic human life and a well-grounded respect for the proven human capacity to misuse newly acquired powers, in this case, the power to manipulate, reshape, dissect and redesign the developing human embryo.

However, having no doubt discovered through focus groups and polling that stem-cell research might be a useful reverse-wedge issue against Republicans, who have traditionally enjoyed an electoral advantage on "values," the Democrats showcased it with a prime-time convention speech by the well-known medical expert Ron Reagan. Message? On the one side are the forces of the good, on the verge of curing such terrible afflictions as Parkinson's, diabetes and spinal-cord injury. On the other are the forces of reaction and superstition who, slaves to a primitive religiosity, would condemn millions to suffer and die. Or as Reagan subtly put it, the choice is "between reason and ignorance, between true compassion and mere ideology."

Compassion? There's nothing less compassionate than to construct a political constituency of sufferers (and their loved ones) by falsely and cruelly intimating that their disease is on the very cusp of cure if only the President would stop playing politics with the issue. Why, after all, was Reagan addressing the nation on a subject of which he knows nothing? Because his famous father died of Alzheimer's, and some (including, sadly, Nancy Reagan) have been led to believe that Alzheimer's is curable using stem cells. This is nonsense. Cynical nonsense. Or as Ronald D.G. McKay, a stem-cell researcher at the National Institutes of Health, admitted candidly to the *Washington Post,* a fiction: "People need a fairy tale." Yet Kerry began his radio address with the disgraceful claim that the stem-cell "ban" is standing in the way of an Alzheimer's cure.

When I was 22 and a first-year medical student, I suffered a spinal-cord injury. I have not walked in 32 years. I would be delighted to do so again. But not at any price. I think it is more important to bequeath to my son a world that retains a moral compass, a world that when unleashing the most powerful human discovery since Alamogordo—something as protean, elemental, powerful and potentially dangerous as the manipulation and re-formation of the human embryo—recognizes that lines must be drawn and fences erected.

Primate Parthenotes Yield Stem Cells

Constance Holden

Reprinted with permission from "Primate Parthenotes Yield Stem Cells" by Constance Holden. *Science* 295: 779–781 (1 February 2002). Copyright 2002 AAAS.

A reproductive quirk of some reptiles, insects, and other species may help stem cell researchers sidestep ethical debates over the use of human embryos. Researchers at Advanced Cell Technology (ACT) in Worcester, Massachusetts, report on page 819 that they have isolated the first stem cell lines from primate parthenotes, embryos grown from unfertilized eggs that, in mammals, are not capable of developing into viable fetuses.

In October, Yan-Ling Feng and Jerry Hall of the Institute for Reproductive Medicine and Genetics in Los Angeles showed they could derive stem cells, which later developed into neurons, from mouse parthenotes. Then in November, ACT scientists grabbed headlines with the news that they had created human parthenotes—although the cell clusters died before reaching the blastocyst stage, well before viable stem cell lines could be extracted.

Now Jose Cibelli and colleagues at ACT report that they have been able to culture a variety of cell types, representing all three germ layers, from stem cells taken from monkey parthenotes. To create the parthenotes, the scientists treated 28 macaque ova with chemicals that prevent eggs from ejecting half their chromosomes—as they do when fertilized—and instead spur the eggs to begin dividing. Four of the 28 developed into blastocysts; the team was able to establish a stable stem cell line from the inner cell mass of one of them. From these stem cells, the researchers developed a considerable variety of cells, including dopamine-producing neurons and spontaneously beating cells resembling heart cells.

Other teams have teased primate ova into blastocysts parthenogenically, but this is the first report that such blastocysts can yield stem cells. The implication of this work, says Don Wolf of the Oregon Regional Primate Research Center in Beaverton, who has generated monkey parthenotes in his lab, is that "[embryonic stem] cells can be derived from human parthenotes."

Not everyone agrees. Developmental biologist Davor Solter of the Max Planck Institute for Immunobiology in Freiburg, Germany, says that even though the researchers have succeeded in generating normal-looking stem cells from monkey parthenotes, this reveals little about whether the same can be done in humans: "Every single mammal has its own quirks. If you want to figure out how to make [parthenotes] in humans, you have to make them in humans."

Ethically, however, the option is attractive. As in other primates, human parthenotes cannot develop to full-term babies. If researchers can find a reliable way to derive stem cells from human parthenotes, they could avoid therapeutic cloning, in which a potentially viable embryo is created as a source of stem cells and then destroyed. Bioethicist Glenn McGee of the University of Pennsylvania in Philadelphia predicts that this won't quell all objections, because people uneasy about stem cell research won't be very comfortable with "the idea of producing a creature whose status as a life-form is entirely ambiguous." Nonetheless, he observes that "the arguments against using embryos in research would seem to suggest that the parthenote is the ideal subject to replace the embryo."

Wolf says parthenogenesis would actually be simpler than therapeutic cloning for producing genetically compatible material for a patient—at least one with oocytes. "Of course, with this approach," he adds, "you could not produce your own stem cells unless you could also provide your own eggs. Sorry, guys."

Conversation on Censorship and Youth Culture

On his album, The Eminem Show, Eminem considers the effects of his writing: "How could I predict my words would have an impact like this / I must've struck a chord with somebody up in the office / Cuz Congress keeps telling me I ain't causin nuthin but problems." The congressional testimony and the letter to Senator Lieberman seem to confirm Eminem's supposition: words can cause problematic action. In this context, the opinions reported in the Knight Foundation poll might make sense: if the lyrics of artists like Marilyn Manson and Eminem are so problematic, why shouldn't they be censored? Conservative critic Mary Eberstadt and radical scholar bell hooks offer an answer: such lyrics are a consequence of cultural conditions, rather than a cause. What might lead these very different writers to take similar positions? For example, what distinguishes Eberstadt and hooks despite their similar conclusions: their evidence, their examples, their explanations? And why would young people be more likely to argue for censorship than the other writers here? Taken together, these readings—in their range of genres and perspectives—offer compelling questions about free speech, but they also offer insight into how foregrounding different aspects of an issue can foreclose or open up radically different conclusions. In that light, what alternate analyses of these issues might you offer?

Sexism and Misogyny: Who Takes the Rap?

bell hooks

From Z *Magazine*. Copyright © 1994 by Z MAGAZINE. Reprinted by permission.

For the past several months white mainstream media has been calling me to hear my views on gangsta rap. Whether major television networks, or small independent radio shows, they seek me out for the black and feminist "take" on the issue. After I have my say, I am never called back, never invited to do the television shows or the radio spots. I suspect they call, confident that when we talk they will hear the hard-core "feminist" trash of gangsta rap. When they encounter instead the hard-core feminist critique of white-supremacist capitalist patriarchy, they lose interest.

To white-dominated mass media, the controversy over gangsta rap makes great spectacle. Besides the exploitation of these issues to attract audiences, a central motivation for highlighting gangsta rap continues to be the sensationalist drama of demonizing black youth culture in general and the contributions of young black men in particular. It is a contemporary remake of *Birth of a Nation* only this time we are encouraged to believe it is not just vulnerable white womanhood that risks destruction by black hands but everyone. When I counter this demonization of black males by insisting that gangsta rap does not appear in a cultural vacuum, but, rather, is expressive of the cultural crossing, mixings, and engagement of black youth culture with the values, attitudes, and concerns of the white majority, some folks stop listening.

The sexist, misogynist, patriarchal ways of thinking and behaving that are glorified in gangsta rap are a reflection of the prevailing values in our society, values created and sustained by white-supremacist capitalist patriarchy. As the crudest and most brutal expression of sexism, misogynistic attitudes tend to be portrayed by the dominant culture as an expression of male deviance. In reality they are part of a sexist continuum, necessary for the maintenance of patriarchal social order. While patriarchy and sexism continue to be the political and cultural norm in our society, feminist movement has created a climate where crude expressions of male domination are called into question, especially if they are made by men in power. It is useful to think of misogyny as a field that must be labored in and maintained both to sustain patriarchy but also to serve as an ideological antifeminist backlash. And what better group to labor on this "plantation" than young black men.

To see gansta rap as a reflection of dominant values in our culture rather than as an aberrant "pathological" standpoint does not mean that a rigorous feminist critique of the sexism and misogyny expressed in this music is not needed. Without a doubt black males, young and old, must be held politically accountable for their sexism. Yet this critique must always be contextualized or we risk making it appear that the behaviors this thinking supports and condones—rape, male violence against women, etc.—is a black male thing. And this is what is happening. Young black males are forced to take the "heat" for encouraging, via their music, the hatred of and violence against women that is a central core of patriarchy.

Witness the recent piece by Brent Staples in the *New York Times* titled "The Politics of Gangster Rap: A Music Celebrating Murder and Misogyny." Defining the turf, Staples writes: "For those who haven't caught up, gangster rap is that wildly successful music in which all women are 'bitches' and 'whores' and young men kill each other for sport." No mention of white-supremacist capitalist patriarchy in this piece, not a word about the cultural context that would need to exist for young males to be socialized to think differently about gender. Staples assumes that black males are writing their lyrics off in the "jungle," away from the impact of mainstream socialization and desire. At no point in his piece does he ask why huge audiences, especially young white male consumers, are so turned on by this music, by the misogyny and sexism, by the brutality. Where is the anger and rage at females expressed in this music coming from, the glorification of all acts of violence? These are the difficult questions that Staples feels no need to answer.

One cannot answer them honestly without placing accountability on larger structures of domination and the individuals (often white, usually male but not always) who are hierarchically placed to maintain and perpetuate the values that uphold these exploitative and oppressive systems. That means taking a critical look at the politics of hedonistic consumerism, the values of the men and women who produce gangsta rap. It would mean considering the seduction of young black males who find that they can make more money producing lyrics that promote violence, sexism, and misogyny than with any other content. How many disenfranchised black males would not surrender to expressing virulent forms of sexism, if they knew the rewards would be unprecedented material power and fame?

More than anything gangsta rap celebrates the world of the "material," the dog-eat-dog world where you do what you gotta do to make it. In this worldview, killing is necessary for survival. Significantly, the logic here is a crude expression of the logic of white-supremacist capitalist patriarchy. In his new book *Sexy Dressing Etc.* privileged white male law professor Duncan Kennedy gives what he calls "a set of general characterizations of U.S. culture" explaining that "It is individual (cowboys), material (gangsters), and philistine." Using this general description of mainstream culture would lead us to place "gangsta rap" not on the margins of what this nation is about, but at the center. Rather than being viewed as a subversion or disruption of the norm we would need to see it as an embodiment of the norm.

That viewpoint was graphically highlighted in the film *Menace II Society,* which dramatized not only young black males killing for sport, but also mass audiences voyeuristically watching and, in many cases, "enjoying" the kill. Significantly, at one point in the movie we see that the young black males have learned their "gangsta" values from watching television and movies—shows where white male gangsters are center stage. This scene undermines any notion of "essentialist" blackness that would have viewers believe the gangsterism these young black males embraced emerged from some unique black cultural experience.

When I interviewed rap artist Ice Cube for *Spin* magazine last year, he talked about the importance of respecting black women and communication across gender. He spoke against male violence against women, even as he lapsed into a justification for anti-woman rap lyrics by insisting on the madonna/whore split where some females "carry" themselves in a manner that determines how they will be treated. When this interview was published, it was cut to nothing. It was a mass-media set-up. Folks (mostly white and male) had thought if the hard-core feminist talked with the hardened black man, sparks would fly; there would be a knock-down, drag-out spectacle. When Brother Cube and I talked to each other with respect about the political, spiritual, and emotional self-determination of black people, it did not make good copy. Clearly folks at the magazine did not get the darky show they were looking for.

After this conversation, and talking with rappers and folks who listen to rap, it became clear that while black male sexism is a serious problem in our communities and in black music, some of the more misogynist lyrics were there to stir up controversy and appeal to audiences. Nowhere is this more evident than in Snoop Doggy Dogg's record *Doggystyle*. A black male music and cultural critic called me to ask if I had checked this image out, to share that for one of the first times in his music buying life he felt he was seeing an image so offensive in its sexism and misogyny that he did not want to take that image home. That image (complete with doghouse, beware-the-dog sign, with a naked black female head in a doghouse, naked butt sticking out) was reproduced, "uncritically," in the November 29, 1993, issue of *Time* magazine. The positive music review of this album, written by Christopher John Farley and titled "Gangsta Rap, Doggystyle," makes no mention of sexism and misogyny, makes no reference to the cover. I wonder if a naked white female body had been inside the doghouse, presumably waiting to be fucked from behind, if *Time* would have reproduced an image of the cover along with their review. When I see the pornographic cartoon that graces the cover of *Doggystyle,* I do not think simply about the sexism and misogyny of young black men, I think about the sexist and misogynist politics of the powerful white adult men and women (and folks of color) who helped produce and market this album.

In her book *Misogynies* Joan Smith shares her sense that while most folks are willing to acknowledge unfair treatment of women, discrimination on the basis of gender, they are usually reluctant to admit that hatred of women is encouraged because it helps maintain the structure of male dominance. Smith suggests: "Misogyny wears many guises, reveals itself in different forms which are dictated by class, wealth, education, race, religion and other factors, but its chief characteristic is its pervasiveness." This point reverberated in my mind when I saw Jane Campion's widely acclaimed film *The Piano,* which I saw in the midst of mass-media focus on sexism and misogyny in "gangsta rap." I had been told by many friends in the art world that this was "an incredible film, a truly compelling love story, etc." Their responses were echoed by numerous positive reviews. No one speaking about this film mentions misogyny and sexism or white-supremacist capitalist patriarchy.

The nineteenth-century world of the white invasion of New Zealand is utterly romanticized in this film (complete with docile happy darkies—Maori natives—who appear to have not a care in the world). And when the film suggests they care about white colonizers digging up the graves of their dead ancestors, it is the sympathetic poor white male who comes to the rescue. Just as the conquest of natives and lands is glamorized in this film, so is the conquest of femininity, personified by white womanhood, by the pale speechless corpselike Scotswoman, Ada, who journeys into this dark wilderness because her father has arranged for her to marry the white colonizer Stewart. Although mute, Ada expresses her artistic ability, the intensity of her vision and feelings, through piano playing. This passion attracts Baines, the illiterate white settler who wears the facial tattoos of the Maori—an act of appropriation that makes him (like the traditional figure of Tarzan) appear both dangerous and romantic. He is Norman Mailer's "white negro," seducing Ada by promising to return the piano that Stewart has exchanged with him for land. The film leads us to believe that Ada's passionate piano playing has been a substitution for repressed eroticism. When she learns to let herself go sexually, she ceases to need the piano. We watch the passionate climax of Baines's seduction as she willingly seeks him sexually. And we watch her husband Stewart in the role of voyeur, standing with dog outside the cabin where they fuck, voyeuristically consuming their pleasure. Rather than being turned off by her love for Baines, it appears to excite Stewart's passion; he longs to possess her all the more. Unable to win her back from Baines, he expresses his rage, rooted in misogyny and sexism, by physically attacking her and chopping off her finger with an ax. This act of male violence takes place with Ada's daughter. Flora, as a witness. Though traumatized by the violence she witnesses, she is still about to follow the white male patriarch's orders and take the bloody finger to Baines, along with the message that each time he sees Ada she will suffer physical mutilation.

Violence against land, natives, and women in this film, unlike that of gangsta rap, is portrayed uncritically, as though it is "natural," the inevitable climax of conflicting passions. The outcome of this violence is positive. Ultimately, the film suggests Stewart's rage was only an expression of irrational sexual jealousy, that he comes to his senses and is able to see "reason." In keeping with male exchange of women, he gives Ada and Flora to Baines. They leave the wilderness. On the voyage home Ada demands that her piano be thrown overboard because it is "soiled," tainted with horrible memories. Surrendering it she lets go of her longing to display passion through artistic expression. A nuclear family now, Baines, Ada, and Flora resettle and live happily-ever-after. Suddenly, patriarchal order is restored. Ada becomes a modest wife, wearing a veil over her mouth so that no one will see her lips struggling to speak words. Flora has no memory of trauma and is a happy child turning somersaults. Baines is in charge, even making Ada a new finger.

The Piano seduces and excites audiences with its uncritical portrayal of sexism and misogyny. Reviewers and audiences alike seem to assume that Campion's gender, as well as her breaking of traditional boundaries that inhibit the advancement of women in film, indicate that her work expresses a feminist standpoint. And, indeed, she does employ feminist "tropes," even as her work betrays feminist visions of female actualization, celebrates and eroticizes male domination. In Smith's discussion of misogyny she emphasizes that woman-hating is not solely the province of men: "We are all exposed to the prevailing ideology of our culture, and some women learn early on that they can prosper by aping the misogyny of men; these are the women who win provisional favor by denigrating other women, by playing on male prejudices, and by acting the 'man's woman'." Since this is not a documentary film that needs to remain faithful to the ethos of its historical setting, why is it that Campion does not resolve Ada's conflicts by providing us with an imaginary landscape where a woman can express passionate artistic commitment and find fulfillment in a passionate relationship? This would be no more farfetched than her cinematic portrayal of Ada's miraculous transformation from muteness into speech. Ultimately, Campion's *The Piano* advances the sexist assumption that heterosexual women will give up artistic practice to find "true love." That "positive" surrender is encouraged by the "romantic" portrayal of sexism and misogyny.

While I do not think that young black male rappers have been rushing in droves to see *The Piano*, there is a bond between those folks involved with high culture who celebrate and condone the sexist ideas and values upheld in this film and those who celebrate and condone "gangsta rap." Certainly Kennedy's description of the United States as a "cowboy, gangster, philistine" culture would also accurately describe the culture evoked in *The Piano.* Popular movies that are seen by young black males, for example *Indecent Proposal, Mad Dog and Glory, True Romance,* and *One False Move,* all eroticize male domination expressed via the exchange of women, as well as the subjugation of other men, through brutal violence.

Contrary to a racist white imagination which assumes that most young black males, especially those who are poor, live in a self-created cultural vacuum, uninfluenced by mainstream, cultural values, it is the application of those values, largely learned through passive uncritical consumption of mass media, that is revealed in "gangsta rap." Brent Staples is willing to challenge the notion that "urban primitivism is romantic" when it suggests that black males become "real men" by displaying the will to do violence, yet he remains resolutely silent about that world of privileged white culture that has historically romanticized primitivism and eroticized male violence. Contemporary films like *Reservoir Dogs* and *Bad Lieutenant* celebrate urban primitivism and many less well done films (*Trespass, Rising Sun*) create and/or exploit the cultural demand for depictions of hard-core blacks who are willing to kill for sport.

To take "gangsta rap" to task for its sexism and misogyny while critically accepting and perpetuating those expressions of that ideology which reflect bourgeois standards (no rawness, no vulgarity) is not to call for a transformation of the culture of patriarchy. Ironically, many black male ministers, themselves sexist and misogynist, are leading the attacks against gangsta rap. Like the mainstream world that supports white-supremacist capitalist patriarchy, they are most concerned with calling attention to the vulgar obscene portrayals of women to advance the cause of censorship. For them, rethinking and challenging sexism, both in the dominant culture and in black life, is not the issue.

Mainstream white culture is not concerned about black male sexism and misogyny, particularly when it mainly is unleashed against black women and children. It is concerned when young white consumers utilize black vernacular popular culture to disrupt bourgeois values, whether it be the young white boy who expresses his rage at his mother by aping black male vernacular speech (a true story) or the masses of young white males (and middle-class men of color) seeking to throw off the constraints of bourgeois bondage who actively assert in their domestic households via acts of aggression their rejection of the call to be "civilized." These are the audiences who feel such a desperate need for gangsta rap. It is much easier to attack gangsta rap than to confront the culture that produces that need.

Gangsta rap is part of the antifeminist backlash that is the rage right now. When young black males labor in the plantations of misogyny and sexism to produce gangsta rap, their right to speak this violence and be materially rewarded is extended to them by white-supremacist capitalist patriarchy. Far from being an expression of their "manhood," it is an expression of their own subjugation and humiliation by more powerful, less-visible forces of patriarchal gangsterism. They give voice to the brutal raw anger and rage against women that it is taboo for "civilized" adult men to speak. No wonder then that they have the task of tutoring the young, teaching them to eroticize and enjoy the brutal expressions of that rage (teaching them language and acts) before they learn to cloak it in middle-class decorum or Robert Bly style reclaimings of lost manhood. The tragedy for young black males is that they are so easily duped by a vision of manhood that can only lead to their destruction.

Feminist critiques of the sexism and misogyny is gangsta rap, and in all aspects of popular culture, must continue to be bold and fierce. Black females must not be duped into supporting shit that hurts us under the guise of standing beside our men. If black men are betraying us through acts of male violence, we save ourselves and the race by resisting. Yet, our feminist critiques of black male sexism fail as meaningful political intervention if they seek to demonize black males and do not recognize that our revolutionary work is to transform white-supremacist capitalist patriarchy in the multiple areas of our lives where it is made manifest, whether in gangsta rap, the black church, or the Clinton administration.

Eminem: Reasons for Rage

Mary Eberstadt

"Eminem: It's the Parents, Stupid," from *Home-Alone America* by Mary Eberstadt, copyright © 1994 by Mary Eberstadt. Used by permission of Sentinel, an imprint of Penguin Group (USA) Inc.

A final example of the rage in contemporary music against irresponsible adults—perhaps the most interesting—is that of genre-crossing bad-boy rap superstar Marshall Mathers or Eminem (sometime stage persona "Slim Shady"). Of all the names guaranteed to send a shudder down the parental spine, his is probably the most effective. In fact, Eminem has single-handedly, if inadvertently, achieved the otherwise ideologically impossible: He is the object of a vehemently disapproving public consensus shared by the National Organization for Women the Gay & Lesbian Alliance Against Defamation, William J. Bennett, Lynne Cheney, Bill O'Reilly, and a large number of other social conservatives as well as feminists and gay activists. In sum, this rapper—"as harmful to America as any al Qaeda fanatic," in O'Reilly's opinion—unites adult polar opposites as perhaps no other single popular entertainer has done.

There is small need to wonder why. Like other rappers, Eminem mines the shock value and gutter language of rage, casual sex, and violence. Unlike the rest, however, he appears to be a particularly attractive target of opprobrium for two distinct reasons. One, he is white and therefore politically easier to attack. (It is interesting to note that black rappers have not been targeted by name anything like Eminem has.) Perhaps even more important, Eminem is one of the largest commercially visible targets for parental wrath. Wildly popular among teenagers these last several years, he is also enormously successful in commercial terms. Winner of numerous Grammys and other music awards and a perpetual nominee for many more, he has also been critically (albeit reluctantly) acclaimed for his acting performance in the autobiographical 2003 movie *8 Mile.* For all these reasons, he is probably the preeminent rock/rap star of the last several years, one whose singles, albums, and videos routinely top every chart. His 2002 album, *The Eminem Show,* for example, was easily the most successful of the year, selling more than 7.6 million copies.

This remarkable market success, combined with the intense public criticism that his songs have generated, makes the phenomenon of Eminem particularly intriguing. Perhaps more than any other current musical icon, he returns repeatedly to the same themes that fuel other success stories in contemporary music: parental loss, abandonment, abuse, and subsequent child and adolescent anger, dysfunction, and violence (including self-violence). Both in his raunchy lyrics as well as in *8 Mile,* Mathers's own personal story has been parlayed many times over: the absent father, the troubled mother living in a trailer park, the series of unwanted maternal boyfriends, the protective if impotent feelings toward a younger sibling (in the movie, a baby sister; in real life, a younger brother), and the fine line that a poor, ambitious, and unguided young man might walk between catastrophe and success. Mathers plumbs these and related themes with a verbal savagery that leaves most adults aghast.

Yet Eminem also repeatedly centers his songs on the crypto-traditional notion that children need parents and that *not* having them has made all hell break loose. In the song "8 Mile" from the movie soundtrack, for example, the narrator studies his little sister as she colors one picture after another of an imagined nuclear family, failing to understand that *"mommas got a new man." "Wish I could be the daddy that neither one of us had,"* he comments. Such wistful lyrics juxtapose oddly and regularly with Eminem's violent other lines. Even in one of his most infamous songs, "Cleaning Out My Closet (Mama, I'm Sorry)," what drives the vulgar narrative is the insistence on seeing abandonment from a child's point of view. *"My faggot father must have had his panties up in a bunch / 'Cause he split. I wonder if he even kissed me good-bye."*

As with other rappers, the vicious narrative treatment of women in some of Eminem's songs is part of this self-conception as a child victim. Contrary to what critics have intimated, the misogyny in current music does not spring from nowhere; it is often linked to the larger theme of having been abandoned several times—left behind by father, not nurtured by mother, and betrayed again by faithless womankind. One of the most violent and sexually aggressive songs in the last few years is "Kill You" by the popular metal band known as Korn. Its violence is not directed toward just any woman or even toward the narrator's girlfriend; it is instead a song about an abusive stepmother whom the singer imagines going back to rape and murder.

Similarly, Eminem's most shocking lyrics about women are not randomly dispersed; they are largely reserved for his mother and ex-wife, and the narrative pose is one of despising them for not being better women—in particular, better mothers. The worst rap directed at his own mother is indeed gut-wrenching: *"But how dare you try to take what you didn't help me to get? / You selfish bitch, I hope you f— burn in hell for this shit!"* It is no defense of the gutter to observe the obvious: This is not the expression of random misogyny but, rather, of primal rage over alleged maternal abdication and abuse.

Another refrain in these songs runs like this: Today's teenagers are a mess, and the parents who made them that way refuse to get it. In one of Eminem's early hits, for example, a song called "Who Knew," the rapper pointedly takes on his many middle- and upper-middle-class critics to observe the contradiction between their reviling him and the parental inattention that feeds his commercial success. *"What about the make-up you allow your 12-year-old daughter to wear?"* he taunts.

This same theme of AWOL parenting is rapped at greater length in another award-nominated 2003 song called "Sing for the Moment," whose lyrics and video would be recognized in an instant by most teenagers in America. That song spells out Eminem's own idea of what connects him to his millions of fans—a connection that parents, in his view, just don't (or is that won't?) understand. It details the case of one more "problem child" created by *"His f— dad walkin' out."* "Sing for the Moment," like many other songs of Eminem's, is also a popular video. The "visuals" show clearly what the lyrics depict—hordes of disaffected kids, with flashbacks to bad home lives, screaming for the singer who feels their pain. It concludes by rhetorically turning away from the music itself and toward the emotionally desperate teenagers who turn out for this music by the millions. If the demand of all those empty kids wasn't out there, the narrator says pointedly, then rappers wouldn't be supplying it the way they do.

If some parents still don't get it—even as their teenagers elbow up for every new Eminem CD and memorize his lyrics with psalmist devotion—at least some critics observing the music scene have thought to comment on the ironies of all this. In discussing *The Marshall Mathers* LP in 2001 for *Music Box,* a daily online newsletter about music, reviewer John Metzger argued, "Instead of spewing the hate that he is so often criticized of doing, Eminem offers a cautionary tale that speaks to our civilization's growing depravity. Ironically, it's his teenage fans who understand this, and their all-knowing parents that miss the point." Metzger further specified "the utter lack of parenting due to the spendthrift necessity of the two-income family."

That insight raises the overlooked fact that in one important sense Eminem and most of the other entertainers quoted here would agree with many of today's adults about one thing: The kids *aren't* all right out there after all. Recall, for just one example, Eddie Vedder's rueful observation about what kind of generation would make him or Kurt Cobain its leader. Where parents and entertainers disagree is over who exactly bears responsibility for this moral chaos. Many adults want to blame the people who create and market today's music and videos. Entertainers, Eminem most prominently, blame the absent, absentee, and generally inattentive adults whose deprived and furious children (as they see it) have catapulted today's singers to fame. (As he puts the point in one more in-your-face response to parents: *"Don't blame me when lil' Eric jumps off of the terrace / You shoulda been watchin him—apparently you ain't parents."*)

The spectacle of a foul-mouthed bad-example rock icon instructing the hardworking parents of America in the art of child-rearing is indeed a peculiar one, not to say ridiculous. The single mother who is working frantically because she must and worrying all the while about what her 14-year-old is listening to in the headphones is entitled to a certain fury over lyrics like those. In fact, to read through most rap lyrics is to wonder which adults or political constituencies *wouldn't* take offense. Even so, the music idols who point the finger away from themselves and toward the emptied-out homes of America are telling a truth that some adults would rather not hear. In this limited sense at least, Eminem is right.

Music Violence: How Does It Affect Our Children

U.S. Government

Music Violence: How Does It Affect Our Children Hearning before the Subcommittee on Oversight of Government Management, Restructuring and the District of Columbia.

Testimony of Donald F. Roberts, Thomas Moore Stork Professor of Communications, Stanford University

Mr. ROBERTS. Thank you, Mr. Chairman.

I am here, I think, because I have spent the last 30 years of my life studying children and media—media content of all kinds. A colleague of mine, Dr. Peter Christianson, from Lewis and Clark College in Portland, and I have a book coming out next week called, *It's Not Only Rock n' Roll: Popular Music in the Lives of Adolescents.* The core thesis of this particular book is that it is impossible to understand adolescents in the United States today if you do not understand their relationship with popular music. It is at the heart of adolescent culture.

I have submitted a written statement, and I will let that stand. I am going to skip over a few comments I had to say about the content. We have heard a great deal about the content today.

I just want to stress that we are talking about two genres out of—well, Billboard now charts 20—and that kids are spread out across these genres. By the time they reach adolescence, they generally focus on one or two, and that is where they listen. So there is a large audience for rap and there is a large audience for heavy metal, but it is by no means the largest audience; kids listen across all of the different genres of music.

Most kids hear some of it, but a lot of kids hear just some of it and do not pay a lot of attention. So, who is the audience? Well in a sense, there are two different audiences—heavy metal and rap. They are both very much male-oriented music, but there, the similarities go away.

For heavy metal, the predominance of fans are largely young, white males. By "young," I am talking about early to mid-adolescence and then on up through adolescence. We can find examples of girls and African-

Americans and Hispanics listening, but they really form a minority of that particular audience.

For the most part, the bulk of the audience for heavy metal is probably what we would call fairly normal, pretty good kids, and there is not much problem with them. However, it appears that this particular subgenre of music has a particular attraction for kids who have problems—troubled kids. They are alienated from school, they are alienated from their parents, they have expressed relatively low satisfaction with family relations. They are kids who tend to be risk-takers or sensation-seekers. Heavy metal fans compared to fans of other kinds of music tend to engage in more reckless behaviors, like marijuana use, cocaine use, drunk driving, casual sex. If we look at their beliefs and attitudes, it turns out that, relative to the fans of other kinds of music, heavy metal fans express lower levels of trust in others; they hold libertarian beliefs, which is sort of "anything goes"; they tend to be more Machiavellian, that is, they are engaged in social behaviors that are manipulative or cynical; and they have fewer religious beliefs.

The real heavy metal fan expresses more permissive sexual attitudes, manifests a lower level of respect for women, gives lower estimates of the frequency of date rape and higher estimates of the general rate of sexual activity in the general population.

As I said, troubled youth are particularly drawn to this type of music. I do not mean to imply a causal connection here. Indeed, I think most of the kids who manifest these attitudes and behaviors probably had them before they were even old enough to listen to heavy metal, but once there, they are attracted, and they become the real fans. They are the fans in the true sense of the word. They are "fanatical." They are are highly committed to the music, very involved in it. When you interview them, they identify with the performers. When you ask them who their role models are, they are more likely than fans of any other group of music to label a heavy metal performer.

Knowing that an adolescent is a heavy metal fan does not mean, generally, that he has these characteristics; but knowing that an adolescent is somewhat troubled, is alienated, is at risk, makes it a very good bet that that youngster will in fact be a heavy metal fan.

The problem here is that these are the kids who may be most susceptible to being influenced by the messages in the music. They are at risk in the first place, and they are willing to say right up front, "Those are my role models." So our worry is that they are particularly susceptible.

Now, the rap audience is a little bit different, not surprisingly. Rap is the dominant favorite among African-American males. In the studies I have seen, as many as 75 to 80 percent of adolescent African-American males list this as their favorite.

However, it is not the dominant favorite, but it is a big favorite among young white males—ironically, young white suburban males. The 14- and 15-year-old white males from Edina is very likely to be a real fan of rap.

Girls of both races like the music, but they do not like the lyrics, they do not like the messages. They like rap because it is vibrant, because it is very danceable; that is what appeals to them most.

The kinds of alienated attitudinal things that I just described for heavy metal do not seem to hold up for the fans of rap, but in particular, if you assume that most of the African-American males are there, listening to rap, you would not expect to find these associations because all of the kids are into rap.

African-American youth, when you interview them, love the music for the sound, but they also love the messages, and the more of a fan they are, the more into the messages they are. The white youth love it for the sound; they do not pay a great deal of attention to the messages. However, once they are there listening, it provides them with something that they do not otherwise have access to. For a lot of white suburban youth, rap provides a window to a culture that they do not have a lot of contact with. They are in a sense engaging in something that we have called "cultural tourism." They are getting a sense of "this is what a black neighborhood—this is what a black male is like," from that music. And I think one of the things that we have to be very concerned about when we are talking about 14- or 15-year-old white kids who live in areas of this country that do not have a lot of contact is that if that is the only picture they are getting of the black culture, they are getting quite a distorted picture.

Let me turn to effects, which is what we are really interested in here. I want to note that social scientists recognize that the primary concern is behavior, but when we are talking about the effects of such things as violence and sexuality, it is very difficult to study behavior. We cannot expose kids to the music and then go and see how many fights they start, how many women they attack.

So that what a lot of these studies do is rely on attitudinal measures and perception measures—"What do you believe," and so on.

What I am going to describe to you are experiments. Identical groups of kids are exposed either to the music we consider to be problematic, music that does not carry these messages, or to no music, and then you compare responses after they have gone through this exposure.

When you do this in the studies that have been conducted, you discover that exposure to the music with this kind of message does make a difference in how they perceive social interaction, social relationships, and in their attitudes.

One other qualifier. The effects that are found in the literature are strongest when the kids are exposed to music videos as opposed to just the straight lyrics. The picture brings with it a good deal more information. One of the interesting things about this, however, is that once an adolescent has seen the music video, when he subsequently hears the music, he replays the music video in his head. Those pictures are with one from then on. We tried to run an experiment 2 years ago where we compared kids who saw the video and kids who just heard the lyrics, and we could not run the experiment because all the kids who just heard the lyrics told us, "Well, I could not understand the words at first, so I just remembered the video." So you cannot even do those comparisons anymore.

So a lot of what I am talking about is response to videos. Specifically, videos laced with many violent images have been demonstrated in experiments to make adolescent viewers more antagonistic in their orientation toward women, more likely to condone violence in themselves and in others. That is to say, after viewing, they were likely to say, "I would engage in this kind of behavior, that kind of behavior, I would devalue women a bit more."

Antisocial videos have been shown to increase the acceptance of subsequently observed antisocial behavior. If one watchs a video that is pretty violent, one is more accepting of violence when it is seen later.

Highly gendered stereotype videos increase the acceptance of gender stereotyped behavior subsequent to exposure.

Sexually charged videos have been shown to lead viewers—and in all of these experiments I am talking about for the most part males, although a couple have been run with females, from about the age of 12 or 13 through college; I am talking about late adolescence—sexually charged videos lead viewers to perceive subsequently observed ambiguous behavior as more sexual. They also lead viewers to be more accepting of premarital sex and otherwise sexually permissive.

At least one case study, not an experiment, reported in the medical literature very recently—I just came across it a week ago—reported that in a situation where teenagers and young adults were locked up in a treatment facility, juvenile delinquents and kids with other problems, they were having a great deal of difficulty with violence and kids attacking each other and attacking their caretakers They removed access to any music videos—MTV, VH-1 and so forth—and the reports indicated that over a period of 3 or 4 weeks the violence in this treatment facility went down.

A couple of conclusions, and then I will wind up. Findings and research on all kinds of media content leave little doubt that children, adolescents and adults learn a great deal from what they hear and see in the media, and it does not matter which medium we are talking about. Children, adolescents and adults do not make distinctions. A screen is a screen is a screen, whether it is a television screen, a video, a rental video, a motion picture or a computer screen. It certainly is no different for adolescents and the music media. Indeed, in our book, we contend that music media are probably most important to adolescents.

Popular music is largely for, of, and by adolescents. It focuses on many of the issues that are central to their concern, many of which are taboo topics—for example, sex and cross-sex relationships—that parents, schools and churches do not do a very good job of handling. The media in general and music media in particular fill the void.

Today, studies have shown that adolescents obtain most of their information, for example, about sex and sexuality from peers and from the media—from ignorance and more ignorance. And the music media, because of their focus on topics like that, are very adept at filling this need. They address these kinds of issues—interpersonal relations, how you treat a woman, sex and sexuality, when to use violence—they address those issues frequently, they are reviewed repeatedly, listened to repeatedly, and the consequences of the portrayed behaviors are typically positive and certainly never negative. Sex is usually safe, rudeness is cool, threats toward police or other authorities are rarely punished, violence is rarely punished, and indeed, tattoos are never for life.

Perhaps most important, heavy metal and rap both attract kids to their audiences who may be particularly susceptible to influence—troubled, alienated white males in the case of heavy metal; angry, inner city African-American males in the case of rap.

Given the nature of the content of so much of the music from these two genres in particular, some remarks made by Professor Albert Bandura, who originated what is known as "observational learning theory"—a theory that is probably most potent for explaining how children learn from the media—about the likelihood that youngsters will learn from almost all the media to which they are exposed is particularly chilling. A couple of years ago, he wrote: "After the capacity for observational learning has fully developed, one cannot keep people from learning what they have seen." The literature that we review in our book indicates that you cannot keep them, particularly adolescents, from learning what they have seen or what they have heard.

Thank you.

Senator BROWNBACK. That was excellent testimony from both witnesses. I think that what we need to do is go to questions if we can at this point and some discussion back and forth.

Dr. Roberts, you point to two sections of music that are particularly troublesome out of 20, and that you have really targeted and studied those, and then you said there is a particular group of individuals in those two sections that listen to that type of music that are most susceptible to the message, and I gather from what you are saying, acting out on that message, or at least having an attitudinal change by this message.

What percentage of young people are we talking about? Is there any quantifiable—

Mr. ROBERTS. Not that I know of. I could not hazard a guess. But you raise a very interesting issue, and the issue is: At what percentage do we get concerned? When I teach a course on this, and people say, well, it is just a few kids, I ask my class if they would, for example, change the First Amendment if I could prove—which I cannot—but if I could prove that something in the media caused one killing. And generally, nobody in the class will ever want to change the First Amendment on that basis.

And then, I say, now, if I could prove that each year, something in the media caused 100,000 murders, if I could honestly prove that—and I cannot, but if I could—would you change the First Amendment? And I have discovered that most students in my classes, at 100,000 murders a year, would say yes.

Now we have a couple of boundaries, and the issue becomes where do you start to get concerned. I think that probably, we are talking about a relatively small proportion of kids who are really going to act out, but a relatively small proportion of people commit murders in this country, and yet murder is a concern. A relatively small proportion of kids in this country, or adults, or anyone else, commit suicide, and yet we are concerned about it. So the fact that we might be talking about a couple of percent—and it may be higher, and it may be lower; I simply do not know—is begging the question; it is enough kids to be concerned about.

Senator BROWNBACK. I think you point this out well in studies. Are there going to be other studies that you know of in progress, looking at the impact of music and music violence on culture?

Mr. ROBERTS. Well, there are always studies ongoing, but never enough. I do not want to wag my finger, but a few years ago, social science funding dried up, and a lot of these kinds of studies dried up. And until somebody decides that it is worth running these studies on a systematic basis, rather than have professors get four or five students to volunteer, you are going to get the occasional study. No one has been willing to put up the kind of funding that I think is needed to address these questions, regardless of what the answers are.

Senator BROWNBACK. Senator Lieberman, I think there is a vote coming up. We might want to proceed and wrap this up, so let me turn to you for questions.

Senator LIEBERMAN. Thanks, Mr. Chairman.

First, Dr. Tucker, you have been a real national leader in this. It has been my honor to have worked with you and Dr. Bill Bennett along the way, and I thank you again for your predictably riveting, honest, and for me inspiring, testimony, and I only wish the folks from the record industry would hear and do something about it. But God bless you, and keep on going forward until we get the change we want.

Appendix

Prepared Statement of Raymond and Christine Kuntz,
Parents of Richard Kuntz, Burlington, North Dakota

February 13, 1997

United States Senator
Joseph Lieberman
Senate Hart Bldg. Suite 316
United States Senate
Washington, DC 20510

Dear Senator Lieberman,

As part our families normal daily behavior on the morning of December 12th, 1996, my wife started our son's shower and went to wake him. But our son was not sleeping in his bed, he was dead, he had killed himself. He has left us and is never coming back.

Dear sir, my son was listening to Marylin Manson's "Antichrist Superstar" on the stereo when he died, (I personally removed the distinctive CD with the red lightning bolt across its face from the player) with the rough draft of a 10th grade English class paper about this artist, that his teacher had returned to him that day for final revisions, on the stand next to his body. The lyrics (enclosed) of "The Reflecting God," on that CD, read as an unequivocally direct inducement to take one's own life. Our son's friends tell us that in the end, that this was his favorite song, that this was the cut that was always on whenever they came over.

We are all certainly free to make our own decisions regarding the value of content, but if you were to ask me, I'd say that the lyrics of this song, contributed directly to my son's death.

Additionally, two more of my son's friends, who have been treated for attempted suicide since his death, are/were caught up in Marylin Manson's nihilistic music and are still considered to be at risk.

Sir, this music, because it glorifies inhumane intolerance and hate, and promotes suicide, contradicts all of the community values that people of good will, regardless of faith, ideology, economic or social position, share. Simply put, this music hurts us as a people. Our children are quietly being destroyed (dying), by this man's music, by ones and twos in scattered isolation throughout our nation today.

The artist's own words, in his lyrics and interviews (and his actions), indicate that this injury to society is intentional. The predatory world that Brian Warner markets, through his stage persona as Marylin Manson,* is one no normal (or few in the normal distribution curve of humanity) person would wish to live in.

By their nature, corporations do not have consciences and it is understandable that MCA would wish to defend a product that entered the Billboard 200 chart at No. 3. But even though they are soulless, corporations do have social obligations and responsibilities and MCA in the name of profit, wrapped in the first amendment, is, by producing and distributing this kind of "art," creating the end, resulting from yelling Fire in a theater.

I understand that the lyrics to individual songs and the content of interviews made by artists with obscure magazines and newsletters are below a CEO's event horizon. But somewhere down the hierarchy line, someone who is aware of artistic content and stated intent, is making corporate economic decisions driven by greed. Decision making that kills.

Shaming major corporations into more responsible behavior is nice, but forcing a corporation to divest itself of a socially unacceptable, still functional subset, possibly at a profit, does nothing to rectify the problem or wash clean the hands of those involved.

The proper, responsible way to deal with organizations like Interscope Records, Nothing Records and the like would be to close them and write off the losses, with as much loud self-congratulatorly applause as one can possibly generate.

Because the problems today are several orders of magnitude worse than they've ever been, it may also be time to reconvene the congressional hearings held in the 80's that resulted in the voluntary RIAA "Parental Advisory" sticker program. It appears to be time to make this program mandatory and give it some

---

*Note: Warner's band members usually adopt androgynous, two part stage names, the 1st part derived from a female celebrity, and the 2nd from a convicted male mass murder. And Brian got lucky, as the lead, he got the pick of the litter, "Marylin" as in Marylin Monroe, the female celebrity who committed suicide and "Manson" as in Charles Manson, mass murderer.

teeth, so that states have some kind of objective criteria to use in regulating the exposure of minors to these dangerous materials.

My wife's name is Christine, my son's name was Richard, my name is Raymond. Sir, if there is anything you can do, we will do what we can to help.

Thank You,

Raymond Kuntz and Christine Kuntz
for Richard Kuntz
Rt 1 Box 31
Burlington, ND 58722

Freedom of What?

Copyright 2005 Associated Press. All rights reserved. Distributed by Valeo IP.

First Amendment No Big Deal, Students Say

The way many high school students see it, government censorship of newspapers may not be a bad thing, and flag burning is hardly protected free speech.

It turns out the First Amendment is a second-rate issue to many of those nearing their own adult independence, according to a study of high school attitudes released Monday.

The original amendment to the Constitution is the cornerstone of the way of life in the United States, promising citizens the freedoms of religion, speech, press and assembly.

Yet, when told of the exact text of the First Amendment, more than one in three high school students said it goes "too far" in the rights it guarantees. Only half of the students said newspapers should be allowed to publish freely without government approval of stories.

"These results are not only disturbing; they are dangerous," said Hodding Carter III, president of the John S. and James L. Knight Foundation, which sponsored the $1 million study. "Ignorance about the basics of this free society is a danger to our nation's future."

The students are even more restrictive in their views than their elders, the study says.

When asked whether people should be allowed to express unpopular views, 97 percent of teachers and 99 percent of school principals said yes. Only 83 percent of students did.

The results reflected indifference, with almost three in four students saying they took the First Amendment for granted or didn't know how they felt about it. It was also clear that many students do not understand what is protected by the bedrock of the Bill of Rights.

Three in four students said flag burning is illegal. It's not. About half the students said the government can restrict any indecent material on the Internet. It can't.

"Schools don't do enough to teach the First Amendment. Students often don't know the rights it protects," Linda Puntney, executive director of the Journalism Education Association, said in the report. "This all comes at a time when there is decreasing passion for much of anything. And, you have to be passionate about the First Amendment."

The partners in the project, including organizations of newspaper editors and radio and television news directors, share a clear advocacy for First Amendment issues.

Federal and state officials, meanwhile, have bemoaned a lack of knowledge of U.S. civics and history among young people. Sen. Robert Byrd, D-West Virginia, has even pushed through a mandate that schools must teach about the Constitution on September 17, the date it was signed in 1787.

The survey, conducted by researchers at the University of Connecticut, is billed as the largest of its kind. More than 100,000 students, nearly 8,000 teachers and more than 500 administrators at 544 public and private high schools took part in early 2004.

The study suggests that students embrace First Amendment freedoms if they are taught about them and given a chance to practice them, but schools don't make the matter a priority.

Students who take part in school media activities, such as student newspapers or TV production, are much more likely to support expression of unpopular views, for example.

About nine in ten principals said it is important for all students to learn some journalism skills, but most administrators say a lack of money limits their media offerings.

More than one in five schools offer no student media opportunities; of the high schools that do not offer student newspapers, 40 percent have eliminated them in the last five years.

"The last 15 years have not been a golden era for student media," said Warren Watson, director of the J-Ideas project at Ball State University in Indiana. "Programs are under siege or dying from neglect. Many students do not get the opportunity top practice our basic freedoms."

Conversation on Standardized Assessment

The No Child Left Behind Act is arguably the largest educational reform in United States' history and has intensified a long-standing debate over the value of standardized tests for assessing student learning. The goal of this act is to wipe out achievement gaps between rich and poor students by the year 2017. Similarly, most standardized tests used for college admissions, like the SAT, are presented as offering a supposedly objective standard by which to evaluate students and judge their achievements relative to one another's. However, many see standardized testing for both graduation and college admission as doing the exact opposite—perpetuating the inequities already present in society. In this conversation, three voices enter into these debates. Some of those voices are interested parties—a teacher, Bill Dunn, and two students discussed in Tracy Jan's report—whose jobs and graduation may depend upon the results of high stakes testing in high schools. Mark Franek is also a high school teacher but he focuses on assessing the fairness of the new writing SAT for his students. How do the varying perspectives, investments, and positions of power affect the opinions each of these three writers put forth? Are their positions affected by their personal investments? How do writers with similar positions change the nature of their discussion when they write for an audience of teachers (Dunn) versus a more public audience like readers of *The Christian Science Monitor*? What positions are *not* represented here?

Confessions of an Underperforming Teacher

Bill Dunn

Reprinted by permission of the publisher from Nieto, Sonia, *Why We Teach* (New York: Teachers College Press, © 2005 by Teachers College, Columbia University. All rights reserved.) "Confessions of an Underperforming Teacher."

About a decade ago *Parade Magazine* ran an issue devoted to stress on the job. I was surprised to see teaching listed as the most stressful job in the nation followed by such obvious careers as air traffic controller, policeman, fireman and so on down the line. Our world has changed considerably in the past ten years, and I doubt that teaching would still head the list. The irony for me is that the stress of the job ten years ago seems laughable given the atmosphere and working conditions in schools today. I should mention that I work in an urban vocational high school. Eighty-five percent of my students are Hispanic. Eighty-three percent qualify for free or reduced lunch, and seventy percent are native Spanish speakers. I wish I could tell you that I don't encounter gangs, weapons, poverty, high pregnancy rates, and the other social ills which plague city schools; but these problems are the realities of where I work. These things trouble me, but I understand them because I live with them daily as do my students. I know the cause of these problems, and I also know that the majority of my students are the victims and not the perpetrators. Violence in schools is as real as metal detectors and policemen. The stresses which students and teachers encounter in schools today should evoke compassion and admiration from the public; unfortunately, quite the opposite occurs, and this troubles me even more. Test results are released and inner-city students and their teachers are ridiculed in bold headlines. My favorite label is "underperforming." I sincerely couldn't have come up with a word with nastier connotations to attach to schools and the human beings who inhabit them.

The simple truth about teaching, in my opinion, is that it is an inherently stressful profession. Most students do not want to do what their teachers want them to do. It takes a great deal of patience to spend eight or more hours a day cajoling students who would prefer to socialize and not to be bothered. My strategy used to be to expose kids to interesting ideas that made them wonder about commonly held assumptions. Interested kids cause fewer problems. I used to console myself with the rationalization that I was doing the right thing for my students, but lately I'm not so sure. Over the last ten years my state has very rigidly defined what it means to be an educated student in a Massachusetts public school. There are clear winners and clear losers. Unfortunately even the kids who pass the test in my school are losers because it usually takes them three or four tries to pass the test. Schools throughout the state have been forced to goose-step to the beat of mandated exams, and the result is continuous drill, and in urban schools that drill often goes on for three to four years. Gone are the interesting ideas and intellectual curiosity that made it a pleasure to teach, and they have been replaced with the stress of doing the same thing over and over again. It's a lousy deal all the way around for students, teachers, and schools. Eventually it will be evident that it's a lousy deal for society as well because uninterested kids on the street often cross the line from victim to victimizer.

The major source of stress over the past ten years has come from unexpected places, and the most insidious thing about the march to higher standards and "high stakes" testing is that those leading the charge purport to be doing it on behalf of the students in "underperforming" schools like mine. No Child Left Behind which means *Ninos Dejan Pasar* to Spanish speaking kids, translates into horrendous dropout rates between freshman and senior year; and in schools like mine thirty to forty percent of the students who continue through senior year are still left behind through little fault of their own. The rhetoric of education reform is in itself appalling. Headlines such as, "State threatens takeover of underperforming districts" should insult everyone not just those students, parents and teachers in poor districts. If you're a fascist regime you takeover the states next to you. When you're a state and you takeover schools, you're on the road to being a fascist regime. As I write, my school is being threatened with a state takeover which means a visit from the accountability and targeted assistance team. I am uncertain who comprises this group and what I am going to be held accountable for, but I am dead certain that they are not on my team. I am fairly certain that they have less classroom experience than I have. I am also fairly certain that they do not live in a community like mine, and that their children have not attended underperforming schools like my children have. I am also dead certain that they will not know the realities of living in a community like mine which has the highest rate of poverty, teen pregnancy, drug and alcohol abuse, etc. In fact as a community, we are first in the state in just about all the bad things, and I am certain that they will not see me or my students. They will only see artificial scores which have little to do with anybody's accountability, intelligence or effort except those who made up the test in the first place. Finally I'm a bit queasy about the oxy-moronic "targeted assistance."

Often when I rant about testing and the MCAS in particular, I am accused of making excuses for my students. I refuse to make excuses; I think they're doing fine. Fifty-four percent of our students are passing the ELA part of the test and approximately thirty percent miss by a few points. I have an acute knowledge of the test because I have spent most of the last four years going over the questions again and again and again. The vocabulary on the test is just plain nasty. Recently I was doing an item analysis of last year's test, and to my surprise there was a question that Limited English Proficient kids got right at a much higher rate than regular education students. It was a multiple choice question based on an excerpt of the *Scarlet Letter.*

Most students across the state had trouble with the dense, archaic text. Students had to pick the correct synonym for the word "edifice" from the context of the passage. This was difficult because the usage of the words in the passage was buried with Nathaniel Hawthorne. The correct answer was "building." Obviously Spanish speakers knew the correct answer because the Spanish word for building is "edificio." Did the test makers put in that question as a concession to LEP students? I'd bet the ranch against it. In fact, I think they screwed up. The rest of the test plays with bizarre word connotations that are simply beyond the reach of second language learners. My point is that one question out of thirty-nine favored LEP students, and it was an accident. The other thirty-eight questions favor middle class kids who are native English speakers. Who also tend to have educated parents, and who tend to live in relatively affluent communities. Now there is nothing wrong with any of those things, but there is something very wrong with labeling kids failing because they were born short on cultural capital and on the wrong side of the language tracks.

So why do I teach? I teach because someone has to tell my students that they are not the ones who are dumb. They need to know that only the blissfully ignorant and profoundly evil make up tests to prove that they and people like them are smart. I teach because my students need to know that poverty does not equal stupidity, and that surviving a bleak, dismal childhood makes you strong and tough and beautiful in ways that only survivors of similar environments can appreciate and understand. I teach because my students need to know that in their struggle to acquire a second language they participate in one of the most difficult of human feats. My students also need to know that four days of reading in a second language under highstakes testing conditions would shut down even Einstein's brain. I teach because my students need to know that right and wrong are relative to one's culture, and that even these definitions become laughable over time. I teach because the people who make up these tests don't know these things, or worse, they do.

New SAT Writing Section Scores Low

Mark Franek

From *The Christian Science Monitor.* Copyright © 2005 The Christian Science Monitor. Reprinted by permission.

Answer the questions below on the basis of what is stated or implied in this oped. For each wrong answer, you'll receive a quarter-point reduction. Don't stress. Your score on this test is worth about as much as your entire high school transcript put together. Ready . . . begin!

I've been a high school English teacher for 10 years, and if there's one thing I hate worse than the SAT, it's the idea of a *new* SAT, which, incidentally, hits testing centers next month for the nearly 1.5 million high school students who take it annually.

It's not that I'm against assessing kids. I give my own students eight to 10 assessments each marking period, though my assignments don't look anything like what students encounter on these high-stakes national exams—which kids would like to jettison as quickly as the suggestion that their parents chaperone the prom.

The new SAT consists of three parts: math, critical reading (a new name for the old "verbal" section), and a writing section, which is a misnomer. Each is worth between 200 and 800 points, for a total maximum score of 2400. Quantitative comparison questions have been dropped from the math section; in its place, more Algebra II and geometry. Analogies have been tossed from the critical reading section, leaving room for more reading passages.

The writing section is entirely new—70 percent of it is composed of pesky multiple-choice grammatical questions (where students aren't writing anything—they're blacking in ovals), while the final 30 percent is reserved for a persuasive essay that our teenagers are supposed to draft and complete in 25 minutes.

Put your pencils down. Readers, I'm not kidding.

Gaston Caperton, the ambitious new head of the College Board, which administers the SAT, is not shy about his goal of changing the way that teens are taught: "When I saw what the College Board was and, more important, what it could be, I saw the power to do much more than they were doing in the past to improve education. . . . This [new] test is really going to create a revolution in the schools."

I'm not so sure. Graded solely on its ability to "improve education," the old SAT scored an "F" in my gradebook. The new version doesn't do much better.

The entire "writing" section of this new test is the kind of assessment that most teachers of writing would run away from. First of all, the idea that during the writing of this blitzkrieg essay—from the official SAT exam preparation booklet—"You should take care to develop your point of view, present your ideas logically and clearly, and use language precisely" in under half an hour and under extreme pressure is ridiculous.

We're not talking e-mail here. This article of mine you're reading now, for example, took several hours to compose—not to mention the fruitful give and take between the paper's editors and me.

That's how real writing gets done. It gets interrupted by coffee breaks, frequent trips to the bathroom, and knocks on the door—both literally and figuratively, as new ideas cross the threshold of the imagination and knock around the writer's mind.

Second, the slew of multiple-choice questions about grammar that the College Board calls "improving sentences and paragraphs" is not what Shakespeare had in mind when he dipped his quill in the inkwell before sitting down to edit a draft.

From the board's official Prep Booklet, here's the first example of what to expect (possible errors appear in italics): "The students (a) *have discovered* that (b) *they* can address issues more effectively (c) *through* letter-writing campaigns (d) *and not* through public demonstrations. (e) No error."

This sentence appears OK to me, even if it is a little clunky. According to the College Board, however, the error occurs at (d) because: "When a comparison is introduced by the adverb 'more,' as in 'more effectively,' the second part of the comparison must be introduced by the conjunction 'than' rather than 'and not.'"

Got that?

But if I were to edit this sentence, I might make a few more changes: "The students discovered that they can address issues more effectively by writing letters than by demonstrating publicly." But, hey, I'd be wrong because this is not the portion of the writing section where I'm allowed to write anything.

What the bulk of the writing section of the new SAT is really measuring is acquired skills in *managing style* within the realm of standard written English; however, these skills cannot be taught or coaxed by silly, top-down, multiple-choice questions that, let's be honest, are an effort to trick up kids so that they can be sorted by colleges.

Students would be better served by consistently reading the commentary section of the local newspaper—and then periodically writing letters to the editor—than by sitting through the painfully boring lesson plans that these changes to the SAT are likely to inspire.

If the goal is to improve education, then I propose a portfolio-assessment approach where students are allowed to gradually generate (over the course of the year) multiple writing samples in various genres (the kinds of things found in any real library or bookstore) and then submit them by some agreed-upon due date.

Critics of this approach will say that portfolios are unreliable and that there is no way to guarantee student authenticity. But we teachers know the truth. The College Board would much prefer that their test remain mostly multiple-choice, which is cost-effective to score. Portfolios would require the Board to hire thousands of English teachers each year to read and assess over a million pages of student writing, much of it demonstrating genuine literacy learning. Now that would be a revolution.

After Multiple Attempts, MCAS Success

From *The Boston Globe*. Copyright © 2005 The New York Times Company. Reprinted by permission.

After finishing high school two years ago, Miguel Reyes searched for a job as a security guard. Doors shut in his face, because he didn't have a diploma, even though he had passed all his classes in high school.

He was a member of the Class of 2003, the first group of students in the state that had to pass the MCAS in English and math to get a high school diploma. But Reyes had taken the English part multiple times in high school and afterward. Each time, he failed.

His friends urged him to give up. "You're not going to make it," they would say. Reyes, whose first language is Spanish, had to write a good essay, in English.

In November, he took the test again in the gym of his former high school, Greater Lawrence Technical School in Andover. At age 20, on his sixth try, he passed.

He is one of 14 students from the Class of 2003 in Massachusetts who met the graduation standard after the most recent retest, state education officials said yesterday.

Four of those students took the test eight times. Two years out of school, the former students said they persisted for a shot at a better-paying job, a chance at college, dreams made possible only with a high school diploma.

Their success boosts their class's passing rate to 95 percent. When they first took the tests as sophomores, only 68 percent of students passed. Approximately 3,000 members of their class never passed the Massachusetts Comprehensive Assessment System exam, according to the state Education Department.

Fewer students try as the years march on. The test has been controversial since its inception, partly because many educators feared it would discourage black and Hispanic students from graduating.

Reyes, who aspires to be a police officer, ignored his friends' advice to quit trying. "Hey, you never know. If other people did it, I can, too," he told them.

Current students also would tease him, "Oh, you're here again?" when he would come to take the MCAS yet another time.

"I just kept walking," Reyes said. "It's my future. It's my diploma. It's what I want."

To prepare for the tests each time, he took MCAS tutoring at his old school and read books on his own. He couldn't get help from his parents, who had emigrated from the Dominican Republic and spoke only Spanish. When not studying, he loaded trucks at a Woburn warehouse for $8.50 an hour. He lives with his mother because he can't afford rent.

Classmates who had passed the MCAS were in college, he said. Those who didn't worked at fast-food restaurants.

With a diploma, Reyes knew he could get automatically accepted to a community college and would be able to apply to a four-year university. Community colleges require either a diploma or a GED.

Reyes was frustrated that manual labor was the only job he could get after four years of high school and wanted to do better.

He tried to persuade his friends to join him on his quest for a bonafide diploma, rather than settle for the certificate of attainment many of them had received, indicating they passed their classes, but not the MCAS. They told him the tests were too hard and that they didn't want to waste their time.

The state tries to make it easy for students to retest, requiring them only to get in touch with their former high schools.

"The door is always open," said Heidi Perlman, Education Department spokeswoman. "They can come back whenever they want to try again. They can come back when they're 30."

Melissa Williams, 21, made her eighth attempt at the math MCAS when she was nine months pregnant last fall. She felt awkward in a classroom full of younger students, she said, but knew it was her only option.

"I wanted to get it done and over with, so I could leave in case I went into labor," Williams said. "I wanted to show my children when they got older that their mother graduated from high school and that she went on to college."

Williams now has a 2-month-old daughter as well as a 3-year-old daughter. Her own parents had dropped out of high school after having children, she said. Williams had received training in cooking and nutrition from the Greater New Bedford Regional Vocational Technical High School. After leaving the school, she tried enrolling in college but could not without a diploma. She went to work as a lunch room cook at a day care center.

Williams said she was annoyed that one test stood between her and a high school diploma. Still, motivated by former teachers, she took practice MCAS tests on the computer several times a week.

Williams received her test results in the mail two weeks ago. She opened the envelope in the car while her mother was driving her to the grocery store. She just made it, passing with the minimum score, 220. "I was excited that I finally did it and that I don't have to go back anymore," she said. "It was about time I passed the stupid test."

She called the school that afternoon and asked them to print up her diploma. The next day, she walked into the front office to pick up the piece of paper she had sought for two years and headed to her local college to enroll in accounting courses.

Reyes got a 230 out of a possible 280 on the English exam. He hopes to start community college in the fall to study business, criminal justice, and law.

"I'm going to go and try my best, like what I just did," he said.

Two days ago, he went to a security office in New Hampshire to apply once more to become a guard, which he thinks will help him achieve his dream of becoming a police officer.

The interviewer asked if he had a high school diploma. He answered yes firmly, but confided he first had to go to a small ceremony at his high school to receive the long-awaited piece of parchment.

Reyes got the $12 hourly job guarding office buildings in Salem, N.H. Orientation starts Wednesday.

Student Essay: The Color of Crime

Jonathan Fuller

While at work, an African American and two white employees heard a woman from a nearby gas station scream for help after just being robbed. They all chased the culprit, who was white, and the African American caught and tackled the robber. When the police arrived on the scene, they asked the manager of the gas station, "Did you catch him?" He replied "Yes," and the officers immediately assumed the African American was the robber and grabbed him by the arm and said, "Come with me" ("The Effects"). This is known as racial profiling, the discriminatory practice by police of treating blackness as an indication of possible criminality (Muharrar). In simpler terms, color equals crime. Every day, people of color are racially profiled, whether they know it or not, by police, media, and other people of *non-color,* which can lead to negative behavior.

Imagine this if you will: You get up in the morning, head for work in your new Mercedes Benz on the highway. You notice police sirens in your rear view mirror, so you pull over. When the officer approaches you, he tells you that you fit the description of someone suspected of trafficking drugs. He then handcuffs you and forces you to lie face down while he searches your car. Well, for Sanford Reese, a black minister, he didn't have to imagine this situation because he actually went through it (McCain). This is the most common form of racial profiling that happens by police officers. Many minorities are pulled over by police for *supposed* traffic violations when in fact they plan to search for drugs. Between 1994 and 1998, an alarming 77% of consent searches on the southern end of the New Jersey turnpike involved minorities (MacDonald).

Why is this you may ask? One possible answer might be because according to a Heritage Foundation analysis of FBI data between 1976 and 1999, 64% of the homicide victims in drug turf wars were black (MacDonald). However, according to a police training manual, "Racial profiling is not good police work," ("Mutual Respect" 16) but unfortunately there is nothing illegal about using race as a factor to pull someone over. The DEA taught state troopers alternate ways of identifying signs of drug couriers such as nervousness, no luggage for long trips, lots of cash, and conflicting stories between the driver and passengers in the car about origins and destination, but racial profiling still continues to occur.

Even with the percentages from the data collected, it is still unfair to postulate criminal behavior with all people of color. That's almost like me saying that since many white people in Texas were members of the Ku Klux Klan, most of them probably still are associated with them.

What people don't realize is that for every criminal caught through racial profiling, an innocent person is harassed by it. An example is when I was coming home one night from the park after a long day of basketball. I noticed two officers in a patrol car near my one way street. I tried to avoid making eye contact with them. They left, and I continued to proceed onto my street. Then, all of a sudden, I saw the same police car coming down the wrong direction and one of the officers walking on the sidewalk with a flashlight. When they saw me, I heard one say, "There he is, let's get em!" My mom heard all the commotion and came outside. When she asked what the problem was, they responded, "We're sorry ma'am, we got a lot of calls about car theft in the neighborhood and your son fit the description." When they left, I wondered to myself how a 15-year-old wearing a bright yellow shirt, blue shorts, carrying a backpack, and dribbling a basketball could possibly fit the description of someone who steals cars.

How many times am I going to turn on the television to the news and see another minority convicted for a crime, or flip through the channels and see a black actor playing the role of a drug dealer or drug junkie? Are there any people of *non-color* that commit crimes these days? When the news media over-represents the number of black people committing crime, the issue becomes "black," stigmatized, linked to some form of always-justified, politically-punishing behavior, and in turn, is further racialized (Muharrar). If in fact people of *non-color* constantly see negative images of blacks on TV, then they will link those images to all African Americans and develop a negative stereotype, thus, pushing racial profiling even further.

I came across an example of this phenomenon while watching my local news a few days ago. My boss, who is white, and who I also worked for over the summer at an elementary school, was being convicted of fraud and stealing over $600,000. In disbelief, I anxiously awaited to see his picture, hoping it wasn't my boss, just somebody with the same name as his. Instead, they ended up showing a picture of a black man, his "partner," who didn't even have that much involvement in the scandal. The main story was about my boss, a white male, and they ended up showing the picture of a black man who they spoke of for less than ten seconds.

Media versions like this of racial profiling feed into the everyday situations African Americans have to deal with, such as getting followed around in stores. For example, a special report aired on the local news about the outbreak of mini-mart and gas station robberies, mostly committed by black males. I knew because of that I would get followed around in stores by employees even more than usual. A friend of mine (who is white) and I decided to put it to the test. We went into a random convenience store and everything was going "according to plan" as I was being followed and being watched from the corners of the clerks' eyes. They would follow me down the aisle, acting as if they were straightening the items on the shelves. While I had the spotlight on me, my friend managed to take at least nine dollars worth of candy, in broad daylight, with other customers in the store.

Racial profiling is wrong and can have negative effects on the victims. "It violates human dignity by sending a message to the person that he or she is less worthy of consideration and respect as a human being" ("The Effects"). It can cause embarrassment to people, especially if it occurs in front of friends, family members, co-workers, etc. For example, how would white parents feel about sending their kids to a black teacher who they saw get pulled over and handcuffed? It can also change the way you live your life. Some people go as far as avoiding the cars of their choice for fear of being pulled over. Imagine that? You work hard, make good money, but can't even buy the kind of car you want because you don't want to get harassed by the police. Being pulled over repeatedly can make you feel less of a person and lower your self-esteem. It's almost like the police officer is directly saying to me: *I don't care if your parents bought the car for you, or if you're a college student with a 3.5 GPA and never committed a crime; because you're BLACK, you STEAL.* Personally, when the police come around, I undergo a state of being more nervous than safe and feel as though I need protection from the people who are supposed to be protecting me!

In conclusion, racial profiling is a serious issue in the United States that needs to be stopped. Even though it won't go away in a short period of time, one way of handling the situation would be to go after the police by making sure that victims get names and badge numbers if they feel they were being treated unfairly due to race. In Cincinnati, there is a petition for the passage of State House Bill 363, which would require police departments to track the race, vehicle make, and license plate of a motorist stopped for a traffic violation. In addition, the law would make departments list why a vehicle was stopped, whether it was searched, whether an arrest was made, and if illicit items were found. The data would then be analyzed by the state legislature (McCain). More petitions such as this could cut down significantly on police stops based on race. Another way to eliminate this unfair treatment is to boycott stores that racially profile. If everything else fails and nothing changes, victims of racial profiling will have two options: to live in fear and deal with it, or paint themselves white!

Works Cited

"The Effects of Racial Profiling." Ontario Human Rights Commission 14 April 2004 <http://www.ohrc.on.ca/english/consultations/racial-profiling-report_6.shtml>.

MacDonald, Heather. "The Myth of Racial Profiling." The Manhattan Institute. 8 April 2004 <http://www.city-journal.org/html/11 _2_the_myth. html>.

McCain, Marie. "Racial Profiling Perceived." *The Cincinnati Enquirer.* 14 May 2000 <http://www.enquirer.com/editions/2000/05/14/loc_racial_profiling.html>.

Muharrar, Mikal. "Media Blackface: 'Racial Profiling' in News Reporting." 8 April 2004 <http://www.fair.org/extra/9809/media-blackface.html>.

"Mutual Respect in Policing." Washington DC: Office of Orientated Policing Services, 2001.

Student Essay:
The SATs: Is There a Reasonable Use for Them?

Christine Oslowski

Not long ago when I was a senior in high school, my fellow classmates and I had to face the dreadful SATs. The teachers would emphasize how important it was to do well on these exams in order to be accepted to qualified colleges and to receive substantial scholarships. So being the successful student that I am, I knew I had to score well on the exam. It turned out that after taking the exam three times, I could not get anything higher than a 1070.

As a result, I had to apply to less qualified schools and let go of many scholarship opportunities. I was embarrassed when someone asked me what set of schools I applied to because I knew they were expecting to hear Worcester Polytechnic Institute or Boston University from a valedictorian. I was also upset that some of my fellow classmates were going to better schools than I was and receiving full scholarships. I felt like the four years of hard work didn't pay off and blamed myself for not studying hard enough for the exam. But maybe the problem wasn't with me. Maybe it was with the test itself.

First some background information about the SATs. In the 1920's the College Board became interested in developing their own intelligence test "suitable for candidates wishing to enter colleges represented on the board" (Valentine 33) as they observed the usefulness of such tests for college admissions. There are two types of intelligence tests, aptitude, designed to predict a person's future performance, and achievement, designed to assess what a person has learned (Myers 432). The College Board wanted to develop an aptitude test that could predict a student's college performance.

In 1924, the board appointed a committee of three psychologists from some of the nation's finest schools to develop the exam. Whenever psychologists are constructing an intelligence test, it must be standardized so that a person's performance can be compared to others'; reliable, so it yields consistent scores; and valid, so it measures what it is supposed to measure (Myers 437). After careful evaluation, the final product of the SATs consisted of two subtests, math and verbal, each scored on a 200-800 point scale. Along with the exam, the committee also "composed a manual for the guidance of college admission officers" (Valentine 34). The manual warned readers that "the new test would not predict subsequent academic performance of students with certainty" (Valentine 35) and that the test should only be used as a supplement to the admission process.

The board also felt that "it was considered necessary, if the SAT was to function effectively, to standardize all the conditions that might affect test performance other than the aptitude the test was designed to measure" (Valentine 36). This included preventing any familiarity to the exam by such methods as not publishing the contents of the exam and its answers.

Since then, the exam is now a multiple choice timed exam consisting of "analogies, sentence completions, reading comprehension, standard math and quantitative comparison items" ("The SAT"). The scale remains the same. Also there are now practice exams available and answers so that a student can prepare oneself for the exam.

As the SAT's popularity grew, so did the criticism. By the 1970's, two main issues surfaced. One was that the test was "biased against blacks and Latinos who score worse on average compared to whites" and "[t]he other was that the SAT scores only measure the ability to take the SAT" (Cloud). Other problems include the lack of predictability of college performance, the misuse of the results, and that intelligent students who score poorly on the exam could possibly be overlooked.

One issue I would like to focus on is what the SATs measure. They are supposed to measure and predict the student's college performance in the first year. But actually the SAT really measures the ability to take the exam favoring those who can afford the extremely expensive prep courses that could "raise a student's score 100 points or more" *(Fair Test)*. According to some data collected by the Fair Test organization, in 2002 the average total score for a college bound student coming from a family with an income of less than $10,000 was a low 839. Yet a college bound student from a family with an income of more than $100,000 scores an average of 1123 *(Fair Test)*. Thus, just being in a family of low income, I am already likely to perform poorly on the SATs. Why rely on a test that seems to measure how much money one is willing to pay? However some argue that poor students are simply getting a lousy education compared to richer students who attend well-funded schools (Cloud).

This issue also ties into the problem with the SAT's lack of validity as a predictor of college performance. In one study at the University of Pennsylvania, researchers compared SATs, achievement tests such as the SAT II, and high-school class rank as predictors of college performance.

"Consideration of multiple regression coefficients revealed that class rank and achievement tests added significantly to overall prediction, whereas SAT did not" (Baron 1047). In fact, in predicting college cumulative grade point averages, the class rank proved to be most accurate. The predictive power of aptitude tests is fairly strong in the early grades, but later it weakens as the range of student abilities becomes more restricted (Myers 436). Furthermore poor predictive ability of the SATs becomes particularly apparent when considering the college performance of females, Hispanics, African Americans, and older students ("The SAT").

I am a perfect example of the SAT's inability to predict college performance. My score on the math portion of the exam was a 570, which is only 70 points beyond the average female math score according to the Fair Test Organization. So it may be concluded that my math skills are slightly beyond the average. However, on the Massachusetts Comprehensive Assessment System or MCAS test's math portion, my score was in the advanced category. On the Advanced Placement exam for Calculus developed by the very people who created the SATs, I scored a five, the highest possible score. With these two results alone, it is obvious that I am talented in mathematics. Well, what about my performance in college? It so happens I received an A in Calculus II. Thus, the SATs did not measure or predict anything.

Another important issue that I believe tremendously affects students like me is the misuse of the SATs in order to make selections by using cutoff scores despite the warning that the results for the SATs should be a supplement to school records, GPA, teacher recommendations, and other criteria. I actually encountered this very problem of misuse from the University of Massachusetts Amherst. Since I was a valedictorian, I was entitled to a huge tuition scholarship; however, it also included a minimum SAT requirement of 1100. I fell short of the requirement by only thirty points. Other examples include programs such as Stanford University's Education Program for Gifted Youth and Northwestern University's Center for Talent Development that use SAT scores to select participants ("The SAT").

These misuses are a major problem because scholarships and programs could be overlooking intelligent students who do poorly on the exam yet deserve such opportunities. I don't think my thirty point difference should have mattered. If the University of Massachusetts Amherst looked at my 4.0 GPA, the scores on other exams, and some of the challenging courses I had taken, I would think that would be enough to earn the scholarship. Since I come from a family of low income and I am a female, it is proven that my scores will likely be lower than a middle class white male. Thus it seems to me it doesn't really matter how well I did in school; I'm already at a disadvantage and there is very little I can do about it.

Fortunately there have been some actions made against the SATs. More and more schools, after having done their own studies, have shown that "class rank, high school grades, and rigor of classes taken are better tools for predicting college success than any standardized test. The ACT and SAT II are often viewed as alternatives to the SAT I ("The SAT"). As of 2003, there are more than 700 bachelor degree-granting institutions that do not require SATs and many more have deemphasized the results ("The SAT").

Even though some actions have been taken, these problems still persist. There are people out there who believe that the test "maintains standards" (Cloud), and it "remains the only genuinely universal mode of assessment currently available to admissions' committees" (Orland). They argue that each student has a unique school experience. Some schools are ideal learning places whereas others are less funded. Thus "what counts as an A at one school is often not the same as what counts as an A at another" (Orland). Furthermore these SAT supporters claim that even though the test may favor some students over others, "without the SATs, there will no longer be a standard for judging students equally" (Orland) and that the use of grades and such "will result in a system that is even less fair" (Orland).

However, if the SATs provide standards, then why are certain groups like females and African Americans scoring less on the exam? It may help to provide standards for individual groups instead of grouping them all together. Also "most four year colleges accept more than seventy-five percent of their applicants and have limited or no real need for the SAT as an admission tool" ("The SAT").

Providing standards wasn't the actual purpose of the SATs. Its only purpose was to predict first-year college grades, which it doesn't really do a good job of. In my opinion, the only real solution to all of the problems with the exam is to either eliminate the use of the SATs or the scores should be made optional for college admissions until the College Board can come up with a better replacement.

What I think colleges should use as criteria for admissions are high school grades, GPA, class rank, achievement tests like the Advanced Placement exams and the SAT II, and teacher recommendations. These have been proven to be better methods of predicting a student's college performance and determining that the student is college bound.

More importantly, I believe nothing should prevent a well-achieved student from receiving a good scholarship or attending a qualified school. It's upsetting that more and more students like me who deserve such privileges are being turned down due to what they score on a test. Why should a test with so many flaws continue to do this to students? It just isn't right.

Works Cited

Baron, Jonathan and Norman M. Frank. "SATs, Achievement Tests, and High-School Class Rank as Predictors of College Performance." *Educational and Psychological Measurement* 52 (1992): 1047–1055.

Cloud, John. "Should SATs Matter?" *Time* 4 March 2001. 10 April 2004 <http://www.time.com/time/education/printout/0,8816,101321,00.html>.

"The SAT: Questions and Answers." *Fair Test University Testing: Main* 12 April 2004 <http://www.fairtest.org/univers.html>.

Myers, David G. "Intelligence." Psychology. Holland: Worth Publishers, 2004. 432–437.

Orland, David. *The SATs: Affirmative Actions' Last Frontier.* 10 April 2004 <http://www.boundless.org/2000/features/a0000409.html>.

Valentine, John A. *The College Board and the School Curriculum.* New York: College Entrance Examination Board, 1987. 31–44.

Suggested Exercises and Activities for Adding to a Conversation

Examining a Conversation by Charting, Marking, and Drawing

1) Fill out the chart below for each essay in the conversation. Keep in mind there may be more than one answer to each question.

	Title & Author	Title & Author	Title & Author
Purpose: What is the author's position on this issue? What is she trying to communicate? For what purpose?			
Assumptions/Beliefs: Do you know why it is important for this author to express the views that are voiced in this article? What is at stake for the author? What assumptions and beliefs does he bring to the text that seem to be unquestioned?			
Audience: Who does the author seem to be addressing with the text? What does the author seem to think this audience believes/ assumes about the topic?			
Context: What other positions does the essay refer to and/or imply are "out there" about this issue? What other solutions to the problems? What might other groups not included in the audience think?			

2) Once you have laid out the articles according to these categories, work across the rows horizontally. Mark points of connection where authors have the same or a similar response, either by using a highlighter, or by marking them with a circle. Then indicate points of conflict, or opposition, with a different color highlighter or by marking them with a square.

3) Follow the same process diagonally. Are there any areas of agreement between, say, the purpose of one piece and the audience's position of another? Where are the conflicts?

4) Coding by color or shape will give you an idea of where these authors stand in relation to each other and to an issue. Write a paragraph explaining what this coding means. What is the nature of the conversation it indicates?

Reading to Write

Read through all the essays on a given conversation as if you might be writing about this topic. Your goal, as a potential contributor to the conversation, is to understand all the different ways people understand the issue and why they understand it in this way. This kind of analysis would allow you as a writer to better understand how people are already thinking about the topic so you can better decide both (a) how you want to frame the issue for yourself, and (b) how to address others concerned about the topic.

Part I—The Problem

What is the problem to be solved? What questions are important to answer to develop a position on this topic? Be sure to look not only at the author of the essay's way of framing the problem but also other people's opinions embedded in the discussion. Also, feel free to extend from what the author actually says to issues that might be *implied* and/or issues that you think should be added to what the essay actually addresses. Make a list from each essay of all the different issues involved with the topic.

Part II—Previous Knowledge

Reread the essays looking for what you can *assume* people already know about the topic. What seems to be common knowledge in all the pieces? Are there any premises everyone seems to agree with?

Part III—Individuated Positions

List all the potential audiences for an essay of your own on the topic (i.e., the people you can see as invested in the topic, care about the issue, or can take action on the issue). Next to each audience include a full sentence about *why* they care about the issue. What's their stake in it?

Analyzing Publishing Context and Audience

Part I—Define the Publishing Context

If the text was originally published as a print-based text (e.g., in a magazine or journal), what publication did it appear in? What is the journal's stated purpose? What political/cultural bias does this journal seem to have? If a speech, what event prompted the speech? Who was the event's sponsoring organization, and what was the purpose for the event? When was the text published or first presented? What social, political, and cultural events (broadly speaking) were happening in the United States (or the world) that might have influenced the purpose for writing the text? For either a speech or print publication, who was the intended audience (or audiences)? What views might the audience hold about the issue being discussed? Why might this audience be interested in the issue being discussed? What types of appeals (e.g., emotional, logical, ethical) and/or examples might be most effective for this audience and this context?

Part II—Explore the Audience

- Mark places in the text where the author most seems to tailor his writing to the audience and context.

- Mark places in the text where the author explicitly addresses a particular audience.

- Write down passages of the text where the author seems to address issues of audience extremely well and say why they are successful.

- Write down passages where the author makes poor choices about context or audience and explain what fails.

- Given the context the author is writing for, is there any bias in the way she presents information? How can you tell? How would a different audience respond to the situation?

Student Essay for Reflection on Writing

Hui Mike Zhang

And It Was All a Dream

I woke up suddenly one night, and it was the strangest sensation. It felt like waking up from a dream, but the transition was seamless. I sat there thinking about sitting there . . . thinking. It was odd, to say the least, that I discovered the subject and topic of my final reflection paper in the middle of the night. As I sit here writing this, and reading my previous writing, I realize that I am writing a story. Not just any story, almost, in a sense, the story of my life.

In my room, there are two posters on the wall. One is a picture of an island, a cascade of ephemeral light shines from the heavens, reflecting off the silent and calm waters. It says: "Perfection, the difference between ordinary and extraordinary is that little extra." The other poster has written on it: "Truth, Beauty, Freedom, and Love," in traditional Chinese characters. I have two computers, one desktop and one laptop hooked up to each other, which pretty much takes up all of my desk. On my bookcase, there are books on biology, chemistry, Chinese, Japanese, as well as smaller textbooks on math and writing. Below that, are cartons of protein and creatine powders. The air is constantly filled with the sound of music, ranging from hip-hop, rock, pop, rap, to classical and traditional. Everything in my room, everything that belongs to me, and everything I have ever written, thought, or said aloud, has a story behind it. They represent my past, my hopes, my wishes, and my dreams.

And it was all a dream, wasn't it? Every morning I wake up, and I am saddened, as if I am saying goodbye and leaving behind another world, a world of dreams, and a dream of worlds. Sometimes I am ripped away from it, torn suddenly as if life fell apart abruptly and without warning. Sometimes it fades away, slowly out of focus and I can feel my own regret even as it slips out of the reach of my mind. And there are times when there is nothing at all. But I know it was there, wonderful and fantastic, dreams of worlds that I explored and took part in. And then, I am filled with an inexplicable sense of loss, a frustration impossible to mitigate. Invariably, I wake up to my life once more. Day after day, there is little change. There are times when I try to stop it, or hold onto each day a little bit more. It's interesting, you would think it's a lot easier to hold onto waking moments than the fleeting passing of dreams, but it feels even harder. And each slow day that life gives me, I have learned to treasure. These days are often the hardest to forget, thank god.

There is probably a look of complete shock and disbelief on my face right now. I am staring at my journal once more, after reading it over fully for the first time. Thirty short pages that chronicled three months of my life. I stare at it, and I cannot believe it. I think to myself, how could this be all? There must have been more that happened. And there was, but I cannot remember. Anything not mentioned directly or explained in detail feels utterly absent. One entry sticks out like a dark shadow in the corner of my mind, blocking out the light of that day. *Weekend was great, a lot of things happened. Filled with hope and joy, my memories will fill in the rest . . . I will remember.* Those were my words exactly, but I cannot remember. My memories will not fill in the rest. Even with my journal, that weekend feels just like another dream, hazy, unclear, and broken. I know it was wonderful; I think I even remember that it was wonderful, but without the memory itself, it is difficult to convince myself. How I wish I could close my eyes one more time and be transported back to that day, to feel the joy of that day once more.

To live in the past is often dangerous and unwise, but in a way, I believe when we think of the past, it is only to lament our own mortality. But it would be equally foolish to not grieve for the passing of our time. We do not have an eternity to live, and a year feels to many of us, like days, hours, even minutes. We often say time passes too quickly, but perhaps it isn't time that passes too quickly, but the part of our human existence that races past time. And the last part of us that seeks to draw us back and slow us down are our memories, and our memories always seem to lose until it is too late, when we have crossed the finish line, where there is little to do but look back upon the race track of our lives. Often, here is where we truly split as human beings. In life, people may be divided into countless identities and groups on issues of society, but all life must come to an end. At the end of the road, there are only two kinds of people. Those who see the end as the end, or those who see the end as the beginning. Only faith and the choices we make in life will decide what we see.

Today, I live at a university far away from many people I love and care for. I know I am not living in the real world, for there is little responsibility I must carry for myself and for others. I have no long term or skilled work experience, and absolutely no experience being financially independent. Truly, I even sound to myself like a dreamer. Each day passes like the passing of a dream, sometimes too quickly and abruptly, sometimes slowly and intangibly. And it was all a dream, wasn't it? No, that is not true, for we are not living in a dream. But each day that has not come, will come to become just a memory, and as the memories grow distant, there is little real difference.

Through thinking about and writing this self reflection, I have realized why people write. When I look around this university, it is finally obvious that everyone writes, regardless of their major. And it is true, everyone writes, from scientists to homemakers, no matter what you do in life, how old you are, or where you may live. From the moment humanity realized, collectively and perhaps subconsciously, that the power of our memories are limited, and that our memories do not transcend our mortality. So you see, we all write for one purpose, whether we realize it or not, and that is to remember. Taking notes for classes, groceries, finances, and whatever else life may demand is an obvious and literal form of writing to remember. Books, fiction or nonfiction, scientific or creative, are all written for us to remember, whatever the point, thesis or lesson the respective work may have. Journals are the most obvious example, where the entire point is to help the writer remember. No matter whom the audience of any written piece may be, writing is ultimately to remember. All writers, then, must seek to write something truly unforgettable. For too many of us, however, we have no idea what we are writing about, or why, and therein lies the difference, and where we often fail to make use of writing's greatest potential.

Writing is only one of many powerful tools that humanity possesses for the benefit of our past, present, and future. However, the written language has been the basis of all technological, scientific, and literary advancement in human history. Today we have high tech telescopes, cameras, and camcorders to record the actual images of life.

Tomorrow we may be able to record the images of our mind itself. But all human knowledge that we have inherited through the thousands of years of our heritage can trace its roots to the written language, and even if the physical act of writing ever fades from society, words will always exist. They say that a picture is worth a thousand words, but one word can conjure a thousand more pictures. In the end, a picture may just be a word, and a word just a picture, synonymous in every practical respect but name.

I write for the same reason that everyone writes. Now that I know and understand that reason, I am confident in my ability to direct my writing to even greater meaning. Writing is something that can only be done in the present, and right now, I am writing for the future, all in an effort to remember the past.